WITHDRAWN

HARVARD LIBRARY

WITHDRAWN

*Monographs of the
Hebrew Union College
Number 29*

———

*Happiness in
Premodern Judaism:
Virtue, Knowledge, and
Well-Being*

Monographs of the Hebrew Union College

1. Lewis M. Barth, *An Analysis of Vatican 30*
2. Samson H. Levey, *The Messiah: An Aramaic Interpretation*
3. Ben Zion Wacholder, *Eupolemus: A Study of Judaeo-Greek Literature*
4. Richard Victor Bergren, *The Prophets and the Law*
5. Benny Kraut, *From Reform Judaism to Ethical Culture: The Religious Evolution of Felix Adler*
6. David B. Ruderman, *The World of a Renaissance Jew: The Life and Thought of Abraham ben Mordecai Farrisol*
7. Alan Mendelson, *Secular Education in Philo of Alexandria*
8. Ben Zion Wacholder, *The Dawn of Qumran: the Sectarian Torah and the Teacher of Righteousness*
9. Stephen M. Passamaneck, *The Traditional Jewish Law of Sale: Shulḥan Arukh, Ḥoshen Mishpat, Chapters 189–240*
10. Yael S. Feldman, *Modernism and Cultural Transfer: Gabriel Preil and the Tradition of Jewish Literary Bilingualism*
11. Raphael Jospe, *Torah and Sophia: The Life and Thought of Shem Tov ibn Falaquera*
12. Richard Kalmin, *The Redaction of the Babylonian Talmud: Amoraic or Saboraic?*
13. Shuly Rubin Schwartz, *The Emergence of Jewish Scholarship in America: The Publication of the Jewish Encyclopedia*
14. John C. Reeves, *Jewish Lore in Manichaean Cosmogony: Studies in the Book of Giants Traditions*
15. Robert Kirschner, *Baraita De Melekhet Ha-Mishkan: A Critical Edition with Introduction and Translation*
16. Philip E. Miller, *Karaite Separatism in Nineteenth-Century Russia: Joseph Solomon Lutski's Epistle of Israel's Deliverance*
17. Warren Bargad, *"To Write the Lips of Sleepers": The Poetry of Amir Gilboa*
18. Marc Saperstein, *"Your Voice Like a Ram's Horn": Themes and Texts in Traditional Jewish Preaching*
19. Emanuel Melzer, *No Way Out: The Politics of Polish Jewry, 1935–1939*
20. Eric L. Friedland, *"Were Our Mouths Filled With Song": Studies in Liberal Jewish Liturgy*
21. Edward Fram, *Ideals Face Reality: Jewish Law and Life in Poland 1550–1655*
22. Ruth Langer, *To Worship God Properly: Tensions Between Liturgical Custom and Halakhah in Judaism*
23. Nili Sacher Fox, *In the Service of the King: Officialdom in Ancient Israel and Judah*
24. Carole B. Balin, *To Reveal Our Hearts: Jewish Women Writers in Tsarist Russia*
25. Shaul Bar, *A Letter That Has Not Been Read: Dreams in the Hebrew Bible*
26. Eric Caplan, *From Ideology to Liturgy: Reconstructionist Worship and American Liberal Judaism*
27. Rina Lapidus, *Between Snow and Desert Heat: Russian Influences on Hebrew Literature, 1870–1970*
28. Howard L. Apothaker, *Sifra, Dibbura deSinai: Rhetorical Formulae, Literary Structures, and Legal Traditions*
29. Hava Tirosh-Samuelson, *Happiness in Premodern Judaism: Virtue, Knowledge, and Well-Being*

Happiness in Premodern Judaism

Virtue, Knowledge, and Well-Being

Hava Tirosh-Samuelson

HEBREW UNION COLLEGE PRESS
CINCINNATI

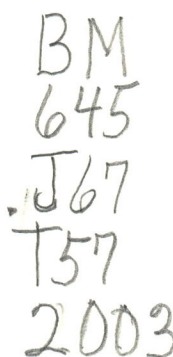

© Copyright 2003 by the Hebrew Union College Press
Hebrew Union College-Jewish Institute of Religion

Library of Congress Cataloging-in-Publication Data

Tirosh-Samuelson, Hava, 1950–
   Happiness in premodern Judaism : virtue, knowledge, and well-being / Hava Tirosh-Samuelson.
      p. cm. –(Monographs of the Hebrew Union College ; no. 29)
   Includes bibliographic references and index.
   ISBN 0-87820-453-9 (alk. paper)
   1. Joy—Religious aspects—Judaism. 2. Happiness—Religious aspects—Judaism. I. Title. II. Series

BM645.J67T57 2003
296.3'6—dc21

2002191909

Printed on acid-free paper in the United States of America
Distributed by Wayne State University Press
4809 Woodward Avenue, Detroit, MI 48201
Toll-free 1-800-978-7323

Contents

Acknowledgments — ix
Abbreviations — xi

Preface — 1

1. Thinking Happiness: Greek and Hellenistic Views — 9
2. *Ashrei*: Torah, Wisdom, and Living Rightly in Ancient Judaism — 55
3. The Happy Life of Torah in Rabbinic Judaism — 101
4. Happiness and the Cultivation of Character in Islam — 143
5. Perfectly Happy: Maimonides' Conception of Happiness — 192
6. The Maimonidean Controversies: Debating the Meaning of Happiness — 246
7. The Kabbalistic Prescription for Happiness — 291
8. Intellectual Perfection and Jewish-Christian Rivalry — 343
9. Religious Perfection and the Interplay of Philosophy and Kabbalah — 394

Postscript — 439

Notes — 450
Bibliographic Essay — 550
Index — 574

אַשְׁרֵי אָדָם מָצָא חָכְמָה   וְאָדָם יָפִיק תְּבוּנָה
כִּי טוֹב סַחְרָהּ מִסְּחַר־כָּסֶף   וּמֵחָרוּץ תְּבוּאָתָהּ
יְקָרָה הִיא מִפְּנִינִים   וְכָל־חֲפָצֶיךָ לֹא יִשְׁווּ־בָהּ
אֹרֶךְ יָמִים בִּימִינָהּ   בִּשְׂמֹאולָהּ עֹשֶׁר וְכָבוֹד
דְּרָכֶיהָ דַרְכֵי־נֹעַם   וְכָל־נְתִיבוֹתֶיהָ שָׁלוֹם
עֵץ־חַיִּים הִיא לַמַּחֲזִיקִים בָּהּ   וְתֹמְכֶיהָ מְאֻשָּׁר

Proverbs 3:13–18

❧ ❧ ❧

*To Norbert, my partner
in the pursuit of wisdom and happiness*

Acknowledgments

This book has been in the making for over a decade. It began in a paper delivered in 1991 in a conference on Jews in Iberia commemorating the 500th anniversary of the expulsion of the Jews from Spain. The article presented at that conference appeared in print in 1998 in *In Iberia and Beyond: Hispanic Jews Between Cultures*, ed. Bernard Dov Cooperman (Newark: University of Delaware Press, 1998). Parts of this paper are now found in Chapters Eight and Nine of this study, reconfigured into a new context. Since that conference I have published several articles, and sections from them are included in this book. Most of Chapter Five appeared as "Maimonides' View of Happiness: Philosophy, Myth and the Transcendence of History," in *Jewish History and Jewish Memory: Essays in Honor of Yosef Hayim Yerushalmi*, ed. Elisheva Carlebach, John M. Efron and David N. Myers (Brandeis University Press for the University Press of New England, 1998). Chapter Eight includes material from "Jewish Philosophy on the Eve of Modernity," published in *History of Jewish Philosophy* ed. Daniel H. Frank and Oliver Leaman (London and New York: Routledge, 1997) and Chapter Nine includes material published in that essay as well as in "The Ultimate End of Human Life in Postexpulsion Philosophic Literature," in *Crisis and Creativity in the Sephardic World: 1391–1648,* ed. Benjamin Gampel (New York: Columbia University Press, 1997). I thank these publishers for allowing me to use this copyrighted material in this study.

A grant from the Amado Foundation enabled me to access pertinent texts extant only in manuscripts. I thank Dr. Abraham David of the Microfilmed Hebrew Manuscripts Institute in the National and University Library in Jerusalem for helping me to obtain relevant manuscripts over the past two decades.

Most of the work on this text was carried out while I was on the faculty of the Department of Religious Studies of Indiana University. A release from teaching duties in Fall 1994, Fall 1995, and the academic year of 1997/98 enabled me to write the first three chapters. Conversations with my colleagues in the department of Religious Studies, especially the late Professor J. Samuel Preus and the recently retired Professor James Hart, helped me sharpen my presentation and analysis. Also helpful were the questions and comments of those who listened to my talks at the American Academy of Religion, the Association of Jewish Studies, the University of

Chicago, the University of Iowa, University of Virginia, and Oxford University, England, where I presented sections from this project. Similarly, the comments and insights of my students at Indiana University and at the University of Pennsylvania stimulated and clarified my thinking. The final writing of the book took place at Arizona State University, where I now teach in the Department of History and where I benefited from a research grant and from the assistance of Ms. Mary Egel and Mr. Paul Tzimihades, who helped prepare the manuscript for publication.

My good friend Dr. Martin Levin read the entire manuscript and helped me to present my arguments and personal point of view with greater clarity. My friends Jill Nathanson Astrow, a painter who wrestles with the challenges of creative art, and her husband, Dr. Alan Astrow, a physician who understands the close connection between the well-being of the body and the well-being of the soul, strengthened my resolve to publish the book. On a recommendation of another friend, Eve Shulmeister, I found a good reader, Dr. James Peck, whose stylistic corrections improved the text immeasurably. The two anonymous readers for the Hebrew Union College Press went far beyond the call of duty reading the manuscript very carefully. Their intelligent and insightful comments enabled me to correct mistakes, provide additional support, and rethink some of my claims. I am grateful to all of them.

Finally, my deepest thanks are reserved to my husband, Professor Norbert M. Samuelson. His analytic mind and challenging questions enabled me to present the material as cogently as I can. I dedicate the book to Norbert with love and appreciation.

Abbreviations

Abr.	*De Abrahamo*	On Abraham
Cher.	*De Cherubim*	On the Cherubim
Decal.	*De Decalogo*	On the Decalogue
Det.	*Quod Deterious Potiori insidiari Solet*	The Worse Attacks the Better
Ebr.	*De Ebrietate*	On Drunkenness
Leg. All	*Legum Allegoriarum*	Allegorical Interpretation
Mig.	*De Migratione Abrahami*	On the Migration of Abraham
Vit. Mos.	*De Vita Moses*	On the Life of Moses
Op.	*De Opificio Mundi*	On the Creation
Praem.	*De Praemiis et Poenis*	On Rewards and Punishments
Quaest. in Gen.	Questions et Solutiones in Genesin	Questions and Answers on Genesis
Quis. Her.	*Quis rerum divinarum Heres sit*	Who is the Heir
Quod Deus	*Quod Deus sit Immutabilis*	On the Unchangeability of God
Quod Omn. Prob	*Quod omnis Probus Liber sit*	Every Good Man is Free
Spec. Leg.	*De Specialibus Legibus*	On the Special Laws
Sob.	*De Sobrietate*	On Sobriety
Som.	*De Somniis*	On Dreams
Virt.	*De Virtute*	On the Virtues
Vit. Cont.	*De Contemplativa*	On the Contemplative Life

Preface

From Plato to the present, Western philosophers have debated the meaning of "happiness":[1] Is it a feeling, a subjective psychological state, a general disposition, or a regulative idea? What are the conditions necessary for the attainment of happiness? Does it mean an overall satisfaction with one's life or an intense joy and a momentary rapture? What is the connection between happiness and virtue, and how does happiness relate to pleasure? Western philosophers have given diverse and conflicting answers to these questions, reflecting the evolution of Western philosophy and culture. This book presents a relatively unknown perspective on Western reflections on happiness: namely, the views of premodern Jewish thinkers.

That Jews were interested in happiness may appear odd to most people: According to conventional thought, its pursuit hardly seems like one of the major tenets of our religion. Three main factors may explain why this is so.

First, Jewish history itself is replete with political defeats, bloodshed, persistent hatred, and most recently, a systematic attempt to annihilate the Jewish people. More commonly, then, people say that Judaism is about survival under very difficult conditions, about suffering, or about hope for the ideal future.

Second, traditional Judaism is grounded in the belief that God revealed to Israel the Law, the Torah, which specifies the commandments (*mitzvot*) that Jews must observe. The primary values of the Jewish religious tradition include joy in the fulfillment of the commandments, devotion to and desire for intimacy with God, and recognition that one is constantly judged by God. In a religious matrix that presupposes awareness of human sins and expectation of reward and punishment, individual happiness somehow seems to be incongruent with the values of the tradition. Indeed, whereas the pursuit of happiness is an individual endeavor, the Jewish religious tradition understands itself in collective terms: both the revelation at Sinai in the remote past and the Messianic Age in the remote future are viewed as communal events that organize Jewish life through peoplehood rather than the pursuit of individual happiness.

Third, and most important, since the Utilitarian philosophers of the nineteenth century, happiness has been equated with pleasure from the satisfaction of desires. Rejecting Kantian ethics and Christian morality, the Utilitarians defined the human good as the Greatest Happiness Principle ("maximum happiness to maximum number of people"), and based it on a calculus of pleasure and pain. As a result, it has become commonplace that "happiness" means being content, being free of worries, having one's desires fulfilled, or obtaining what one wishes. This is the "happiness" that most Americans consider an inalienable human right promoted in the Declaration of Independence. In industrialized Western democracies, where capitalism is the dominant economic system, having what one wants is associated with the possession of material goods. Against this view, living a Jewish life seems either irrelevant or a direct obstacle to the attainment of that state.

This book argues to the contrary. Not only did Jewish thinkers not disregard the concept of happiness. They devoted considerable attention to it. Moreover, I claim, Judaism understood itself as the best path to a happy life. In fact, one reason Jews remained loyal to their tradition despite their suffering, I contend, was that they were deeply convinced that their tradition secured their happiness. This is precisely what the liturgy affirms each time Jews return the Torah to the Ark during a worship service, saying "It [the Torah] is the tree of life and those who hold fast to it are happy." Obviously, to make sense of Jewish self-understanding and of my claims about Judaism, it is necessary to change the way we think about happiness.

Properly understood, I contend that in Judaism happiness does not mean possessing material goods, having fun, feeling content, or enjoying physical pleasures, although some of these elements may be part of the happy life. Happiness is not a subjective feeling manifested in a given moment or for a short period of time. Instead, it means flourishing, thriving, and experiencing well-being appropriate to human beings. It is an objective state of affairs that pertains to human nature and to the quality of a human life as a whole, from the perspective of its entire duration.

Moreover, the intrinsically good life is inseparable from a set of religious beliefs, the most important of which is that God, the creator of the world, has a special relationship with the People of Israel, to whom God revealed His Wisdom and Will in a form of law: the Torah. The challenging question, then, is not "How can Judaism be concerned with happiness?" but rather, "Can the notion of happiness in Judaism make sense independent of the belief in Torah and the life that flows from it?" I answer that question in the negative. Until Baruch (Benedict) Spinoza in the mid-seventeenth century, all premodern Jewish thinkers held that Jews could flourish only if they lived the life of Torah and devoted themselves to fathoming God's Wisdom. Nonetheless, their views were not all struck from one mold. Over time, those thinkers gave different answers to the basic questions "What does Torah mean?" "How does the Torah ensure human happiness?" "How does Torah relate to Wisdom?" and "What results from following Torah and pursuing Wisdom?"

To be sure, the objectivist understanding of happiness was not uniquely Jewish. It was shared by other ancient intellectual and religious traditions and was analyzed systematically by Aristotle in the *Nicomachean Ethics* and the *Eudemian Ethics*. Aristotle's philosophy remained influential throughout antiquity and dominated the history of Western philosophy throughout the Middle Ages and well into the seventeenth century. Our study will show that Aristotle's reflections on happiness were very much a part of Jewish intellectual history and of Judaic reflections on happiness, despite important differences between Judaism and Greek philosophy. The absorption of Aristotle's ethics began, not in the Middle Ages, as is commonly thought, but already in the late Second Temple period. The Jewish philosophers in the Hellenistic period, most notably Philo of Alexandria (c. 20 B.C.E.–c. 50 C.E.), showed how the Jewish Scriptures could be read in light of the Greek conception of happiness and how virtue is related to knowledge. The fusion of Greek and Judaic perspectives reached its zenith during the Middle Ages, especially in the works of Moses Maimonides (1138–1204) and his followers.

Most of this book, therefore, concerns the reception of Aristotle's *Ethics* in medieval Jewish philosophy, and the concept of happiness (in Hebrew *hatzlaha*, or *osher*) can be seen as the point of intersection between Greek philosophy and Judaism. Indeed, Jewish thinkers framed their attitudes toward life and death, individual and society, body and soul, good and evil, male and female, Jews and non-Jews, religion and philosophy, virtue and knowledge in their reflections on the meaning of human happiness. Put differently, the discourse on happiness was the most comprehensive context for the articulation of Jewish self-understanding outside of the legal reasoning of halakhah (i.e., normative Jewish law). Analysis of the history of the discourse on happiness can, therefore, shed light on our understanding of the history of Jewish thought and the evolution of Jewish culture. It can, as well, document the dynamics of unity and diversity, continuity and change in Jewish self-understanding while showing how Judaism interacted with surrounding non-Jewish civilizations.

Tracing the evolution of the discourse on happiness from antiquity to the seventeenth century, this book is arranged chronologically, showing the correlation between a given notion of happiness and Jewish history and culture at a particular time. These changing conceptions of happiness were propelled by an internal dialectic between two dimensions: in Western culture their code words are "*mythos*" and "*logos,*" Greek terms that capture the shift from sacred narratives to systematic philosophy, as much as they capture two ways of being in the world, or two approaches to the interpretation of reality. In Judaism, *mythos* is the sacred narrative about the eternal covenant between God and the People of Israel and the obligations that follow from it, i.e., Torah. *Logos* is expressed in Judaism in the term *hokhmah* meaning "wisdom." Thus the discourse on happiness is a dramatic interplay between Wisdom and Torah, between philosophy and religion, between reason and faith. This dialectic is exhibited *within* Greek culture and *within* Judaism as much as it governs the relationship *between* Judaism and other civilizations and cultures. In each chapter we shall see how the drama took shape within a given historical epoch and its unique cultural sensibilities.

Why should one wish to tell the story of the premodern discourse on happiness? My answer is four-fold. First, I believe that if we seek to be happy we must hold a correct notion of happiness. I maintain that the ancient and medieval philosophers—Jews and non-Jews alike—have raised all the important questions about the human pursuit of happiness, even though many of their metaphysical, cosmological and biological assumptions have proven to be mistaken or debatable. Despite these serious limitations, I maintain that there is still much to learn from ancient and medieval thinkers about how to approach the pursuit of happiness. They were correct to think about happiness in terms of flourishing or thriving as a human being, rather than in terms of feeling good or having fun or owning things, and they were right to place self-control at the core of moral conditioning. I hope that the encounter with the ancient and medieval approaches to happiness will enable readers to reexamine their own views and struggle with the right kinds of questions.

Second, I want to tell this story because it presents Judaism as a multivocal and multifaceted tradition that harbors many perspectives and viewpoints. Most broadly it is true that the three main forms of Jewish self-understanding were halakhah, philosophy, and kabbalah. In this book I highlight the story of Jewish philosophy, broadly defined as "the Wisdom tradition," in order to challenge certain contemporary misperceptions. Today it is rather common to dismiss the philosophic strand in Judaism as a product of a small group of elitist intellectuals who talked only amongst themselves and who engaged in "un-Jewish" activities—studying non-Jewish texts and theorizing within non-Jewish paradigms. Since Judaism centers on halakhah, so the argument goes, philosophic inquiry was marginal, insignificant, or downright heretical. I challenge this perception by showing not only how the philosophers shaped Jewish culture, especially in Mediterranean communities, but also how that philosophical reasoning expressed one of the deepest religious commitments of Judaism: the commitment to the pursuit of truth—a commitment that was fully in place by the second century B.C.E. when Torah became inextricably associated with Wisdom. That association implied that commitment to God's revealed law was also the commitment to pursue the truth about the world created by God, resulting in knowledge that brings one closer to God. While the scope and content of "Wisdom" changed over time, the main point remained the same throughout the premodern period: to be happy, Jews had to live in accordance with Torah *and* become wise. Thus for premodern Jewish thinkers, the pursuit of truth about the world became a religious obligation that encouraged them to devote their lives to the pursuit of knowledge about the world, about humanity, and about God.

Third, I want to show how this commitment to the pursuit of truth made premodern Judaism particularly open to conversation with non-Jewish cultures and civilizations. The Judaism that emerges from my reconstruction is by no means parochial or self-absorbed; it is remarkably curious about other intellectual and religious traditions and open to truths regardless of the ethnic and cultural identities of those one who utter them. From its inception, Judaism evolved by adopting and adapting parts of prevailing modes of thought into its own peculiar religious self-understanding. As a result, Judaism has constantly changed, exhibiting a remarkable elasticity without losing its unique identity.

Finally, I maintain that the discourse on happiness is a very useful prism from which to grasp the dynamic of intellectual life in pre-modern Judaism. Various themes, ideas, texts, trends, debates, and literary genres that seem unrelated cohere more meaningfully once they are recognized as part of one discourse. More specifically, reflections on happiness provide the best lens from which to view the history of Jewish philosophy because it shows how metaphysics, cosmology, psychology, and ethics were intertwined, giving medieval Jewish philosophy a unique coherence.

For whom is this book written? My most immediate audience will consist of scholars of Jewish Studies who write about the history of Jews and Judaism. For them, the book's contribution lies in the way it presents Jewish intellectual history from a contextual, interdisciplinary, and crosscultural approach. Those familiar with my publications know that I have been writing primarily about medieval philosophy and kabbalah. However, to understand the medieval reflections of happiness I had to venture outside my specialization and explore biblical, postbiblical, and rabbinic texts. Because I am not an expert in these areas, I had to rely on the scholarship of others to formulate my own views.

I believe that Western culture cannot be understood without the study of Jews and Judaism, and that therefore the exploration of Jewish intellectual history is relevant both within and beyond the field of Jewish Studies. This book, then, is also written for scholars in those disciplines that have shaped my own intellectual development: religious studies, history, philosophy, and medieval studies, although I cannot claim to be fluent in all of them to the same degree. I believe, however, that the interdisciplinary approach to intellectual activity is appropriate because it reflects the complexity of human life. Interdisciplinary work, however, has become difficult given the fragmentation of the academy, where outside of one's immediate specialization, many scholars are nonexperts. Thus in order to make my material accessible to a broad range of academic readers, I had to provide data that the specialist in a given area would find unnecessary, and I deliberately glossed over nuances of ongoing academic debates that were not germane to my story.

Ethicists and historians of Western ethics may find this book particularly interesting for its focus on virtue ethics.[2] Since 1958, philosophers have noted renewed interest in Aristotle's ethics, new studies of Hellenistic philosophical schools,[3] and a plethora of theoretical essays and books about the differences between ethics of virtue and ethics of duty.[4] Theories that place virtue at the center of their concern are now promoted as a serious alternative to theories originating with Kant or those based on Utilitarian ethical theories.[5] Unlike modern ethical theories that attempt to solve problems and test beliefs through a step-by-step decision-making procedure in which a general, abstract, universal rule is applied to specific moral dilemmas, virtue ethics focuses on the agent. Concerned with how one should live, it has a psychological and anthropological orientation, and its model for decision-making is perceptual rather than rule-based. Because the revival of virtue ethics reflects a general critique of Enlightenment ideals of objectivity and universality, it has been labeled as a type of "anti-theory."[6]

Be that as it may, this book clearly fits into the current revival. Yet instead of seeing virtue ethics as a secular response to questions of morality, my study highlights its religious dimension in Judaism, where there is no tension between the two types of ethical theories and where the recommended virtues are those that enable one to fulfill the divinely revealed commands as stated by its sacred narrative. I thus join those who take a narrative approach to ethics, where the morally admirable dispositions of agents cannot be divorced from moral practices and traditions. A meaningful life, then, is one that has a narrative unity, and the virtues are the traits needed to impose a narrative on the life of an individual and community as the agents simultaneously tell and enact the narrative. Since this book is written as an exercise in intellectual history rather than philosophical ethics, it does not provide theoretical arguments in favor of one approach over another and does not judge whether a given philosophical position is true or not. The philosophical work of recovering virtue ethics in Judaism remains to be done by others.

I hope that nonacademic readers interested in Judaica will also find this work useful. In the Postscript I spell out the implications of the premodern discourse on happiness to contemporary Jews and to all who seek happiness. And throughout, I have made an effort to make rather dense and technical material accessible to readers who do not devote their lives to academic research.

Chronologically, conceptually, and methodologically, then, the scope of this book is broad indeed. It is a synthetic work that reflects my own intellectual development over time and my particular bent of mind. The broad scope, of course, has merits and demerits: it allows for a comprehensive overview of an entire discourse, but it does not allow for a deep analysis of individual texts, authors, or ideas. An analogy will clarify the principle that guided my attempt to strike a certain balance. This book is like an organized tour, and the travelers include individuals with varied academic and nonacademic backgrounds At each stop an overview arises from a close look at selected sites. The tour does not intend to be exhaustive—only seductive. It hopes to tempt the tourist to revisit these sites in the future or to travel to related terrain and linger longer.

1

Thinking Happiness: Greek and Hellenistic Views

Written for nonspecialists in Greek philosophy, this chapter focuses on Aristotle's analysis of happiness in the *Nicomachean* Ethics. It exposes the teleological framework of his philosophy, his rationalist understanding of human nature, the role of reason in molding the good character, the place of pleasure and friendship in the virtuous life, and the relationship between contemplation and action in human flourishing.

Why do we begin with Greek and Hellenistic notions of happiness, rather than with the Bible? First, in order to be able to understand how Judaism could be viewed as a pursuit of happiness, we need to move away from contemporary popular notions of happiness and adopt the view of the ancient philosophers who posited a causal connection between virtue, knowledge, and human flourishing. By clarifying the Greek philosophical approach to happiness, especially as articulated by Aristotle, this chapter provides an overarching conceptual vocabulary for the entire book. Second, all Western reflections on happiness in the ancient and medieval periods were shaped by the Aristotelian legacy. Not only is it impossible to understand how medieval Jewish thinkers thought about happiness without the philosophic schemata of Plato and Aristotle. The biblical and rabbinic material come into sharper focus only when viewed through the lens of the Greek and Hellenistic philosophy. Third, while the Bible refers to events that happened prior to the rise of Greek philosophy, it became a canonic text, or Scripture, during the Hellenistic period. Especially in the Writings, which reached closure after Aristotle, we find explicit reflections about human happiness, manifesting the encounter between Israelite culture and Greek modes of thought. Finally, the dynamic of the entire discourse on happiness in Judaism makes sense once we understand the tension between two conceptions of the happiest life discussed in detail by Aristotle: the life of contemplation of philosophic truth versus the life of moderate action in the sociopolitical sphere. We are not interested in arguing for one or the other here, but only in tracing the interplay between them in Jewish reflections on happiness.

Mythos and Logos in Greek Philosophy

Even though Greek philosophy could not fully extricate itself from myth,[1] Greek philosophical reasoning (referred to briefly as *logos*) grew out of the religious myth it attempted to displace. Like all religious myths, the Greek myths did not seek to explain the world but rather to disclose a sacred one. They defined the culture of their believers by establishing social and educational values, prescribing daily tasks and ceremonial responses, inspiring cultural patterns, and giving meaning to lifecycle events. Like other traditional narratives, the Greek myths were comprised of telling (which is one meaning of *logos*), but they told about that which is beyond telling. Instead of *explaining* reality, the myths *presented* the existential meaning of a lived world. Put differently, the myths were not intended as speculation, whose objective meaning could be translated into conceptual language, but as expressions of irreducible, existential meaning.

With the emergence of Greek philosophy, *mythos* was devalued to the status of fiction or unreal tales, while *logos* was understood to consist of abstraction, analysis, synthesis, and judgment—all tools by which one could discover the permanent, unified, immovable and unchanging principles that underlie all change.[2] The mental activities that characterize philosophy reflect the assumption that the human mind is separate from the world it perceives and seeks to know. At least in principle, the mind is able to grasp the structure of reality—namely, to classify it by means of abstract principles. Thus with the rise of philosophy, the traditional myths were distrusted and even viewed as an obstacle to knowledge of truth.

The Sophists

Systematic philosophical thinking began in Greece with the philosophers of nature who sought to define the most general principle or principles that explained why things are what they are. But systematic *ethical* thinking, which is relevant to our story, began with the Sophists in the fifth century B.C.E., roughly at the time of the canonization of the Torah by Ezra. The Sophists, a group of professional educators (26 of them are known by name), sought to establish educational practices congruent with the democratization of the Greek polis. They promoted themselves as teachers "of the art of living successfully within the public sphere (*politike techne*)"[3] and marketed their expertise in rhetorical skills that were very valuable in a society organized and governed by the medium of direct speech.[4] Brilliant oratory and argumentative dexterity were the tools they used to make a case for any opinion, be it true or not. Rhetoric, the art they taught, was linked to the epistemological view that "knowledge could only be relative to the perceiving subject."[5]

The Sophists marked a change in Greek ethics. The moral values of the ancient Greek city-states had heretofore reflected the ethos of a military elite that valued proficiency in combat, superiority in weaponry, and physical skills.[6] Since only wealthy men could possess the costly arms and the leisure necessary for military training, only the wealthy could train their children in requisite fighting skills that included horsemanship, gymnastics, and hunting. In the warrior code of this military elite, the coveted excellence, *eudaimonia*, was defined as "doing well in reference to wealth, power, and honor."[7] A man was considered good (*agathos*) in accordance with his honor, and the principal means of gaining honor was to perform great deeds that publicly demonstrated his *arete*, namely, "excellence" in some concrete capacity.[8] This was the craft or skill that was "at once the business and the virtue of the sophist to teach."[9] And it was no longer strictly military and physical.

By the time of the Sophists, public success was determined by victory not on the battlefield but in law courts, councils and assemblies; and the Sophists provided the skills that assured such success. Ever searching for students who could pay their fees, they traveled throughout the Greek mainland, where they encountered diverse customs and cultural conventions. This experience led to reflection on the distinction between nature (*physis*) and convention (*nomos*). The most extreme Sophists judged human conventions to be an imposition on true nature, a position that led to cultural relativism as well as the belief that gratification of desires is the road to human well being. Moral and legal conventions are but "fetters on nature," obstacles that should be overcome by superior individuals whose talents entitle them to have a greater share of wealth, power, and sensual pleasures.

Socrates

The Sophists' moral counsel was no more than a reworking of the aristocratic warrior code, now coupled with the claim that "man is the measure of all things." The most serious challenge to Sophism came from Socrates (b. ca. 470 B.C.E.) whose position was anything but a reaffirmation of aristocratic moral values.

The first to pose the question "How should we live to be happy?"[10] Socrates introduced a philosophical view that identified human well-being with the internal quality of one's soul (*psyche*). In order to achieve a clear and correct understanding "of the way a person ought to live," one must pursue wisdom, namely, engage in philosophy."[11] Applying the argumentative skills of the Sophists, Socrates examined moral terms and ethical actions in order to discover within them some common or universal quality.

Socrates argued that if knowledge is virtue, then ignorance is vice, and all moral transgressions are ultimately a form of ignorance. His most important contribution to ethics, then, was the equation of virtue and happiness with the possession of knowledge or wisdom. All moral knowledge is some form of knowledge, which sometimes is practical (*phronesis*) and at other times is theoretical (*sophia*). Furthermore, "all moral excellences are in some sense parts of a single whole that he calls 'true *arete*', with each particular aspect marked by distinct capacities or functions."[12]

Plato

The students of Socrates—the most famous of whom was Plato—perpetuated their teacher's notion that the life of moral excellence consists of "care of the soul," an intrinsic good that does not require other external sanctions or rewards. For Plato the soul (*psyche*) was understood to be a fallen spirit (*daimon*) that was entombed in the body for a series of reincarnations in various life forms.[13] Release from this cycle of rebirths could be achieved only through a life of ritual and dietary purity, ascetic practice, ethical conduct, and mathematical study; only these would restore the soul to its original divine state. At the same time, Plato's psychology was closely linked to his metaphysical theory of Forms—the eternal, immaterial, supersensible entities apprehensible only by reason. The Forms alone, Plato held, were objectively real; all other things known to us in the phenomenal world were only reflections of these objective standards. The *psyche* possesses knowledge of these Forms prior to its association with a body whose vices and passions cause souls to forget their initial knowledge. Only the lovers of wisdom, the philosophers who keep themselves pure, can "recollect" that knowledge, which they can achieve only through dialectical inquiry and the pursuit of virtue. Thus, in Plato's philosophy, the happy life is one spent in pursuit of wisdom—that is, in the acquisition of logically necessary and universal truths.

For Plato, however, philosophy was not merely a subject for solitary study but a way of life to be shared by friends in the common pursuit of wisdom. One product of this group endeavor was *The Republic*, a dialogue in which Plato constructs a model social structure of a three-tiered state governed by those who are suited for it "by nature." He calls these rulers "the Guardians." Two character traits distinguish them. One is "high spiritedness," which is conducive to courage in war. The other is an inherent love of wisdom, which is associated with friendship with and gentleness towards one's fellow citizens.

According to Plato, the role of the Guardians is not to favor the happiness of any one group within the ideal community over another group, but rather to serve the good "for the polis as a whole." True well-being requires functional excellence where each part performs its appropriate task without interfering with the performance of the others. What is true for the collective as a social organism is true of the individual as a healthy psyche. Hence, happiness is understood both psychologically and socially to be a harmony of constituent parts that is identical with justice (*dikaisune*), one of the four cardinal virtues, the other three being wisdom, courage, and temperance.

In the "completely good" community, which is to say, the properly organized and ruled society, all four cardinal virtues are manifested. Wisdom belongs essentially to the ruling Guardians, who possess the requisite "science" or "knowledge" to lead others. Courage is the essential trait of the warrior-Auxiliaries, whose education has been carefully controlled to exclude false beliefs. Temperance (*sophrosune*) exerts a kind of control (*enkrateia*) over our indulgence in certain pleasures—a mastery of one's self that emerges when reason, "the naturally better part" of the human psyche, governs the appetitive part, "the worst" part of us. In the social sphere temperance is evident when each individual performs the one service in the polis for which his nature is best suited.

Like society, the human *psyche* is composed of diverse elements or parts: the rational element (*logistikon*) that reasons; the spirited (*thumoides*) that moves one to action; and the "appetitive" (*epithumetikon*), the seat of passions and desires. Ideally the rational part should rule because it is "wise and exercising forethought on behalf of the entire soul"; the spirited part should function as an "ally" to the ruling principle, implementing and enforcing its decisions, while the appetitive part must be disciplined and controlled by the two superior elements. Wisdom is manifested in the individual when the rational element governs in accordance with the knowledge of what is beneficial for each of the parts and for the common whole; courage is on display whenever the spirited element "preserves in the midst of pains and pleasures the commandments of reason: while temperance occurs whenever there is "friendship and concord among the elements" (*Republic*, 441c–42d). Justice turns out to be nothing more than the proper internal ordering of the *psyche* wherein each of the elements performs its own functions.

For Plato, then, human well-being, or happiness, is analogous to health. When the internal parts of the *psyche* are properly ordered according to nature, one experiences well-being. Conversely, when parts are not properly ruled by reason, the result is disorder, discord, and ugliness.

Plato provides the transition from myth to philosophy in Greek culture. Though he attempted to extricate philosophy from traditional myths, he repeatedly resorted to them, either to illustrate a philosophical doctrine or to point out the limits of human understanding. Thus the precise relationship between mythos and logos in the Platonic corpus is still a matter of scholarly debate.[14] Some hold that in Plato's works mythos is at odds with logos, while others understand myth as a necessary corollary to dialectical and logical reasoning. Still others insist that mythos reconciles the irrational and the rational aspects of man, in the process of which myth transcends knowledge. Be this as it may, Plato constructed "likely stories," i.e., narrative representations of aspects of the cosmos and the place of humans in it, in order to transform the culture and politics of his time. At the same time he criticized the poetic myths of his generation and banished their creators, the poets, from the ideal republic of the Philosopher-King. He allowed only those stories that were carefully formulated and vigilantly regulated by the Philosophers/Guardians for the moral benefit of the common folk and for civil guidance.

Plato's theories occupy a privileged place of influence in the development of Jewish ethics, and we will return to his understanding of myth when we discuss Maimonides' philosophy. For now let us turn to Plato's student, Aristotle, whose analysis of *eudaimonia* ("flourishing") provided the conceptual vocabulary of the discourse on happiness for all subsequent reflections in Western civilization. The reception of Aristotelian ethical theory in Jewish thought, then, is key to the understanding of the Jewish view of happiness.

Aristotle on the Human Good

Unlike Plato, Aristotle attempted to completely omit the use of myth in his presentation of philosophy, and, some scholars view him the founder of scientific philosophy in the West. However, even though he departed from Plato by shifting the focus to the empirical study of nature, Aristotle retained the Platonic criterion for knowability, according to which only universals are intelligible. Criticizing Plato's theory of transcendent Forms, to which we shall soon return, Aristotle held that observation of things by the senses and proper classification of their properties enable us to discover what explains a thing, namely, its essence. Essences are not universals that exist beyond the realm of ordinary experience. Rather, they are the common classes that disclose what things are, and they must be discovered in sense experience.

For Aristotle, philosophy was the vehicle for the transcendence of the process of change in human life, and in this he manifested his continued allegiance to Plato. However, unlike Plato, who treated poetic *mythoi* pejoratively because they distort the truth, Aristotle regarded poetry as "deriving from and satisfying the impulse to understand the world of human action by making and enjoying representations of it."[15] Aristotle's theory of mimesis in general [imitative activity] and his conception of linguistic mimesis in particular reflect his view of human beings as rational creatures who are rooted in the natural order. Thus, whereas for Plato mimesis was the attempt to mirror reality, that is, to reproduce objects as faithfully as possible, for Aristotle "mimesis reflects reality by embodying universals, but without necessarily mirroring the world accurately in all respects."[16] With a more positive view of the mimetic arts, including poetry, Aristotle minimized the conflict between *poeisis* and philosophy and understood *mythos* to mean not a fictitious fable but a "plot," or better still, a "plot-structure."[17] Accordingly, he held that

> the artist aspires to produce plot-structures, or images, or forms of some other kind, which are consistent with reality, above all with that level of reality perceived through universals, which are also the concern of the philosopher.[18]

That Aristotle viewed poetry (and *poeisis* in general) as rooted in human nature (both the human need for pleasure and the propensity to take pleasure in the products of imitative activity) reflects his broad understanding of human nature, and, in turn, of human happiness.

The Teleological Framework

Aristotle's *Nicomachean Ethics* opens with his statement, "Every art and every inquiry, and similarly every action and pursuit, is thought to aim at some good; and for this reason the good has rightly been declared to be that at which all things aim."[19] These words capture Aristotle's naturalistic, objectivist, and teleological conception of the good and of human happiness.[20] He believed that each being is so constructed in its nature (*physis*) that it acts only according to a single particular pattern. Everything naturally aims toward an end (*telos*), and that end determines the direction of the individual's development.

In common parlance, "nature" means "what there is." Empirically observed, it is the innate impulse toward movement. Aristotle's own language is more technical. In the *Physics* II:1, he distinguishes between things that "exist by nature" and things that are "not constituted by nature." "Nature" is defined as "a source or cause of being moved and of being in rest in that to which it belongs primarily, in virtue of itself and not in virtue of a concomitant attribute."[21] Aristotle equates the very power of movement with nature as form, that is to say, the mode of structure of a thing by virtue of which it "moves, grows, and alters and comes to rest when it has reached the terminus of its movement."[22] For Aristotle "the world of nature is thus a world of self-moving things. . . . It is a living world: a world characterized not by inertia . . . but by spontaneous matter."[23]

Nature as such is a process of growth and change, which Aristotle explains as the interplay of four causes: Some underlying substratum (the *material* cause) acquires a new specification or perfection (the *formal* cause) through the action of an agent (the *efficient* cause) that is moved to act by the attraction of some good (the *final* cause, or *end*). Through change, a thing acquires a higher level of perfection (*entelechia*).[24] Thus all change is a process in which a thing is transformed from potentiality to actuality through which the thing actualizes itself. The goal of self-actualization is thus intrinsic to the process, in which each thing strives toward its own perfection.

Aristotle's conception of the end (*telos*) overlaps his conception of the good. A thing reaches its natural perfection when it has all its parts, when the parts function well in their own characteristic activity (*ergon*),[25] and when the thing reaches the end of its proper development and so becomes fulfilled. To know what is the proper perfection of a given thing we need to know not only what is its *telos* but also what is its characteristic activity or function. Thus every thing (including the human) acts in order to attain a desired end. When that end is fully and most completely realized, then that given thing reaches its perfection.

Aristotle developed his conception of the good as a critique of Plato, who claimed that good things or actions are good because they partake in the Idea or Form of the Good. The Idea of the Good is to the world of particular goods as the sun is to the universe. It is both the source of all good things as well as that thing that makes it possible for us to recognize goodness in things. The self-subsistent Idea of the Good is separate from individually good things and transcends the world of change and flux.

Plato explains the relationship between goodness and human persons through an analogy with health and its relation to a body.[26] Health cannot be defined in hedonistic or utilitarian terms. Rather, it is a guide to what we shall become. Likewise the Good can neither be defined as a set of rules about what to do; nor is it to be identified with the useful or pleasant. Instead, it is an absolute standard for becoming a certain kind of person.

As Plato explains in the *Phaedros*, the soul is capable of "seeing" the absolute, eternal, ethical standards that are independent of human beings. These standards yield norms for us to live by, norms that tell us what to be. Having grasped these absolute standards through the study of philosophy, we live by them healthfully and harmoniously.

In the *Ethics* I:6 Aristotle adduces several arguments to refute Plato's theory of the Good.[27] First, the good is not a substance but a quality of a given substance in relation to another substance. Second, the good is not one but many, encompassing several categories such as quality, quantity, and relation. Third, if there were one Form of the Good in which all things partake, there would have been one science of the Good. However, there are in fact many sciences, each of which studies a distinct type of good things. For example, the science of medicine is concerned with good health and the science of military strategy studies the good in war, namely, victory. Fourth, in reality there is no entity that corresponds to the Idea of the Good that exists apart from the particulars that are good. The Idea of the Good is no more than a concept that forms in our mind, whose truth depends on something other than itself corresponding to it. Finally, Plato's Idea of the Good has little practical relevance to human life. Precisely because it is presumed to be transcendent, the Idea of the Good is unattainable and unrealizable. When a craftsman wishes to perform well in his craft he does not look for the Idea of the Good but rather for the specific circumstances of his craft. In short, what is good would vary from one set of circumstances to another in accordance with the purpose of the activity.

Aristotle claims in opposition to Plato that there are good things, good activities, and good intentions, and that goodness varies in accordance with his so-called "categories."[28] The good we are seeking is not a self-subsistent Form, antecedent to good things, but the end for the sake of which each and every act is done. The human good in action is the subject of the science of ethics, and since the good cannot be conceptualized apart from the reality of particular existents, the good is like a "moving target" in that science.²⁹ Its measure has to adapt itself continually to changing circumstances.

The measure of practical truth—the truth discovered by the practical science of ethics—is correct desire. In the sphere of human action it is the goodness of the agent that provides the measure of the good. The good person is the one who is properly trained and educated so that his good character traits lead him to perform the good act.

In the earlier books of the *Ethics*, Aristotle used the word *kalon* to refer to the desired good. As J. Owens explains, in the Greek of Aristotle's day the word *kalon* had a very broad range of meanings, encompassing not only "the morally good" but also "the physically beautiful" as well as "the right." The words "noble" or "fine" come closer to the meaning of *kalon*, capturing not only the aesthetic dimension of the term but also the moral notion that it is "the right thing to do." The right thing to do is not fixed by nature but varies from one set of circumstances to another. It is the wise man himself, who has reached the proper balance of the soul's functions, who determines what ought to be done in a given situation. Hence, in Aristotle's ethics the goodness of the agent logically and temporally precedes the goodness of the act.

The Final Good

Teleological Ethics

Aristotle's teleological ethics is both descriptive and normative. When he says that A is pursued for the sake of B, he means that B provides a norm that guides A because B is more desirable than A.³⁰ Whatever is done for the sake of something else is inferior to that for the sake of which it is done. Although Aristotle did recognize that certain goods promote each other and that there are intrinsic goods that can also function as a means for yet a higher good, in general he envisioned the sphere of human affairs (and indeed reality as a whole) as a hierarchy of interlocking means and ends.

The hierarchy of meaningfully connected ends, however, cannot go on *ad infinitum*. Aristotle argues that the chain of goods must come to an end. "If, then, there is some end of things we do, which we desire for its own sake (everything else being desired for the sake of this), and if we do not choose everything for the sake of something else (for at that rate the process would go on to infinity, so that our desire would be empty and vain), clearly this must be the good and the chief good" (I:1 1094a 18–22). Put differently, there must be one thing that we seek above all else because we seek it only for its own sake, or else there would be nothing desired for its own sake. If the chain goes on forever, then desire is empty and futile; but since nature "does nothing in vain," desire is not empty and futile and the chain must have an ultimate end.

Although Aristotle rejected, on metaphysical grounds, the possibility of an actual infinite regress of causes, in the *Ethics* he bases his argument on ordinary experience rather than metaphysics. As J. Annas has shown, the concept of a final end arises naturally from any intelligent reflection on what we normally do and the implications of human action.[31] If we stopped to reflect on our conduct, we would realize that we do certain things according to a certain priority, because we see that they contribute to a final end that is our final good. The very fact that our actions are ordered this way suggests that the teleological structure must culminate in a final end.

For something to qualify as a final good it must satisfy two formal conditions: it must be "a good without qualification" and it must possess "self-sufficiency" (*autarkeia*). Aristotle describes the first prerequisite as follows:

> Now we call that which is in itself worthy of pursuit more final than that which is worthy of pursuit for the sake of something else, and that which is never desirable for the sake of something else more final than the things that are desirable both in themselves and for the sake of other things, and therefore we call final without qualification that which is always desirable in itself and never for the sake of something else (I:7 1097a 30–34).

In other words, the hierarchy of ends must terminate in something that has three properties: a) it is desirable in itself; b) it is not desirable for the sake of something else; and c) everything else is desirable for its sake. Aristotle simply says that if there is some single end for the sake of which all others are pursued, then this will be the final good.[32]

The Ambiguity of the Final Good

Aristotle's characterization of the final good was rather ambiguous. Is the final good a member of a class of intrinsically good things that are desirable for their own sake or does the final good constitute a class all by itself in which it is the only member? The fact that Aristotle called the final good the "most complete" (*teleion*, literally: "most goal-like" or "end-like") further complicates matters.[33] It is possible to interpret the word "complete" (or "perfect" as some scholars prefer) in at least two ways. According to the first interpretation the final good is "complete" because it includes or contains all other things that are intrinsically good. This is the "inclusive" or "comprehensive" interpretation of Aristotle.[34] On this view, the final good is an aggregate of intrinsic goods that are desired for themselves, and it is "complete" because it includes all other goods. According to the second, "exclusive" interpretation, the final good is the point of termination for a hierarchically ordered series of intrinsic goods.[35] It is "complete" or "perfect" because it admits no further activity; all actions and pursuits are completed and perfected in it. The final good is therefore the dominant end that creates the internal structure of a hierarchy of intrinsic goods. All goods receive their value to the extent that they promote or contribute to the attainment of the final good.

No less ambiguous is the second formal characteristic of the final good as self-sufficiency. Aristotle defines "self-sufficient" (*autarkes*) as "that which when isolated makes life desirable and lacking in nothing" (I:7 1097a 34). The condition of self-sufficiency means that the final good for humans must be an activity that by itself and without anything else makes life worthy and complete. Those who endorse the "inclusive" interpretation understand Aristotle to mean that the final good is self-sufficient and worthy for its own sake, because it contains all goods, both those which are pursued for their own sake and those which are pursued for the sake of something else. Self-sufficiency is thus synonymous with comprehensiveness.[36] By contrast, those who hold the "exclusive" interpretation understand self-sufficiency to mean that the final good is so outstanding in excellence that nothing else can be added to it to make it better or to impact it directly. It is unique and cannot be numbered together with other goods because it is qualitatively different from them.[37] It is precisely because the final good is so outstanding in quality that it organizes all other things into a meaningful structure of subordinate ends and serves as the absolute standard by which all goods are evaluated. The full implication of the formal characteristics of the good will be clarified in the last section of this chapter.

The Meaning of "Eudaimonia"

By Aristotle's day it was already a commonplace to hold that *eudaimonia* is the name for "the highest of all goods achievable by action" (I:4 1095a 16–17). The word literally means "having a good spirit."[38] In ancient Greek usage one could have a good spirit only if one's soul was in a good condition. Thus the quality of one's soul determined the well-being of one's life as a whole.³⁹ *Eudaimonia* is commonly translated as "happiness" and I will retain this translation throughout the book. For Aristotle (as for all ancient Greek, Hellenistic, and Roman philosophers) happiness was not a temporary feeling of contentment or a psychological state of joy, but rather a stable pattern of living. *Eudaimonia* thus connotes "well-being," "flourishing," or "doing well" and it pertains to one's life as a whole over a long period of time.⁴⁰

For Aristotle to say that *eudaimonia* is the final good of human life, however, the good that all human beings seek, tells us very little. In J. Annas' words, *eudaimonia* is no more than a "thin specification" of the highest human good.⁴¹ Most people, according to Aristotle, identify *eudaimonia* with the life of pleasures that are derived from gratification of bodily desires such as eating, drinking, and sex (I:5 1095b 19–20). Although he does not reject pleasure as a component of the good life, he adamantly dismisses the notion that the life of bodily pleasures is the highest life for humans.

He goes on to say that a better sort of people equates happiness with a form of political life in which we strive for honor (I:5 1095b 24–9). However, honor depends more on the giver than on the receiver, whereas happiness must characterize the agents themselves. Since honor does not belong to the person, it cannot qualify as the final good of human life. Moreover, honor is something people aim at because it assures them of virtue. Hence, virtue and not honor is the proper end of the political life. But Aristotle argues that virtue cannot be the highest end of human life, because it is compatible with inactivity (for example, during sleep) whereas happiness must be an activity.⁴²

The final candidate for the title of *eudaimonia* is the life of contemplation. Aristotle defends this, the philosophic activity in Book X of the *Nicomachean Ethics*, as the highest end of human life.

Human Nature

Nature itself, according to Aristotle, the consummate biologist, dictates the meaning of the good life for humans. By *human nature* Aristotle understood those inescapable facts about humans that place certain constraints on the organism, determine its development, and specify its mature functioning or well-being.⁴³ Since the objective facts about the nature of the human species reveal the basic human potentialities and the limits of what humans can do and can expect of themselves, human flourishing is the full functioning of the mature member of the species. When Aristotle discusses human nature, then, he tells us not only what human beings are like but also what they *should* try to become if they are to flourish or excel as members of the human species.

To explain our nature Aristotle has to articulate a psychological theory that accounts for the relationship between the physiological, emotional, mental, and cognitive facts of the human animal. He elaborates such a theory in his *De Anima,* and his ethical theories must be interpreted in light of it.[44] In fact, the most problematic aspect of Aristotle's conception of happiness stems from the ambiguity of those pronouncements on the human intellect in the *De Anima*.[45]

Aristotle held that we are a composite of body (*soma*) and soul (*psyche*). The soul is "a substance qua form of a natural body which has life potentially" (*De Anima* 2:1 412a19–21). That is, qua form, the soul is the substance of an organic natural being.[46] Unlike Plato, who believed that forms exist independently of matter, Aristotle held that the form is the form of a particular "this" that arranges its associated particular in a certain way. As a substance the soul is an actuality or fulfillment (*entelechia*) of a certain potential. In other words, the soul is the actuality of the natural body.

Aristotle distinguishes two senses of the term "actuality." The first is a level of organization that can emerge directly in the activity. The second is an actual use or exercise of a capacity.[47] Aristotle calls the soul the first actuality of a natural body in both senses of the term—namely, as that potentiality of the body that possesses life and as its virtuous activity, i.e., its happiness or flourishing. Aristotle explains many of the functions that constitute being alive in this two-fold way. These functions include nutrition, reproduction, growth, sensation, movement, imagining, dreaming, desiring, and cognitive activities. Aristotle grouped them into three clusters, which he named as three types of souls: the nutritive soul (i.e., physical activities necessary for survival of the organism); the sensitive soul (i.e., perceptions, sensations, feelings, emotions, and desires that account for the movements of the organism); and the rational soul (i.e., cognitive activities).

Humans share a nutritive soul with plants and animals, and they share a sensitive soul with animals. However, only humans possess the capacity to reason. Other animals possess the power of perception and can recognize and remember particulars, but they lack the capacity to grasp the universal features of these particulars. Therefore, animals cannot deliberate, cannot make rational decisions, and cannot conceptualize what is good for them.[48] Reasoning, then, is the characteristic activity or function (*ergon*) of human beings that distinguishes them from all other species.

Once Aristotle identified this characteristic function, he had to conclude that human excellence is the mature functioning of the capacity to reason. The good life for humans is "a life in accordance with the rational principle." That is to say, the rational soul must rule over the irrational functions of the soul and structure all human activities in accordance with reason. To flourish we must live in accordance with the governing element within us, the element that defines our uniqueness as human beings—reason.

Put differently, the pursuit of happiness is a rational endeavor. Grounded in our nature as rational animals, the pursuit of happiness is the human striving for self-realization through the acquisition of true knowledge. Aristotle's reasoning goes like this: If nature does nothing in vain, and if we are naturally inclined toward truth, it follows that we do, for the most part, attain the truth.[49] Since to flourish as a human being consists of perfecting the characteristic function of the human species to reason, the happy or flourishing life is one in which rationality is realized in accordance with the excellences appropriate to it.

THE VIRTUES: EXCELLENCES OF CHARACTER

For Aristotle, as for all philosophers in the Greco-Roman world, the question "How ought I to live my life?" was intrinsically linked to the question "What sort of a person ought I to be?" Thus, Aristotelian ethics is concerned not simply with "How I am to conduct myself in my life? but "How am I to become the kind of person who is readily disposed so to conduct myself?" The dispositions to behave in a certain way are the virtues (*aretai*), the excellences that constitute the happy, well-functioning person. Virtue (*arête*) then is a form of human excellence, a state of character pursued for its own sake, as a constituent of one's good. Virtue is not a means for the attainment of the good, but a central element of the human good. In Aristotle's ethics of virtue, the rightness of the act is derived from its contribution to human well-being, and the primary bearers of moral epithets are character and character traits (i.e., qualities of persons). Thus, for Aristotle, the science of ethics was not viewed as a theoretical discourse about abstract, universal rules of conduct, but as a practical guide to life.

Character

Aristotle's ethics of virtue focuses on the moral quality of the agent rather than on the moral quality of the act or on the abstract, general rules that obligate the agent to act in a certain way. And at the core of this virtue-ethics stands the concept of character (*ethos*) and the life that expresses that character. Character, to use N. Sherman's succinct definition, "has to do with a person's enduring traits: attitudes, sensibilities, and beliefs—that affect how a person sees, acts, and indeed lives."[50] As noted above, Aristotle divides the soul into two parts, the rational and the irrational. Within the irrational part of the soul Aristotle distinguished between the nutritive soul, which has nothing to do with virtue, and another part that is "the seat of the appetites and of desire in general" (I:13 1102b 30). That part has both rational and irrational aspects. It is irrational to the extent that it "opposes and reacts against" the dictates of the rational element in the soul, and it is rational "insofar as it complies with reason and accepts its leadership."[51] Thus, even though the non-rational part of the soul does not engage in reasoning, it can listen to reason and can thus be controlled, persuaded, and shaped by the rational part. Accordingly, character is a quality of the non-rational part of the soul that has the capacity of following reason in accordance with a prescriptive principle.

The cultivation of character involves a long process of moral training, habituation, and practice, in which the rational aspect of the soul shapes the irrational aspect to do that which is fine and noble. Ethics is thus the science of the moral education that enables us, through deliberation and choice, to develop the psychological traits that incline or orient us toward the objective good.

The psychic power in us that orients us toward the good is called "desire" (*orexis*), which simply means wanting that which appears to us to be good. Aristotle distinguished between rational and irrational desires. The irrational ones are those that follow sensation and imagination and are closely related to the physical functions of the body.[52] The most irrational of all is appetite (*epithumia*), a biologically determined function close to the modern concept of impulse. Yet even the appetites can obey the command of reason. More removed from the physical functions of the body is "rational desire" (*boulesis*), which is concerned with intelligible objects. In between rational desires and the appetites are the passions (*pathe*), which have both rational and irrational aspects. The passions can listen to the voice of reason though they often, so to speak, miss what they hear.

The desiring part of the soul reaches its excellence if and only if it is managed by reason. In Aristotle's psychology we do not have direct control over feelings and passions. We can only control the actions that establish the dispositions that are the source of the feelings. Therefore, moral training consists of mastering the irrational aspects of the soul through habitual practice and thus attaining stable states (*hexis*). Through acquired self-control the agent learns to delay gratification and condition his feelings in such a way that he will act rightly in concrete situations. Only in the reasoned control of our passions do we find our freedom to flourish as we truly are—rather than being enslaved to the cravings of the body or the whims of the irrational soul.[53]

The reasoned control of the passions must not be understood as a recommendation to suppress feelings and emotions, which, in fact, Aristotle recognized for their value in the formation of the good character.[54] Even though emotions and feelings by themselves cannot lead us to act in the right way, they do not blind us; they do help us to "see" the morally salient features of a given situation, and should be transformed or converted under the guidance of reason. If properly cultivated, the emotions can enhance our moral perception and benefit the formation of character. L.A. Kosman summarizes this point by saying that "Aristotle's moral theory is not only a theory of how to act well but also how to feel well. The art of proper living includes the art of feeling well as the correlative discipline to the art of acting well."[55]

The cultivation of character—the melding systematically of the elaborate set of psychological traits—is a rational process. To acquire the virtues, the dispositions to act rightly, one must act knowingly; one must choose virtuous acts for their own sake, namely, find the actions themselves valuable. Repeated choices and the development of habits of choice add to the consistency and rationality of one's conduct and to the stability of one's character. The virtuous agent is reliable precisely because his conduct flows from fixed character traits that manifest a degree of personal maturity and integrity.

The formation of character must start at an early age and is essential to a good upbringing. The moral beginner first imitates or impersonates the mature virtuous person by following examples and taking advice. Through repeated acts of choice the moral trainee develops those dispositions that enable him to immediately grasp the moral significance of a given situation, act appropriately, and take pleasure in so doing. Habituation is not a mindless drill of prescribed actions, but a cognitive shaping of desire through perception, belief, and intention.[56] Once the virtues are acquired, the agent is naturally repelled by wrongdoing. The virtues are, therefore, not the opposites of vices, but are rather the way to avoid the vices that are themselves the opposites of virtues.[57]

Aristotle compares the acquisition of virtues to learning an expertise or a skill.[58] Like skill, virtue requires experience, practice, and a certain level of understanding. Yet virtue is not itself a skill, because skill is concerned with *making* things (*poeisis*) whereas virtue (or excellence) is concerned with *doing* or action (*praxis*).⁵⁹ In the case of skills, the products have their goodness in themselves, so that it is enough that they be of a certain character. The skilled person does not have to possess the goodness of the thing. Occasionally it happens that even a poorly trained person makes a good product. But in the case of virtue, more is required to make the products, i.e., actions, good. To do a virtuous act the agent himself must be virtuous. He must possess well-entrenched traits of character and exercise them at that time. Virtue is more accurate than skill and its intellectual aspect is more developed. The virtuous person cannot become so without being critically reflective about his actions.

In short, to acquire a virtue one must have knowledge of the aim of each act; one must consciously choose to do the act; and one must choose to do the act for its own sake. Through knowledge of ends, exercise of self-control, rational deliberation, and habitual practice of good deeds, the agent acquires the virtues. The good person is the kind of person for whom proper conduct emanates characteristically from a fixed disposition, and the good life is a life of activity in which such dispositions are realized and not simply possessed by persons of worth. The virtuous person acts rightly out of character, because the virtues are like second nature to him or her.

Because character emerges through years of moral training and experience, it cannot be divorced from the socio-cultural context in which the agent is situated. The judgments that go into the training of character thus connect a network of perceptions, reasoning, values, beliefs, choices, desires, emotions, feelings, capacities, sensitivities, and actions.⁶⁰ Contemporary moral philosophers such as Stanley Hauerwas and Alasdair MacIntyre, who hold that the emergence of character is possible only within a certain moral tradition, build on an Aristotelian insight even though they develop it in a different context and with a different intent.⁶¹ The full significance of this point to the discourse on happiness in medieval Jewish philosophy will be appreciated later on when we explore the conversation between the Aristotelian and Jewish conceptions of the good life.

The Doctrine of the Mean

The thrust of Aristotle's *eudaimonian* ethics is to develop the moral personality that lives intelligently by curbing desires and practicing virtuous acts governed by a worthwhile end. The good character is fashioned through the rational cultivation of moral virtues by practical reason, which will be discussed below. The moral virtues emerge from the grasp of the mean, the intermediate, "just-right" point between two extremes—one an excess and the other a defect—and the application of the mean to concrete situations.[62] The perfectly virtuous man is the one who not only exhibits the mean in his acts, but who has internalized or incorporated the mean into his character so that it takes hold of his feelings.

The doctrine of the mean is part of the definition of the excellence of character (*ethike arete*). As Urmson explains, the doctrine of the mean is not a doctrine of moderation that tells where the mean lies.[63] Aristotle is not interested in a mathematically fixed point that lies between extremes. He also does not say that for every emotion the right amount of is always the moderate amount. Instead he holds that virtue

> . . . is a state concerned with choice, lying in the mean relative to us, this being determined by a rational principle, and by that principle by which the man of practical reason would determine it (II: 6 1107a 1–3).

The mean is about having the right feeling toward the right object, at the right time, for the right reasons, under the right circumstances, and acting accordingly. The fact that the mean is relative to us and to be determined by the wise man distinguishes excellence of character from other settled states. For example, if one is generous one has a settled disposition to enjoy acting generously. Yet what constitutes generosity varies from one situation to another and depends on a full appreciation of all the factors involved in light of knowledge of general principles. That type of knowledge is provided by the faculty of practical reason, to which we shall soon turn. The mean links desire, emotions, and actions. An action manifests some emotion such as anger, fear, confidence, envy, joy, longing, and pity, and involves pleasures and pain (likes and dislikes) (II: 4 1105b 21). For each excellence of character there will be a specific emotion; the emotion to be exhibited in "just right" amount.

Aristotle inherited from Plato the formulation of four cardinal virtues that were recognized in his day: wisdom, courage, temperance, and justice.[64] Plato, however, interpreted these virtues very widely so that they nearly overlapped, and his analysis of wisdom and justice tended to identify these two virtues with virtue as a whole. Aristotle moved beyond Plato to speak of twelve virtues, but his list is neither exhaustive nor logically ordered. Its gist, however, is quite clear: each virtue is the mean with regard to excess and defect of feelings and actions.

The details and critique of Aristotle's list of moral virtues need not concern us here.⁶⁵ All we need to establish is that moral virtues arise from the control of desire by the practical intellect. Only the one who has acquired the excellence of the practical intellect can discern the mean between excesses and defects.

Practical Reasoning

To be virtuous, Aristotle believed, as did all ancient moral philosophers, that one has to have *phronesis*, practical wisdom, or prudence (VI:13 1144b 17–1145a6; X:8 1178a 16–19).⁶⁶ *Phronesis* is an intellectual virtue, the perfection or excellence of practical reason (*praktikos logos*). The practical intellect is the calculative or logistical aspect of the human intellect. It is concerned with guiding action with respect to things that can be otherwise than they are.

Practical intellect is distinguished from theoretical intellect (*theoretikos logos*), the epistemic faculty that is concerned with knowing the truth about what cannot be otherwise than it is. The perfection or excellence of theoretical reason is wisdom (*sophia*)—the philosophic activity of contemplating necessary, universal, and eternal objects. Practical wisdom and theoretical wisdom constitute two of the five intellectual virtues that Aristotle regards as superior in value to the twelve moral virtues outlined above. Since theoretical wisdom is not directly involved in the formation of character, Aristotle postpones its analysis to the last book of the *Ethics*, where he equates it with the final good of human life.

Practical reasoning is a cognitive activity that combines universal and particular aspects. The universal aspect of practical wisdom is knowledge of the good life in general, namely, what is good for a human being in general, unconditionally, qua human being (VI:5 1140a 25–31). The particular aspect of practical reasoning is the ability to recognize how particular circumstances fall under general categories (VI:7 1141b15; VI:8 1142a14; 20–22; VI:11 1143a29; 32–34). To make intelligent decisions the man of practical wisdom (*phronimos*) must rely on general principles, but he must also always be sensitive to the complexities of particular situations. So the man of practical wisdom perceives what virtue requires of him in a particular case and instructs him to act accordingly.

The aspect of the practical intellect that enables the agent to hit the proper mean in action and feeling is *orthos logos*, i.e., right reason. *Orthos logos* remains close to particulars and enables the agent to improvise ends on the basis of past experience and the specific features of a given situation.[67] It is this ability to recognize how general ends of good living are manifested in particular situations that makes practical wisdom analogous to perception and has led some scholars to understand *phronesis* as moral insight. Indeed, practical reasoning is like the "the eye of the soul," with which the virtuous person "sees" what are the morally salient features of the given situation and what should be done in order to promote the good life. The moral insight of the practically wise, however, does not mean an intuition or a feeling about what needs to be done. Rather, it means a discernment of the morally relevant facts in view of the good for humans. Practical wisdom thus specifies or concretizes the components of human flourishing and guides the agent toward particular actions that secure the good life. Ideally, practical reasoning and virtue work in tandem: virtue provides the emotional basis for adopting an end, and practical reason both conceptualizes and determines the action that will satisfy the good end (VI:13 1145a 5–6).

The primary activity of practical reason is directed towards things that can come to be through our actions. Aristotle teaches that we do not deliberate about those things that we know completely, such as first principles of a science or the ends of a given enterprise or profession. Nor do we deliberate about those things that we can wholly predict, such as truths of mathematics or of nature, because they are necessary and eternal. Rather, we deliberate about things "in relation to ends," namely, about those things that we need to do in order to promote certain ends (III: 2 1111b 20–33; III:1 1112a 30–b8; III: 3 1112b 15 ff; III: 3 1113a 9–11).

The deliberation of practical reason culminates in a reasoned choice (*prohairesis*), a decision to do virtuous deeds for their own sake. Through choice the rational soul is realized and the non-rational part of the soul is brought into harmony with and under the control of the rational part. The practically wise person chooses the act both as an instance of a certain virtue and for the sake of being virtuous. Aristotle's notion of rational choice must be understood in the context of his distinction between voluntary and involuntary acts.[68] The criterion of the voluntary is that the source of the action is to be found in the agent himself and not wholly in things that are external to him. Hence, Aristotle defines the voluntary act as "that of which the moving principle is in the agent himself, he being aware of the particular circumstances of the action" (III:1 1111a 23). Conversely, acts are involuntary if they are brought about through external force or through ignorance.

All voluntary acts are chosen (III:3 1112a 14–15), because it is "the thing men have done from reason" (and so from choice) that is thought most properly their own and voluntary (IX:8 1168b 35). As A. W. Price put it, "the chosen is the paradigm of the voluntary."[69] Choice is a matter of desiring to do what deliberation has shown to be conducive to our goal. Thus, deliberation shapes choice. A good choice is one that is based on a proper understanding of the end of human life, i.e., happiness, and the way in which a particular state of affairs promotes the ultimate end.

The cultivation of the habit of choice requires experience over time. Experience helps the practically wise to "see" or recognize the relevant features of a given situation and to decide on the best action in light of general principles. On the basis of experience, which includes both deliberation and emotional sensitivity, the man of practical wisdom can also learn to revise ends relative to other desired ends and to tailor ends through action. Thus, the end that sets a deliberative process in action may itself be considerably transformed by the process of deliberation that adapts to changing circumstances. The practically wise man, therefore, must be immersed in the everyday life of his community. Both the formation of good character and the exercise of virtue require of him to be deeply involved and interacting with other people.

The primacy of practical reasoning in the formation of character entails that one cannot be wise without being good, and, vice versa, to be morally good one must be practically wise. Moreover, the operation of practical wisdom in virtuous activity suggests that all the virtues are structurally similar and that they must be consistent and reciprocal (VI: 13 1144b30–1145a 2).[70] If an individual genuinely has one virtue constitutive of goodness, then he has them all. The agent must have a correct grasp of and the right attitude towards every act in life in light of what is the best life for human beings. Each virtue contributes to the quality of one's character and to the overall good of the agent. Making right judgments and decisions in an ever more unified and coherent way both presupposes and encourages development of the appropriate feelings and emotions. In the ethically virtuous man, the man of practical wisdom, the reflection of the good life as a whole adds up to a unified picture of the best life. The practically wise aims at an overall end—a good to be achieved in life as a whole. He makes long-term plans and decisions about the quality of his life as a whole and takes specific actions to realize that life plan. In this way the virtuous man of practical wisdom lives a happy life.

Virtue and Pleasure

Learning to be virtuous is learning to take pleasure in virtuous activities.[71] Aristotle rejected the thesis that pleasure is in itself bad and that it is a hindrance to the good life.[72] Instead, he held that the good person must take pleasure in acting well and the good life must be, at least to some extent, pleasant. Pleasure points the agent in the right direction because pleasure proper to the activity encourages the performance of the activity. Since pleasure perfects the activity, the moral worth of pleasure is dependent on the activity. For Aristotle there are objectively good and bad pleasures.

It is right for the good man to seek pleasure: It augments the activity in that people who engage in the activity with pleasure are more exact and discriminating (X: 5 1175a 30–b1). Moreover, the stronger the pleasure, the more it prevents people from attending to other activities (X:5 1175b1–13) and the longer and better the activity goes on (X:5 1175b 14–16). Yet one must distinguish between real pleasures and apparent ones. Pleasure reflects the perfection of the desired object and the excellence of the operating faculty. When a perfect faculty is operating on a perfect object, there is the highest pleasure. Pleasure can indeed occur in less perfect conditions, but the degree of enjoyment is a function of the degree of excellence of actualization, which, in turn, is a function of the degree of excellence of faculty and object. If neither of the latter has any excellence, then there is no pleasure. Thus, one can distinguish between good and bad pleasures. Furthermore, the very existence of a desire for a bad pleasure indicates a sickness or deformity of the desiring soul.

The connection between virtue and pleasure is best understood through the classification of various moral types. At the top of the scale of excellence is the ethically virtuous person who has acquired the moral and intellectual virtues through habituation and practice. He consciously chooses to do what is virtuous for its own sake, namely, because it is fine or noble. This virtuous man has acquired the virtue of temperance (*sophrosune*). Therefore, his thoughts and feelings work together in harmony: he feels in ways appropriate to circumstances and immediately "sees" what he should do in order to act rightly. His actions are in the mean, because they naturally flow from his emotions that are also in the mean. Therefore, the virtuous person experiences no internal struggle, friction, or distress. He likes the acts that he performs for their own sake and takes pleasure in doing them.

This temperate man of practical reason does have passions, but he has them in the mean and he performs right actions in their regard. He does not desire sensual pleasure more than he ought to, and such desires are not manifested at the wrong time or when they are "contrary to what is noble or beyond his means" (III: 11 1119a 14–18). He does not have to use knowledge in order to resist the lure of pleasures, because his pleasures coordinate with his knowledge; acting from knowledge is pleasurable to him (VII:1 1145b 13–14). He will not be attracted to the type of pleasure enjoyed by a child or by a beast, but will naturally seek those that come from higher activities of the soul such as learning and thinking. He thus takes pleasure in activities that are intrinsically good, and finds the wicked man's pursuits not merely wrong but repulsive.

The second best person is the self-controlled, or continent person (*enkrates*). This person wants to act badly but makes himself act as the good man does. In terms of actual conduct there is no difference between the virtuous man and the continent man,

> for both the continent man and the temperate man are such as to do nothing contrary to the rule for the sake of the bodily pleasures, but the former has and the latter has not bad appetites, and the latter is such as not to feel pleasure contrary to the rule, while the former is such as to feel pleasure but not to be led by it (VII: 9 1151b 34–1152a 3).

However, internally the two types of agent differ greatly. The self-controlled man experiences inner conflict and anguish because he acts contrary to his emotions. The internal struggle indicates that the self-controlled man has not yet acquired the virtues as stable, well-entrenched states of character.

Less virtuous than the self-controlled man is the incontinent man (*akrates*). He lacks self-control.[73] He knows the right thing to do and tries to act properly, but cannot because of a perceptual failure. He fails to see how a given situation falls under the description of what is good (VII: 7 1150b 19). Or, if he does think about what he is doing, the uncontrolled man does not see the particular case properly; he misperceives the morally salient points, either because he fails to see how the specific situation fits the general principles, of which he is aware, or he fails to draw the right conclusions. The incontinent man goes wrong in matters that concern pleasure because he acts impulsively. As a result, the conduct of the *akrates* is very similar to that of the self-indulgent man (*akolastos)*, who allows the appetites and the passions to govern his life. As Aristotle put it: "And the incontinent and the self-indulgent man are also like one another; they are different, but both pursue bodily pleasures—the latter, however, also thinking that he ought to do so, while the former does not think this" (VII:9 1152a4–6).

"The self-indulgent man"(*akolastos*) differs from the uncontrolled man in that the former has no regrets and stands by his choice, where as the incontinent (*akrates)* man is subject to regrets (VII:8 1150 b 29–31). In general the presence of regret indicates a poor moral quality. "If a man cannot at the same time be pained and pleased, at all events after a short time he is pained because he was pleased; and he could have wished that these things had not been pleasant to him; for bad men are full of regrets" (IX:4 1166b 22–5). He would have wished that these things had not been pleasant to him (IX:4 1166b 23–4). However, since the acts of the incontinent man emerge from within the agent, they are still classified as voluntary and punishable.

At the bottom of the hierarchy of moral types is the vicious man (*kakos*). He is ignorant of the general principle of the good for humans. He does have ends but they are mistaken ones; they do not accord with human nature. The vicious man also has the intellectual capacity to revise his ends, though he rarely does so. He follows those aspects that humans share with animals rather than the functions that are characteristically human. The extreme cases of brutishness can hardly be considered human. The brutish man hardly knows what he is doing and can barely be held responsible for his actions.

Aristotle's hierarchy of moral agents indicates that the good life must contain pleasures, but that it is very important to be correct about the nature of pleasurable activities. The virtues themselves ensure that the right kind of pleasure is enjoyed for the right reason, at the right time, in the right way. Because Aristotle held an objectivist conception of the good, he also subscribed to an objectivist conception of pleasure. Only appropriate pleasures lead in the right direction, namely, towards human happiness or well-being.

Aristotle's attitude toward pleasure explains why he thought that the good life must include some external goods, such as a modicum of wealth, good health, a family, good fortune, and above all friends. Whether these factors are constituent ingredients of happiness or only its necessary conditions is a matter of dispute, to be discussed below. For now suffice it to say that for Aristotle the good life cannot be a solitary life. His analysis of friendship in Books VIII and IX and in parts of Book X highlights the social aspect of his notion of happiness. The very fact we are social animals dictates that we need other people not only for survival but also in order to cultivate the virtues and live the good life. And friendship (*philia*) is the highest context in which virtues are cultivated and exercised.

HAPPINESS AND FRIENDSHIP

The teleological assumptions that guide Aristotle's philosophy are manifested in his theory of friendship.[74] Like Plato, Aristotle assumed that nothing can be loved or desired unless it appears to us as a good. Thus to love something does not mean to bestow a special value on the desired object, but to be attracted to the object because its goodness elicits our love or desire, whether the goodness of the object is real or apparent and whether the object is desired for its own sake or for the sake of something else.[75] The perceived quality of the object itself is the source of our desire or love.

Types of Friendship

In Aristotle's day the concept of friendship was used very broadly to apply not only to relations within the family but also to all sorts of civic contacts. Different contexts and circumstances give rise to different forms of friendship. Aristotle distinguished between three types: friendship of utility, friendship of pleasure, and friendship of goodness. He says:

> Therefore those who love for the sake of utility love for the sake of what is good *for themselves*, and those who love for the sake of pleasure do so for the sake of what is pleasant *to themselves*, and not insofar as the other is the person loved but insofar as he is useful or pleasant. And thus these friendships are only incidental; for it is not as being the man he is that the loved person is loved, but as providing some good or pleasure (VIII:3 1156a 14–19).

Whereas the other two forms of friendship are derivative and secondary, friendship among "good men qua good" is friendship "firstly and in the proper sense" (VIII:4 1157a 30–1). Aristotle defines the highest form of friendship as follows:

> Perfect [*teleios*] friendship is the friendship of men who are good, and alike in virtue; for these wish well alike to each other *qua* good, and they are good in themselves. Now those who wish well to their friends for their sake are most truly friends; for they do this by reason of their own nature, and not incidentally; therefore their friendship lasts as long as they are good—and goodness is an enduring thing (VIII:3 1156b 7–11).

Perfect friendship then exists only among good men, because they are interested in one another as persons rather than as instrumentalities for something else (advantage or pleasure).

In IX:4 Aristotle lists five marks of friendship exhibited in the relationships between virtuous men. A friend is taken to be (1) someone who wishes and does good or apparent goods to his friend for the friend's own sake; (2) one who wishes the friend to be and to live for the friend's own sake; (3) one who spends his time with his friend, and (4) one who makes the same choices or (5) shares his friend's distress and enjoyment.

Virtuous friends enable us to be the best we can be in our moral activities. Such friendship is characterized by trust (VIII:3 1156b 28–9). Virtuous friends help each other develop in character (IX:9 1170a 11–12). They correct each other (IX:12 1172a 12) and confer in difficult situations (III:3 1112b 10–11). The virtuous friend offers valuable advice and in many other ways helps one develop character and improve moral skill (VIII:1 1155a 14–16; IX:12 1172a 10–12). The good person profits by having friends because they make his virtuous activities more continuous (IX: 9 1170a 4–8), and he learns from them.

Virtuous friendship differs from the other two types of friendship in the following ways: First, virtuous friends are friends without qualification. "Those who wish well to their friends for their sake are especially friends" (VIII:3 1156b 9–10). Each person is a friend to the other because of that person's intrinsic goodness. Second, virtuous friendship is not self-interested. In derivative forms of friendship there is a mixture of self-seeking and non-self-interested well-wishing and well-doing. Within virtuous friendship the friends are linked directly by the relation of loving for its own sake. In the other forms of friendship the same relation links the parties, but only indirectly. Third, virtuous friendship is enduring because it involves both absolutes and relative goodness and pleasantness. In contrast, friendships of pleasure and utility are transient because they depend on changing circumstances (VIII: 3 1156a 19–21; VIII:4 1157a 14–15; VIII:6 1158b 9–10). Fourth, virtuous friendship alone is immune to slander (VII:4 1157a 20–2), because it requires long familiarity. In contrast, the other two types of friendship can easily dissolve under the pressure of slander, because they are based on superficial familiarity. Fifth, virtuous friends usually live together sharing the virtuous activities that enhance their good character. Useful friends and pleasant friends do not find a need to share their life with each other beyond the immediate reason for their association.

Virtuous friendship is a matter of a deliberate rational choice. Aristotle states: "mutual love involves choice and choice springs from a state of character; and men wish well to those whom they love for their own sake, not as a result of feeling, but as a result of a state of character" (VIII: 5 1157 b

30–32). When good men discern the moral virtue in one another, they naturally decide to be friends. They delight in each other's character, admire one another's goodness, and they mutually benefit from overlapping interests.

Friends promote each another's virtue in several ways. Each is for the other an object on which to practice virtuous actions (IX:9 1169b 10–13). Consequently, they provide one another with virtuous actions to contemplate a model for self-comparison. Pursuing activities in company with those who share one's ends is pleasanter than doing so alone and increases one's ability to keep them up (IX:9 1170a 5–8). Friends engage together in those activities "for since they wish to live with their friends, they do and share in those things that give them the sense of living together" (IX: 12 1172 a 5–7). By doing so they become better. Since virtue is produced by training under the influence of those who possess practical wisdom, friendship is the setting in which good dispositions are formed and maintained by continuous activity.

Virtuous friends naturally seek to live together (though not necessarily in the same household) because they take delight in each other's company. Virtuous friends agree about the meaning of the good life and have a commitment to pursue the noble ends, though they need not agree about the specific ways of achieving it. Over a long period of time their lives become intertwined in a coherent pattern of good living. Ideally virtuous friends live in a small society of their choosing where they function as partners in virtue. The good and happy life is a shared life.

The Friend as Another Self

Aristotle's analysis of friendship points out an intrinsic linking of virtue, knowledge, and love. Through shared living, virtuous friends contribute to each other's self-understanding. When we choose a person as a friend we do so on the basis of his and our own firm and stable character. Since our choice of a friend manifests our character, in selecting a friend we select "another self" (*allos autos* or *heteros autos*) (IX:4 1166a32; IX:9 1170b 6–7). In Aristotle's words: "as a man is to himself, so he is to his friend" (IX:12 1171b 33–4). The friend becomes "another self" to us when we wish him to enjoy every kind of good we value for ourselves.[76] In this regard virtuous friends become "a single soul" (IX:8 1168b7).

In loving and valuing the other person for his own sake one becomes able to love and value oneself. A.W. Price explains that this notion of the friend as a mirror of the self stems from Aristotle's theory of perception,[77] according to which the eye takes on whatever form is needed for a man to see color. In perception we become transparent to what we are perceiving, so that perceiving it and perceiving ourselves are the same mental acts. It is a way of being aware of oneself even though there is no self-consciousness.[78] And it is in order to achieve the latter that one's fellows are so valuable, since "to perceive a friend must be in a way to perceive oneself." When we join our projects with a friend we become conscious of his pursuing them and in turn we become conscious of a new way of pursuing them ourselves. Friendship is thus the context in which we become explicitly aware of ourselves not just abstractly as an agent, but as an agent with a certain character. In this way we achieve real self-knowledge, and to retain that knowledge we need to retain our friends. We will come back to these ideas about friendship when we discuss the ethos of the rabbinic academy.

TWO IDEALS OF HAPPINESS

Social Activity Or Contemplation?

Aristotle's discourse on friendship focuses our attention on the inherent ambiguity of his conception of happiness. If friendship is only a means to the supreme good, then human happiness *per se* does not consist of interacting with other people in the ideal way. Friendship may in some way contribute to human happiness, but no more than other external goods, such as health, strength, good fortune, and wealth. If friendship is a constituent ingredient of happiness, then human happiness is a composite good which contains all those goods that are desired for their own sake. However, in Book X chapters 7 and 8, Aristotle appears to have made an about-face. After convincing us that the happy life consists of virtuous activity in the social sphere, he endorses the life of contemplation as the best life for humans. All other activities, including the attainment of moral virtues, must be subordinate to it. So, which is the best life for man, the moral life of virtue and friendship or the theoretical life of contemplation? Did Aristotle plainly contradict himself or is there a way of interpreting him that will reduce the apparent inconsistencies? Let us look more closely at Aristotle's portrayal of contemplation as the best form of life, since it will be central to the debate about happiness.

In Book X: 7–8 Aristotle equates *eudaimonia* with the activity of contemplation (*theoria*) and relegates the life of ethical virtue and practical reasoning to a mere second best. Contemplation is the activity of the best part of the soul, the theoretical reason (*logos theoretikos*); it is directed to the best objects that are necessary and eternal; it is the most continuous activity in which humans can engage over a long period of time; it is the most pleasant because it perfects the most noble part in us; it is self-sufficient, for nothing can be added to it to make it better; it is leisurely, because it is done for its own sake, aiming at no end beyond itself; and it is the one activity that makes human beings become most like gods, thereby transcending the limits of human nature. Therefore Aristotle encourages us to make ourselves immortal by cultivating that which is divine in us:

> But we must not follow those who advise us, being men, to think of human things, and, being mortal, of mortal things, but must, so far as we can, make ourselves immortal, and strain every nerve to live in accordance with the best thing in us; for even if it be small in bulk, much more does it in power and worth surpass everything (X:7 1177 b 31–1178b 1).

Wisdom (*sophia*) is the excellence or perfection of the theoretical intellect. It encompasses knowledge of things that are necessary, unchanging, eternal, self-contained, and noble. In contrast to the practical wisdom (*phronesis*) that pertains to practical matters, theoretical wisdom is metaphysical. It is the knowledge of first principles, of fundamental truths about reality. But how can knowledge of theoretical truths enable humans to become like the gods or God? To answer this question we turn once more to the theory of knowledge developed in the *De Anima*.

According to Aristotle, when we think about something our mind possesses the objects about which it thinks. Thinking is indeed very much like sensing (*De Anima* II:4) and in particular like seeing (*De Anima* III:5). Like perception, thinking involves a passive part of the intellect capable of receiving a form without being subject to any change. The intellect is capable of receiving all forms (as intelligible universals) because it does not have a form of its own and because it is unmixed with the soul's functions. Similarly, the intellect cannot be intermingled with the body, or else it would be affected by the various qualities of the body. And because the intellect is unmixed with the body, it must be simple and separable from the body.

Aristotle recognized passive and active aspects of the human intellect. The active aspect is analogous to light. As light "makes potential color into actual colors" so does the active intellect make it possible for a human to grasp intelligibles. In this sense the active intellect is the efficient cause of cognition in two respects: because it "illumines" the objects making them accessible to the intellect, and because the agent intellect prepares the material intellect for the reception of intelligible forms. It is especially in the latter sense that the active intellect is regarded as "separable, impassible, unmixed," because activity is its nature.

In the final passage of this difficult chapter in the *De Anima,* Aristotle further distinguishes between knowledge in general and the knowledge of individual persons. Whereas knowledge in general, or wisdom, is eternal and unchanged, knowledge possessed by the individual is temporal, proceeding sequentially from potentiality to actuality. However, since Aristotle also holds that the agent intellect of individuals is "separable, impassible, and unmixed" (*De Anima* III:5 430a 17) he appears to suggest that the human intellect of individuals is "immortal and eternal." What exactly Aristotle had in mind became the center of heated academic controversies during the Middle Ages and the Renaissance, as we shall see in later chapters. At this point we need to explain the connection between contemplation and the imitation of God.

In Book VI chapter 7 Aristotle described Anaxagoras, Thales, and other wise men as those who contemplate things that are "excellent, admirable, difficult, and divine, but useless; viz. because it is not human good that they seek" (1141b 4–8). The word "divine" is the crucial one in this sentence. Aristotle maintains that knowledge is divine only under two conditions. First, it must deal with things divine, and second, it must be worthy of God's possession.

The knowledge necessary for human happiness is knowledge of divine reality, which is indeed the subject matter of metaphysics, or first philosophy. By virtue of philosophical knowledge, or wisdom, humans may be called divine because they become like God. By extension, everything associated with this knowledge—the understanding that nurtures it, the life that it controls, the happiness it inspires, and even the man who devotes himself to it—may share the same epithet, "divine." Aristotle then says that the human capacity to cognize eternal truths enables the wise man (*sophos*) to be like the gods, that is, transcend the natural order and participate in the divine order.

We must keep in mind that Aristotle's conception of God is very different from the conceptions of monotheistic religions. For Aristotle the divine order was the eternal support system of the universe; without it the universe would not exist. Aristotle's God is an impersonal thought in pure actuality; it thinks itself in eternal self-contemplation (*Metaphysics,* Book 12). As a perfect thought, God alone is truly self-sufficient, requiring no interaction with anything outside itself. Because God is perfect, God desires nothing; God has no intentionality, and God has no knowledge of extra-divine reality. Indeed, God is the First Cause of the universe, and as such is the terminus of the chain of causes. God's relationship to the universe is a passive one; as the most perfect being, God is the object of thought and desire. God is a Prime Mover because by being loved God causes change (*Met.* XII: 7 1072 a 26). The goodness of the Prime Mover's life lies in the possession of the formal characteristics of the good, especially self-sufficiency. By saying that the Prime Mover is an object of desire and love, Aristotle ensures that the Prime mover can cause motion without itself being in motion. So all things in some way are oriented toward God, but God's relationship to a thing is not personal, because Aristotle's God is not a person. Herein lies the substantive difference between the Jewish and Greek views of happiness emerging in this book. As Jonathan Lear put it, "God is a principle of heaven and nature: Aristotle calls him a way of life. And it is a way of life that is 'such as the best which we enjoy,' though because of our natures we can only live it for short period of time.[79]

Thus the unqualified endorsement of contemplation as the best life for human beings raises serious problems. First, it appears to negate Aristotle's own understanding of the human species. If happiness is predicated on the actualization of that which is divine in us, then one becomes most human by virtue of realizing that which is not human in us. Second, Aristotle was seeking an absolute standard that qualifies for the well-being of the human species as a whole, but the philosophical life is realizable only by a tiny number of people. Not all people are capable of philosophizing, and of those who are, only a small number possess the material conditions necessary for the cultivation of reason. Therefore, contemplation cannot be posited as the natural perfection of the human species. Third, contemplation is said to be best because it is self-sufficient and long lasting. However, contemplation requires in fact solitude and disengagement from daily human affairs. Aristotle himself insists on our social nature. Hence the life of contemplation conflicts with the natural human need for social interaction. Fourth, by equating man with the immaterial, separable active intellect, Aristotle comes full circle to hold a Platonic position in accordance with which the intellect is an incorporeal form *in* the body rather than the organizational principle *of* the psycho-physical composite.

The Ambiguity of Happiness

So what was Aristotle's conception of happiness? Contemporary Aristotelian scholarship is divided into two interpretative approaches. One endorses the "inclusive" interpretation and the other advances the "exclusive," or "dominant" interpretation. I have already introduced these two interpretations when discussing the formal conditions of the final good.

The bone of contention between the two interpretations focuses on the following questions: Does happiness consists of a single good that serves as a dominant end, or does it consist of all goods? Can happiness be improved by adding to it or is it a unique kind of activity to which nothing can be added? What are the most important facts about our species that dictate the nature of happiness? Did Aristotle speak about the good life or about the best life? Glossing over the nuanced differences among the various interpreters of Aristotle, I will sketch the major features of each of these interpretations without passing judgment about their correctness.

The Inclusive Interpretation

The proponents of the "inclusive" interpretations include, among others, J. Ackrill, W. F. R. Hardie,[80] J. Cooper, T. Irwin, K. Wilkes, R. Sorabji, L. A. Kosman, N. Sherman, J. Annas, J. Kekes,[81] and S. A. White.[82] They hold that Aristotle was fully cognizant of the difficulties of locating happiness in contemplation of the eternal. Even though he regarded it as the highest virtue, he did not propose it as the best life for man. Contemplative life is beyond the reach of most people, and beyond more than occasional reach even for those who are capable of it. Moreover, Aristotle regarded human beings as social animals who require association with other persons not only for physical survival but also for faring well. The "inclusive" interpretation emphasizes that happiness must be an "activity of the complete life in accordance with complete virtue." It cannot consist in just one activity—contemplation—but must include all excellences, both practical and theoretical. Thus happiness is the most worthy good because of its all-inclusive structure. All intrinsic goods are included within it, so that there is no way to make it more desirable by adding something else to it.

Aristotle's major insight, according to this interpretation, was that the happiest life consists of just and decent living in a political sphere. Good actions spring from and appeal to good states of character, and they are good because they are a healthy and balanced condition of being human. The happy, well-functioning person is the well-rounded one who cultivates a wide range of virtues, including generosity, temperance, and courage as well as the more down-to-earth qualities of wit, humor, and conviviality. The life that cultivates these excellences, jointly with other human virtues, is the happiest life. The happy man who lives well and flourishes (I: 8 1098b 21) is not only the one who possesses ethical and intellectual virtues, but the one who expresses his balanced character in action toward other persons (I:8 1099a 1–6). The happy man will occasionally engage in contemplation, but even contemplation, which is truly the most noble activity for us, is better done if pursued in concert with the other virtues (X:7 1177b). The theoretical activity of contemplation will enhance and perfect the sort of happiness and pleasures of which the happy are capable, but it will not be in itself at the core of human happiness.

No single good alone can constitute happiness, since none is entirely perfect or complete (*teleion*) in itself and each is sought beyond its own intrinsic value for the sake of happiness. Neither is any one good self-sufficient (*autarkes*), for the realization of virtues presupposes some good fortune no less than good fortune presupposes virtue, since the two are mutually dependent. Only a combination of all of these otherwise distinct goods can be something complete (*teleion*) and self-sufficient. The composite is complete when it is chosen for its own sake, when it consists of organized patterns of preferences and pursuits that make up the virtuous life, and when it includes the necessary essential goods, chosen for their own sakes. The composite is self-sufficient when it is a way of life that is entirely worthy, when it meets basic needs, and when goals central to life can be pursued.

The good and happy life is a shared life precisely because we are not gods and we are not self-sufficient. The self-sufficiency of the human good is characterized not by a solitary existence but by life lived in social relations with others. The worthy life, the life that is lived for its own sake and is lacking in nothing, is the life of action and a form of contemplation that includes friendship with other virtuous persons. That life must include the leisure for contemplation, but contemplative activity neither supplants nor takes precedence over the more worldly virtues. Contemplation must be conjoined with the other virtues in a life that remains political and communal. Hence, human happiness cannot be attained without attention to the political institutions that govern our social life. Therefore, the science of ethics is an integral part of political science.

On this reading, Aristotle's conception of happiness is indeed a critique of Plato's. Aristotle recommends that we renounce the pursuit of the perfect Good because it is beyond our human reach. Instead, we should look for something good that lies within our reach, something that we can share in as human beings. The proponents of the inclusive interpretation admit that Aristotle labeled the mixed life of moral and philosophical excellences as "secondary" in value to the pure life of *theoria*, but it is the only life possible for us, given the limits of human nature.

The Exclusive Interpretation

In contrast, several contemporary scholars, among them A. Kenny,[83] R. Kraut, T. Nagel, and R. Heinaman,[84] interpret Aristotle "exclusively." The best life for humans consists of one type of activity: the exercise of the theoretical part of reason. Every other good is desirable to the extent that it contributes to this activity. The life of moral action in the political sphere is the second best life. The philosophic life and the moral life indeed share a lot in common but the philosophic life is happier than the political life that is devoid of contemplation. The "exclusive" interpretation can also be characterized as an "intellectualist" approach to human happiness.

The "exclusive," or "intellectualist" interpretation focuses on the *ergon* argument in I:7 where Aristotle states that "the good for man is activity of soul in accordance with virtue, and if there is more than one virtue, according to the best and most perfect"(I:7 1097a 26). This line of argument recognizes the possibility of several virtuous activities, but it insists that only one activity is the best. The most perfect or happiest life must, therefore, be of a kind that manifests the highest excellence of humankind. Aristotle declares that the intellect, the faculty perfected by philosophic wisdom, more than anything else is man himself. Therefore, while the lower functions of the soul serve reason and are under its control, the dominant character of being human must refer to reason. All functions, including the practical employment of reason itself, provide support for the highest activity, but they are not component factors of our proper excellence. Human happiness resides in the perfection of the highest part in us, i.e., speculative reason, and consists of contemplation of the eternal. Contemplation is the ultimate end of human life. It is the pinnacle of a hierarchy of goods, and every good is to be located somewhere within a hierarchy created by that dominant, single end.

No less than the "inclusive" interpretation, the "exclusive" interpretation roots Aristotle's conception of happiness in his conception of human nature. Whereas the first interpretation emphasizes the limits of human nature, the second brings to the fore the inherent capacity of people to transcend their nature as social animals. The capacity to think theoretically is the divine element in us that enables us to think about things higher than ourselves and thereby to go beyond our human limits and become like the gods. It is in this capacity that mature persons are capable of *eudaimonia*, whereas animals are incapable of it, children have not yet achieved it, and certain adults such as slaves are by nature prevented from reaching it. Even free women cannot be truly happy, because their deliberative power lacks authority.[85]

Essential to the exclusive interpretation is Aristotle's aforementioned distinction between activity (*energia*) and process (*kinesis*). Happiness must be an *activity* rather than something that develops over time toward a stage of completion. So what sort of activity is the theoretical life of contemplation? Aristotle did not equate contemplation with meditation or with mental gazing, although Hellenistic and medieval commentators tended to read him in this way. As R. Kraut explains, for Aristotle contemplation is simply the activity of bringing to mind truths that have already been discovered through the systematic study of the theoretical sciences, chief among which is metaphysics.[86] Contemplation occurs when we reflect silently upon these metaphysical truths as well as when we write, read a book, listen to a book being read, and when we lecture and teach. Since *philosophia* is another name Aristotle gives to contemplation (X:7 1177a25), we may say that contemplation is the activity of philosophizing.

Contemplation is an activity of such outstanding quality that there is no upper limit to it. One cannot philosophize too much or too long. In fact, the more one philosophizes, the better one's life is. Concomitantly, the philosophical activity of contemplation is not affected by other goods. No increase or decrease in the degree to which we possess other goods by themselves constitutes an increase or decrease in happiness. The presence of other goods—such as health, wealth, and friends—creates the *preconditions* for the most virtuous activity, but it does not include them. Contemplation is not an alternative to the other goods; it is a standard for the organization of our activities and goals into a coherent system.

According to the exclusive interpretation, the unqualified praise of contemplation in Book X does not contradict the rest of the *Ethics* and does not invalidate the claim that there are several types of life that are desirable in themselves. Aristotle acknowledged the existence of two modes of life that are both good and happy—the civil life and the philosophic life—but he claimed that the philosophic life is superior. Indeed, to engage in a philosophical life one indeed needs health, wealth and leisure; one must possess a virtuous character, and one must live in the company of virtuous friends with whom he can philosophize. The philosopher will need all the virtues and a measure of external good in order to lead the life that is regularly devoted to theoretical activity over a long period of time. However, since contemplation is the *dominant* end of human life, it dictates that the philosopher will engage in ethical activity only for the sake of contemplation and that the best amount of lower goods to have is the amount that contributes most to contemplation.

The life of the statesman who focuses on the cultivation of moral character and the acquisition of practical wisdom will be a good and happy life but neither the best nor happiest. Devoid of contemplation, the rational activity of the statesman is neither continuous nor leisurely, for it pertains to changing particulars rather than to universals, it concerns the bodily-related aspects of the soul, and it is affected by external circumstances. The man of mere moral virtues and practical wisdom is unable to transcend the natural order and imitate the divine life that could endear him to the gods, to the extent that the gods have any concern for human life. In other words, the man of moral virtue will live merely a human life, without the possibility of sharing in the divine life. Aristotle thus concludes that in order to improve the quality of our lives so as to transcend our human limitations we need to add the philosophical activity of contemplation. Primary happiness is, therefore, superhuman and a thing apart, not because it implies a divine intervention transcendent over men, but because the pursuit of contemplative practice elevates happiness above all inferior powers.

How to Make Sense of the Ambiguity?

The differences between the inclusive and exclusive readings of Aristotle must not obscure the elements that they share. For Aristotle, happiness pertains to one's life as a whole and not to a momentary feeling of satisfaction or contentment. Happiness is not subjective; it is rooted in the teleological structure of reality and the objective facts of the nature of the human species. It requires a conscious effort to cultivate the virtues, the stable character-traits that direct us toward the good. The objectively happy life can be attained only if we allow our rational selves to govern and control the irrational aspects of our souls through practice and habituation and bring about the mean in emotions and actions. The good life is thus predicated on self-mastery and self-control rather than on an impulsive gratification of bodily needs or emotional cravings. Human flourishing takes place in a social context, rather than in isolation, but it must include a certain measure of philosophical activity; without contemplation of eternal truths we cannot be fully human. Finally, the happy man is the well-rounded person who engages in philosophy. Thus far the two interpretations are in full agreement.

The difference between them boils down to the following questions: What is the role and value of philosophical contemplation in the happy life? and What is the role and value of involvement in the political sphere?

Two major explanations have been offered to resolve the ambiguity. According to the first, the *Ethics* is not technically speaking a book; rather, it is comprised of the notes of Aristotle's live lectures delivered in the Lyceum over a long period of time and later edited by his son, Nicomachus. The very nature of the live discourse precludes absolute consistency in its argument. Any attempt to impose such consistency on the *Ethics* and solve its internal tensions is thus misguided. According to the second explanation, Aristotle was vacillating between two psychological theories. The tension in the *Ethics* arises from the fact that he could not fit his account of separable reason (which is *not* the form of the body) into his general theory of the soul as the form of the body. Thus he could not make sense in the *Ethics* of the nature of man as a compound composed of something divine with much that is not divine.[87]

Both explanations are plausible, and they are not mutually exclusive. My own position is that Aristotle was conflicted about the human predicament precisely because he understood the complexity and uniqueness of human animals as sentient creatures aware of their own mortality and valiantly attempting to overcome pending death. For him, theoretical contemplation was the only way to transcend human finitude. Therefore, he presented the two models of good life—the moral/political and the philosophical—as two poles of human existence, the ideal and the real, respectively. Aspiring to the attainment of the philosophic ideal endows human life with meaning and fuels the relentless human striving toward self-perfection. It is the very struggle to approximate this philosophic ideal that makes us better human beings, according to Aristotle, and enables us to live happier, more flourishing lives. Aristotle's teaching on happiness is ridden with conflict, then, because human life itself is so burdened with the tension between the ideal and the real.

Such ambiguity may be very frustrating to a philosopher who aspires for utmost clarity and consistency. Especially if one takes Aristotle as an authoritative author, one would attempt to remove the inconsistencies and resolve the tension in Aristotle's teachings. Thus over the centuries philosophers and historians of philosophy have marshaled arguments in favor of one or the other of these readings, or proposed yet a third reading to reconcile the differences between them.[88] However, Aristotle's ambiguity is not a problem for the intellectual historian. It is precisely because Aristotle left for posterity an ambiguous legacy that the process of creative interpretation was possible, giving rise to the Aristotelian tradition in Western philosophy. The richness of Aristotle's argument, his ability to see the inevitable tensions of the human predicament, and the subtlety of his language with its endless shadows of meanings have all facilitated the multiple interpretations and creative readings and misreadings that enable us to speak about Aristotelianism as a distinct intellectual tradition.

I do not, therefore, attempt to prescribe which reading is the correct one but argue instead that the tensions between the possible readings of Aristotle shaped the history of the discourse on happiness in the premodern period among Jews, Muslims, and Christians. Thus the following chapters will trace the interplay between the "inclusive" and "exclusive" interpretations of Aristotle's conception of happiness in medieval Jewish philosophy.

HAPPINESS IN POST-ARISTOTELIAN PHILOSOPHY

Transition from Greek Polis to Hellenistic Empire

Aristotle followed his teacher Plato in presupposing that happiness can be attained only within the well-ordered society of public-spirited citizens. The polis is regarded as the ideal social arrangement, and in his ethical theory it is the citizen of the polis who is the carrier of human value. But already during Aristotle's own lifetime, the Greek polis was undergoing profound transformation brought about by the rise of Macedonia to power. His own student, Alexander, would conquer vast territories, thereby changing not only the political structure of the Near East but its prevailing intellectual climate. In the Hellenistic empires that came to power after the death of Alexander, new philosophical schools emerged, attempting to address the new reality of a population uninvolved in the political process. With these political changes came a shift in the conception of human happiness. Since Aristotle defined the human as a "political animal," the polis had priority over the particular make-up of a given individual. Thus whereas Aristotle held that human happiness required first the well-functioning society, the Hellenistic philosophical schools—Cynicism, Epicureanism, and Stoicism—focused on the well-being of the individual with little regard to politics and civic activity. Hellenistic philosophical schools were all familiar with Aristotle's views, even though they developed their moral theories independently of the Peripatetic school.[89] Some of the motifs and social ideals of the Hellenistic schools permeated the views and attitudes of Jewish philosophers in the Hellenistic period and of the framers of rabbinic Judaism.

The Cynics: The ideal of Self-Sufficiency

Socrates, we recall, placed the cultivation of the *psyche* at the core of the philosophical life and devalued or subordinated worldly standards of value such as wealth, status, power, and the like. He maintained that "to have no wants is divine, and to have as few as possible is nearest to the divine."[90] One of Socrates' disciples, Antisthenes of Athens (c. 446–366 B.C.E.), based his own ethical teachings on the Socratic principles of self-sufficiency (*autarkeia*) and self-mastery (*enkrateia*). "True wealth and poverty do not pertain to externals, but to the condition of one's *psyche* and all that the body requires is a basic satisfaction of essential needs: simple food, clothing, shelter, and periodic sex."[91] For him moral virtue was sufficient for *eudaimonia*, which he equated with a disposition of independence or freedom from worldly needs and passions.

The austere and ascetic tendencies of Socrates' teachings and life style were fully developed by the Cynics, who regarded Diogenes of Sinope (c. 400–320 B.C.E.) as the founder of their school. Diogenes followed the ascetic tenor of Antisthenes' philosophy to its logical conclusion and assumed the life style of a beggar and a wanderer. He scorned wealth, status, luxury, and political aspirations as "ornaments of vice" that rob one of the freedom to live the simple life. Instead of a civic association, Diogenes proclaimed himself "a citizen of the world" and "assumed an anarchic position of extreme individualism."[92]

Diogenes recognized "nature" as the only source of ethical guidance, distinguishing between "natural" and "unnatural" conduct. Teaching and preaching in the agoras, bathhouses, and street corners, he personally demonstrated his view that the pursuit of self-sufficiency is the only remedy for the vicissitudes of fortune and the oppression of conventions. His message of voluntary austerity as the path "toward least burdened existence" had a unique appeal to the individual inhabitants of the cities and empires of the Hellenistic Near East. Though other Cynic teachers were less radical in their ridicule of prevailing social standards and conventions, the ascetic tenor of Diogenes' teaching was endorsed by the other philosophical schools. Thus Hellenistic ethics was decidedly apolitical, in contrast to the legacy of Aristotle. This distinction will become relevant to our discussion of rabbinic ethics.

The Epicureans: Moderate Hedonism

More significant philosophically was Epicureanism, a philosophical school founded by Epicurus (b. 341 B.C.E.), who established himself as a teacher in

Athens about 311 B.C.E. and founded the Garden, a community of intimates sharing a way of life in accordance with the teachings of their master.[93] Epicurus perpetuated the Socratic notion that philosophy is a therapeutic activity, but the ultimate goal of human life for him was a life of "untroubledness" (*ataraxia*) or "tranquility" (*euthemia*). For him, "tranquility is a state of mind of the happy person, a part of happiness, but not happiness itself."[94] Happiness itself was conveyed in language of private contentment in negative forms. One should aspire to imperturbability (*a-taraxis*), an absence of toil or suffering (*a-ponoia*), painlessness (*a-lupia*), living without fear (*a-phobos*), being uninvolved in public affairs (*a-pragmosune*), being unburdened by liturgical services (*a-leiturgia*), and, in short, living the undisturbed life (*a-thurubus zen*).

To attain these goals one had to get rid of erroneous beliefs and misconceptions that cause mental distress and emotional disturbance. False notions, including beliefs in "vengeful gods, mythical monsters, animate celestial powers or postmortem sanctions,"[95] are the cause of the suffering of the soul, but they can be dispelled through rigorous philosophical analysis. Departing from the Platonic-Aristotelian metaphysics, Epicurus adopted the atomistic physics of Democritus, in which all natural phenomena and all motions are explained as spontaneous interplays of countless atomic compounds of varying size, shape, and weight. Their temporary arrangement in the infinite void dissolves in time through a ceaseless process of change. In this worldview of random change, there is no room for divine involvement, be it by the mythical gods of popular beliefs, the Divine Demiurge of Plato, or Aristotle's First Cause. By rejecting any form of supernaturalism, Epicurus believed he could liberate humans from unnecessary fears.

The consequence of Epicurean atomistic physical theory was a pervasive empirical orientation that focused on sensory experience (*aisthesis*). In that experience, various organs of sense come into contact with objects of physical reality. All sensations are accompanied by feelings of pleasure or pain, and it is indeed the presence of the former and the absence of the latter that all people seek. Since all living creatures from the moment of birth are well disposed to pleasure and opposed to pain, naturally and without the aid of reason,[96] Epicurus reexamined the importance of pleasure, which he declared to be "our first and inborn good." Studying human needs and desires, he considered some pleasure to be natural and necessary (for example, food, shelter, and security), others to be natural but unnecessary (for example, sex and fine foods), and still others unnatural and unnecessary (for example, public status and riches). For Epicurus, then, the "life of blessedness" (*to makarios zen*) was not an endless pursuit of material pleasures, but a life restricted to the satisfaction of natural and necessary needs that establishes the atomic equilibrium of bodily health and mental tranquility. In this regard Epicurus' teachings were consistent with the ascetic sentiments of the Cynics. Contrary to contemporary misperceptions, he was no crude hedonist.

Epicurus equated full pleasure with painlessness (the repose of our atomic body-soul complex) and hence adopted certain ascetic elements inherent in the ideal of self-sufficiency (*autarkeia*). He counseled his audience to develop moderate desires in conformity with natural and necessary needs and to entertain natural but unnecessary pleasures only if they bring no disturbance in their wake. In practical terms this resulted in a modest life style for Garden members. The recourse to any ascetic stance is strictly instrumental. The virtuous living is conducive to pleasure in the form of health of body and tranquility of mind. "It is not possible to live pleasantly without also living prudently, nobly and justly, nor is it possible to live prudently, nobly and justly without living pleasantly."[97]

While Epicurus proposed a form of moderate or tempered hedonism, opinions of him in intellectual and popular circles was negative. The call to pleasure was viewed as a radical attack of anti-religious and antipolitical quality, because Epicurus rejected the belief in the punitive divine powers that he regarded as the primary cause of human anxiety and distress. Likewise Epicurus rejected the fear of death and all dualistic positions that accorded the *psyche* transcendent status as the solution to the human fear of death. Accordingly, he repudiated all eschatological notions of personal immortality, ranging from the religious-mythical tales of postmortem sanctions in Hades and paradisiacal bliss in Elysium to the cycle of rebirths proclaimed by various philosophies. He denied otherworldly existence and radically negated the conventional religious-mythical belief. It is for these reasons that Epicurus was perceived in rabbinic literature as the worst sort of dangerous pagan philosopher,[98] even though the rabbis, as we shall discuss in Chapter Three, actually adopted some of his advice and lived their own lives very much like members of Epicurus' Garden.

That philosophic community provided the ideal social context for the pursuit of happiness. Free to renounce the burdens of public service in favor of the personal rewards of friendship, the Epicurean philosopher pursued wisdom in the company of like-minded friends. The possession of friendship was declared the greatest means for the "attainment of blessedness throughout the whole of life."[99] Epicurus' Garden became an alternative community to the polis and a model to other "uninvolved" segments of the Greco-Roman world, for whom ethics had to be separated from politics. His apolitical hedonism was a program of personal escape and disengagement. It diverged from the Aristotelian project not only in rejecting the transcendental aspects of earlier thought, but in subordinating abstract theorizing to practical wisdom. Reason was not allowed to soar beyond the mundane reality of sensory experience to any speculative higher realm of truth or being. And by severing ethics from politics, Epicurus pointedly restricted his concerns to the private sphere, though he still regarded philosophy as therapeutic. The sages' reasoning is reduced to the calculation of risks and the pursuit of private pleasures within the constraints imposed by existing conditions.

The Stoics: Virtue as the Only Good

The most influential Hellenistic philosophical school was Stoicism.[100] It permeated Hellenistic culture and was adopted by the ruling elite of republican Rome. The Old Stoa was founded by Zeno of Citium (b. 333 B.C.E.) at the close of the fourth century, but its doctrinal consolidation was carried out by Crisippus in the second half of the third century B.C.E. Establishing his school in the *Stoa Poikile* in Athens about 300 B.C.E., Zeno was associated with the Cynic philosopher Krates, and from his influence Zeno adopted many Cynic overtones while toning down their radicalism. The Stoics adopted the Cynic ideal of self-sufficiency while repudiating the Cynic "shamelessness" in behavioral practice and rejecting the Cynic indifference to dialectics and natural science. Most importantly, Zeno anchored his ethics in the very nature of things. For him, "the search for the human good, for *eudaimonia*, was to be conducted with reference to a universal cosmic Nature, the ordering principle of all the particular entities encompassed therein."[101]

The Stoics postulated a monistic pantheism in which God, matter, and cosmos form a unitary continuum. God is its "active" principle, extending throughout the whole as "creative fire" or "thermal *pneuma*," rationally fashioning each existing thing. Matter is the "passive" substance through which the Logos that is God immanently operates. The cosmos is divine, rational, and animate, because of the pneumatic penetration of the whole by God who also is in some sense the *psyche* of the universe.

The Stoics viewed God, Logos, Mind, Destiny, Zeus, and Nature as parts of the same pantheistic principle. Their overriding belief was that the universe is rationally organized, complete, and providentially arranged by a divine power with whom human beings enjoy privileged kinship on account of their possession of reason, which itself was said to have the same nature as the Divine Logos, as part to whole. The Stoics thus anchored their ethics in a comprehensive ontology and provided for a fundamental redefinition of personal identity and meaning with reference to a divine and universal order. It is this view, as we shall see in the next chapter, that made Stoicism compatible with Jewish religious belief in a world created by a personal God.

The Stoic *telos* was "living in accordance with *physis.*" Life in conformity with Nature is at once a virtuous life, "since *physis* leads us to *arete.*"[102] Since human nature is distinctly endowed with reason, living in accordance with nature means living rationally. Because of corrupting personal associations and the pursuit of false externals, most people do not live consistently with their own natures and with universal cosmic nature and thus fail to attain virtue and true *eudaimonia*. The Stoics retained the Socratic equation of virtue, reason, and happiness, but they modified it in many ways. For example, they absorbed the Cynic's inventory of things into good, bad, and indifferent. The good include the four cardinal virtues of practical wisdom, temperance, justice, and courage, along with all that partakes of these virtues or stems from them. The bad include thoughtlessness, intemperance, injustice, and cowardice and all that partakes of vice or stems from it. Finally, what is indifferent includes life and death, honor and dishonor, pain and pleasure, wealth and poverty, sickness and health, and all things similar to these. Most natural goods were to be regarded as "indifferent"—namely, as that "which can be used both for good and for bad and is not itself a good." Furthermore, since strength, beauty, wealth, power, etc. can be used for both virtuous and vicious ends, the Stoics regarded them as ethically indifferent.

The Stoics retained the Socratic equation of virtue with knowledge, but they defined the content of the virtues in epistemic terms. Thus practical wisdom is the knowledge of good and evil, of things to do and not to do; courage is knowledge of what is and is not terrible, or of things to endure and not to endure; temperance is the knowledge of things to be chosen and avoided; and justice is the knowledge of allocating things in accordance with the worth of the object and its recipient. The corresponding vices are analogously defined as forms of ignorance. The result was that the Stoics radically internalized morality and *eudaimonia*, thereby shielding the individual from the external world. For them the goal of the happy life is the "absence of passions" (*apatheia*), not because they are emotions per se, but because they manifest mistaken judgments by the ruling reason. Instead of accepting things as "indifferents," reason mistakenly accords the wrong values to them and thereby causes disturbance in the soul. The goal of the Stoic sage, then, is to extirpate these "excessive impulses" by reasoning correctly about their true value.

Stoicism became the most popular philosophical school in late antiquity because it was more attentive to the social dimension than Cynicism or Epicureanism were. Given that human beings are naturally constituted to live in communities, it follows that ethics must be attuned to the imperative of social life.

But whereas Stoic moralists avoided the antisocial excesses of other postcivic philosophies, they remained essentially abstract. In the Stoic sources of this Roman period (Cicero, Seneca, Epictetus and Marcus Aurelius), there is a universalistic ethos based on unity or brotherhood of mankind and the notion of an inhabited world in which universal norms of Divine Physics and Natural Law apply. Zeno, for example, described the ideal polity as the ideal community of the virtuous, in which they alone are citizens, friends, kindred, and free. In this ideal society, many standard institutions of the polis are excluded—for example, law courts, gymnasia, currency, temples and religious statuary, traditional family units, and sexually differentiated clothing. These radical proposals bear the influence of Cynicism. For the Stoics, too, only the virtuous are true citizens, for they alone are members of the *cosmopolis* and adhere to the *nomos* of Divine Nature; they alone live consistently with *orthos logos* of Zeus, i.e., with nature. For the Stoics, the true polis is the cosmos or heaven that embodies logos or Nature; the earthly polis and constitutions are dismissed as ridden with vice and error. On earth the true citizen is the wise man; all others are "exiles, enemies, unjust and lawless."

Summary

To provide a conceptual foundation for our entire book, we have exposed the teleological framework of Aristotle's philosophy, his rationalist understanding of human nature, the role of reason in the molding of character, the place of pleasure and friendship in the virtuous life, and the relationship between contemplation and action in human flourishing. We noted that Aristotle's analysis of happiness could be interpreted in two different ways: one that regards the best life as one filled with contemplation of philosophic truth, and the other that views the best life as one of moderation in the socio-political sphere. In the coming chapters we shall show how these philosophical terms, concepts, and ways of reasoning became an integral part of the Jewish discourse on happiness, albeit under different forms. Indeed, the Greek and Hellenistic reflections on happiness were absorbed into Judaism, beginning already in the Second Temple period, even though Israelite religion developed in a very different society and held very different beliefs about human well-being. As we shall see, the absorption of Hellenistic ideas are most evident in the writings of Jewish authors from the second century B.C.E., both canonical and extra-canonical, since they were developed in a Hellenistic cultural environment. We shall begin to trace that distinctly Jewish perspective in the next chapter, where I will highlight the basic parameters of the biblical approach to the life of well-being as it developed over time.

2

Ashrei:
Wisdom, Torah, and Living Rightly in Ancient Judaism

We now turn to the Bible, the canonic Scripture of Judaism. The Bible, of course, is not a work of philosophy. It does not contain sustained logical argumentation, and no topics are presented systematically. Moreover, on any given theme, the Bible speaks in more than one voice, reflecting not only the diverse literary genres of which it is comprised and the long and convoluted process that brought its text into existence, but also the complexity of ancient Israelite civilization. Thus we cannot expect to find in it a fully articulated theory of human happiness. Nonetheless, I submit that the Bible itself provided the basis for the Jewish conception of happiness.

Contemporary ethical theorists, as we noted in the Preface, usually present Judaism, and later Christianity and Islam, as traditions based on ethics of duty. In these traditions the rightness of the act is derived from doing what one is *obligated* to do, and moral epithets are actions that can be labeled as "right" or "wrong." Because ethical standards are derived from the commands that God makes known to the believer through revelation, the human good is thus defined in terms of obligations and duties to a divine legislator rather than in terms of human self-fulfillment.

This book argues that in Judaism a radical separation between ethics of duty and ethics of virtue is not tenable. The two are not in conflict because between 516 B.C.E. and 70 C.E., when the Second Temple was functioning as the administrative and religious center of the Jewish people and when Judaism was gradually shifting its focus from a Temple-centered, sacrificial cult to a book-centered religion, a fusion of ancient Israelite religion and covenantal theology took shape. According to covenantal theology (the *mythos* dimension of Judaism), God, the creator of the universe, entered into an everlasting covenant with one group of people—Israel—to whom He revealed His will in the form of Law, the Torah. Only the one who lives in accordance with God's will and who observes His commandments can enjoy a happy life of security, longevity, material prosperity, and peace. The ancient Wisdom tradition (the foundation of *logos* in Judaism), by contrast, maintained that the moral order and in turn, human well-being, are located in the very structure of the universe. Only the wise man—he who grasps that structure and lives in accordance with it—can flourish, i.e. experience happiness. Stephen A. Geller holds that the Book of Job, which he dates to the sixth century B.C.E., is the earliest manifestation of the fusion of those two dimensions—specifically, of the Wisdom tradition in Israel with the covenantal theology of the Book of Deuteronomy.[1] Even if one does not accept the details of Geller's reading of Job, the scholarly consensus is that, by the beginning of the second century B.C.E., the identification of the Torah with Wisdom was fully in place, taking shape in the cultural matrix of the Hellenistic world.

That identification, this book argues, is central to the history of the discourse on happiness. It established a shared ground between Judaism and other intellectual traditions and enabled Jewish intellectuals to interpret the meaning of God's Torah through the pursuit of Wisdom. Put differently, the identification of Torah and Wisdom confirmed the centrality of the pursuit of Wisdom in Judaism, on the one hand, and the ability of Judaism to converse with other civilizations without losing its distinctive identity, on the other hand. However, what exactly constituted "Wisdom" and where it could be found would change over time, reflecting the varied historical experiences of the Jewish people. This chapter explains how the Judaic conception of happiness was rooted in the fusion of Torah and Wisdom and how Jewish thinkers in the Second Temple period understood the meaning of happiness in light of their encounter with Greek and Hellenistic philosophy. That encounter marks the beginning of Jewish philosophy

PRUDENTIAL WISDOM AND TORAH PIETY

Near Eastern Wisdom

The Wisdom literature of Israel belongs to a larger Near Eastern Wisdom tradition whose roots may be traced to Egypt and Mesopotamia as far back as the third millenium B.C.E.[2] The orientation of this literature was universal and human-centered in the sense that it paid little attention to national myths and heroic narratives and reflected on human life as a whole. It assumed that what is good for humans can be inferred from observations of nature. Thus rules of human conduct were derived from judgments about the place of humans in the cosmic order, and the purpose of those rules was to assure the attainment of human destiny. These universal concerns were expressed in a distinctive style: short proverbs, parables, riddles, and didactic poems.

In Egypt, Wisdom literature emerged in the royal court, where schools for training the children of future rulers and bureaucrats were housed.[3] Accordingly, that literature was concerned with the proper speech and correct etiquette that were "indispensable to aspiring rulers."[4] In Mesopotamia, formal teaching took place in the Temple cult, and its goal was to train scribes in special skills of mantic arts. Mesopotamian Wisdom literature, therefore, focused on the expertise of the sage in interpreting signs and omens, since the wise men earned their livelihood from this activity as well as from the scribal duties they performed either in government service or for private wealthy individuals.

Ensconced between the great civilizations of Egypt and Mesopotamia was ancient Israel. Modern Bible scholars still debate how this Wisdom tradition emerged in Israel and who its bearers were.[5] Some associate the origin with the reign of King Solomon, who had strong diplomatic and commercial ties to the royal courts of neighboring states.[6] His palace housed foreign scholars, and therefore his court might have had a formal school for training future administrators.[7] Thus, the traditional Jewish association of Solomon with non-cultic, scientific, and artistic learning might contain some historical truth.[8] However, since there is limited evidence for the existence of a lay school during the period of the First Temple, other scholars believe that in ancient Israel the Wisdom tradition emerged neither in the royal court nor in the Temple but in the family or the clan.[9] Parents transmitted to their children folk wisdom and lore in short, memorable maxims, whose major goal was the formation of character in preparation for life. Nevertheless, at least some of the material recorded in Proverbs clearly is the product of a courtly environment. It includes advice on proper table manners, eloquence, propriety, humility before superiors, fidelity, skills and modes of conduct useful at the court or in a bureaucratic setting.[10] The reference to conduct in the presence of a king and the emphasis on the king's responsibility for ensuring justice are further indications that at least some wisdom teachings were refashioned for the court.

Prudential Morality in Proverbs

In style, Wisdom literature is very different from prophetic, priestly, epic, or historical strata of the Hebrew Bible. Unlike the prophet, the teacher of wisdom intended in his advice (*etzah*) to elicit assent through persuasion rather than through obedience and transformation of conduct. Unlike the priest, he focused on universal themes of human life and conduct rather than on the procedures of the cult or the perpetuation of the national myth. The sage spoke in cool words based on practical experience, instructing his listeners on right behavior in the right place at the right time for the right reason. He did evoke authority, but not the authority of the Law (as did the priest) or the authority of the word of God (as did the prophet). Instead, he spoke in the name of the sapiential tradition, with the authority of his own convictions and knowledge of what Wisdom demands.

The ancient Israelite Wisdom tradition was practical and pragmatic. Based on the observation of nature and human conduct, it was concerned with ordering life so as to maximize success and prosperity. Its teachings enabled the learner to master his environment and cope with the dangers and vicissitudes of life. By hearkening to the counsel of the wise, the adherent of Wisdom could obtain the concrete components of the good life—health, wealth, fame, honor, longevity, and progeny—by skillfully avoiding dangerous pitfalls. Those who listened to the wise person would be rewarded, and those who ignored his counsel—the fools—would lose life itself. In short, the main concerns of Wisdom literature were human well-being, the timeless problems of human existence, and the destiny of human life. We may therefore justifiably call this literature "eudaimonistic."

The Israelite sapiential tradition presupposed that reality is meaningfully ordered and that human intelligence is capable of deciphering that order so as to orient human life in accord with it.[11] Wisdom was thus defined in terms of an attempt to discover and maintain order in both the personal and social arenas of life. The wise man, then, is the one who harmonizes his life with the universe. Because he knows its secrets and lives in accordance with them, he benefits from the well-ordered, happy life. In contrast, those who refuse to acknowledge the cosmic order suffer grievous consequences; their lives are ruled by chaos. This concern with the underlying order of reality explains the emphasis of the sapiential literature on propriety. The one who lives in harmony with the principles of the universe is blessed with health, fame, wealth, longevity, and remembrance.[12]

We may do well to realize that the focus on propriety and orderliness has much in common with the Greek emphasis on self-mastery, self-control, temperance, and doing what is "just right." The wise man of Proverbs is not that different from the *phronimos* (practically wise) of Aristotle's *Ethics*. In Proverbs the wise man is diligent, prudent, trustworthy, patient, generous, modest, peaceable, and self-controlled (Pr. 10:17; 11:15; 13:17; 14:29; 15:18; 16:32; 17:27; 19:17; 20:13). In other words, the sapiential tradition in Israel, no less than Greek philosophical tradition, was concerned with character formation in preparation for life.[13]

The counsel of the wise man was meant to cultivate the good agent, whose good actions flow effortlessly from the well-established good character. Since character formation begins by avoiding any excess, even of those things that are good in themselves, Proverbs warns against excessive drink and gluttony and against too much talk and bad company. In this prudential mentality, good things carried to excess yield negative consequences, a view that Aristotle shared and articulated philosophically in the doctrine of the mean.

To live in harmony with the ordered universe, the wise person must acquire the virtue of self-control. He subordinates his passions (Pr. 16:32), whereas the fool is governed by them.[14] He acquires the virtues by avoiding dangerous temptations that lead one to become wicked. Thus he knows that drunkenness, laziness, and gossip are dangers that lure young people and adults away from the path of life. Self-control is most evident in the way the wise person speaks, since the tongue is the most difficult thing to master. The wise person speaks the right words at the right time, so that he expresses himself eloquently as much as he appreciates the value of silence. Proper speech enables the wise to treat friends and enemies appropriately and to present himself competently with dignity in front of superiors.

Prudence Fused with Torah Piety

Though the Wisdom tradition in Israel originated in the pre-exilic period, the literary documents that have reached us are all post-exilic.[15] After the breakdown of the Judean monarchy in 587 B.C.E. and the emergence of a Jewish diaspora, the need to preserve allegiance to the Jewish people in a gentile world gave rise to a new type of instruction in the ancestral tradition. That tradition was gradually associated with a sacred text, the Torah, which itself developed out of the pre-exilic reforms of King Josiah in 622 B.C.E. and the literary activity of the scribal school that produced the Book of Deuteronomy and Deuteronomic history.[16]

First under Persian rule and more so during the Hellenistic period, the wise man became the scribe of Torah. In this capacity, he inculcated the teachings of the Wisdom tradition as the revealed teaching and instruction of God. In the context of teaching Torah, the old prudential Wisdom was increasingly theologized, culminating in the final identification of Torah with Wisdom by the second century B.C.E.

Specifically, the idea of Torah as Wisdom proper for Israel can be traced to Deuteronomy 4:5–8. The Torah scholars, the carriers of the sapiential tradition, facilitated the development of a comprehensive outlook on life that transformed the old prudential outlook by providing "fundamental abstract notions such as 'the fear of the Lord' and 'the way of wisdom' [which] were used to co-ordinate and integrate a variety of inherited traditions."[17] The "fear of God" (*yir'at YHVH*) became readily identified with the way of Wisdom (Pr. 9:10; 14:27; 15:33; and Job 28:28), and the underlying order of the universe was now ascribed to an all-benevolent Creator. He who practices the fear of God as practical piety avoids doing evil, which presents itself in various forms, from drunkenness to adultery (Pr. 3:7; Job 1:1). The one who holds aloof from evil and carefully avoids it because he fears God embarks on the path of Wisdom and the good life (Pr. 2:6).

As ancient Wisdom traditions were blended with the legal, priestly tradition, the ethics of virtue and the ethics of obedience to divine commands began to be fused. The two parts of the Hebraic traditions converged, as Brevard S. Child put it, giving a unified expression of the good and obedient life. Both the Proverbs and the Law call for a commitment to God and his divine order. Both parts of the canon call for man to love justice and honesty, to care for the poor and needy, and to accept life as a cherished gift from God.[18] Since the Torah is to be regarded as the true source of sound ethical conduct that leads to happiness, right conduct now meant following the divine Law as the wise person interprets it. Thus, Proverbs insists that right conduct is a matter of reverence and dedication as much as it is a matter of inner disposition (Pr. 16:23). It is not surprising, therefore, that Proverbs (23:23) holds, as did Aristotle, that virtue or inner disposition cannot be lost once it is acquired.

The fusion of the legal and sapiential traditions yields a human ideal that combines the qualities of the wise person—the one who cultivates the proper inner dispositions according to wisdom—and the righteous person (*tzaddiq*)—the one who behaves justly according to the teachings of a just God. The righteous person is the wise one who delights in meditating on the wisdom embodied in the sacred writings that reveal the will of God, namely, the Torah. His antithesis is the "wicked" (*rasha*), who foolishly ignores God's teaching and whose life is therefore marked by a poor quality. Since God's Torah is now regarded as the true source of sound ethical conduct (Ps. 19:7, 119:98), the unwise person is not only a fool but a person who offends against God. By contrast, the wise person has the inner religious insight to know that God rules the world (Dt. 32:6). He understands the words of the prophets and the way and gracious acts of God (Ps. 107:43). The wise man is also aware of his own sin (Ps. 51:6) and the way in which life is circumscribed by God (Ps. 90:12). This type of insight breeds humility (Pr. 11;2; 13:10), the most cherished virtue in rabbinic ethics. But it is also the basis of true faith and trust (Ps. 90:12). In short, already in the biblical Wisdom literature edited in the late Second Temple period, living by the Torah was understood as its own reward because through it one enjoyed the good life.

WISDOM PSALMS

Like Proverbs, the Book of Psalms includes very ancient material, even though it probably received its final editing in the third century B.C.E. or even later.[19] In its entirety, the Book of Psalms does not belong to the Wisdom stratum of the Bible, but several Psalms have long been recognized as sharing linguistic, thematic, and stylistic features with the Wisdom tradition.[20] Hence, they were called "Wisdom poems" (*Weisheitgedichte*), or "Wisdom Psalms." The most commonly thus designated " are Pss. 1, 19 (divided by scholars into 19A and 19B), 32, 34, 37, 49, 73, 78, 112, 119, 127, though there are other lists as well. These Psalms are didactic in style, and those whose main topic is instruction, namely, *Torah* of God, were also named "Torah Psalms."[21]

The identity of the authors and the setting in which these Psalms were written cannot be determined with certainty. Most scholars accept the view of Gunkel and Mowinckel that they were written by learned men or skilled scribes who were concerned with teaching Scripture. Whether these sages composed the "Wisdom Psalms" for private instruction in their lay scribal school, as Gunkel, Mowinckel, and Von Rad have speculated, or whether they were priestly authors who gave the originally cultic Psalms a sapiential character, as Herman Jensen has suggested, need not concern us here.[22] It is also unclear whether or not these "Wisdom Psalms" fulfilled any cultic function in the Second Temple.[23] However, it is likely that the Jerusalem Temple did play an important role in the transmission of the Wisdom tradition during the post-exilic period, especially since there was no king and no official royal court or scribal school. Thus the "Wisdom Psalms" signify the gradual transformation of Israel into a Scriptural religion.

Who is Happy? Critical Terms in the Bible

Ashrei

One of the formal features of the "Wisdom Psalms" is the formula *ashrei* (happy is the one who . . .), although this formula also appears in Psalms that do not share the technical vocabulary of Wisdom literature.[24] The actual *Sitz im Leben* of the formula is very difficult to reconstruct. Since most of the Psalms were originally composed for Temple worship, it stands to reason that the formula *ashrei* could have been uttered during the pilgrimage to the Temple, where the worshippers expected to find happiness.[25]

A closer look at the word *ashrei* will give us a deeper understanding of the Judaic approach to the well-lived life. The Hebrew stem *'-sh-r* means "to walk, to advance" (Is. 3:12; 9:15; Pro. 4:14; 9:6; 23:19). From this stem comes another Hebrew noun—*ashur*—(as in Ps. 17:5; 11; 37:31; 40:3; 44:19; 73:2; Job 23:11; 31:7) which means "footsteps."

The most common form of the stem *'-sh-r* is the construct *ashrei*, which appears over forty times in the Bible, twenty-six of them in the Psalms.[26] Biblical scholars have debated the etymology of the construct. Some lexicographers connect it with two Akkadian roots *wasaru*, which means "to be upright," and *eseru* which means "to be in order (right, correct)."[27] Others find its roots in the Egyptian word that means "prosperity," "good luck," and "happiness." And still others associate *ashrei* with the Egyptian root that connotes "to go straight, lead, guide."[28] In the Psalms, as will become clear below, the term *ashrei* functions as an exclamation uttered by an observer about the state of being of another person.[29] Nahum Sarna explains that this exclamation is based on "the discriminating judgment of an observer who expresses wonderment and admiration over another's enviable state of being."[30] If so, *ashrei* can best be translated as "Oh for the happiness of that person," or "How fortunate is the person who. . . ."

Derekh

The fact that the stem *'-sh-r* pertains to walking explains why in several Psalms the term *ashrei* is associated with the word *derekh* (literally meaning "path" or "way"). Indeed, in the Wisdom tradition *derekh* is understood most generally to denote life as a whole, or a pattern of living of a certain kind (for example, in Ps. 118:25). In the epic tradition, *derekh* generally refers to a specific endeavor that one is about to undertake and for whose successful completion the individual requests divine support. Thus we find the word in Genesis 24, when Abraham sends his servant to seek a wife for his son Isaac, and the servant prays to God for success in his *derekh*. In this chapter the term appears in conjunction with the verb *tz-l-h* that means "to do well," or "to prosper." When a particular task is completed successfully, it is understood to be due to divine involvement. The request for divine blessing is evoked when one bids farewell to another and bestows a good wish for future success (as in I Kings 22:12; II Chronicles 18:11). In some cases the verb *tz-l-h* appears in agricultural metaphors (e.g., Jer. 22:30; Ez. 17:9–10) and is associated with the stem *tz-m-h* ("to grow," "to give rise to").[31] In these cases the verb should be translated as "thriving" or "flourishing," a meaning that survived in rabbinic Hebrew and in Hebrew liturgy. In short, in the biblical religion, no less than in Greek morality, human well-being meant flourishing throughout one's life. Appropriately, the Bible uses organic imagery to capture the notion of human flourishing. We shall turn to this point below.

Barukh

In the epic tradition of the Bible, human flourishing was understood in concrete terms, pertaining to life in this world and to tangible goods. Thus the blessings that Isaac confers on his son Jacob include the abundance of grain and wine (Gen. 25), as do the blessings that Jacob will promise to his descendants. They all reflect the values of an agrarian rural society—one that must struggle with the unpredictability of nature. Blessing (*berakhah* in Hebrew) is an expression of God's gift to the recipient. The one who is blessed (*barukh*) by the power of God flourishes and his/her dealings with other human beings turn out to be successful.[32] The source of success and prosperity, however, is not one's own calculation or manipulation, but the very presence of divine blessing. The blessed person who receives God's divine power is de facto a person whose life goes well. This is why Sigmund Mowinckel held that *ashrei* was synonymous with *barukh*; both functioned as forms of blessing or being blessed. Mowinckel states:

> . . . blessing is identical with the very powers of life and their manifestations in external and internal happiness and welfare: in health, a long life, fertility, power of victory, of happiness, peace, and joy and power and integrity of mind in fellowship with the clan, and in a life in conformity to "justice" and "law" and "tradition." To have "blessing" includes whatever the Israelite understood by the term *shalom*,

"wholeness," "welfare," "harmony," or "peace," as it is usually translated.[33]

For Mowinckel, then, the blessing is "health-giving power, creating and promoting life, the power of blessing, blessedness.'" '"The blessed one" (*barukh*) is a person "having in himself blessing.'"[34]

Other scholars agree that in the Bible human well-being manifests being blessed by God, but they argue that *ashrei* and *barukh* are not identical. Hans-Joakhim Krauss, for example,[35] has pointed out that *ashrei* is never used in the Bible in reference to God, but only in reference to an individual, people, or land; it is never used in the sense of conferring some good on another, as one does in a blessing. And, as Nahum Sarna put it, the formula *ashrei* is "always employed to describe an existing situation, never one that is desired or promised."[36] These differences in usage led Krauss and others to talk about *ashrei* as a "secular" formula whereas *barukh* has religious denotations. Yet, as will soon become clear, this distinction is not maintained in the so-called Torah Psalms, where the term *ashrei* is associated directly with the Torah of YHVH.

Psalm 1: The Truly Happy Person

The nexus of Torah and Wisdom is captured in Psalm 1, which was composed rather late but placed at the opening of the collection to provide a lens through which Jews should engage in the life of Torah. The opening word—*ashrei*—stands at the core of the Jewish religious understanding of happiness: the best lived life for Jews is one devoted to the Torah of God; through it one can become righteous as God is. The life of Torah, however, requires the cultivation of moral virtues as well as knowledge about the relationship of Torah to God's created world.

According to Psalm 1, the study of God's Torah itself constitutes the life in which humans can best flourish. If we read it in light of the Greek understanding of happiness, we may be able to see what the Judaic and Greek approaches have in common and where they differ. This is not to say that its author was familiar with Aristotle's *Nicomachean Ethics* (such a claim is in principle unverifiable and quite implausible), but rather that the Hebrew poem and the Greek philosophic text share a similar definition of happiness. In both cases, it pertains to the quality of life as a whole rather than to a momentary sensation of pleasure; it is an activity rather than a static condition; it is predicated on the acquisition of inner dispositions to behave in a certain way, and it requires knowledge about the nature of human beings and their place in the cosmic order. The Hebrew and Greek traditions differ not in their definitions of happiness but in their assumptions about the nature of the universe and the place of human beings in it, assumptions that color their respective views of happiness.[37]

Psalm 1 portrays both the happy life and its opposite, but instead of analyzing them conceptually and theoretically, as did Aristotle, the poem depicts types of persons—the "righteous" (*tzaddiq*) as opposed to "the wicked" (*rasha*)—in order to make a point about the ideal way of life. Like the *Ethics,* which begins by stating what happiness is not, so Psalm 1 opens with a description of what the happy person has not done. He "has not followed the counsel of the wicked [*resha'im*] or taken the path of sinners [*hataim*], or joined the company of the insolent" [*letzim*] (v.1).

The righteous person who lives the happy life is referred to in the singular (*ha-ish*) while his antithesis is discussed in the plural: "wicked ones" (*resha`im*), "the sinners" (*hatta'im*), and "the scoffers" (*letzim*). Aristotle's insights about happiness might shed light on this linguistic discrepancy. We recall that for Aristotle there can be, in principle, only one type of life that is the best life for the human species. It is a life that is intrinsically good; it is good not for anything else but itself; it is a path taken for its own sake rather than for the sake of someone else. Similarly the term "*ha-ish*" refers to "humankind" regardless of gender. He/she is the ideal person who actualizes the one and only best way of life. By contrast, there are many ways to fall short of the ideal, or that prevent one from attaining it. Hence the Psalm speaks of "wicked," "sinners," and "scoffers" to represent various forms of imperfect life and various degrees of moral development.[38] Furthermore, we can say that not only is there but *one* good life, the good life itself manifests internal unity. It exhibits no conflicts and turmoil; it is a life in which a single, overarching purpose endows everything with meaning and makes the various parts of the life fit into an organic whole. Thus, the individual of Psalm 1 personifies the ideal way of life, the happiest life, which is both singular and unitary.

The notion that happiness is a pattern of living, a kind of activity that flows from who we are, is conveyed in Psalm 1 by the use of verbs that describe the happy person's activities. He does not "walk" (*halakh*) with the "wicked ones," or "sit" (*yashav*) with "the sinners," or "stand" (*amad*) with "the scoffers." Indeed, he lives a life of internal integrity reflected in everything he does. The most general term for this type of activity is the word *derekh,* which In Wisdom literature as well as in prophetic text denotes a life as a whole, a pattern of conduct of a certain quality. Thus, the prophets demand that Israel repudiate its "evil way" and return to God, and in the Wisdom literature the wise man advises the listener about the components of the good life. The right or straight path, according to the Psalter, can be taught; in fact it is taught by God directly, without intermediaries, as we learn from Psalm 27:11 when the poet requests: "teach me, God, your Ways" (*horeni YHVH derakhekha*). Through His Torah, God acts as a teacher.

The ideal way of life, according to Psalm 1, is charted by the Torah of God, which the happy man studies "day and night" (*yomam va-lailah*). *Torah* is here understood as the teachings or instructions of God, and it refers both to the legal tradition that specifies the laws God gave to Israel and to the Book of Psalms itself, which has become God's teachings to Israel.[39] The righteous person studies the Torah of God not only as a subject matter of meditation or contemplation, but through active oral recitation.[40] And the wholehearted devotion to God's Torah involves no compulsion or duress. On the contrary, the righteous man "delights in the Torah of YHVH" (*be-torat YHVH ḥeftzo*) because it is the source of everything good, joyful, and pleasant. (Cf. Ps. 37:31; Ps. 40 vv. 2–13)

Again, if we read this statement in light of Aristotle's analysis of happiness, we can say that the study of the Torah of God functions in the happy life of the righteous person just as philosophy functions in the life of the Greek lover of wisdom. Both are understood as delightful pleasurable pursuits, to which there is no limit, because the activity itself is good for its own sake. A main difference between the two pursuits, however, concerns their accessibility. In the philosophic culture of Aristotle's Greece, philosophy was reserved for a small elite of male citizens, whereas the admonition to engage in the constant study of Torah is addressed to all members of the community of Israel.[41]

The total immersion in the Torah of God contains its own reward. The righteous person who so acts is "like a tree planted besides streams of water/which yields its fruit in season/whose foliage never fades/and whatever it produces thrives"(v.2). This elaborate analogy was an adaptation of a prevalent metaphorization in Near Eastern literature in which trees symbolically represented the King.[42] Here, the evergreen represents the flourishing of the righteous person who leads the morally perfect life because he is focused on the Torah of God.[43] Like a tree that enjoys a constant flow of water and grows deep roots, so the righteous man enjoys the life of rootedness, stability, and security. As the tree lives in accordance with the rhythm of nature, bearing fruit at proper times (literally "in its time" [*be-itto*]), so the happy man enjoys an ordered life wherein things happen exactly at the appropriate time, not too early and not too late. Finally, as the tree is always green and its foliage never wilts (*yibbol*), so the happy person is able to respond to the challenges of life in a healthy and flexible manner. In short, every endeavor of the righteous person thrives ("*ve-khol asher ya`aseh yatzliaḥ*"), because he possesses internal integrity. Success and prosperity (*hatzlaḥah* in Hebrew) are the outcome of internal integrity, viz. virtue, which results in the overall wellness of the righteous man's life.[44]

In contrast to the happy life of the righteous man, the poem depicts the insubstantial life of the "the wicked," "sinners," and "scoffers." The poem does not detail their conduct, but if we read it in conjunction with other references to the "wicked" in Psalms and the Book of Proverbs, as does N. Sarna, a composite portrait of those unfortunates emerges.[45] In Psalm 1, the "wicked" are the godless, either those who deny that God has any interest in or knowledge of human action, or those who brazenly defy what they know God demands of humankind. Either way, the wicked ignore God's Torah and "plot against the righteous" (Ps. 37:12) or "seek to slay him" (Ps. 37:32).

Psalm 1 takes for granted the traditional view of retribution—the view contested in the Book of Job. Along with other Psalms, it assumes that God's eyes "are toward the righteous" (Ps. 34:15) and that He will intervene on their behalf (Ps. 7:9; Ps. 37:17). At the same time, He will cut the cords of the wicked (Ps. 129:4).

Psalm 1 is clearly aware that there are many who seem to prosper even though they do not conduct themselves righteously. Those people will not escape retribution, however, for they are "like chaff that the wind blows away" (v. 4). In other words, they may prosper for a while, but they will not succeed in weathering the winds of life because their lives are insubstantial. Nor will they survive judgment (*mishpat*) (v. 4b). Although we do not know when this "judgment" will take place (in this life, after death, or in the remote eschatological future), the Psalm clearly affirms that God rules justly and punishes those who deserve punishment.

"Righteous" (*tzaddiq*) is one of the epithets of God, who loves righteousness and justice (Ps. 33;5; 99:4). Indeed, the authors of the Psalms tell us that God is "just in all His ways" (Ps. 145:17) and that "His judgments are just" (Ps. 119:137). God judges righteously (Ps. 7:9, 11)—that is, He assists those who are the victims of injustice by punishing the wicked who perpetrate injustice.

God's people are expected to imitate His righteous actions. The righteousness (*tzedaqah*) of human beings, however, is not a matter of behaving in accordance with an abstract, ideal norm. Rather, it arises out of the relationship between God and those who are faithful to Him. It is defined within the boundaries of the covenantal relationship itself, the mutual promises and obligations between God and His chosen people, Israel. For the author of Psalm 1, the happy life is a life of justice and righteousness that involves faithfulness to God and willingness to follow His Torah.

The association of human well-being with divine justice (*tzedeq*) and righteousness marks the major difference between the Greek and Judaic approaches to happiness. Aristotle, as we saw in the previous chapter, held that right conduct does not flow from observing a general rule or behaving in accordance to laws, but from cultivating the proper dispositions that subordinate the passions and the appetites to the rule of reason. An act is good if it is performed by a good person, namely, one who possesses the virtues. In Psalm 1, by contrast, the goodness of the agent is directly linked to the degree to which he/she conforms to the will of God as expressed in God's Torah. The "righteous" *(tzaddiqim)* who are most happy conduct themselves according to "justice" (*be-mishpat*) as defined by the Torah, whereas the actions of the "wicked" ignore God's Torah and conflict with its just teachings. By contrasting the two types of individuals as two different ways of life, the poem makes it patently clear that the path to human flourishing is constituted by the life of Torah. This message is the foundation of the philosophic discourse on happiness.

The Interdependence of Wisdom and Creation

Ps. 119: The Saving Power of the Revealer of the Torah

The best or happy life is articulated most eloquently in two other Psalms—Pss. 19 and 119—that also belong to the Wisdom tradition and share similar language and themes with Psalm 1. These two poems[46] capture a theme that Jewish philosophers in the Middle Ages developed conceptually on the basis of the science of their day.

Psalm 119, the longest of all the Psalms, instructs the student in the rudiments of obedience to Torah by devoting each stanza to a letter of the Hebrew alphabet. The speaker asks God to deliver him from his suffering and his persecutors, a justified plea based on the devotion of the speaker to the Torah. He also asks God for additional wisdom so that he might more closely and rigorously follow the divine commandments, the source of his wisdom.

Precisely because the Torah is the locus of true wisdom, the one who lives by it experiences the happy life. The poem thus opens with the exclamation: "How happy those of blameless way [*temimei derekh*] / who walk in the Torah of YHVH." Referred to in various forms—"law," "decrees," "statutes," "commandments," "ordinances"—the Torah is presented as all-encompassing; no human concern, crisis, or issue remains outside its purview. It charts the "path" (v. 15) or "way" (vv. 3, 37) of the happy life. Faithfulness and obedience to it, however, do not entail a burden, but instead utter joy and delight.[47] Indeed, over and over (vv. 16, 24, 47, 70, 77, 92, 143, 174), the speaker associates Torah with the very "*sha'ashu'a*" that means "delight," "joy," or "pleasure," making it clear that obedience to Torah is a joyful activity because the Torah is life-giving, nourishing, and enlightening.

The speaker's total devotion to the Torah of God, however, does not mean that his life is free of difficulties. On the contrary, he speaks of the adversaries (e.g., vv. 61, 68, 69, 84, 95, 122, 153, 161) who pursue him. However, he is able to find support and rescue through devotion to Torah, which "revives the soul" (vv. 25, 28). The speaker's love of Torah (vv. 97, 163, 127) thus contains its own reward; because he is constantly oriented toward God, he rightfully enjoys His saving presence (v. 77). The poet's devotion to Torah is not focused on its formal study, however, but, as in Psalm 1, on the constant meditation and reflection about God's ways (v. 15). Adherence to Torah is thus both the end of the happy life as well as the very medium through which the speaker experiences his daily interaction with God.

Although the Torah is God's gift to the community of Israel, to which the speaker belongs, observing its commandments is personal for the speaker, and the happy life is possible because he totally internalizes God's teachings. The Torah becomes his portion (*ḥeleq*) (v. 57), a teaching that the speaker treasures in his heart (vs. 11, Cf. Ps. 40:7–8). It "distinguishes good from bad, clean from bad, holy from profane, whole from imperfect,"[48] so that by virtue of internalizing it, the poet is able to steer away from sin and in return justly hope for and expect God's salvation (v. 123). Living by God's instruction, then, does not automatically exclude pain and suffering, since human beings are not perfect. However, those made happy through Torah possess the means to overcome tribulations and enjoy the Torah's saving power.

Ps. 19: The Saving Power of the Creator of the Earth

God's life-giving Torah is good (*tovah*) because God is good.[49] In Wisdom literature, as von Rad has observed, "*tov*" is a beneficent power, a life-giving force that creates "well-being" and "life" in terms of possessions, fortune, name, children, longevity, etc. for the wise/righteous and for his community.[50] According to Psalm 119, God's gracious kindness (*ḥesed*) is expressed not only in the welfare of the individual but also in the very existence of the created world (*eretz*).[51] Indeed, the Book of Psalms presupposed the theology of creation even though it expresses this theology through poetic speech rather than through reasoned discourse. The Psalmists take for granted that YHVH, the God who revealed the Torah to Israel, is the creator of the cosmos who intervenes in its affairs through providence. Thus, if Psalm 119 highlights the intensely personal and intimate tie of the individual to God through observance of Torah—the speaker is God's servant (vv. 17, 125)—Psalm 19 glorifies the Torah of God by praising His splendid creation and governance of the world. The created world itself manifests the glory of God, the giver and teacher of Torah.

Indeed, Psalm 19 can be viewed as a sustained polemic against the deification of nature in neighboring pagan religions.[52] In contrast to prevailing paganism, our author states: "The heavens proclaim the glory of God/ and the sky manifests the work of his hands" (v. 1). Created by a transcendent God, nature praises God's glory by its very internal order, majesty, and splendor, thus extolling God's greatness without employing "speech" (*omer*), "words" (*devarim*), and "voice" (*qol*). Even the sun, which neighboring cultures worshiped as divine, is here portrayed as a servant of God, its creator. Contrary to pagan mythologies in which the Sun-God rests during the night in the sea, lying in the arms of his beloved, here the sun is like a "bridegroom leaving his chamber," and a "warrior [*gibbor*] who runs his course."[53]

If nature can speak of God's greatness without language, humans cannot; they are constituted through language. Therefore, the second part of the poem shifts its focus to the Torah of God, a linguistic structure through which divine-human communication is made possible. Not coincidentally, the way Torah functions in human life is similar to the way the sun functions in nature. As the sun provides vital heat and light, so the Torah is "radiant" (*barah*), and enlightens the eyes (*me'irat einayim*) (v. 8). As a life-giving force, it "revives the soul" (*meshivat nefesh*): its reviving power is rooted in the wisdom contained in its teachings. Hence, the Torah makes the fool wise (*maḥkimat peti*) and gladdens the heart of those who adhere to it. Its vitality makes it "more desirable than gold" and "sweeter than honey," two natural elements that share the same color as the sun and remind us of those admonitions in the Book of Proverbs that praise Wisdom above all material possessions, such as gold and silver.

The moral lesson from all this is self-evident: one should pursue only Torah rather than waste one's life in pursuit of commodities or pleasures that only lead to crime (*pesha*). The Torah itself constitutes a quality of life that is its own reward (v. 11). In short, it is not a static entity but an active power that transforms the lives of those who adhere to it. If God can be heard to speak through the "instruction," then one's life is revived (Ps. 19:7) and one's heart rejoices (Ps. 19:8). Light shines forth from the Torah (Ps. 119: 105, 130). The relationship of the individual to the Torah is characterized not by rigid observance but by joy, love, and eagerness. The Torah is the stream of life that makes human existence fruitful in wholesome, successful activity.

Creation Theology and the Foundation of Wisdom

A well-developed creation theology underlies the notion that the Torah of God is life giving. A full analysis of biblical creation theology will steer us away from our focus on happiness.[54] However, as some have argued, "the notion of God as Creator must be the formative and co-ordinating idea that holds together a biblical theology. Of all sections of biblical literature it is the Wisdom writings that give pride of place to the presupposition of a world governed by a single all-wise, all-seeing, and all-powerful Creator."[55]

While biblical creation theology differs from Aristotle's understanding of the relationship between the world and God, it shares with Aristotle the fundamental assumption that the universe is a purposive whole.[56] Both Aristotle and the biblical authors presuppose a teleological or purposeful structure in which everything occupies its proper, natural place. Thus Psalm 104 describes the assignment of beings to their local and temporal realms: the badger to the rocks, the stork to the cedar trees, the lion to the night, and man and his work to the day. Unlike in Aristotle, the teleological structure of the universe is ascribed in the Bible not to necessity, but to a purposeful creative act that brings everything into existence "in wisdom." Therefore, creation itself is intelligible to those who possess the wisdom to discern its internal order. The all-encompassing order of creation even has room for evil. As Proverbs 16:4 states: "The Lord has made everything for its purpose / even the wicked for the day of trouble."

That God created the world in Wisdom means not only that the world is governed by regularity and order, but also that the created world is founded upon a justice established by God in creation.[57] It follows that those who go against the created order of God, as do the wicked and the fool, sin against God. Thus Proverbs 14:31 warns us that "He who oppresses a poor man insults his Maker/but he who is kind to the needy honors him" and "he who mocks the poor insults his Maker" (17:5). Since the created order itself reflects divine justice, "knowledge of the world and education of man belong together."[58] The good life means a life of intrinsic goodness in which the good person imitates God's justice.

The identification of Wisdom and Torah made it amply clear that the right attitude to life—the attitude that guaranteed security, prosperity, and happiness—was "based on a religious commitment."[59] Character formation could not be based solely on human self-reliance; complete trust in God was advised, as we find, for example in Proverbs 3:5. The universal concerns of the sapiential tradition—such as the enigma of undeserved suffering, the inequities of life, and the finality of death—would now be viewed within the particularistic prism of Torah, the specific set of instructions by which the Israelite community would interact with God, interpret its past and present, and orient itself toward the future.

THE EMERGENCE OF JEWISH PHILOSOPHY

Hellenism and Hellenization

The fusion of prudential morality with a belief in the Torah as God's revealed word occurred during the Hellenistic period, after the conquest of the Near East by Alexander the Great and the establishment of the Hellenistic kingdoms of the Ptolemies in Egypt and the Seleucids in Syria. Greeks settled into newly established cities, and imported their material culture, political institutions, leisure patterns, educational system, civic religion, customs, and cultural sensibility. As the Greek language became the lingua franca of the Near East a process of Hellenization took place, gradually producing a syncretism between Greek culture and local traditions.

From the third century B.C.E. onward, the question that faced all Jews in Palestine and in the diaspora was not whether or not to Hellenize, but how much to Hellenize.[60] In Palestine this process began when the Ptolemies of Egypt established Greek cities that promoted Greek culture.[61] Jews studied Greek, visited the gymnasium, assumed Greek names, and absorbed other Greek cultural patterns. During the heyday of the Second Sophistic movement,[62] Greek orators established schools in Palestine. Since some of these cities, for example, Gedera and Ascalon, could boast thriving philosophical academies by 150 B.C.E., educated Jews in Palestine also had access to Greek *paideia,* including philosophy and rhetoric.[63]

Scholars have long debated the depth and scope of the Hellenization in Palestine.[64] While the debate is not fully settled, it is safe to say that the Hellenization of Palestine was an uneven process. Some regions (for example, the Coastal Plain) and some social classes (for example, the priesthood in Jerusalem, urban businessmen, and learned intellectuals) were more Hellenized than others. In general, the Hellenization process accelerated over time. After Palestine was conquered by the Seleucids of Syria in 198 B.C.E., the desired attitude toward Greek culture divided the Jerusalemite priesthood and the upper classes into radical and moderate factions. The most radical group wished to make Jerusalem into a Greek polis and support the policies of Antiochus IV, who prohibited the practice of Judaism as part of his attempt to consolidate his vast empire under the banner of a unified Hellenistic culture. His interference in the internal affairs of the Jews in Jerusalem led to the rebellion of the Maccabees, and eventually to the establishment of an independent Jewish state in 141 B.C.E. Yet as soon as the state was established the Hasmonean rulers conducted their affairs as typical Hellenistic rulers, further accelerating the process of Hellenization in Jewish Palestine. The details of these affairs and the religious diversity of the Jewish population in the Hasmonean state cannot concern us here. Suffice it to say that in the late Second Temple period, allegiance to the Jewish religion did not preclude profound Hellenistic acculturation. This point is made clear by looking at three examples: Ben Sira, the anonymous author of The Wisdom of Solomon, and Philo.

Ben Sira: The Equation of Torah and Wisdom

Jeshua (Jesus), son of Elazar, son of Sira was a Jeruselamite sage who headed his own "school of exegesis" (*beit midrash*), where instruction was imparted to individuals who wished to pursue Wisdom as a scholarly vocation.[65] His teachings, which were an example of a nationalist Jewish response to Hellenism,[66] were collected in a book known as "The Wisdom of the Son of Sirach," or "Ben Sira," or "Ecclesiasticus."[67] Writing in Hebrew between 198 B.C.E. and 175 B.C.E., this member of a priestly family articulated a view of happiness that characterized the life of the upper classes in Jerusalem in a period when Jerusalem's aristocracy was deeply divided. The faction that was allied to old Ptolemaic power condoned a moderate Hellenization, while the faction that pursued alliance with the Seleucids supported a more rapid and thorough Hellenization. As a member of the wealthy establishment in Jerusalem, Ben Sira supported the Temple cult that the priests administrated, but he rejected the separatist tendencies of Ezra and Nehemia who forbade intermarriages.[68]

Ben Sira's upper class posture is evident in his decision to write under his own name and promote the scribal profession over all other professions (51:13–30). Like Aristotle, he disdained commerce and menial labor[69] and portrayed the ideal life as an ongoing search for Wisdom; that search included extensive travel, cosmopolitan learning, association with the elite, and counsel to kings. Also like Aristotle and Plato, among other ancient philosophers, Ben Sira understood the relationship between the seeker of knowledge and the object of his search—Wisdom—as a form of love. For him, therefore, the lifelong preoccupation with Wisdom/Torah, was a Jewish *philosophia*.

In Ben Sira's academy, students of the scribal profession studied Scripture along with ancient Wisdom tradition, especially the Book of Proverbs. Ben Sira's aphorisms and didactic poetry also indicate his familiarity with the writings of the Stoics, Homer, Theogonis, and the Greek epideictic literature.[70] Since in the Hellenistic world the scribe (*grammateus*) functioned officially as a government official who performed administrative, financial, or judicial duties, it is probable that Ben Sira held a similar position. He pointed with pride to his profession as a "scribe" (*sofer*), however, and demonstrated his readiness to borrow Greek expressions and ideas only as long as they were subjected to a thorough Hebraizing. His allegiance to the ancestral tradition meant adherence to the basic worldview of the sage of the monarchical period—that is, the worldview expressed in the Book of Proverbs. However, unlike Proverbs, Ben Sira's writings are the first Wisdom text actually to quote Scripture, referring to primeval history (Gen. 1–11), the covenant with Noah (17:2), the Patriarchal narratives, and King David. Ben Sira does not mention particular laws, but speaks of Torah as that specific conduct that is guided by traditional sagacity.

The main purpose of Ben Sira's writings was to defend Judaism against competing philosophies. Judaism, according to him, is a comprehensive mode of life that is rooted in its own Wisdom, which is superior to that of the Greeks, because Jewish Wisdom literally is divine. Not only does Wisdom come from God, it is synonymous with God. Later, in the first century C.E., Josephus would employ this line of argument in his apologetic defense of Judaism, *Against Apion*, and throughout the Middle Ages it would resurface in a variety of forms, theoretical and practical, as we shall see later in this book.

The Glorification of Wisdom

Elaborating on Proverbs 8:22–31, Ben Sira speculates about Wisdom, praising it as the first of all created things and the principle that informs the created order: "It is He [YHVH] who created her / He saw her and took her measure/He poured her out upon all his works" (1:9). Like Proverbs, Ben Sira personifies Wisdom (chap. 24) as a female who seduces her pursuers as, for example, when she says: "Come to me, you who desire me/and eat your fill of my fruits / For the memory of me is sweeter than honey / and the possession of me sweeter than the honeycomb" (24:19–20).[71] But Ben Sira goes beyond Proverbs when he equates Wisdom, who was with God at the creation of the world, with the Torah of the sacred tradition: "All this is the book of the covenant of the Most High God / the Law that Moses commanded us as an inheritance for the congregations of Jacob" (24:23). As a member of the assembly of the Most High, Wisdom proceeded from the mouth of God at the beginning of time, before anything else was created. She came down from her throne on a pillar of cloud to wander through the world in search of a resting place, a search that ended when she came to rest in the sanctuary of the "beloved city," Jerusalem (24:1–12).

Scholars have noted that Ben Sira's depiction of Wisdom is very similar to that of the Egyptian goddess Isis, whose cult was very popular during the Ptolemaic Empire and long afterwards.[72] There are speeches in which Isis lists her accomplishments and titles in the first person, stating how she presided over Creation as the eldest daughter of Re and how she came down from her heavenly abode to search throughout the world for a place in which to establish her cult. She was also known by the title "lawgiver" and was identified by her theologians with *Maat*, principle of both cosmic and social order. In this capacity Isis/Maat proclaimed laws for humanity, maintained justice and righteousness, and sustained the social order.

Apparently Ben Sira was familiar with these liturgical texts of the cult of Isis and made use of them in his portrait of Wisdom,[73] seeking to endow Torah with universal significance. In language reminiscent of Psalms 1 and 119, he depicts the Torah as the source of vitality that irrigates his own plot, namely, his school, and becomes in the process a source of life and growth for others (24:31–32).

The root of Wisdom and the ultimate source of human happiness, according to Ben Sira, is the Fear of the Lord (1:11–20; 19:20; 25:10–11; 34:13–17). In accord with the teaching of Proverbs, he portrays the ideal sage: "Better is the God-fearing man who lacks intelligence / than the highly prudent man who transgresses the Law" (19:24). Such fear, leading primarily to observance of Torah or the commandments, is also associated with reverence for the Temple service. Thus Wisdom, Fear of the Lord, and Torah are intricately interrelated in the teachings of Ben Sira. "All wisdom is the fear of the Lord / and in all wisdom there is the fulfillment of the law" (19:20).

The Fear of God, then, is the bridge between the theoretical or speculative aspects of Wisdom and the prudential ethics recommended by Ben Sira. His ideal sage, who follows Dame Wisdom, is the one who knows how to conceal his thoughts and how to retain secrets; he shuns the temptations of adultery while being married to a sensible wife; he is able to control his appetites (especially for wine), while enjoying moderate physical pleasures;[74] he is careful in the selection of friends and counselors and avoids slander and hasty speech; he practices generosity and kindness, but without the zeal of the prophets who spoke against injustice. In general, the prudentialist ethics of Ben Sira are pervaded by caution and careful concern for a balanced life.[75]

An "Inclusive" Interpretation of Happiness

For Ben Sira the main virtues of the wise man are self-control and temperance. He speaks more favorably about the external goods such as wealth (31:8) than did Proverbs, but recognizes their dangers and how they may lead one to stray from the right path. Likewise, Ben Sira recommends sensual pleasures such as drinking wine, as long as one indulges in moderation (31:27). His general attitude toward life is one of joy (30:22), rejecting jealousy, anger, anxiety or vengefulness as negative attitudes or vices that shorten one's life (30:23–24).

Ben Sira's view of the happy life accords with the "inclusive" interpretation of Aristotle's conception of happiness. That is to say, the good life includes certain external goods such as wealth, family, friends, and attentive listeners. This bourgeois view, which Gordis characterized as "proto-Sadducean,"[76] entails a moderate and prudent enjoyment of life in this world. It ends with death, after which all that remains is one's reputation. Ben Sira's concern for a lasting reputation is linked to his view of shame, which he absorbed from Greek philosophical sources, especially Plato's philosophy.[77]

However, unlike Plato and his followers, Ben Sira did not share the belief in the immortality of the soul that was endorsed by the Pharisees and by Jewish philosophers in the Egyptian diaspora.

THE FIRST JEWISH PHILOSOPHERS

In the Egyptian diaspora, Jews constituted a distinct *politeuma* (i.e., a quasi-independent and self-regulating communal organization) with the freedom to observe their own religious rites. Still, their adoption and adaptation of Greek culture was profound. The Greek language quickly replaced Hebrew and Aramaic, necessitating by the third century B.C.E. the translation of the Bible into Greek. The Septuagint assured the continued allegiance of diaspora Jews to their sacred tradition as well as the emergence of Jewish creativity in the Greek language. Writing for Jews, gentiles, or for a mixed audience, Jewish authors adopted Greek literary modes, which gave rise to new Jewish literary genres, including chronography, romance, drama, epic, lyric poetry and, most relevant to us, philosophy.[78]

The first Jewish philosopher known to us by name was Aristobulus, a Jew who "worked as an adviser on Jewish affairs to the pro-Jewish Ptolemy IV Philometer (180–145 B.C.E.)."[79] Between 176 and 170 B.C.E. he published *An Explanation of the Mosaic Scripture,* which he dedicated to Ptolemy VI Philomotor in an attempt to answer that latter's questions about the Torah. This earliest attempt to reconcile the Bible with Greek philosophy by means of allegorization survived only in references of the Church Fathers, Clement, and Eusebius, who used it to support Christian teachings.[80]

Aristobulus wanted the reader to understand the Torah philosophically and to demonstrate the rationality of the Jewish religion, which is indeed presented as a type of philosophical school (*hairesis*).[81] His intention, however, was not to merge the Jewish religion with Greek philosophy, but to make sense of his ancestral culture through the prism of Greek philosophy. In fact, Aristobulus argued that Judaism is superior to other philosophical schools because "Plato and the philosophers borrowed from Moses."[82] Indeed, the God of the Jews and the God of the gentile philosophers, according to Aristobulus, are one and the same, a view that would become commonplace in medieval Jewish philosophy.

The extant writings of Aristobulus indicate that Jewish thinkers were familiar with Greek virtue ethics. Aristobulus in particular was at home in the works of Aristotle, including his analysis of happiness in the *Ethics* and the debate about virtue between the Peripatetics and the Stoics.[83] He sided with Aristotle and the Stoics in their claim that moral virtue has value and that external goods such as wealth or material success do not constitute happiness. However, unlike the Greek philosophers, Aristobulus held that right conduct was ordained by God. Hence, he made piety (*eusebeia*), the Septuagint translation of "Fear of God," a cardinal virtue that alone leads to the knowledge of good and evil and the desire to fulfill the divine law.

What makes Aristobulus' teaching thoroughly Jewish is his identification of Torah with the rational wisdom of the philosophers. In his view, since the Torah teaches philosophical truths, it must not be taken literally. Those who cling to the letter of Scripture are devoid of intelligence and unable to understand the thoughts of Moses. For example, Aristobulus interprets the Sabbath as the beginning of intellectual light in which all things are beheld, making the inner meaning of the Sabbath identical with Wisdom. The seventh day is holy because it refers to the proportion of seven, thereby giving us knowledge of all things, human and divine.

The allegorical method enabled Aristobulus and other educated Jews in the Egyptian diaspora to explain to themselves and to non-Jews the meaning of the Jewish practices, beliefs, and sacred texts that kept the Jews a people apart in the Greco-Roman world—and that elicited admiration and respect for them as well as suspicion and hatred.[84] One contemporary of Aristobulus was the anonymous author of the "Letter of Aristeas to Philocrates," which illustrates that loyalty to Judaism was compatible with immersion in Greek culture. It was written most likely in Alexandria as a supposed account of how the Egyptian king commissioned a Greek translation of the Hebrew Bible and how the seventy-two translators discussed matters of kingship. For our purposes it is instructive that the text depicts the translators as "excellent" or virtuous people who were well-versed in Greek scholarship (*paideia*). Most importantly, their excellence was to be found in their ability to act in accordance with the "mean," as Plato and Aristotle's virtue ethics taught.[85] They were neither uncouth nor conceited in dealing with others; they could listen and comment appropriately. The description of the group thus fits the scribal ideal of Wisdom literature and has much in common with Ben Sira.

The Wisdom of Solomon

The author of the *Wisdom of Solomon* was thoroughly conversant with Middle Platonism (a philosophical school that flourished from 80 B.C.E. to 220 C.E. and that was steeped in Stoicism), the Egyptian cult of Isis, and the Jewish Wisdom tradition. Composed as an exhortatory discourse (*logos protreptikos*),[86] the Wisdom of Solomon is an attempt to place the Jewish religion within a broad philosophical context, intelligible to educated contemporaries who are steeped in Hellenistic philosophy. The author identifies himself with King Solomon and, on the basis of I Kings 3, presents Solomon as having achieved a union with Wisdom through searching and praying (7:7–9; 9:1–18). Thus, the *Wisdom of Solomon* perpetuates the existing Jewish tradition that made Solomon the prototype of the sage and the patron of arts and sciences, a tradition further developed by medieval Jewish philosophers.

The major focus of the book is praise to Wisdom. Like the World-Soul of the Stoics, Wisdom is understood as a principle of order that "reaches mightily from one end of the earth to the other, and she orders all things well." (8:1). Inspired by a Stoic *Hymn to Zeus*, the author of *The Wisdom of Solomon* lists 22 attributes of Wisdom. It is a spirit (*pneuma*) that is "intelligent, holy, unique, manifold, subtle, mobile, clear, unpolluted, distinct, invulnerable, loving the good, keen, irresistible, beneficent, humane, steadfast, sure, free from anxiety, all powerful, overseeing all and penetrating through all spirits that are intelligent, pure and altogether subtle" (7:22). Its portrayal as a "reflection of eternal light / a spotless mirror of the working of God / and an image of his goodness" (7:26) betrays the ontology of Middle Platonism. As a spiritual entity, it is more real than its reflections. Wisdom exists on its own as an emanation of God's glory and as His agent in creation. Its brightness is more radiant than the sun. Like the sun, Wisdom possesses generative powers—"she can do all things / while remaining in herself" manifested, especially in the life of humans, since "in every generation she passes into holy souls / and makes them friends of God, and prophets" (7:27)."

In a language that suggests familiarity with Neo-Pythgoreanism as well as with Middle Platonism, the author turns Wisdom into a hypostasis, that is, "a quasi-personification of certain attributes proper to God, occurring in an intermediate position between personalities and abstract beings."[87] On the basis of emanationist ontology, Wisdom is portrayed as a force that pervades the entire cosmos while remaining intimately close to God (7:24; 8:1, 3). Because it is identical with the Divine Mind through which God acts (9:9), it contains the paradigmatic patterns of all things (9:8) and serves as the instrument in their creation of the universe out of formless matter. In this sense, Wisdom is identical with Divine Providence over the created cosmos.

Notwithstanding the supernal status of Wisdom, human beings who are devoted to her pursuit can easily find her (6:12–16) because they are endowed with the rational mind, the foundation of kinship between humanity and God's Wisdom (8:17;7:23–24). The lover of Wisdom makes her his "bride" and "spouse," enjoying intimate kinship with her (8:9; 7:28; 8:16). However, since she is an attribute of God, intimacy with her entails a mystical union with God. In the *Wisdom of Solomon*, then, for the first time in Jewish texts, supreme happiness, the ultimate end of human life, is characterized as a mystical union between God and the lover of Wisdom. Thus Wisdom is both immanently present in us while at the same time transcendent to the cosmos and temporal human life. This outlook becomes the cornerstone of the philosophical conception of happiness in the Jewish Middle Ages, even though those later philosophers did not have access to the Wisdom of Solomon.

The pursuit of Wisdom, according to our text, yields an encyclopedic scope of knowledge, including the natural sciences, all human arts and crafts, logic and rhetoric, the divinatory arts, and all moral knowledge (8:7). The possession of such a vast storehouse bestows on the possessor not only joy and riches in this world, but the greatest boon of all, the immortality of the soul (8:9–13). To my knowledge, the *Wisdom of Solomon* is the first Jewish text to associate happiness with immortality of the soul.

Unquestionably, the author of *Wisdom of Solomon* derived the doctrine of immortality of the soul from Platonic sources. However, whereas Plato spoke about the pre-existence of the soul, the author of *Wisdom* builds on the biblical notion of creation in the image of God. Since the soul is created in the image of the immortal God, it too is potentially immortal, even though it associates with the perishable body for the duration of one's life (8:19–20; 9:15). The soul can overcome death by acquiring wisdom, which restores it to its original integrity (6:17–20; 8:13. 17).

Those who pursue Wisdom are granted the four cardinal virtues—self-control, prudence, justice, and courage (Wis. 8:7). This is Plato's list of virtues (*Phaedro* 69c; *Republic* 427e; *Laws* 631c), which Zeno, the founder of Stoic philosophy, had adopted and the author of *Wisdom* endorsed wholeheartedly.[88] To obtain the cardinal virtues, the ideal sage must abstain from the enjoyment of good things—such as "costly wine and perfumes" (2:7)—that are the concern of the ungodly "who reason unsoundly" (2:1). By cultivating the virtues—that is, taming the body's passions—the soul can regain immortal life.

With the doctrine of immortality of the soul, the conception of happiness takes a new turn. True happiness is not only predicated on the condition of the soul (7:8–10); it is also the ultimate goal of human life and the culmination of the pursuit of Wisdom (6:17–20). To accomplish the ultimate end, the soul must live a life of righteousness and justice, since only the righteous will enjoy immortal life. The life of righteousness means a process of purification or purgation. The soul must rid itself of fraudulence, cunning, arrogance and any form of injustice that prevents the pursuit of Wisdom. Moreover, the pure soul requires a trusting heart, one that does not seek to test the Lord. It avoids every trace of murmuring against God, while obeying His commandments. The process of purification thus enables the soul to become holy as it fulfills God's holy ordinances in holiness.

For the author of *Wisdom of Solomon*, the righteous one who lives this holy life will be able to survive the death of the body and live forever, which is the ultimate reward for righteousness (Wis. 5:15). Death is now understood as an entrance into a life of blessed eternity. The *Wisdom of Solomon* thus departs from the views of Ben Sira to endorse an idea that became the hallmark of Pharisaic-Rabbinic Judaism. Unlike the Pharisees and their rabbinic heirs, however, it is silent on the resurrection of the dead, another important tenet of rabbinic Judaism.

A link between the purification of the soul, a life of virtue and righteousness, and immortality is common in Middle Platonism, but these ideas were given a Jewish "twist" when the author connected Wisdom and prophecy. *The Wisdom of Solomon* never explicitly identifies Wisdom and Torah, as does Ben Sira, but it does speak of Wisdom as the source of prophecy and suggests that Wisdom is the direct bearer of revelation. In the last part of the book (chaps. 10–19), the author discusses the role of Wisdom as an active principle in history, especially in the history of Israel, from creation to the exodus. While his discussion does not identify Wisdom specifically with Torah, he implies that Wisdom is the archetypal Torah of which Mosaic Law is an image.

The observance of Israel's Law is therefore no longer a parochial affair. Instead, it is Israel's way of being true to the God-bestowed order and harmony of the world. The laws in question, that is, Wisdom's laws, include biblical laws, but they are placed in a broader context by being derived from Wisdom as a cosmic principle. Even when the author speaks of Moses' leadership of the Israelites in the wilderness, he presents Moses as a prophet rather than as a lawgiver (11:10).

PHILO: HAPPINESS AS THE IMMORTALITY OF THE SOUL

The Judeo-Hellenistic philosophical culture reached its culmination with Philo of Alexandria (15 B.C.E.–50 C.E.). Scion of one of the wealthiest and most prominent Jewish families in Alexandria,[89] Philo belonged to the social elite that educated its members privately in institutions of its own.[90] Most Jewish members of the upper social class did not renounce Judaism. At the same time, however, they did not engage in ideological battles to defend their lifestyles. But when some Jews expressed disbelief in divine providence and interpreted biblical texts strictly as philosophical allegory, Philo spoke against them, arguing that they wanted to assimilate into Hellenistic-Roman society and abandon Judaism. This was precisely what his own brother, Alexander Lysimachus, did when he became chief inspector of customs on the Eastern border of Egypt and guardian of the Emperor Tiberius' mother. Philo's son Alexander also became an apostate, and his public career took him to the highest post of a Roman official in Egypt, that of a prefect. Philo himself headed the delegation of five sent by the Jewish community of Alexandria to the emperor Gaius Caligula after anti-Jewish riots broke out in Alexandria in 39–40 C.E. As a member of the Jewish aristocracy in Egypt, Philo enjoyed recreational activities that were part of the cultural life of a Greek polis—theater, concerts, boxing, wrestling, and horseracing. Still, he counseled against participating in public festivals because they often turned into unpleasant public displays of anger, rivalry, and licentiousness.

Although Philo was thoroughly proficient in the philosophy of Plato, Aristotle, the Stoics, and Pythagoreanism,[91] his allegiance to Scripture was never in question. Drawing on the Jewish Wisdom tradition (including Proverbs, Ecclesiastes, Song of Songs, the Wisdom of Ben Sira, and the Wisdom of Solomon),[92] Philo contributed to the discourse on happiness by working out both philosophically and exegetically the details of the association of happiness (*eudaimonia*) with Torah (*nomos*) and reason (*logos*). Indeed, the nexus of virtue, knowledge, and well-being in Philo presaged many of the attempts of later medieval Jewish philosophers to reconcile Judaism and Greek philosophy. This is why Harry A. Wolfson was correct to regard all of medieval Jewish philosophy as a continuation of Philo.

Philo agrees with the Greek philosophers that only a life lived in accordance with reason leads to human happiness. However, Philo distinguishes between shallow philosophy or empty rhetoric and the genuine pursuit of Wisdom when he speaks about those who

> ... giving up their time for the study of philosophy, not of that sort of philosophy which word catchers and sophists seek to reduce to a system, selling doctrines and reasonings as they would any other vendible thing in the market ... but who, applying themselves to the kindred philosophy, which they make up of these components parts, namely,

of intention, and words, and actions, all united into one species, in order to the acquisition and enjoyment of happiness (*Vit. Mos.* II XXXIX. 212).[93]

The true philosophic life consists of a harmonious blend of theoretical, linguistic, and practical activities. For Philo all three are to be found in the divine Law of Moses, which leads its adherents to the attainment of the ultimate end of human life—the seeing of God. True happiness, Philo tells us, combines virtue and the philosophic life as follows:

> Hope is the source of all happiness; hope excites those persons who are filled with an admiration of virtue to study philosophy, under the idea that by her means they will be able to obtain a clear sight of the nature of all existing things, and to do things which are in accordance with and consistent with the perfection of those who most excellent modes of life—and contemplative and the practical [sic], which he who attains to is at once truly happy (*Praem* II. 11).

Theology

Philo's conception of happiness is predicated on the identification of the biblical God with the God of the Greek philosophers. The former is the Creator of the universe who entered into a historical relationship with one nation, Israel. The latter is the perfect Being who is truly self-sufficient. The Creator is the "transcendent source of all that exists" (*Deus Imm.* XXV. 116), "the Highest of causes" (*Som.* Book I XXXIII.190), or the "Being who is uncreated and everlasting, and maker of the universe" (*Decal.* XIV. 64). Echoing Aristotle, Philo also holds that God is perfectly self-sufficient. God "possesses all things and needs nothing" (*Vit. Mos* I XXVIII. 157); "He gains benefit from nothing, seeing that he is neither in need of anything nor does any exist capable of adding to his superiority of all things" (*Det.* XVI. 54). As Pure Being, God is "the first and most perfect of all things; from whom, as from a fountain, all particular blessings are showered upon the world, and upon the things are people in it [sic]" (*Decal.* XVI. 81)

The language is undoubtedly Platonic, but Philo seems to go beyond Plato by insisting that God is "beyond the Good itself and the Beautiful itself." As the primal Good, "[God] alone is happy and blessed, having no participation in any evil whatever, but being full of all perfect blessings. Or rather, if one is to say the exact truth, being Himself the good, who has showered all particular good things over the heaven and earth." (*Spec. Leg.* II XIV. 53). God's perfection is complete, "for the blessed and most happy One does not admit any likeness or comparison or parable; nay, rather He is beyond blessedness itself and happiness and whatever is more excellent and better than these."

By combining the views of Plato and Aristotle, Philo explicitly delineates the connection between perfect goodness, self-sufficiency, and happiness. The source of God's perfection is His totally incorporeal nature. God "is free from all pain, and free from all fear; He has no participation in any evils, He yields to no one, he suffers no sorrow, He knows no fatigue, He is full of unalloyed happiness; His nature is entirely perfect, or rather God is Himself the perfection, and completion, and boundary of happiness" (*Cher.* XXV 86). The Creator God who is the source of all existents is therefore both the origin of human happiness as well as the ultimate end which men seek. If God is perfect happiness, the happy life must be a life that seeks to imitate God. Such a life is what the Bible calls "holy," a life that Israel must be called to lead by observing God's law. Philo's religious ethics follows from his conception of God as the source of all goodness and the perfection of Good.

Logos: a Bridge between God and Creation

God created the world as an expression of His unbounded goodness. Philo states: "For God is both all good, and is also the maker and creator of the universe; and He also created it having a foreknowledge of what would take place, and being its preserver and most blessed benefactor, full of every kind of happiness." (*Spec. Leg.* I XXXVIII. 209). As the "Father" and "Maker" of the universe, God continues to care for the world after its creation through "invisible powers" that hold the universe together (*Mig. Abr.* XXXII. 181). Divine providential care sustains and nourishes everything, as the biblical manna in the wilderness illustrates figuratively. Yet, though God's love extends to His creation, God is not in the world.

God is ontologically and temporally prior to the world, transcending time and space. The ontological gap between the all-perfect source of Being and the created universe is bridged by the Logos, a "rational thought of mind expressed in utterance or speech."[94] The Logos is present in God, in the created order of the universe, and within man, who is "created in the image of God." Philo's Logos doctrine can be traced to both Jewish and Greek sources. It is undoubtedly indebted to the Stoic doctrine of Logos, which Philo divested of its pantheistic connotation by identifying it with the Word of God by which the world was created. However, Philo's doctrine of the Logos can also be traced to the Jewish Wisdom tradition of Proverbs, Ben Sira, and the Wisdom of Solomon, all of which present the Word of God as revealed in the Law. With his Jewish predecessors, Philo personified the Logos as the rather masculine counterpart to the feminine figure of Wisdom.

Philo's Logos is not a separate entity but rather the thought of God that is expressed in the rational order of the universe, intelligible to the human mind. God "has stamped with a particular character that which previously had no character, and has endowed with form that which had previously no distinctive form, and having perfected the entire world, he has impressed upon it an image and appearance, namely, his own word" (*Som.* Book II VI. 45). Logos is that stamp. In this regard Logos is an *eikon* of God that is to be found in the rational order visible in the universe. That order is accessible to human beings, because they are created in the "image of God," namely, because they are created with a reasoning power, the soul (*Quest. Gen* II. 62). Philo states:

> but man, who is the most excellent of all animals, in respect of that predominant part that is in him, namely, his soul, is also most closely related to the heaven, which is the purest of all things in its essence, and as the common language of the multitude affirms, to the Father of the world, inasmuch as he has received mind, which is of all the things that are upon the earth the closest copy and most faithful representation of the everlasting and blessed idea (*Decal.* XXV 134).

The Human Being

Since God Himself is Light, and the archetypal source of every other light, the Logos, as an emanation of divine light, enables the human mind to "see" the pattern of the created world. Not surprisingly Philo would define the ultimate purpose of human life in visual language, namely, the "seeing" of God. Whether this is an ecstatic experience or the highest form of rational knowledge proper has been long debated by scholars.[95] God, of course, is not to be seen with the eyes of the body but with the eyes of the soul, or mind (*Abr.* XII. 57). Yet, "seeing" God is the goal of human life.

According to Philo, the creation "in the image of God" is a figurative expression for Plato's doctrine of the soul, and the human ability to "see" God is explained in that context. Human beings are a composite of corporeal body and spiritual soul, two substances that unite for the duration of one's life and then separate at death. Originally, says Philo,

> the Creator made no soul in any body capable of seeing its Creator by its own intrinsic powers. But having considered that the knowledge of the Creator and the proper understanding of the work of Creation would be of great advantage to the creature (for such knowledge is the boundary of happiness and blessedness), He breathed into him from above something of His own divine nature (*Det.* XXIV. 86).

The same idea is spelled out in another place when Philo says "Moses affirms that this man was an image and imitation of God, being breathed into his face in which is the place of the sensations" (*Op.* XLVIII. 139). The presence of the divine breath in the first created human being, Adam, would have enabled him to be as happy as God. However, Adam chose to turn away from God and focus instead on the pleasures of his body:

> [Adam] deliberately chose what was false and disgraceful, and evil, and despised what was good, and honorable, and true; for which conduct he was very fairly condemned to change an immortal for a mortal existence, being deprived of blessedness and happiness, and therefore he naturally was changed so as to descend into a laborious and miserable life (*Virt.* XXXVII. 205).

For Philo, the biblical creation narrative posits the human reality that the body is the source of passions and temptations that lead one away from focusing on God. Echoing the Orphic motifs of Platonic psychology, Philo speaks about the body as a "tomb of the soul" (*Spec Leg.* IV XXXVI. 188). The body is "an evil thing, and one that plots against the soul and that is at all times lifeless and dead" (*Leg. All.* III XXII. 69). Thus the association of the divine soul with the corporeal body poses both a danger and a challenge to the soul. If the soul is ruled by the passions of the body, it will fail to become like God, but if the Soul properly controls the body, directing it to the ultimate goal of human life, one can participate to some extent in the life of the Logos, and thereby escape the body. In this respect, all humans are "allied to the divine Reason, having come into being as a copy or fragment or ray of that blessed nature." Therefore, Philo exhorts his readers to leave the body and its passions: "Be alienated from them in your mind, allowing none of them to cling to you, standing above them all" (*Mig. Abr.* II. 7).

The purpose of Philo's ethical teachings, then, is to direct his readers on the path that leads the human soul to become Godlike, culminating in the mystical experience of "seeing God." To attain the ultimate end of human life, we must devote ourselves to the acquisition of virtue. As Philo says with Aristotle, "For it is the use and enjoyment of virtue that is happiness, and not the bare possession of it" (*Det.* XVII, 59). In other words, "Happiness is the employment of perfect virtue in a perfect life" (ibid. 60).

Ethics: Virtue and Virtues

Philo had at his disposal two distinct Greek definitions of virtue. According to Aristotle, we recall, it is a mean between the two extremes of an excess or a deficiency. Virtue emerges through habitual practice when reason controls the emotions and the passions in accordance with the doctrine of the mean. Thus the Peripatetics acknowledged that some emotions are useful, recognized degrees between virtues and vices, and counseled moderation. In contrast, the Stoics held that virtue is the only good, that between virtue and vice there is no middle ground, and that virtue is acquired by extirpation of passions (*apatheia*).[96] They called for the obliteration of all feelings and emotions in order to become free of them, denied differences in importance between various virtues and vices, and held that humans are either perfectly virtuous or perfectly wicked.

On the nature of virtue, Philo, as did the author of IV Maccabees,[97] sided with the Peripatetics against the Stoics. Philo did not regard all emotions as negative, because they were given by God. Indeed, some are good and virtuous—for example, "righteous anger," about which Aristotle speaks in the *Ethics* (IV: 5 1125b 26–1126b10), and pity and compassion, which are absent from Aristotle's analysis. Philo also believed that some sins involving emotions and feelings are less grave than others. Furthermore, he did not believe that human beings are either perfectly virtuous or perfectly wicked. Instead, he considered life as a process of self-improvement through the gradual acquisition of virtues. Philo, therefore, adopted the Aristotelian doctrine of the mean, which he understood as a doctrine of moderation.

According to Philo, for most human beings, moderation between excess and deficiency is the best path; it is "the straight path" prepared by God for men of virtue (*Migr. Abr.* XXVI.146). Following the "midmost line" is the proper way to develop virtue, a position that was shared by other Jewish intellectuals of the Judeo-Hellenistic diaspora, such as the anonymous author of the *Letter of Aristeas*, who described the "middle course" as "the best course to pursue."98 To attain the middle road, self-control is particularly necessary in order to combat desire. Thus, for most people virtue does not mean the absence of emotion and feeling, but their moderate control.

However, the Stoic view of virtue is not totally absent in Philo's writings. His description of exceptional individuals such as Moses resonates with the Stoic doctrine that the emotions must be extirpated.99 In the case of Moses, anger must be cut out completely, "for no moderation of passion can satisfy him," a rendering that clearly changes the plain meaning of the biblical text.100 The complete absence of passions was possible only because Moses received special assistance from God. His share of "surpassing excellence" includes even the power to cut out the passions. Moses is therefore called divine and holy since he was "perfectly wise" (*Leg. All.* III XLVIII. 140). But again, Philo does not remain a consistent Stoic. Contrary to the early Stoic teacher, Chrisippus, who held that hatred of evil is not appropriate to the wise man, Philo holds that Scripture does teach us to feel the hatred of evil and even describes the hatred of evil as a virtue that Moses possessed.101

By Philo's day the Aristotelian division of the virtues into moral and intellectual virtues was a commonplace. We recall that the moral virtues come from habitual practice through "experience and time," while the intellectual virtues come from instruction. According to Aristotle and Plato, the inculcation of moral and intellectual virtues is the duty of the state, which must build the proper educational system to train its citizens in those virtues. For Aristotle the laws that can accomplish the desired education are the patterns of nature that can be discovered by reason. Knowledge of the laws of nature, then, is necessary for the cultivation of virtue and the formation of the good character. The Stoics lived in a period of breakdown of the city-states, and therefore de-emphasized the role of the state in the acquisition of virtue. Instead of the enacted laws of the state, they substituted the unwritten law of nature, discoverable by human reason as the law that one must follow in order to cultivate virtue.

Philo presents Aristotelian and Stoic themes in an interesting fusion and then gives it a distinctly Jewish interpretation. On the one hand, he endorses the claim that the good life is a life shaped by a law that is rooted in reason and in nature. However, he did not believe that human reason could discover the laws of nature on its own. Only a law that was revealed by God, the creator of nature, can be in accordance with nature, "for such a law, being the work of God, is like nature itself, and like nature it is universal and eternal and immutable."102 That law, Philo would insist, is the Law of

Moses. It alone would lead one to the attainment of happiness by inculcating true beliefs and good deeds.

Philo's classification of the virtues combines elements from Plato and from Aristotle, to which he added his own religious contribution. One classification of the virtues, based on Platonic ontology, is the distinction between generic Virtue and specific virtues. That distinction is the core of Philo's allegorical interpretation of the Garden of Eden narrative (Gen. 2:10–14). Eden stands for the Wisdom of God, the Logos; and the trees in the Garden are "trees of Virtue God plants in the soul" (*Leg. All.* I XVII, 56). The "tree of Life" is generic Virtue, from which all specific virtues flow, and its pre-eminence is denoted by its location in the middle of the garden, which is the Soul. In Philo's interpretation of Genesis. 2:9, God caused every theoretical and practical virtue to spring out of the Soul. Along with the biblical text, Philo wrestles with the origin of evil in a world created by a benevolent God, and with the difference between the two trees. He explains the difference by alluding to the potentiality of the soul. The Soul, Philo explains, "resembles wax, which is capable of receiving every impression, whether good or bad." (*Leg. All.* I XVIII, 61). Philo further explains that when the soul "receives the impression of perfect virtue, it has become the Tree of Life; but when it has received the impression of vice, it has then become the Tree of the Knowledge of Good and Evil, and vice and all evil have been banished from the divine company." Without solving all the exegetical and theological difficulties of the biblical text, Philo concludes that the Tree of Knowledge of Good and Evil is not in Paradise, properly speaking (*Leg. All.* I XXXII, 100).

Generic Virtue, namely goodness, is represented in the biblical narrative not only by the Tree of Life but also by the River (*Leg. All.* I XIX. 65). The Virtue that issues forth out of Eden is an aspect of divine reason. In this regard Philo follows the Wisdom literature (Prov. 8: 1 ff. and Wisdom 9–12). Philo contrasts Wisdom with its opposite, Pleasure. If Eden represents the Wisdom of God and the River stands for generic Virtue, the four rivers that flow from it represent the four cardinal virtues of the Platonic list that were adopted by the Stoics. The Pishon represents prudence (*phronesis*), the Gihon stands for courage (*andreia*), the Tigris is the virtue of self-control or temperance (*sophrosyne*), and the Euphrates stands for justice (*dikaisyne*).[103]

Philo's reading of the text illustrates how he subordinates Greek virtue ethics to the biblical text by paying close attention to the meaning of Hebrew words, refracted through the Greek translation. For example, the Tigris, which "flows in front of Assyria," symbolizes temperance (*sophrosyne*). Philo reasons that in Greek, the name "Assyrians" is translated *euthynontes*, meaning "directors." Appropriately, the virtue of temperance attempts *to direct* the course of human weakness by restraining pleasure (*hedone*). Philo finds further support for this allegorical reading by likening desire to a tiger, "the most untamable of beasts," and it is indeed with desire that the virtue of temperance is "most conversant."

Philo notes that whereas the Pishon and Gihon are said to "surround" their respective territories, the Tigris and the Euphrates do not. The reason is that *phronesis* and *andreia* can encompass and overcome folly and cowardice, but *sophrosyne* cannot "encircle" appetite and pleasure. Even those who practice self-control (*enkrateia*) must resort to food and drink. Hence, Philo rejects Stoic *apatheia*, except in the case of Moses, who was purified by divine Grace (*Vit. Mos.* II XIV. 68). Ordinary people can expect to achieve only *metriopatheia* (*Leg. All.* III XLVIII, 140), which means "medium-level pathos." Significantly, Philo's identification of the four rivers with the four virtues became very popular with the Church Fathers.

In accordance with the Platonic doctrine of Ideas, Philo distinguishes between "heavenly virtues" and "earthly virtues." The latter are the copy and imitation of the former. The four virtues symbolized by the four rivers constitute the "heavenly virtues," namely, the virtues of the soul, which lead the one who cultivates them to heaven (*Sobr.* XIII. 61). Among the "earthly virtues" Philo enumerates bodily excellence such as "health, efficiency of the sense, dexterity of limb and strength of muscle and such as are akin to these."[104] These excellences are to be differentiated from external advantages such as wealth, which do not properly belong to ethics because they do not pertain to character per se.

Side by side with this Platonic classification, we also find the Aristotelian distinction between moral and intellectual virtues, which in the Stoic parlance was transformed into the distinction between contemplative virtues and practical virtues. The intellectual virtues have God as their object. They embrace correct opinions and beliefs about Him, His nature, and His activity as Creator. One such virtue is the belief that God exists; another is the belief that He exercises providential care over what He has created. The first four of the Ten Commandments are intended to inculcate intellectual virtues. To possess all of the intellectual virtues is to possess Wisdom, which is knowledge of all the teachings contained in the Law (including revealed doctrines and ethical laws). Wisdom is also defined in terms of its four constituent virtues: piety, godliness, holiness and faith. These religious virtues indicate Philo's original thought, which transformed Greek virtue ethics into a Jewish religious ethics.

For Philo, the properly ordered life, the life that is lived in accordance with nature and with divine reason, requires the virtue of piety (*eusebia*). Piety is Wisdom in the service of God. It is claimed to be "the source of virtue" as God is the source of Being. For Philo the function of piety is similar to the "Fear of God" in the work of Ben Sira; it is a guide that distances one from the potential sources of sin. Since he does call prudence (*phronesis*) the "first among the four cardinal virtues," it seems reasonable to assume that Philo considers piety analogous to prudence, which tells one what not to do and paves the way to a life of faith.

In Greek philosophical literature, faith is an epistemological category. For Plato it means "opinion about real things"; for Aristotle it means a "vehement assumption," and for the Stoics it is a "strong assumption."[105] Philo turns faith into a virtue, indeed the outstanding virtue that he exhorts his readers to possess. Though Philo uses the term faith (*pistis*) to denote four different things,[106] both religious and non-religious, his most prominent use of the term is trust in God alone—namely, faith in the revealed truths of Scripture.

The virtue of faith has a cognitive aspect; it signifies a commitment to the belief that God is One and above all, and that He provides for His world. Accordingly, Philo presents Abraham as "the first person who is said to have believed in God, since he was the first who had an unswerving and firm comprehension of this, apprehending that there is one supreme cause, and that He it is that governs the world by His providence, and all the things that are therein" (*Virt.* XXXIX. 216). Faith is also defined as belief that there is one God, who is the God of Scripture, and that there is no other. Faith too is called "the queen of virtues," because it involves belief in revealed truth and trust in God's promises. Having faith means putting trust in God rather than in high office, fame, or other external goods (*Abr.* XLV. 263). Philo concludes:

> Therefore, the only real, and true, and lasting good is trust in God, the comfort of life, the fulfillment of all good hopes, the absence of all evils, and the attendant source of blessings, the repudiation of all unhappiness, the recognition of piety, the inheritance of all happiness, the improvement of the soul in every respect, as it thus relies for support on the cause of all things, who is able to do everything but who wills only to do what is best (*Abr.* XLVI. 268).

Thus the virtues of piety and faith, or trust, capture between them the virtues of godliness and holiness.

The religious virtues clearly indicate where Philo departed from his Greek teachers. He differed from them as well in regard to moral virtues that are experienced in the social sphere. Philo pays a lot of attention to the virtue of humanity (*philanthropeia*), which he links to the virtue of justice (*Decl.* XXX.164; *Vit. Mos.* II II.9). Under the headings of justice and humanity come all the particular lessons and doctrines relating to the tasks of body and soul (*Spec. Leg.* II XV. 63–64). The virtue of humanity means giving help to those in need; a "virtue nearest in nature to piety" (*Virt.* IX. 51). Indeed, piety (*eusebia*) is "a sister and twin" of the virtue of humanity, because "the love of God involves the love of man."[107] In narrating the stories of the Patriarchs, Philo first gives examples of their piety followed by examples of their justice. Moses, too, is said to have possessed humanity and fellow-feeling through "a happy gift of natural goodness." The pious man is the humane man. Fellow-feeling and just dealings with others go hand and hand, and both derive from acknowledgment of the holiness of God, although these virtues are not identical with piety. Other virtues related to humanity and justice are concord, equality, grace, and mercy.[108]

Judaism: Moses and the Perfect Law

Like Plato and Aristotle, Philo holds that virtues can be implanted through laws that induce one to act in a certain way. The ideal Platonic lawgiver is the philosopher who knows the Good and can enact laws based on that superior knowledge. Like Socrates, Moses was a real human being and not just a symbol of some virtue. However, Moses was superior to all other human beings in that he was "the all-wise." Philo provides a highly idealized account of Moses' life, illustrating his outstanding moral and religious qualities. Loved by God as few others have been, Moses was a man of "special holiness" (*Virt.* XXXVII.201), even the holiest of men. He is described as "the most perfect of men" (*Ebr.* XXIII.94), with reference to his priestly piety (*Vit. Mos.* II XIII. 66) and his constant and unbroken nobility and other virtues (*Vit. Mos.* I. V. 24; I, VI. 29; *Vit. Mos.* II X. 58). There was no sin or imperfection in Moses. He was "king, and lawgiver, and high priest, and prophet" (*Vit. Mos.* II LI. 292) and "in each function he won the highest place."

Moses' highest excellence was his knowledge. Philo adopted Plato's theory of Ideas, which distinguishes between the world of Ideas and the sensible world. The former is a "world that only intellect can perceive" and that was "framed from the eternal Forms," whereas the latter is the world "discerned by the senses," which merely reflects the paradigmatic Idea. The world of Ideas can be apprehended only by passing on to it from this world. No Idea can be obtained from incorporeal existences "except by making material objects our starting point."

Philo applies the Platonic doctrine to his interpretation of Mosaic prophecy. On top of Mt. Sinai, according to Philo, Moses was shown the wholly incorporeal "paradigmatic essence." Using the language of allegory, Moses recorded what he had seen of the incorporeal world of real essences. The intellectual study of "mental things and real existences" is the allegorical study of Scripture.[109] In accordance with the Platonic schema of the *Republic*, Philo portrays Moses as the philosopher-king who "attained the very summit of philosophy" (*Vit. Mos.* II I. 2), and he should be credited with discoveries wrongly attributed to others. For example, it was Moses, not Heraclitus "who long ago discovered the truth that opposites are formed from the same whole." While Moses was not a god, he was not merely human either. Philo applies to Moses the same title—*theos*—that he applies also to the Logos. Indeed, Moses received a "divine communication," which meant that "all that follows in the wake of God is within the good man's apprehension while he himself alone is beyond it." Moses rescued mankind from the bondage of matter: As the embodiment of Logos, he is called "the law-giving Word," by which humanity could be rescued from the bondage of matter. Thus, Moses is the supreme High Priest, who bestows "a blessing that nothing in the world can surpass (*Vit. Mos.* II XIII. 67).

Philo distinguished between unalterable laws of nature, which are discoverable by human reason, and enacted laws, which may be altered. In pre-Mosaic times, a few individuals—Enosh, Enoch, Noah, Abraham, Isaac, and Jacob—discovered unwritten natural law, by which they could live virtuous lives. That law is the incarnation within the natural order at the time of creation of the pre-cosmic Logos. At creation the incorporeal Logos was implanted in nature to act as its Law. The Pre-Mosaic Patriarchs followed the Law, the Logos, implanted in nature as a whole.

> . . . for these first men, without having been followers or pupils of any one, and without ever having been taught by preceptors what they ought to do or say, but having embraced a line of conduct consistent with nature from attending to their own natural impulses, and from being prompted by an innate virtue, and looking upon nature herself

to be, what in fact she is, the most ancient and duly established of laws, did in reality spend their lives in making laws, never of deliberate purpose doing anything open to reproach (*Abr.* I. 6).

But for Moses the natural law is manifested in the Torah, making it possible for all those who live by the Law to become virtuous, because the Torah addresses the human condition—in which the multitudes are neither perfectly good nor utterly bad. In the Ten Commandments, God revealed to Moses in the form of Law a virtue ethics from which are derived all the special laws, which emanate from the Ten Commandments.

The Law of Moses is the ideal, divinely inspired Law, the perfect natural law sought by the philosophers. As David Winston put it, the Mosaic Law is "the truest reflection of the Logos which is embodied in the physical universe and constitutes its immanent natural law."[110] The Ten Commandments are the supreme catalogue of virtues; they are the headings of the special laws, and they inculcate the highest standard of virtues. The ten "generic commandments" "train men and encourage them to prudence, and justice, and piety, toward God and all the rest of the company of virtues, connecting sound words with good intentions, and virtuous actions with wise language" (*Spec. Leg.* IV XXV.134). Those who "take pains to cultivate virtue" are those who "set the holy laws before them to guide them in all they do or say" (*Praem* I. 20; XX. 119). Thus, those who conform to these laws "ought to be free from all unreasonable passions, and from all wickedness; and most especially ought all men to be so, who are either appointed by lot or elected to judge between others" (*Spec.* Leg. IV IX.55).

Philo's fusion of ethics of virtue and ethics of duty is conveyed through his allegorical interpretation of the biblical text. He applied to Scripture the same method that the Stoics used to interpret Homer and Greek mythology.[111] The Hebrew Scriptures for him are the inspired Word of God. Moses' utterances were "manifestations of the whole of the divine virtues, and especially of that merciful and bounteous character by means of which he trains all men to virtue, and especially the race that is devoted to his service, to which he lays open the road leading to happiness" (*Vit. Mos.* II XXXV. 189). The Hebrew Scriptures were composed in a state comparable to that of the philosopher when he is inspired to recall intelligible Ideas beyond the world of sense and matter. That means that, for Philo, Moses and not God was the author of the Torah, a heretical notion indeed as far as later rabbinic Judaism is concerned.[112] The same inspiration also guided the

Septuagint translators who preserved the true meaning of the mysteries conveyed by Moses.[113]

At Sinai, Moses' purified soul was engraved or inscribed by God. By virtue of this divine impression of knowledge, Moses was a "living law" even before he composed the written laws. In his own person Moses functioned as a kind of seal designed to impress the law in the shape of his life on those who would become his followers (*Vit. Mos.* I XXVIII. 158–59). Moses expressed his extraordinary knowledge through the act of writing (rather than speaking) when he composed the Pentateuch, which contains laws for proper conduct and facts about the structure of the cosmos. However, the language at his disposal was post-lapidarian and no longer the original Adam language, which was mimetic. Whereas Adam's language presented reality by giving names to things on the basis of direct apprehension of their essence (*Leg. All.* II II.15), Moses could only use an imperfect language. Moreover, since Moses addressed all of Israel, who were by definition imperfect and ill-prepared, he had to use audio-visual aids to convey his conceptual message. The result was the anthropomorphic language of the Bible, which requires allegorical interpretation.

The Allegorical Reading of Scripture

The main task of the reader of Mosaic Scripture is to uncover the message that, for pedagogic reasons, Moses conveyed indirectly through the use of figurative language. A careful reading of the Mosaic Torah must develop on two levels of meaning, one below the other. The literal meaning needs to be peeled off so that the deeper meaning of Scripture can become accessible. Philo's allegorical exposition of the Bible is meant to expose the intrinsic relationship between the moral education of the human soul, on the one hand, and the order of the cosmos in which the soul's journey from vice to virtue takes place. Only in the context of the divine Law, the Law revealed by the Creator of nature, are knowledge of nature and attainment of virtue causally linked. Presumably only those "who live with the soul rather than with the body" can understand this link, as does Philo, because "they have access to facts stripped of the body and in naked reality." As a result, Philo's allegorical interpretation evades the temporal character of historical events and minimizes the spatial aspect of ordinary "literal" descriptions as well.[114]

The biblical text imparts moral education in a variety of ways. Some narratives pertain to the career of the soul and its path toward perfection. Others exemplify through a story the theoretical components of virtuous life, and in still others the biblical hero exemplifies a model for desirable conduct to be emulated by the reader. Though these are not always consistent readings of biblical narrative, Philo's assumption remains the same: "Scripture is able to make ethical proclamations, because Moses, the author of Scripture, embodied all virtues and transferred them from the person to his writing."[115] The upshot of the Philonic analysis is that only the Mosaic Law enables those who follow it to live by the Stoic mandate of life in accordance with nature.[116]

Underlying Philo's exposition of biblical narratives and biblical laws is the assumption of Greek and Hellenistic virtue ethics that the good life requires control of passions and, more generally, the curbing of desire. Indeed, this is the main purpose of the tenth commandment. Desire is a kind of emotion that is understood to be like a "fountain of all evil" (*Spec. Leg.* IV IV.16). In order to attain perfection and happiness, "men should discard this passion, detesting it as the most disgraceful thing and the cause of most disgraceful actions" (*Spec. Leg.* IV XVI. 95).[117]

Philo follows the Stoics when he uses desire and pleasure interchangeably. He also followed the Stoic definition of emotions as "immoderate and violent impulse" and as an "irrational and unnatural" movement of the soul (*Spec. Leg.* IV XIV. 79). However, he did not follow them blindly. For example, he considered desire to come from ourselves and to be voluntary (*Decal.* XXVIII. 142), in direct opposition to the Stoics.

Philo's distinction between desire and all other emotions may seem to be based on Aristotle's discussion of the voluntary and involuntary, but with an important difference: in Aristotle's case all the emotions are said to have their origin in the agent. If some emotions are involuntary, it is because the agent is ignorant of particular circumstances. For Philo, by contrast, all the emotions, with the exception of desire, are "coming from the outside and assaulting from the outside" (*Decal.* XXVIII. 142).

Philo departed from Aristotle in order to accommodate a religious position: voluntariness is the freedom to do either good or evil, which is the gift of God to man. At the foundation of such choice there is desire (*orexis*), which is a species of appetency that moves human beings in opposition to reason. Freedom and choice require both will and desire. A rational appetency is freedom to do good, while irrational appetency is freedom to do evil. The opposite of desire is temperance, or continence (*Spec. Leg.* I XXIX. 149). Philo declares it to be the "most pure and unblemished virtue" (*Spec. Leg.* I XXIX. 150). The virtue of temperance is taught by the tenth commandment as well as by special laws.

Consequently, Philo can classify the law under the headings of the various virtues that are meant to be implanted in men by performing these laws. The performance of the law, however, should not be construed too narrowly. Philo is by no means a narrow legalist; he insists on the congruence of thoughts, deeds and intentions:

> For when such as the words are, such also is the mind; and when such as the counsels are, such likewise are the actions; then life is praiseworthy and perfect. But when these things are all at variance with one another life is imperfect and blameable, unless some one who is at the same time a lover of God and beloved by God takes it in hand and produces this harmony (*Virt.* XXXIV. 184).

A similar idea is expressed in another place, where Philo links the congruence of intention, actions, and words to happiness:

> For if such as the designs are, such also are the speeches; and such as the words spoken, such also are the actions; and if these things are bound up with each other, reciprocally preceding and following one another through the indissoluble bonds of harmony; then happiness prevails, and this is the truest wisdom and prudence. For wisdom has reference to the service of God, and prudence to the regulation of human life (*Praem.* XIV 81).

The Zenith of Happiness: Mystical Union

Philo's discussion of the zenith of happiness illustrates the extent to which he transformed the philosophic concept of *eudaimonia* into a religious concept. For him, the goal of happiness is "being loved by God," a *relational* concept that suggests an interaction between God and those who seek Him. As Philo puts it: "For those whose ally is God are consummately happy, but those to whom he is an enemy are sunk in the lowest depth of misery" (*Virt.* VIII.50). In other words, it was a particular conception of God as Creator that led Philo to understand happiness as a love linked to knowledge, a love that is very different from the emotions we associate with earthly love. Those who live the virtuous life—in which reason governs the emotions and passions—enjoy happiness in this life and participate, to some extent, in God's perfect happiness. Philo teaches:

> And if any were able in all his parts to live to God rather than to himself, looking by means of the external senses into those things which are their proper objects, for the sake of finding out the truth; and through the medium of the soul, investigating in a philosophical spirit the proper objects of intelligence, and those things which have a real existence, and by means of his organs of voice, singing hymns in praise of the world and of its Creator, he will have a happy and a blessed life (*Quis Her.* XXII. 111).

The zenith of the happy life, then, is an individual, ecstatic, unmediated coming to know the transcendent and immaterial God. It is a contemplative, mystical experience in which the "eye of the mind," or the soul, comes to "see God." Philo says: "But he to whose lot it falls, not only by means of his knowledge, to comprehend all the other things which exist in nature, but also to behold the Father and creator of the universe, has advanced to the very summit of happiness" (*Abr.* XII. 58). As the *telos* of human life, this mystical experience governs the direction of the happy life, organizing all human activities so as to attain it. Since for Philo the revealed Law of Moses is the ideal Law, which God implanted in nature at creation, the universal goal of "seeing God" is achievable only for those who live by the Law of Moses, since it alone guides humanity in accordance to nature. Hence, the experience of "seeing God" constitutes the community of "Israel," which for Philo is a intellectual-religious category ("those who see God") rather than an ethnic or national category. This view would enable Christian readers to adopt Philo for their own needs, making him into a Church Father.[118]

The question is whether or not the mystical experience is available in this life. Philo's answer is ambiguous. On one hand, he holds that ordinary men cannot in fact "see God" in this life because they are governed by their bodies. Only exceptional persons such as Moses and a few other biblical figures could claim such an experience. Presumably, the mystical experience itself remains an ideal that will be realized only in the afterlife, after the soul is separated from the body. On the other hand, Philo clearly teaches that the meaning of the name Israel is "he who sees God." The community of "Israel" thus constitutes those who live the ideally happy life in which they come to know God in this life as much as God is knowable through "thoughts, words, and deeds." The name "Israel" may therefore denote not all of those who constitute the historic, ethnic group known by that name, but a small, select group of those who live by the Law of Moses and who devote themselves to the contemplation.

One group of Jewish people—the Theraputae of Lake Mareotis in Egypt—in fact enacted Philo's ideal program for the happy life. Philo describes this group of unmarried men and women as follows:

> This then is what I have to say of those who are called therapeutae, who have devoted themselves to the contemplation of nature, and who have lived in it and in the soul alone, being citizen of heaven and of the world, and very acceptable to the Father and Creator of the universe because of their virtue, which has procured them his love as their most appropriate reward, which far surpasses all the gifts of fortune and conducts them to the very summit and perfection of happiness (*Vit. Cont.* XI. 90).

These men were viewed as "free by nature, and not subject to the frown of any human being." They "have celebrated their manner of messing together and their fellowship with one another beyond all description in respect of its mutual good faith, which is an ample proof of a perfect and very happy life" (*Quod Omn. Prob.* XIII. 91).

Scholars have regarded Philo's statements about the Theraputae to be an accurate account of an existing community devoted to the contemplative life within the context of Mosaic Law. Philo's description, however, was definitely construed to fit his ideal of happiness: the life of virtue that leads to a mystical "seeing" of God. Philo says:

> But the therapeutic sect of mankind, being continually taught to see without interruption, may well aim at obtaining a sight of the living God, and may pass by the sun, which is visible to the outward sense, and never leave this order which conducts to perfect happiness (*Vit. Cont.* II. 11).

Whether or not the group actually attained mystical experiences, it is clear that their life style was the happiest way of life. Others who were not members of the community but followed Philo's prescription were to be rewarded by the joy derived from orienting themselves toward God rather than toward the pursuit of external goods or the temptations of the passions. Their ultimate reward would take place after the death of the body.[119]

SUMMARY

By the Second Temple period, the ancient Wisdom tradition ("Logos" in short) and covenantal theology (the "Mythos" of Judaism) were fused already in the later stratum of the canonic Scriptures. The opening poem of the Book of Psalms captures this fusion most succinctly, and other Psalms make explicit how Wisdom is related to Torah and to God's created world. These ideas frame the emergence of the Jewish response to Hellenistic cultures. The *Wisdom of Solomon* and the writings of Jewish intellectuals such as Ben Sira and Philo reflect the retelling of the Jewish Scriptures in light of Greek philosophy. The views of these writers did not become part of normative Judaism, but they represent an integral strand within Jewish culture.

Philo illustrates the extent to which a first-century Jewish intellectual could creatively reconcile the Greek philosophical tradition, especially its virtue ethics, with Scripturally-based Judaism and its ethics of duty to divine commands. In Philo's time the nexus of happiness, wisdom, and virtue was taken for granted by Jewish intellectuals and was common not only in philosophical texts but in popular prose literature as well. For Jewish intellectuals who continued to swear allegiance to the Torah of Moses, there was no conflict between the virtue ethics of the Greeks and the ethics of obedience to divine commands. By the same token there was no conflict between philosophical reasoning (or "Logos") and the narratives of Scriptures (or "Mythos"). Both were reconciled with the belief in the Torah, which specifies both what one should do and the true beliefs one must hold in order to live the best kind of life in accordance with God's created nature. The life in accordance with nature requires self-control and mastery of bodily-based passions and appetites, and its rewards are to be experienced both in this life and in the afterlife.

Not long after Philo's death the Jews faced a major catastrophe—the destruction of the Temple in 70 C.E. and the collapse of Jewish political independence. Five decades later Alexandrian Jewry was destroyed when the Roman authorities quelled Jewish rebellions that had flared throughout the Empire (115–117 C.E.). By the early second century, Judaism underwent a major transformation when rabbinism became the dominant voice of Jewish self-understanding in the increasingly Christian Roman world. Whether or not the rabbis were familiar with Philo's philosophy and whether or not Philo and the rabbis shared the same hermeneutical principles is a hotly debated topic among Philo specialists.[120] Since I take a historical-cultural approach to the story of Judaism, Philo and other Jewish intellectuals in the Hellenistic world are no less part of Jewish culture than the rabbis.

3

The Happy Life of Torah in Rabbinic Judaism

With the physical destruction of Alexandrian Jewry in the early second century C.E., Judeo-Hellenistic philosophy came to an end. The Judaism that became normative came into existence after the destruction of the Second Temple in 70 C.E. It was the creation of the rabbis, a small intellectual elite in Palestine and Babylonia that emerged as the dominant variant out of multiple and conflicting viewpoints about the meaning of being Jewish. In this chapter I will argue that despite the diversity and multivocality of rabbinic literature, its texts share a coherent outlook that I will call "the happy life of Torah." Elaborating upon the motifs of Wisdom literature, the texts state forthrightly that for Israel, the Chosen people of God, happiness is to be found in adherence to God's revealed Torah as interpreted by the rabbis. For the rabbis, the love of Torah was *philosophia,* literally speaking—namely, love of wisdom—but the ultimate end of life was the attainment of holiness through the imitation of God. The rabbinic understanding of virtue was thus inseparable both from rabbinic theology and from the context of the rabbinic academy, where virtue was cultivated through interpersonal relationships among its members. In the organic web of rabbinic values, the very observance of Torah's commandments constituted the best way to live and flourish so as to become holy as God is holy. Simply put, those who live by the Torah are happy; they enjoy well-being in this world, and everlasting life in the world to come. This chapter, then, situates this rabbinic outlook in its proper historical context and explains both what the rabbis shared with Greek and Hellenistic philosophies and where they significantly differed.

RABBINIC JUDAISM IN ITS HISTORICAL CONTEXT

The Great War and Its Aftermath

Rabbinic Judaism emerged out of the crisis of the Great War (66–70 C.E.) and the need to make sense of a catastrophic defeat for Israel and her God.[1] In 70 C.E. Jerusalem was captured by the Romans and the Temple in Jerusalem, the cultic and administrative center of the Jewish people, was destroyed. It spelled the end of Jewish political sovereignty, the demise of the sacrificial cult, the massive economic ruin of Judea, the frustration of Jewish apocalyptic dreams, and the breakdown of Jewish social institutions.[2] The Great War also marked the end of Jewish sectarian diversity, and in its aftermath a new form of Judaism, the Judaism of the rabbis, emerged.

Prior to the Great War, the Jewish community in Palestine consisted of a plethora of religious groups, each possessing its own interpretation of Jewish Scriptures, ideals of piety, and norms of conduct.[3] Josephus described the various sects as "philosophical schools" that differed from each other in regard to theoretical issues such as free will and determinism, the immortality of the soul, and the resurrection of the dead. However, sectarian disputes apparently focused on law more than theology. More specifically, the Temple itself served as the bone of contention between the various sects. The Sadducees, who comprised priestly families in charge of Temple administration, were a deeply Hellenized segment of the Jewish society, but they also were fiercely loyal to the interests of the Jewish nation. They considered Scriptural legislation as stated in the Written Torah and administered by the Jerusalem priesthood to be the only source of authentic divine legislation for the community of Israel.

The Pharisees, whose adherents included all social strata in Jewish Palestine, focused on the laws of purity and tithing in an attempt to extend holiness outside the precincts of the Temple. Originating most likely in a table fellowship that sought to replicate the altar of the Lord in the privacy of the home, the Pharisees articulated a way by which all members of Israel, and not only the priests, could become holy through the performance of divine commandments, encompassing all spheres of life. The Pharisaic interpretation of the Written Scripture claimed for itself a status of "Torah," developing the ideology of the two-fold Torah, one Written and the other Oral, both of which were believed to be revealed by God at Sinai.

The Essenes, especially the group that settled in Qumran, rejected the Jerusalem Temple and priesthood and looked forward to the time when they would be able to observe the cult, the offering, and the sacred calendar in the True Temple erected by God. Another faction, the Zealots, were an amalgam of militant groups who were opposed to Rome's control of the Land of Israel, and who reflected the social concerns of the oppressed lower classes and the peasantry. Finally, there were the Christians, apocalyptically-oriented Jews who regarded the Temple as profane and hoped to replace its current controllers with their own followers, who viewed Jesus as messiah, high, priest, and/or atoner.

Only two groups survived the Great War—the Christians and the Pharisees. The Christians would gradually change their ethnic make-up from a messianic Jewish sect to a gentile Church. The Pharisees became the dominant intellectual elite in Jewish Palestine but ceased to exist as a sect. After 70, the scholars who perpetuated their traditions (though they never explicitly identified themselves as Pharisees),[4] were called "rabbis."[5] Their views and lifestyle would eventually become normative Judaism; the views and practices of the rabbis would be regarded as obligatory for all Jews and not only for members of the rabbinic class.

Rabbinic Academies

The locus of rabbinic activity was the academy (in Hebrew, *yeshivah*; in Aramaic *mativta*), which was originally a loosely organized voluntary association between masters and students. After the redaction of the Mishnah in about 200 C.E., however, the rabbinic academy became a permanent institution of higher learning with a fixed hierarchical structure and well-established social roles. With the failure of the Bar Kokhba revolt in 135 C.E.—the last Jewish attempt to regain political sovereignty in Palestine before the twentieth century—the rabbinic academies in Palestine moved from Judea to the Galilee and many of their scholars fled eastward to Babylonia, ruled by the Parthians until the mid-third century and then by the Sassanians.[6] In due time, the academies of Babylonia would eclipse the academies of Palestine in importance, and their literary output, the Babylonian Talmud, would dominate Jewish law and lore to this day.

In the Tannaitic period (prior to the editing of the Mishnah), the rabbinic academy in Palestine shared certain features with the philosophical schools of the Greco-Roman world.[7] Each of these schools had a founder who was considered an exemplary wise man or a good man; his virtues were extolled by members of the schools, the disciples, in both oral and written traditions. The common activities of the philosophical schools and the academies were studying, teaching, and writing—all with the intent of promoting fellowship and friendship. Each school had a distinct social identity apart from the rest of society and the organizational means to perpetuate its existence. Most importantly, neither the Greco-Roman period nor the Jewish schools were preoccupied only with speculation. The Greco-Romans considered the theoretical life to be the foundation for a certain way of life (*praxis*) conducive to happiness.[8] And the all-encompassing way of life articulated and practiced by the rabbis was regarded by them to be the happiest life—the intrinsically good life that benefits its practitioners both in this world and in the afterlife.

The similarity with Hellenistic philosophical schools was less pronounced in the Babylonian academies, which came into their own only in the third century C.E., after the promulgation of the Mishnah. Their formal structure was much more complex. They functioned not only as academic centers for the learning of Torah, but also as courts, as legislative bodies, and as institutions for public teaching.

In both Palestine and in Babylonia the rabbis constituted a very "small closely knit coterie of savants, whose very numbers allowed for a high degree of social and religious cohesiveness."[9] The rabbinic code of conduct regulated all actions toward other members of the rabbinic class as well as toward non-members (often referred to in rabbinic sources as *am ha-aretz*).[10] The purposes of the rabbinic moral code were to shape the character of the wise men, the sages who devoted their lives to the study of Torah, and to create a cohesive community that extended a wide range of social services to its members. Members of the rabbinic class were expected to care for each other's physical needs—especially in times of decline in economic status, illness, or death, as much as they were called on to facilitate and participate in joyful events.[11]

The basis of the rabbinic way of life was the personal tie between the master and his disciples.[12] The teacher was regarded not only as a scholar famed for his learning of Written and Oral Torah, but as a model of one whose very daily conduct embodied and exemplified Torah. It was presupposed that success in the study of Torah came only from actual association with a sage, since he was the embodiment of Torah in and out of the academy, privately and publicly, day and night (B. Berakhot 47b; B. Ketubot 111a). How the rabbis embodied Torah in their conduct was illustrated in numerous tales about the merits of named rabbis. This semi-hagiographic material, found throughout the rabbinic corpus, should not be taken as documentation of what the rabbis actually did or said. Rather, it portrays the sages as idealized models for emulation by other rabbis, reflecting the values of the redactors of the documents concerning desirable character traits and the actions that flow from them. As William Scott Green put it, these documents were produced for an "internal audience. They are of rabbis, by rabbis, and for rabbis."[13] By the same token, the rabbinic sources portrayed biblical characters as role models who attained the ideals of the rabbinic movement.[14]

The personal association of a disciple with a master was a hierarchical relationship in which the disciple rendered many services to the master. Serving a sage (*shimush hakhamim*) included accompanying the master in travel, going with him to the market, attending to his meals, taking care of him in time of sickness, and insuring his physical safety and well-being. Students were to treat their masters with utmost respect and deference, rising when he entered the room and never embarrassing him in public. Disciples were expected to be sensitive to their masters' feelings and to anticipate their reactions in future circumstances. In this institutional setting all aspects of the sages' deportment, from table manners, through speech patterns, to bodily cleanliness, were highly regulated within an authoritative, hierarchical structure. The special deportment of the rabbis was intended to distinguish them from members of other segments of the society.

The Cultivation of Virtues

The rabbinic academy was the social setting for the cultivation of virtues. The desired character traits emerged from the actual lived experience both "vertically" (i.e., in the relationship between disciples and their superiors) and "horizontally" (i.e., in the relationship between disciples and their peers).[15] The student with the virtuous character thus cultivated would be disposed to both *act* and *feel* in a certain way. His appropriate actions and corresponding attitudes emanated from his observance of God's Will as expressed in the Torah. All his ethical values reflected religious assumptions, and many of his religious precepts had an ethical dimension. In the case of the divine Law, there was no conflict between law and morality: the commandments had a force of law in addition to being morally good and good for the human recipients.[16]

Though exceedingly small in number,[17] the rabbinic elite played a crucial role in Jewish self-government both in Palestine and in Babylonia. With the political support of the Patriarchate in Palestine and the Exilarchate in Babylonia—the institutions that represented the Jewish minority in the non-Jewish government—the Amoraim staffed Jewish courts for litigation among Jews, supervised the collection of taxes, organized Jewish education, and provided spiritual leadership.[18] The involvement of the rabbis in the administration of Jewish communal life justifies our seeing them as "scholars-bureaucrats," not unlike Greco-Roman rhetors and teachers who were active in political life. Over time, especially in Babylonia, the rabbis came to be regarded both as practitioners of wisdom who taught the most valued part of higher education, and as holy men possessed with supernatural powers.[19]

Thus rabbis were believed to be capable of bringing about rain, making the fields plentiful, healing the sick and helping women in childbirth, and, in general, affecting the quality of interaction between Israel and God.

Rabbis as Philosophers

If the rabbinic academies resembled Greco-Roman philosophical schools, can the rabbis be called "philosophers?" The question is difficult because of the ambiguity of the term "philosophy" in the ancient world. If by "philosophy" we mean syllogistic reasoning in pursuit of truth about first principles, i.e., the type of inquiry that characterized the philosophy of Aristotle and the Peripatetic school, then rabbinic discourse was not philosophical.[20] Instead, rabbinic intellectual energy was devoted to elucidating principles of law and their application in concrete situations. While this reasoning employed logical procedures—the so-called thirteen rules (*middot*) of R. Yishmael—its goal was hermeneutic. Logical procedures were employed in the interpretation of sacred texts (biblical and rabbinic) rather than in the service of formulating abstract, general, first principles. It is not surprising, therefore, that rabbinic sources do not refer to Aristotle and that his technical philosophical vocabulary was absent.[21] In fact, of all the Greek, Hellenistic, and Roman philosophers, only two are mentioned by name in rabbinic literature: Onemous of Gadara, who was considered the greatest of all philosophers because of his sympathetic attitude toward the Torah, and Epicurus, whose views were seen to be the epitome of heresy.[22]

The rabbinic sages, however, were neither totally ignorant of Greco-Roman philosophy nor unequivocally hostile to it. Even though rabbinic sources include an exhortation to "withhold the study of *higayon* (logic) from children" (B. Berakhot 28b), rabbinic sources attest some familiarity with Hellenistic philosophical schools.[23] This is not surprising, since in the heyday of Pharisaism and rabbinic Judaism, philosophical education was well represented in Palestine and Trans-Jordan. Ascalon, Gaza, Gadara, Caesarea, Sebastia, Gerasa, and Petra all boasted philosophical academies in which all branches of Hellenistic philosophy were studied in some syncretistic fashion.[24] Furthermore, Palestine produced some distinguished philosophers. For example, there was Antiochus of Askalon (ca. 130 B.C.E.—ca. 69 B.C.E.), who was originally a member of the Skeptical Academy, but who rejected Skepticism in favor of an eclectic synthesis of his own, based on Platonic, Aristotelian, and Stoic elements.[25] No less important were the itinerant teachers of the Second Sophistic movement who popularized

Greco-Roman philosophy and rhetoric in public places throughout Palestine.²⁶ Whether rabbinic sages availed themselves of written collections of Greco-Roman rhetoric or absorbed information about the lives and views of the philosophers through oral communication only, rabbinic literature has many intriguing parallels with Greco-Roman rhetorical traditions.²⁷

Henry Fischel in particular has portrayed the rabbinic sages as a Jewish version of the Greco-Roman *Sophos*. Like them, the rabbis taught without pay, attached themselves to particular disciples who followed them around and served them, and looked to gifts for support. As did other intellectual elites in the Hellenistic world, the rabbis distinguished themselves by walk, speech, and peculiar clothing, and they demanded for themselves a privileged status, especially in terms of exemption from taxation. To legitimize their intellectual activity, the rabbinic scholars created "a chain of tradition," a list of teachers (rather than ancestors) modeled on Hellenistic philosophical schools.²⁸

Most importantly, the rabbinic scholars viewed the wise man as a hero of virtue who possesses encyclopedic knowledge, both of which are components of the happy life. In fact, the rabbis absorbed the Stoic catalogues of virtues and vices as well as specific social values such as self-sufficiency, self-knowledge, the simple life, nonconformity, imperturbability, and equanimity.²⁹ In the rabbinic portrayal of the ideal life, one can find a strong anti-vanity and anti-luxury posture that is concomitant with moral discipline based on self-control. Furthermore, the rabbinic sage, like his Greco-Roman counterpart, made wisdom his ultimate concern and considered its pursuit (as expressed in the Torah) to be the road to personal fulfillment in accordance with an eternal pattern.

The latter point in particular is relevant to the rabbinic conception of happiness. I propose that, because these rabbis constituted an educated, intellectual elite in a Greco-Roman world, they absorbed Greco-Roman virtue ethics into the biblical ethics of obligations to divine commands. As learned men, the rabbis took for granted that the pursuit of wisdom is both theoretical and practical, that the life of wisdom requires the cultivation of a good character that possesses specific virtues, that character requires self-control and mastery of passions, and that the life of the virtuous person constitutes human happiness.

However, precisely because the virtue ethics was determined by *function*, the rabbinic religious ethos differs significantly from the virtue ethics of Greco-Roman philosophical schools. In rabbinic Judaism, ethics were in the service of a *personal relationship with God*, a religious value that is conspicuously missing in Greek virtue ethics.

Rabbinic Literature: Diversity and Unity

Rabbinic literature, that is, the literary documents produced by the rabbinic scholars from the fall of the Temple in 70 to the redaction of the Babylonian Talmud about 600 C.E., originated in actual oral deliberations that were gradually committed to writing, editorial selection, and final redaction. The first literary document of the rabbinic movement was the Mishnah, redacted about 200 by Rabbi Judah I (Judah Ha-Nasi, or "the Patriarch"). Whether the Mishnah was intended to serve as the first code of Jewish law, a digest of laws to guide actual Jewish litigation, an ideal constitution for the eventual renewal of Jewish sovereignty, or an eternal, ideal paradigm of perfection to substitute for the broken historical reality, is still a matter of dispute.[30] Be this as it may, once it was published, it served as the basis of further textual interpretations, which anchored the document, now defined as Oral Torah (*torah she-be-al-peh*), in the Written Torah of the canonic Scriptures.

In the four centuries after the Mishnah's redaction, the literary output of the rabbinic scholars that constituted Oral Torah would encompass—in addition to the Mishnah—the Tosefta, the halakhic (i.e., legal) and aggadic (i.e., non-legal) midrashim, as well as the Palestinian and Babylonian Talmuds. After the redaction of the Palestinian Talmud (ca. 400 C.E.) and the Babylonian Talmud (ca. 600 C.E.), the literary output of the rabbinic movement continued to be studied, interpreted, and committed to writing, giving rise to post-talmudic rabbinic documents, legal and non-legal, that perpetuated the classical sources in the Middle Ages and further expanded the tradition.

Given the length of time involved in the production of this literature and the diversity of its literary genres, any attempt to generalize about *the* rabbinic outlook on any given topic is fraught with methodological difficulties.[31] First, the various documents of rabbinic literature vary in style, organization, and intent, so that each document is quite autonomous and must be understood on its own terms. Second, the documents at our disposal have been subjected to a long and uneven editorial process. Since the final, redacted product contains several layers of earlier material, one can at best speculate about the intent of the authors who redacted the documents, rather than about the original intent of the rabbis whose names are cited in the documents. Third, even though much of rabbinic non-legal material is ascribed to individually named sages, one cannot assume that the saying attributed to a given sage or a tale told about him in fact reflects his actual words or deeds. Very often what is attributed to a given sage in one document appears in another text under a different name or with changed details. The name of a given sage, then, functions more like a code for a certain literary tradition than as the actual opinion of a real person.[32] Finally, rabbinic speculations on matters of beliefs and doctrines were intended to be inconclusive. The framers of the documents deliberately left these issues open-ended in order to prevent creedal disputes, a lesson that the rabbinic scholars learned from the catastrophic results of the Great War.[33] Consequently, rabbinic sources recorded a variety of opinions, moods, and viewpoints, which were often in conflict with one another.

Despite the dominant reticence to generalize about rabbinic Judaism, however, I hold that this literature is not so fragmented or disjointed that any generalization is vacuous. After all, the framers of all rabbinic documents considered themselves to have stood "in the chain of tradition from Sinai and uniquely disposed to possess the oral part of the Torah, revealed by God to Moses at Sinai for oral formulation and oral transmission, in addition to the written part of the Torah possessed by all Israel."[34] Rabbinic pronouncements were thus presented as "Torah," namely "complete and exhaustive statements of God's will for Israel and humanity."[35] The rabbinic sage saw himself first and foremost as an exegete of the divine word, an interpreter of an already revealed truth. Rabbinic discourse was therefore hermeneutic, whether the rabbis presented their views through a verse-by-verse commentary on the canonic texts or as a free-standing homily that creatively employed Scripture as its proof-text. While the hermeneutic style contributed to the lack of terminological precision and consistency, it also conferred a certain degree of coherence on the vast rabbinic literature.

In accord with the work of Max Kadushin, I believe it is legitimate to talk about rabbinic Judaism as an "organic" system in which the whole is larger than the sum of the parts and the parts are intrinsically connected to each other. I cannot here reproduce Kadushin's rather intricate way of classifying the various components of rabbinic ethical reasoning.[36] What is relevant for us is his claim that rabbinic Judaism articulated a coherent, text-based religious ethos in which ethical values were to be gleaned from the concrete setting of rabbinic scriptural exegesis, anecdotal tales, parables, and homilies. In Kadushin's reconstruction of rabbinic Judaism as an "organic tradition," moral values, social attitudes, literary motifs, and theological postures are dynamically and intricately related, even though rabbinic ethical thinking was not governed by abstract rules.

This chapter cannot do justice to this complex and dynamic value system. My presentation is, admittedly, selective, partial, and tentative. I draw my material primarily from aggadic rather than halakhic sources, and I highlight the ethical strand of rabbinic Judaism. I refer particularly to Tractate Avot of the Mishnah,[37] the Hebrew commentary on it—*Avot de-Rabbi Natan* (The Fathers According to Rabbi Nathan) in its two versions,[38] the minor tractates of the Talmud known as *Derekh Eretz Rabbah* and *Derekh Eretz Zutta*,[39] and the midrashic lore from the school of R. Elijah, *Tana debe Eliyahu*.[40] In style, content, and outlook these texts perpetuated and elaborated the Wisdom tradition of the late Second Temple period, as they fused the ethics of (legal) obligation to divine commands with the ethics of virtue that permeated Hellenistic philosophy. Of course, the rabbinic view of the well-lived life is not limited to these texts, but expressed in many forms throughout the rabbinic corpus.

Given the hermeneutic nature of rabbinic discourse, it is no surprise that rabbinic texts do not provide systematic reflections on the meaning and nature of human happiness. Such rabbinic views can be gleaned from the numerous statements that begin with the biblical formula *ashrei* ("happy is/are . . .") and from rabbinic homilies on the language of the Psalms. In rabbinic sources the term *ashrei* functions as an antecedent to a cohortative statement that expresses approval of a certain conduct or that promotes a certain religious value. By looking at these statements throughout the corpus we can piece together a network of inter-related ethical-religious values that constitute the life of Torah. Rabbinic texts develop the linkage between happiness and righteous conduct posited by Psalm 1, either by using the biblical verses as proof-texts for homilies on other Scriptural texts or by elaborating upon the meaning of that Psalm. In the Babylonian Talmud Avodah Zarah 18a, for example, we find such midrashic elaboration in the midst of a halakhic discourse on the legal status of visiting Roman institutions of entertainment. Through pondering the lessons to be drawn from Psalms, the interlocutors of the conversation in fact reflect on the quality of the happy life, doing so through text commentary rather than by topical elaboration. The use of the Psalms as a point of departure for rabbinic speculation is, of course, what *Midrash Tehilim* (Midrash on Psalms) is all about.

For example, the imagery of the happy man as a flourishing tree appears in several places in the rabbinic corpus, most importantly for our purposes in Tractate Avot 3:22 and in *Avot de-Rabbi Natan* chapter 39. The image conveys the rabbinic understanding of happiness. Human flourishing throughout life is predicated on internal goodness rather than on the possession of external goods, and the former requires adherence to Torah. This view so captured the rabbinic perspective that it became part of the synagogue worship service that replaced the Temple sacrifice. Similarly, the causal relationship between human happiness and Torah is expressed when the rabbis ascribed Proverbs 3:18 (originally referring to Wisdom) to the Torah. Whenever the Torah scroll is returned to the Ark during the service the community recites: "It [i.e., the Torah] is a tree of life and those who hold fast to it are happy." Likewise, the linkage between happiness and the life of Torah is affirmed by the so-called Ashrei hymn—Ps. 145—to which are appended two verses from the Psalms that open with the formula *ashrei*.[41] The rabbis decreed that this Psalm be recited at least three times a day, reminding Jews that happiness depends on commitment to Torah.

THE RABBINIC MYTHOS OF TORAH

The Covenant: God, Torah and Israel

The Torah-centered life of the rabbis consisted of an assiduous study of sacred texts, close attention to the master-disciple relationship, and a range of communal activities. This comprehensive way of life was rooted in a fully developed sacred narrative, or mythos, about the eternal covenant between Israel and God. This interpretative story endowed rabbinic life with meaning and served as the prism through which Israel was to interpret all human affairs—past, present, and future. The rabbinic mythos has three components: God, Israel, and Torah, which intersect in the following manner:

From sheer benevolence, God created the world out of His own free Will. Divine creative activity was neither capricious nor arbitrary. It was guided by Wisdom and tempered with justice. Ordering the created world hierarchically and functionally, God placed human beings—created in His own image—at the summit of the created order. He endowed them with the ability to think and to make wise or unwise choices: a wise choice is one that accords with God's will; an unwise choice is one that goes contrary to God's will. The personal God of rabbinic faith is a communicative creator who continually provides for His creatures and responds to their changing needs. Periodically He intervenes in the natural order and in human affairs.

The personal God of rabbinic Judaism has a special relationship with one group of people—Israel. That relationship is construed in terms of an eternal covenant (*berit*), a perpetual interaction that cannot be abrogated. The zenith of the relationship is a historical event—the theophany at Sinai—in which God revealed His Will to the entire people of Israel in a form of law, the Torah, through the mediation of the prophet Moses. The Torah defines the terms of the covenantal relationship: God commands and Israel obeys. Failure to observe God's commandments is understood as sin, which incurs appropriate punishment. Conversely, loyalty to God's commandments is amply rewarded, both in this world and in the world to come.

The covenant establishes a communal way of life dedicated to holiness (*qedushah*). By giving Israel the Torah, God makes Israel holy, and through the performance of the Torah's commandments Israel affirms and realizes that holiness. In the life of holiness there is no separation between ritual and ethical imperatives. Moral failings are offenses against God, for Israel's life is to be consecrated to God as part of doing what God wants of Israel. Israel is called to strive to be like God, to walk in His ways so as to attain the holy life.

The covenantal relationship expresses God's love for Israel. God chose Israel to receive His revelation not because the people merited it but as an expression of His unbounded benevolence. In turn, Israel is called upon to love God unconditionally and to respond to the gift of revelation by observing its demands. Indeed, God's revelation places on Israel a set of obligations and duties whose fulfillment expresses Israel's love for Him. Like all love relations, the covenant between God and Israel is dynamic and ever changing, but it cannot and will not be abrogated. When Israel turns away from God (collectively or individually) by neglecting to live in accordance with His will, it is chastised and punished. Repentance brings Israel back to God, the eternal lover, and the covenantal relationship is renewed. Thus, precisely because humans, like God, are able to choose, the love relationship between them is very stormy; both partners make mistakes that they later regret and that are forgiven so that the relationship is never abrogated.

In the rabbinic mythos of the covenant, Israel's well-being or happiness (collectively and individually) reflects the quality of the relationship with God, a relationship that is centered on "Torah." Here lies the main difference between the rabbinic and the Greek approaches to happiness. Whereas for the Greek philosophers human well-being is a direct result of human efforts through the acquisition of virtues, in the rabbinic perspective happiness is relational; one is happy to the extent that one is properly related to God and, through God, to other persons.

As much as the rabbis perpetuated and elaborated the covenantal model of biblical religion, so did they continue the association of Torah and Wisdom. Absorbing the ontology of Middle Platonism, the rabbis claimed that

God created the world while consulting the primordial Torah, which functioned as the blueprint of the created cosmos.[42] Because the primordial Torah served as a paradigm of the universe, there is a structural correspondence between the Torah and the created universe. The theoretical implications of this idea would be developed in the Middle Ages, both by Maimonides and by the kabbalists. Accordingly, these implications will have important ramifications for their respective conceptions of human happiness.

Torah and Derekh Eretz

The term "Torah" in rabbinic literature is multivalent. It encompasses both the revelation of God's will to Moses at Sinai in the form of a Written Torah—which includes not only the Pentateuch but the entire Scriptural canon—and the deliberations, decrees, and homilies of the rabbis, which constitute the Oral Torah. The Written and the Oral Torah complement each other. Whereas the Written Torah is fixed and unchangeable, the Oral Torah continues to grow through exegesis. Whereas the Written Torah only spells out the principles of the Law, the Oral Torah particularizes these principles in response to ever-changing historical circumstances. Together, the Written and Oral Torah encompass all aspects of life—public and private, communal and individual, intellectual and legal. Time, space, the human body, social institutions, and ritual are all organized and made meaningful within the framework of Torah, both Written and Oral. No aspect of human life remains outside its scope, including the opposite of Torah—that is, the mundane worldly pursuits common to all human beings, which the rabbinic sources called *derekh eretz* (literally the "way of the land" or "way of the earth," i.e., the way of most people who inhabit the earth).

The concept of *derekh eretz* is at the center of a modern debate over whether or not rabbinic Judaism recognizes an extra-legal realm of ethics. Its interlocutors answer the question according to their location on the spectrum of modern Judaism.[43] Those who align themselves with Orthodoxy tend to answer the question in the negative; for them, halakhah is broadly conceived and encompasses ethical injunctions, and thus in Judaism there is no meaningful separation between religion and ethics. At the other end of the spectrum, liberal thinkers argue that the rabbinic tradition is but a historical product that does not dictate all moral precepts for Jews. Instead, some of those precepts are articulated by human reason and are known universally. Thus the historical sources of Judaism do not exhaust universal ethics. In between these two extremes is the position of Conservative thinkers who state that rabbinic sources recognize the existence of moral issues not directly stated by halakhah, which entail a proper interaction between "Torah" (i.e., the divinely revealed Law) and *derekh eretz* (universally recognized ethics, or worldly wisdom). Since the present work is an exercise in intellectual history rather than philosophical ethics, I will not attempt to resolve the theoretical issue by providing arguments in favor of one or the other positions. Nonetheless, one comment is in order.

Because of their view of rabbinic Judaism as a rule-centered religious system, modern Jewish philosophers have framed this issue in the context of Kantian deontological ethics. Thus both Orthodox and Reform theologians have employed Kantian ethics to reformulate Judaism for modern times, even though for the former Jewish law is heteronomous, and for the latter Judaism posits human autonomy. Both groups, however, have minimized the degree to which the goodness of the moral agent, i.e., virtue, is crucial to assessing the rightness of the act because they were not sufficiently informed of Greek and Hellenistic moral theories that dominated the moral outlook of antiquity for Jews and non-Jews alike. In highlighting the presence of virtue ethics in rabbinic Judaism, I am trying to show that the rabbis did not believe that following divine commands is possible unless one cultivates the right virtues. The list of virtues itself, I maintain, reflected the lifestyle of the rabbinic academy, the sacred narrative of the Jewish tradition, and the social values that the rabbis shared with other learned men in antiquity. In that context, I question the notion that in Judaism halakhah is the only source of ethics, and find Kadushin's analysis of the interplay between Torah and *derekh eretz* germane to our discussion.

Kadushin has shown that the term *derekh eretz* in rabbinic texts is a dynamic concept that pertains to four distinct areas: modes of behavior common to all of mankind, practical wisdom with moral overtones expressed in concrete advice and admonition, rules of good manners about the proper way to act, and ideals of ethical behavior.[44] Under this broad category of *derekh eretz,* then, rabbinic texts refer to natural sexual behavior, business practices, parental training, universal human traits necessary for human survival, good deeds, acts that express reverence and respect, attitudes and viewpoints essential to the good life, proper and improper conduct, attitude and conduct toward God, and other ethical practices that God Himself will reward or punish.

It is safe to say that while rabbinic sources recognized the existence of a realm of a universally applicable ethics, they also insisted on the interdependence of Torah and *derekh eretz.* The Torah itself teaches *derekh eretz,* and one who studies Torah must also study *derekh eretz*.⁴⁵ While knowledge of *derekh eretz* came even before the revelation of Torah, its practice after the revelation is enhanced by the observance of mitzvot. Thus he who practices both *derekh eretz* and mitzvot can avoid transgression and enjoy divine rewards. Conversely, infringement of the principles of ethical *derekh eretz* leads to misfortunes.

Virtue as Duties

Avot 4:14 summarizes the interplay between Torah and *derekh eretz* in the name of Rabbi Eleazar ben Azarya: "If there is no Torah, there is no *derekh eretz*; if there is no *derekh eretz*, there is no Torah." This famous but rather ambiguous maxim can be reasonably read to mean that in the life governed by the Torah, one's duties to God and one's worldly concerns, including ethical behavior toward one's fellow human beings, are two sides of the same coin. As the revelation of a commanding God, the Torah makes known what God wishes His believers to do in the form of Law. Obeying His will as expressed in the commandments is therefore the duty of all those who stand within the covenantal relationship to God. However, the ability to follow God's revealed law is predicated on the acquisition of specific virtues, character traits that dispose one to be open to observe His will as revealed in the Torah. Thus, the conduct that the rabbinic texts consider as *derekh eretz* is itself predicated on virtues that create a personality well-disposed to observe God's commands. Furthermore, since rabbinic teachings were themselves considered normative Torah, the virtues that the rabbis found desirable were not mere recommendations or guiding principles for behavior, but duties that carried obligatory force. In other words, one *must* strive to emulate those values.

If this reading is correct, then rabbinic sources posit a reciprocal relationship between duties and virtues: only those who possess the character traits that dispose one to accept willingly the Torah as obligatory can perform the commandments of God, but the very performance of the commandments constitutes the practice that makes one further willing to obey God's will and hence to become more virtuous. The halakhic system, then, operates as a prescribed regimen for life, a perpetual "diet" (in the original sense of the Greek term) that molds a coherent pattern of living that contains the mechanism for growth in virtue.⁴⁶ Since the halakhic system includes moral obligations, I side with those scholars who claim that in rabbinic Judaism there is no conflict between law and ethics.

The Value of Torah Study

Aristotle argued that to qualify as happiness a certain good must be self-sufficient, complete, and desired for its own sake rather than for the sake of something else. This is precisely how the rabbis understood the study of Torah. It was to be cultivated "day and night," a perpetual preoccupation in intellectual activity that had practical ramifications: it leads one to doing good deeds and, in turn, it constitutes the best or happiest life. Rabbinic sources are replete with praise of the study of Torah as the highest religious activity, equivalent in worth to the performance of all the commandments. *Avot de-Rabbi Natan* expresses this common viewpoint in stating: "the study of Torah is more beloved by God than burnt offerings. For when a man studies Torah he comes to know the will of God."[47] One should study Torah daily, and the rabbis recommended weekly and monthly study quotas. A break in one's study schedule could only lead to forgetfulness, which was to be avoided at all costs.[48] One must not postpone the study of Torah, lest one be prevented from it completely by an early death (Avot 2:3). The study of Torah itself is the cause of one's prosperity in this world, because God rewards those who do it.[49]

Most importantly, the study of Torah must be carried out "for its own sake" (*li-shemah*); it must not be undertaken as a means for something else, be it social status, wealth, or fame. Avot 4:6 states in the name of Rabbi Zaddok:

> Do not make them [Torah and mitzvot] a crown to aggrandize yourself with them nor a spade to dig with. And so Hillel used to say, he who makes a worldly use of the crown [of Torah] shall pass away.

The same counsel is expressed in Avot 1:3 in the name of Antigonos of Sokho who received the tradition from Simon the Righteous:

> Do not be like servants who serve their master in order to receive a reward; be like servants who serve their master without expecting to receive a reward, and let the fear of heaven be upon you.

The study of Torah "for its own sake" reflected the believer's unconditional love and devotion to God, which could result in the readiness to sacrifice oneself to Him. The student of Torah was expected not only to give up comforts and luxuries, which were viewed as dangerous incitements to sin, but to be ready to give up life itself for Torah. Martyrdom (*qiddush ha-shem*) for the sake of "sanctifying God's Name" exemplified the supererogatory tendency in rabbinic thought, one that took the pursuit of perfection to its ultimate conclusion, as we shall see below. However, while certain rabbinic heroes—for example, R. Aqiva and R. Hannina ben Tradyon—gave their lives for God's Torah during the Bar Kokhba revolt, the dominant ethos of rabbinic Judaism was more moderate.

The study of Torah for its own sake was not to result in the denial of life but rather in its affirmation. Indeed, the world is believed to be sustained by Torah (Avot 1:2), which is referred to as a "drug of life" (*sam ḥayyim*).[50] Similarly, although rabbinic sages were an intellectual elite, they presented the ideal of Torah study as obligatory for all Jews. In short, the possibility of studying Torah is open to all who seek to be happy.[51] This dominant outlook of rabbinic religious ethos is stated succinctly:: "Happy is the man who possesses the words of the Torah and who keeps them safely (literally, "in his head") and knows how to give a proper answer concerning them."[52] "Happy is the man that studies much at an academy and troubles much in study, and lessens his business activity, that sits and meditates on the words of the Torah every day continually."[53] "Happy is the man that maketh himself like unto an ox for the yoke and like unto an ass for the burden, and sits and meditates upon the words of Torah every day continually."[54]

Clearly the commitment to Torah constitutes the happy life, and accepting the demanding life of Torah is an act of love of the highest order. It is to be done passionately, relentlessly, and with total devotion. Not accidentally the rabbis employed erotic language to describe such total devotion. The Torah, imaged as a woman, is the object of desire and love for the male student, and the act of Torah study is conceived as a form of adoration and worship.[55] Such intense study produces intimacy and nearness with God. Indeed, it is a form of human love of God. The rabbinic ethos, then, was but a Jewish version of the erotic language that Socrates and his disciples used to express their love of wisdom, namely, *philosophia*. In both cases the result of the erotic pursuit of wisdom is an intense joy and delight that accompanies pure theoretical activity.[56]

TORAH AND THE CULTIVATION OF THE VIRTUOUS CHARACTER

The Upright Path

Perpetuating the Wisdom tradition, the rabbinic sages took for granted that the happy life is predicated on the possession of certain virtues.[57] Only the one who possesses good character traits, which dispose one to do good deeds (*ma'asim tovim*), can experience the happy life. Rabbinic Hebrew, however, has no word that is equivalent to the Greek *arête* (virtue). The word that comes closest is *middah*, namely "quality" or "attribute," and it is a neutral term that lacks the specific connotation of excellence. A *middah* may be either good or bad, either a virtue or a vice, depending on its content and its function within the rabbinic value system. Instead of analyzing what makes a trait good or bad, the rabbis used figurative language in which the goodness or badness of the trait is defined by its context. Thus in their figurative discourse, "a good heart" (*lev tov*) or "a good eye" (*ayin tovah*) connotes generosity, kindness, open-mindedness, and friendliness, which are exemplified in a wide range of actions. Conversely, "a mean heart" (*lev ra`*) or a "bad eye" (*ayin ra`ah*) connotes a hateful, unfriendly, unkind posture.

By the same token, the rabbinic sources exemplify desirable traits through talking about a person or a personality type. Thus Avot speaks about "the courageous" (*gibbor*), "the temperate," (*kovesh et yitzro*), "the shy" (*bosh panim*), "the humble" (*anav*), "the modest" (*tzanu`a*), "the lowly" (*shefal ruah*), "the patient" (*savlan*), and so forth. Conversely, the rabbinic sources do not theorize about vices but discuss undesirable traits that lead one to commit sinful acts that produce a certain personality type. Thus the sources speak about "the rigid" (*qapdan*), "the "prideful" (*ga'avtan*), "the brazen" (*az panim*), "the coarse" (*gas lev*), and other descriptive terms that characterize the "wicked" person (*rasha*). Out of these and other positive and negative figurative expressions emerge the personality types that can experience the good life because they follow the Torah of God.

In continuity with biblical usage, rabbinic sources employ the term *derekh* ("path" or "way") to denote a coherent pattern of conduct. The desirable path—in Hebrew *derekh tovah*—is an intricate nexus of deeds and attitudes that is intrinsically good because it follows God's will as revealed in the Torah. *Derekh tovah*, or *derekh yesharah*, are thus figurative expressions of the happy life, the choice-worthy life. Avot 2:8 is a typical example of rabbinic reflection about the good life:

> He [Rabban Yohanan] said to them: "Go out and see which is the good way that a man should adopt." Rabbi Eliezer said, "A good eye." R. Yehushua said: "A good friend." Rabbi Yosi said: "A good neighbor." Rabbi Shimon said: "One who foresees the result of an action." Rabbi Eleazar said: "A good heart." He said to them: "I accept Eleazar ben Arakh's opinion, because his includes all of yours."

This stylized conversation and its parallels in *Avot de-Rabbi Natan* 14[58] are literary traces of what could have been actual scholarly conversations. The interlocutors of this exchange attempt to identify the essential components of the happy life. For the first sage, a "good eye," namely the virtue of generosity, is the underlying principle of a good life; for the second, it is close personal relations with a "friend";[59] for the third scholar, it is proper social relations (i.e., "the good neighbor"); and for the fourth, prudence is the core of the good life.

The Mishnah presents the final position—"good heart"—as the best answer to the leading question because it is the most inclusive. It stands to reason that it is chosen because it is most vague. A "good heart" is a metaphor for a wide range of related attitudes, virtues, and acts that the Mishnah does not specify because they are embedded in a presupposed religious outlook.

The Mishnah then approaches the question by looking at the converse of the good way, namely, "the bad way a person should avoid." The same sages listed in the same order now cite "a bad eye," "a bad friend," "a bad neighbor," "one who borrows and does not pay back," and finally a "bad heart" as the vices and wicked conduct that one must shun in order to enjoy the good path. For the rabbis, no less than for their Greco-Roman counterparts, happiness means the experience of well-being or flourishing that emerges from a virtuous pattern of living, a pattern rooted in the nature of humans.

Taming the Evil Impulse

Like their Greco-Roman counterparts, the rabbis took it for granted that the good life requires self-control.[60] They were aware that devotion to the life of Torah was not an inborn proclivity; but it was acquired through a highly disciplined regimen that inculcated good moral habits from early childhood. Rabbinic ethics, like Aristotle's, is behavioristic: the desired character emerges through habitual practice that disposes the person to act and to feel in a certain way, and to choose to do the good and avoid that which is bad. However, whereas for Aristotle the acquisition of virtues involved rational deliberation, for the rabbis (as for the Stoics) the acquisition of good character traits involved the conditioning of the human will (*ratzon*). The Torah, then is *the* character-forming agency; it specifies what one *must* do in order to condition the human will through taming or subduing the evil impulse. By means of Torah one not only learns to do what is right, but becomes so tempered as to find it characteristic to do good and to avoid evil. The Torah weaves good conduct into one's personality.

Although rabbinic sources are replete with subtle insights about human motivation,[61] these do not add up to the kind of systematic psychological theory that we find in Greek and Hellenistic philosophical literature, or in Philo. Rabbinic texts do distinguish between body and soul (referred to in Hebrew as either *nefesh*, *ruah*, or *neshamah* interchangeably), but offer no philosophical analysis of these principles or discussion of the internal structure of the human soul. Early in the Tannaitic sources, the soul and the body are presented as part of one organic unity, even though the soul is considered responsible for the functioning of the body.[62] Both the soul and the body constitute the living human person, and both are involved in one's orientation toward or away from God. Only later, in the Amoraic sources, does a more dualistic position emerge, according to which the body and the soul are differentiated. In this view, not only does the soul pre-exist the body in a realm all its own, but during its temporary dwelling in the body the relationship between them is conflict ridden: the body is regarded as the source of sin and as a hindrance for the well-being of the soul. Yet both the Tannaitic and the Amoraic sources take it for granted that the body needs to be controlled and curbed if one is to attain moral perfection. This is not to say that the body is perceived negatively; created by God, it is definitely good; however, it can be used sinfully when the person commits unlawful acts.

The origin of sin, according to the rabbis, is internal, and can be found in the natural inclination that the rabbinic sources call the evil impulse (*yetzer ha-ra*).[63] Created by God and found in us from infancy, the *yetzer ha-ra* is a tendency or an inclination located "in the heart," the rabbinic metaphor for intentional action. Unlike the passions and the appetites in Aristotle's psychology, it is not itself a physiological function, but rather a type of wanting or desiring. It functions like an inner voice that can lead a person to negate God's commanding Will unless one learns to curb it. The task of the moral life is precisely that: to subdue or control the evil impulse so that the other natural inclination, the good impulse, can dominate one's actions.

The rabbinic sages recognized that self-control is difficult to achieve. In fact, for them, to control the evil impulse is the highest expression of the virtue of courage (*gevurah*). As Avot 4:1 tells us, the truly courageous or heroic person (*gibbor*) is not the one who is physically strong, as in Homeric ethics, or the one who fearlessly faces anticipated danger, as Aristotle held, but the one who controls the temptation to sin and to act contrary to God's will. A parallel statement in *Avot de-Rabbi Natan* teaches that the true hero is the one who is strong, swift, and brave "to do the will of thy Father who is in heaven."[64] To inculcate this outlook, rabbinic midrashim include tales about famous rabbis who faced temptations, often related to sexuality, and who overcame them by controlling their evil impulse.[65] Undoubtedly, for the rabbis heroism is self-control and willingness to submit oneself to God.

The Torah itself, according to the rabbis (B. Berakhot 5a), is considered the best antidote to the instigations of the evil impulse. Presumably, "the mind that becomes preoccupied with Torah excludes temptations from without and evil devising within."[66] *Avot de-Rabbi Natan* states this point in a form of analogy: The evil impulse is like iron that one holds in a flame. So long as it is in the flame one can make of it any implement he pleases. So too the evil impulse: its only remedy is in the words of the Torah, for they are like fire.[67] The very preoccupation with the Torah acts like a medicine that preserves life, since the decision to turn to Torah restores one to God, the source of life.[68]

Though submission to the Torah manifests the overcoming of the evil impulse, it cannot uproot the human inclination to sin. The evil impulse continually asserts itself throughout one's life, which means that the cultivation of virtue takes place through a perpetual struggle between the evil impulse and the good impulse. Those who overcome and control their evil impulse are the righteous or virtuous ones, whereas the wicked are those who are controlled by their impulse: "The wicked are controlled by the heart . . . but the righteous control the heart," says an anonymous dictum.[69]

The continued struggle with the evil impulse suggests that most of Israel never attains total righteousness or moral perfection. Thus R. Yosse the Galilean divides Israel into three categories: the righteous ones, whose actions are governed only by the good impulse; the wicked, who are ruled by their evil impulse; and the intermediate ones, the majority of Israel, who are ruled alternatively by the good impulse and by the evil impulse (B. Berakhot 61b).

The Power of the Will

When Greek, Hellenistic, and Roman philosophers discussed self-control, they unambiguously assigned to reason, the best part of the human soul, the control of the passions and the appetites. But how does one submit oneself to Torah so as to control the evil impulse? Because rabbinic sources did not articulate a systematic theory of the soul, their answer remains vague. On the basis of Scripture, rabbinic sources consider human beings to be created with the power of choice, a power they locate in the human will (*ratzon*).

In their recognition of the will as a distinct human function, the rabbinic sages radically differed from Aristotle and were much closer to the Stoics, who believed that "man's entire deliberative process is . . . also subject to the causal nexus."[70] Recognizing human will as a psychological function, however, does not illuminate how the will works and how it relates to what one knows to be good. That kind of explanation will emerge only in the philosophical sources of the post-Maimonidean tradition. Similarly, while the rabbinic sources recognized the potential conflict between divine determinism and human will, they did not deal with it theoretically; instead, they left the tension unresolved.[71] This issue became a major focus of philosophical analysis in the fourteenth century, and we will discuss it in Chapter Eight. For now, according to rabbinic sources humans are able to choose by exercising their will, and their choice reflects their orientation toward God and His Torah.

Avot 2:2 states this point most succinctly in the name of Rabban Gamliel: "Make your will like His will so that He should make His will like your will; nullify your will before His so that He may nullify the will of others before your will." This laconic statement reduces the complexity of religious life to the alignment of the human will with the will of God, an activity that leads one to perform God's commandments and be amply rewarded. The Mishnah does not explain the psychological mechanism by which one can in fact align the human will with God's will; nor does it draw out the psychological implications of the demand to minimize one's willfulness. It only intimates that because human beings are empowered to train their wills by cultivating the virtues, they are also responsible for their willful actions. Indeed, the rabbinic doctrine of retribution, an aspect of rabbinic theodicy, is predicated on the belief in the power of the human will.

The conditioning of the human will begins with the "fear of Heaven" (*yirat shamayim*), "fear of God" (*yirat ha-shem*), and "fear of sin" (*yirat ḥet*). Such fears act as deterrents against temptations to commit sinful acts and as guides to avoid all sort of potential pitfalls. Recognizing, as did Psalm 1, the powerful influence of human associations on one's moral conduct, Avot 2:8 exhorts its reader not to associate with "the evil neighbor" who may cause one to deviate from the upright path. *Avot de-Rabbi Natan* would enlarge this category to include "the evil wife," who is also governed by the evil impulse.[72] This view of women as potential detriments to the righteous life persists throughout the discourse on happiness in the Middle Ages.

The human fear of God begins with the fear of punishment, whether the punishment is meted out in this life or after death, in the world to come. By avoiding sinful acts and pursuing the life of good deeds, the believer comes to a higher level of fear, namely, the reverence and awe that arise when one recognizes God as the creator of the universe. Avot 2:1 captures this perspective in the name of Rabbi, i.e., the editor of the Mishnah, Rabbi Judah ha-Nasi. "Consider three things and you will not come to sin: know what is above you—a seeing eye and a listening ear and that all your actions are written in a book." A parallel position is stated in Avot 2:13. "Know also before whom you are laboring and who the employer is who will pay you the wages for your labor."

The awareness of God as the executor of ultimate justice, then, constitutes the cognitive dimension in the training of the will and the acquisition of virtues. When one recognizes God as the ruler of the universe and the giver of the Torah, one accepts "the yoke of the Kingdom of Heaven" (*ol malkhut shamayim*), and this acceptance is manifested in the performance of God's commandments. In sum, the rabbinic list of virtues is meant to inculcate the personality type disposed to fulfill God's will as revealed in the Torah.

Virtues and Good Deeds

Rabbinic virtues reflect the ethos of Torah as practiced in the hierarchical structure of the rabbinic academy. In serving their masters, disciples acquired desirable character traits such as humility, meekness, modesty, patience, and loyalty.[73] These traits enable an individual to function in a hierarchical social setting that hallows authority, insists on respect for both superiors and peers, and uses kingship as the primary model for the worship of God. Accordingly, the rabbinic sources unambiguously reject arrogance, haughtiness, brazenness, coarseness, envy, and jealousy—all of which promote selfishness, which in turn undermines the social cohesion of the rabbinic academy. Indeed, the very vices that corrode human relations are also the ones that make it impossible for one to accept the kingship of God and the authority of God's revelation in the Torah.

The rabbinic academy functioned also as an extended family that provided a broad range of social services to its members. The rabbinic sources, therefore, highlight character traits that sensitize the individual to the needs of others, especially the weak, the socially marginal, and the poor. Fusing the prudential values of the Wisdom literature with prophetic moral concerns, the rabbinic sources extol patience, generosity, compassion, kindness, and attitudes that lead their possessor to acts of lovingkindness (*gemilut ḥasadim*) such as giving hospitality to the stranger and charity to the poor, visiting the sick, comforting mourners, feeding the hungry, facilitating marriage, and redeeming prisoners. These good deeds (*ma'asim tovim*) toward other persons constitute what Walter Wurtzburger appropriately called, "ethics of responsibility," an ethics in which care for the well-being of the other is integral to the well-being of one's own.[74] By contrast, rabbinic sources unambiguously denounce vices—such as impatience, short-temperedness, irascibility, envy, jealousy, greediness, niggardliness, hatefulness, and arrogance—that diminish the capacity of the individual to serve others, and, by extension, prevent one from worshiping God. In an ethics of responsibility a failure to respond to the material and spiritual needs of others is a failure to worship God. A talmudic statement summarizes this point as follows: "Happy is the man to whom there is no transgression, and in whom there is no deliberate trespass or sin, in whom there are good deeds and the study of Torah, lowly and humble."[75]

Put differently, in rabbinic Judaism the virtues emerge in the actual relationship with other persons and are exemplified in specific actions that address both material and emotional needs of the other. The very activity of Torah study in the social context of the academy facilitates the conditioning of the will in which the acquisition of virtue takes place. Such moral conditioning occurs both "vertically" (that is, in the relationship between disciples and their superior masters) and "horizontally" (that is, in the relationship of the disciple and his peers, or colleagues).

Avot 1:6 calls on a person to "to take a master [*rav*] and to acquire a friend [*ḥaver*]." The range of desired behavior toward one's superiors, discussed above, is complemented by the intimacy that emerges with one's friend, or study partner. The rabbinic insistence that one should not study alone but with a friend echoes the recognition of friendship in the acquisition of virtue that Aristotle analyzed and that the members of Epicurus' Garden practiced. This is not to say that rabbinic sages derived their views about the value of a friend from reading Aristotle's analysis of friendship in the *Ethics*. Rather, I conjecture, the ideal of virtue-friendship permeated the rabbinic understanding of Torah study because it was a popular value in the philosophic culture of the Greco-Roman world.

Learning Torah, like the study of philosophy, is not a solitary activity, but a life-long preoccupation that is undertaken with a like-minded person who is equally devoted to the life of study. Given the desirability of shared study, it is clear why rabbinic sources speak against such vices as being short-tempered, irascible, rigid, jealous, or bearing a grudge, all of which are traits or conduct that undermine friendship.

The life of shared study and caring for others brings about a gamut of emotional dispositions. Rabbinic sources, no less than Aristotle, understood that virtues are not only dispositions to *act* in a certain way but also permanent dispositions to *feel* a certain way. Thus Avot 3:12 exhorts one to perform God's commandments out of joy (*simḥah*), a cheerful countenance (*ma'or panim*), and wholeheartedness (*lev tov*) toward God and other human beings. Melancholy, bitterness, or pettiness, are all emotional postures considered incompatible with the performance of mitzvot. These dispositions express a self-centeredness that excludes the other from the purview of the self, whether the other is the rabbinic fellow or the Wholly Other—God. Conversely, openness to the needs of others indicates an ability to derive satisfaction (*qorat ruaḥ; naḥat ruaḥ*) from benefiting others and from witnessing their well-being. Rabbinic ethics, then, not only denies the ideal of self-sufficiency. It considers the need to act with lovingkindness toward others as the highest expression of emotional well-being.

Torah and the Pursuit of Truth

The virtuous rabbinic personality encompasses certain intellectual traits that emerge from the very text-based nature of rabbinic learning. Thus, its sources portray the ideal student of Torah as diligent (*ḥarutz*), patient (*savlan*), cautious (*zahir*), and honest (*yashar*), all of which are traits that enable one to devote one's life to Torah study for its own sake. Their opposites—impatience, hastiness, forgetfulness, and sloth—are incompatible with the total devotion required by Torah study.

Since rabbinic education was primarily oral, it required memorization of a vast body of textually-based interpretative traditions, transmitted from generation to generation within the academy. The rabbinic sources accordingly praise keen memory and retention power as characteristics of the ideal student (e.g., Avot 5:12; 5:14). However, mere retention of what one has learned is not sufficient. The ideal student must delve in depth into the divine teachings and be able to analyze them, draw inferences, and make connections. The person who possesses cognitive talents such as sharpness, cleverness, wit, and quick grasp is highly esteemed in rabbinic ethical teachings.

The exercise of these traits yields intelligence (*da'at*) and understanding (*binah*), which are the primary intellectual excellences of the ideal student.

Avot 3:14 indicates that the rabbis considered them to be two distinct virtues: "If there is no intelligence there is no understanding; if there is no understanding there is no intelligence." However, this aphorism does not define these intellectual excellences or specify how the two relate to another intellectual virtue—wisdom (*ḥokhmah*). It will remain for the medieval Jewish philosophers, who articulate an elaborate philosophical psychology, to give these vague terms more precise meaning.

The life of Torah is dominated by the search for truth, since truth is one of the attributes of God. Thus intellectually the pursuit of truth is manifested in the perpetual and even zealous attempt to fathom the depth of God's Will as revealed in the Torah and interpreted by the halakhic process itself. This pursuit accounts for the intellectualism that pervades the halakhic discourses of the Talmud, where human reason is placed in the service of worship as the student explores the meaning and scope of the revealed Law.

Torah study, then, is a form of worship that, as the pursuit of truth, extends to encompass all forms of human interaction. Conducting one's affairs truthfully and honestly is a form of imitating God. Hence, rabbinic sources consider honesty (*yosher*) vital, and speak out against any sort of pretense and misrepresentation as a violation of truth. There must be no disparity between words and intentions, between reality and appearance. Thus truthfulness is not only an intellectual virtue; it is also a social virtue that facilitates proper family life, friendship, and business relations.

In the academic context, devotion to truth leads the student of Torah to admit when he does not know or when he makes mistakes. The recognition of fallibility constitutes modesty (*anavah*) and contributes to a posture of lowliness that the rabbis praise. They warn against boasting "with the words of Torah" or ascribing one's intellectual accomplishments solely to one's own natural talents or intellectual efforts. He who does so "will be uprooted from the world."[76] The low of spirit or meek person (*shefal ruaḥ*), by contrast, knows that all his accomplishments are ultimately due not to his own efforts but to God's benevolent gifts.[77]

The all-consuming nature of Torah study could easily undermine involvement in performing good deeds toward others. Not unlike Aristotle, the rabbis were aware of the potential tension between intellectual or speculative activity (*iyyun*) and action (*ma`aseh*), as we learn from long discussion on the subject recorded in the B. Qiddushin 40b and in Sifre on Deuteronomy # 41 (Finkelstein, ed. p. 85). The majority opinion is that "the study of Torah is greater because it leads to good deeds." However, the superiority of good deeds over Torah study is recognized in Avot 3:9, which states that "whoever's deeds are more abundant than his wisdom, his wisdom will endure, but whoever's wisdom is more abundant than his deeds, his wisdom will not endure."

The debate itself suggests that the rabbis recognized the complementary relationship between the theoretical and practical aspects of the life of Torah. Study of God's revealed Will that does not lead to action is vacuous, because God's will concerns action toward others; conversely, a life of good deeds that is not rooted in proper knowledge and understanding gained through Torah study lacks appropriate depth. Only when Torah study is undertaken for its own sake does the scholar becomes "a beloved friend" of God.

> He loves God; he loves mankind; he gives joy to God; he gives joy to men. It [the Torah] clothes him with humility and fear, and it makes him fit to be pious, righteous and faithful; and it removes him far from sin, and brings him toward virtue [*zekhut*]. And men profit from him in counsel, wisdom, understanding and strength.[78]

In short, the rabbinic sources exhibit the same tension between *theoria* and *praxis* that concerned Aristotle in his analysis of happiness, and the rabbinic resolution of the tension was no less ambiguous than Aristotle's.

Humility: The Overarching Virtue

While Aristotle and the rabbis share that ambiguity, the rabbinic emphasis on humility identifies a major difference between them. In Chapter One we noted that for Aristotle, "greatness of soul" (*megalopsychia*) is the crown of all the virtues. Indeed, he suggests that it is a beautifully ordered pattern of the virtues.[79] The magnanimous man has "what is great in every virtue" (NE IV:3 1123b 30), and he practices them on a grand scale. The great-souled person has a sense of his own goodness. Because he knows that he has complete virtue, he feels no need to be honored for it by men of practical wisdom (1124 a 5–9)—unlike other men, who pursue honor "in order to convince themselves of their own virtue" (1095 b 26–8). With this inner sense of his own goodness, the great-souled man is fundamentally undisturbed by changes in his material and physical circumstances and in his external relations. He is like an aristocrat who is economically self-sufficient and therefore able to engage in giving gifts on a large scale; his "greatness of soul" results in magnanimous conduct.

In contrast, the rabbis made humility the overarching virtue of the ideal sage (B. Avodah Zarah 20b),[80] and several rabbinic sages are depicted as extremely humble persons. B. Eruvin 13b states that "Everyone who humbles himself, God exalts; and everyone who exalts himself, God humbles; one who runs around for greatness, greatness flees from, and one who flees from greatness, him greatness runs after." In the same source, the rabbis give humility a role in settling the disputes between the schools of Hillel and Shammai and name it as one of the attributes of God, the exemplar of all moral conduct. God's humility is shown in His election of Israel, a lowly people, and in the manner in which God chooses to manifest His presence. Instead of the lofty mountains, God causes His Presence (*shekhinah*) to dwell upon an unimpressive Mount Sinai; and instead of beautiful and towering trees, He chooses to dwell in a thornbush (B. Sotah 5a). Moses, the greatest of all prophets, indeed comes closest to God by being the most humble of men, and humility is the character trait that the rabbis ascribed to Abraham, Moses, David, and Nimrod.

Even though some rabbis were wealthy (as was Rabbi, the redactor of the Mishnah), the virtue of magnanimity and the acts of giving on a large scale are never mentioned in rabbinic sources. In fact, in accord with Cynic and Stoic morality, the rabbis counseled against the accumulation of wealth. The truly wealthy, says Avot 4:1, is the one who knows how to be content with his portion in the world (*sameaḥ be-ḥelqo*). The happy person is the one who is able to find satisfaction (*sippuq*) in whatever life brings to him or her. In contrast, the desire to accumulate material goods indicates that one is controlled by the evil impulse and that one has not yet reached quietude of mind. The full meaning of the counsel to be content with little cannot be simply reduced to the influence of Stoic virtues. It is a feature of the religious outlook of rabbinic Judaism.

Humility, meekness, and lowliness of spirit are virtues that emerge when one reflects on the human condition. The wisdom that one needs to become virtuous is the recognition that human life begins with a "putrid drop" and ends in "a place of worm and maggot" (Avot 3:1). In between, one's life is carried out under the watchful eye of God, who knows and records human deeds and metes out just rewards and punishments (Avot 2:1). The awareness that one is constantly subject to divine inspection and that one is accountable to God is diametrically opposed to the attitude of the "great-souled" man of Aristotle, who does not need to be accountable to

God because in the Aristotelian worldview God is not involved in human affairs. God is an impersonal foundation of the universe, and to the extent that it acts, its activity is self-contemplation to the exclusion of anything else. But the God of rabbinic Judaism is personally concerned with and influenced by human activities. Put differently, it is *theology* that dictates the difference between the ethics of Aristotle and the ethics of the rabbis.

HAPPINESS AS A RELATIONSHIP WITH GOD

Holiness and the Pursuit of Perfection

If the central goal of the rabbinic religious ethos is relationship with God, the same virtues that dispose us to behave righteously toward each other are the character traits that dispose us to relate properly to God. In accord with the teachings of Leviticus 19, the goal of rabbinic Judaism is to be holy as God is holy. This goal is understood to be attainable, in principle, because God has revealed to Israel the teachings that chart the path of holiness, namely, the Torah.

Furthermore, as Gen. 1:26 states, all humans are created in the "image of God" (*tzelem elohim*), though the meaning of that concept is open to interpretation.[81] In some rabbinic texts, it was taken to be "the foundation of fundamental human equality and the recognition of human worth." According to Mishnah Sanhedirn 4:5, "It is the duty of everyone to say: 'For my sake the world was created.'" This Mishnah recognizes that human beings are both individually unique and, at the same time, stamped with the one seal, the image of God, which makes them share something very profound. By virtue of the divine image, human beings are equal to and bear responsibility for one another. Other rabbinic texts interpret creation in the divine image to mean the inviolability and sanctity of all human life as well as human dignity. The prohibition against murder is derived from that belief, and destroying the other is akin to destruction of the divine image. The same applies to the prohibition of activities that diminish human worth, such as shaming a person in public. An entire range of ethical directives in concrete circumstances is spelled out to specify this general principle of human dignity grounded in the belief that we are created in the divine image.

For the biblical authors, the concept meant that God looks, acts, and feels like a human being. Biblical depiction of God is thus blatantly anthropomorphic and anthropopathic. Not at all disturbed by this depiction, the rabbis further fleshed out the all too human portrayal of God. In a recent article, David Stern argued that the more the rabbis could talk about God in personal terms, the more they could enter into a personal relationship with Him.[82] Projecting onto God their own insecurities and anxieties after the destruction of the Temple, they portrayed Him in rather "undivine" terms. For example, in *Lamentations Rabbah*, the text Stern chose for his discussion, God appears as insecure, indecisive, and weak, an obvious projection of rabbinic anxieties and fears.

I endorse Stern's insight but wish to expand on it from the perspective of virtue ethics. The intensely personal depiction of God in rabbinic sources also manifests the rabbinic preoccupation with cultivation of character, an activity that requires interaction with other persons. In human interaction, the other is the recipient of acts of lovingkindness (*gemilut ḥasadim*). At the same time, in the performance of good deeds one acquires the virtues in an attempt to imitate God's character traits. Thus, God functions like a mirror in which one can see oneself and strive to improve what one sees by improving one's conduct towards other persons.

How, then, do the rabbis know the personality traits of God? Lamentations Rabbah, the basis of Stern's analysis, is by no means our only source for how the rabbis depicted Him. Far more common than the indecisive God is the just and compassionate God. The biblical appellation *Elohim* (as in Ex. 22:8) reflects the attribute of justice (*middat ha-din*) and expresses the remote, transcendent, and unfathomable aspects of divine reality—God as creator of the universe, supreme judge of humanity, and redeemer of Israel. In contrast, the rabbis associated the Tetragrammaton with the divine attributes of mercy and compassion (*middat ha-raḥamim*), using Ex. 34:6 as their proof-text to portray the personal, intimate, and caring aspect of God as He is known to the believer through His myriad deeds of lovingkindness. It is this divine attribute in particular that the rabbis expected Israel to imitate in order to attain holiness. Midrash *Tana debe Eliyahu* thus interprets the biblical injunction "You shall walk in His way" (Deut. 28:9) as follows:

> Man must imitate God, i.e., imitate aspects of God's lovingkindness; Just as Heaven is merciful and compassionate toward the wicked and receives them in repentance, so ought ye to be compassionate toward one another; just as Heaven is gracious, giving free gifts both to those that know Him and to those that do not know Him, so ought ye to give gifts to one another; just as Heaven is long-suffering, patiently biding with the wicked and receiving them in repentance, so ought ye to bide patiently with one another in (a spirit) of kindliness and not bide patiently with one another in a spirit of retaliation; just as

Heaven is abundant in lovingkindness, leaning toward lovingkindness, so ought you to lean toward the good to do it more than to the bad."[83]

Both aspects of God are brought to mind in the liturgy, especially in the *Pesuqei de-Zimrah,* the preliminary prayers of the morning service, which consist of selections from the Psalms. These carefully selected hymns mention both aspects of God: His magnificent creation and mighty deeds in human history make us aware of God's greatness and radical otherness and elicit our awe, wonderment, respect, adoration and praise. Concomitantly, the liturgy dwells on the compassionate and merciful aspects of God, who takes care of His creatures by healing the sick, raising up the fallen, feeding the hungry, clothing the naked, and protecting the orphan and the widow—in short, doing all the morally good acts that Israel can and must do if its society is to be just. It is precisely this sort of compassionate conduct that renders the people of Israel a happy community, a community that lives the intrinsically good life when it imitates God's attribute of lovingkindness.

The point is affirmed liturgically in Psalm 145, which the rabbis incorporated into the liturgy, supplemented by two verses from other Psalms that open with the word *ashrei.* The rabbis, then, understood happiness as a *relational* category. Through moral action toward other persons, those who recognize God, namely Israel, become His holy co-partners in the management of the world. Conversely, to sin against God would result in the loss of holiness, experienced as God's hiddenness (*hester panim*). Therefore, the synagogue service, as all other forms of worship in rabbinic Judaism, was the context in which the ideal personality type could emerge so as to perpetuate Israel's eternal covenant with God.

That covenant of Israel is an on-going love affair. Indeed, the commandment to love God "with all your heart and all your might" (Deut. 6:4) forms the core of the *shema,* the Jewish declaration of faith in the unity, oneness, and uniqueness of God. The virtuous or righteous person who studies Torah for its own sake, controls the evil impulse so as to avoid sin, and cares for other people is called "a friend" (*re'a*). He is both "a lover of God" and a "lover of people" (Avot 6:1), and that friendship with or love of God is possible precisely because the righteous person has acquired the requisite virtues. Recall Aristotle's analysis of friendship (*philia*), where we see some interesting similarities between the Greek and Judaic perspectives. Aristotle distinguished between friendship based on pleasure, friendship based on utility, and the friendship of virtue. The first two can be collapsed into one category—conditional friendship—as opposed to virtue friendship, which is unconditional. This distinction was prevalent in Hellenistic reflections on friendship, so it is no surprise that we find it echoed in Avot 5:19, where the anonymous author distinguishes between *ahavah she-hi teluyah ba-davar*, namely love that is motivated by a concern other than itself, which is destined to disappear, and *ahavah she-einah teluyah be-davar*, namely, love that has no external motive, which lasts eternally. Israel's relationship with God must be of the latter kind. Only with God, the ideal virtuous friend, can Israel (individually and collectively) grow in virtue as it attempts to emulate God through acts of mercy and compassion. Loving God as the virtuous person loves a virtuous friend constitutes worshipping God for God's own sake (*le-shem shamayim*) rather than for any other motive. It is because both God and Israel grow in virtue in their ongoing relationship that the covenant is perpetual but ever changing, as Scripture itself teaches and the rabbinic homilies confirm.

Perfection: Moderation or Supererogation

The ideal of *imitatio Dei* involves rabbinic religious ethics in a tension between two operational modes: moderation and supererogation. All rabbinic ethical teachings are rooted in the notion of self-control and self-mastery of the passions, and all presuppose that cultivation of the ideal character requires discipline and habitual practice. Yet the notion that Israel is to be as holy as God is holy calls one to excellence and perfection, which raises the question: Does acting righteously mean following the moderate course of action and avoiding excesses, or does it mean going beyond the call of (legal) duty and engaging in saintly acts of supererogation? If one is to be perfect like God, in what does perfection consist? The logic of the ideal of perfection dictates a certain zealous disposition that does not rest until perfection is attained. Such perfectionism is quite contrary to the ideal of moderation and self-restraint.

The underlying assumption of biblical religion was that God's creation is good, though not perfect. All material things, including the human body and its physical needs, are therefore considered good, and satisfying these goods is viewed as part of the covenantal relationship with God. However, the fusion of the Wisdom tradition with Torah piety in the Second Temple period entailed an emphasis on self-discipline and self-control in the cultivation of desired character traits. For the sages of the Wisdom literature, the good life did not mean denial of the body, but rather the proper training of emotions and the curbing of desires. However, it was the notion of self-discipline that facilitated the development of an ethos of saintliness (*hasidut*), which linked righteousness to renunciation of material goods, abstinence from physical pleasures, frequent fasting, and even self-sacrifice, all in the name of the search for spiritual perfection. We have mentioned the ethos of abstinence in our discussion of Philo. His position was common in the extra-canonic texts and in several Apocalypses. The renunciatory ethos was particularly strong among the Essenes of Qumran, who went as far as endorsing celibacy in their pursuit of holy perfection.

Most importantly, it was the Pharisees, the precursors of the rabbis, who associated the ideal of holy living with renunciatory practices. The Pharisees, as Steven Fraade put it, were

> noted for having been scrupulous in the practice of ritual purity, especially at meals: they ate their common meals as though they were priests eating sanctified offerings, being especially careful to protect the table from impurity. They [were] also reported to have been particularly careful concerning Sabbath observance and tithing and were known for their fasting, simple living, and close-knit communities.[84]

To constitute the holy nation outside the precinct of the Temple, the Pharisees required separation (*perishut*) from the impure environment around them. Thus the Pharisaic ideal of perfection is clearly in accord with an ethos of supererogation rather than one of mere moderation. The destruction of the Temple would further legitimize the Pharisaic ideal of abstinence and self-denial as ways to express mourning and penitence over the catastrophic loss of Israel's goodness.

After 70 C.E. some Pharisees continued to promote the ideal of saintliness as the ultimate goal of spiritual perfection. A passage from B. Avodah Zarah 20b captures this form of extreme pietism.

> It is taught: Be on your guard against anything evil (Deut. 23:10). A person should not have impure thoughts during the day, lest he encounter impurity at night. From here R. Pineas ben Jair says: Heedfulness leads to cleanliness, cleanliness leads to abstinence (*perishut*), abstinence leads to purity, purity leads to holiness, holiness leads to modesty, modesty leads to fear of sin, fear of sin leads to saintliness,

saintliness leads to the Holy Spirit, the Holy Spirit leads to the revivification of the dead.

In this interpretation saintliness combines ritual purity, moral perfection, and holiness. In theory, ritual cleanliness does not necessarily entail self-denial or physical hardship, but this connection was apparently made by the early Hasidim in the second century B.C.E. and their pietistic ideals were perpetuated by some Pharisaic and rabbinic teachers.[85] For them, the ultimate commitment to Torah required minimizing physical comfort. It is impossible to discern the original impetus of the statement:

> This is the way of Torah: a morsel of bread with salt shalt thou eat and water by measure shalt thou drink and on the ground shalt thou sleep, and a life of hardship shalt thou live, while thou toilest in the Torah.[86]

But this attitude toward material goods could be easily combined with the anti-luxury and anti-vanity posture of Cynicism and Stoicism. Whether physical hardship is understood as a preventive measure against the temptations of the evil *yetzer ha-ra* or as a punitive attitude toward the body is open to interpretation. What is clear is that the rabbinic endorsement of modesty and simplicity could easily slip into a program of self-denial; what begins with moderation could end in supererogation.

With the development of rabbinic halakhah the question of moderation vs. supererogation was subsumed by another question: Does halakhah itself define the limits of moral excellence, or is moral excellence or perfection to be attained by going *beyond* the limits of the Law (*lifnim mi-shurat ha-din*)?[87] The question is not resolved in rabbinic texts, where the various positions are given equal weight. On the whole, however, the literature appears to shun extreme asceticism. It is very likely that the very changes after 70 C.E. made the rabbis, the perpetuators of Pharisaic traditions, tone down the ideal of saintliness. When the Pharisees ceased to exist as a sect and took an active role in the administration of the Jewish community in Roman Palestine and in Babylonia, moderation appeared to be the norm. The happy life of Torah was then understood as a life of simplicity and modesty, even though some rabbis were famed for their wealth. The tension between the devotion to Torah and the pursuit of wealth and physical pleasures, then, was recognized though not resolved:

He who eats much and drinks much impoverishes himself in Torah and so also he that loves sleep, for the words of the Torah are devoured only by him who is physically weary because of them.[88]

Joy and Suffering in the Life of Torah

Any form of self-discipline minimally requires some curbing of appetites and ideally yields a transformation or reshaping of desire. Since the taming of desire minimally involves delay of gratification and maximally abnegation and self-denial, there can be no moral training without a measure of pain and suffering. For the ancient philosophers, especially the Cynics and the Stoics, such discomfort was regarded as totally necessary and compatible with both human flourishing and freedom. Conversely, the individual who shuns pain and is dominated by the human penchant for physical comfort and pleasure will become a slave to the passions. *Avot de-Rabbi Natan* indicates that the rabbis shared this outlook: they regarded the strictures of Torah as limitations that produce greater freedom.

> He broke the tables of the Commandments. What is that? It was said: When Moses went up on high to receive the tables of the Commandments, which had been inscribed and put away since the six days of Creation—as it is said, "And the tables were the work of God, and the writing was the writing of God, graven upon the tables" (Ex. 32:16): read not "graven" (*harut*) but "freedom" (*herut*), for whosoever studies Torah is a free man.[89]

For the rabbis, then, the Torah is indeed a system of commands having little to do with convenience or comfort, but it is only this program of moral training that frees individuals from pursuit of illusory goods and trivial concerns, directing them to devote their lives to what matters most, relationship with God.

The association of Torah and suffering is stated several times in the Tana debe Eliyahu. For example: "Happy is the man that maketh himself like unto an ox for the yoke and like unto an ass for the burden, and sits and meditates upon the words of Torah every day continually."[90] The same sentiment is expressed in another text from the same source: "Happy is the man that wears himself down [through laboring] in the words of the Torah and that sits and plows in them like the cow plowing in the field." This Midrash concludes with the statement, "The Torah is given only to him who suffers over it."⁹¹ Clearly, voluntary suffering for the sake of Torah is very much part of the righteous life.

Human suffering, especially unmerited suffering, was already articulated as a theological problem in the Wisdom literature. The Book of Job, of course, is the first systematic struggle with the question "Why do the righteous suffer and the wicked prosper?" The question was not resolved by the Book of Job, but its intricate literary structure and rich poetic style made it the classical text for all future reflections on the problem in Judaism.⁹² The meaning of human suffering came into sharp relief with the destruction of the Temple in 70 C.E., requiring innovative emotional and theological responses. In rabbinic sources the defeat of 70 was taken to be a kind of death for which one is in a perpetual state of mourning. The midrashic sources expounded upon the meaning of the tragedy, its causes and ramifications, and the halakhic sources created the rituals that enabled Israel to deal with the loss.⁹³

The dominant explanation of suffering saw a causal connection between suffering and sin. The Temple was destroyed because of Israel's transgressions, chief among them being baseless hatred (*sin'at ḥinam*). Suffering was not only merited; it also fulfilled an important didactic function—it was a kind of chastisement from God that leads to self-correction: "When a man sees that he is being chastised let him examine his ways" (B. Berakhot 5a; B. Sanhedrin 27b). Through suffering one embarks on a path of self-examination, remorse, renunciation of one's sinful past, and finally repentance (*teshuvah*), the return to God and the renewal of the divine-human relationship.

The positive view of suffering suggests that God does not act capriciously or abusively. Rather, like a loving parent who cares for erring offspring, God leads His children, Israel, back to the "right path" by allowing them to experience the negative consequences of their errors. These are called "chastisements of love" (*yissurin shel ahavah*), and their goal is repentance.

Thus the positive notion of suffering is totally compatible with happiness, if happiness is properly understood. Moreover, the very aspiration to religious perfection supposes a causal connection between suffering and the acquisition of virtue. If suffering cleanses or purifies the sinner, then there is reason to conclude that the more one suffers the more holy one becomes, and the closer one can get to God. This is the logic of the extreme pietism that leads not only to asceticism, but to sacrificing one's life for the sanctification of God's name—*qiddush ha-shem*. The ideal of martyrdom was undoubtedly an integral part of rabbinic Judaism, especially during the Bar Kokhba revolt in 132, the last Jewish attempt to overthrow Rome.

Although *qiddush ha-shem* did define the limit of acceptable asceticism in rabbinic Judaism, life was not to be intentionally lived at the limit. The Torah is a regimen for life and not a prescription for death. Thus the rabbis articulated a program for living, after the loss of the Temple, in a broken, imperfect world. The cessation of the sacrificial cult made it impossible to fulfill a central commandment of the Torah—to rejoice three times a year during the seasonal festivals (Deut 16:15). The rabbinic response to the trauma of 70 was the substitution of prayer for the sacrificial cult. God is now worshiped in the heart rather than through animal sacrifice. With this transformation, as Gary Anderson has shown,[94] came a reinterpretation of the commandment to rejoice, along with the injunction to mourn the destruction of the Temple and the tension between the two commandments.

In the Tannaitic period the commandment to rejoice was expanded to include nonsacrificial activities such as "drinking of wine, wearing special garments, and even preparing nonsacrificial meal." Later, in the Amoraic period, the very obligation of Torah study was equated with the obligation to rejoice before God. The life of Torah study itself was now promoted as the most joyful one—a concept frequently expressed by the rabbis: "What joy can a man have in this world except only in words of Torah."[95] The joy of Torah study is an inkling of the bliss to be enjoyed in the world to come, since God is the author of the words and phrases over which the rabbinic scholars pore. In another statement we read: "For just as Israel obeys the Torah in this world and rejoices in it, so the Torah rejoices in them forever."[96] And J. Berakhot 9:5 states in the name of Hillel: "Torah is loved by the Jews and all are glad [*semeḥin*] with it." In fact, God Himself was joyful (*sameaḥ*) when He gave Israel the wondrous gift of Torah (B. Berakhot 5a).

Torah study is to be undertaken with a cheerful attitude, as is prescribed in B. Berakhot 31a: "One should not prepare to pray while immersed in sorrow, or idleness, or laughter, or chatter, or frivolity, or idle talk, but only while still rejoicing in the performance of some commandment [*simḥah shel mitzvah*] (B. Berakhot 31a). In *Tana debe Eliyahu*, the same idea is expressed regarding fulfillment of certain commandments:

> Let a man give his charity with joy and it will be credited to him as righteousness; let a man set aside with joy the heave offering that is due the priests from him and it will be credited to him as righteousness; let a man give his tithes with joy and it will be credited to him as righteousness.[97]

All these citations and many others testify to the centrality of joy in the rabbinic conception of the good life, a joy that emerges from the very life of Torah.

Interestingly, while the joy of Torah is spiritual, its intensity can be expressed verbally only through sensual metaphors.[98] Sometimes it conjures up delights of exquisite food: "The Torah given to Israel was 'like goblets filled with water ... and tables full of all the delicacies of the world.'" Elsewhere it is not unusual to find that erotic metaphors are used to delineate the pleasure of Torah study, which is an act of love. Whether the rabbis eroticized the spiritual act of Torah study or, conversely, spiritualized their erotic energies depends on how one understands the meaning of eros and need not be decided here. What is clear is that for the rabbis the pursuit of perfection through Torah study was analogous to the love of *sophia* in the Greek academies of philosophy.

In one respect, however, the rabbinic and the philosophic delight in intellectual activity are not the same. In the Greek setting, the pursuit of wisdom amounts to self-fulfillment, for excellence in it constitutes the full realization of the human potential. Though this process takes place through interaction with others, ideally through virtue-friendship, the delight that completes moral excellence is centered on the self. It is the pursuer of wisdom who experiences the delight of intellectual activity, and the delight ultimately derives from his own activity. In contrast, in the rabbinic context, the joy in performing the mitzvot is derived from pleasing another person, from fulfilling the needs of the other—and ultimately, the Wholly Other, God. The "joy of commandment" thus focuses on the other rather than on the self, and ethical-spiritual perfection is the desired result of that relationship with the other.

The Rewards of Torah

Happiness, Aristotle taught, is a self-sufficient good because it is desired for its own sake and not for the sake of anything else. The life of Torah was understood in the same way:

> Do not be like servants who serve their master in order to receive a reward; be like servants who serve their master without expecting to receive a reward, and let the fear of heaven be upon you (Avot 1:3).

Precisely because the life of Torah is intrinsically good, living in accordance with Torah enables one to enjoy its intrinsic goodness. In this regard, the one who follows the prescriptions of Torah is de facto rewarded by God, even though one cannot compel God to reward him or her for living rightly.

These rewards, which Israel prays for and hopes to receive, are granted only if Israel worships God for God's sake (*le-shem shamayim*). They can be divided into three related categories: personal, social, and political. For the individual, the goods include health (*beri'ut*), longevity (*orekh yamim*), dignity (*kavod*), livelihood (*parnasah*), a loving family (*shelom bayit*), satisfaction (*qorat ru'ah*) and joy (*simhah*). Since these goods are experienced in human interaction through doing acts of lovingkindness (*gemilut hasadim*), the rewards of Torah pertain not just to the individual but to the community at large. A life in devotion to Torah, then, yields a community that enjoys justice (*tzedeq*), friendliness (*re`ut; ahavah*), compassion (*rahamim*), and peacefulness (*shalom*). In this ideal life, there is no strife, no conflict, no unnecessary hatred, no fraud, and no deception; human relations are properly conducted. Israel, however, is but one of the nations. When the Jewish people lives in accordance with God's will, it prospers vis-à-vis the nations. After the destruction of the Temple, that meant that its political enemies would be subdued, its exiles would be gathered to the land of Israel, and Jerusalem and the Temple would be rebuilt. Thus Israel's status among the nations ultimately manifests the quality of its relationship with God, on an individual and on a collective level.

The rabbis, however, were very aware that the reality in which they lived was inherently imperfect and incomplete. The Temple was destroyed; the people of Israel were in exile, social relations between Jews were anything but peaceful and just, and individual actions were often controlled by the evil impulse. So, it was reasonable to ask, "When will the life of Torah be fully rewarded?" and the rabbis' answer was, "In the remote future." The postponement of reward to the future life was another rabbinic way to solve the problem of suffering and evil in a world created by a benevolent God who revealed His goodness to His chosen people, Israel.

Rabbinic speculations about the remote future are an amalgam of themes, sentiments, and views reflecting the complex eschatological and apocalyptic heritage of the Second Temple period as well as the profound crisis brought about by its destruction.[99] Rabbinic reflections included extra-canonical and often sectarian Judaism of the late Second Temple period as much as they absorbed Greek psychological theories. Generally speaking, the rabbinic literature that deals with these themes focuses on the "Days of the Messiah" (*yemot ha-mashiah*), when Israel's political tribulation will come to an end and it will be redeemed. A human military leader, the

Messiah (or Messiahs) will herald the arrival of that Messianic Age. Although the sources affirm the causal connection between observance of the commandments and the coming of the messiah (e.g., B. Shabbat 118a), the precise nature of the Messianic Age is not clear. From the apocalyptic literature, mostly of a sectarian nature, the rabbinic tradition absorbed a catastrophic depiction of it: the victory of righteous Israel will come about only after cataclysmic wars with its enemies and a significant deterioration in its quality of life (B. Sanhedrin 97a), but thereafter the ideally good life will be significantly better than the historical reality known in the present.

The destiny of the individual was no less a part of speculations about the remote utopian future, especially vis-à-vis overcoming death and the perpetuation of life in the world to come. The belief in personal survival after death was pre-rabbinic, but it became very prominent in rabbinic Judaism because of the absorption of psychological dualism, namely, the distinction between body and soul. The more the rabbis absorbed Platonic themes that recognized the soul as a separate entity from the body, the more they could talk about the immortality of the soul, as did Philo before them. The details of the career of the soul after death, however, remained open to question, giving rise to various rabbinic rituals of mourning.[100] Be that as it may, in general rabbinic sources affirm a close causal connection between the life of virtue in this world and the survival of the individual soul. For the righteous (*tzaddiqim*), death is not to be feared because life does not end with it. In fact, the truly righteous ones: Abraham, Isaac, Jacob, Aaron, Moses and Miriam (B. Baba Batra 17a), merited the easiest of deaths—"death by a kiss," a painless departure of the soul reserved for them alone.

The souls of the righteous continue to exist in the world to come, enjoying a blissful intimacy with God and knowing no want, need, strife, or conflict. It is a life of bounty and peace, of joy and delight (Berakhot 17a; Exodus Rabbah 52:3; Genesis Rabbah 62:2). Imagining this ideal existence, the rabbis depicted the world to come in their own image—a place where the righteous will study Torah and experience the intense pleasure that accompanies intellectual activity. Indeed, entry into this reality is the highest reward Torah can offer, reflecting the justice of God who rewards the righteous and punishes the wicked.

The status of the body remains unresolved. Does it disappear completely? Not according to rabbinic eschatology. Absorbing Persian beliefs in the resurrection of the dead[101] articulated first by the prophet Ezekiel, rabbinic sources posited the revivification of the dead as part of the eschatological future. At that post-historical phase, the body and soul of the righteous will be reunited, and the final triumph over evil will be accomplished.

Understood as a miraculous activity by God, that revivification is the ultimate reward of the intrinsically good life and the ultimate affirmation of the nexus of Torah and life. The commitment of the rabbis to belief in resurrection is made clear in the Mishnah of Sanhedrin, Chapter 10, where affirmation of this belief is stated to be a precondition for entering the world to come. The belief in resurrection was indeed disputed in the Second Temple period, but the Pharisaic-rabbinic tradition made it a central tenet, affirmed in the liturgy, and provided exegetical support for it (Sifre Deuteronomy 306; B. Sanhedrin 91b).

Belief in the efficacy of the righteous life for overcoming death was not just a matter of theoretical speculation. Saul Lieberman has shown that the term *me'ushar* (the "happy one") and *mevorakh* ("a blessed one") were common epitaphs on tombstones in the land of Israel. These terms were synonymous with the phrase *ḥelek tov* (literally "good portion") and "fortunate" (*ba'al mazal*).[102] Other virtuous personality types—*tzaddiq* (righteous), *ḥasid* (pious), *yashar* (upright) and *ne'eman* (loyal, faithful, or reliable)—are also common in tombstones in Palestine, and they appear in *Avot* as the virtues that one acquires through the study of Torah. In fact, the sages ascribed the last listed virtue, *ne'eman*, even to good non-Jews who led the morally good life by being loyal and honest.

SUMMARY

This chapter discusses the rabbinic claim that the life of Torah is the best-lived life because it enables one to become most like God. Although the rabbis were organized like a philosophical school of the Hellenistic period, they articulated their views hermeneutically rather than systematically, linking Torah, virtue, and human happiness through an intricate network of related religious values, beliefs, and practices. Still, the rabbinic tradition was suffused with Hellenistic culture and shared important general themes with Aristotle. Both held an objectivist, teleological approach to the valuation of human life. For them, all existence is organized purposefully, and human life in particular has a clear end that enables humans to know how they ought to live. Both Aristotle and the rabbis presuppose that to live in accordance with human nature one must be good, and that goodness requires the acquisition of virtues through deliberate, habitual practice of good acts. Moreover, both systems of thought hold that an individual can flourish only through social interaction, and such interaction is to be guided by the principle of moderation. Finally, both believe that human nature is such that humans not only aspire to transcend mortality, but that the good life itself is a necessary condition for the fulfillment of such aspiration.

The two perspectives diverge, however, in the rabbinic view that happiness is framed within the myth of Torah and the eternal love relationship between God and Israel. For the rabbis, happiness, or well-being, emerges as a personal relationship with God, manifested in the life of Torah. That relationship involves first and foremost the will and the ability to chose to either orient one's life toward God or to rebel against God. The best life is a life of unconditional love of God in which the believer lives the life of Torah for its own sake and strives to imitate God through good deeds toward others. Not an exercise in futility, the life of Torah is a pleasant, hopeful, and joyful activity in which the practitioner benefits from doing God's will both now and in the remote future, when the ultimate reward and ultimate pleasure of the life of righteousness will take place in the world to come.

Medieval Jewish philosophy, to which we shall now turn, did not simply impose Greek categories on the received nonphilosophic religious tradition, but developed and elaborated the Wisdom facet of the Torah/Wisdom nexus. "Wisdom" now would encompass a very broad range of sciences, whose cultivation was regarded to be a religious obligation. With the expansion of the content of wisdom and the rise of new philosophic ethos unique to Islamic culture, the discourse on happiness was transformed once again.

4

Happiness and the Cultivation of Character in Islam

By the seventh century, when the rabbis' exposition of Scriptures was accepted as normative Judaism, Jews found themselves living in a new religious civilization—Islam. For the Jews in the Near East, the Mediterranean Basin, and Iran, the Muslim conquests of the seventh century spelled profound economic, social, and cultural changes. While persecution was not totally absent from the Muslim world, it was sporadic and short-lived. Jews were recognized as *dhimmis*—members of the legal pact, the *dhimma*—and enjoyed legal protection of life and property and the freedom to practice their religion in return for the payment of taxes.[1] However, although their status afforded them "regular and continuous security,"[2] in reality they were second-class citizens and the actual payment of the poll tax (*jizyah*) was burdensome and intended as a humiliating act. In addition, they were subject to a wide range of legal disabilities. By law Jews had to wear distinctive garb, could not own Muslim slaves, build synagogues higher than mosques, ride horses, or hold positions of power in Islam. Nevertheless, in the High and Late Middle Ages, the Jews in Muslim lands thrived economically and culturally, leaving for posterity some of the most enduring legacies of Jewish civilization.

Jewish economic life was thoroughly transformed when Jews became urbanized, engaged in commerce, trade, and a vast range of arts and crafts.[3] They established domestic and international trading firms specializing in luxury goods such as silk, spices, and precious gems, and they invested their accumulated wealth in credit-based financial ventures. Notwithstanding legislation to the contrary, by the tenth century there were Jewish merchant-bankers who extended loans and financial advice to the Muslim administration and were granted an official position in the imperial bureaucracy.

The wealthy Jewish merchant-banker became an influential leader in the Jewish community, though his authority was derived not from expertise in rabbinic sources but from social position in the Muslim state. In Baghdad, the capital of the Abbasid Empire, in the Andalusian caliphate of Cordoba, and in the subsequent petty kingdoms that replaced it, outstanding Jews rose to power as diplomats, financial advisers, and even viziers and heads of the army. These leaders served as the foundation of a new Jewish culture that was shaped by Muslim paradigms, even though it was distinctively Jewish. In philosophy and poetry that took for granted the link between virtue, knowledge and human well-being, members of this class reflected most intensively on the meaning of human happiness.

The medieval Jewish discourse on human happiness should be understood in the context of the rationalist Jewish culture that emerged in the late ninth century in response to Islamic rationalism, which in turn came into being after the translation of Greek and Hellenistic philosophy and science into Arabic. Islamic rationalism compelled Jews to reexamine the rabbinic mythos and to think through the meaning of Judaism as a belief system. Like Plato and Aristotle, the new Jewish philosophers defined a human being as a rational animal; consequently, they equated human happiness with the well-being, or activity, of the rational element, i.e., the soul, or the intellect. Because this intellectualist focus was itself predicated on the view that God is an abstract, noncorporeal, changeless, eternal being, absorbed in self-contemplation, it necessitated a new interpretation of the Wisdom/Torah nexus posited in biblical and rabbinic Judaism. The Wisdom of God contained in the revealed Torah would now be studied in terms of what was known to be true through the sciences, and the Jewish sacred narrative would be recast into intellectual categories.

In this chapter I examine the encounter between rabbinic Judaism and philosophic rationalism and with it the rise of a systematic discourse on happiness. I shall focus on the ideas of three Jewish philosophers—Saadia Gaon (881–942),[4] Solomon ibn Gabirol (d. 1057), and Bahya ibn Pakuda (fl. ca. 1050)—as well as on the secular poetry and rhymed prose of Samuel ibn Naghrella (993–1055/6). Saadia Gaon showed why commitment to the mythos of rabbinic Judaism does not conflict with knowledge of philosophy and science. He also explained how rabbinic theology and ethics must be reinterpreted in light of what is known to be true in philosophy and science. His discussion becomes clearer if read against Aristotle's *Nicomachean Ethics* and its reworking by Islamic moral philosophers. Ibn Gabirol went further to show how the well-being of the body is related to the well-being of the soul. Linking individual character traits, or virtues, to parts of the body and to aspects of the physical universe, ibn Gabirol made explicit the connection between physics, psychology, and ethics. And ibn Paquda taught that one's obligations to God involve both "duties of the limbs" (i.e., the physical performance of the mitzvot) and the "duties of the heart" (i.e., holding certain beliefs and cultivating certain dispositions.) The ideas of ibn Gabirol and ibn Paquda can be fully understood only in the context of the culture of the Jewish courtiers in Muslim Spain. By looking at the poetry and rhymed prose of Samuel ibn Naghrella, this chapter illustrates the congruity between medieval Jewish rationalism and biblical Wisdom literature and the transformation of rabbinic virtue ethics under the impact of Islamic culture. In short, the religious philosophers discussed in this chapter created a Jewish philosophical discourse on happiness.

SAADIA GAON: THE FOUNDATION OF PHILOSOPHICAL ETHICS

In Defense of Rabbinic Judaism

Saadia Gaon was the first rabbinic Jew to defend Judaism against the challenge of Islamic religious rationalism. A century before Saadia, Christian converts to Islam, chief among them Hunayn ibn Ishaq (d. 873), headed a translation movement that rendered the classical heritage into Arabic. Articulating a technical philosophic-scientific vocabulary, the translators compelled Muslim thinkers to address the theological problems that arose from the encounter between Greek/Hellenistic philosophy and the beliefs of Islam. The texts selected for translation were mainly those studied by the Peripatetic school of the Hellenistic world—namely, the writings of Plato, Aristotle, and their Hellenistic commentators, such as Alexander of Aphrodisias (fl. 198–209 C.E.) and Themistius (fl. 340–384 C.E.). It is to these works that we shall return throughout the rest of the book.[5] Also important were the astronomical works of Ptolemy, the medical corpus of Hippocrates, Galen, and Dioscorides, and the religio-philosophic writings of the Neoplatonists, Plotinus and Proclus. These newly translated works were further enriched and made more accessible by the Muslim philosophers who built on them, giving rise to Muslim philosophy and science.

Islam's encounter with Greek and Hellenistic philosophy and science necessitated the delineation of the relationship between the philosophical sciences and the study of Muslim sacred texts. For the next two centuries Muslim authors composed numerous catalogues that offered several distinct classifications of the sciences.[6] In general, most authors distinguished between two kinds of sciences and their respective methodologies. The first was the study of sacred texts including Quranic exegesis, the science of *hadith*, and Muslim jurisprudence—with the preparatory disciplines that secured the skills necessary for jurisprudence. The second was the study of "foreign" or rational sciences, also called "the sciences of the ancients." The relationship between the two classes of sciences varied from one thinker to another, but the division itself indicates that *from the start, philosophy was viewed as non-indigenous.* The distinction between the two types of sciences will play an important role in the discourse on happiness among Muslim thinkers, and will reverberate as well among Jewish philosophers.

The most relevant development for our understanding of Saadia was the formulation of Islamic speculative theology, known as *Kalam* (literally, meaning "speech,'" or "discourse'"). It originated in meditations on the meaning of Quranic statements and is closely related to early Sufi mysticism and to the Muslim legal science of jurisprudence (*fiqh*). Out of the encounter with Christian theologians, Muslim thinkers began to systematize the religious beliefs of Islam and explain their meaning by using rational reasoning and philosophical vocabulary.[7]

Kalam theology produced two main schools—the Mu'tazilah and the Ash'ariah. While the former was declared official theology under the Abbasid Caliph al-Ma'mun (813–33) and his three successors until the 850s, the latter school would become the Orthodoxy of Sunni Islam. For the history of Jewish philosophy and the beginning of the philosophic discourse on happiness, the Mu'tazilite were crucial. Saadia Gaon, the founder of Jewish philosophic ethics, was a Jewish version of a Mu'tazilite theologian.

The Mu'tazilites' conception of reason was quite different from that of Aristotelian Muslim philosophy. Instead of syllogistic demonstration of the Peripatetics, the Kalam theologians appealed to what is "reasonable" to maintain given empirical knowledge of the world and the knowledge of human language.

Mu'tazilite speculations focused on five themes: the unity of God, the justice of God, reward and punishment, the classification of all human actions according to religio-ethical criteria, and the admonition to do the good and avoid evil. These Muslim theologians were convinced that the apparent tension between philosophy and religion was due to the shortcomings of human language and devoted most of their efforts to exegetical considerations of sacred texts rather than to metaphysical systematization. They resolved most of the apparent conflicts between the revealed tradition and human reason by giving the tradition a nonliteralist meaning and thereby protecting the radical incorporeality and otherness of God.

Mu'tazilite theology was absorbed by Jewish thinkers in the Muslim East as early as the ninth century. God, for the Mu'tazilite theologians, was first and foremost the creator of the universe. They contended that God's existence could be rationally proven, and they adopted various atomistic physical theories, which were quite different from ancient Greek physics, in order to show the total dependence of the world on God.[8] Along with the incorporeality of God, the Mu'tazilites emphasized God's self-sufficiency, which for them entailed His absolute benevolence. Because God is totally just, it is humans who are fully responsible for their actions and are rewarded and punished accordingly. Human reason alone is capable of discerning most of the rules that must guide social interaction, but these rules are not sufficient for human well-being. Out of divine justice, God comes to assist human reason by revealing ritual laws that complement ethics. It is the observance of these ritual laws for which we are rewarded. Rational knowledge and revealed knowledge are acquired in different manners: the former is acquired through unmediated discernment of reason planted in human beings; it is thus universal and objective. The latter is received through hearing and is particular and tradition-specific. Between rational and revealed knowledge there is a dialectical relationship: reason can and should be employed to interpret religion either in defense of certain beliefs or as a critique that is meant to clarify the correct meaning of these beliefs. The logical inquiry into religion is thus a religious obligation imposed on the true believers, though only a few can actually attain it.

Jewish rationalism emerged in Islam because the very identification of Torah and Wisdom in rabbinic Judaism required that Jewish intellectuals be informed about other intellectual and religious traditions with their respective truth claims. In practice, too, Jews had to respond to sophisticated Islam because Jewish scholars were often invited to public debates with Christian and Muslim theologians. Rabbinic Judaism, of course, was rife with theological and ethical reflections, but the midrashic style precluded systematic theology. The rabbis, who elaborated on the relationship between God and Israel, depicted God in very personal language, describing how God's personal traits are reflected in divine actions. Moreover, within the rabbinic tradition there was a strong ecstatic, visionary strand that posited seeing God seated on the Throne of Glory as the goal of Jewish religious life.[9] Under the leadership of the Geonim (i.e., the heads of the rabbinic academies in Baghdad), the literary tradition that captured these visions and religious speculations—known as Heikhalot and Merkabah literature—was consolidated and edited along with the editing of midrashic collections. Thus, the literature that depicted the transportation of religious practitioners (usually personified as famous rabbis) to the celestial realm to gaze at the awesome greatness, majesty, and beauty of God was no longer strictly esoteric.[10]

The experience of gazing at the beauty of God yielded descriptions of the fantastic measurements of God's stature (*shi`ur qomah*).[11] This text and other cognate fragments from the literature of Heikhalot and Merkabah tradition fused exegetical, ecstatic, and visionary modes of rabbinic Judaism. The measurements of God's Body, revealed to the select visionary within the context of an ecstatic experience, were presented as the esoteric meaning of the Song of Songs. The figure of the beloved, which the rabbis already understood allegorically to represent God, was now described in great detail with astronomic measurements. Moreover, the Torah reposed on the Body of God, suggesting that the revealed Torah that Israel possessed mirrored God's body.[12] It was this literature that inspired much of the Karaite criticism of rabbinic Judaism, and, in turn, Saadia's defense of it against the Karaites.

Muslim rationalism, understandably, posed problems for the visionary and ecstatic strands in rabbinic Judaism. In the new intellectual climate the detailed description of God's Body became an intellectual embarrassment, especially in confrontation with Muslim theologians and philosophers. However, while Muslim rationalism inspired the Karaite critique of the rabbinic dogma of the dual Torahs (the Written Law and the Oral Law), the social causes of Karaite sectarianism go far beyond the dissemination of rationalism.[13] They included the opposition of the Jews in the periphery of the Abbasid Empire to the centralization of power in the hands of the Gaonate of Baghdad, a refusal to accept the rabbinic accommodation to life in exile, a power struggle about succession to the office of the Exilarch, and messianic agitation by Jewries in central Asia. All these factors resulted in sustained efforts to invalidate rabbinic Judaism through rationalist philosophical concepts and arguments.

In place of the doctrine of dual Torahs, the Karaites declared Scripture to be the exclusive source of religious obligation in Judaism, and, in accord with the rationalist spirit of their day, they claimed that reason (rather than imagination) must be the only tool applied to the search for the meaning of Scripture. Modeled after Mu'atazilite theology, the Karaite theologians regarded rational speculation as religious obligation and launched a rationalist biblical exegesis that differed greatly from the midrashic procedures of the rabbis.

Along with the rationalist analysis of Scriptures, and aided by the emerging science of grammar and philology, Karaite scholars also systematized the tenets of Scriptural Judaism. They were the first to define the dogmas of Judaism and to articulate a philosophy of law based on the distinction between rational and ceremonial precepts. The Karaite rationalist interpretation of

Scripture had a strong ascetic bent, since it rejected the halakhic tradition that adapted biblical law to changing conditions. As a point of fact, Karaite legal reasoning established its own type of oral law, but its tenor was much less accommodating to human comfort and more infused with awareness about the destruction of the Temple. Indeed, certain groups within the Karaite movement called themselves "mourners of Zion" and absorbed some of the ascetic practices of the Sufi movement.

Responding to the Karaite critique, Saadia Gaon defended rabbinic Judaism and transformed it from within by using the categories of Mu'tazilite Kalam. An Egyptian born rabbinic scholar, he assumed the leadership of the Sura academy after his successful campaign against the leadership of the Palestinian Geonim.[14] Writing in Judeo-Arabic (that is, Arabic language written in Hebrew characters and interspersed with Hebraisms and citations of Hebrew texts), Saadia adopted the style and content of the Mu'tazilite Kalam, claiming that there is nothing in the rabbinic tradition that is contradictory to reason when the Written Law and the Oral law are properly interpreted. To prove the claim he composed linear commentaries on many books of the Bible, and was the first to compose a thematic collection of halakhot. In his main theological treatise, *Kitab al-Amanat wa-'l I'tiqadat* (The Book of Doctrines and Beliefs), Saadia delineated the circumstances that legitimize a nonliteralist understanding of the biblical text.[15]

This theological *Summa* had a clear polemical intent. It was written to refute all forms of Jewish skepticism and disbelief rife in Saadia's time and to place rabbinic Judaism on a firm rationalist foundation. Saadia's method of reasoning was not significantly different from that of the Karaites, but his conclusions were very different. Like them he regarded the rationalist inquiry into the meaning of the received tradition by human reason to be a religious obligation. However, unlike the Karaites, Saadia's rationalist inquiry was meant to show that the revealed tradition included not only the Written Torah but also the Oral Torah. He firmly believed that his method of exposition could help turn religious beliefs, affirmed on the basis of tradition, into firmly held convictions corroborated by rational proofs. With Saadia begins the medieval philosophical analysis of human happiness.

The Tenth Treatise: Style and Purpose

Saadia Gaon's views on human happiness are to be found in the Tenth Treatise, entitled "Concerning How It is Most Proper for Man to Conduct Himself in this World."[16] Contrary to the view of Joseph Dan and in agreement with Eliezer Schweid,[17] I hold that the Tenth Treatise does not stand in opposition to the rest of the book. There is no contradiction between Saadia's religious views and his concern for human conduct in worldly affairs. Rather, the principles that guide Saadia's advice concerning human worldly conduct are religious. These principles are grounded in Saadia's understanding of God as creator and in his view (which accords with the theology of the Mu'tazilite Kalam) that ethical principles are objective and immediately accessible to human reason. Saadia's scriptural references are no mere "ornamentation" to a secularist ethics, but part of his sustained argument for the rationality of the revealed tradition. While Dan is correct to note that the literary style of Saadia's Tenth Treatise differs from rabbinic ethical discourse, my sense is that Saadia's ethical views are not a radical departure from the rabbinic tradition. This scholarly dispute is not trivial. It goes to heart of the claim about the place of philosophy in rabbinic Judaism.

The purpose of the Tenth Treatise, as Schweid has already stated, is to prove that "all the paths, to which the Torah directs students and observers of its commandments, legitimize it as an ideal constitution."[18] In other words, Saadia was the first rabbinic scholar to articulate a rationalist religious ethics in which human reason is placed in the service of Torah observance. However, Schweid failed to discuss the degree to which Saadia's Tenth Treatise echoes Aristotle's *Nicomachean Ethics* or its reworking by Saadia's Muslim contemporaries.

The *Ethics* was translated into Arabic by Ishaq ibn Hunayn (d. 911), and Saadia's younger contemporary Abu Nasr al-Farabi wrote a commentary on it.[19] As Marshall G.S. Hodgson has stated, "It was Aristotle's *Ethics*, out of all the corpus of the Falsafah, that gained the greatest vogue" among the Muslim gentlemen who translated rationalism into a socio-cultural program known as *adab*.[20] Even though it is impossible to prove that Saadia in fact read the *Nicomachean Ethics*, we can establish that Saadia's ethical reflections convey the teleological understanding of human happiness offered in that work—and that Saadia Gaon was the first rabbinic philosopher to illuminate the teleological assumptions underlying rabbinic reflections on human happiness.

The purpose of Saadia's Tenth Treatise comes into a sharper focus when the text is situated within the moral philosophies of his Muslim and Christian contemporaries.[21] For example, Yaakub al-Kindi (d. 866) wrote several ethical treatises, including *Paving the Way to Virtue* and *Exhortation to Virtue*, which are no longer extant. Abu Bakr al-Razi (d. 925) expounded his ethical views in his *al-Tibb al-Ruhani* (Spiritual Physics), analyzing vices such as "arrogance, envy, anger, falsehood, miserliness, gluttony, drunkenness, erotic passion, frivolity, avarice, worldly ambition, and fear of death."[22] Abu Nasr al-Farabi (d. 950) wrote not only a commentary on Aristotle's *Nicomachean Ethics*, but also *The Attainment of Happiness*, a text that creatively fuses Plato's political theory with Aristotle's ethics. Yahya ibn Adi (d. 974), a Jacobite Christian, composed *Tahdhib al Ahlaq* (Refinement of Moral Character), which provides a classification of moral traits, including "temperance, contentedness, dignity, forgiveness, composure, modesty, friendliness, compassion, loyalty to friends, trustworthiness, confidence-keeping, humility, cheerfulness, truthfulness, purity of intention, generosity, courage, competitiveness, fortitude, magnanimity and justice" all of which are necessary for the attainment of intellectual perfection.[23] A less known thinker, Abu'l Hasan al-Amiri (d. 991), wrote *al-Sa`adah wa'l-Isad* (On Happiness and Making Happy), and the most famous contributor to Islamic ethics, Ahmad Miskawayh (d. 1030), wrote the *Tahdhib al Ahlaq* (Refinement of Moral Character), which is virtually a summary of Aristotle's *Ethics*, as well as *Tartib al-Sa'adat* (The Grades of Happiness).

The theme of human happiness and the cultivation of the moral qualities necessary for it would continue to engage Muslim thinkers for another two centuries in the works of ibn Sina (d. 1037), al-Ghazali (d. 1111) ibn Bajja (d. 1138), ibn Rushd (d. 1198), Fakhr al-Din al-Razi (d. 1209), Nasir al-Din al Tusi (d. 1274) and others. We should note, however, that the Muslim philosophical discourse on happiness was indebted not only to Aristotle's *Ethics* but also to non-Aristotelian Hellenistic sources based on the *Ethics*. Indeed, much of the information about the moral character of the ideal person came to Muslim thinkers from the ethical treatise of Galen (d. c. 200) entitled *Peri Ethon* (Traits of Character), (whose Greek original is no longer extant), in which he harmonized the ethical teachings of Plato and Aristotle.[24] We need to recall as well that Aristotle's *Ethics* itself was translated into Arabic from a commentary of the Neoplatonic philosopher Porphyry (b. c.232 –d. c. 306 C.E.), and that Plotinus' preoccupation with the purification of the soul shaped much of Islamic philosophical ethics.[25] In other words, in Islamic civilization the discourse on happiness was an amalgam of several philosophical traditions, including Aristotelianism, Stoicism, and Neoplatonism. This is not the place to analyze how these elements were fused in Islamic thought. All I want to establish is that Saadia's Tenth Treatise joined an existing philosophic conversation on the cultivation of moral virtues and the attainment of happiness and that this philosophic discourse gives the Treatise its so-called secular coloring, even though Saadia's work is anything but "secular."

What is the Final Good of Human Life?

In accord with the Aristotelian way of reasoning, the Tenth Treatise is empirical. It begins with observations on actual human conduct and with citations of various opinions about human happiness. Saadia subjects these opinions to close examination, and refutes or modifies them in order to establish a rational consensus that he then examines in light of the revealed tradition.

Saadia claims that human beings exhibit certain "likes" and "dislikes," namely, they are by nature attracted to some things and feel repelled by others, precisely as Aristotle claimed in the *Ethics*. These natural proclivities are not "virtues," as Colette Sirat renders the term.[26] Rather, they are tendencies that people transform into all-consuming pursuits because they regard the attainment of these things as a final good. In a teleological universe, since the goal determines how one would spend one's life, it is crucial to be correct about the goal or the end of human life. This, however, can be determined only if we possess knowledge of the nature of human beings, for the goal of human life must accord with that nature. What is novel about Saadia's Tenth Treatise is not its "secular" tendencies, but the systematic exposition of human philosophical anthropology as the basis for Jewish ethics.

In the Sixth Treatise, Saadia examines eleven theories about the nature of the soul and its relationship to the body, culled from Aristotelian, Neoplatonic, and Stoic sources,[27] showing what is problematic about them as a prelude to his own theory. After refuting them all, Saadia presents his own theory, according to which human beings are a temporary combination of two substances—body and soul. Both are created by God, and both are united by Him (*Beliefs and Opinions*, 241–42).

The substance of the soul is refined, "comparable in purity to that of the heavenly sphere [and] like the latter, it attains luminosity as a result of the light which it receives from God" (*Beliefs and Opinions*, 242). The association of the soul with luminous substance can be traced to Plato, who was the first to link knowledge to visual perception and who initiated the tradition that speaks about knowledge in visual metaphors.[28] Yet for Saadia the soul is not strictly-speaking a noncorporeal substance; rather, it is made of a refined substance that is not devoid of matter altogether, even though it is qualitatively different from the corporeal body, a "dark place" in which the luminous soul is imprisoned for the duration of its life on earth (*Beliefs and Opinions*, 243). It is also true that the human soul needs a body as its instrument of action, for "the soul performs its functions only by means of the body, since the act of every created being requires for its execution some instrument" (*Beliefs and Opinions*, 243). That Saadia distinguishes between the appetitive, impulsive, and cognitive faculties or parts of the soul (*Beliefs and Opinions*, 360) and that he regarded the body as an instrument of the soul, indicate the impact of familiar Platonic themes on his psychological theories.

This psychological dualism has important ramifications for Saadia's view of human happiness. First, it must take into consideration both the well-being of the body and the well-being of the soul, in such a way that the well-being of a person involves control of the body by the soul. To allow the body to take the lead would result in the soul's destruction. Second, the interdependence of body and soul explains why Saadia insists on the doctrine of resurrection. Although the two substances separate at death and the soul of the righteous person continues to live on as an immortal substance, in the end of time, as a result of divine intervention, the individual soul will be recombined with its corresponding body. Third, for the duration of human life on earth, a proper balance between soul and body constitutes the morally good life, for which one is rewarded with eternal life and the recombination of body and soul in the eschatological, remote future. The good life is thus a *balanced* life in which all the aspects of the human composite are given appropriate expression within a hierarchy of goods.

Critique of Commonly Accepted Goods

As Aristotle did in the *Ethics*, Saadia provides a list of the activities that, in his view, people commonly view as "good." He includes the following items: 1) abstinence; 2) eating and drinking; 3) sexual intercourse; 4) love; 5) accumulation of wealth; 6) begetting of children; 7) habitation of the world; 8) longevity; 9) political power; 10) the need for revenge; 11) knowledge; 12) worship; and 13) rest. Schweid has already noted that this list is not haphazard and has an internal coherence congruent with the purpose of the Tenth Treatise. I agree with much of what Schweid says, but with certain modifications that emerge from reading this list against its Aristotelian underpinning and Islamic ethical philosophy.

The items listed by Saadia were all goods that moral philosophers in antiquity have discussed with reference to human happiness. His list begins with the value of "abstinence" and ends with the value of "rest." As we saw in the previous chapter, these were two of the ideals that the Cynic and Stoic moral philosophers endorsed in their attempts to define the happiest life. In Saadia's own day, these ideals were endorsed by various communities, including Christian monastics and Sufis, and were given a philosophical exposition by al-Kindi. Saadia rejects these ideals on the grounds that to endorse them as the exclusive goal of human life results in the denial of the body created by God. A human life governed by these ideals would suffer from great imbalance. The sages who advise abstinence as a means for attaining wisdom cause the "abandoning of the amenities of civilized existence": they ignore that which makes us human, and as such, requires attention. Saadia specifically rejects those who in the name of abstinence counsel against marriage (clearly a critique of Christian celibacy), because for him marriage is a necessary institution for the perpetuation of the human species. Furthermore, it is likely that Saadia's refutation of the denunciatory life was one more expression of his polemic against the Karaites.[29]

For Saadia, the body no less than the soul is God's creation, and as such its well-being must be an integral part of human happiness. Because denial of bodily needs or its harsh treatment through radical extreme asceticism does not accord with God's creation, moderation would thus be the ideal practice to yield the good life. By the same token, Saadia rejects the ideal of total rest, the last item on the list, because it too is contrary to the well-being of a living human organism. When rest becomes the ultimate end of human life, it necessarily results in illness, since one would neglect activities necessary for the care of the body. Hence, a life of total rest, practiced by hermits of various religious and intellectual traditions, cannot be a correct understanding of the commitment to reason.

Saadia's Classification of Goods

In between the first and last items on the list, Saadia examines other "goods" that human beings tend to mistake as the ultimate end of human life. Schweid has already noted correctly that they can be classified according to the functions of the soul. Physical pleasures derived from food, drink, and sex (items # 2 and # 3) correspond to the appetitive part. Social goods correspond to the "impulsive" or desiring function of the soul (items # 4 through # 10). Finally, cognitive activity, such as the pursuit of wisdom and devotion to God (items # 11 and # 12), fall under the rubric of the rational faculty of the soul. Each of these ideals may be either a necessary activity or even a good activity, but taken by itself, to the exclusion of the other goods, each can lead to an imbalanced life that prevents human well-being.

The tenor of Saadia's moral advice is the ethics of moderation and self-control. Observation of actual human conduct and practical experience, characteristic of learned men, are the basis of his claims. According to Saadia, physical pleasures derived from food, drink, and sex are the most obvious activities that people mistake as the ultimate ends of human life. When one devotes life solely to the pleasures derived from eating, one suffers from "indigestion and heaviness of limbs." Gluttony produces a "coarsening" of the mind and leads one to neglect duties. The same may be said of wine. Furthermore, if one derives satisfaction only from food and drink, one would eventually devote all economic resources to them and even commit crime to procure them. Ideally, one should eat and drink only as much as secures the "sustenance of the body," but not more. Likewise, sexual intercourse is a necessary human activity that produces pleasure, but excessive engagement in sex "makes the body flabby, wears it out quickly and hastens senility" (*Beliefs and Opinions*, 372), and it often brings shame and disgrace. Sex is a positive activity only if it is carried out for the purpose of procreation. Saadia examines common theories that link erotic attraction to the positioning of the stars and rejects the view that sexual desire has a physiological foundation controlled by external forces knowable through astrology. On the contrary, Eros is located in the human soul and can be controlled by reason.

The best context for such control is heterosexual marriage. Husband and wife "should be affectionate to each other for the sake of the maintenance of the world." Within the context of the marriage the husband "should give vent to his desire for his wife in accordance with the dictates of reason and religion and to the extent required in order to bind them closely together, but restrain it vigorously and forcefully beyond that point." That counsel is in accord with the rabbinic perspective on sex.

As Aristotle has noted, next to the physical pleasures most people usually consider the accumulation of wealth as the ultimate end of human life, since wealth facilitates the possession of things that provide comfort and pleasure. Saadia exposes the fault in such devotion to material prosperity. It leads to "quarrels and contentions and animosities" (*Beliefs and Opinions*, 379). It causes social injustice by impoverishing others, and leads to "loss of honor and the disappearance of trust." When wealth becomes the exclusive goal of human life, it destroys the integrity of the person and corrodes human society, which flourishes only if its members show compassion for the needs of others. This awareness of the fickleness of wealth is in accord with the teachings of Proverbs and Ben Sira.

A functioning society is essential to human well-being, but some people mistakenly identify social activities, such as raising a family or simply being productive, as the ultimate goal of life. Having children is necessary and good, but one must not idealize or "romanticize" it. Family life, beginning with pregnancy, Saadia informs us correctly, includes pain and hardship. Children can often be disobedient and rebellious, and raising them requires discipline and control. They cannot be made the sole preoccupation of one's life. Likewise, devoting all of one's energy to production and construction of things is satisfying on some level, but it cannot be taken to be the highest goal. The life of the engineer or the farmer is full of anxiety and heartache, since success is not totally within human control. One has to engage in manual labor for the sake of producing those things necessary for survival, but one should not glorify the life of production.

Honor and power are the social values to which many people devote their lives. Although in traditional society honor comes with old age, Saadia shows that longevity per se cannot be a good desired for its own sake, since "the longer a person lives the greater are his cares and worries and troubles. Also the toll of his iniquities and sins increases and the computation and summation thereof becomes longer" (*Beliefs and Opinions*, 386).

Leadership is good when it is carried out with wisdom, but political power over others is by no means an intrinsic good. Such ambition leads to haughtiness, boastfulness, exploitation, self-centeredness, and self-importance. This mindset often leads to social trouble, because one becomes too argumentative and too self-assured to the point of being oblivious to the needs of the very social hierarchy in which one seeks success. If that success is understood as power over others, it also results in envy, which leads to intrigue and destruction, all of which result in a desire for revenge.

Saadia shows how the satisfaction derived from revenge cannot be taken to be a good to be pursued for its own sake. Vengefulness makes one hateful and blind to the needs of others; it leads to destructive behavior that results in the ruin of not only enemies but also close associates, and often to self-destruction. The vengeful person is solely preoccupied with his own misfortune, which in itself worsens the quality of his social life.

Having shown that none of the social "goods" can be pursued for its own sake, Saadia concludes the list by turning to intellectual "goods"—knowledge and devotion to God. This is the most intriguing part of the Tenth Treatise. In essence, Saadia rejects *theoria* as the exclusive end of human life. Contemplation is good, but it cannot be pursued to the exclusion of other needs, both physical and social, which are necessary for the survival and flourishing of the human being. Instead, Saadia advocates an "inclusive" approach to human life because it is more consonant with human nature as God created it. However, lest one would say that "the highest endeavor of the servant of God in this world ought to be to dedicate himself exclusively to the service of his Lord," Saadia proceeds to show that even this kind of activity is wrong. "The service of God," says Saadia, "consists in [the fulfillment of] all the rational as well as the revealed precepts of the Torah" (*Beliefs and Opinions*, 396).

Humans are created with body and soul, and the well-being of both is necessary, as the Torah itself recognizes. Thus serving the Lord must not be taken to mean a denial of the body and the affairs of this world. Saintliness entails radical asceticism, which is contradictory to nature as created by God. If taken to its logical conclusion, asceticism amounts to death in this world, because the hermit's life of isolated piety ignores the pleasures and beauty of the world and undermines the communal life presupposed by observing the Torah's commandments. For Saadia, then, the ideal life is not based on the stilling of the body to the utmost but on giving it its proper due through self-control and the curbing of desire.

Philosophical Ethics and the Rationality of Judaism

The ideal life, according to Saadia, is a life rooted in balance. He does not tell us the details of how such balance is to be achieved: this has already been specified by the precepts of the Torah as interpreted by the rabbinic tradition.

Saadia claimed that the revealed tradition is totally compatible with reason. Human reason can and should be applied to the received tradition, to remove mistaken opinions about a range of things, to clarify the meaning of the sacred texts, and to make sense of beliefs and practices that may seem either inexplicable or nonsensical.

Why then is there a need for revelation? While all are endowed with the capacity to reason, not all people develop this capacity in the same degree. For example, all children and women, as a class, lack the requisite cognitive power; and uneducated adult males do not actualize their cognitive potential. A revelation of the truth by God, then, is needed to make the truth known to all those who cannot fathom it on their own.

If being endowed with reason means that some can successfully discover the truth on their own accord, it follows that eventually philosophers could discover the reasons for the commandments and make revelation redundant. Thus Saadia distinguished between the "rational commandments" and the "ceremonial commandments." In the former there is a complete overlap between the rational content and rational discovery; but the latter class of commandments is to be known only through revelation.[30] Saadia then acknowledged that there are limits to the scope of human reason and a range that humans cannot know independently—viz., the specific details of worshipping God are known to God alone and require a revelation to be communicated. This applies also to the particulars of ethics.

On the other hand, the employment of reason to the sacred tradition reduces both misinterpretation and skepticism, which according to Saadia were rife in his day. Reason can articulate the main principles that should guide human conduct by understanding human nature and the position of man in the order of things. Thus reason can fathom the principle of self-control and moderation, which excludes obsessive preoccupation with illusionary good. The real conflict between reason and revelation, Saadia correctly understood, lay in the question whether the world is created by God or is eternal.[31] Because Jewish philosophers had to struggle first with the problematics of creation, it is no coincidence that in the first few centuries of the Middle Ages physics and metaphysics were their main focus of interest, and ethics occupied a secondary status. Following Saadia's example, however, medieval Jewish philosophers correctly understood that the moral philosophy of Aristotle and his Hellenistic followers was generally congruent with the ethos of rabbinic Judaism.

After surveying various theories about the origin of the world and finding them deficient, Saadia proved to his satisfaction the rationality of the doctrine of creation, confirming the existence of a creator by employing proofs articulated first by the sixth-century Christian philosopher, John Philoponus.[32] On the basis of the proof that a creator exists, Saadia proceeded to derive His attributes, which are separated in human language but not in reality: God is one, living, powerful, and wise—all presupposed by the notion of "creator."

God's essence is reflected in God's actions, which include the revelation of the Law and the retribution for obedience and disobedience of the Law, all of which manifest God's justice. To compensate both the body and the soul, divine retribution must ensure not only the immortality of the soul after the death of the body, but the resurrection of the body and reunification with the immortal soul in the end of time.

The very duality of human nature means that we are citizens of two worlds: the embodied life of this world (*ha-olam ha-zeh*) and the life after the disintegration of the body (*ha-olam ha-ba*). These two modes of existence are interdependent; life after death is causally determined by the quality of life in this world. In this case, the quality of character and the goodness of one's deeds determine the ability to survive the deterioration of the body. The soul, therefore, needs the body for its own perfection, and it matters greatly how one conducts oneself in this life. Neither excessive indulgence in bodily pleasures nor extreme abstinence from satisfying bodily needs are good; rather, balance in this life is necessary if one is to attain the afterlife; such balance is accomplished in fact by living within the strictures of the Law, for many of its teachings can be reasoned out and found useful to human well-being.

The dual nature of human existence dictates that the afterlife does not end with the separation of the soul from the body. That the body eventually will be revived in a post-historical future is also a dictate of both reason and revelation. To God, the creator of life, the revivification of the dead is not a hardship; it is an expression of the power of giving life. Logically, the belief in resurrection of the dead follows from the belief in creation: if the first can be proven rationally, so can the last.

"The ultimate end of human life" is thus ambiguous. For life in the world as we know it through the senses, the ultimate goal is proper harmony between the various functions of the soul. This leads to proper management of the body, just social relations, and a correct balance among various human pursuits. However, this life is only a preparation for yet another life, a life in which both body and soul will receive their due rewards. Saadia does not describe the details of the life in the world to come, but it is obvious that it, rather than the worldly life, is the ultimate end of the human life. This fervent assertion of an afterlife is as much an argument for theodicy as it is an affirmation of the rabbinic eschatology that the Karaites found problematic.[33]

Emotionally, the affirmation of the afterlife and the resurrection of the dead as the ultimate reward of correct religious life is satisfying, instilling hope and trust in the religiously observant without denying or ignoring the mundane life in this world.

Implications for Subsequent Medieval Jewish Philosophy

Our discussion of the Tenth Treatise has important implications for the discourse on happiness in the Middle Ages. First, the rationalist tradition did not stand in opposition to religion, but was an attempt to deepen and strengthen religious commitment. It is thus a mistake to view philosophical ethics as a "secularist" endeavor. Second, the discourse on human happiness was always related to prior philosophical assumptions about the structure of the universe and the place of mankind in it. Thus, it is impossible to understand a thinker's view of happiness without reference to his judgment about a range of ontological, cosmological, psychological, and epistemological positions. Third, the philosophic discourse on happiness combined theoretical and practical reasoning, viewing the former as pertinent to life in this world and the latter as relevant to the afterlife. Fourth, undoubtedly Saadia had some views about human character, but did not develop them. Instead, he focused on the notion of religious obligation as the core of the pursuit of religious perfection.

What is novel in Saadia's philosophical ethics is not the nonreligious character of his thought, but the expansion of the scope of "wisdom." The tools of human reason were now to be applied to any claim, whether made by authoritative sacred texts or articulated on the basis of scientific information. If properly interpreted, so Saadia held, in principle these claims cannot contradict each other. The goal of Saadia's philosophical ethics was ultimately religious—viz., relationship with God. However, the interaction with God places a premium on the power of the intellect over the body or the emotions. To worship God and to live the morally and religiously good life, then, one must employ reason, by which one can provide both for the well-being of the body and the well-being of the soul.

COURT CULTURE AND THE ETHOS OF SELF-CONTROL

Jewish Courtiers in Muslim Spain

During the first two centuries of Islam, Jewish life was thoroughly transformed. In both the Muslim East and West, Jews became urban people and adopted the Arabic language. Particularly in Muslim Spain, Jews cultivated philosophy and its related sciences. Accordingly the history of the discourse on happiness is primarily the story of Spanish Jewry.

Although Jews were present in Spain as early as Roman times, very little is known about their life there except that they were subject to periodic persecutions under Visigothic kings.[34] Then in 711 Spain fell to the Umayyads and a governor was installed there by the caliph in Damascus. The persecuted Jewish minority in Spain apparently cooperated with the Muslim conquerors, thereby establishing the Jewish alliance with the royal power that would remain intact until the fifteenth century, when Ferdinand and Isabella expelled the Jews from Spain.[35] The Abbasid revolution of 750 shifted the orientation of the Empire eastward and made the Muslim West less prone to control of the caliphs in Baghdad.

An Umayyad Prince, Abd al-Rahman I, arrived in Iberia in 756 and established an independent government at Cordoba. Over the next two centuries, the caliphate of Cordoba, supported by thriving agriculture and commerce, launched a cultural renaissance that would have lasting impact on Jewish culture.

In the multi-ethnic and multi-religious Cordoban caliphate, ambitious individual Jews could rise to power in the administration of the Muslim state and even hold the highest position of *vizier* (prime minister), even though in theory a Jew could not have authority over a Muslim. After the dissolution of the Cordoban caliphate and the rise of the petty kingdoms, the Jewish courtiers were especially appreciated by the ruling power, to whom they were personally loyal. Individual Jews rendered a range of services to these Muslim rulers: they were financial advisors, tax collectors, treasurers, diplomats, translators, land surveyors, astronomers, and physicians. As a class, these professionals would serve as the social foundation for the cultivation of philosophy in Muslim Spain, the core of which was devoted to reflections on happiness.

The Adab Culture in Islam

The culture of the Jewish courtiers in Spain was a Jewish version of the *adab* cultural program, which in turn was the Arabic equivalent of the Greek philosophical *paideia*.[36] Along with philosophic and scientific compositions, the translators made available in Arabic a vast anecdotal literature about the life of the *sophos*, the learned man who devotes his life to the pursuit of wisdom.[37] This biographical information not only enlarged the storehouse of tales to be told for social entertainment; it also created a philosophic ethos (a philosophic *derekh eretz*, if you will) concerned with manners and social decorum. The major themes of this ethos, known as *adab*, were the values of moderation and self-control common in the Greco-Roman world, tailored to fit the civil service structure of the Muslim state and the peculiarities of the Muslim religion. Thus the list of virtues would be adapted to address the needs of the Muslim civil service. For example, mastery of calligraphy, which is essential to Arabic language, and fluency in the art of poetry were added to the requisite virtues of the learned man.

In the urban, mercantile environment of the Abbasid Empire, the *adib* (the man schooled in *adab*) was a highly refined person who was expected to be conversant in many topics in order to add brilliance to the court. Therefore, the key to success was possession of rhetorical skills, poetic eloquence, and calligraphic ability, all of which were cultivated through the study and production of prose and poetry. The *adib* culled his knowledge from prose books whose contents encompassed tales, fables, anecdotes, practical advice, and popularization of scientific information, all gleaned from the philosophical-scientific heritage of the Hellenistic world, interspersed with some material from India. *Adab* prose had a strong didactic tendency. Its goals, however, were not the moral values of the Muslim revealed Law, the *Sharia*, but the worldly values of refinement, beauty, wealth, leisure, and pleasure.

In its attitude toward happiness, *adab* culture encompassed two seemingly contradictory tendencies, often expressed by the same author. On the one hand, it gave rise to a robust worldliness that celebrated the pleasures of the senses and viewed advancement in the court as the goal of human life. In this regard *adab* aphorisms counseled utilitarian ethics for success in society and enjoyment of bodily pleasures. On the other hand, *adab* culture also promoted literary reflections on the human condition that diminished the value of all temporal endeavors. In poetry and prose, *adibs* taught that worldly pleasures and social success are only illusory, preventing one from attaining genuine happiness. True reality lies not in this world but in the next life, and it can be attained through focusing on God alone. These Sufi-inspired reflections, expressed in sententious poetry and rhymed aphorisms, were suffused with an acute awareness of human mortality, of the transience of wealth and political success, and of the profound insecurity of all human affairs. While they lacked technical philosophic rigor, they were psychologically astute and emotionally subtle.

Hebrew Adab: Poetry and Prose

Although the *adab* culture was primarily associated with the life-style of a certain class connected with the court and the bureaucracy of the state, it was particularly useful and appealing to the Jewish courtiers in Muslim Spain. Moreover, the *adab* literature facilitated the emergence of a social ethos that enabled a resourceful and ambitious social climber to survive in a court. For the non-Arab and non-Muslim, the only claim to aristocracy one could display before his Muslim superiors were excellence of character, breadth of knowledge, and the usefulness of his specialized skills. For the Jewish courtier, then, the *adab* culture was the vehicle for advancement in state administration.

As part of the administration of the Muslim state, these Jewish civil servants not only lived in material opulence; they also attracted to their court a coterie of Jewish poets and scholars whose style was governed by the etiquette and aesthetic sensibilities of their Muslim counterparts. The Jewish courtiers occupied two worlds—the world of the Jewish minority and the world of the state bureaucracy—and occasionally the two cultural orbits could have been in some tension with each other.[38] For example, when Samuel ibn Naghrella led the army of Granada to war against the army of Seville,[39] it is reasonable to assume that he encountered situations in which commitment to Jewish law conflicted with his responsibilities as a commander of an army. Yet for Samuel ibn Naghrella, the most successful of all the Jewish courtiers, service to the Muslim state did not entail a loss of Jewish religious-ethnic identity. In a society that defined formal legal status by religious affiliation, the only way a Jewish courtier could renounce his Jewishness was through formal conversion. Many Jews apparently converted to Islam in the first few centuries, but those who chose to remain Jewish could not and did not wish to forget their identity. Samuel ibn Naghrella and his cohorts were not interested in "assimilation" or "acculturation," as these are understood today. Rather, they sought to define their distinctive Jewish commitments in the cultural vocabulary of their time. Thus the adaptation of Muslim modes of culture was carried out for the sake of expressing Jewish uniqueness, often in competitive opposition to the dominant culture.[40]

One of the hallmarks of the courtier culture was the writing of so-called secular poetry (*shirat ha-ḥol*).[41] For the first time in Jewish history, Jewish poets wrote about nature, wine, sensuous love, politics, war, and physical objects, rather than the religious themes in Jewish liturgy, such as the relationship of Israel and God.[42] The explicit references to physical pleasures in this poetry might lead one to believe that in Muslim Spain Jews identified happiness with hedonism, simplistically understood as a pursuit of vulgar, uncontrolled sensual pleasure. I argue against this view, although an elaborate proof of my claims will take us beyond the confines of this study.

The Ethos of Self-Control

Hebrew secular poetry did not endorse bodily pleasures as the ultimate end of human life. First, the same poets who rhapsodized about their passion for a beautiful woman or a young lad also composed poems lamenting the shortness and precariousness of human life, the fickleness of worldly affairs, and the heartless cruelty of fate. Second, the very same poets who reflected about the meaning of human life also composed exquisite poetry for use in the synagogue, where they used their linguistic skills to describe the eternal love relationship between God and Israel, the difficulties of exile, and their hope for the coming of the Messiah. This religious poetry expressed the sacred narrative of Judaism in terms of the journey of the individual soul and its struggle with the body.

Third, and most important, secular poetry was rooted in the ethos of self-control and posited a hierarchical relationship between body and soul in which the latter must govern the former in order to yield or promote the good life. The highly stylized poems about nature, love, and wine do not advocate the raw sensations of physical pleasures (whether they are derived from food, drinks, or sex), but instead call, through stylized language, for the refinement of sensations. Only those who already tamed their desires could recline on their sumptuous sofas and derive pleasure from listening to elegant poems about bodily pleasures. The intricacy of courtly poetry and its ambience of refinement and sophistication themselves presuppose that the Jewish bureaucrats cultivated an ethos of self-control.

This is how I understand, for example, the wine poetry of Samuel ibn Naghrella.[43] With utmost subtlety, he describes the excellence, fragrance, color, texture, temperature, and taste of the wine, or conveys the intricate beauty and delicacy of the wine cup or the goblet from which the wine is served. In other wine poems he conveys the gay atmosphere of the party and meditates about the impact of wine—the sensations it evokes, and the pleasure that arises from a mild intoxication.[44] This discussion of pleasure is conveyed through puns, metaphors, and thematic development, all of which can be understood and appreciated only if one is fully alert and not inebriated. Furthermore, in none of the poems do we find a valorization of drunkenness or advocacy of imbibing of wine in order to numb the senses. I suggest, therefore, that this wine poetry does not glorify the bodily pleasure of drinking; rather, the real pleasure and joy come from talking about wine in a highly refined and stylized manner.

The same applies to sensuous love poetry, heterosexual or homosexual. What matters is not the actual raw experience of the passionate lover, but the delicate, witty, and playful control of the emotions through poetry that depicts real or imagined experiences. Though the suffering of the male lover is described in great detail, what is celebrated is not enslavement by passion and desire, but the ability of the poet to free himself from enslavement through a linguistic recounting that gains him the admiration of the audience. The artistic composition itself is the medium of gaining self-control and refining the senses.

Finally, poets such as Moses ibn Ezra, Abraham ibn Ezra, Solomon ibn Gabirol, and Judah Halevi were all philosophers who claimed that a human being is more than just a physical body, and that human life is not limited to one's affairs in the mundane world. Precisely because these poets took it for granted that we are composed of both body and soul and that after the death of the body another mode of life awaits the soul, they could frame their jolly poetry about the senses in a proper perspective. The sententious poetry and rhymed aphorisms these poets wrote reflected a deeper, psychologically more mature understanding of human life than their subject matter would suggest. Regardless of the particular life experience described, awareness of human mortality and the precariousness of worldly affairs framed the sensuous poetry in a proper perspective.

Practical and Theoretical Wisdom

Hebrew sententious poetry and prose are fine examples of the ethos of self-control that permeated the court culture. This ethos and the virtues that resulted from its cultivation were predicated on knowledge, both of worldly affairs and of the place of human beings in the cosmic order. The first kind of knowledge was practical, utilitarian, and based on actual life experience; the second was speculative or meditative, reflecting on human life as a whole. Samuel ibn Naghrella's *adab* collections, *Ben Mishlei* (The Son of Proverbs) and *Ben Qohelet* (The Son of Ecclesiastes) illustrate this point. They indicate not only how much educated Jews have absorbed the Arabic *adab* culture, but also how much they perpetuated the nexus between virtue and knowledge in their understanding of the well-lived life.[45] These collections, copied and edited by ibn Naghrella's sons Yehosef and Aliasaf, derived their inspiration and much of their content from the most comprehensive *adab* thesaurus in Muslim Spain, the *Al Iqd al-Farid* (The Unique Necklace), written by Mahmud ibn Abd Rabih (860–940). Like their Arabic sources, ibn Naghrella's collected rhymed aphorisms, epigrams, short sententious poems, and witty riddles all have a strong didactic character; they are obviously meant to teach wisdom to their listeners/readers in order to shape their conduct.

That Samuel ibn Naghrella named his edited collections after the biblical books of Proverbs and Ecclesiastes indicates how much he saw his own wisdom as a continuation of biblical wisdom. Moreover, unlike the intricate ornamentation of the poetic genres, the language of the aphorism is simple and direct and its style is markedly similar to the Wisdom literature of the Bible, where ideas are often expressed in pairs of opposites. Thus laziness is contrasted with activity, rest with a life of wandering, silence with talking, keeping a secret with disclosing it, a king's usefulness with the harm he can cause, wealth with poverty, and generosity with miserly conduct.[46] These dichotomies express not only an awareness of the diversity of human behavioral patterns, but also the ethos of moderation that warns against extremes.

The wisdom that Hebrew *adab* imparts to its listener/reader is both practical and theoretical. The aphorisms and short poems contain practical counsel and utilitarian advice about success in worldly affairs. The wise counsel is rooted not only in the accumulated practical wisdom of the ancients, but in the actual experience of the seasoned Jewish courtier who has seen it all—court intrigue, war, glory, and failure. The advice is prudential, intended to direct the recipient in the management of actual affairs, often related to government. However, while the advice presumes active involvement in worldly affairs, it is anything but vulgar. Mobility and survival at the top of the social ladder are possible only to those who exercise caution, delay of gratification, moderation, self-control, intelligent management of resources, and foresight. These values can be achieved only if one makes reason the ruling part of one's soul through habitual practice of deeds that lead to virtue. Although Bahya and Judah Halevi found faults with the court culture, the works of Samuel ha-Nagid indicate that involvement in that culture and the pursuit of moral perfection were not mutually exclusive; rather, social success depended on the cultivation of specific virtues.

The virtues that Samuel ibn Naghrella recommends are patience, dedication, tenacity, loyalty, moderation, silence, and magnanimity (or generosity). These virtues are not new. We have encountered them both in biblical Wisdom literature and in the teachings of the rabbinic sages. What is new is their application to the new social setting—most notably the virtue of magnanimity. Generosity in giving is a biblical and rabbinic value, the very foundation of Jewish social ethics. Now the Jewish courtiers were expected to act on a large scale, either as patrons of arts and sciences, through which they glorified themselves, or in their involvement on behalf of their Jewish religious-ethnic minority. For these purposes, material wealth was necessary. Thus if in rabbinic literature we noted a clear anti-luxury and anti-vanity tendency, in the aphorisms of Samuel ibn Naghrella we find a positive attitude toward material wealth. In agreement with Aristotle, ibn Naghrella understood that the virtue of magnanimity requires the ability to give on a large scale. He therefore advises his addressee to travel to great length to find wealth and to manage it properly so one does not lose it.

Yet ibn Naghrella, who was a wealthy man, was familiar with the difficulties of accumulating wealth and the ease with which it can be lost. Accordingly, he never once recommended that the accumulation of wealth be the ultimate end of earthly human life. On the contrary, many of his aphorisms emphasize the ephemeral nature of material goods, and the fact that wealth provokes envy and causes anxiety. Thus the prudential wisdom of the aphorisms is in full accord with the ethics of moderation and self-control. A certain modicum of material goods is both enjoyable and even necessary for the virtuous life of magnanimity, but the prudential wisdom and utilitarian morality of *Ben Mishlei* and *Ben Qohelet* are based on a deeper reflection about the meaning of human life. Ibn Naghrella's speculative poetry is rooted in his awareness of human mortality as well as in his understanding of the place of human beings in the cosmic order. He was familiar with the speculative *adab* poetry that absorbed the values of the Sufis, and his sententious poetry reflects skepticism about worldly success and deep suspicion toward the trap of worldly affairs, which prevents one from enjoying the unlimited bliss of the afterlife. Life on earth is represented through poetic depiction of "world" (*tevel*) and "time" (*zeman*); the first captures the spatial, corporeal, and material aspect of human existence; the second concerns the temporal dimension—viz., the brevity of human life and the inevitability of death.

That temporal dimension is reflected in the metaphors of *adab* sententious poetry. The world is no more than a house that one occupies for a short time, a hotel that one rests in between birth and death. Life is a dangerous voyage in which this world is not more than a bridge to death. There is a certain unreality to the life in this world. It is no more than a dream, an illusion from which one must awake by means of wisdom. Moreover, the corporeality of the physical world means that everything in it is subject to change, decay, and ultimately disintegration. Therefore, the world is profoundly unstable. Nothing in it is everlasting; everything in it is doomed to die. This knowledge must lead one to reject material goods as a source of security and turn instead to more lasting values.

These somber reflections on the nature of the human condition were not meant to produce despair and grief, but rather to lead the listener/reader toward the only thing that gives comfort and consolation, the pursuit of wisdom. Human freedom is to be found not in pleasures of the body, which only enslave men further, but in gaining a true understanding of human life and cultivating an internal goodness that is unaffected by external circumstances. The real *telos* of human life lies not in this world, but in the afterlife. The way to enter it is through the cultivation of virtues, which require renunciation of worldly temptations. Only wisdom can awaken the soul from the corporeal illusions and blindness of the world, making it alert and truly alive. The soul can be fully awake only when it departs from this world to the incorporeal, blissful, eternal life of Gan Eden. True happiness lies not in this world, but in the afterlife, provided one acquires the virtues and exercises the ethos of self-control.

Is there an unbridgeable conflict between prudential wisdom and the speculative meditations about the human condition? Not really. It is not that one is active and the other passive; one optimistic and the other pessimistic; one pro material goods and the other suspicious of them; one promoting political activity and the other against it. Both practical advice and meditations on the human condition complement each other as the two dimensions of the human composite, a being composed of body and soul who goes through two phases in life, this world and the world to come. What unites these aspects into a coherent whole is the ethos of self-control, which is necessary for prosperity in this life as well as for proper understanding of the limitations of the earthly part of the human journey.

Ibn Gabirol: The Moral Training of a Jewish Adib

A professional poet in the court of the patron Yequtiel ibn Hasan in Saragossa (to whom the poet composed one of his most laudatory poems and whose death was commemorated in one of his most moving elegies), Solomon ibn Gabirol was a perfect example of a pious Jewish *adib*. He possessed extensive knowledge of the *adab* prose literature and mastered its poetic conventions and ideals. For this reason, a collection of Arab moral aphorisms, circulating in the Hebrew translation under the title of *Mivḥar ha-Peninim* (Choice of Pearls), was ascribed to him.[47] From the vast encyclopedic knowledge of Arabic learning, ibn Gabirol culled his philosophical and scientific knowledge, molding it all into his own Weltanschauung, which had a strong Neoplatonic tinge, although it departed from the prevailing Neoplatonism on some important points.[48]

From this court Jew in Muslim Spain came the first systematic attempt to spell out how the well-being of mankind is linked to the structure of the universe and to the composition of human beings. Ibn Gabirol's moral treatise *Islah al-Akhlaq*, translated into Hebrew as *Tiqqun Middot ha-Nefesh* (The Improvement of the Moral Qualities),[49] delineated the connection between cosmology, psychology, and ethics. Ibn Gabirol's treatise should be viewed as a distinctive Jewish contribution to the philosophic "science of moral qualities" (*ilm al-Akhlaq*), as ethics was called in the Muslim world, even though it is hard to pinpoint one particular text that influenced him most. Like Saadia before him, ibn Gabirol joined an existing philosophical discourse on the cultivation of virtues but gave it a Jewish "twist" by anchoring it in Scriptures.

The Purpose of the Book

Originally written in Arabic, though transmitted among Jews only in its Hebrew translation by Judah ibn Tibbon,[50] *The Improvement of the Moral Qualities* is in many respects a continuation of Saadia Gaon's philosophical ethics discussed above.[51] Here again, I must take issue with Joseph Dan's interpretation, which presents the treatise as a "secular" scientific text.[52] According to Dan, ibn Gabirol's work departed radically from rabbinic precedents in style and content, stood in tension with the religious philosophy of ibn Gabirol, and marked a radical new beginning in the history of Jewish ethical writings.

I agree with Dan that the style of ibn Gabirol's text is novel. It conspicuously lacks the features of rabbinic homiletics still present in Saadia's Tenth Treatise, and it makes no references whatsoever to rabbinic personae as models for emulation. Instead, ibn Gabirol provides a systematic, scientific analysis of the human temperaments that serve as the physiological basis of moral training. To the extent that he adduces exempla, they are taken either from the Bible or from the *adab* literature of his day. (He mentions Greek and Arabic sages and cites tales about illustrious kings.) Ibn Gabirol's text breathes the culture of the court, both actual and literary, and among its sources, in addition to those mentioned above, was Hunayn ibn Yishaq's collection of aphoristic, biographical, gnomic, anecdotal literature entitled *Adab al-Falasifa,* translated into Hebrew as *Musrei ha-Filosofim* (The Moral Teachings of the Philosophers).[53]

The novelty of ibn Gabirol's book, however, is to be found not so much in its omission of rabbinic references but in its content. This is not a manual on moral training but a theoretical treatise on the physiological principles that underlie the ethos of self-control, which permeated courtier culture. To the extent that the text advises actual conduct, the advice flows from a certain understanding of how the body works, knowledge that indicates ibn Gabirol's indebtedness to the medical ethics of Galen and Hippocrates.[54] His ethical counsel is grounded in human biology and conforms to what is known scientifically. For ibn Gabirol, then, scientific knowledge does not stand in conflict with religion, but instead is necessary for religious decision making—namely, how should one live one's life in a world that emanates from God and in which the soul yearns to return to God.

Human Nature

Ibn Gabirol devoted his main philosophical work, *Meqor Ḥayim* (Fountain of Life), to the exposition of the metaphysical principles that account for the structure of reality as a great chain of being in which matter and form interact on all levels of reality. In his view, the human being is composed of a corporeal body and a non-corporeal soul and stands at the top in the hierarchy of beings of the world known through the senses. Comprising the peak of the created order, the human constitution manifests intentional design, orderliness, and beauty. The human species is "the most proportioned, as regards constitution of all living beings; and, in addition to this, most perfect and most beautiful form and most completely fashioned" (*Improvement*, 29). Echoing the common theme in Neoplatonic literature, ibn Gabirol presents the human species as a microcosm, with "the blood corresponding to air, the yellow gall corresponding to fire, black gall corresponding to earth and white moisture corresponding to water" (*Improvement*, 32), while the four elements and the four humors reflect the mathematical assumptions of the Pythagorean tradition, which privileged the number four, the first square number.[55]

The ultimate evidence that the human species is superior to all other beings in the perceptible world is that man alone is endowed with a "a rational soul, elemental, wise, everlasting, which does not perish with him" (*Improvement*, 29). Ibn Gabirol does not provide the reader much information about the nature of the rational soul, though he does state that "the Deity hath created the soul pure, stainless, and simple," adducing Ecclesiastics 7:29 as his proof text.

Moreover, since the rational soul is a pure substance, it is not capable of producing evil, for "that is the work of the vegetative soul, i.e., the natural impulse" (*Improvement*, 45). We are not told how exactly the rational soul is linked to the vegetative soul that is in charge of all the physiological functions, but it is clear that proper management of the body by the soul should exhibit the control of the rational soul.

Human well-being in this life thus requires the hegemony of reason over the passions and appetites of the body. If reason fails, one falls prey to the irrational desires of the body and loses the "enduring happiness which [man] can reach in the intellectual world, the world to come" (*Improvement*, 31). The principles that underlie proper human conduct constitute the "medicine of the soul," analogous to the "medicine of the body."[56] Indeed, the wise man is like a "skillful physician who prepares prescriptions, taking of every medicine a definite quantity" (*Improvement*, 34). However, the ultimate end of this medical management is not life in the temporal order, but rather the everlasting existence of the rational soul in the intelligible realm. In the final analysis the ethos of self-restraint and moderation should serve the immortal life of the soul in the afterlife.

Embodied human beings encounter the physical world through the mediation of the five senses, each of which is associated with specific human dispositions arranged in pairs of two, one positive the other negative, resulting in a total of twenty human dispositions.[57] While his data is taken from the vast scientific-philosophic literature composed by non-Jews, ibn Gabirol insists that the Bible itself teaches it. He turns primarily, though not exclusively, to Proverbs and Ecclesiastes to find proper proof-texts for his physiologically based ethics, and his reading of the biblical sources is decidedly nonexegetical. His point of departure is scientific-philosophic truth rather than the biblical text, which is asserted in support of the former without much elaboration. Ibn Gabirol takes it for granted both that the biblical text is true and that, as such, it cannot contradict the truths of science. His approach to the biblical text is not different from that of Saadia Gaon.

Virtues and Vices

The ideal person is the one who reaches a well-balanced condition of body and soul: he makes the rational soul govern his passions. If we put together the characteristics that ibn Gabirol finds laudable, we could easily recognize the ethos of the *adib* who works in the service of princes and kings. His prudential values are suffused with the spirit of caution and moderation. The list of laudable character traits includes meekness, modesty, capacity to love, compassion and mercy, cheerfulness and good disposition, good will and contentment, alertness, generosity, and valor. The negative dispositions or vices include pride, impudence, capacity to hate, cruelty, wrath, envy, sloth, niggardliness, and cowardice.

These character traits are generally in accord with the rabbinic tradition with one exception—viz., ibn Gabirol's emphasis on valor or magnanimity. Instead of the rabbinic emphasis on control of the passions (*kibbush ha-yetzer*) as true heroism, he clearly praises the nobleman who can perform on a grand scale. Citing non-Jewish courtiers for emulation as well as biblical judges and kings, ibn Gabirol, as did Samuel ibn Naghrella, makes room for a new virtue, nobility, in his list of commendable traits.

The Jewish courtiers' ethos of self-control reached its zenith in religious poetry and systematic philosophy, both of which ibn Gabirol was the greatest master. In his *Meqor Ḥayim*, he employed the form of Platonic dialogue to present a Neoplatonic metaphysics and cosmology whereby the entire universe is a hierarchy of being that emanates from God, the most supreme being and the source of all existents, in a dialectical interaction of matter and form. He expressed the same theoretical principle in poetic form in his *Keter Malkhut* (Kingly Crown). That for his contemporaries there was no tension between philosophy and faith is manifested in the fact that *Keter Malkhut* was incorporated into the liturgy.[58] In both works the goal of human life is intimacy with God, which can be attained only if one has acquired the moral virtues and, in addition, possesses theoretical knowledge about the structure of the universe. Through the conditioning (or, in ibn Gabirol's language, the "improvement") of human raw energy, or desire, the human soul can approximate God. By perfecting oneself morally and intellectually, the human soul can attain the ultimate (religious) goal of human life. This outlook is expressed most beautifully in the works of a younger contemporary of ibn Gabirol—Bahya ibn Paquda.

HAPPINESS AS RELIGIONS PERFECTION: BAHYA IBN PAQUDA

Intellectual Piety

Ibn Gabirol and ibn Paquda were prime examples of a new intellectualist piety that emerged in Jewish life in Muslim Spain. Locating the relationship between God and Israel in the noncorporeal aspect of the human, referred to either as "soul," "mind,'"or "intellect," this religious intellectualism predicated worship of God on human *understanding* of God's relationship with the created universe, and put a premium on human interiority rather than on the performance of deeds through the limbs of the body.

To equate Jewish worship solely with action without a concomitant internal intention was considered to be empty religious posturing. For pious intellectuals in Muslim Spain, the study of philosophy and its related sciences did not stand in conflict to religious worship; rather, study itself was taken to be a religious obligation, a duty imposed by God in order to enable the individual to come closer to Him.[59] The human mind was viewed as the vehicle for the worship of God. Through it, the love of God could be expressed in the most refined manner—noncorporeal, consistent with God's nature. The goal of the philosophic life was deeply spiritual—viz., intimacy with God, a spiritual being, with whom the human mind or soul could interact because it too was spiritual.

This emphasis on the rational aspect of the human soul, the intellect, had important ramifications for their conception of human happiness. For the religious philosophers, it was evident that happiness cannot be found in material prosperity, bodily pleasures, and social success. These values belong to the corporeal body and do not reflect the essence of being human. If the essence of being human is possessing intellect, then human well-being must belong to the excellence of the intellect. Furthermore, since the rational soul is not a corporeal substance, the happiness of the soul cannot be experienced in this world, but only in the afterlife, in the world to come. The quality of one's life in this world, however, determines whether or not the individual rational soul will attain the desired perfection. For this reason, it is essential to know how to conduct one's life, so as to attain the happiness of the soul. This is why Bahya ben Joseph ibn Paquda felt a need to compose his *al-Hidaya ila Faraid al-Qulub*, known in Hebrew as *Hovot ha-Levavot* (The Book of Direction to the Duties of the Heart).[60] Bahya's avowed reason for writing this work is most relevant to our study. He explains:

> Having studied these books [i.e., by the Babylonian Geonim Saadya Gaon, Hefetz ben Yazliah and David al Mukammatz] I could not find among them even one dealing exclusively with the esoteric knowledge. When I found that this knowledge, the knowledge of the duties of the heart, was neglected, not contained in any book comprising all its origins, forsaken, with none of its chapters collected in one work, I was deeply astonished (*Duties*, p. 88).

This quotation is interesting for two reasons. First, it indicates that Bahya considered himself to be the first author to write a systematic analysis of the science of inner "Duties of the Heart." Apparently, he was either unfamiliar with ibn Gabirol's work, even though they were contemporaries, or he rejected ibn Gabirol because he did not provide the appropriate foundation for a rationalist Jewish ethics. Second, while Bahya chides the Geonim for failing to produce a systematic analysis of the virtues, he notes that the "ancient righteous forefathers" were in fact quite aware of the inner duties of the heart and understood the connection between the striving for perfection and the cultivation of the proper moral dispositions (*Duties*, p. 96). Clearly

Bahya saw himself not only in direct accord with the rabbis but also as an innovative philosopher who deepened rabbinic Judaism by explicating its philosophical import. The inner science of the Duties of the Heart, then, is not an imposition from without but integral to the revealed tradition itself.

The Historical Context of Bahya Ibn Paquda

The dating of Bahya's life and *Duties of the Heart* has generated considerable scholarly dispute, although by now most would agree that he lived in the second half of the eleventh century, most likely in Saragossa,[61] and that he held a position of judge (*dayan*) in the Jewish community. Bezalel Safran has conjectured that the total absence of further information about Bahya's life and social activities might be accounted for by the fact that his work consists of a scathing critique of the courtier educational program and social ethics.[62] Regardless, *Duties of the Heart* became a classical text of Jewish religious ethics, among the first texts to be printed in the late fifteenth century.

Safran was correct in noting that Bahya's work contained a critique of a certain type of educational program, common among the Jews who wished to find a place in the bureaucracy of the Muslim state. Furthermore, Bahya did reject the pursuit of worldly success underlying that educational program. However, he should not be viewed merely as a critical outsider to the court culture, since he was himself well versed in the *adab* culture and utilized its treasures of literary anecdotes illustrating philosophical and religious values. I suggest that Bahya did not criticize the *adab* culture per se, but only the superficial and partial adaptation of it by those Jews who made social advancement their first priority. Being motivated exclusively by the desire for worldly success, these people looked at learning as a means to worldly ends, focusing exclusively on those useful skills that prepared one to become an *adib*.

Bahya ibn Paquda rejects the educational program of the would-be courtiers by describing it in a dramatized speech by the evil instinct. Tempting the would-be *adib*, the evil instinct says:

> Do not preoccupy your mind with any studies except those through which you can ingratiate yourself into the favor of your contemporaries and through which you can become acceptable to the great ones of your generation—the vizier, the chief of the royal police, the royal finance officer and political dignitaries. [These are studies of] the unusual feature of language, the laws of prosody, the principles of

grammar and poetry. [Know the] choice anecdotes, exotic parables and strange tales. Frequent the sessions of eloquent men; learn to communicate with all sorts of people. Master the science of the stars, on the basis of which the appropriate course of action for the public and for individuals can be determined (*Duties*, 254).

The evil instinct tempts the ambitious person to master only those linguistic and rhetorical skills, together with the science of astrology, that were deemed necessary for success in court. Such an approach to knowledge is mistaken for scholarly and religious reasons. From a scholarly perspective the focus on penmanship, eloquent speech, poetry, and refined style is wrong when it becomes its own end rather than the launching pad for reaching the higher sciences of logic, mathematics, physics, and metaphysics. The social climbers, then, acquire only the externals of learning, neglecting the core of the scientific curriculum.

Absorbing the teachings of Sufi teachers,[63] Bahya insists that human happiness can be properly understood only when one fully apprehends the meaning of being created by God. The purpose of *Duties of the Heart* is to spell out that meaning and draw the necessary conclusion for human happiness (*sa'adah* in Arabic). In line with the Sufi mentality, Bahya would argue that true happiness is to be found only in total submission to the service of God.

Intellectual Service to God

The full joy and delight of intimacy with God are to be experienced not in this world but in the next life, a noncorporeal reality in which the soul regains its initial perfection. However, to attain the ultimate felicity, one must first possess the correct knowledge of God and His creation. In short, Bahya's critique of the courtiers of his day is a critique from within the *adab* culture in the name of true wisdom, a wisdom that comes from mastering all the sciences and leads to proper understanding of the created universe and the place of God in it. In this critique, intellectual commitments are religious by nature.

From the Brethren of Purity, a religio-philosophic society, Bahya adopted a classification of the sciences.[64] For him philosophy properly speaking contains three main subjects: physics, mathematics, and metaphysics (*Duties*, 86). Physics and the mathematical sciences (arithmetic, geometry, astronomy, and music) are closely connected, enabling us to understand the "secrets of the world" as well as to know what is necessary for the proper functioning of the human body. The science of physics pertains not only to the perceptual world, the world dominated by the laws of generation and decay, but also to the celestial realm in which heavenly bodies were then understood to be moved by noncorporeal intelligences or separate intellects. To this realm, according to Bahya, belongs as well the human soul, a spiritual substance whose essence is light. The knowledge about noncorporeal entities, says Bahya, leads to the science of metaphysics, which culminates in knowledge about God and God's relationship to the world (*Duties*, 86).

As Saadia Gaon stated before him, Bahya holds that the same knowledge that philosophers could deduce in their inquiries is conveyed in its own unique language by revealed Scriptures. Much of Bahya's work attempts to illustrate the correspondence between human reason and the Hebrew Scriptures, in an obvious polemic against the emphasis on the divine in the Quran. While he occasionally refers to rabbinic sources, especially Tractate Avot of the Mishnah, it is the Bible that stands at the center of Bahya's intellectualist re-reading of Judaism. Many of his proof-texts are gleaned from the Wisdom stratum of the Bible, especially the Psalms, in an attempt to show both that the Hebrew Scriptures teach philosophic truths and that its teachings are conducive to the attainment of felicity in the next life.

The "duties of the heart," Bahya tells us "belong to the field of metaphysics" (*Duties*, 102). Modern Orthodox readers of Bahya have tended to ignore this statement, classifying Bahya's work simply as a "devotional work" or a popular work of Jewish ethics, and failing to appreciate the connection between ethics and metaphysics. Bahya's ethical exhortations pertain to the management of the soul as a spiritual substance created by God that combines temporarily with the human body for the duration of one's life. Bahya's work is offered as instruction or directions to protect the soul and ensure its well-being. Since most people—and according to Bahya, the Jewish courtiers in particular—do not take care of the soul, favoring the body instead, they suffer the resultant consequences. Bahya's *Duties of the Heart,* then, is offered as a therapeutic program that can either prevent the sickness of the soul or heal it in case sickness takes root. However, a proper care of the soul, Bahya holds, is feasible only for those who possess an accurate knowledge of the structure of the universe created by God and a correct understanding of the human condition.

Classification of Duties: Duties of the Heart and Duties of the Limbs

Knowledge of God and His created world is one of the "duties of the heart," namely, obligatory beliefs that one must affirm and understand in the mind. These duties include:

> To believe in the creator of the world, who brought the world into existence from nothingness; to believe in pure monotheism, free from a belief in any other gods; to assent to obeying God in our hearts; to meditate upon the wonders of creation in order to arrive at the knowledge of Him; to rely completely upon Him; to be humble and submissive before Him; to exhibit a constant care and attention to our deeds lest we be ashamed before his constant scrutiny of all our acts and secrets; to feel a desire to please him and consecrate all our work for His sake; to love those who love Him and hate those who hate Him.

These obligatory beliefs are not associated with physical activities that involve body parts and can be contrasted with the obligations that involve body actions, which Bahya calls "duties of the limbs" or "duties of the members." The latter are divided into two sub-categories: a) "duties imposed by the mind if they had not been imposed by the Scriptures," and (b) "duties imposed by revelation only, duties neither imposed nor forbidden by the mind."[65] Both "duties of the heart" and "duties of the limbs" involve both positive obligations as well as prohibitions, both forbidden deeds (which constitute most of the Jewish law) and forbidden feelings and the behavior that flows from them, such as "envy, rancor, and vengeance against people of our creed" (*Duties*, 87).

Evidently, Bahya was aware of the perceived tension between religion and philosophy, and was dismayed by the prevalence of this false dichotomy in his own day. If the practitioners of the *adab* culture mistakenly separated the rhetorical sciences from physics and metaphysics, the talmudic scholars of the time focused exclusively on the study of the Law, through exegesis of the biblical text or the details of halakhic practice, paying little attention to the foundations of the Law. Bahya felt that both groups were mistaken: they ignored what matters most in human life, the wisdom that leads to submission to God. His intent was to spell out that foundational knowledge in a language that was accessible to the learned Jewish men of his time, even though they may have lacked proficiency in the philosophical sciences, which could clarify for them the meaning of the foundational wisdom. In this respect, Bahya anticipated and perhaps even influenced Maimonides' articulation of the Thirteen Principles of faith.

SUMMARY OF DUTIES OF THE HEART

Happiness and the Science of Metaphysics

Bahya's approach to happiness is clearly non-Aristotelian, reflecting the impact of his Neoplatonic and Sufi sources. The question of human happiness, he argues, belongs to the science of metaphysics because happiness concerns the well-being of the human soul. As mentioned, *Duties of the Heart* is devoted to an explanation of the nature of the soul and the dangers it faces in the duration of human life. To address these dangers the book also includes the prescribed therapy that ensures the soul's well-being, either as preventive measures or as remedies to sickness already in place. For Bahya that begins with a correct understanding of reality, i.e., the fact that whatever exists is created by God. Following in the footsteps of Saadia and the Mu'tazilite Kalam, Bahya devotes the First Treatise to proving the existence of one creator and the peculiar attributes that belong to that unique being (*Duties*, 116–17). What matters to Bahya most is not that the existence of a creator is a rational belief, but that that belief establishes the radical otherness of God.

The First Treatise focuses on the Unity of God (*tawahid*). It asserts that God is one and not many, whole and not composed of parts, unique and unlike any other created thing. Bahya distinguishes between the "absolute oneness" of God and "relative oneness" of all other entities (*Duties*, 127–29), a distinction that he probably derived from the scientific encyclopedia of the Brethren of Purity and its Neoplatonic philosophic sources,[66] and which paves the way for a negative theology.

Because God is unlike anything else, absolutely simple, unique, and real, no ordinary term derived from our perception of the world can apply to Him positively. Since God is an absolute unity, the distinction between substance and accidents does not pertain to Him. Therefore, ordinary language that is rooted in the distinction between them (linguistically expressed in the distinction between subject and predicate) is not applicable to God.

Anticipating Maimonides, Bahya states that it is appropriate to talk about God in positive attributes only if we "consider the attributes as the denial of their opposites." Bahya cites Aristotle as the author of this notion, but it is not clear whether he consulted the original Aristotelian source or rather (as I tend to believe) encountered this definition in the writings of the Brethren of Purity. He does not develop the notion on logical grounds, most likely because he had not as yet absorbed Aristotle's logic. What Bahya did absorb from his sources were the religious ramifications of the divine otherness. If "the Creator is the only one who is real" (*Duties*, 103)—that is, if God alone is the ideal paradigm of unity so that every other creature is deficient by comparison, then God alone must be worshipped; to worship anything other than God is a form of idolatry.[67] The mistake of most people is to pursue the unreality of temporal goods, thereby ignoring the true and the real, i.e., God.

In the first chapter Bahya focuses on the transcendence of God, highlighting His remoteness and inaccessibility. However, the transcendent deity is also ever-present, because He created the world and manages it with care and concern. The second chapter of *Duties of the Heart* shifts the focus to God's created universe, which manifests God's omnipotence and benevolence. In the created world, human reason can discern intentional design, order, harmony, and purposefulness, all of which are marks of God's wisdom. The evidence for these discernible marks is produced both by scientific inquiries and by revealed Scriptures, and can be illustrated further by universal, common knowledge recorded in the tales of *adab* literature.

The creative act consists of an interplay between matter and form. Their compositional degree varies from the most pure and universal to the most base and corporeal. The result is a hierarchical cosmology in which all beings are arranged, divided into levels of reality: God, the Universal Soul, the celestial world, and the sublunar world. These levels are linked to each other by divine effluence, a kind of energy that penetrates all levels of reality and holds the universe together.

In the created world, which lies "under the moon," and is hence referred to as the sublunar world in the hierarchy of medieval cosmology, the human being is the supreme creature. Man is a blend of two distinct substances, the body and the soul, which belong to two difference ontological orders. The human composite itself manifests the duality of spirituality and corporeality in the created world, and the structure of the human being mirrors in miniature the structure of the world. Man is a microcosm of the macrocosm. Thus knowledge of the world and knowledge of man are two sides of the same coin.

Bahya's main interest is the human soul, since its well-being constitutes the ultimate end of human life. He defines it as follows: "The soul is a simple spiritual substance, which inclines by its nature to the spiritual beings that are like itself, and rejects by its nature the coarse bodies that are unlike it" (*Duties*, 427). This definition indicates Bahya's commitment to the

Platonic psychological schema that views the soul and the body as two substances combined temporarily for the duration of a person's life. Bahya does not provide a detailed philosophical analysis of the combination of the soul and the body; for this reason, it is understandable that the anonymous text *Kitab mani al-nafs* was ascribed to him.[68] It provides the philosophical theory that Bahya presupposed but did not include. Since his work was meant to exhort his listeners to live a certain type of life, he focused on the religious ramifications of psychological dualism rather than on their philosophical justification.

The Relationship of Soul and Body

Although both body and soul were parts of God's creative act, exhibiting purposefulness and wisdom, Bahya's attitude toward the corporeal body is ambivalent (*Duties*, 427). The body itself is a manifestation of divine wisdom and grace, and as such it is good. Indeed, the more one knows about its intricate structure and complex operation as understood by the best available scientific knowledge of the time, the more one can appreciate the greatness of God, who placed the human soul in this "well-built palace" (*Duties*, 214). However, the fact that the human body is a corporeal substance means that it occupies a lower status in the hierarchy of beings and that as such it is antagonistic to the soul. Hence, along with admiration for the human body, Bahya also speaks negatively about it as the seat of the desire, passions, and appetites that lead to sin and that hinder the soul's "search for deliverance." Ideally, the soul should take control of the body and restrict it to necessities.

What is crucial to Bahya is that the better one knows oneself, the better one can fathom the secrets of the world and vice versa. Knowledge of the physical world is essential to knowledge of oneself, and, in turn, to human happiness, precisely as Socrates and all the Greek philosophers thereafter had asserted. Bahya indeed cites the Socratic maxim "philosophy is man's knowledge of himself," attributing it to "one of the philosophers" (*Duties*, 160). However, unlike the pagan philosophers, Bahya gives the maxim a religious twist. Proper knowledge of oneself means knowledge of "the creator through the marks of His wisdom" (*Duties*, 160). Knowledge of the human body and its complex operation and development only yields awe and wonderment at the greatness of God's wisdom (*Duties*, 161–62), which is the foundation of Bahya's emphasis on humility. Philosophy and the sciences associated with it are thus vehicles for producing attitudes and virtues that constitute the happy life of service to God.

While Bahya's commitment to a two-substance theory is clear, his discussion of the "soul" suffers from vagueness because the term is used both broadly and narrowly. Broadly speaking the "soul" pertains to an wide range of mental acts, emotional dispositions, feelings and modes of conduct such as

> joy, sorrow, happiness, grief, remembering and forgetting, knowledge and ignorance, bravery and cowardice, tyranny and justice, shame and impudence, hope and fear, love and hate, enjoyment and pain, vanity and modesty, self-conceit and self abasement and all the others you feel within you (*Duties*, 215).

In this sense, the term "soul" denotes interior life as opposed to an exterior, physical or physiological aspect of the human composite, denoted by the term '"body."

Yet Bahya also holds, in accord with Aristotelian psychology, that the body does not generate its own physiological activities; these are the result of a soul. He reasons that the capacity to crave both food and sex, which are the activities of the "appetitive faculty," were designed by God for the survival and propagation of the human species. These cravings are intended by God to be a source of pleasure, which are part of the "well-being of the body" (*Duties*, 403). The problem arises when people make the well-being of the body their primary focus, leading their *souls* to desire excesses that result in the "downfall of [one's] affairs and the decay of his body" (ibid.).

Narrowly and more appropriately defined, the term "soul" applies specifically only to the intellect (or, in Mansoor's translation, the "mind") and its cognitive capacity manifested in human speech. To the human intellect belongs both "the distinction between falsehood and truth," as well as the capacity to make moral judgment—that is, "the preference for justice and avoiding of inequity, rewarding the good with goodness and thankfulness and requiting the bad with evil and reproof." (*Duties*, 199). Thus, the rational capacity that God "implanted" in human beings is the foundation of all philosophical-scientific activity as well as all moral sensibility. It is by virtue of this magnificent rational capacity that God made the human species "superior to all the creatures" (*Duties*, 158). The human intellect belongs to the noncorporeal order:

The mind, a fine spiritual substance derived from the upper and spiritual world, is a stranger in this world of coarse bodies . . . The mind, however, is not only a stranger in this world, but has nothing to support it and nothing to keep it company. Rather is everything against it (*Duties*, 181).

This definition echoes the Pythagorean-Platonic myth of the soul that was absorbed by Neoplatonism (both ancient and Muslim), Gnosticism, rabbinic thought, and Sufism. The "descent" of the soul is understood teleologically. The soul has a "task" to complete. She can return to her origin only if she controls the body and curbs its desires. Again, what is crucial for Bahya is not the explanation of how the intellect interacts with the lower functions of the soul, but how to draw correct moral-theological conclusions from the fact that intellect/mind is a stranger in the corporeal world.

Asceticism: The Control of Desire

In accord with the prevalent ethos of self-control, Bahya held that the task of religious-intellectual life is to ensure that mind or intellect rules over the body to facilitate the process by which the intellect regains its initial perfection. On these premises, human life is understood as an on-going test and challenge that God devised at creation. The one who passes the test successfully is rewarded accordingly by God with the everlasting joy of the afterlife. The fate of the mind in the human body is thus in human hands. One can either ensure that the mind controls the body directing itself toward the proper goal, or, conversely, one can allow the body to control the mind.

For Bahya, human drives, impulses, and cravings are lumped together under the category of "desire" (*ishq* in Arabic). Desire is a raw energy, located in the body (or more specifically in the liver). In itself desire is a positive force, "implanted by God" in humans, enabling them to propagate so as to ensure the perpetuation of the species. It becomes a negative force only when it produces excesses, be they in possessions, status, or pleasures. The reason desire can so easily turn into a negative force is that it is "close to man's soul from his childhood" (*Duties*, 181), for desire is a natural propensity toward sensual pleasure that all animals have. Thus people who devote their lives merely to the gratification of bodily needs are no better than beasts or infants. Since, like the body itself, it grows stronger the more one exercises it, "desire," Bahya states, is "always active, feeding the body incessantly, night and day," (*Duties*, 181). If it takes control of human actions, then "the mind grows weaker, being given so little use and limited exercise in the role for which it was created."

The Law as Therapy of the Soul

To protect the soul against sickness and to ensure that human beings enjoy the afterlife, we need a regimen to control the body, its appetites, and its cravings. This therapeutic function is provided by the Law revealed by God to the prophets. Bahya states that "the Law is the medicine for this sickness of the soul and this malady of nature" (*Duties*, 181). It creates a structure for the taming of desire through the cultivation of religious virtues that orient human beings toward God rather than toward the pursuit of transient and illusionary worldly success. The Law (or "religion") helps to "fortify and purify the mind" from the controlling influence of desire. For support, Bahya cites Psalm 19:8, a text that we have already discussed in Chapter Two.

Submission to the Law of God has two distinct levels. It begins with a fear of punishment and an expectation of reward. Fear ensures that one will avoid doing forbidden things and will perform only that which is permitted. The fear of God and expectation of reward pertain primarily to "duties of the limbs," and are not the highest form of worship. Yet avoiding sin and doing good works prepare the soil in which the seed of intellectual perfection can take root (*Duties*, 183).

From this beginning one can proceed to cultivate the intellect, whose obligations are limitless, in contrast with the "duties of the limbs," whose number is finite. Ascending to the level of intellectual obedience to God, the worshiper transcends fear of punishment or expectation of reward. His worship becomes an expression of reverence for and awe of God, which can occur only when the worshiper fathoms God's uniqueness and benevolence. Thus, the revealed Law is the vehicle for religious growth, moving the believer toward that which is most real, true, and good.

The Law, Bahya says, following Saadia Gaon, includes obligations whose rationale is accessible to the human intellect as well as obligations that remain inscrutable. No such distinction is made explicit in the Torah itself, because of the actual level of intellectual development of the human race at the time the Law was given. Again, anticipating one of Maimonides' famous views, Bahya maintains that at the time that the Law was revealed, the human race was ruled by their animal desires then, with mind and discrimination too weak to grasp most of the intelligible things. So the Law treated them in the same way, making both intelligible duties and those imposed by revelation equal in their force. Whoever has a strong enough mind and understanding was aroused by both means to undertake their performance upon himself. He whose mind was too weak to understand his obligation in both ways undertook to perform them by way of the Law only, regarding them all as duties imposed by revelation (*Duties*, 188).

Understanding the rationales for the commandments is itself a religious obligation, since understanding is a path for religious perfection. Those who equate piety with mere observance of the Law to the exclusion of understanding doom the practitioner to a superficial and imperfect religious life.

Asceticism (*zuhd* in Arabic, or *perishut* in Hebrew)—the discipline, training, and control of the instinctual urges—is the very purpose of the Law (*Duties*, 405). While asceticism's goal is the soul's nearness to God, it serves a broader purpose and stands for the wide range of directives by which one gains control over desire and achieves intimacy with God in this world and felicity of the soul in the next.

Bahya clearly rejects extreme asceticism as a regimen that is not prescribed by the Law, again anticipating the position of Maimonides. The fact that God created us as embodied creatures means that the needs of the body are good in themselves and therefore require attention. He holds that the Law favors only a "moderate asceticism," one that is this-worldly and life affirming. It rejects luxury and excessive bodily pleasure, but not involvement in society. Moderate asceticism means that one must be concerned with both the well-being of the body and the well-being of human society.

The practice of moderation is thus governed by knowledge of what the body really needs, as opposed to pursuing what is unnecessary or harmful. The same principle of moderation also governs social relations. It directs the individual to practice self-control in all of his affairs, guided by the virtues of compassion, mercy, gratitude, sensitivity to the needs of others, patience, truthfulness, and forbearance (*Duties*, 410–11), which are all manifestations of religious virtues that are rooted in a correct understanding of the human condition.

Religious Virtues

Most of the *Duties of the Heart* (chapters four through eight) is an elaborate discussion of the virtuous person who draws the correct conclusions from the awareness that the world is God's creation and that God alone is the true sovereign of the affairs of the world. Reflection on these doctrines can lead, according to Bahya, to only one conclusion: that there is only one proper object of worship or service, God. Everything else is secondary, derivative, or illusory.

If God is the only object of worship, the proper posture of the religious person is total reliance on Him. It is more than a virtue; it is the total orientation of the practitioner of virtue from which all other virtues—especially humility—arise. Trust in God is contrasted with reliance on one's own natural talents and worldly accomplishments. The one who trusts God "ceases submitting to others, never beseeching men for anything, neither humiliating himself nor flattering them." Most importantly, he never follows them in the worship of someone other than God. Therefore, whoever relies on God never fears others, and never is afraid to oppose them. Rather, he is "happy to remove the robe of their honors, to get rid of the obligation of gratitude to them and the duty of rewarding them."

Bahya's criticism of the Jewish courtiers and their social ethics is directed toward their treatment of other human beings as objects of worship. Real power lies with God rather than with social superiors. Having attained high positions, the courtiers take credit for their own social success, cultivating arrogance, the highest mark of human superficiality.

While humility is the religious virtue that follows necessarily from trust in God alone, reliance on God yields a long list of benefits, or "advantages." The one who relies on God "can free his mind from the affairs of this world and purify his soul for works of worship, so that in the peace of his mind and the tranquility of his soul, in his little concern with the affairs of this world, (he) is very like the master of alchemy who is well-versed in both theory and practice." (*Duties*, 223) Moreover, reliance on God does not mean that one must refrain from involvement in worldly affairs. As we noted above, Bahya does not recommend departure into a life of seclusion and isolation, but encourages his readers to be involved in a wide range of social activities, all conducted with proper moderation. Nor does reliance on God necessarily entail rejection of worldly goods. A person who trusts in God and happens to be wealthy remembers that his wealth is not his own and "hastens to fulfill his duties to God and men with a generous soul and a happy disposition" (*Duties*, 226). If, on the other hand, he happens to be poor, he "considers poverty a grace bestowed by God upon him, in that he is not bound by the duties to God and men that money imposes on him because his mind is free from the trouble of preserving and managing it" (Duties, 226–7). Since neither wealth nor poverty is the doing of human beings, one must not be proud when one is wealthy or ashamed when one is poor.

Bahya, then, offers a view of generosity in conflict with the one practiced by the Jewish courtiers and suggests that true generosity is to be understood along the lines of traditional rabbinic ethics. The generous person is the one who possess "a good disposition" (*lev tov*) toward all people rather than one who supports artists in order to increase his own fame and social influence.

The one who relies on God possesses "a tranquil heart, free of worldly interest, a peaceful soul, undisturbed and unworried by the loss of bodily desire, a state of rest, ease and security in the world." While Bahya cites Jeremiah 17:7 as his proof-text, we may note that this set of dispositions could be found as well in the Epicurean and Stoic traditions, which regarded imperturbability and peace of mind as the ideal virtues of the sage, and in the Sufi masters who taught that in God alone can one find security. The sage who relies on God is not obsessed with attaining goods and is not perturbed by material losses or decline in social status. The inevitable vicissitudes of worldly affairs simply do not disturb the one who finds shelter in God and who submits himself to God's demands rather than to human caprices.

Bahya is fully aware that reliance on God is difficult to attain because of the constant instigation of the "evil instinct" (*yetzer ha-ra*). The "instinct," Bahya notes, is one's "worst enemy in this world," because it uses the weapon of skepticism to undermine reliance on God. The "instinct" attempts "to make you suspect your truths, to perplex your established certainties. He tries to confuse you, leading you away from your true welfare, confounding your firm faith and beliefs" (*Duties*, 276). Doubts about the existence of the Creator, the existence of prophecy, the validity of the tradition, future rewards and punishments, or that God and nothing but God is the object of worship, are all the instigation of the "instinct." These doubts would misdirect focus to worldly affairs for their own sake at the expense of focus upon the afterlife. They lead to a human pride that equates happiness with worldly success rather than with submission to God. That the doubts are all forms of untruth suggests that there is a necessary connection between knowing what is true and cultivating the appropriate religious personality intent on pleasing God and none else. Affirming the centrality of humility in rabbinic ethics, Bahya states that humility is the root of all worship . . . it distinguishes servitude from sovereignty; it is the affirmation that sovereignty may be attributed to God alone . . . Humility may also drive away one's haughtiness and arrogance, vanity and self-conceit, vainglory and self-esteem, one's sense of loftiness and self-importance, one's desire to prevail over the weak, one's presumptions toward what is above oneself and other kinds of pride similar to this (*Duties*, p. 304).

Since it involves a "meekness of the soul," the trait can be found at three ascending levels, not all of which constitute true humility. In terms of human embodiment, a kind of "humility" is exhibited in the ability to endure misfortune and suffer pain. This trait is common to both men and other animals, and therefore cannot be regarded as genuine humility. In fact, it is often based on ignorance, because the more one knows the easier it becomes to avoid misfortune. A higher degree of "humility" is one that pertains to social relations. It is rooted in "true understanding of good and evil traits" (*Duties*, 305) and involves the ability to accept the authority of social superiors (masters, employers, rich patrons). However, this too does not constitute the true trait and cannot be considered a virtue.

It is only in reference to God that one can possess true humility, which is the result of constant self-examination, or self-reckoning, in which a person brings to mind, meditates and reflects on, the human condition. In his chapter six, devoted to the trait, Bahya cites seven themes that one must meditate upon in order to cultivate humility. The list is extended in chapter eight to include thirty items that should be at the forefront of one's concern. These are, we should note, very similar to those that Samuel ibn Naghrella discussed in his sententious poetry and aphorisms. In both cases we can trace them to Sufi influences.

Through meditation on particular themes, the religious practitioner can renounce the pursuit of fame, pleasure, and power, as well as the arrogance that comes with them. He can develop humility and modesty, which are manifested in two distinct ways: he will treat other people with compassion, patience, and mercy; and he will submit himself to God and obey God's Law. With such submission, the truly humble man can sustain any mishap or calamity, endure social disgrace, and remain immune to both praise or blame (*Duties*, 319–20). The life of the humble man is a happy life.

The Ultimate End: A Mystical Union with God

Bahya's religious ethics played an important role in the development of Jewish reflections on happiness.[69] He insisted that happiness does not lie in material goods, bodily pleasures, fame, or power. Since it is the soul and not the body that defines man as distinctly human, happiness pertains to the soul. The well-being of the soul must be a non-corporeal existence that we can experience only after the death of the body and its separation from the soul. Bahya's focus on the afterlife thus complements this psychological dualism. The next life is the world where the soul can enjoy the delights it deserves. In this world, the soul has a task to fulfill; it must control the natural inclination of the body toward excesses and direct itself toward the True, the Good, and the Real—God. Life in this world is thus understood as at best a preparation for the felicity of the soul in the next life.

In accordance with the Platonic myth of the soul, its happiness is understood in the context of the soul's descent to the world and its ascent to its heavenly origin. The spatial categories of the Platonic/Neoplatonic worldview were matched with the temporal categories of rabbinic Judaism, which separate this world from the world to come. The soul that acquired the appropriate religious virtues is able to survive the death of the body and enjoy the bliss of a mystical integration, absorbed into the divine reality from which it came. The ultimate end of the intellectual piety is the mystical absorption into divine reality, which can come only to the one who possesses a "strong understanding of his Lord and [meditates] upon the perpetual graces that He has given him and upon his obligation to obey Him and follow His commands and prohibitions" (*Duties*, p. 339). Bahya calls the man who returns to God in this fashion "the happiest" and to the conduct that facilitates it "the path of happiness" (*Duties*, p. 425).

Bahya does not describe this mystical embrace of the soul exactly: the experience transcends the corporeal order. However, in the poetic admonition (*tokheḥah*) that concludes the book, he summarizes its content as an address to his own soul and says the following: "The king perhaps will desire your beauty/And raise His face toward you/and give you peace" (Duties, 450). The mystical moment, then, is a face-to-face encounter between God and the perfected soul—one that has sought God through righteousness and humility. It is reasonable to conclude that Bahya saw *Duties of the Heart* as a guide for his own soul's attainment of happiness.

Though the ultimate mystical union could not be described, Bahya discusses the wise persons "who love God" and who experience well-being in this life:

The people who know their God understand His purpose with them, His control over them, and His wise management of their affairs; those who have observed His care for them, His rule and mastery of everything He has permitted them to do or choose, both in the affairs of this world and in religion, those who have verified and established with certainty the fact that all their affairs follow the course of the creator's decree and will, these people cease to prefer one situation to the other, and they put their trust in God, knowing that He will choose for them the best and most advantageous of all situations (*Duties*, 440–41).

Since the lovers of God are in the world, they still have to pay attention to the needs of their bodies and to social relations. However, they do so only to the least extent possible, for "their bodies belong to this world, but their souls are heavenly and spiritual." Their relative liberation from material conditioning is achieved by focusing exclusively on their obedience to God, "out of deep concern for His commandments and prohibitions" (*Duties*, 441). The perfect religious worshippers, those who possess the knowledge of God in the heart,

> worship Him as if they were with the holy angels in the heavenly spheres. All their desires are utterly eliminated, all their passion for pleasure is uprooted, as their hearts are filled with the yearning to obey God and imbued with love for Him (*Duties*, 441–42).

In short, Bahya presents an intellectual-mystical vision of human excellence. It is a life directed toward an ultimate goal, the mystical union with God, which takes place within the parameters of Jewish Law. When the prescriptions of the Law are properly understood and performed with the appropriate mental posture, the human soul is able to purify itself by acquiring moral, intellectual and religious virtues that enable the soul to control the body. While the full reward of this perfect life is to be experienced after the death of the body, already in this world the lover of God enjoys the profound benefits of obedience to God. The lover of God is relatively free from the limitations of the corporeal world, experiencing the bliss of spiritual life.

SUMMARY

During the first five centuries of Islam, Jewish life and culture were thoroughly transformed. Adopting Muslim modes of thought and cultural patterns, Jewish intellectuals "transposed" rabbinic Judaism into a philosophical key, so to speak. The new philosophical culture was by no means antithetical to rabbinic Judaism. Focus on reason, the mark of being human, provided the philosophers with a clear knowledge of what they considered to be the truth, thereby enabling them to come closer to God and provide a deeper justification for allegiance to the revealed tradition. The religion of the philosophers was bold, not because it was "secularist," but because it conceptualized God in impersonal abstract concepts that privileged the intellect as the vehicle for interaction with God. In this regard, their understanding of God differed markedly from the naive or corporeal understanding common to the uneducated Jewish masses.

Indeed, the intellectualization of rabbinic Judaism presupposed that the educated elite was socially superior to the uneducated. This elitism was not new in Judaism, since the Judaism of the rabbis itself was a product of what a small intellectual elite imposed on all Jews. The philosophers, however, changed the focus of rabbinic elitism when they shifted the emphasis from mastery of the halakhic tradition to mastery of philosophy and its related sciences. To be good Jews, all had to aspire to become good philosophers who *know* God appropriately.

It goes without saying that those who lacked a natural ability to engage in philosophy were at a disadvantage in this intellectualist religious culture of the philosophers. However, since all human beings are endowed with the capacity to think, in principle it was possible to educate the entire society, provided these philosophic truths could be properly presented. With this goal in mind Bahya concluded his philosophical-religious treatise with a summary of its main tenets in a poem, joining Solomon ibn Gabirol and others who composed poetry as a didactic tool for the dissemination of intellectual piety.

The intellectualization of rabbinic Judaism also meant that human well-being was now understood to have two distinct levels—that of the body and that of the soul. The two were qualitatively different but not diametrically opposed. Only when the soul properly controlled the cravings of the body could the individual enjoy fully the well-being of the body, which was itself a necessary condition for the well-being of the soul. The conditioning of the body was to be achieved through the cultivation of the moral, intellectual, and religious virtues possessed by the soul, culminating in its excellence.

This intellectualist ethos of self-control was in full accord with the biblical Wisdom tradition as well as rabbinic Judaism. Now, however, it expressed itself in the new cultural setting of the refined courtiers, utilizing new modalities, taken from *adab* or Sufi literature. Moreover, the religion of the philosophers gave the rabbinic tradition a strong individualistic slant, further emphasizing the interiorization of Jewish religious life. This is not to say that the philosophers denied the collective dimension of Jewish life or that they disregarded the centrality of halakhah. Some of the philosophers (e.g., ibn Gabirol, Moses ibn Ezra, Abraham ibn Ezra, and Judah Halevi) produced impressive religious poetry, which the entire Jewish community used for expressing their deepest religious sentiments. Others (e.g., Saadia Gaon, Samuel ibn Naghrella, and Bahya ibn Paquda) were leading halakhists of their generation. Indeed, the philosophers also considered themselves *responsible* for the education and edification of the community at large, even though their vision of human well-being was primarily individualistic. Yet, the philosophers viewed the life of *action* to be only a means to a higher life of intellectualist *contemplation*, culminating in the knowledge and love of God.

This view received its most elaborate articulation in the works of Moses Maimonides, to whom we devote the next chapter. Many of the elements of Maimonides' position could already be found in Abraham ibn Daud's *Emunah Ramah* (Exalted Faith) composed in 1160/1.[70] In the opening of the third part of that work he declares the attainment of happiness (*haga`at ha-hatzlahah*) to be the ultimate end of human life. Echoing the teachings of ibn Sina on happiness (along with many other topics),[71] ibn Daud asserts that happiness means perfection of the human soul, attainable by those who cultivate the virtues through the observance of the Torah and who also actualize their rational potential. The happy life culminates in intellectual perfection, which ibn Daud identifies with the love of God. But only the one who possesses a correct knowledge of the world can come to love God, since love is commensurate with knowledge, and knowledge of God leads to imitation of God in one's interaction with others. There is, then, no conflict between Torah and philosophy. Instead, philosophy transforms belief from simple faith to exalted or sublime faith.

The Jewish philosophers' focus on the human intellect required them to articulate psychological theories that could explain how the intellect knows external reality and how it relates to the human body. They articulated these theories only after they had absorbed Aristotle's philosophy, which they read with the help of Muslim commentators. At the same time, the more familiar they became with Aristotle's philosophy, the more it became necessary to demonstrate that Aristotle's logos and the rabbinic mythos were truly compatible. This task dominated the writings of Moses Maimonides, the most important and possibly the most subtle of all the medieval Jewish philosophers.

5

Perfectly Happy: Maimonides' Conception of Happiness

Moses Maimonides (1138–1204) was the first to show systematically how the rabbinic notion of religious perfection (*shelemut*) could be understood in the context of Aristotelian virtue ethics, Plato's political theory, and the cosmology and psychology of Islamic rationalism. Believing rabbinic Judaism to be true because its foundation is divinely revealed and Greek philosophy to be true because its central claims are rationally demonstrable, Maimonides sought to show that there is no necessary conflict between Judaism and philosophy, if both are properly understood. Maimonides' conception of happiness was the crux of his comprehensive and subtle integration of religion and philosophy, of Torah and Wisdom, of mythos and logos.

By Maimonides' day, Islamic philosophy produced extensive theoretical literature. Nevertheless, "the philosopher qua philosopher had no recognized social status."[1] Philosophers did not have schools of their own and did not hold official governmental or clerical positions as philosophers. They earned their livings primarily by offering rulers a particular service that required some specialized knowledge such as medicine or mathematics. This arrangement enabled the philosophers to develop their own views with relative independence from political pressure, but it also corroded the classical tradition of Plato and Aristotle, which assigned an important political role to the philosopher. Muslim philosophers such as al-Farabi, ibn Sina, and ibn Bajja—who were Maimonides' main sources—solved the problem by articulating a new theory of prophecy as a cognitive state. Accordingly, to be a prophet one first had to be a philosopher. Conversely, the theoretical wisdom of the philosopher could and had to be translated into political action. Still, the role of the philosopher in Muslim civilization was quite problematic.

Broadly speaking, all the scientific disciplines were considered part of the training of the wise man. But in a stricter and more technical sense '"philosophy" pertained only to the theoretical sciences, physics and metaphysics, and the other disciplines were considered preparatory to it. All medieval philosophers who absorbed the Aristotelian legacy took it for granted that theoretical knowledge of the sciences was distinct from but not unrelated to practical knowledge. Accordingly, knowing how the universe works (knowledge gained through the natural sciences) was relevant to knowledge about human conduct, and conversely, the personal qualities of the individual were deemed a necessary condition for determining the degree of knowledge that an individual could attain. Thus for the Muslim philosophers and for Maimonides, as for their Greek and Hellenistic predecessors, knowledge, virtue, and happiness were necessarily linked.

Wisdom about God was the zenith of philosophical knowledge and, for the philosophers, the ultimate goal of human life. However, the philosophers' reflections on God greatly differed from the thought of other believing Muslims. For al-Farabi, ibn Sina, ibn Bajja and ibn Rushd, God was not the personal creator of the world and revealer of the *Sharia*, but an abstraction understood within the categories of Greek philosophy. Their philosophical speculations, therefore, differed greatly from the scholastic theology of Kalam, discussed in the previous chapter. Appropriately, the philosophers' conception of happiness was also intellectual, for the ultimate end of human life was the perfection of the human intellect, a process that led to knowledge of God, to the extent that God could be known by human beings. The details of this claim will become clear in the following chapters. For now suffice it to say that the identification of happiness with intellectual perfection was one of the main reasons the leading Muslim theologian, al-Ghazali (d. 1111), opposed the prevailing philosophic conception of happiness and endorsed Sufism as the authentic Muslim path to human fulfillment. He composed *Kimia-yi sa'adat* (The Alchemy of Happiness) in an attempt to articulate a Muslim alternative view to the one proposed by al-Farabi.[2]

Following al-Farabi's reconciliation of religion and philosophy,[3] Maimonides significantly advanced the discourse on happiness by explicitly interpreting rabbinic Judaism, especially its ethics, in terms of Aristotle's ethics. Maimonides could do so because of the shared ground between the rabbinic and Aristotelian definitions of happiness. Both held an objectivist, teleological approach to the valuation of human life. Both presupposed that the good life springs from the very nature of human beings. Both maintained that the good person must acquire virtues through deliberate, habitual practice of good acts. Both held that the good life requires social interaction, and that such interaction must be guided by the principle of moderation. Finally, both believed that human nature is such that human beings can aspire to transcend mortality, and that the good life itself is a necessary condition for the fulfillment of that aspiration.

Although rabbinic ethics reflected the prevailing social values of the Stoics and the Epicureans, Maimonides pushed back to the Aristotelian foundation of Hellenistic moral philosophy. He, in agreement with Plato and Aristotle, viewed human beings not only as rational animals but also as political animals. Therefore he insisted that to experience well-being human beings require a just social order. Even though the ultimate goal of human life transcends politics, Maimonides believed that the well-lived life requires the appropriate political setting, The political aspect of Maimonides' conception of happiness makes sense if we recall that during the Middle Ages, especially in Muslim society, the Jewish minority enjoyed extensive self-government, and Maimonides himself served as a leader of the Jewish community in Egypt.[4]

The core of the Muslim marriage of philosophy and religion focused on the phenomenon of prophecy. To be a prophet one first had to become a philosopher and reach moral and intellectual perfection. Having attained the knowledge of truth, the philosopher, as Plato argued, is compelled to communicate his perfect knowledge to others in order to establish a just polity in which all people can aspire to a higher knowledge of God. Maimonides, however, read Plato through the commentaries of his mentor al-Farabi, and was influenced by the latter's reworking of Plato's political theory in which the founder of the most perfect regime is a philosopher-prophet-legislator who "translates" philosophical truths into the metaphoric language of religious expression. Furthermore, Maimonides also agreed with al-Farabi that the ones who know truth—the philosophers—are epistemically and socially superior to the ignorant masses. For Maimonides, a religion (meaning, a legal system) founded by a philosopher-prophet-legislator is the ideal social order: it enables those who live within its circle to attain both well-being of the body and well-being of the soul. Therefore, in the case of a true (i.e., philosophic) religion, there is no conflict between religion and philosophy, or between mythos and logos. Religion is but the rhetorical expression of philosophic truth. It is this model that undergirds Maimonides' conception of happiness, making him both central and controversial in the history of Judaism.

In this chapter I shall argue that Maimonides the Jewish philosopher-jurist had one consistent message to his Jewish readers: because the Torah of Moses creates the best social order in which we can attain the perfection of the intellect, Judaism is the best possible program for the happy life for humanity. Maimonides stated this claim as one of the dogmas of Judaism and conveyed it through elaborate narratives (or "plot-structures") about the origins, development, flourishing, and ultimate purpose of the human species. Yet because he also inherited the ambiguity of Aristotle's conception of happiness and believed that philosophy should be taught through hints and parables, he left for posterity an ambiguous legacy whose meaning is still being debated.[5] I will not be able to solve the Maimonidean enigma, but I hope to propose a well-argued and plausible reading of his conception of human perfection.[6]

INTERPRETING MAIMONIDES

Sources of Ambiguity

Maimonides wrote legal, philosophical, and theological works that vary greatly in style, content, and intent. His main legal work—the *Mishneh Torah* (Code of Jewish Law)—is a legal digest, written in Hebrew and addressed to all Jews who were students of Jewish Law. In contrast, his *Dalalat al-Ḥa-irin* (The Guide of the Perplexed) is a philosophical-theological work composed in Judeo-Arabic and addressed to a relatively small and well-defined audience of Jews who were perplexed by the seeming tension between the claims of philosophy and Judaism. To determine the relationship between the legal works and the philosophical-theological works of Maimonides, the reader must not only coordinate what Maimonides says in both types of works but also determine Maimonides' theoretical view of the relationship between philosophy and religion. What makes this task especially difficult is the particular style of the *Guide of the Perplexed*.

Maimonides intentionally obfuscated his views by composing the *Guide* as an esoteric work.[7] Those views are consciously obscured through various rhetorical techniques.[8] For example, his discussion of any given topic is dispersed through several different places in the work, and in each case the different context affects the meaning of what he says. Sometimes what Maimonides states in one place appears to conflict with his pronouncement on the topic in other places. The reader has to pay careful attention to his choice of words, the order of the presentation, and the context in which each statement is embedded. Indeed, Maimonides himself specified how he wished the reader to proceed. The ideal reader of the *Guide* should

> connect its chapters one with another; and when reading a given chapter, [the reader's] intention must be not only to understand the totality of the subject of that chapter, but also to grasp each word that

occurs in it in the course of the speech, even if that word does not belong to the intention of the chapter.[9]

As the body of Maimonidean scholarship amply proves, even the most careful readers differ with one another in their readings of the *Guide*. The task of interpretation involves many judgment calls, all of which reflect the readers' assumptions about Maimonides, the nature of Judaism, and the purpose of philosophy. A close reading of the *Guide* alone is thus no guarantee of certain understanding of Maimonides' intent.

The manner in which Maimonides employed sources is a second reason for the ambiguity of his message. In accordance with the medieval style of writing that defers to the authority of past authors, Maimonides cites many philosophic sources—Greek, Hellenistic, and Muslim—without telling the reader how he is using the sources at his disposal.[10] Not all of them can be identified with certainty; some citations are not named by title, and others that are listed by title refer to works no longer extant. Also, Maimonides often lists sources with which he disagrees in order to juxtapose them with others, but the reader must determine whether Maimonides agrees with, disagrees with, or qualifies any given source. Moreover, Maimonides' sources may be equivocal themselves and may even be conceptually incoherent. It remains for the reader to interpret each one and determine which of them best reflects Maimonides' position. This difficulty is most evident with regard to his view of human happiness.[11]

A third source of ambiguity is the tension in Aristotle's own analysis of happiness. Aristotle can be read to claim either the "exclusive" view that happiness consists in the contemplation of necessary, abstract truths, or the "inclusive" view that human happiness is experienced as a composite of goods, experienced in a social-moral sphere by the person who acquires moral and intellectual virtues.[12] Maimonides, who was familiar with the *Nicomachean Ethics*, reproduced Aristotle's teachings on happiness, transmitted by Muslim commentators,[13] and Maimonides accentuated their inherent ambiguity in his own discussion.

We noted that Maimonides was deeply indebted to al-Farabi, but as far as human happiness is concerned, al-Farabi himself vacillated between the "exclusive" and "inclusive" readings of Aristotle's views on happiness. Miriam Galston has persuasively argued that, by and large, al-Farabi endorsed the "inclusive" interpretation of the good life.[14] If so, human well-being is a composite of all good ends. It includes both practical and theoretical activities, and most importantly, it pertains only to life in this world. The happy life comes to an end at death, and there is no life after death. The accounts of personal immortality, which Islam clearly asserts, are dismissed as "old-women's tales."

Had Maimonides simply reproduced al-Farabi's views, it would have been difficult for him to protect himself against Jewish charges of heresy. However, the story is more complex because Maimonides was no less influenced by ibn Bajja, who, by contrast, favored the "exclusivist" interpretation of happiness.[15] The emphasis of his philosophy was on the link between metaphysics and epistemology. Within a Neoplatonized-Aristotelian metaphysics, ibn Bajja attempted to show that the human intellect is able to grasp disembodied forms and that the knowledge of them constitutes ultimate felicity, which he equated with the knowledge of God.[16]

Since the views of al-Farabi and ibn Bajja are both present in Maimonides' works, the interpreter has to decide which of them is closer to Maimonides' original intent. To make matters even more complicated, Maimonides borrowed very heavily also from ibn Sina[17]—although in the *Guide* he never mentions this Persian philosopher-physician-poet by name. Moreover, in his famous letter to Samuel ibn Tibbon, Maimonides speaks somewhat dismissively of ibn Sina.[18] To sort out how Maimonides employed his diverse sources requires the reader to determine which of their views is most plausible. This determination, in turn, necessarily reflects a host of other assumptions about Maimonides and about Judaism.

If this were not enough, a fourth source of ambiguity is found in the very concept of perfection employed by Aristotle and giving rise to both the "inclusive" and "exclusive" interpretations. Aristotle's idea of human well-being, we now know, was teleological. The *telos* or end determines the development of every living being that is transformed from the potential to something actual. When a thing actualizes its potential, it reaches its perfection (*entelechia*). However, to situate the notion of "perfection" in this kind of teleological metaphysics necessarily produces ambiguity. Perfection can mean either that a thing *has the end within it*, or that the thing is *at the end* of a process of self-actualization. According to the first meaning, wherein a thing contains the end within it, the perfected entity exhibits an internal harmony or equilibrium. This was how Plato and his student, Aristotle, both understood "perfection." However, according to the second meaning, in which perfection is the termination or completion of a process of actualization, the perfection of a thing simply means that it has attained its mature form, which is a second sense in which Aristotle uses the term. Consequently, when the concept of perfection is linked to human well-being, happiness is either the mark of the balanced life or it is the destiny, the termination point, of the process through which human beings actualize their potential as rational animals.

Aristotle tried to dispel some of the confusion by distinguishing between activity (*energia*) and process (*kinesis*), as we noted in Chapter One. Happiness (*eudaimonia*), he told us, is an activity (*energia*) in accordance with virtue, and virtue is determined by the *telos* of the species. For Aristotle happiness is activity rather than something that develops over time toward a stage of completion.[19] For the human species to be happy means that all parts of the human composite function properly and its rational part exercises control over the whole. When a harmony of the parts is attained, the result is human well-being or happiness. Hence, happiness, for Aristotle, is not a process.

Maimonides, I maintain, blurred the distinction between activity and process. His description of the happy life includes the process by which one becomes perfect, the goal (*telos*) that directs the process, and the state experienced when the *telos* is realized. I believe that blurring the distinction between activity, end, and process was necessary in order to bring about his fusion of Aristotelian philosophy and rabbinic Judaism. In the teleological metaphysics of Aristotle, well-being pertains to a static condition, namely, what the thing is when it functions most fully. However, rabbinic Judaism views all forms of life dynamically and relationally. Whatever is, is so because of its relationship to and interaction with God. This is especially so in the case of divine-human relationship.

The sources of ambiguity noted above do not exhaust the complexity of Maimonides' message. Throughout the chapter I will note other instances in which Maimonides' legacy can be given diverse interpretations. While I will attempt to clarify the ambiguity, I will not be able to remove it. Indeed, it was precisely because Maimonides could be read in more than one way that the discourse on happiness took the various twists and turns that it did in the centuries after him.

The Interplay of Logos and Mythos

Modern scholars on medieval Jewish philosophy have written more about Maimonides than about any other thinker, and for a good reason. Maimonides not only spelled out the meaning of the Torah-Wisdom nexus, or the interplay of logos and mythos in theory, he also used his authority as a halakhist to legislate his views and make them obligatory on all Jews. No attempt to interpret Judaism after Maimonides can ignore his legacy. Building on existing scholarship, I would like to propose a reading of Maimonides' writings that situates his views on human happiness in the context of the interplay between logos and mythos. So far I have used the word *mythos* to denote an interpretative story that constitutes social identity and legitimizes norms of conduct.[20] In Chapter Three I presented rabbinic Judaism as an elaborate mythos about God, the creator of the universe, who willingly entered an internal love affair with the Jewish people to whom He revealed the Torah. The rabbis embellished this covenantal myth in numerous midrashim and halakhic deliberations, from which they drew legal and practical implications for the way Jews must actually live.

Kenneth Seeskin summarized the consensus in modern scholarship when he said that Maimonides "demythologized" rabbinic Judaism.[21] For example, Maimonides depersonalized the Jewish conception of God, rejecting anthropomorphic and anthropopathic God-language and positing instead a negative theology of divine attributes. He identified the will of God with God's wisdom, limiting the freedom of God to that which God knows. He interpreted "creation in the image of God" to mean that the intellect is the essence of man and that rationality is the foundation of divine-human relations. He insisted that the goal of Jewish worship is the knowledge of God and that the love of God is commensurate with such knowledge. He presented prophecy as the zenith of a natural process of cognizing intelligibles and insisted that all true prophets are philosophers. He systematically explained the reasons for the commandments, highlighting their underlying rationality and accessibility to the human mind. Finally, he identified the perfection of the intellect with the ultimate end of human life and the sole cause of immortality.

I suggest that when Maimonides is said to "demythologize" Judaism, the term *myth* signifies non-rational or nonphilosophical aspects of Judaism. Maimonides attempted to explain away these aspects by transposing Jewish beliefs into philosophical parlance or by providing rational explanations for various Jewish practices. There is no doubt that he enhanced the intellectualization of rabbinic Judaism begun two centuries earlier. Yet he did not rid it of its mythic structure. Instead, he recast the rabbinic myth in a new logocentric version. By this I mean to say three things. First, Maimonides reinterpreted rabbinic Judaism to argue that Judaism is a revelation of philosophic truths whose knowledge leads to happiness. In his philosophic retelling, the sacred text of Judaism—the Torah—is a philosophic document; it teaches philosophic truths indirectly through narrative language.

Second, Maimonides himself introduced his re-reading of Judaism through narratives that he either constructed himself or adapted from existing sources. In so doing he followed the Muslim thinker ibn Sina, who taught philosophy by composing philosophical tales.[22] Third, in using the phrase "logocentric myth," I intend to indicate that Maimonides believed that the grasp of certain issues, such as the origin of the universe, are beyond human understanding. Truth about them cannot be proven through syllogisms. They can only be expressed through "likely stories," as Plato had already taught.

Maimonides' View of Myth

Like Plato, then, Maimonides employed narratives to convey abstract truths that exceed human reason. But like Aristotle, Maimonides did not believe that the narrative had to *mirror* reality. Instead, it only had to *correspond* to the way things are, as Aristotle understood "plot-structures." Maimonides' view of human well-being can be deciphered when we highlight the four "plot-structures" he employed. These narratives tell the story of the human species—that is, of human well-being, or happiness—from creation, through revelation, to redemption.

The first narrative concerns human origins and consists of a retelling of the biblical account of the Garden of Eden. As Maimonides tells it, the story is a philosophic parable that prescribes both how humans as a species ideally should act, and how they tend to act when they fall short of the ideal. The second narrative traces the development of human society, especially the move from paganism to monotheism. Reworking midrashic materials based on Genesis and Quranic materials about the Sabians, Maimonides depicts Abraham as a departure from the pagan environment of his day, thereby moving the human species one step higher in its pursuit of happiness. The third narrative focuses on the giving of the Torah to Moses at Sinai. The fourth, from the end of the *Guide*, is Maimonides' own invented parable about a royal palace. It teaches truths about the destiny of human life.[23]

As Leo Strauss has helped us to see, Maimonides wrote the *Guide* in a style and structure that mimic the Torah itself, as Maimonides understood it.[24] The Torah of Moses corresponds to the structure of reality, the nature of human beings, and the functions of language.[25] Maimonides believed, as I will argue, that the Torah of Moses contains the most perfect relationship between logos and mythos. In that perfect relationship, the linguistic veils of poetic speech, narratives, and laws adequately conceal deep philosophic truth. When the Torah "speaks in the language of human beings" (B.

Yebamot 71a; Baba Metzi'a 31b) it reveals the "golden apples" of philosophy by concealing them behind the "silver leaves" of figurative speech. Maimonides attempted to do the same when he conveyed his philosophic logos by wrapping it in his four "plot-structures."

That the Torah, according to Maimonides, teaches truth through narratives makes it very similar to ancient philosophy. Maimonides repeatedly reminds the reader that the "ancients"—notably, Plato and Aristotle—used metaphoric and parabolic speech to convey philosophic truths. The rabbis too, Maimonides claims, were enamored with parables and employed them to convey their deeply held beliefs.

Why did Maimonides believe that truth should be conveyed in that manner? Several modern scholars, such as L. Berman, A. Ivry, and J. Macy, follow the lead of Leo Strauss and provide a political answer to the question. They claim that Maimonides, like a long line of philosophers before and after him, concealed his philosophical outlook for fear of political persecution. This interpretation assumes that there is a conflict between philosophy and revealed religion. Whereas philosophy (or "Athens" for short) is rooted in natural human reasoning and relentlessly pursues the knowledge of universal truth, religion ("Jerusalem") is rooted in an authoritative, particularistic, received tradition.[26] Even though the received tradition may claim to be revealed by God, it is no more than a collection of accepted opinions that cannot be demonstrated philosophically. Since the masses lack philosophical competence, they are unable to grasp the teachings of the philosophers. To protect themselves from the hostility of the masses, the philosophers are compelled to conceal their true views through various means of rhetorical dissimulation. According to these scholars, Maimonides' resort to intentional obfuscation is the paradigm of such philosophic writing.

My view is otherwise. I suggest that Maimonides' esoteric style of writing, and especially his teaching philosophy through these elaborate "plot-structures," was not a conspiracy or a ploy to hide philosophy from the ignorant masses.[27] Rather, it was an attempt to place himself within the received tradition and in continuity with rabbinic esotericism.[28] At the same time, it was an expression of the underlying metaphysical principles to which Maimonides adhered.

MAIMONIDES' PHILOSOPHICAL ASSUMPTIONS[29]

Metaphysics: Matter and Form

Maimonides employs the two main categories of Aristotelian metaphysics to explain the structure of reality. All existents, except for God, exhibit the duality of matter and form. Matter is the substratum that has the capacity to become something, and form is that which makes a thing into what it is. While matter and form can be distinguished from each other conceptually, in reality they are inseparable. This is true first and foremost in the world known to us through the senses. In that world, things come to be and pass away. In the corporeal realm matter and form are both present as aspects of concrete particulars. Form determines *what* a thing is, namely, the essence of a thing, and matter specifies *that* a thing is, namely, its existence. The duality of matter and form thus parallels the duality of essence and existence.[30]

This duality applies as well to the higher level of the ontological order—namely, to the celestial sphere. Even though Maimonides believed that Aristotelian astronomy was flawed in its details,[31] he accepted wholeheartedly the cosmology of medieval Aristotelianism, whose basic premise was the distinction between the earthly and the celestial realms. The world as we know it from our senses is a world that literally is "under the moon," the last of the planets that revolve around a stationary earth. The sublunar world of physical sensual reality is dominated by the processes of coming-to-be ("generation" in Aristotle's language) and passing away ("corruption" in Aristotelian parlance). In the *Guide* III:8, Maimonides articulates the hylomorphic principle as follows: "All bodies subject to generation and corruption are attained by corruption only because of their matter; with regard to form and with respect to the latter's essence, they are not attained by corruption, but are permanent."[32] This is another way of restating Aristotle's view that universals do not exist *in* particulars and are not *separate from* them (as are Platonic forms). Matter is governed by form—or, better still, as Lenn Goodman put it, "Matter becomes articulate to the extent that it is governed by form.[33]

We recall that according to Aristotle's philosophy, the corporeal world is constantly subject to change, and the processes of change move toward the actualization of their end (*telos*). Thus for Aristotle and for Maimonides, change is not a random or spontaneous event, but a purposeful process determined by a particular privation, namely, lack or absence that determines the trajectory of every process of becoming. A particular lack determines how a particular substratum—i.e., the material cause—is transformed from potentiality to actuality by an agent that functions as the formal cause of change. Below we shall see how these metaphysical principles relate to the question of human well-being. For now we need only establish that in the corporeal world, according to Maimonides, everything is comprised of matter and form and a relative privation.

In continuation of the above-cited passage from the *Guide* III:8, Maimonides provides further information about matter:

> The nature and the true reality of matter are such that it never ceases to be joined to privation; hence no form remains constantly in it, for it perpetually puts off one form and puts on another.[34]

According to this definition, matter is, in principle, inherently unstable, because it is not a thing, or better still, not anything. To be something, matter requires form, which transforms it from potentiality to actuality. Maimonides already told us that in the sublunar world, matter, form, and privation are relative principles. A particular matter is actualized by a particular form because of a particular privation. If so, in the world as we know it, one can distinguish between different kinds of matter, depending on the specific privation that inheres in them. *The hierarchy of being emerges because matter assumes different degrees of corporeality.* Thus, some matter is more "base," i.e., corporeal than other matter, and, conversely, some matter is more capable of receiving form. Note that this is not an accurate reading of Aristotle, but a Neoplatonized version of Aristotle's metaphysics that Maimonides absorbed from his Muslim sources, especially from Avicenna.[35]

Physics: The Heavens and the Great Chain of Being

In the Aristotelian worldview metaphysics was closely related to physics. The interdependence of matter and form pervades all aspects of reality, with the exclusion of God, but it is exhibited very differently in the celestial spheres. Like all medieval Jewish philosophers, Maimonides subscribed to a certain picture of the universe, a certain cosmology that was a mixture of Aristotelian and Neoplatonic elements. It was a hierarchical world view in which everything occupied a "natural place," determined by the *telos* of the species, and all species were ranked hierarchically, from the least corporeal at the top of the hierarchy to the most corporeal at the bottom of the so-called Great Chain of Being.

In the hierarchy of beings there was a qualitative difference between the terrestrial world—composed of various mixtures of the four elements (i.e., air, fire, earth, and water)—and the celestial realm. The celestial bodies that constituted "the heavens," which were arranged as concentric spheres around the stationary earth, were themselves considered to be animate beings. Their "bodily" aspect was the spheres (*galgalim*), and their souls were rational intellects or intelligences (*sekhalim*), which functioned as the principle of motion of the spheres.

The intelligences came into being in a process of emanation from God, their first cause, and the process was understood in cognitive terms. The first intelligence was the product of God's thinking, but as a thought conscious of itself it gave rise to a second intelligence—one that thinks both itself and its cause.

Whether God is the First Intellect or rather an intellect that stands beyond the series of emanated intellects was hotly debated in medieval Aristotelian cosmology.[36] Maimonides (following ibn Sina) wished to protect the transcendence of God, and made a qualitative distinction between God and the first intellect. God's existence is unlike anything else, because God exists necessarily and in God there is no distinction between essence and existence. In all other beings, including the emanated intellects, existence is superadded to essence.[37] However, there were other medieval Aristotelians, notably ibn Rushd, who wished to remain closer to the assumptions of Aristotle's philosophy, where God is the first intelligence precisely because God is the first cause. As such God is the ultimate cause of all things, indeed the *telos* of all existents, both individually and collectively. However, according to ibn Rushd, God does not transcend the cosmos that emanates from Him.

Regardless of the debate about the first intelligence, Maimonides and the Jewish Aristotelians who followed him agreed that there was a total of ten intelligences, one responsible for the motion of the sphere of the "fixed stars," seven others for the corresponding seven known planets, and the last for the motion of the terrestrial, corporeal world. This intelligence was referred to as the Active Intellect, indicating that it functioned, in the final analysis, as the efficient cause of processes in the sub-lunar world.

The Active Intellect and the nine intellects "above" it were regarded by Maimonides as "pure forms," namely, forms devoid of matter. Thus, the medieval Aristotelians retained the Platonic legacy. That is to say, even though in the corporeal, terrestrial world there were no disembodied forms, they did exist as the sources of motion in the translunar world. This entire philosophical-scientific explanation was said to be in full accord with the Jewish tradition. What the philosophers call "separate intelligences," the Jewish tradition calls "angels," and the tenth intelligence that is in charge of the sublunar world is the angel known as "Ishim" in rabbinic writings.

Psychology: The Human Being as Composition of Body and Soul

Maimonides tells us that humans also must have material and formal aspects. The duality of matter and form is crucial to Maimonides' conception of human happiness because it means that human well-being must pertain both to the material aspect of the human species—the body—and to its formal aspect—the soul. In the *Guide* III: 8 Maimonides applies the metaphysics of matter and form to human beings in the following manner:

> Similarly every living being dies and becomes ill solely because of its matter and not because of its form. All man's acts of disobedience and sins are consequent upon his matter and not upon his form, whereas all his virtues are consequent upon his form. For example, man's apprehension of his creator, his mental representation of every intelligible, his control of his desire and anger and all bad habits found in him, are all of them consequent upon his matter. Inasmuch as it is so, and according to what has been laid down by divine wisdom, it is impossible for matter to exist without form and for any of the forms in question to exist without matter, and as consequently it was necessary that man's very noble form, which we have explained is the *image of God and His likeness*, should be bound to earthy, turbid and dark matter, which calls down upon man every imperfection and corruption" (Pines ed., p. 431).

Relevant to our interest in the underlying Aristotelian assumptions of Maimonides' ethics, we learn three important things from this passage. First, human beings are to be distinguished from all other animals by virtue of their form. Second, the form of the human species is the rational capacity of the human soul, namely, the intellect. Third, the intellect is what makes us in some way similar to God. The Torah expresses that similarity by stating (Gen 1:26) that God created humans in the divine image (*tzelem elohim*).

How does the "divine image," the intellect, relate to the other aspects of a human being? If the intellect constitutes the essence of a human being, how does the intellect relate to other aspects or functions of the soul? More importantly, how does the intellect relate to the human body? Does the intellect require the body for its own perfection, or is it totally independent?

The crux of Maimonides' view of human happiness revolves around his understanding of human rationality. To convey his truth-claims about human rationality, and thereby to lay the foundation for his understanding of human well-being, he turned to the Genesis narrative of the Garden of Eden, the first of his four "plot-structures" about the human species and its appropriate well-being.

HUMAN NATURE AND THE ORIGINS OF HUMANITY

The Human Intellect: The Form of the Human Species

Like Aristotle, Maimonides thought about human happiness in terms of the well-being, or proper functioning, of the species as a whole. Maimonides also agreed with the philosophic tradition that claimed that the capacity to reason is what distinguishes human beings from other animals. These commitments informed Maimonides' reading of the Garden of Eden narrative as a parable that should be understood both prescriptively and descriptively. The story teaches how God intended us to be by describing the human form. Additionally, it indicates how actual human beings tend to behave and why they fail to realize the form of their species. It thus speaks about how human beings should be, as God so intended them, and how they in fact fail to follow God's intention. Hence, Maimonides' reading of the biblical narrative is yet one more source of ambiguity.

Maimonides frames his retelling of the narrative as an answer to a question concerning some of its contradictions,[38] all of which he resolves by focusing on the meaning of the expression "divine image" (*tzelem elohim*). The apparent difficulties arise because of a misunderstanding of the term "image" (*tzelem*), which refers not to physical shape but to the "natural form" of a thing, "in virtue of which a thing is constituted as a substance and becomes what it is" (*Guide* I:1, Pines ed., p. 22). If the natural form of a human being is the intellect, then the biblical statement that God created man "in the divine image" means not that human beings are physically shaped like God but that they possess intellectual apprehension that makes them *in some way* similar to God. An additional problem arises from the equivocal nature of the term *elohim* in the Torah.

By associating humanity with rationality Maimonides clearly places himself within a philosophical tradition that goes back to the ancient Greeks. However, the information Maimonides provides about the status of human intellect is by no means simple or straightforward. In the *Book of Knowledge* of the *Mishneh Torah*, Yesodey ha-Torah 4:8, he combines the philosophic and religious understandings of the soul. He states that "the vital principle of all flesh is the form which God has given it." At the end of the passage Maimonides says that the Hebrew terms for the form of the human species are *nefesh* and *ru'aḥ*, but when he goes on to characterize the form of the human species, it becomes evident that only the rational function of the soul—the intellect—is the specific form. It is the intellect that makes human beings distinct from all other animals and in some way related to God. He says:

> The superior intelligence in the human soul is the specific form of the mentally normal human being. To this form, the Torah refers in the text "Let us make man in our image, after our likeness" (Gen. 1:26). This means that man *should* have a form that knows and apprehends idealistic beings that are devoid of matter, such as the angels which are forms without substance or that (intellectually) man is like the angels" (Yesodei Ha-Torah 4:8).[39]

The word "should" in the above passage is crucial to my reading of Maimonides. The form that constitutes us as distinct beings spells out the *end* toward which we must aspire if we are to be fully human. The actualization of the human form involves the apprehension and contemplation of the intelligences devoid of matter (and therefore are known in medieval cosmology as "separate intelligences"). This is the highest level of human intellectual development, which as such serves as the goal or ultimate purpose of human life. When this form is attained, the human intellect is no longer dependent upon the body, and thus can survive its death. Hence the human intellect can become immortal when it contemplates necessary abstract truths.

Maimonides makes the connection between intellectual perfection and immortality in the following passage (Yesodei Ha-Torah 4:9):

> This form of the soul is not compounded of elements into which it would again dissolve.... But it comes directly from God in heaven. Hence when the material portion of our being dissolves into its component elements, and physical life perishes—since that only exists in association with the body and needs the body for its functions—this form of the soul is not destroyed, as it does not require physical life for its activities. It knows and apprehends the intelligences that exist without material substance; it knows the creator of all things, and it endures forever.[40]

Here Maimonides teaches that immortality is possible when the human intellect reaches a certain level of perfection. What makes the language difficult is that the final perfection is presented as something that comes "directly from God" rather than something that is achieved through human effort. Whether the highest form of knowledge comes from God or from man will continue to concern the interpreters of Maimonides for centuries. Those who wish to read him as a traditionalist will emphasize the move "from the top down," so to speak, and those who read him as a naturalist philosopher will highlight the efforts of the human intellect. In any case, all interpreters agree that Maimonides identifies the well-being of the human species with the perfection of the human intellect.

The Human Capacity to Know: The Material Intellect

According to Maimonides' metaphysical principle, matter and form are interdependent. If so, we still need to learn precisely how the human intellect, the rational faculty of the soul, relates to the other functions of the soul.

In Maimonides' day there were basically two approaches to the question of the relationship between body and soul. Plato's position was that the soul is itself a separate substance whose existence is independent of the body even though the soul requires the body for its operation. At death the soul and the body separate, and the soul returns to its pre-existent state of being. Aristotle, who denied the two-substance theory, viewed the soul as the life force of the body, so that death means the end of both participants in the composition, soul and body. However, Aristotle re-introduced the Platonic view in his ambiguous teachings linking the intellect's attainment of human knowledge to immortality.

The Hellenistic commentators on Aristotle's writings, who regarded him as a follower of Plato, continued to struggle with this problem. Alexander of Aphrodisias, mentioned in Chapter Four, held that the intellect is but a *disposition* to cognize intelligibles and that what survives death is only the actualized intellect. By contrast, Themistius, another Hellenistic commentator mentioned in Chapter Four, interpreted Aristotle along Platonic lines, viewing the intellect as a separate substance.[41] Viewed from a religious perspective, which asserts the immortality of the individual soul, the position of Alexander is more problematic than the position of Themistius.

Of the medieval Muslim philosophers, al-Farabi and ibn Bajja were closer to Alexander's view, whereas ibn Sina adopted the view of Themistius. Thus much of the debate during the late Middle Ages about Maimonides' views on happiness and their implications for Judaism hinged on judging whether Maimonides followed Alexander or Themistius. Since Maimonides' language is so richly ambiguous, it was possible to argue both ways.

I concur with Herbert Davidson, who has shown that Maimonides endorsed the view of ibn Bajja when he defined the human rational faculty as "a power in a body."[42] The term "power" is understood as a disposition or capacity to become something. That capacity is actualized during the process of thinking. Since in Aristotelian metaphysics a capacity to be something is characteristic of matter, it is appropriate that Maimonides calls the disposition to know "the material intellect" or "hylic intellect" (*hyle* means matter in Greek). Like Alexander of Aphrodisias, then, Maimonides thought that the rational human soul is created as a "disposition" in the human organism, "inseparable from its body," although, as Herbert Davidson put it, "it is not inseparable in the sense of being distributed through the human body."[43]

At birth, then, the human intellect is no more than a capacity to know; the process of learning actualizes that capacity, transforming it from potentiality to actuality. When learning takes place, however, the intellect is no longer just a disposition to know; it also is a "store house" of bits of knowledge. The human intellect, Maimonides says, in accord with Aristotle, actually possesses within itself the intelligible concepts it comes to know. When we actually think about what we know, the human intellect is a unity of knower, known, and the act of knowing. The original state of the intellect is called a "potential intellect," the achieved final state an "acquired intellect," and the intermediate state when the intellect is in the process of realizing knowledge is called an "actual human intellect."[44]

In Aristotelian metaphysics the transformation of anything from potentiality to actuality requires an agent that functions as a cause. In Aristotelian philosophy something can act as an agent of change only if it already possesses the relevant characteristics in actuality. In other words, only what already is actual can move something else from potentiality to actuality. Following the Muslim interpreters of Aristotle, Maimonides would say that the efficient cause of human intellection is another intellect. More specifically, it is the intellect or intelligence that governs all processes of change in the terrestrial world, which he calls the "Active Intellect" (*ha-sekhel ha-po`el*). It is at this level that Maimonides' Aristotelian cosmology, introduced above, becomes relevant to his theory of knowledge.

The Active Intellect

The Active Intellect, the lowest in the chain of intelligences, is the cause of human knowledge. Like a lamp that sheds light and makes physical things visible, so the Active Intellect makes things accessible to the human intellect. As an intelligence separate from corporeal matter, the Active Intellect is engaged in thinking, and the objects of its thinking are the laws that govern the processes in the terrestrial world.[45] Because the Active Intellect is itself actualized thought, it can bring about the transformation of the human intellect from potentiality to actuality. In this manner, the Active Intellect acts as the efficient cause of the actual human intellect. According to Aristotle's theory of knowledge, when the intellect thinks, the subject, the object, and the act of thinking become one and the same. For the Active Intellect this is true all the time, but for the human intellect this is true, according to medieval Aristotelians, only when it "unites" or "conjoins" with the Active Intellect. The Active Intellect is thus both the agent of human knowledge and the goal toward which the human intellect strives. When the human intellect achieves unity with the Active Intellect, the human intellect will know all that can be known about the terrestrial world.

All medieval Jewish and Muslim Aristotelians thought about human knowledge within these cosmological categories. The Christian Aristotelians, however, advanced a different reading of Aristotle. For them the "active intellect" was an internal function of the human intellect and not an external entity. In Chapter Eight we will see how these differing views played a role in the Jewish-Christian confrontation concerning the meaning of happiness. The Active Intellect matters because for Jewish and Muslim Aristotelianism it was another way of talking about the laws that govern the corporeal world. To speak about Active Intellect in the Middle Ages is like speaking about Wisdom (or Sophia) in the ancient world.

According to Maimonides, a person obtains intelligible thoughts through "conjunction (*ittisal; hidabbeq*) with the divine [Active] Intellect, which emanates upon him and from which the form [the intelligible] thought comes into existence."[46] The word "emanate" indicates that Maimonides operated within the metaphysical and cosmological parameters of medieval Neoplatonized Aristotelianism. By applying the term to the acquisition of knowledge, Maimonides indicated that knowledge is a process that proceeds in two directions, from the bottom up and from the top down. From the "bottom up" the acquisition of knowledge involves the extraction of intelligible universals from data gathered by the senses. In this direction the human disposition to know is actualized and the human intellect is engaged in thinking. The highest type of cognitive activity occurs when the human intellect becomes one with the Active Intellect and exercises thinking on the most abstract level. At that point the human intellect is like a "vessel" that receives an overflow, which emanates from "above"—that is, from the Active Intellect. The more refined the human intellect is, i.e., the more independent it is from corporeality, the more it can receive the "overflow" from the Active Intellect.[47]

Since the Active Intellect consists of the formal principles that govern all processes in the terrestrial world, the highest form of knowledge for humans is to know what the Active Intellect knows. What prevents human beings from uniting with the Active Intellect is their corporeal body. The body and the bodily-dependent functions (nutrition, sensation, desire, and imagination) serve as obstacles to the conjunction with the Active Intellect. The more one can overcome corporeal embodiment, the more one can actualize the potential of the human intellect to conjoin with the Active Intellect. The process of acquiring knowledge is one in which the potential to know is actualized. In it the "potential intellect" or "material intellect" becomes an "acquired intellect." Since for Maimonides the human intellect is initially no more than a disposition to know, the process of actualizing also is the process through which the disposition becomes a substance (*etzem*). Much of the debate over Maimonides' words in the three centuries after his death revolved around this point. To what extent does the actualization of the disposition to know constitute a new substance?

The Acquired Intellect

Maimonides was ambiguous about the status of the human intellect. On the one hand he held that, unlike the "potential intellect," the "acquired intellect" is "not a power in a body," but rather is "completely separate from the body and emanates upon it." If so, it appears that the cognizing intellect has an identity of its own, and its life is independent of the body in which it functions. On the other hand, Maimonides also states that there is a nexus between the intellect and the body, such that the intellect relates to an individual person as "God is [related] to the world."[48] This is a highly opaque statement. The relationship between God and the world is one of the most problematic issues in Maimonides' legacy. Critical to solving the problem is a determination of the status of the "acquired intellect."

In several places in Maimonides' writings it seems that the "acquired intellect" is an incorporeal substance that exists independently of the human body. In the *Mishneh Torah*, for example, he equates the advanced stage of human intellection with "final perfection" and states:

> Of this form [the acquired intellect] it is said in the Law: "Let us make man in our image, after our likeness." That is to say, he should have a form which knows and apprehends the intellect devoid of matter, like the angels, which are form devoid of matter, and that he should come to resemble them.[49]

The state of "final perfection" is attained when one "knows everything a man can know about all existent things." Maimonides understands this final perfection to be a conjunction of the human intellect with a semi-divine Active Intellect, and describes the intellectually perfect man as follows:

> His mind is always faced upward, bound beneath the [celestial] throne, to understand the holy pure forms and to behold the Wisdom of the Holy One, blessed be He, in its entirety, from the first form until the center of the earth, and knowing from them His greatness; at once, the Holy Spirit rests upon him, and his soul commingles with the rank of the angels called *Ishim* [viz. the Active Intellect] and he is turned into another man [*ish aḥer*] and he understands in his mind that he is not as he was but that he has risen above the rank of the remainder of the wise man, as it is said of Saul, "And thou shalt prophesy with them, and shalt be turned into another man" [I Sam. 10:6].[50]

We now learn that the highest form of human cognitive activity is prophecy.[51] Prophecy is an "overflow" from the Active Intellect onto the human intellect that is prepared to receive it. Because the prophet conjoins with the Active Intellect and attains knowledge of abstract laws that govern the terrestrial universe, he is the wise man whose intellect reaches perfection. The more perfect a person is intellectually, the more he is able to receive the overflow and become a prophet. Indeed, prophets differ among themselves in their degree of dependence on the body. The most superior prophet-philosopher is the one who is least dependent on his bodily functions, such as the prophet Moses. Since Maimonides declares the intellect (the rational function of the soul) to be the form of the human species, it follows that the well-being of the human species is to be identified with the act of thinking in which abstract, necessary truths are themselves objects of thought. This statement indicates that the ultimate end of human life is the act of contemplation in which the intellect thinks about the principles of reality—i.e., the thinker contemplates metaphysics.

Accordingly, Maimonides will portray the ultimate end of human life as the activity of contemplation. Moreover, he links this act, which he posited as the highest perfection of human life, with the attainment of immortality. Contemplation of necessary truths is declared to be "in true reality the ultimate end; this is what gives the individual true perfection, a perfection belonging to him alone; and it gives him permanent perdurance, through it man is man."[52] The "final perfection" attained through intellectual activity is the "sole cause" of human immortality.[53] To be fully perfect, the human intellect must transcend the feature that makes it human, namely, its association with the body. By cognizing the intelligible order of reality, the human rational potential is both actualized and substantialized. The perfected intellect—the "acquired intellect"—is a substance separable from the body, as Aristotle hinted in *De Anima* III:5.

Knowing God and Imitating God

Maimonides' understanding of the human intellect seems to suggest that he adopted the "intellectualist" or "exclusive" interpretation of Aristotle on human happiness. Only when we engage in contemplation of eternal truth do we become one with the form of the human species, i.e., with the universal "man." Maimonides' view on whether mankind in principle can have metaphysical knowledge should be understood against the background of his ontology, cosmology, and epistemology.

Maimonides (like ibn Sina) was adamant that human beings, who are contingent, can never know the essence of God, the necessary being. As a simple unity whose essence is identical with His existence, God transcends the limits of human knowledge. We can only know *that* God exists, but not *how* God exists. The ontological gap between the created and the creator can never be bridged—not even by the prophet Moses, whom Maimonides called "the master of all wise men."[54]

What else we can know is limited to how God governs the terrestrial world. This is, according to Maimonides, what the Torah means when it speaks in Exodus 23:19 about revealing to Moses the "ways" (*derakhim*), but refusing to reveal God's "face" (*panim*). According to Maimonides, the "ways" are the eternal forms of things, the patterns of all things, which the philosophers call Active Intellect.[55] So although humans cannot know

God's essence, they can comprehend God's "ways" when their own intellect unites with the Active Intellect that governs the sublunar world.

The knowledge of God's "ways" is accessible (in principle) to humans. Though this knowledge is in and of itself theoretical, it pertains to what God *does*. These are God's attributes of action that pertain not to the essence of God but to God's operation in the world. However, Maimonides' analysis of God's attributes of action is itself ambiguous. On the one hand, the actions of God are to be learned from the way the natural world operates. On the other hand, when the Torah refers to God's attributes of action, it uses terms that pertain not just to nature but to the moral sphere. The prophet Jeremiah speaks specifically about God's "lovingkindness, justice, and righteousness," all of which are moral attributes that human beings are called to imitate.[56] Now it appears that Maimonides identifies human perfection not with the possession of abstract, theoretical knowledge, but rather with *action*, as the Torah itself prescribes when it enjoins humans "to walk in God's ways."[57] If so, Maimonides' endorsement of the "exclusive" reading of Aristotle's *eudaimonia* is less clear than previously presented. The emphasis on other-directed action as the sphere for human flourishing (action that Maimonides analyzes and codifies in his halakhic works), appears to support the "inclusive" reading of Aristotle's view on human happiness.

I contend that Maimonides does not hopelessly contradict himself. He presents the one case in which the tension between contemplation and action is resolved. That case is Judaism, a philosophical-legal system rooted in the divine Law, the Torah of Moses, both Written and Oral. In the case of Judaism, the intellectual life of contemplation and the moral life of action coincide to yield the best livable life as well as the approximation of the human ideal. Maimonides makes his case for Judaism in the *Mishneh Torah*, where he provides what he considers to be empirical data about the Torah of Moses. He presents his case dogmatically in the *Commentary on the Mishnah* in the Introduction to Sanhedrin Chapter Ten by articulating Thirteen Principles that assert the superiority of the Mosaic Torah, and he does so rhetorically by constructing the four myths or "plot-structures" to convey truths about the human condition. His interpretation of the Garden of Eden narrative presents truths about what humans beings *should be* as well as how they normally *are*.

THE GARDEN OF EDEN: TWO MODES OF HUMAN EXISTENCE

"Adam": Species Descent from Theoretical to Practical Wisdom

Maimonides believes that human happiness means living in accord with the form of the human species. But given his philosophical assumptions, forms do not exist separate from matter. In reality human beings exist as a composition of matter and form. What follows from it? Maimonides' view has to be discerned from the way he interpreted the meaning of *Adam*, the first human being in the biblical Garden of Eden narrative, which is explained to the perplexed reader thus:

> For the intellect that God made overflow unto man and that is the latter's ultimate perfection, was that which *Adam* had been provided with before he disobeyed. It was because of this that it was said of him that he was created *in the image of God and in his likeness*. It was likewise on account of it that he was addressed by God and given commandments, as it says: *And the Lord God commanded, and so on.* For commandments are not given to beasts and beings devoid of intellect. Through the intellect one distinguishes between truth and falsehood, and that was found in [*Adam*] in its perfection and integrity. Fine and bad on the other hand, belong to the things generally accepted as known, not to those cognized by the intellect. . . . Similarly one expresses in our language the notions of truth and falsehood by means of the terms *emeth* and *sheqer*, and those of fine and bad by means of the terms *tov* and *ra*. Now man in virtue of his intellect knows truth from falsehood; and this holds good for all intelligible things. Accordingly when man was in his most perfect and excellent state, in accordance with his inborn disposition and possessed of his intellectual cognitions—because of which it is said of him: *Thou hast made him but little lower than Elohim*—he had no faculty that was engaged in any way in the consideration of generally accepted things, and he did not apprehend them. So among these generally accepted things even that which is most manifestly bad, namely, uncovering the genitals, was not bad according to him, and he did not apprehend that it was bad. However, when he disobeyed and inclined toward his desires of the imagination and the pleasures of his corporeal senses—inasmuch as it is said: *that the tree was good for food and that it was a delight to the eyes*—he was punished by being deprived of that intellectual apprehension. He therefore disobeyed the commandment that was imposed upon him on account of his intellect and becoming endowed with the faculty of apprehending generally accepted things, he became absorbed in judging things to be bad or fine. Then he knew how great his loss was, what he had been deprived of, and upon what a state he had entered.[58]

In this reading, the Garden of Eden talks about the human condition from two perspectives: the theoretical and the practical. Initially, that is, prior to the sinful act of disobeying God, *Adam* was engaged in pure cognitive activity, making distinctions between what is true and what is false. Because a reasoning capacity entails an ability to choose, the Torah states that *Adam* was commanded by God and exercised choice when he disobeyed God's command. Maimonides understands the sin of disobedience to be an epistemic shift from the knowledge of truth and falsehood to knowledge of good and evil, which in Aristotelian terms is a shift from *theoretical* to *practical* knowledge.[59] Whereas the latter concerns deliberations about doing something for the sake of something else, the former concerns knowledge for its own sake. Prior to the sin, *Adam* was preoccupied with pure thinking, the activity that constitutes the formal end of the human species. After the sin, *Adam* was engaged in practical reasoning that involves actions toward other persons in the social sphere.

How are we to understand the connection between these two modes of being? If read as a philosophical tale, the biblical narrative proposes both a prescription for the human condition—namely, the human ideal—as well as a description of how human beings in fact conduct themselves in the terrestrial world. On this reading, both the proper name *Adam* and the noun *Ish* (man) stand for the human species. Accordingly, prior to the sin *Adam* is the human ideal, whereas the post-lapsarian *Adam* stands for the actual condition of humans. The ideal is a-temporal; it denotes a state of existence that real human beings should aspire to attain so as to be truly human. Whether or not they pursue the ideal is a matter of choice, the same kind of choice that *Adam* had in the biblical narrative. Exercising choice is a feature of rationality.

But how are we to explain a bad choice? In the language of the biblical narrative, why did *Adam* sin? Maimonides' answer is provided in terms of the relationship between matter and form. Because matter is irrational, all sins can be ascribed to the material aspect of persons, namely, to their body or their various bodily aspects that are non-rational. The biblical narrative expresses this point when it discusses the relationship between *Adam* and *Eve*. The gender distinction between "male" and "female" in the Bible, according to Maimonides, is but a parabolic way to convey the metaphysical difference between form and matter respectively.[60] In this regard the Bible did precisely as did "Plato and his predecessors [who] designated matter as the female and form as the male."[61] Thus when the biblical narrative speaks about the creation of the first human being as a unity of "male" and "female," it teaches that we are a composition of matter and form. The material aspect of the human being is the body and the formal aspect is the soul, or more precisely, the rational faculty of the soul, the intellect.[62]

For Maimonides the actual relationship between matter and form is riddled with conflict and tension. Our material aspect, the human body, is the source of passions, desires, and emotions that cause us to sin by pursuing the wrong ends and pulling away from contemplation of necessary truth that leads to God. The body is not only an obstacle in the attainment of human perfection in this world; it is also a hindrance in the attainment of immortal life, since immortality is predicated on knowledge of eternal truth. The body must die, since it is a material entity that is subject to the laws that govern all growth and decay. It is only the rational power of the soul, the intellect, that can survive the death of the body, provided that one has devoted one's life to the acquisition of knowledge. If, by contrast, one devotes life solely to the satisfying of bodily needs and desires, one will fail to actualize the intellect, and will surely die. This is the meaning of the Garden of Eden story in which *Adam* lost life eternal when he listened to *Eve* and disobeyed God.

In Maimonides' first "plot-structure," then, he absorbed Aristotle's teleological metaphysics, but ascribed it to a wise Creator rather than to "nature." Accordingly he interpreted the biblical narrative both as an explanatory *description* of why things are the way they are, and as a *prescription* of what men must do in order to attain God's original intent for the human species. Put differently, the narrative in the opening chapters of Genesis explains why human beings tend to behave as they do and specifies how they should behave. *Adam* prior to sin represents the human ideal, a being preoccupied with the contemplation of abstract truths, because his intellect, the form of the human species, rules over the material body. The sin of Adam reflects the choice that most people in fact make. Instead of devoting their lives to contemplative activity, they are focused on moral action, which is based on knowledge of what is "good" and "evil," rather than on knowledge of what is "true" and "false."

THE EVOLUTION OF HUMAN SOCIETY

The Socio-Political Nature of Mankind

Adam prior to the sin stands for the human ideal; it is the post-lapsarian *Adam* that represents the human species as we know it in time-space.[63] Furthermore, according to Maimonides, this human species has evolved over time from holding mistaken views about reality to grasping a more correct understanding of it. Maimonides relates the evolution of the human species in his reconstruction of the myth of the Sabians.

In the *Guide* II: 40 Maimonides explains the political nature of humanity by appealing to diversity He recapitulates the views of Plato and Aristotle that human beings live in organized societies and that they are not self-sufficient. They need others in order to survive and, with the use of thought and foresight, they can accomplish what is needed for self-preservation. Since the use of tools requires specialized skills, human beings also must divide themselves into specialized groups, each group mastering different skills. These divisions in turn promote conflicting interests, which leads to the further institution of laws by which to resolve these differences in a peaceful, constructive way. Human beings therefore are not only social animals by nature: they are also political, for without laws no human society can endure.

People also differ from one another in temperament and aptitude—essential differences whose ultimate source is matter. In any social context these natural differences will promote conflict in which natural human tendencies, such as anger and cruelty, will be realized. By definition no human society can be perfect, because human beings are corporeal beings who can easily be ruled by desire. For human beings to live peaceably with each other, society requires a

> ruler who gauges the actions of the individuals, perfecting that which is deficient and reducing that which is excessive, and who prescribes actions and moral habits that all of them must always practice in the same way, so that the natural diversity is hidden through the multiple points of conventional accord and so that the community becomes well ordered.[64]

In other words, a rule of law imposed by a just ruler is necessary for the proper functioning of society.

What kind of law should that be? One that is conducive to the attainment of the ultimate end of the human species is best. And for Maimonides, such law is divine. In the *Guide* III:27 he defines it exactly: a law is divine if it perfects both the bodies of human beings and their souls. The well-being or perfection of the body, according to Maimonides, is regulated by law in both negative and positive ways:

> This is achieved through two things. One of them is the abolition of the wrong doing toward each other . . . The second thing consists of

the acquisition by every human individual of moral qualities that are useful for life in society so that the affairs of the city may be ordered.[65]

A law that secures the well-being of the body is a law that, by placing limitations on human action, forbids people to harm each other and forces them to curb their desires (especially the desire for power). In addition to negative prescriptions, a law that secures the well-being of the body also prescribes the moral virtues that human beings must acquire through habitual practice. The moral virtues can be acquired when moral agents practice the mean between excesses.

The well-being (or "welfare" in Pines' translation) of the body (*tiqqun ha-guf*) is but the basis for the well-being (or welfare) of the soul (*tiqqun ha-nefesh*). The latter is attained only through the "procuring [of] correct opinions," by means of learning (Pines ed., p. 510). In other words, the well-being of the soul can be attained only when we know truth, thereby actualizing the human rational potential and making the intellect "rational in *actu*" (Pines ed. p. 511). The "ultimate perfection" of the soul, i.e., its most excellent functioning, is "knowing everything concerning all the beings that is within the capacity of man to know." This is the intellectual perfection that is the "only cause of permanent preservation" (ibid.).[66]

The precise relationship between the well-being of the body and the well-being of the soul was yet another source of debate among the interpreters of Maimonides' writings. Maimonides' perplexing discussion of human perfection contributed to the difficulty of interpreting his views. In *Guide* III: 27, for example, Maimonides posits the perfection of the body as prior to perfection of the soul "in nature and in time." By that he means that concerns for health, security, and self-preservation are pre-requisites to acquisition of knowledge; if one has to worry all the time about food and shelter, one has no energy left for the thinking and reflection that lead to the well-being of the soul. That does not mean that one has to be wealthy in order to live well. While he rejects asceticism,[67] Maimonides does highlight the value of finding contentment with little food, the minimum necessary for the health of the body.[68] A healthy body can be the foundation of a healthy soul—that is, a soul that possesses those true views of reality that constitute its perfection and well-being.

But the pursuit of the well-being of the soul is itself a process that culminates in the "final perfection." We already noted that final perfection "consists in his knowing everything concerning all the beings that it is within the capacity of a man to know in accordance with his ultimate perfection."[69]

This is, indeed, a highly opaque, and perhaps even a circular, statement. While Maimonides posits the knowledge of "everything concerning all the beings" as the ultimate knowledge to which we should aspire, he also reminds us that, by virtue of being human, our knowledge of reality in its totality is, by nature, limited.[70]

In the *Guide* I: 34 Maimonides severely limits this kind of knowledge to a very small class of individuals. While all human beings are born with the potential to know, this ability varies among individuals because of their material make-up (i.e., the particular mixture of elements). We are not by nature equal; only those who are able to grasp abstract, necessary truths can realize the well-being of the soul. Moreover, the possession of abstract knowledge is extremely arduous, requiring considerable investment of both time and effort. Only the most dedicated and devoted among those who are naturally inclined to possess abstract knowledge can in fact attain it. Most importantly, to attain theoretical knowledge an individual must possess the moral virtues, which, in turn, requires an individual to live in a society governed by good laws. As we have noted, the properly ordered society is that one whose laws express truths and whose practices ensure that humans will flourish in accordance with the *telos* of the human species. Regimes whose laws can be shown to be morally corrupt or based on falsehoods cannot direct the members of the body politic toward the attainment of human well-being. In short, the two dimensions of human well-being—the well-being of the soul and the well-being of the body—are closely intertwined. Human well-being cannot be considered outside the social and political context in which people find themselves, since no one can live alone and survive, let alone, thrive. Human flourishing requires a society that is rooted in a divine law.

Maimonides argued that only one such law in fact exists—the Torah of Moses. That Law was given to Israel because it reached a higher stage of human development than any other nation. Israel departed from the false opinions of the pagan world, which posited a plurality of corporeal deities, and came to the recognition of a more correct opinion: there is only one God and that God is qualitatively different from any other existent. Maimonides' argument about the divinity of the Torah of Moses, which is its intrinsic perfection, follows from his reconstruction of the evolution of the human species.

A legal system is good or bad depending on whether or not those who frame it and/or interpret it know what is true and how to distinguish it from what is false. The value of a legal system also depends on whether the laws in question prepare one or prevent one from attaining knowledge of the truth as opposed to falsehood. Maimonides believed that because human beings possess rationality, they can determine which laws are true and which false. A legal system rooted in mistaken beliefs about the cosmic order and the place of mankind in it cannot secure the well-being of body and soul. This is Maimonides' basic argument against pagan societies. Their members hold mistaken beliefs about reality that prevent them from achieving human well-being because ultimate perfection consists in knowledge of truth. To attain human perfection, paganism therefore has to be eradicated and replaced with a truer worldview—monotheism. Maimonides creatively and imaginatively reconstructs the evolution of the human species as a transformation in human consciousness from paganism to monotheism. Thus his "plot-structure" focuses on the ancient nation of the Sabians and the departure of Abraham, the father of the Jewish nation, from the paganism that was then prevalent.[71]

From Paganism to Monotheism: The Sabians

From our perspective Maimonides' retelling of the story of the Sabians is itself a construction of a historical fiction according to which the history of Israel is part of a cosmic history that narrates the gradual evolution from polytheism to monotheism. For Maimonides, however, the story was part of a philosophic exposition of how humanity evolved from mythos to logos. While formally it is not a parable with inner and outer meanings, it still is a story that teaches philosophic truths. The raw material for the narrative came from various literary Arabic sources—primarily the Quran, Islamic heresiology, and universal histories that Maimonides transformed.[72]

Maimonides depicts the Sabians as the dominant religion in the time of the biblical ancestors of Israel. They are portrayed as the archetypes of idolatry, engaged in magical conjuring of celestial bodies, astrology, orgiastic cults, reverence for blood, and sacrifice of children. In addition to these pernicious practices, the Sabians are alleged to have endorsed a fundamental error about the structure of the universe—viz., "they believed in the eternity of the world, since in their opinion heaven is the deity."[73]

Why did Maimonides choose the Sabians as the archetype of polytheism? I suspect that it is a veiled polemic against the Quran.[74] In his attempt to distinguish sharply between Judaism and all other religions, Maimonides represents the Sabians in a negative light, and insists that the religion of Israel was a rebellion against and a departure from Sabian practices and beliefs on behalf of monotheism, the belief in the existence of a transcendent God who willfully created the universe.[75]

The hero of Maimonides' "plot-structure" is Abraham, "the pillar of the world," who marks the shift from polytheism to monotheism in human history, a shift that facilitates true human happiness. Abraham is portrayed as the pivotal figure in the fight against idolatry, both ritually and doctrinally.[76] The struggle against idolatry has shaped the history of the Jewish people, a history that Maimonides reconstructs for his readers on the basis of a creative misreading of biblical, aggadic, and Arabic sources.

The purpose of Maimonides' own version of universal history is to show that the nation of Israel is a nation of philosophers, that philosophy is genuinely Jewish, and that the study of philosophy is the only path to human perfection. Reframing the myth of the chosen people, Maimonides presents the Jewish nation as a

> community that is full of knowledge and is perfect as He, may He be exalted, has made clear through the intermediary of the Master who made us perfect saying: *Surely, this great community is a wise and understanding people* [Deut. 4:6].[77]

In other words, Maimonides insisted that philosophy, which ultimately originated with pre-Lapsarian Adam, flourished among the ancestors of the Children of Israel, notably Abraham, was fostered by Moses and the Law, and even reached a high point among the ancient Israelites with Solomon. It declined, however, during the exile when Jews took on the ignorant opinions of the nations among whom they dwelled.[78] Moreover, the Jews' poor material conditions made it difficult for them to cultivate philosophy, since form requires the presence of appropriate material conditions. Maimonides' literary endeavor, then, was intended to reverse this situation. His code of Jewish Law projects the kind of ideal social order he felt was necessary for the cultivation of philosophy and the attainment of the ultimate purpose of human life. Concomitantly, he specified the philosophic meaning of this Law in his *Guide*, providing the knowledge he deemed necessary for the attainment of intellectual perfection.

In my view, Maimonides' reformulation of the Sabian myth resembles Plato's myth of the three metals in the *Republic*[79] more than it anticipates the historical awareness of the seventeenth century, as Amos Funkenstein claims.[80] Like Plato, Maimonides constructed a story that posits a moral standard by which to evaluate the quality of individuals and societies rather than accurately depicting events in the remote past. More specifically, the story of the Sabians contains an implicit claim about the nature of human happiness—namely that the Sabian idolaters could not have enjoyed such happiness because they did not cultivate the intellect, the divine spark whose actualization defines humanity.

More advanced religious polities—Christianity and Islam—have progressed further in the attainment of human happiness. However, they too have failed to attain it, because their beliefs and practices are still not completely free from idolatry. Maimonides thus argues that only those who live in the ideal polity of Judaism can approximate human happiness. One might argue against my reading saying that if I am correct, nobody is ever happy, since Jews only approximate it and gentiles have no way of experiencing it. My answer is that since for Maimonides human well-being is indeed a process that is never fully achieved in this world, Jews have a better chance of experiencing it than gentiles, because Jews live a more just life.

Why then did Maimonides find it necessary to tell the story of the Sabians to the members of the perfect polity? The answer is that he believed that interpreting the story would redirect his audience back to the pursuit of the proper goal, a cultivation of philosophy that culminates in humanly accessible knowledge of God. In Maimonides' "likely story," all human affairs—especially those of the Jewish people—can be construed as part of a dramatic progression from idolatry to monotheism, from corporeality to spirituality, from a simplistic understanding of the Jewish myth to a correct, philosophical reading of it. Collectively and individually, Jews could assess their place in this process by comparing themselves to the negated Sabians.

MOSES' PHILOSOPHIC TORAH

Torah and Moses: A Perfect Law and a Perfect Law-Giver

Maimonides' conception of human happiness is in complete accord with the rabbinic perspective: only those who live by the Torah of Moses can experience the well-being of the body and the well-being of the soul and be truly happy.[81] Maimonides expresses this claim through his philosophic rereading of the foundational myth of Judaism: the revelation of the Torah at Sinai.

In accord with Jewish tradition, Maimonides holds that the qualitative difference between Israel and all other nations is that Israel possesses a divinely revealed law—the Torah of Moses. Maimonides presents Moses as a perfect philosopher-prophet-legislator who has attained "intellectual prophecy" and whose laws thus reflect the structure of reality. Maimonides imaginatively depicts Moses not only as the "master of all prophets" and "the master of all wise men," but also as a unique human being who was so perfect, he could cognize the intelligible principles of reality *almost* directly, i.e., with almost no corporeal mediation whatsoever. At the same time, he could achieve this high degree of intellectual excellence without losing his humanity.[82]

In the *Mishneh Torah* Maimonides dogmatically asserts the qualitative difference between Moses and all other prophets, and in the *Guide* he takes pains to differentiate between the "intellectual prophecy" of the Muslim philosophers and the uniqueness of Mosaic prophecy. These assertions are meant to single out the Torah of Moses as the one and only divine Law, whose cognitive content is identical with the structure of reality.[83] Because Moses comprehended the pattern of the laws of nature—i.e., his intellect conjoined with the Active Intellect—the Torah of Moses "enters into what is natural," including human nature. Put differently, the esoteric, abstract content of the Torah is identical with the laws of nature; it manifests the order of things.[84]

The Uniqueness of Moses' Prophecy

Maimonides considered the uniqueness of Mosaic prophecy as *the* most central principle of the Jewish faith and placed it in the middle of his list of Jewish dogmas. Thus it is the seventh in Maimonides' thirteen principles of faith, listed in the Introduction to *pereq ḥeleq* of Tractate Sanhedin in his *Commentary on the Mishnah*:

> We are to believe that he [Moses] was the chief of all other prophets before and after him, all of whom were his inferiors. He was the chosen one of all mankind, superior in attaining knowledge of God to any other person who ever lived or ever will live. He surpassed the normal human condition and attained the angelic. There remained no veil he did not rend and penetrate behind, nothing physical to hold him back, no deficiency, great or small, to confuse him. All his powers of sense and fantasy were repressed, and pure reason alone remained. This is what is meant by saying that he spoke to God without angelic mediation.

After this statement Maimonides goes on to explain the biblical verse "God spoke to Moses mouth to mouth" [Numbers 12:8], and he then enumerates four differences between Moses and all other prophets, supporting each with biblical prooftexts.

Maimonides considered the prophecy of Moses to be the foundation myth of Judaism in two senses. First of all, cognitively, it is a myth in the Platonic sense of the term, namely, a true story about reality that makes known that which cannot be known in any other way. Maimonides employed this notion of "myth" whenever he constructed parables or interpreted those of the Torah. In this regard he followed in the immediate footsteps of ibn Sina, notwithstanding the disparaging remarks he made about Persian philosophy in his letter to Samuel ibn Tibbon, already mentioned above. From the fact that Maimonides listed the uniqueness of Moses as the central dogma of Judaism, I infer that he did not think it could be proven syllogistically; it can only be asserted, and then supported by evidence from its effect, namely, from the Torah of Moses.

Does the seventh principle *present* truth or *construct* truth? Within the second sense of "myth," I believe that it does both things simultaneously. The seventh principle, I would argue contra Strauss and his followers, is not a myth in a sense of a fictitious story that the philosopher must tell the ignorant masses in order to hide the dangers of philosophy to the established political regime. Rather, it is a myth in the sense of a privileged, truth-telling narrative that presents truths that ordinary philosophical demonstration cannot in principle establish. The seventh principle functions as an axiom for the true religion that can and must employ philosophy in order to explain the myth. However, the use of syllogism on the basis of a myth is valid only because the myth itself corresponds to the way things are. Thus the myth of Mosaic prophecy both presents truth about reality and provides true data for Judaism as a philosophical-legal system.

The seventh principle asserts the supreme excellence of Mosaic prophecy as well as the difference between Moses and all other prophets. Maimonides makes the same point in the *Mishneh Torah*, Hilkhot Yesodei Ha-Torah, 7:8. Moses was addressed by God immediately, whereas all other prophets were addressed through an intermediary; Moses received his prophecy in broad daylight, whereas others prophesied while being less awake; Moses experienced no fear and trembling, whereas the other prophets were overcome with dread; finally, Moses could prophesy whenever he wished, whereas others were totally dependent on God's will for their prophecy. These differences are all ascribed to the fact that Moses transcended human corporeality and "attained the angelic." Moses transcended his human embodiment, suppressing his senses, appetites, and desires to their utmost minimum, so that his body no longer functioned as a "veil" between him and God. Transcending human corporeality, Moses apprehended the way things are in the spatio-temporal order.

So the seventh principle links Mosaic excellence to transcendence of human corporeality. However, what does that mean in a philosophical system that defines perfection as the *telos* of the human species? Did Moses' excellence suggest that he had attained the perfection of the species? Or was Moses so superior to all other human beings that he really was in a class by himself? We should recall that Maimonides, in accord with Muslim sources, regarded the prophets to be the most excellent class of people, superior to the class of the philosophers, who are more excellent than ordinary people. To say that Moses was the most supreme of all the prophets of Israel is thus to assert that Moses was also superior to all philosophers and other prophets. He was, in short, the most excellent human being. However, since Maimonides also states that Moses transcended that which makes one a human being, it follows that Moses' excellence can be attributed to that which is not human, or more than merely human.[85] Maimonides remains vague about the meaning of such transcendence.

One way to reach a greater degree of clarity is to highlight the distinction Maimonides makes between the prophecy of Moses at the gathering at Mount Sinai and Moses' prophetic activity before and after that theophany. Sinaitic prophecy was qualitatively different from all other prophecy, and, therefore, it is not enumerated in the eleven ranks of prophecy in the *Guide* II:45. At Sinai Moses was able to experience what no one else did because he transcended the limitations of the corporeal world.

Phenomenologically, I think Maimonides understood Moses' prophecy at Sinai in terms of what we would call today a near-death or out-of-body experience. For the Israelites present, however, the Sinaitic event lasted 40 days and 40 nights, a number that the Bible employs to convey perfection. For Moses, however, that experience was, literally speaking, a moment that had no duration.

Precisely because at Sinai Moses went beyond the limits of the terrestrial, corporeal world, Maimonides states that "we [who are still conditioned by corporeality] are incapable of grasping its true reality" (*Guide* II:35). In other words, ordinary human beings who are bound by corporeality can only deduce the existence of this experience from the evidence of its effect, namely, from the Torah of Moses. The essence of the experience, that is, how Moses prophesied and what it was like for him in that moment, remain inscrutable for us. It is a mystery, one of *sitrei torah*, the most subtle and difficult matters. The Torah tells the existence of these mysteries without explicating their essence.

Although he highlighted the otherness of Mosaic prophecy, Maimonides refused to make Moses an angel, let alone God. Moses reached "the level of the angelic" only with respect to cognition. Since Maimonides equated the angels with the Separate Intellects, it means that at Sinai Moses cognized as do the separate intellects, namely in a singular grasp of structural unity. However, the body that Moses transcended was human, not celestial. Hence, in the post-Sinaitic experience, Moses employed human faculties, refined as they were, and engaged in human activity. By virtue of his continued corporeality he could author the Torah and govern his people. Employing the imagination, an embodied function in Maimonides' Aristotelian psychology, Moses "translated" his cognitive apprehension into written language and promulgated a law that perfects the body and soul of those who live by it.

The ambiguity of Moses' status reflects Maimonides' ambivalent attitude toward matter, which we have already noted above. On the one hand, Maimonides, as a good Aristotelian, insisted on the interdependence of matter and form. In the spatio-temporal order, form does not exist without matter and there is no matter that is not in-formed. On the other hand, Maimonides regarded matter negatively as the principle of chaos, instability, indeterminacy, and unintelligibility that stands in opposition to the rationality, order, stability, and intelligibility of form. For Maimonides the tension between the material and formal aspects of the temporal order is conveyed not through a dualistic struggle of two independent principles, as in kabbalah, but in his rather ascetic posture toward the body, its needs and pleasures. The prophet Moses was the most superior human being because he stilled his bodily functions, but since Moses was a historical human being, he could not but be human. Maimonides adopted neither docetism nor incarnationism to explain the uniqueness of Moses, even though his depiction of Moses may resonate with some views of Jesus.

Was Moses a prophet? Maimonides answers: yes and no. In the *Guide* II: 35 he tells us that the term "prophet" applies to Moses "amphibolously" (*be-sippuq*). It is important to note that Maimonides used this word rather than *be-shittuf* or *be-shittuf gamur,* meaning "equivocally" or "with absolute equivocation." "Amphibolous" terms, according to Maimonides in the *Guide* I: 56, are those that apply to different things that are similar in some non-essential respect. That similarity makes it proper to use a given term in relation to things that differ from each other in essence but share some accidents in common. The term "prophet" applies to Moses amphibolously because in his non-Sinaitic activity Moses was somewhat like other prophets, while at Sinai Moses' prophecy was of a different essence altogether. In short, Moses both belonged and did not belong to the class of prophets. The seventh principle pertains only to Mosaic prophecy at Sinai, which yielded the Torah.

Maimonides tells us that we cannot know the "true reality" of Moses' apprehension because we are in time and Sinaitic prophecy was a-temporal. We only know about the singularity of Mosaic prophecy from its effects, namely, the Torah of Moses. Just as we learn about God from the effects of God's work, i.e., the created world, so do we learn about Moses' prophecy at Sinai from the Torah that Moses gave to Israel. Indeed, our knowledge about the origin and end of the universe—creation and redemption respectively—are analogous to our knowledge of Moses' prophecy at Sinai. Since both the origin and the end are a-temporal, we must remain in the dark about their essence.

The Perfection of the Torah of Moses

Moses' perfection includes as well the perfection of his imaginative faculty. In accord with Plato and Aristotle, Maimonides regarded the imagination with suspicion because it could create situations that have no objective correlative, thus leading the knower to commit errors about reality.[86] Therefore, Maimonides insisted that the imagination played no role whatsoever in the attainment of Moses' prophecy, which was strictly conceptual. It only played a part in the transmission of Moses' prophecy to the Israelites. Alfred Ivry, therefore, is correct to note that "Maimonides believes that the Torah as we have it is the result of Moses' religious imagination."[87] This view is not far from the position of Philo, as we discussed in Chapter Two.

The perfect imagination of Moses indicates that the Torah is the most perfect *poetic* text, one in which there is a perfect fit between the cognitive, esoteric core of philosophic truths and the figurative language of the Torah's narratives, a fit that justifies *allegoresis*, i.e., the hermeneutical act.[88] The linguistic perfection of the Torah means that its narratives, poetic imagery, and laws function as matter for the cognitive truths, which are their form. As a perfect artist, Moses produced his perfect knowledge of reality in "the language of men" so that embodied, historically-situated Israelites would have access to the truth, albeit through the veils of figurative speech. Moses' perfect prophecy thus resulted in the most perfect fit between matter and form, between the "silver leaves" of figurative speech and the "golden apples" of cognitive, philosophic content. It is this perfect speech that facilitates, nay demands, interpretation, and it is this act of interpretation that constitutes human happiness for the recipients of the Torah. Since Maimonides did not sharply distinguish between activity and process, as did Aristotle, it is reasonable to conclude that for him the happiness human beings can have is to be found in the very pursuit of happiness through the hermeneutics of the Torah of Moses.

How, according to Maimonides, do we know the perfection of the Torah of Moses? First, because of its function; it is a Law that as a matter of fact perfects body and soul. Second, the Torah is perfect because of its rationality, since its inner order is intelligible and graspable by human reason. Third, the Torah has the most accurate expression; Moses grasped universals and was able to choose the most appropriate images and metaphors, leave out what was unnecessary and know what kind of combinations would produce the best results. And finally, because the Torah of Moses is the only Law whose abstract, universal, general principles can address ever-changing particulars. The Torah of Moses alone both defines the *telos* of human life and specifies how to attain that *telos*.

As a divine Law, the Torah of Moses mediates between the historicity of corporeal creatures, who are subject to change, and the timelessness of philosophical truths. Whereas the exoteric, historically-bound narratives and laws of the Torah facilitate the attainment of bodily and moral perfection, the esoteric, philosophic truths of the Torah perfect the body and the soul by actualizing the human rational potential, the divine element in humans. Thus only those who live by the Torah of Moses—namely, the Jews—can transcend the corporeal/historical dimension of human life and attain immortal life. To do so, the Jew who seeks happiness must strip the Torah of its corporeal/historical wrappings to disclose its philosophical, abstract, and a-historical truths. By studying the Torah the seeker of perfection acquires first the moral virtues (through habitual practice of actions in the mean) and then the intellectual virtues (through cognizing true beliefs), culminating in the attainment of the ultimate end of human life—the intellectual love of God.

Mosaic Prophecy and Negative Theology

It would have been enough for Maimonides to say that Moses' prophecy was perfect because the Torah is perfect. However, he also explains the perfection of the Torah in terms of unique features of Mosaic apprehension, and at the same time insists that that apprehension is essentially unknowable. The root of the problem is Maimonides' negative theology and his understanding of transcendence. What we know about God can be inferred from what we know about God's universe, but the essence of God remains in principle unknowable, because of the ontological gap between the creator as a necessary being and everything created as contingent beings. The radical negative theology of Maimonides sees all terms applied to God in the Torah as absolute equivocations, which would suggest that the term "prophecy" as applied to Moses and any other prophet is also absolutely equivocal. However, as we have seen, this is not the case. Maimonides would have been more consistent had he said that the term "prophet" applies to Moses equivocally (*be-shittuf*), but he does not say so, because he cannot deify Moses.

Precisely because he insisted that Moses was human and the Torah rationally intelligible, Maimonides had to explain in what sense the Torah is from God. This is the purpose of talking about "divine ruse" in the *Guide* III:30 and 32. In God, will and wisdom are the same, since God is an absolute unity. What God wills and what God knows are the same, and both are manifested in the way God governs the world. Since God governs through nature, divine management of human affairs takes into consideration the particular conditions of humanity. The "divine ruse" was to give Israel the Torah through the intermediacy of Moses at a level that Israel could accept. Given the prevalence of idolatrous practices and beliefs, the "divine ruse" was evident both in forcing Israel to live in the desert in order to improve its character and in using Moses as the intermediary to address Israel at a level where it could comprehend God's word.[89]

In the *Guide* III: 32, we read:

> And just as the deity used a gracious ruse in causing them to wander perplexedly in the desert until their souls became courageous—it being well known that life in the desert and lack of comforts for the body necessarily develop courage whereas the opposite circumstances necessarily develops [sic] cowardice—and until, moreover, people were born who were not accustomed to humiliation and servitude—all this having been brought about by Moses our Master by means of divine commandments.

Concomitantly, in order to make sure that we will not conclude erroneously that the Torah of Moses is merely contingent, Maimonides spelled out in his

Eighth Principle why the Torah cannot change. Hence, I believe that Maimonides' Thirteen Principles function as an addendum to Maimonides' radical negative theology in order to nuance his apparent agnosticism.

What then does Maimonides mean when he identifies the Torah as "the Torah of Moses?" The term "Torah" is no less ambiguous than Maimonides' other key theological expressions. When the term refers to the canonic biblical text, it is used both narrowly to denote the Five Books of Moses and broadly to denote the entire Bible, including the Prophets and even the Writings. However, in many cases the Law of Moses includes not only the Written Law but also the Oral Law. At its most general level, the "Torah of Moses" refers to the Law "in its totality," namely, the abstract, inner structure of the Torah that corresponds to the way things are in reality.

"To live by the Torah of Moses" involves all four senses of the term. However, specific determinations of the expression's meaning vary with context, and Maimonides does not spell out for us what these determinations are. His lack of clarity was not intended to tease or frustrate his readers. Rather, he sought to imitate the very nature of the Torah itself, whose meaning is to be disclosed through an on-going, never-ending process of interpretation. The well-lived life can only be experienced by those who live by the Torah of Moses, and that life devotes much time to this activity of interpretation.

THE TORAH AS A REGIMEN FOR HUMAN WELL-BEING

The Interdependence of Body and Soul

The pursuit of happiness is analogous to being on a perpetual "diet,"[90] speaking literally about the body and metaphorically about the soul. The "diet" specifies the proper rules for proper bodily conduct and internal emotions and thoughts, whose observance leads to acquisition of moral and intellectual excellence. By living according to the regimen articulated in the Torah, we can attain the well-being of body and soul. Maimonides illustrates (but does not demonstrate) this point in his halakhic works. In his *Commentary on the Mishnah*, he composed an introduction to tractate Avot—the *locus classicus* of rabbinic ethics—in which he articulates the principles that inform the ethical teachings of the rabbis. The principles largely correlate with and overlap the ethical teachings of Aristotle, though they do not duplicate them. The so-called "Eight Chapters" include many of the themes also discussed in the Book of Knowledge of the *Mishneh Torah*, in Hilkhot De'ot (Laws Concerning Character Traits), although there are some differences in nuance and emphasis between the two sources.[91]

We have already noted that for Maimonides the body is the material aspect of human beings and that the soul is the formal aspect.[92] Maimonides, like Aristotle, held that the soul is the organizational principle of the living body, the aspect of the human composite that accounts for various physiological and rational functions. Maimonides identified five such functions and arranged them in a hierarchical order, ranging from the most bodily-dependent functions of nutrition, growth and reproduction, through the functions of sensation, appetite, and imagination, which combine corporeal and non-corporeal elements, to the least physically-dependent function of cognition.[93] To fully live as a human being both body and soul must function well together, and Maimonides understood this proper functioning hierarchically. It occurs only when the rational soul or intellect governs the lower functions of the soul. Only then can the human organism enjoy well-being. Maimonides ordered all intellectual functions hierarchically, putting a premium on theoretical activity. Furthermore, because he insists on the interdependence of soul and body (and in general on the interdependence of matter and form), his view of human well-being must be hierarchical as well.

Human well-being is grounded in physiology; a healthy body is a prerequisite for the well-lived life.[94] In his halakhic works Maimonides, the celebrated physician of the Egyptian court, shared his knowledge of the human body in order to explain how specific laws of the Torah ensure a healthy lifestyle.[95] Eating too much, eating harmful foods, eating at the wrong time of day, or avoiding exercise are all factors that contribute to poor health and prevent one from flourishing as a human being. In Hilkhot De`ot 3:3 Maimonides states that

> If one conducts himself in accordance with the [art of] medicine and sets his heart only upon making his body and limbs perfect and strong and upon having sons who will do his work and labor for his needs, this is not a good way. Rather, he shall set his heart upon making his body perfect and strong so that his soul will be upright to know the Lord. For it is impossible for him to understand and reflect upon wisdom when he is sick or when one of his limbs is in pain. He shall set his heart upon having a son who perhaps will be a wise and great man in Israel. Whoever follows this way all his days serves the Lord continuously, even when he engages in business and even when he has sexual

intercourse, because his thought is everything to fulfill his needs so that his body will be perfect to serve the Lord.[96]

The illness of a soul is caused by errors of judgment. To possess a healthy soul, a person must possess correct judgment about what is objectively good, which, in Aristotelian metaphysics, is determined by the *telos* of the species. A healthy soul is one that possesses a proper inner balance, or harmony of parts, which results in desiring what is objectively good for the person. By contrast, a sickness of the soul, manifested in improper conduct of the wicked person, indicates that the soul suffers from imbalance, leading the individual to desire what is not objectively good. Hence, Maimonides was not only a physician of the body, but also a "physician of the soul" who could determine how to train it to acquire the virtues, and how to remedy it if it was was out of balance. These are also the tasks of the wise who use their knowledge of ethical principles to "cure their disease by means of the character traits that they teach them, until they make them return to the middle way." (Hilkhot De'ot, 2:1, *Maimonides' Ethical Writings*, p. 31). Thus ethics performs a therapeutic function.

Whereas the moral virtues concern the functions of the soul, in the *Guide* II:40 Maimonides enumerates those virtues as part of the well-being of the body as well. Indeed, the training or conditioning of the appetitive function of the soul is inseparable from bodily functions. To desire something, to have passion for something, to like or dislike something, are all activities of the soul that cannot be separable from bodily functions. Because the human being is a unified whole, desires and feelings are not disembodied mental acts but activities of the soul that have physical manifestations. The proper training of the desiring aspect is thus necessary for the maintenance of bodily health.

The training of desire cannot be accomplished without knowledge. In the previous chapters we established the close connection between wisdom and moral goodness in the ancient Israelite Wisdom tradition and its parallels in Greek philosophy. Maimonides was aware that Hebrew does not have a word for "ethics." The Bible and the rabbis employed the word *middot* to talk about those characteristics, especially the characteristics (or attributes) of God, that mankind is called to imitate. In the *Mishneh Torah*, Maimonides introduced the word *de'ot* (sing. *de'ah*)—which captures the cognitive dimension of character molding—to denote those traits that are to be acquired through habitual practice. To acquire good traits, one must *know* what is objectively good for the human species; holding an incorrect opinion about ends, and especially about the ultimate end of life, will necessarily result in the acquisition of vices rather than virtues.

The Cultivation of Character: The Moral Virtues

Maimonides tells us (Hilkhot De`ot 1:7) that human beings are to become morally virtuous by habitually practicing the middle way (*derekh ha-mitzu`a*). Though born with certain dispositions, due to their particular material make-up, they can still possess good character traits by habitually practicing good deeds. What makes a certain act good is the mean between two equally bad extremes, the "too much" and the "too little."[97] When people habitually practice doing things "just right," they become good, which is to say that they acquire intrinsic states of character out of which flow good actions. The acquired virtues thus become ingrained, a "second nature" of sorts, so that one does the good without experiencing internal tension or conflict.

When Maimonides reinterpreted rabbinic teachings in light of Aristotle's doctrine of the mean, he too had to work out the tension between the ideal of moderation and the call for supererogation. He does so by asserting that the middle between extremes characterizes God's mode of operation. He uses the biblical phrase "the ways of God" to describe those moderate traits. Thus the Torah's command to walk in God's path should be understood as choosing the mean between extremes. Maimonides asserts: "We are commanded to walk in these middle ways, which are the good and right ways. As it is said, 'and you shall walk in His way' [Deut. 28:9]" (Hilkhot De`ot 1:5). Referring to the conduct of Abraham (Gen. 18:19), Maimonides states that "whoever walks in this way brings good and blessing upon himself" (Hilkhot De`ot 1:7). The Torah itself, then, secures the intrinsically good life, and those who adhere to it enjoy well-being. While this is not a literal reading of the biblical text (which often describes God's actions as anything but moderate), it is a reading that highlights the major claim of the rabbinic tradition, viz., that the Torah is the exclusive path to the happy life.

In the *Nicomachean Ethics* Book IV, Aristotle illustrated how specific virtues are themselves the middle between two extremes. It is easy to recognize Aristotle's teachings in Maimonides' Eight Chapters: IV where the following virtues illustrate the doctrine of the mean:

> Thus, moderation is one of the good actions, and the state of the soul that produces moderation is a moral virtue. Lust is the first extreme

and total insensibility to pleasure the other extreme; both of them are completely bad. The two states of the soul necessarily giving rise to lust (the excessive state) and insensibility (the deficient state) are both moral vices. In like manner, liberality is the mean between miserliness and extravagance; courage is the mean between rashness and cowardice; wit is the mean between buffoonery and dullness; humility is the mean between haughtiness and abasement; generosity is the mean between prodigality and stinginess; contentment is the mean between greed and laziness; gentleness is the mean between irascibility and servility; modesty is the mean between impudence and shyness; and so too, with the rest of them (*Maimonides' Ethical Writings*, p. 67).

In the body of the *Commentary on Avot*, to which the Eight Chapters is the Introduction, Maimonides illustrates these principles in some detail. He could justifiably do so because Tractate Avot is indeed suffused with the virtue ethics that prevailed in ancient philosophy.

Maimonides Versus Aristotle

Maimonides' portrayal of the virtuous, well-balanced person seems to depart from the Aristotelian ideal in three important respects.[98] First, Maimonides counsels that in certain cases wherein a person suffers from sickness of the soul, it is actually advisable to "look to which side it inclines in becoming unbalanced, and then oppose it with its contrary until it returns to equilibrium" (*Maimonides' Ethical Writings*, p. 68). Accordingly, Maimonides teaches that to treat a person with a miserly soul, it is necessary that he "repeatedly act in an extravagant manner until the condition that makes him miserly is removed from his soul, and he just about acquires an extravagant disposition or comes close to it. Then we would make him stop the extravagant actions and order him to perform liberal actions continuously. . . . Similarly, if we were to see him acting in an extravagant manner, we would order him to perform miserly actions repeatedly" (*Maimonides' Ethical Writings*, pp. 68–69). Consideration of the particular propensities of people, which for Maimonides are often based in a particular material composition, brings Maimonides closer to Aristotle than it may appear. Maimonides does not go as far as Aristotle to hold that the mean is relative to the agent, but he does concern himself with the particular needs of the agent.

The second difference between Aristotle and Maimonides concerns the virtue of magnanimity, or spending on a large scale. For Aristotle, the virtuous gentleman possesses a great-soul (*megalopsyche*) by virtue of which he performs benevolent acts on a large scale. In contrast, Maimonides says that people err when they think that "extravagance and prodigality are among the praiseworthy actions." (Eight Chapters: IV, *Maimonides' Ethical Writings*, p. 68). Like the rabbis, he did not consider magnanimity a virtue and instead counseled modesty in terms of giving and contentment with little in terms of receiving. While Maimonides considered the trait to be a departure from the "proper mean," Jewish philosophers in the fifteenth century—who were more at home in the culture of the court—treated this virtue more favorably. They too returned to Aristotle's *Ethics* but articulated a different rationale for their social class.

The third difference between Maimonides and Aristotle has to do with self-control. For Maimonides it clearly is a virtue. To acquire virtue one needs self-control, or self-restraint, which is possible only when one allows reason, the highest function of the soul, to subdue and control the appetites and passions that originate in the body. Self-control can be realized only when reason properly grasps the *telos* of human life (that is, the theoretical aspect of human reasoning) and devises the proper means to accomplish that end (i.e., the practical aspect of reasoning). For Aristotle, on the other hand, the very exercise of self-control or continence indicates that a person has not yet reached the highest level of moral excellence and still experiences conflicts between desire and reason. Still wishing to do what what is not objectively good, he acts in ways that are not conducive to human well-being. By contrast, the truly wise person experiences no such conflict; naturally recoils from doing what does not contribute to human well-being, and is not tempted by evil.

Maimonides admits there is a surface disparity between the position of the Aristotelians and the judgment of his rabbinic sources. In apparent contradiction of Aristotle, the rabbis consider the one who overcomes temptations to be "more praiseworthy and perfect than the one who feels no torment at refraining from evil." The very resistance to evil is itself considered a source of moral worthiness, contrary to the position of the philosophers. Nevertheless, he holds (Eight Chapters: VI) that on this point "what appears in the speech of the Law [is] in agreement with what the philosophers have said" (*Maimonides' Ethical Writings*, p. 79). Maimonides resolves the tension by distinguishing between two types of desires. The rabbis and the philosophers are in agreement with regard to "things which all people commonly agree are evils, such as the shedding of blood, theft, robbery, fraud, injury to one who has done no harm, ingratitude, contempt for parents and the like." In these cases the one who does not experience any desire to commit these acts is clearly superior to the one who is tempted by these evils but manages to control himself. The merit that the rabbis assign to self-control pertains not to internal conflict concerning these evils, but rather to self-control with regard to prohibitions specified by the Law.

The Torah refers to this category of law as "statutes" (*huqqim*). The medieval Jewish philosophers referred to them as "ceremonial laws." Their observance is a source of joy to the virtuous Jew who must exercise self control in their observance. In this case to subdue passion (*kibbush ha-yezter*) is more praiseworthy than to observe these laws with complete emotional abandon and without reservation. The rabbis were correct, according to Maimonides, to assign a higher rank to the one who, confronted with temptation, admits "I do indeed want to, yet I must not, for my father in heaven has forbidden it" (*Sifra Leviticus* 20:36).

Intellectual Perfection

These differences between Aristotle and Maimonides should not be exaggerated. Behind them is a fundamentally shared agreement that human ethics is grounded in rational activity, that the mastery of virtues is for the sake of achieving perfection, and that perfection is intellectual. For Aristotle theoretical reasoning pertained to knowledge of causes, and its excellence (or virtue) was the contemplation of necessary, abstract truths that are not subject to change. Practical reasoning, by contrast, consists of deliberation about the means for the attainment of good, and requires consideration of changing circumstances. Practical reasoning is involved in the acquisition of moral virtues and its excellence is the virtue of practical wisdom (*phronesis*).

Maimonides partially follows Aristotle in regard to intellectual virtues as shown in Eight Chapters chapter II:

> (i) wisdom, which is knowledge of the remote and proximate causes and which comes after knowledge of the existence of the thing whose causes are being investigated; and (ii) intelligence, which includes (a) theoretical intellect, I mean, the first intelligibles, which we have by nature; (b) the acquired intellect, but this is not the place for that; and (c) brilliance and excellent comprehension, that is, excellent grasp of a thing quickly, in no time, or in a very short time (*Maimonides' Ethical Writings*, p. 65).

The two intellectual virtues listed are "wisdom" and "intelligence," both of which belong to theoretical reasoning, not practical reasoning. Similarly, at the end of the *Guide* (III:53) Maimonides describes the fourth and highest form of human perfection. There he says,

> The fourth species is the true human perfection; it consists in the acquisition of the rational virtues—I refer to the conception of intelligibles which teach true opinions concerning the divine things. This is in true reality the ultimate end; this is what gives the individual true perfection, a perfection belonging to him alone; and it gives him permanent perdurance, through it man is man (Pines ed., p. 635).

In these two places Maimonides does not speak about practical wisdom as a distinct intellectual virtue. However, as Howard Kreisel has demonstrated, this does not mean that Maimonides devalued it.[99] On the contrary, practical wisdom is at least as central to Maimonides' virtue ethics as is theoretical wisdom. The integration of the two is a function of the integration of Maimonides' philosophic and halakhic writings. The ideal person who cultivates moral and intellectual virtues has to be a Jew who is equally rooted in both the Jewish religious tradition and in philosophy.

HAPPINESS AND THE TRANSCENDENCE OF CORPOREALITY

Naturalizing the Messianic Age

The quest for perfection takes place in the corporeal world, but its ultimate end is the transcendence of the corporeal human condition and the attainment of the human ideal. The ultimate end of human life is to be as close as possible to the way God created man, i.e., an intellect in actuality, as exemplified in the Bible in *Adam,* prior to his sin. The life of Torah is thus a life in pursuit of the ideal. This pursuit is understood in the rabbinic literature as a striving for the messianic age.

Rabbinic speculation about the messianic age was very diverse. Some rabbis presented it simply as the end of human history, while others described the catastrophic events that would constitute the final end of all human life, and yet others highlighted the discontinuity and dissimilarity between life as we know it and the messianic age. Maimonides diminished its catastrophic quality because he believed in the stability of nature. The corporeal world does not need to be improved through apocalyptic upheavals in which nature itself is transformed.[100] For Maimonides, then, the messianic age will witness only a change in the realm of human history—

namely, the liberation of Israel from foreign domination. Free to control their own affairs, the Jews will live in peace in their sovereign polity, governed by the Torah, which will enable them to attain the intellectual love of God, i.e., attain the "final perfection" of human life.[101] In the messianic age Jews will truly experience human well-being. Properly directed toward the ideal, they will benefit from the presence of its material conditions.

Maimonides' de-emphasis of the miraculous quality of the messianic age became a major source of contention in the controversies about his legacy. Even more controversial is his view on the meaning of *olam ha-ba*, one of the most ambiguous concepts in rabbinic Judaism. For the rabbis, *olam ha-ba* ("world to come") was both an ideal toward which humanity must strive and a post-historical epoch that will be experienced by those who live according to God's Torah. When Maimonides gave rabbinic Judaism an Aristotelian interpretation, he identified *olam ha-ba* with the perfection of the intellect by virtue of which human beings can attain immortality. He characterized *olam ha-ba* as the "ultimate end toward which all our efforts ought to be devoted, . . . the ultimate and perfect reward, the final bliss that will suffer neither interruption nor diminution."[102]

Maimonides explicitly divorced *olam ha-ba* from its original association with the apocalyptical and eschatological drama of the messianic age when he stated: "The sages and prophets did not long for the days of the Messiah . . . [but] that Israel be free to devote itself to the law and its wisdom . . . and thus be worthy of life in the world to come."[103] The world to come then is not a specific phase in the post-historical messianic drama, but a distinct mode of existence for the perfected rational soul. The only difference between the pre-messianic and the messianic age, then, lies in the attainability of that mode of existence. Whereas in the pre-messianic, historical era only the select few will enjoy the bliss of immortality, in the messianic age all of Israel will attain the ultimate end of human life effortlessly, enjoying the bliss of immortal life.

That at least some select Jews could and can transcend history by virtue of intellectual perfection is the message of the myth of the king's palace in the *Guide* III:51. As an accomplished teller and inventor of *mythoi*, Maimonides employed his creative imagination to communicate what he thought was true, to the extent that the truth can be known to temporal/corporeal human beings.[104] To ensure that readers understand the myth of the king's palace correctly, Maimonides also supplies its appropriate interpretation.

The Myth of the King's Palace[105]
The Intellectual Love of God as the Final Perfection

Maimonides concludes the *Guide* with an invented parable about a king who is ensconced in his palace and the people who stand in proximity to the king. The parable divides human beings into classes arranged in a hierarchical order. Each class represents a certain phase in the perfection of knowledge, from utter ignorance (represented by those outside the gate of the city), through several levels of intellectual perfection in an ascending order that corresponds to the hierarchy of the sciences. The ladder of perfection culminates in the knowledge of God by the prophets who "direct all the acts of their intellect toward an examination of the beings with a view to drawing from them proofs with regard to Him." [106] In the language of the parable, the highest phase of the knower of God is the intimate presence of the knower in the inner chambers of the king's palace. The meaning of the parable is that those who live by the Torah can attain moral and intellectual perfection, culminating in the final perfection: the intellectual love of God. The life in accord with the commandments of the Torah but without proper speculation does not lead to the attainment of the final perfection. One reaches it only through holding the correct opinions, acting in accord with the Torah's prescriptions, and acquiring thorough scientific knowledge of all that exists.

Maimonides equates the highest stage of intellectual perfection with the love of God. He describes the true lover of God as one who has attained

> such apprehension of true realities and his joy in what he has apprehended, achieves a state in which he talks with people and is occupied with his bodily necessities while his intellect is wholly turned toward Him, may He be exalted so that in his heart he is always in His presence, may He be exalted, while outwardly he is with people (Guide III:51, Pines, ed. p. 623).

This lofty state is articulated in the Song of Songs 5:2 in a "poetical parable" that according to Maimonides describes the heroes of the monotheistic drama—Abraham and Moses. In a language reminiscent of Plato's simile of the sun in the *Republic*, Maimonides says of the perfect lover of God that

> he who apprehends and advances with his whole being toward the object of his apprehension is like one who is in the pure light of the sun. He who has had apprehension, but is occupied, is while he is occupied

in this state like one who has a cloudy day in which the sun does not shine because of the clouds that separate it and him (*Guide* III:51, Pines, ed. 625).

This language reminds the reader to return to the Introduction of the *Guide* where Maimonides says:

> But sometimes truth flashes out to us so that we think that it is day, and then matter and habit in their various forms conceal it so that we find ourselves again in an obscure night, almost as we were at first. We are like someone in a very dark night over whom lightning flashes time and time again (*Guide*, Introduction, Pines ed., 7).

The perfect lover of God, then, is the one "for whom the lightning flashes time and time again, so that he is always, as it were, in unceasing light."

Perfection and the Limits of Language

At the conclusion of the *Guide*, Maimonides links ultimate perfection to the hermeneutical process in a very personal way. Speaking in the first person, he interrupts the flow of his discussion to explain how he himself arrived at a profound insight about God's relationship to the world. His language suggests that the very act of interpreting the Torah in the process of composing the *Guide* led him to the desired illumination described above. He states: "A most extraordinary speculation has occurred to me just now through which doubts may be dispelled and divine secrets revealed" (III:51; Pines ed., p. 624).

Maimonides likens dispelling of doubts to the clearing of the clouds, which makes the sun (i.e., truth) shine forth. The truth that was revealed to him in that moment of clarity, after he had succeeded in removing his own veils of ignorance and corporeality, was

> that providence watches over everyone endowed with intellect proportionately to the measure of his intellect. Thus providence always watches over an individual endowed with perfect apprehension whose intellect never ceases from being occupied with God. On the other hand, an individual endowed with perfect apprehension, whose thought sometimes for a certain time is emptied of God, is watched over by providence only during the time when he thinks of God;

providence withdraws from him during the time when he is occupied with something else (*Guide* III:51, Pines, ed. 624).

Rabbinic Judaism, I suggested, centers on the myth of the eternal love affair between God and Israel. Maimonides reinterpreted this love with reference to both partners. God's love to Israel is manifested not in the passionate concern for Israel and periodic, miraculous interventions, but in the regularity of nature's fixed laws and their accessibility to the human intellect. These are the "ways" of God, i.e., the attributes of God's action, which are knowable by the human mind through the study of physics and metaphysics. The better one understands the laws of nature, the more one avoids mishaps and error, thereby appearing to enjoy a special favor from God. Correspondingly, human love of God is manifested first in the imitations of God's "ways" by virtue of which humans can acquire the moral and intellectual virtues, and it culminates in the intellectual love of God. At its highest phase, the human love of God is not the gushing outburst of emotions and bodily affections, but the serene, self-controlled, silent joy of contemplation that is commensurate with one's knowledge of God.[107] Maimonides replaced the rabbinic understanding of Eros with the philosophic conception of Eros, the non-personal, intellectualist love of wisdom.

For Maimonides, when human perfection is finally attained in the act of contemplation, not only is the corporeal dimension of human life transcended, but also language itself, since language befits the temporal/corporeal modality of creation. When perfection is attained, silence is the only appropriate response. In the *Guide* I:50, Maimonides reminds us that the Torah itself understood the significance of silence in divine worship when it stated that "silence is praise to you" (Psalm 65:2). It is only fitting, then, that the myth of the king's palace be placed at the end of the *Guide,* after which Maimonides and his readers are left with silence. When the human temporal/corporeal modality is transcended, words become redundant and inadequate, leaving us to contemplate the disclosure of logos through the linguistic veils of mythos in the attainment of human happiness.

The Pursuit of Happiness as a Midrashic Activity

Let me summarize Maimonides' logocentric rendering of the rabbinic notion that the life of Torah is the happy life by retelling it as a musical parable. The Torah is the most perfect score of human happiness ever composed because its composer was the most perfect musician that ever lived and that will ever live. In order to reproduce the perfect score, the performer must be in perfect physical and mental shape. Body and soul must be well-tuned and harmonically balanced so as to match the inner balance of the score. Since the excellence of the performer-interpreter determines the quality of the production, each individual performance reproduces the score to varying degrees of excellence.

Precisely because it is only a reproduction, however, the product (no matter how good) always falls short of the ideal. In the created world of time-space there is only relative happiness. What is crucial, however, is that for those who live by the Torah and understand it correctly (as Maimonides claims to do), the pursuit of happiness is not in vain. In full accord with the rabbinic tradition, Maimonides holds that the pursuit of happiness within the boundaries of halakhah is the most reasonable, joyful, and delightful activity available to mankind. Those who live by the Torah are the happiest of all human beings, to the extent that humans can be happy.[108]

Maimonides' use of "plot-structures" (either invented or appropriated) did not demythologize Judaism but exchanged a logocentric myth for the rabbinic one. Myth, he seems to tell us, is inevitable in human life because human beings are a composite of matter and form. Consequently, the process by which we come to know truth is necessarily hermeneutical. Hermeneutics is the essence of Judaism because it accords with the structure of reality. In this conception of happiness, hermeneutics and happiness converge.

Because of this identification, Maimonides could argue that the life of Torah perfects the life of those who adhere to it, which is precisely what the rabbinic tradition asserts liturgically. For the Jews who live by the divine law, the ongoing process of self-perfection comprises the gradual removal of veils, be they veils of corporeality in the thing known, the veils of ignorance in the knowing subject, or the veils of language in the medium that communicates between them. The perfecting quest for happiness and truth are thus one and the same. Both require a disciplined regime of habitual practice in the social-moral sphere, as both Aristotle and the rabbis claimed.

Maimonides' philosophic portrayal of the happy life of Torah resolves the apparent tension within the *Nicomachean Ethics* along the lines proposed by R. Kraut, as discussed in Chapter One. The theoretical life and the practical life are not necessarily in conflict with each other. Rather, they are complimentary components of one type of life—a life that organizes all activities according to one *dominant* principle, the contemplation of God. The happy or perfect life consists of both *praxis* (*ma'aseh*) and *theoria* (*iyyun*), appropriately reflecting the duality of matter and form, of body and soul, respectively. For

Jews, the practical life consists of imitating the "ways" by which God governs the universe—namely, with lovingkindness, justice, and righteousness as the Torah prescribes and the rabbinic tradition elaborates. Maimonides' recognition of the importance of action in the social-political sphere rejects the earlier tendency to withdraw from the world and cultivate *apathia* or *ataraxia*, which the Stoics counseled in the ancient past and the Sufis practiced (albeit in a different setting and under a different myth) during Maimonides' own time.[109]

Summary

Maimonides left for posterity an intentionally ambiguous legacy that shaped the course of Jewish philosophy until the seventeenth century. Because of that ambiguity it was possible to read Maimonides in various and conflicting ways. I have presented one plausible reading, according to which he postulates that only a life lived within the enclosure of the divine Torah of Moses can lead one to attain both the well-being of the body and the well-being of the soul. The Torah of Moses is the "diet" that leads to perfection, but it does not yield necessary, automatic results to those who follow it. Both the perfection of the Law and the perfection brought about by the Law are ideals; in the spatio-temporal order of particulars their pursuit is frustrated by material conditions and individual choices. The approximation of the ideal is thus reserved for very few individuals under very specific conditions.

Nonetheless, the pursuit of perfection within the strictures of the Law of Moses is neither trivial nor an exercise in futility. What it promises is not a shortcut to a desired end, but a quality of life that is superior to any other: it alone corresponds to the way things are and is directed toward the right end—namely, toward the knowledge and love of God. To understand properly the "diet" of the Torah one must study it and interpret it. One must strip away the linguistic veils of the Torah's narratives and laws (i.e., the material aspect of the Torah) in order to reach its philosophic, conceptual core. By interpreting the Torah with the help of Maimonides, the corporeal, figurative veils of the Torah are gradually removed, and its incorporeal, philosophical core is exposed. Thus, hermeneutics discloses the necessary, immutable truths whose knowledge guides the knower to transcend corporeality and attain the bliss of immortal life.

Maimonides was fully aware that his claims about the Torah of Moses as the exclusive path to happiness could not be proven philosophically. Hence, he presented it as a foundational dogma of Judaism and provided empirical support for it in his Code of Jewish Law. Most importantly, he conveyed his vision of human happiness through sophisticated rhetorical means that, like the Torah itself, were intended to reveal philosophic truths by concealing them. By purposefully creating a veil of ignorance, Maimonides called on his readers to remove that veil. To unlock the philosophic secrets of the Torah, which is its meaning, one has first to decipher the secrets of the *Guide* (i.e., its structure and Maimonides' intent). By writing a riddle or a mystery (namely, the *Guide*) about another riddle or mystery (namely, the Torah), Maimonides created a context he thought appropriate for the pursuit of truth and the attainment of human happiness. He thus launched his readers-interpreters-students on a search for truth and happiness that endows life with meaning. To be happy, that is to live well, a Jew needs to decode the Torah of Moses with the help of Maimonides.[110]

6

The Maimonidean Controversies: Debating the Meaning of Happiness

After Maimonides, all Jewish philosophers reflected about happiness within the contours he left for posterity. Whether they agreed with him, elaborated upon the meaning of his views, or took issue with him, they all held that happiness could be attained only within the confines of the perfect political order, that such order must be founded on the divinely revealed Law, and that the Torah is the one and only such Law. However, the Maimonidean approach was by no means universally accepted. In fact, it became the focus of a very intense controversy that lasted throughout the thirteenth century and resurfaced during the fifteenth and sixteenth. Significantly, Maimonides was so controversial not because he held heretical views, but because he captured the deepest problematics of Judaism: the interplay of Torah and Wisdom, of mythos and logos. After him, all Jewish attempts to make sense of the identification of Torah and Wisdom posited in the Bible required wrestling with his legacy.

As we have shown, Maimonides' views on the ultimate end of human life were spelled out in his *Commentary on the Mishnah* and in the *Mishneh Torah*. His logocentric reformulation of rabbinic Judaism necessitated a response precisely because he presented it as legally binding in terms of what all Jews must think and must do. Understandably, as soon as Maimonides' teachings became known, they aroused criticism that erupted into a series of heated debates and generated ad-hominem attacks, bans, counter-bans, Jews informing on other Jews, and even an invitation for the papal Inquisition to become involved in Jewish cultural affairs.

The Maimonidean Controversy engaged Jewish communities in several countries, but its main arena was Spain and its cultural offshoot—the Jewish communities of Provence. Thus the history of the discourse on happiness until the end of the Middle Ages is inseparable from the history of Spanish Jewry, which during the twelfth century underwent profound changes due to the reconquest of Spain by the Christians. With the shift of

Jewish life from Islam to Christendom, the debate about the meaning of happiness intensified both within the Jewish community and between Jews and Christians.

This chapter will focus on the internal polemics during the thirteenth century. I argue that the various phases and themes of the Maimonidean Controversy become coherent if viewed as a debate about the *meaning of happiness within Judaism*. Arguments about the fate of the human soul after death and the resurrection of the body (phase 1), about the composition of Jewish education (phase 2), about the allegorical interpretation of the Torah (phase 3), and about the validity of astrology (phase 4) were all aspects of a larger question: *What is the necessary and sufficient knowledge for the attainment of the ultimate end of human life?* Since that ultimate end was defined in terms of the individual soul, this was a debate that pertained to *personal salvation*. For this reason the Maimonidean Controversy should not be viewed as a cool academic disagreement about theoretical matters, but as a series of passionate and often acrimonious personal and communal conflicts about the orientation of Jewish culture, the desired interaction with other religious and intellectual traditions—indeed, even the boundaries of Judaism.

In emphasis and focus, this chapter is quite different from the preceding five and the subsequent three. The narrative is historical rather than philosophical and takes into consideration not only ideas but also individual personalities, political agendas, cultural sensibilities, and social institutions. This shift in focus is necessary for two reasons. First, it provides support for my claim that reflections on happiness are not merely academic or theoretical. One's notion of happiness shapes how one lives and acts, and especially what kind of education one deems desirable. By defining the cultural context in which Jews debated the *meaning and ramifications* of certain conceptions of happiness, we can see how the concept was central to Jewish self-understanding. Second, this chapter sets the stage for the issues discussed in the subsequent chapters: the kabbalistic alternative to a rationalist conception of happiness, the interreligious dimension of the discourse on happiness, the reception of Aristotle's *Nicomachean Ethics* among both Christians and Jews, and the transformation of the Maimonidean tradition due to the interaction with kabbalah. These and other themes could not be understood without the information provided in this chapter. Thus, while it does not add another analysis to our discussion, it is essential to our reconstruction of the evolution of the discourse on happiness in premodern Judaism.

THE CULTURAL SETTING: FROM ISLAM TO CHRISTENDOM

Maimonides' own life reflected the dramatic ending of the so-called Golden Age of Judeo-Arabic cultural symbiosis. With other Andalusian Jews, his family was forced to flee the region in 1148, when Jewish life was destroyed by the Almohads, a militant North-African Muslim dynasty that temporarily halted the advance of the Christian conquest of Iberia. While Maimonides eventually found his way to Egypt, many Andalusian Jews migrated northward to the Christian kingdoms of northern Spain and the principality of Provence in Southern France, bringing the illustrious culture of Muslim Spain to Jewish communities in Christendom. The transition of Jewish life from the orbit of Islam to Christendom would have a profound impact on the history of Jewish philosophy and its reflections on human happiness.

The Christian takeover of Spain from the Muslims was one aspect of the Crusading movement, whose goal was to reassert Christian supremacy over Islam and to oust Islam from control of the Holy Land.[1] During the last quarter of the eleventh century, the Christian kingdoms in northern Iberia took advantage of the political weakness of the thirty petty Muslim kingdoms in Andalusia, who were governed by rival Berber dynasties that exhausted each other's power.[2] The conquests reflected the expansionist policies of the recently united Christian kingdoms of Castile, Galicia, and Leon under one crown in 1037.

When Toledo fell to the Christians in 1085, the Muslim ruler of Seville enlisted the Almoravid kingdom of Morocco for assistance. The Almoravid ruler Yusuf ibn Tashufin (1090–1106) temporarily succeeded in uniting the feuding Muslim kingdoms under the banner of an ascetic form of Islam. Half a century later another fanatic Islamic movement, the Almohads, intervened in the struggle and devastated Andalusia, imposing conversion on non-Muslims. They failed, however, to halt the Christian reconquest of Iberia. Except for the small kingdom of Granada, which remained Muslim until 1492, the entire Iberian peninsula was Christianized between the eleventh and thirteenth centuries.

The Jewish population in Iberia was deeply affected by these changes. In the initial stages of the Christian reconquest, the Jews fared well. Already in 1063 Pope Alexander II extended the traditional papal policy of protection to Jews and warned the knights not to harm them. Such protection was rooted in the notion that the Jews were "the witness people" to God's revelation in Christ, and therefore their life must be protected, albeit kept inferior. The main concern of the Spanish monarchs, however, was utilitarian.

The Jews were viewed as an important factor in the colonization of the previously Muslim territories, and were not only allowed to stay but were "offered special inducements to replace the fleeing Muslim population: land grants, elective privileges, and tax exemptions."[3] In some cases the Jewish communities were exempt from paying taxes and duties for several years.

As in other parts of Christian Europe, the legal but precarious status of the Jews was defined in charters granted to individuals or to specific Jewish communities.[4] On the one hand, these charters assured protection to Jewish life and property. On the other hand, they delineated the total dependence of the Jews, politically and physically, on the rulers (monarchs or emperors) who granted them privileges.

Any harm to Jews was considered to be an offense against the ruler to whom they legally belonged. The charter given to the Jews of Teruel in 1176, for example, summarizes the royal attitude toward them when it states that "the Jews are the slaves of the crown and belong exclusively to the royal treasury." The alliance of the Jews with the kings would prove to be a double-edged sword. It both facilitated the economic growth of Jewish life in Christian Spain during the twelfth and thirteenth centuries, and it undermined the Jewish presence in Iberia. When opposing institutions—the municipalities, the nobility, and the Church—grew strong enough to challenge the royal protection of Jews, it would be in the interest of the monarchs to dispose of them. The final expulsion of the Jews from Iberia in 1492, when their presence was deemed detrimental to the state, was a logical conclusion to their total dependence on royal power. Even the Jews who were expelled did not challenge the legality of the expulsion.

In the second half of the twelfth century and the first half of the thirteenth, however, the Jews of Christian Spain enjoyed immense economic growth. In addition to engaging in both agriculture and a wide variety of crafts, Jews played an important role in the administration of the state. Their knowledge of the Arabic language and culture, and especially their knowledge of specialized sciences, made them particularly valuable in the administration of the expanding Christian kingdoms. The Jews were instrumental in setting up the commerce, industry, and bureaucracy of the expanding Christian kingdoms, rendering to monarchs their special expertise as tax collectors, treasurers, personal physicians, translators, diplomats, land surveyors, astronomers, and astrologers. Though in theory Jews could not exercise power over Christians, in Iberia the monarchs hired many Jews to serve in state bureaucracy and granted them extensive personal privileges. The courtiers constituted a distinct Jewish aristocracy that transmitted to

Christian Spain many of the values, ideals, and sensibilities of the Jewish courtier class in Muslim Spain, including the discourse on happiness.

In return for heavy taxation and total dependency on the monarchs,[5] the Jewish community in Spain was given a large measure of legal autonomy and religious freedom. Each community was responsible for the payment of taxes levied on Jews collectively and for the orderly conduct of its members. Litigation among Jews was to be adjudicated by rabbis according to Jewish law, and Jewish penal power included imprisonment, fines, flogging, excommunication, and even capital punishment. The affairs of a given Jewish community were managed by a small council of appointed officials, all of whom came from a well-knit oligarchy that retained its social identity and power by carefully planned marriages.

The Jews' economic diversity in the thirteenth century led to the emergence of three distinct social classes: a small oligarchy that worked in the service of the crown; a middle class of merchants, successful craftsmen, and educated Jews such as scribes, teachers, and physicians; and a lower middle or upper lower class of artisans and community clerks. The very poor, who earned their living by domestic service to the rich, paid no taxes and hence were not considered as a distinct class. Toward the end of the century the middle class demanded a greater share in the management of the Jewish community, and in some cases (for example, in Catalonia) their demands erupted into open revolt.[6] These social differences would also play a role in the ideological debates that constituted the Maimonidean Controversy.

Culturally the transition from life under Islam to life in Christendom was quite a smooth one. In both Spain and Italy, Jewish scholars collaborated in the translation of Hebrew philosophical texts into Latin. But most of the translation went the other way around. In the thirteenth century, especially in Italy, a few philosophical texts were translated from Latin into Hebrew. And the Jews who migrated from Andalusia northward to Aragon, Catalonia, and Provence brought with them their Judeo-Arabic cultural paradigms and were determined to perpetuate them in Hebrew. The families of ibn Tibbon and Kimhi, who settled in Provence, were crucial in the transmission of the Judeo-Arabic philosophic tradition to Christian Europe. By translating the philosophical classics of Saadia Gaon, Bahya ibn Pakuda, Solomon ibn Gabirol, and Maimonides, they created a language for Jewish philosophy. Though Arabic continued to be studied by educated Jews, from this time on Jewish philosophy would be written exclusively in Hebrew. It was precisely the diffusion of the Judeo-Arabic philosophy and its cultural success that caused the intense debates about the status of philosophy in Judaism and the validity of the philosophic conception of happiness.

PHILOSOPHY AS A CULTURAL FORCE

Modes of Studying Philosophy in the Thirteenth Century

How was a Jew to study philosophy in the thirteenth century? Unlike in medieval Christendom, where this kind of learning had a clear institutional setting, in medieval Judaism it remained largely a private, autodidactic affair.[7] The interested individual had to purchase manuscripts of philosophical and scientific texts or have them copied for his own use, which produced a form of patronage for Jewish philosophy. Some students would use these texts to write texts of their own that were either commentaries on or summaries of their original authoritative texts. This study was a bookish, private activity, where the student hired a private tutor rather than attending a school. Those who were inclined to pursue philosophic knowledge were willing to travel great distances to procure manuscripts or find a qualified instructor. Given the cost of manuscripts and the time required for its study, it is understandable that philosophy was cultivated generally only by those who had leisure and means, even though we do know of individuals who devoted themselves to this kind of life despite their poverty.[8]

The study of philosophy and its related sciences was particularly appreciated by Jews who pursued social mobility through serving the crown as physicians, diplomats, translators, state administrators, and tax collectors.[9] For this purpose, Jewish students of philosophy continued to study Arabic even after it ceased to be taught within the closely-knit, aristocratic families of their patrons. During the thirteenth century, the group of those interested in learning philosophy was enlarged to include not only these social circles, but also the newly emerging middle class. The scribes who copied manuscripts for wealthy patrons, physicians, pharmacists, successful merchants, and skilled artisans were all interested in access to philosophic-scientific knowledge for various reasons and with diverse levels of expertise.

The corpus of Aristotle's works was the basis of scientific-philosophical education. It included as well a few dialogues of Plato (the *Republic* and the *Timaeus*), the *Isagoge* of Porphyry, and a few Neoplatonic works that circulated under the name of Aristotle.[10] In 1210 Samuel ibn Tibbon translated Aristotle's *Meteora* into Hebrew, thereby inaugurating a vibrant, Jewish translating effort that, by the mid-fourteenth century, reproduced the entire Aristotelian corpus in Hebrew.[11]

The selection of these texts was no coincidence. The translators understood correctly that in order to legitimize Maimonides' claim that the Torah teaches philosophy, Aristotle's physics had to be mastered. Otherwise, for example, they could not make philosophic sense out of the biblical creation narrative.[12] Since Greek philosophy was known to Jews only in its Arabic version, the study of philosophy involved as well a mastery of the philosophical works of al-Farabi, ibn Sina, al-Ghazali, ibn Bajja, ibn Tufayl, and ibn Rushd, all of which became available in Hebrew and were studied with summaries and commentaries.[13]

During the thirteenth century, the study of Aristotle's philosophy was carried out primarily through the commentaries of ibn Rushd, who was known in the Latin West as "the Commentator." He composed three types of commentaries to each of Aristotle's works: a short paraphrase and summary of Aristotle's arguments; a mid-length version that included the original text and some commentary; and a long version that consisted of a detailed, linear commentary on Aristotle's full text.

During the thirteenth and early fourteenth centuries, those who aspired to technical philosophical knowledge translated the commentaries of ibn Rushd into Hebrew and composed their own super-commentaries to them.[14] The primacy of the commentary as the mode of producing philosophy meant that the Jewish philosopher did not aspire to originality. Believing that the truth already had been revealed or discovered by earlier philosophers, the main task of the Jewish philosopher was to interpret what was already known and to reconcile apparent difficulties either between religious and philosophic texts, or between various philosophical authorities.

The expansion of philosophical knowledge during the thirteenth century necessitated some attempt to gather the accumulated knowledge in a form convenient to study. Jewish philosophers were familiar with two main classifications of the sciences, one taken from al-Farabi the other taken from ibn Sina.

For Muslim philosophers, "philosophy" was the queen of the sciences. Al-Farabi was the first to systematize the philosophico-scientific knowledge of his day into a coherent overall picture. His *Ihsa' al-Ulum* (Catalogue of Sciences) would have a major influence on Jewish scholars because "Wisdom" would now include all of these sciences. He divided them as follows: 1) The linguistic sciences (grammar); 2) logic (namely, the eight books of Aristotle's *Organon*); 3) mathematics (including arithmetic, geometry, optics, astronomy, music, mechanics); 4) physics (reproducing the topics of Aristotle's books on the natural sciences); 5) metaphysics; 6) politics; 7) jurisprudence; and 8) theology.

Ibn Sina altered the classification of the rational sciences by distinguishing between speculative sciences (those disciplines that seek truth), and the practical sciences (those disciplines that seek well-being). In the former class ibn Sina included physics (i.e., the eight basic sciences drawn from the work of Aristotle and the seven derivative sciences: medicine, astrology, physiognomy, interpretation of dreams, talismans, charms, alchemy); mathematics (which included arithmetic, geometry, astronomy and music, plus ten derivative sciences); and metaphysics (comprised of the five great divisions of the Metaphysics of Aristotle and two derivatives—prophetic inspiration and eschatology). The practical sciences were composed of ethics, economics, and politics.

Medieval Jewish philosophers became familiar with both classifications and produced their own enumeration of the sciences as variations on these themes.[15] In addition, in the thirteenth century Jewish scholars composed philosophical anthologies and encyclopedias, summarizing technical knowledge. *Reshit Ḥokhmah* (Origin of Wisdom) by Shem Tov Falaquera, *Sha'ar ha-Shamayim* (The Gate of Heaven) by Solomon of Arles, *Ya'ir Nativ* (Lighting the Path) by Judah ibn Abbas, and *Midrash ha-Ḥokhmah* (The Exposition of Wisdom) by Judah ben Solomon ha-Cohen ibn Matqah are examples of this genre.[16] These encyclopedias presented an architectonic structure of all the various academic disciplines, the major themes of each discipline, and the references to authoritative views of Greek and Muslim philosophers. While the bulk of the information in these philosophical digests was gleaned from non-Jewish sources, the texts bear a clear Jewish stamp: discrete philosophical ideas were introduced alongside references from biblical and rabbinic sources. The Jewish student of science and philosophy was thus expected to read philosophy in the light of the rabbinic tradition and rabbinic texts in the light of philosophy, on the presumption that both sources of truth were in agreement with each other.

The philosophers' claim that Torah teaches philosophic truths reached its highest expression in philosophical biblical commentaries. Maimonides, we have already shown, had articulated the hermeneutic principles that should guide the philosophic interpretation of the Torah, but he did not produce biblical commentaries. In the thirteenth century, the followers of Maimonides carried out their master's exegetical program and applied his general principles to details of the biblical text.

While philosophers composed commentaries on the Pentateuch as well as on select prophetic books, they particularly favored the books of Proverbs, Ecclesiastics, Job, Song of Songs, and Daniel. Proverbs and Ecclesiastics provided them with biblical support for the pursuit of wisdom and for philosophic morality. The Book of Job was read as a philosophic reflection on the problem of evil and divine providence. The Song of Songs was taken to be the source of metaphysical information about the destiny of the soul and its attainment of intellectual perfection, and the Book of Daniel was a key text for reflections on eschatology.

As Marc Saperstein has aptly put it, a commitment to the philosophical curriculum by no means entailed "a weakening attachment to the Jewish tradition."[17] Since in Judaism Torah study is part of Jewish communal worship, it is not surprising that the philosophers wished to disseminate their philosophic knowledge and interpretation of Torah by delivering sermons on the biblical text from the pulpit.[18] The truth of Torah had to be made explicit to the community at large so as to elevate the quality of Jewish religious life. However, it was precisely the philosophical rendering of biblical texts (in written and oral forms) that caused the major opposition to philosophy from people who regarded it to be an alien intrusion into Judaism.

To defend themselves against these opponents, some philosophers attempted to make the case for philosophy and to enlarge its appeal to the general Jewish public by composing philosophical novels or dramatic dialogues. Typical of this genre were *Sefer ha-Mevaqesh* (The Book of the Seeker) and *Iggeret ha-Vikuah* (Epistle of the Debate) by Shem Tov Falaquera. In *Sefer ha-Mevaqesh* Falaquera dramatized the pursuit of philosophic knowledge through the literary figure of the wandering student who pursues first practical knowledge from various craftsmen and professionals and then embarks on the pursuit of theoretical knowledge by studying the various disciplines with different teachers for specific lengths of time.[19] In *Iggeret ha-Vikkuah*, Falaquera discussed the desired relationship between religion and philosophy by personifying them in the figures of the Pietist and the Scholar, respectively.[20] Both works were written in rhymed prose interspersed with short poems. Their goal was not to impart technical philosophical knowledge, but to inculcate the values of the philosophic life in a larger audience.[21]

The Philosophic Curriculum: Expanding "Wisdom"

The thirteenth century witnessed the explosion of scientific-philosophic learning in the Jewish world. For the philosophers, the expansion was rooted in the initial identification of Torah with Wisdom articulated in the books of Proverbs and Ecclesiastes, both ascribed to Solomon. The famed wise king was now portrayed as the ideally wise man, and his wisdom adduced as proof that philosophy had been cultivated among the Jews before it was co-opted by the Greeks or lost in the travails of life in exile.[22] The alleged Jewishness of philosophy thus legitimized the gleaning of philosophical knowledge with no attention to its origin. Whether the truth is uttered by a Jew or by a non-Jew makes little difference, since truth is one and its source is God.

A quick look into *Reshit Ḥokhmah* by Falaquera illustrates the ambitious scope of the scientific-philosophic curriculum of the thirteenth century. Falaquera recapitulates from the writings of Muslim philosophers the Aristotelian division of the sciences,[23] whose main categories were grammar, logic, mathematics, physics, metaphysics, and politics. Each of these was further subdivided into specialized topics that constituted their own distinct academic subdisciplines. The study of language was subdivided into seven subcategories that encompassed linguistics and semiotics. The study of logic was subdivided in accordance with the topics of Aristotle's *Organon*: *Categoriae, De Interpretatione, Analytica Priora, Analytical Posteriora, Topica,* and *De Sophisties Elenchis,* supplemented by the *Rhetorica* and the *Poetica*.[24] The mathematical sciences included arithmetic, geometry, algebra, mechanics, optics, astronomy (sub-divided into mathematical astronomy and astrology), and music (divided into harmony and musical performance). The discipline of physics was subdivided in accordance with the various topics covered by Aristotle's physical works, such as *Physica, De Caelo et Mundo, De Generatione et Corruptione, Meteora, Parva Naturalia,* and *De Anima.* One of the branches of natural science was medicine, which included the topics of anatomy, pathology, diagnostics, pharmacology, dietetics, hygiene, and therapeutics. Other related natural sciences included physiognomy, alchemy, and talismanics.[25] Metaphysics was subdivided into various topics including the principles of causality, the attributes of God, the separate intelligences, and their relationship to the celestial bodies. Based on these studies in natural philosophy, the discipline of metaphysics was credited with the ability to provide information about the more distinctly religious topics of prophecy, miracles, and the reward and punishment for the soul in the afterlife. Finally, the practical science of politics included ethics, politics, jurisprudence, and dialectics.[26]

Jewish philosophers in the Middle Ages produced other classifications of the sciences, varying from one another in details. Generally speaking, however, they regarded the study of the linguistic and mathematical sciences to be preparatory to the study of the theoretical sciences physics and metaphysics. Thus, especially in Italy, we find that Jewish philosophers formally used the scholastic division of the liberal arts into the three linguistic sciences of the trivium (logic, grammar, and rhetoric) and the four mathematical arts of the quadrivium (arithmetic, geometry, astronomy, and music). These ancillary sciences were necessary before one could embark on the study of the theoretical sciences.

In accord with the organization of medieval encyclopedias, the theoretical sciences were formally distinguished from practical philosophy, which was concerned with types of human management or government (*hanhagah*). The study of ethics dealt with management of the soul, while the management of the household and the interaction among its members was the subject matter of economics, and the management of the city-state was assigned to the science of politics. For Maimonides, as we have seen, practical philosophy also included the "government of the great religion," namely the government of the ideal state by religious laws. In the thirteenth century the disciples of Maimonides, such as Falaquera, continued to regard the study of revealed law as part of political science, but in the fifteenth century Jewish philosophers would declare it to be part of theology, which they would formally distinguish from philosophy.

It is important to note that the identification of Torah with Aristotelian philosophy as posited by Maimonides could lead one to draw opposing conclusions, each emphasizing a different aspect of the Maimonidean legacy. One could say that since the Jews are in possession of the Torah, they do not need any other source of wisdom. Conversely, one could argue that because the Torah contains all forms of human wisdom, Jews are not only permitted to glean true knowledge from all available sources regardless of origin, but have a religious obligation to do so. According to this view, there can be no conflict between the teachings of the sciences and the teachings of Torah, and when apparent conflicts arise, they should be "explained."

Another reasonable consequence of the identification of Torah with philosophic wisdom was a focus on the claim that philosophy is the inner, or hidden, meaning of Torah. If that is so, the goal of human life is to go beyond the "external" expressions of philosophic truth to the "internal" significant core. On this reading, the plain meaning of Torah and the practices it commands are only a means to a higher, cognitive end. At best, the Torah creates the social order that enables one to engage in philosophy; however, what really matters is the perfection of the intellect, culminating in the knowledge of God.

The Status of Aristotle's Ethics

Falaquera's classification of the sciences indicates the immense scope of scientific-philosophic learning. What matters for our discussion is not the precise content of the classification of the sciences, but the ramifications of this curriculum for reflections about the meaning of happiness. In agreement with Greek, Hellenistic, and Muslim philosophers, the followers of Maimonides insisted that the acquisition of philosophic knowledge constituted human happiness. Through the study of philosophy one could acquire correct knowledge about the world and the proper ways of conducting oneself in it. The attainment of moral perfection, however, did not itself constitute the ultimate end of human life. In accord with the exclusive, or intellectualist, reading of Aristotle's *Ethics*, that ultimate goal was declared to be the contemplation of necessary truths, culminating in the knowledge of God. Philosophy, then, was a means to a religious end, and ethics was the science that explained what that ultimate end of human life is.

Following the Aristotelian schema, Jewish philosophers in the thirteenth century regarded ethics as part of political science, but their formal knowledge of this discipline combined the study of Aristotle's *Nicomachean Ethics* with the political teachings of Plato in the *Republic* and the *Laws*. In accord with al-Farabi and Maimonides, the Jewish philosophers in the thirteenth century presupposed the congruence of Aristotle and Plato in regards to ethics. This assumption was not totally wrong, since Aristotle's *Ethics*, as we have seen, evolved out of the problematic set forth by Plato. However, it was primarily the Muslims who presupposed this congruence: they had limited access to Aristotle's *Politics*, a work in which he broke new ground and departed from the theoretical assumptions of his teacher.[27] Therefore, when ibn Rushd discussed Aristotle's political science, he did so by composing a commentary to Plato's *Republic* alongside his commentaries on Aristotle's *Nicomachean Ethics*.[28] For Jewish philosophers such as Falaquera, whose *Reshit Ḥokhmah* recapitulated the teachings of al-Farabi, Plato's political works and Aristotle's *Ethics* complemented one another. They both taught that the ultimate goal of human life is intellectual perfection, which can be attained when humans live in a social order grounded in the knowledge of philosophical truth, namely a state founded by a philosopher. In his commentary on the *Guide*, entitled the *Guide to the Guide*, Falaquera cited from the *Ethics* seven times. It appears, however, that he did not have access to the original text but to an Arabic summary of it.[29]

During the thirteenth century, then, Jewish scholars derived their knowledge of Aristotle's *Nicomachean Ethics* primarily from the works of al-Farabi and from the references to the *Ethics* in the works of Maimonides. Only in the early fourteenth century did they begin to acquire a more systematic knowledge of the work. Two Jewish scholars in Provence were crucial in this regard: Samuel ben Judah of Marseilles and Joseph ibn Kaspi. As Lawrence Berman has shown, Samuel ben Judah introduced Jewish readers to the *Nicomachean Ethics* in stages.[30] First he translated into Hebrew ibn Rushd's short commentary on Plato's *Republic*, which he completed on November 24, 1320. Then he translated ibn Rushd's *Middle Commentary* on the *Ethics*, which he finished at Beaucaire on February 9, 1321. Since Samuel ben Judah was more at home with the disciplines of logic and physics, he found the Arabic translation of the *Ethics* particularly difficult; he left many blank spaces and revised the original translation twice. On September 21, 1321, while imprisoned in the Fort of Rodorta at Beaucaire for being a Jew, he finished his first revision of the translation and indicated that he intended to get the help of Christian scholars who had the commentary of al-Farabi on Aristotle's *Ethics*. Between June 17 and July 16, 1322 he made the second and final revision of his translation of Ibn Rushd's *Middle Commentary on Aristotle's Ethics*, but he proceeded without making contact with the Christian savants because of "the magnitude of the annoyances and persecutions which have overtaken us on the part of this nation which exiles us." This translation became known to Joseph ibn Kaspi, who summarized it in a more elegant and accessible form in his *Terumat ha-Kesef*, which is no longer extant.[31]

Ibn Kaspi, like Samuel ben Judah, was a well-to-do student of philosophy who traveled extensively in Provence, Spain, and North Africa, and devoted his life to the pursuit of philosophic wisdom.[32] Ibn Kaspi's philosophical commentaries were another major vehicle for the popularization of learning about the *Ethics* in Jewish philosophy. Interested in the text for didactic purposes, he read the *Ethics* as a practical guide for the urbane sophisticated Jews who wished to harmonize rabbinic Judaism and philosophy. Thus the work was added to a body of non-halakhic medieval ethical literature initially patterned after the Arabic *adab* literature, which as we have seen in Chapter Four, shaped Sephardic Jewish culture. While this literature is not technically philosophical, it does embody and popularize many philosophical notions, thereby contributing to the dissemination of philosophy among the Jews.

Even though Aristotle's *Ethics* was partially known in Hebrew translation during the thirteenth century and the full text was available by the early fourteenth century, the science of ethics received relatively little attention during these centuries from Jewish philosophers,[33] who at the time focused mainly on physics and metaphysics, relegating ethics to secondary status in their activities. Why? The answer, I believe, is threefold.

First, with respect to ethics, there was little conflict between Greek philosophy and the rabbinic tradition. Since the pursuit of wisdom, the ethos of self-control, and the ideal of moderation were shared by both, the Jewish philosophers did not have to focus their energy on proving their compatibility. Not so with Aristotelian physics and metaphysics, whose assumptions stood in stark contrast to the beliefs of rabbinic Judaism. Thus during the thirteenth and fourteenth centuries, Jewish philosophers had to devote their attention to neutralizing these difficulties.

Second, in the Aristotelian schema of the sciences, ethics was classified as "practical philosophy." In principle, as Aristotle has shown, the science of ethics lacked conceptual clarity: it was closely aligned to the changing conditions of lived human experience. Since in Greek philosophy, that which was subject to change was lower in epistemic value than that which was necessary and unchanging, the theoretical sciences of physics and metaphysics were more important in the hierarchy of sciences. The principles of ethics were relevant to the pursuit of wisdom either as the preparatory acquisition of the virtues, or in the application of theoretical knowledge to social reality. In either case, ethics itself was not the ultimate end of human learning.

Third, in Judaism the praxis of religious life was determined by halakhah itself. The Jewish philosophers all lived by the strictures of the Jewish law and accepted the belief that it (both Written and Oral) was revealed—even though after Maimonides few of them made significant contributions to the study of halakhah. Thus it was more logical to absorb the science of ethics into the philosophy of Jewish law, as Maimonides did, than it was to view ethics as an independent science that charts its own praxis.

For these reasons the study of ethics remained marginal during the first century and a half after Maimonides. For his followers, there was no conflict between philosophy and religion. On the contrary, the ethical teachings of the philosophers supported and deepened religious commitment. At the turn of the fifteenth century, however, Jewish philosophers renewed their interest in the *Ethics* for reasons that will become clear in Chapter Eight.

Philosophical Elitism and Esotericism

Beginning with Saadia Gaon in the tenth century and culminating in Maimonides in the late twelfth century, the Jewish philosophers made the case that the acquisition of philosophical knowledge was a religious obligation. Since reason can verify and concretize the teachings of Scriptures, which are accepted on faith, "it was permissible to interpret Scripture and even negate its literal meaning on the basis of reason.[34]" To the extent that philosophy and rabbinic Judaism appear to contradict each other, the difficulties could be explained in light of the rabbinic principle that the "Torah speaks in the language of human beings." Maimonides, as we have seen, expanded that principle and argued that the Torah itself is a philosophic text that uses figurative language to convey truths. To uncover the hidden philosophic truths of the Torah, one had to read the Bible allegorically or submit its language to close logical and philological scrutiny. Maimonides, however, was also very aware that the esoteric, philosophic truths of divine revelation may be both disturbing and dangerous for the uneducated. Philosophy therefore should not be taught to the masses but should remain the privileged knowledge of the elite.

In the thirteenth century, however, the followers of Maimonides were struggling with the problematic status of the intellectual in the community. On the one hand, they agreed with Maimonides that human beings are not equal in their intellectual proclivities and that "these sciences and especially the divine science cannot be endured by the mind of every man."[35] Defending Maimonides' views on esoteric writing and the elitist tendencies involved in it, the writings of the philosophers were suffused with condescension toward the uneducated masses, who were perceived to be either unwilling or unable to follow the philosophic path and who pursued instead the pleasures of the body. In so doing, the masses forfeited the possibility of enjoying the eternal bliss of the soul.[36] Echoing Maimonides, Falaquera continued to endorse esotericism when he said the following:

> it is improper to reveal to all men the profound matters of wisdom . . . It is possible that they will harm whoever has not engaged in the study of the sciences and is not perplexed, to the point that they will fall into a perplexity from which they cannot be saved . . . The same food which may be poison to one kind of animal is food for another kind of animal . . . Whoever holds that all opinions are suitable for all mankind is as he who holds that all foods are suitable for all kinds of animals.[37]

On the other hand, the philosophers made claims about human nature and posited the ideal of the human species as such (or, in the language of

Maimonides, "man qua man"). To be fully human, all people had to actualize the rational potential through the study of philosophy. In the thirteenth century, then, the philosophers were urged to make the case of philosophy for the rest of society and to spread the knowledge of philosophy through education. Compelled to compromise esotericism, they wrote commentaries on the *Guide of the Perplexed,* in effect explaining the secret teachings of Maimonides. The philosophic, hidden truths of the revealed tradition had to be exposed and communicated to the many so that all would be able to attain the ultimate end of human life. One way of mitigating the tension between esotericism and reaching the masses was to teach philosophy through parables, riddles, figurative speech, and other analogical modalities. While these rhetorical means could safeguard the truths of philosophy, they could not conceal the "missionizing" intentions of the philosophers. The more philosophy spread among the educated classes of Jews, the more heated the debate about the place of philosophy in Jewish traditional society became.

The philosophers made a case that the knowledge of philosophy is necessary for the correct and complete understanding of the Law. According to them, perfect faith requires knowledge of the sciences. However, if one can attain human perfection through the study of philosophy, it is not clear what function the revealed Law has to play in this attainment. Does the Law have any cognitive value for achieving an adequate understanding of the higher demonstrative sciences of physics and metaphysics? Even if the true content of religious Law overlaps that of philosophy, what is the epistemic value of the revealed texts? Moreover, if there is a conflict between the two sets of truth claims, how is one to determine which teachings are correct? These questions and more were hotly debated during the so-called Maimonidean Controversy, to which we now turn.

THE MAIMONIDEAN CONTROVERSY: AN OVERVIEW

In the context of debating the correctness of Maimonides' views and their implications, Jews sorted out an entire range of philosophical and theological questions concerning the origin of the world, the attributes of God, God's providence, the nature of miracles, the nature of man, and the destiny of the human soul. *Since the data upon which Jewish thinkers theorized was articulated by non-Jews, the debate about these questions became inseparable from the debate on the cultural boundaries of Judaism and the desired interaction between Judaism and other religious traditions.* Cultural matters, however, are never merely academic; they necessarily reflect social and political factors. Thus, the debate about Maimonides was inseparably intertwined with a power struggle within the Jewish world that reflected different cultural sensibilities in diverse Jewish communities.

My goal is neither to provide a definitive account of the events, nor to analyze the content of all the treatises involved in the Maimonidean Controversy. This would require a separate book. I wish only to establish that the various phases of the Controversy were linked to each other as aspects of the debate about the meaning of happiness within Judaism, and that the events of the thirteenth century would determine the development of the discourse on happiness in the centuries that followed. Specifically, during the Controversy, kabbalah emerged as an alternative program for conceptualization of human happiness in Judaism. We will discuss this development in the next chapter.

The Maimonidean Controversy of the thirteenth century had four distinct phases.[38] The first phase—the so-called Resurrection Debate (1202–1204)—pertained to the definition of happiness and focused on the definition of the human soul. The second phase (1232–1235) shifted the focus from the definition of the ultimate end of human life to the way in which human well-being is to be attained, bringing to the fore the question of Jewish education—viz., which books should constitute the Jewish curriculum, how they should be studied, and what their relative importance is. The third phase of the debate (in the late 1280s and early 1290s) pertained to the legitimacy of philosophical biblical exegesis. By that time, kabbalah had emerged as an alternative mode of biblical exegesis and interpretation of the commandments, presenting itself as the protector of rabbinic Judaism from the radical interpretation of the philosophers. The final phase erupted in 1303 when Abba Mari of Lunel, an opponent of philosophy, turned to the kabbalist R. Solomon ibn Adret, who was also the halakhic leader of the Jews in Catalonia, urging him to place the study of philosophy under a ban. After a long negotiation, during which the main issues were rehashed once more, a ban was issued on July 31, 1305 on anyone under the age of twenty-five studying philosophy. The interdiction, however, excluded the *Guide of the Perplexed* as well as the practical disciplines of astronomy and medicine.

Idit Dobbs-Weinstein has stated that the Maimonidean Controversy was a struggle between "two fundamentally opposed, essentially ethical world views, namely the nature of the highest human good and the best means to achieve it."[39] This statement is true concerning the core of the controversy, but it is also somewhat misleading. In truth, the Maimonidean Controversy involved more than the two camps of "Maimonists" and "anti-Maimonists":

each of the feuding camps in turn consisted of those who advocated different positions, each of which reflected its own social, political, cultural and personal concerns.

Phase 1: The Debate about Resurrection and the End of Human Life

The Debate in the East

The debate about Maimonides began while he was still living. His intellectualist interpretation of rabbinic eschatology was the first aspect of his thought to draw criticism. The critique came first from Samuel ibn Ali, a Gaon of Baghdad, who represented the continued tradition of Jewish Kalam in the East. Maimonides was extremely critical of the institution of the Gaonate and openly challenged its authority for determining Jewish law. Because he judged it to be mistaken about science and epistemology, Maimonides regarded the tradition of Jewish Kalam to be intellectually inferior in theological matters and devoted many pages in the *Guide* to disproving the position of Kalam theologians (Muslim and Jewish) with regard to the origin of the universe, the attributes of God, and divine providence. Aware of Maimonides' attack on Gaonic authority, ibn Ali was especially threatened by Maimonides' code *The Mishneh Torah* because it undermined the dialectic method of talmudic studies in the Gaonic academies. He and other Babylonian scholars attempted to discredit the code by finding flaws in it.

Samuel ibn Ali was the first to charge that Maimonides' interpretation of *olam ha-ba* was heterodox: it denies bodily resurrection.[40] The information about this charge was communicated to Maimonides by his beloved disciple, Joseph ben Judah ibn Sham'un, who was at the time in Baghdad and was involved in a political battle with Samuel ibn Ali. Joseph ben Judah summarized the claims of the Gaon and attempted to refute them. Maimonides defended his views in a letter that he sent to Joseph ibn Gabir of Baghdad, in which he insisted that the Gaon of Baghdad had misunderstood him, the Torah, and philosophy. To clear himself from further charges, Maimonides composed *Iggeret Tehiyat ha-Metim* (the Epistle on Resurrection).[41] For Maimonides the opposition of Samuel ibn Ali presented what was worst in Jewish Kalam: a half-baked exposure to philosophy that resulted in conceptual blunders. Maimonides' purpose in the Epistle on Resurrection was to show that he did affirm the centrality of the miracle of bodily resurrection in the Jewish belief system. He argued, however, that the precise nature of the miracle is, in principle, unknowable, and that it does not contradict the belief in the intellectual nature of *olam ha-ba*, which according to him constitutes the ultimate end of human life.

Maimonides' Epistle on Resurrection

Maimonides' apologia is anything but straightforward. The problem lies in the fact that to understand his view on bodily resurrection one must consider as well his views on miracles and on the creation of the world, which are themselves unclear. Maimonides reiterates that his belief in bodily resurrection is literal. It is included in the Thirteen Principles of Judaism and thus, no one can accuse him of heresy. Yet, when one turns to his explanation of that resurrection, its precise nature remains elusive. In the *Epistle on Resurrection* Maimonides presents it as a singular miraculous event that exceeds normal human experience. While it is neither naturally impossible nor unbelievable, the bodily resurrection of the dead is not to occur in this world (*ha-olam ha-zeh*) and we have no knowledge of any world other than this one. Hence, in principle we can have no knowledge of bodily resurrection. It cannot be demonstrated rationally and must be accepted on the authority of the tradition.

To clarify his views, Maimonides grudgingly explained the difference between miracles that are naturally possible and those that are naturally impossible miracles. The former class consists of singular events that are predicted by prophets and persistent. They interrupt the regular order of things, but their persistence makes it clear that they cannot be explained as chance events. They are "programmed" into stable nature by God. In contrast, a *naturally impossible* miracle is a singular, non-enduring event; such an event cannot be imagined or thought of prior to its occurrence. We can believe these events have happened only after they have occurred once, but we cannot conceptualize them. Maimonides thus affirms the belief in bodily resurrection, but it makes clear that bodily resurrection is not the ultimate end of Jewish life. That proper end is the immortality of the perfected intellect.

The Debate in the West

While Maimonides was defending himself in the East, his *Mishneh Torah* made important headway in Spanish Jewish culture in the West. In Christian Spain, the nascent Jewish community did not have a longstanding history of involvement in halakhic studies. Maimonides' *Mishneh Torah* summarized all of Jewish law without providing the antecedent legal discourse for it. Furthermore, it specified what all Jews must believe in order to enter *olam ha-ba*. Maimonides was the first to list the obligatory dogmas of Judaism, in which he did include the belief in the resurrection of the dead.

However, given what he said about *olam ha-ba* in his *Commentary on the Mishnah*, it was reasonable to doubt that he regarded resurrection as the ultimate end of human life and the reason for Jewish commitment to the performance of the commandments.

In the end of the twelfth century the *Mishneh Torah* was rapidly gaining acceptance among the Jews who preferred its eminently clear, highly organized, and succinct formulation of rabbinic Judaism. It was not only useful in litigation; it was particularly effective as an educational program. Yet, the more one became acquainted with it, the more one could be disturbed by its intellectualism. This was the response of R. Meir Halevi Abulafia of Toledo, who was the first to understand the full implication of Maimonides' intellectualist conception of human happiness.

The Critique of R. Meir Halevi Abulafia

Bernard Septimus has analyzed the activities of R. Meir Abulafia (known by the acronym Ramah) in the first phase of the Maimonidean Controversy.[42] Our reconstruction is based on his findings. Ramah was born in Toledo about 1165 to one of the aristocratic families of Andalusia that migrated to Castile in flight from the Almohads. On his maternal side, Ramah's family was linked to the upper class leadership of the Jewish community in Provence, a tie central to the development of the Maimonidean Controversy. Ramah correctly understood that Maimonides' identification of *olam ha-ba* with perfection of the rational soul conflicted both with traditional talmudic eschatology and with the view of the ideal life shared by ordinary Jews.

Ramah's opposition to Maimonides was twofold: first, he argued that the Maimonidean vision of the salvation of the individual rational soul did not emerge from the plain meaning of talmudic literature. The Jewish tradition depicts the ideal end of humanity in corporeal, collective terms, which includes the resurrection of the body. It says nothing about the cognitive perfection of the individual soul. Second, Ramah was concerned that Maimonides' understanding of human perfection would jeopardize religious commitment among the Jewish masses. If the ultimate end of human life is an intellectual perfection gained through the study of philosophy, then the causal relationship between observance of the mitzvot and reward and punishment in the afterlife is jeopardized. Given the intellectualism of Maimonides, his stress upon observance of the law was not at all self-evident. Maimonides could thus bring about religious laxity and skepticism, which were most deleterious to Jewish life.

Responses to Ramah

As Ramah began to raise public objections against Maimonides, he turned for support to the scholars of Lunel, where he received his halakhic training and had familial ties. In Provence, the *Mishneh Torah* was already well known to scholars, and their leader, R. Abraham ben David of Posquèire (known in the acronym of Rabad), had already raised serious objections to its conception of Jewish law. Indeed, much of Ramah's halakhic critique of Maimonides was simply an elaboration of issues raised or anticipated by Rabad.[43] However, to Ramah's disappointment, he failed to enlist the support of the scholars in Lunel. Their leader, R. Jonathan ha-Cohen, chose to remain silent rather than compromise the authority of Rabad.

The other scholar who did respond to Ramah's letter, R. Aaron ben Meshulam, had a very different perception of Maimonides. If for Ramah Maimonides was no more than first among equals, for Aaron ben Meshulam and other scholars in Provence, the *Mishneh Torah* was "an oracle of sorts,"[44] whose authority must not be challenged. As Septimus has shown, the Spanish talmudist (Ramah) failed to assess the degree to which Maimonides had already become a cultural icon among the Jews of Provence.

Ramah's critique of Maimonides, respectful as it was, was perceived to be an inappropriate response by a young, talented, but proud upstart who had to be put in his proper place. Aaron b. Meshulam, who composed the response, lectured Ramah about proper conduct and clipped his proud wings. The Provençal scholar went on to give a moderate interpretation of Maimonides' view of *olam ha-ba*, undermining the validity of Ramah's critique.

Ramah's public criticism of Maimonides drew even heavier opposition from a more formidable force—Sheshet ben Isaac Benvenisti of Barcelona, who, like Ramah, came from an old Andalusian aristocratic family. In opposition to Ramah, the Jewish leader from Barcelona straightforwardly endorsed the noncorporeal conception of the ultimate end of human life that Maimonides had proposed. Sheshet was also the first to note that the *Mishneh Torah* was bringing about an educational revolution among the ignorant Spanish masses, and he claimed that scholars were jealous of Maimonides: the *Mishneh Torah* was undermining their exclusive legal hegemony.[45] In Sheshet's view, the talmudic statements that depict corporeal resurrection were all written for the "benefit of the masses who cannot grasp anything that is not physical."[46] The intellectuals, by contrast, understood that the ideal end of human life pertains to the eternal life of the wise soul, and they lived in accordance with this ideal. For Sheshet Benvenisti, Maimonides' noncorporeal interpretation of human perfection deepened the intellectual quality of Jewish life. Hence Ramah's insistence on bodily resurrection was judged to be a defense of a more primitive view.

Ramah felt rebuked, and in 1203 he sought support from the Ashkenazi scholars of Northern France, where rationalist philosophy was not known and where Maimonides was not taken to be the exclusive authority of Jewish law. However, again, to Ramah's disappointment, the French scholars refused to get involved. They agreed that Maimonides' view of *olam ha-ba* was erroneous, but they regarded the difference as merely a legitimate internal Jewish debate about a point of Jewish law. Failing to connect the dispute on the meaning of *olam ha-ba* with the status of philosophy and science in Judaism, they did not perceive the theological implications of the topic as Ramah did. That connection would be made in Northern France during the subsequent three decades, and it would lead to the involvement of the French Tosafists (i.e., the authors of glosses on the Talmud) to become involved in the second phase of the Maimonidean Controversy, during the 1230s.

The debate on resurrection ended once Ramah got hold of Maimonides' *Epistle on Resurrection*, which Maimonides sent to Samuel ibn Tibbon with the express request that it be translated and distributed.[47] Ramah softened his criticism of Maimonides. However, he did not completely withdraw his objection to Maimonides' position, which he regarded as "willful misinterpretation" of rabbinic Judaism.[48]

As was often the case in the Maimonidean Controversy, the opponents of Maimonides understood the depth and subtlety of his views better than his enthusiastic fans did. Ramah correctly grasped the implications of philosophical esotericism for traditional Jewish practice and the ramifications of a cognitive conception of human perfection for the uneducated masses. Ramah was right to perceive that Maimonides' conception of human perfection privileged the intellect over the body and that his rationalist interpretation of miracles, which stressed the perdurance of irregular events, went contrary to the traditional view of miracles. Maimonides' emphasis on the immortality of the soul was in accord with his emphasis on the regularity of natural events, but it compromised God's omnipotence and restricted God's ability to interfere with and suspend natural laws.

PHASE 2: THE DEBATE ABOUT JEWISH EDUCATION

During the first three decades of the thirteenth century, the study of philosophy continued to make inroads into the culture of the Jewish educated class in Spain and Provence. Samuel ibn Tibbon's *Ma'amar Yiqavu ha-Mayyim* (A Treatise on [the verse] "Let the Water be Collected") and his *Commentary on Ecclesiastes* were written to specify the philosophic meaning of the biblical text. The former text concerned the creation narrative of the Bible, articulating a distinct philosophic ethos. As reflected in the works of the ibn Tibbon family and its associates, Maimonidean rationalism was no longer confined to the views of the outstanding savant but became a distinct variant of Judaism, with its own educational program. Moreover, the very success of philosophy among the educated class in Provence precipitated a debate about its place in Jewish culture and necessitated a delineation of boundaries between Judaism and other cultures. Since philosophical knowledge was derived from Greek, Hellenistic, and Muslim texts, it became apparent to the opponents of Maimonides that philosophy was "alien" to Judaism.

Historically, of course, the status of philosophy in Judaism was much more complex, as we have seen in Chapters Two and Three. A superficial knowledge of Hellenistic culture was shared by broad segments of the Jewish population in Palestine and the diaspora, but a deep knowledge of Greek and Hellenistic literature was limited to a relatively small, educated elite. We have noted how the ethical teachings of the rabbis absorbed certain sentiments and ideals of Hellenistic philosophical schools, despite the fact that some rabbinic sources reflect a manifest distrust and suspicion of Greek culture. Thus, the Babylonian Talmud Menahot 64b includes the statement "Cursed is the one who teaches his son Greek wisdom," even though another source in Tractate Sotah 49b and Baba Kama 83a relates that the school of Raban Gamliel in Yavneh taught "Greek wisdom" to "five hundred children." What exactly "Greek wisdom" meant here is a matter of dispute. Dov Rapel's conjecture that the term referred to rhetoric is the most convincing to me.[49] The suggestion that the study of Greek rhetoric could have a deleterious effect on one's religious commitment was not unreasonable: it was the exposure to the dominant culture that challenged commitment to the ancestral tradition. The Talmud therefore does contain statements that causally link heresy with the study of "external books."

By the thirteenth century the scope of "Greek wisdom" grew exponentially with the absorption of the Aristotelian corpus. As more Aristotelian texts became available in Hebrew, it became necessary to define the scope and content of the Jewish curriculum. The cultural issues that were brought about by the transformation of Iberian Jewry during the twelfth century finally came to a boiling point in 1232.[50]

Conflict between Divergent Views of Jewish Culture in Provence

It was no coincidence that the second phase of the Maimonidean Controversy erupted in Provence, which was a unique meeting ground for diverse

Jewish subcultures. In the twelfth century its Jewish communities boasted a thriving talmudic culture, as is evident in the quality of the biblical exegesis, midrash, and halakhic expertise produced there during this period.

For one thing, after 1148 Provence absorbed many Jewish émigrés from Andalusia who were active in promoting their distinctly philosophic culture through Hebrew translation. Concomitantly, the talmudic scholars of Provence were tied to the halakhic traditions of the French talmudists, who, as we noted above, had little knowledge of philosophy but were familiar, through contact with the Jewish communities in Europe, with the mystical teachings and ethical ideals of German pietism, which developed rabbinic esotericism into a full-fledged and distinct worldview. These speculations, conscious attempts to reassert authentic rabbinic Judaism over and against the perceived deviations of Maimonides and his followers, were later crucial in the emergence of kabbalah in Provence.

The controversy began when R. Solomon ben Abraham of Montpellier, the main opponent of philosophic education, started to agitate against the spread of philosophy in Provence, while, at the same time, defending the elevated stature of Maimonides. Directing his ire instead at the intellectual followers of Maimonides, especially Samuel ibn Tibbon, Solomon charged that they spread confusion and weakened allegiance to Judaism. To bolster his position, he decided to take the case outside the boundaries of Provence and enlisted the aid of talmudic scholars in the Jewish communities of Northern France. Solomon sent his student R. Jonah Gerondi to France to bring about a public condemnation of philosophic education and to ban the study of Maimonides' *Guide* and his Book of Knowledge in the *Mishneh Torah*. The French scholars did get involved; they publicly rebuked those who studied philosophy, yet avoided any personal attack on Maimonides. Though the original text of the ban (*ḥerem*) did not survive, a letter that apparently accompanied it[51] indicates the main charge against the philosophers. Because they were influenced by Maimonides, and because they studied philosophic texts by non-Jews,[52] they were accused of doubting the veracity of biblical narratives and traditional Jewish eschatology.

Responding to the public stance of the Northern French rabbis, the leaders of Narbonne and Lunel described the "men of Tzarfat" as unenlightened, superstitious, and impulsive.[53] Furthermore, they attempted to isolate R. Solomon ben Abraham and his disciples by issuing a counter-ban of excommunication. To gain further support for the counter-ban, the Maimonists dispatched to Spain R. David Kimhi—the grammarian, biblical exegete, poet, and translator who had introduced Spanish Jewish philosophy to the Jewish communities in Provence. Kimhi had complete success in

Aragon, a partial success in Catalina, but little success in Castile,[54] all of which indicates the complexity of Jewish culture in Spain, where there was no clear correspondence between cultural and social status.

In 1232 a cautiously conditional ban was issued by the Aragonese Maimonist community of Saragossa, which was led by the family of Bahya Al-Constantini, a Jewish courtier of King James I. Other communities in Aragon (Huesca, Monzon, Clatayud, and Lerida) supported a somewhat weaker version of the ban. However, in the Catalan communities of Barcelona and Gerona there were indications of strong sympathy for Solomon's cause, reflecting social conflicts within those communities.[55] Philosophy aside, a new middle class resented the aristocratic control of the old Andalusian families and demanded greater participation in communal decision-making.

The Role of Nahmanides in the Debate

As the ideological struggle began to involve issues of political power, it also became personal. The aristocratic leaders of Barcelona attacked the character of R. Jonah Gerondi, charging that he was a descendent of an illegitimate marriage.[56] R. Jonah was the cousin of R. Moses ben Nahman (Nahmanides) of Gerona, perhaps the most complex of all the acting personae in the Maimonidean drama.[57] Culturally Nahmanides stood at a crossroad: he was born in a Christianized environment but was educated both in the Judeo-Arabic scientific tradition of Andalusia and in the talmudic culture of Franco-German Jewry. Moreover, he was instrumental in the emergence of kabbalah at the turn of the thirteenth century as an alternative, parallel program to philosophical spirituality. In Gerona he was linked to a small group of kabbalists who began to write down the principles of kabbalistic theosophy and apply them to biblical exegesis.[58] Nahmanides is also associated with the social upheaval in the Jewish communities of Barcelona caused by the rise of a new social class in the Jewish community of Catalonia that challenged the control exercised by the Jewish aristocrats from Andalusia.[59] In the dispute during the 1230s, however, he played a moderating role. In Septimus' words, Nahmanides

> attempted to defend the Montpellier anti-rationalists from the ban of a Provençal communal establishment for whom Maimonides had become sacrosanct. At the same time he wrote a classic open letter to the Tosafist schools of northern France in defense of Maimonides and

sought (apparently with some success) to have their ban against *Sefer ha-Madda* and the *Guide of the Perplexed* withdrawn.[60]

Hence Nahmanides was instrumental in rallying the communities of Barcelona and Gerona against David Kimhi, openly challenging the local Jewish aristocracy led by the brothers Abraham and Judah ibn Hasdai. Conversely, Nahmanides was helpful in showing that the study of "Greek wisdom" was not forbidden by the rabbis, and that Jews had to resort to the books of the Greeks only because they had lost their own philosophic tradition when they were exiled,[61] which became a standard legitimization of its study. Substantively, Nahmanides' position indicates how the debate during the 1230s linked the question of happiness to three other issues: the nature of miracles; the status of rabbinic *aggadot*, especially about the eschatological end; and the destiny of the human soul in the afterlife.

As regards the first topic, Nahmanides objected to the naturalism of Maimonides, which highlighted the regularity and stability of the natural order. As far as Nahmanides was concerned, Maimonides' view of nature was not any different from Aristotle's, for both held that the laws of nature were necessary and unchanging. In truth, Maimonides' position on miracles was much more complex.[62] He departed from Aristotle most significantly when he affirmed creation and made room for divine voluntaristic activity. Indeed, for him, the occurrence of miracles attested to the creation of the world.[63] Maimonides speaks about miracles in three difference ways: 1) as ex nihilo creations or incursions of God, which reflect God's ability to mold nature according to His will;[64] 2) as stipulations with natural processes at the close of creation to unfold in extraordinary ways at appointed times in the future;[65] and 3) unanticipated natural anomalies.[66] Furthermore, while Maimonides affirmed the possibility of all miracles related in Scripture, he did not interpret them all literally. When the literal meaning of the biblical text plainly conflicted with Aristotelian physics—for example, in the case of Joshua's halting the course of the sun, which denies the perfect motion of the celestial bodies—Maimonides opted for a figurative interpretation of the biblical text. That Maimonides insisted on the inviolability of the natural order once it was fixed and that he regarded the activity of divine will to be consequent upon God's wisdom suggests that his views on miracles in fact coincided with the naturalistic Aristotelian worldview—where miracles are in complete harmony with nature and are a product of God's impersonal governance of the world.

Nahmanides reached this conclusion as well when he rejected the notion that miracles are exceptions "programmed" into the natural order at the point of creation. He argued instead that all things in the created order constitute "hidden miracles" and "have nothing to do with 'nature' or 'the customary order of the world.'"[67] For Nahmanides, then, the very existence and operation of the created world is a result of constant divine activity. The extraordinary events that the Jewish tradition considers as "miraculous" are manifestations of God's creation, God's knowledge of particulars, providence, and hidden miracles.[68] By denying the necessary aspect of "nature," Nahmanides wished to insist on direct divine involvement, especially with regard to the affairs of Israel. As such, there is nothing "natural" about human affairs, especially not human well-being. Rather, happiness can be understood only with reference to God's creative activity.

On the status of talmudic aggadot, Nahmanides also developed a very subtle position that validated a nonliteral interpretation and even recognized limits on the legal force of aggadah. This position would be the crux of his defense of Judaism against Christian polemics in 1263.[69] In the Maimonidean Controversy the aggadot, which vividly depict the world to come in corporeal terms, were hotly debated. The Maimonists insisted on giving them a nonliteral interpretation, whereas the anti-Maimonists insisted that at least for the Jewish masses the literal meaning carried important emotional force that should not be taken away. Nahmanides' rather subtle endorsement of a nonliteral interpretation would make him much closer to the rationalist camp than some of his own cohorts would have preferred.

With regard to the third issue, the destiny of the soul, Nahmanides' view was no less spiritual than the view of the philosophers. In *Sha'ar ha-Gemul* (Gate of Retribution), the last segment of his *Torat Adam* (Laws about Humans), he developed a doctrine of the soul that absorbed many features of Platonist ontology and psychology. Presenting the soul as an immaterial substance whose perfection, i.e., holiness, is possible only through obedience to God's commands,[70] Nahmanides saw the perfected soul as attaining a level of divinity superior to the status of the perfected intellect. He thus reaffirmed traditional Jewish eschatology and elaborated on the destiny of the human soul in the afterlife. Although he rejected the intellectualization of Judaism, his views on the afterlife indicate that he too reflected on the ultimate end of human life in regard to the perfection of the individual soul. What Nahmanides and other kabbalists proposed are alternative programs for individual salvation. We will explain those alternatives in the next chapter by looking more closely at the views of *Sefer ha-Zohar* (Book of

Splendor), the central text of Spanish kabbalah produced during the third phase of the Maimonidean Controversy.

The struggle to find the proper balance between philosophy and kabbalah in regard to human salvation was manifested in the works of Nahmanides' close associate, the poet Meshulam Da Piera, who used his poetic talent to defend the aggadot against the views of the Maimonists. His polemical poetry—written in the stylistic norms of the Andalusian school, now transported to Christian Spain—used irony and satire to reject the philosophic view of salvation and to defend the traditional Jewish perspectives on corporeal resurrection and the miraculous nature of Torah.[71] Da Pierra's commitment to kabbalah undergirded his approach to the biblical text as well as his rejection of both philosophical allegorization and the philosophic conception of happiness.

No less than for Nahmanides, Da Piera's conflict was intense and personal. When Da Piera would later learn about Nahmanides' moderate stance, he composed a poem depicting Nahmanides as a convert to the rationalist camp![72] Eventually he withdrew from the public debate. The complex confluence of themes in the Maimonidean Controversy illustrates that a division of the feuding camps between "rationalists" and "anti-rationalists" is much too simplistic.

The Involvement of the Church

The tone of the Maimonidean Controversy during the 1230s became exceedingly shrill when Maimonides' *Guide* and the Book of Knowledge of the *Mishneh Torah* were denounced (allegedly by Solomon ben Abraham) to church authorities in Montpellier and subjected to inspection. While the Jewish community was struggling with a proper response to the writings of Aristotle, the Christian West was undergoing a parallel struggle regarding their place in the curricula of the universities. In 1210 and again in 1215, the study of Aristotle's works in natural philosophy (i.e., physics and metaphysics) were placed on ecclesiastical ban by the University of Paris.[73] Books by philosophers such as David of Dinant were publicly burned, and students of philosophy were charged with heresy and subject to imprisonment or burning at the stake.[74]

In 1231 Pope Gregory IX himself renewed the prohibition on the study of Aristotle and appointed a special censorship commission to expurgate all heterodoxy from his works. These bans were unable to halt the spread of Aristotelianism in European universities, but they do suggest that the absorption of Aristotle's natural philosophy in the Christian West did not occur without struggle. Whoever denounced the works of Maimonides to the clergymen in Montpellier apparently knew what he was doing.[75] Thereafter the Christian authorities became involved in internal Jewish affairs, compromising the cultural autonomy of Jewish communities. This trend was exacerbated as the century progressed, and soon Jews were forced to submit themselves to sermonizing by Christian friars.

What precisely was done to Maimonides' works is still not entirely clear. The more cautious reconstruction of events, as related by Jeremy Cohen, is probably close to the truth. It seems likely that the books were indeed inspected by the special commission and certain pages perhaps recommended for public burning. But there is no direct evidence that the works were actually consigned to the flames in a public spectacle,[76] as was the fate of a Talmud publicly burned in 1248 in Paris, having been found "guilty" of blasphemy against Christianity in two Inquisitorial proceedings.[77] Be that as it may, the very fact that Maimonides' books were denounced to the Christian clergy was viewed in the Jewish world as an act of treason, and the pro-Maimonists were determined to punish the culprits. David Kimhi, who was at the time in Avilla but confined to bed due to illness, publicly accused Solomon ben Abraham of Montpellier of informing on Maimonides. However, Kimhi failed to rally the Jewish communities in Castile (especially in Toledo and Burgos) to support appropriate punishment of the alleged culprit.

Alfakar's Critique of Maimonides: The Social Dimension of the Debate

The aristocrats in Toledo and Burgos turned to Meir Halevi Abulafia (Ramah), the pivotal figure of the first controversy on resurrection. Although Ramah proposed that both sides of the controversy should come together before him and submit their claims to adjudication, this did not happen. Instead, another member of the same social class, the physician Judah ben Joseph Alfakar, forcefully argued the anti-Maimonist case against the pro-Maimonides position of David Kimhi.

Alfakar's critique focused on a disputed issue in the legacy of Maimonides that was directly related to happiness. Maimonides' rationalist exposition of the mitzvot stated their rationales in terms of the intellectual development of the human species. Thus the laws about sacrifices were necessary because at the time they were given, sacrifice was the common mode of worship. The historicization of the mitzvot indicated their value was merely instrumental, which made it reasonable to assume that in the future, when humanity reached a higher intellectual development, the mitzvot would not be necessary. Alfakar rejected Maimonides' rationalization of the mitzvot because it took human well-being as its standard. For Alfakar, the Maimonidean understanding of nature was also problematic because "biblical teachings and Greek naturalism are irrevocably opposed and irreconcilable." According to Alfakar, Maimonides'

> intention was [to explain the Bible such] that the laws of nature not be abrogated, so that the Torah might be at one with Greek philosophy. And he imagined the former and the latter to be twin gazelles. But [instead] there is mourning and lamentation; for the earth cannot bear them dwelling together as sisters; for not like unto the Egyptian women are the Hebrew women! This Torah declares: "Not so—my son is the live one and your son is the dead!" And her rival vexes her sorely.[78]

Alfakar's rebuttal of Kimhi shows that he fully understood the connection between modes of biblical interpretation and the attainment of happiness. For Alfakar the nonliteral interpretation of the rabbinic tradition, which was practiced in his own day (especially by David Kimhi!), introduced naturalism into Judaism, which was contrary to the rabbinic tradition. For the philosophers, the exclusive road to salvation lay in the natural self-actualization of the human intellect. The attainment of philosophic perfection, then, had nothing to do with the efficacy of the Torah's commandments; it was strictly determined by nature.

The Inter-Communal Struggle

Kimhi, in his response to Alfakar, attempted to defend the philosophic perspective by revisiting the issues of noncorporeal resurrection and the incorporeality of God. He insisted that a philosophic understanding of the tradition helped to confirm his allegiance to the faith, and that philosophy had never led him to forsake the halakhic life.

When Kimhi failed to convince Alfakar and other members of the aristocracy in Castile, he turned to Meshulam ben Kalonimus, the *Nasi* of Narbonne,[79] requesting further support from the elder statesman. Meshulam issued a moderate letter of recommendation to Kimhi and a moderate defense of the *Guide*. However, all this was to no avail. Kimhi was eventually expelled from Burgos, having failed to gain support for the condemnation of Solomon ben Abraham of Montpellier for allegedly denouncing the works of Maimonides to the Church. Alfakar later modulated his position and regretted the blanket condemnation of the Provençal rationalists. However, it was too late. The controversy had become charged with ad hominem attacks and vicious rumors that were spread abroad through letters.

The Provençal scholars in Lunel and Narbonne wanted the Jewish community in Spain to ratify the excommunication of Abraham ben Solomon and his associates. However, now it seemed that the anti-rationalists in Montpellier would go unpunished and would be able to flee southward. Indeed, Barcelona had become the refuge for excommunicated anti-rationalists from Montpellier. There they were welcomed by Nahmanides and another talmudic scholar, Samuel ha-Sardi.

The attempt to defame the reputation of Jonah Gerondi was revived by the leaders of the aristocratic, pro-Maimonist camp—Abraham and Judah ibn Hasdai—who turned to Judah Alfakar, expecting him to express the same view on grounds of social solidarity, but Alfakar and other members of the aristocracy in Burgos and Toledo aligned themselves with the anti-Maimonist camp, and ibn Hasdai failed to rally the old families around the banner of philosophy.

The Debate in Egypt

While inter-communal struggles in Europe grew more intense, knotted, and vindictive, in 1235 the Maimonidean controversy spread to Jewish communities in Egypt when a physician in Montpellier, Isaac ben Shem Tov, reported the events to Abraham, the son of Maimonides, who was the official leader of Egyptian Jewry. In his *Milḥamot ha-Shem* (The Wars of the Lord), the son of Maimonides recapitulated the events of the controversy, which for him hinged on acceptance of the noncorporeal nature of God. He accused the Provençal anti-Maimonists of being "confused in their knowledge, corrupt in their faith, barren of understanding" because they took the aggadic depiction of God to be literally true.[80] For the son of Maimonides, such literalism, which Maimonides had appropriately rejected, was the cause of confusion about the nature of the world to come and about God. It was, therefore, a mistake to depict the ideal end of human life in corporeal terms, since neither God nor the human soul is of corporeal substance. For Abraham, this corporealist approach of the Northern rabbis was itself evident influence of their Christian cultural environment, which he regarded as inferior to Islam.81 His own religious philosophy indicates how Sufi mysticism, rabbinic piety, and intellectual rationalism can coalesce in the pursuit of human perfection.82

Evaluation: The Core Issue in the Debate

This entire controversy—with the bans, counter-bans, emissaries, propaganda letters, and ad hominem attacks—eventually subsided, even though its underlying issues continued to simmer in Jewish culture and would erupt at least twice more before 1306. I conjecture that the debate on Maimonides was acrimonious precisely because at its core the salvation of the individual soul was at stake. All of its other issues—anthropomorphism, the origin of the world, the meaning of miracles, biblical exegesis, the rationales for the commandments, the composition of Jewish education, and the viability of astrology—led back to that central one: the salvation of the individual soul as the ultimate end of human life. It is no coincidence, then, that during the controversy Nahmanides composed *Sha`ar ha-Gemul* to articulate a Jewish perspective on personal salvation that differed from the philosophers' view and that Hillel ben Shemuel of Verona, a major player in the third phase of the Controversy, wrote *Sefer Tagmulei ha-Nefesh* (A Book on the Rewards of the Soul), reformulating the philosophic position and showing that it is in full accord with the rabbinic tradition. Defining the end of human life in terms of personal salvation divided Jews among themselves no less that it separated them from Christians, for whom belief in Christ was the only path to salvation.

PHASE 3: THE DEBATE ABOUT BIBLICAL EXEGESIS

The controversy of the 1230s resolved nothing. The theoretical and cultural disputes continued to simmer for the rest of the century as Jewish philosophy and kabbalah developed side by side as parallel programs for the attainment of human perfection.

The Debate in Italy

During the 1240s the translation of philosophic texts into Hebrew was intensified, championed by members of the ibn Tibbon family, who continued to generate translations of Aristotle's works into Hebrew. One member of the family, Jacob Anatoli, took the enterprise to Italy in the 1240s. Invited to the court of Frederick II in Naples, he collaborated with Michael Scotus in the translation of Aristotelian philosophy into Latin. Anatoli also inaugurated, as we noted above, the delivery of sermons based on philosophical principles, which was one of the reasons for the eruption of the third phase of the Maimonidean controversy in 1289–1291. The Maimonidean program of biblical interpretation was no longer confined to the written word; it spread orally through the main oral mode of Jewish education—preaching. And for those listeners who opposed philosophy, philosophical biblical interpretation was the cause for religious laxity and even an incitement to conversion.

Meanwhile, Anatoli's student Moses ben Solomon of Salerno translated the *Guide* into Latin and consulted the monk Nicholas of Giovinazzo in the project.[83] This translation was used by Thomas Aquinas when he attempted to resolve the tension between Aristotelian philosophy and the Christian faith. While indebted to Maimonides' philosophy, Aquinas pursued a different way to harmonize religion and philosophy, which will be discussed in Chapter Nine. Interestingly, when Jewish scholars became familiar with the Thomistic model, they found it suitable for reconciling reason and religious faith. The first to recognize this value was the Italian Jewish philosopher Hillel ben Samuel of Verona, who was deeply involved in the third phase of the controversy during the late 1280s.

Hillel came from a French family and received a traditional rabbinic education along with his study of medicine and philosophy. In Rome he befriended Zerahya ben Sheltiel, a scholar from Barcelona who settled in Rome and was instrumental in the dissemination of Aristotelianism among Italian Jews. Zerahya translated from Arabic into Hebrew the works of Aristotle, Themistius, al-Farabi, and ibn Rushd as well as the Neoplatonic text *Theology of Aristotle*, and placed Jewish Aristotelianism on a firm footing in Italy.[84] Other associates of Hillel were Isaac ben Mordecai, the physician of the Pope Nicholas IV, and Abraham Abulafia, a mystic who developed his idiosyncratic speculative theories about the meaning of Maimonides' *Guide*.[86] Prior to Abulafia, Zerahya ben Shaltiel composed the first linear commentary on the *Guide*, making it a canonic text that should be studied with great care so as to be applied correctly to the interpretation of the biblical text and rabbinic literature.

The Debate Moves to the East

In the late 1280s the agitation against Maimonides was renewed, this time by another French Tosafist, Solomon Petit, who settled in Acre, Palestine. There he spread the "signed letters" of French scholars lobbying against the study of Maimonides' philosophical works. When news about Solomon's campaign reached Hillel ben Samuel, Hillel wrote to his influential friend at the Papal court, R. Isaac ben Mordecai, asking him to use his political influence to bring an end to this anti-Maimonist campaign. Hillel's attempt was successful. In separate decrees the rabbinic leadership in Babylonia (Iraq), Palestine, Egypt, and Italy issued bans of excommunication against those who sought to curtail the study of the *Guide*.[86]

By the late 1280s the accusation that adherence to Maimonides' philosophy was detrimental to Judaism could not stick. In 1291 Hillel of Verona completed his *Sefer Tagmulei ha-Nefesh* (A Book on the Rewards of the Soul), where he would prove that intellectual perfection is personal. Sorting out the psychological theories of Aristotle, Alexander of Aphrodisias, Themistius, al-Farabi, ibn Sina, ibn Rushd, and Maimonides,[87] Hillel argued that what survives the death of the body is both spiritual and individual, a position articulated two decades later by Thomas Aquinas.[88] According to Hillel, "eternal happiness" (*haztlahah nitzhiyit*) involves not just the perfected intellect, as Maimonides held, but also the sensitive power (*ha-koah ha-margish*), the appetitive power (*ha-koah ha-mit`orer*), and even the imagination (*ha-koah ha-medameh*), provided these functions are perfected through the cultivation of virtues.[89] It is the virtuous life charted by the life of mitzvot that leads to personal survival, contrary to the view of ibn Rushd, for whom immortality was only universal, gained through conjunction between the human intellect and the Active Intellect. Hillel tried mightily to chart a middle course between Maimonides and Nahmanides concerning the nature of the world to come.[90] Even if he was not entirely successful, *Tagmulei ha-Nefesh* makes clear that what was at stake in the Maimonidean Controversy was holding the right views about the ultimate end of human life, i.e., about happiness.

Mitzvot as a Path to Happiness: Philosophy versus Kabbalah

Parallel to the dissemination of Jewish Aristotelianism, kabbalah was cultivated by small groups in Gerona, Barcelona, Toledo, and Burgos—the very places where the Maimonidean Controversy flared. As we shall see in the next chapter, the kabbalists absorbed many philosophical concepts, including the notion of the salvation of the perfected soul as the ultimate end. However, they gave these concepts a very different slant within the context of kabbalistic theosophy and biblical exegesis.

Reasserting the rabbinic myth of the love affair between God and Israel, the kabbalists attempted to delve into the mysteries of God's inner life. The

Torah, they claimed, is not the disclosure of the laws by which the natural world, including the human world, is governed (as the Maimonists believed), but a manifestation of the dynamic life of God. God is a unity within a plurality of ten powers (the *sefirot*), and God's revelation of Himself in the Torah constitutes the path by which Israel can communicate with Him. In contrast to the Maimonidean historical and instrumentalist exposition of the mitzvot, the kabbalists articulated a sacramental view of the commandments, according to which they are themselves the symbols for participation in, and even integration into, the life of God. The path toward human perfection leads through the performance of divine commandments with proper intention.

The first opposition to kabbalah was voiced already in the 1240s, when Meir ben Simon of Narbonne attacked the kabbalistic conception of God as a radical departure from Jewish monotheism.[91] The charge did not stick, however. Kabbalists continued to elaborate their rather daring speculations about God and to present kabbalah as the authentic program for the attainment of human perfection. By the 1280s the *Zohar* began to circulate in Spain, bringing together all the various strands of kabbalistic speculations that had developed since the beginning of the century.

Similar to Maimonides' *Guide*, the *Zohar* presents itself as a revelation of the Torah's mysteries, knowledge of which brings about more than the salvation of just the individual soul. Proper decoding of the Torah according to the directions of the *Zohar* would yield the salvation of society, the cosmos, and even God himself. The *Zohar* would become a credible theoretical alternative to Maimonides' philosophy only in the fifteenth century, and culturally kabbalah would supplant Maimonideanism only by the end of the sixteenth century. Still, the early fourteenth-century kabbalists who fell under the spell of the *Zohar* correctly understood it as an alternative interpretation of the nexus of Torah and Wisdom that undergirded the discourse on happiness.

While philosophy and kabbalah were struggling to define the appropriate approach to the divinely revealed text, Jews had to defend their sacred tradition against mounting pressures from the outside. In 1236 rabbinic Judaism in France confronted a major assault, orchestrated by the apostate Nicholas Donin.[92] He argued that Jews had shifted their loyalty from the Bible to the Talmud, and thereby undermined the place that Augustine's doctrine of the Jews as "witness people" accorded to them in Christendom.[93] The accusation was not totally without basis, but referred to the extensive glosses on the Talmud composed during the twelfth and early thirteenth century by the talmudic scholars known as the Tosafists.

Worse yet, inquisitorial tribunals in 1239 and 1244 found the Talmud guilty of blasphemous statements against Christianity. As a result, copies of the Talmud were collected and consigned to the flames, and the ability of French Jewry to study it was severely curtailed. Two decades later, another apostate, Pablo Christiani in Barcelona, convinced the Dominican order to challenge the Jewish community to a public debate in which the opposite charge was advanced—namely, that the talmudic corpus contains statements that teach Christian truths.[94]

Nahmanides, the leader of Catalan Jewry and a major player in the Maimonidean Controversy, defended Judaism against the claims of Pablo Christiani in the Barcelona debate. Cornered by his skillful opponent, Nahmanides conceded that the homilies of the Talmud had no legal power in Judaism and that they must not be understood literally—a view clearly at odds with his view of aggadah and indicative of the difficult situation in which Nahmanides found himself. Though after the debate he published a report in Hebrew detailing his alleged success, the Dominicans convinced the king, James I of Aragon, to expel Nahmanides from Spain, thus indicating the declining power of Jewish courtiers. By fleeing to Palestine Nahmanides saved his life, but in retrospect the Barcelona debate can be viewed as the beginning of the end of Jewish life in Spain. In Chapter Eight we will see how the confrontation between Judaism and Christianity directly shaped the philosophic discourse on happiness.

In any case, at the close of the thirteenth century, the educated classes no longer endorsed a literalist approach to the sacred tradition. The only question was: Which nonliteral interpretation manifests most deeply the mysteries of divine revelation? By the end of the century there no longer was any doubt about Jewish interest in philosophy and science. Philosophical concepts and terminology were absorbed into Jewish self-understanding by both philosophers and kabbalists. Philosophy and kabbalah were cultivated by people of all social classes, and there was no correlation between social status and allegiance to any specific spiritual program. Against this reality, the only remaining attempt to curb the spread of philosophy was by limiting its study to men over the age of twenty-five.

PHASE 4: THE DEBATE ON ASTROLOGY AND THE BAN ON PHILOSOPHY

Renewed Agitation in Provence—Abba Mari and the Question of Astrology

The last phase of the Maimonidean Controversy began when a Provençal scholar, Abba Mari of Lunel (known as Don Astruk), opened negotiations with Solomon ibn Adret (known as Rashba), the halakhic leader of

Aragonese Jewry, who had considerable influence in Provence. Rashba received queries about Jewish law from the Jewish communities in Perpignan, Montpellier, Narbonne, Carcasonne, Marseilles, and Avignon. His responses were held in high esteem. However, Rashba himself, as Marc Saperstein has noted, had "a clear recognition of the principle of local self-determination and the importance of local custom in deciding the law."[95] When Abba Mari initially turned to Rashba, he actually asked him about a totally different matter—whether or not it was permissible to use a certain kind of amulet, in conjunction with astrological prognostication, to treat a certain kidney disease. Abba Mari's concern was the much broader issue of the rightful place of philosophy in traditional Jewish society. If philosophy could not be eradicated, at least it could be restricted.

Rashba was slow to act: he recognized that the autonomous nature of Jewish communities limited his legal power. Hence he insisted that the initiative for the requested restriction of philosophy should come from the Jewish communities in Provence and not from him; he would only sign a ban cast collectively by Provençal scholars. Abba Mari then had to focus his efforts on gaining support within the broad scholarly Jewish communities there. In Provence, however, a ban of excommunication first had to be authorized by the authorities. Furthermore, such a ban required the full consent of the representative council of the Jews.[96] Because of these roadblocks, Abba Mari focused his effort on the communities of Montpellier, only to find that community divided. For example, Jacob ben Machir (a member of the Tibbonide family) and other scholars of philosophy opposed the restrictions on philosophy, and challenged the very legality of Rashba's interference in Jewish affairs of communities not directly under his jurisdiction.[97]

Ibn Machir's challenge to Rashba reflected the new political reality in Southern France during the reign of Philip the Fair (1285–1314).[98] That Capetian monarch, having gained control over Languedoc and Montpellier, both of which had previously been under the sovereignty of Aragon, had to come to terms with their integration into France. The Jewish community itself was just as divided in its assessment of these external political developments as it was over the value of cultivating philosophy. However, the Christian authorities supported the rationalist camp. Presumably, they believed that exposure to philosophy would make Jews more amenable to Christianity.[99] That expectation made sense only against the background of the scholastic absorption of Aristotelianism into Christian theology, especially in the works of Thomas Aquinas.

The Ban of Rashba on the Study of Philosophy

Abba Mari's unsuccessful attempts to gain support made him turn to Rashba again and propose that a ban on philosophy should be issued first in Barcelona—with the assumption that it would then be accepted in Provence. Events finally moved in this direction when Abba Mari's campaign received the support of a Jewish leader in Narbonne, Calonimus ben Todros, who was apparently kin of Abba Mari. It was the support of this politically influential person, whose position as *Nasi* was still regarded with great esteem, that made Rashba finally agree to impose the ban.

The ordinance to limit the study of philosophy to those over the age of twenty-five was apparently composed by Abba Mari and then signed by Calonimus ben Todros. It led to the formal ban issued by Rashba and other scholars in Barcelona on July 31, 1305. The opponents of the ban issued their own counter-ban in Montpellier, and Abba Mari and his supporters countered with their own counter-counter-ban. The whole affair finally subsided with a rude awakening of the Jews to their precarious political situation. In 1306 the Jews of France were expelled from the royal territories.[100] Many Provençal Jews thus settled in Spain or in Provençal towns still under the Aragonese crown.

Abba Mari settled in Perpignan, where he collected the three years of correspondence that constituted the final stage of the controversy. He entitled the collection *Minḥat Qena'ot* (An Offering of Zeal).[101] Substantively, the correspondence indicates that between 1303 and 1305 there was only one new issue—the charge that the philosophers relied heavily on astrology in their practice of medicine, thereby violating the prohibitions against idolatry.[102] Interestingly, Maimonides himself was unequivocally opposed to astrology and to any association between it and philosophy on theoretical or practical grounds.[103]

Jewish Astrology and Religious Naturalism

Astrology in the Middle Ages was considered a scientific discipline with both theoretical and practical aspects, all of which were directly related to happiness since the location of the stars (i.e., the theoretical aspect of the science) influenced the events and hence the well-being of human beings (i.e., the practical aspect). Jewish interest in astrology during the Middle Ages was occasioned by the ninth-century revival of Hellenistic astrology and magic by the Sabians in Mesopotamia as part of their revival of Neoplatonic, Neo-Phythagorean and Hermetic traditions. Believing that the stars possessed a spiritual power, or energy, these scholars engaged in astral magic for practical and theoretical purposes—to satisfy material needs and to purify the soul of the practitioner (the magician) so as to conjoin with the celestial bodies. These speculations and practices penetrated Islamic thought from the ninth century onward and were prevalent among the anonymous scientist-philosophers who were known as Brethren of Purity and who adapted these scientific pursuits to their Shiite Islam.

For the Brethren of Purity, engagement in astrology and magic was inseparable from the pursuit of intellectual perfection: all pertained to the operation of the natural world. The individual who reached perfection and possessed scientific knowledge of all existents could not only prognosticate future events but could also change natural processes, which is to say, perform miracles. Astral magic was thus the expression of intellectual perfection according to the Brethren, as well as to ibn Sina. In the twelfth century this view was largely adopted by Judah Halevi,[104] Abraham ibn Ezra, and Moses ibn Ezra, albeit with important modifications. These philosopher-poets gave rise to an astrological interpretation of the past, especially the remote biblical past, and introduced astro-magical exposition of the commandments.[105] Fully aware of these practices were considered by many as bordering on idolatry, ibn Ezra presented his astrological views in cryptic comments throughout his biblical commentaries.

Ibn Ezra's older and younger contemporaries, Abraham Bar Hiyya and Moses Maimonides, respectively, rigorously denounced astrology as a pseudo-science and astral magic as an idolatrous practice, which they did their best to prohibit. Their efforts effectively curtailed the dissemination of astrology during most of the 1200s, but toward the end of that century and throughout the fourteenth, astrology and astral magic thrived precisely among the rationalists who sought to understand how the sublunar world works. These scientist/philosophers "rediscovered" Abraham ibn Ezra and composed super-commentaries to his biblical commentaries in which they spelled out the exact astrological meaning of ibn Ezra's esoteric remarks.[106] In Spain during this second half of the fourteenth century this group would include scholars such as Samuel ibn Zarza, Samuel ibn Motot, Joseph Tov Elem, Ezra Gatingo (Astruk Shlomo), Shlomo Franco, and Shem Tov ibn Shaprut. Their systematic exegetical works attempted to prove the total congruence between Torah and what they took to be scientific philosophic knowledge, an eclectic fusion of Aristotelian, Neoplatonic, and Hermetic strands.

Similarly, in Provence during the late fourteenth and early fifteenth centuries, Judah Halevi's *Kuzari* became the subject of new commentaries by Shlomo ben Menachem (known as Prat Maimon) and his disciples Netanel Kaspi, Jacob ben Hayim Farissol, and Shlomo ben Judah of Lunel. Although Halevi argued for the dissociation of religion and philosophy, he was very well versed in the philosophy and science of his day. In part he criticized Aristotelian science by showing that there are various natural phenomena that it fails to explain. Halevi cited astrological and magical notions about the influence of the stars or the hidden, occult qualities (*segulot*) of natural entities that exposed the limits of Aristotelian science. His *Kuzari* thus served both as a source for alternative non-Aristotelian scientific explanations of natural phenomena and as a text that expressed serious reservations about the validity of Aristotelian science.

The Jewish rationalists of the second half of the fourteenth century radicalized Maimonides' rationalism. For them, because of the conjunction between the human material intellect and the Active Intellect, nature was fully knowable by the human mind without divine assistance. If men can know the pattern of the sublunar world, as it is known to the Active Intellect, they can know how nature works and they can intervene or manipulate natural processes by virtue of the spiritual power that they possess. One way to harness the spiritual energy of the stars was to create icons that presumably captured that energy and applied it to heal aflicted people. This practice became so controversial in the beginning of the fourteenth century that Abba Mari of Lunel convinced Rashba to ban it, on the charge that it was idolatrous.

Dov Schwartz has shed much light on the debate over the use of astral magic in the practice of medicine, which was a contentious issue in the last phase of the Maimonidean Controversy. The Jewish rationalists themselves were divided in their attitudes toward the permissibility of astrology in halakhah and the effectiveness of harnessing the energy of the celestial bodies through icons for healing.[107] Levi ben Abraham, the main participant in the final phase of the controversy, believed in the scientific validity of astrology, the effectiveness of drawing spiritual energy, and the halakhic permissibility of astral magic. For him the stars did influence human physical well-being, manifested in health and sickness, and they even determine the forms of corporeal things. Hence the use of talismans and other icons of the stars to draw spiritual energy downward is beneficial and halakhically permissible.

Levi ben Abraham goes further to show that this view is in accord with Maimonides! Later scholars in Provence—such as Isaac de Lattes, Prat Maimon (Shlomo ben Menachem) and his students Jacob Farisol, Netanel

Kaspi, Solomon ben Judah of Lunel—all admired Levi ben Abraham and followed his lead. Prat Maimon, for example, regarded the spiritual energy of the sun to be the source of religious and intellectual virtues, including the attainment of prophecy. To absorb the spiritual energy there is need for proper preparation; a special place and an icon can be used for the purpose of attaining prophetic overflow. This view of prophecy, which links superior knowledge to the performance of miracles, places an intellectually perfect human agent at the center of the miraculous activity. It is what Aviezer Ravitzky dubbed "the anthropological conception of miracles."

This view was common among Jewish Aristotelians in the fourteenth century such as Moses Narboni and Nissim of Marseilles, to whom we shall return in Chapter Eight. For them the intellectually perfect man, the prophet, was empowered to perform miracles by virtue of his sublime knowledge, as explained by the "anthropological conception of miracles."[108] Likewise these two rationalists explained the ancient sacrifices as mediums that enabled Israel's priests to focus their imaginations as they engaged in the prognostication of the future or attempted to draw spiritual energy from the supernal world for the benefit of Israel. In the same vein, Prat Maimon and Netanel Kaspi in the early fifteenth century viewed the Temple as an elaborate talisman that could draw the heavenly energy to earth, and they believed that certain locations were more apt to receive the supernal overflow than others. This notion, however, was not endorsed by Levi ben Abraham, for whom the Temple was strictly a symbol of eternal truths about the heavenly spheres, which should be contemplated rather than used for any benefit.

"Rationalists" vs. "Traditionalists"

Excepting the debate on astrology, both sides in the fourth phase of the Maimonidean Controversy rehashed familiar themes from earlier phases of the controversy using the same rhetorical conventions. The main accusation of the critics of philosophy was leveled against the use of philosophical biblical exegesis to highlight the inner, abstract content of biblical narratives. By 1303, as Gad Freudenthal has argued, the Maimonidean Controversy was no longer about whether to study philosophy but rather about how to define the appropriate relationship between traditional Jewish topics and the various branches of philosophy in the context of the Jewish curriculum.[109] Virtually all the participants in the debate revered Maimonides; they accepted his claim that the doctrinal dimension of Judaism can be expressed in philosophical language and acknowledged that the ancient rabbinic sages themselves had some philosophical knowledge, especially of astronomy and medicine. Freudenthal convincingly maintains that the Controversy was not between "rationalists" and "anti-rationalists" or between "Maimonists" and "anti-Maimonists," but rather between "rationalists" and "traditionalists." Each camp harbored a variety of sentiments and nuanced postures. Most importantly, observes Freudenthal, the "traditionalists" were themselves ambivalent about the study of philosophy: their culture was already suffused with philosophical categories that they themselves internalized, whether they publicly admitted it or not.[110] The desire to limit the scope of philosophy, then, expresses the anxiety of the traditionalists about the "the other within" and a need to curb it. For this reason, it is not surprising that the debate about philosophy employed gender imagery: in a male-dominated society women are the ever present "other within."[111] Furthermore, since the disputing parties often referred to the language of the opposing side *in order to refute it*, gender imagery pervades both camps. Both personified Torah and philosophy as females, both portrayed the negative image of philosophy as "alien women" (*ishah zarah; ishah nokhrit*),[112] and both framed the relationship between Torah and philosophy in terms of power relations between a mistress and her female handmaiden.

Defining the proper relationship between Torah and philosophy was also the concern of Maimonides and his followers. In fact it was Maimonides who originally framed the ideal relationship in hierarchical terms of servitude. Philosophy is justified because it serves as "apothecaries, cooks and bakers" to glorify the beauty of Torah. So long as philosophy is employed as its handmaiden (*shifhah*), philosophy is both necessary and useful to Torah. In the ensuing Maimonidean Controversy, philosophy was commonly portrayed as biblical Hagar, the boastful concubine of Sarah, who improperly challenged the lawful wife, Sarah, and was forced to flee from Sarah's justified wrath.[113] In this imagery, there is nothing wrong with philosophy per se, but with the brazen character of the philosophers who challenge the proper hierarchy between philosophy and Torah and make philosophy their mistress. Inasmuch as Sarah ensured that the son of Hagar, Yishmael, would not inherit the covenant, so do the traditionalists insist that philosophy (associated with Islam) should not be given a rightful place in traditional Jewish life.

The Provençal rationalists, led by Jacob ibn Machir, also acknowledged that the Torah is superior in status and worth to philosophy. They shared the genderized language of their opponents, even though they transformed its meaning. The real protection of "the daughter of Jacob" will come when all Jews acknowledge that the Torah of Moses itself contains all truths, including the truths of philosophy. The gentile philosophers (in ancient Greece or in medieval Islam) merely understand its external aspects, but not its inner core,[114] which is precisely what the Jewish tradition calls "the mysteries of the Torah" (*sitrei Torah*). In this regard the philosophy of the gentiles functions like the narratives of the Torah, namely, as external garments of the inner Torah, an abstract truth. This is why philosophical reading, which views Abraham as the figurative representation of form and Sarah as matter, is proper: it discloses the underlying structure of reality in a manner that is comprehensible to non-philosophers.[115] The Torah, then, is the supreme philosophy because it teaches abstract truth about the way things are.

It is obvious that what the rationalists found valuable in Maimonides' hermeneutics, the traditionalists considered heretical. The rationalists hailed the allegorical approach to the biblical text as an attempt to penetrate the deeper meaning of the revealed text, underlying what seemed to be trivial or inexplicable stories. The traditionalists, by contrast, regarded the allegorical interpretation of the text as an expression of skepticism about the historicity of biblical events. However, neither the traditionalists nor the rationalists found the gender aspect problematic. They both took it for granted that the woman should be subordinated to the man and both presented philosophy and Torah as two rival women.[116]

In Defense of Philosophy

The most interesting document to be composed at this phase of the controversies was Yeda`ya Bedersi's *Mikhtav ha-Hitnatzelut* (A Letter of Apology), a rigorous defense of philosophical education as a program for the attainment of human perfection.[117] Bedersi recounts the history of Jewish philosophy prior to Maimonides, singing the praises of the philosophers who removed anthropomorphism from Jewish belief. He reaffirms the status of Maimonides and defends his interpretation of miracles, which distinguishes between natural and logical impossibility. According to Bedersi, Maimonides' subtle exposition of miracles only glorified Judaism, proving to all the intellectual correctness of the tradition. The charge that philosophy leads to heresy is thus totally baseless.

With regard to allegorical interpretations of the biblical text, Bedersi denied that the philosophic, inner meaning negates the value of the literal meaning. To the extent that the philosophers privileged the allegorical, they did so with specific aggadot and not with the biblical text itself. The simple meaning of the text and its historicity have never been challenged by the philosophers. Furthermore, there is no evidence that philosophic interpretation leads to religious laxity.[118] There is nothing conceptually new in Bedersi's Apologia. Its sole value is that it reflects the cultural ambience of the educated classes.

Another contemporary Provençal commentator, Joseph ibn Kaspi, also showed how the use of philology and logic are essential for the interpretation of the biblical text. In so doing he buttressed the importance of the literal meaning of the text, in contrast to the tendency to read the Bible solely for its abstract, theoretical meaning. At the same time, however, he also defended the centrality of philosophic knowledge in interpretation of the revealed text.

The ban limiting the study of philosophy was finally imposed by Rashba (on July 31, 1305), but it had little impact. During the fourteenth century, philosophy and its related liberal arts and sciences continued to flourish in Provence, Spain, and Italy and dominated Jewish theological self-understanding. Kabbalah did not yet emerge as a viable alternative to philosophy, though kabbalists were among the vocal opponents of the rationalists. By 1350 Aristotle was fully absorbed, as the commentaries of Averroes were translated into Hebrew and stimulated super-commentaries in Hebrew. A few of the philosophers also wrote systematic Jewish theology, using their technical knowledge of Aristotle's philosophy to explain the religious beliefs of Judaism.

While in the short run, the ban had little effect, it did signal the tenuous status of the study of the natural sciences and philosophy in traditional Jewish society.[119] The opponents of these pursuits succeeded in persuading some Jews that science and philosophy were "alien wisdoms" that did not belong in Judaism because they led to heresy. Although three centuries would pass before this position was accepted by large segments of Jewish society, it was the ban in 1305 that already indicated the future marginalization not only of philosophy and science within Judaism, but also of the conception of individual salvation in terms of philosophic wisdom.

SUMMARY

The distinct phases of the Maimonidean Controversy during the thirteenth century can be viewed as variations on a single theme: the debate on the implications of Maimonides' view of human well-being, or happiness, for Judaism. Since all agreed that the attainment of happiness was predicated on knowledge, the operative question was: What type of knowledge is necessary and sufficient for attaining moral and intellectual perfection—Torah and/or Philosophy? The supporters of Maimonides viewed intellectual perfection as the ultimate end of human life, whereas the anti-Maimonists regarded it as an arrogant, self-serving preoccupation that undermined collective Jewish life and negated rabbinic ethical values. The supporters of Maimonides, by contrast, regarded the ideal of intellectual perfection and the education that it required as a profound religious contribution to Judaism. Only if Jews perfected their intellects through the study of philosophy, they argued, could they properly worship God.

What happiness is, this chapter has shown, is not a mere theoretical issue, but one that frames one's self-understanding and cultural choices. The Maimonidean Controversy, therefore, was a fundamental dispute about Jewish education, much like the debate that raged in American academe during the 1980s about the composition of the "canon" of Western civilization and like the current *Kulturkampf* in Israel. Those who viewed the ultimate end of human life as the contemplation of eternal truths insisted that Jewish education should include the study of philosophic works written by Jews and non-Jews alike. Those who opposed the philosophic ideal of happiness rejected those works, fearing the infiltration of destructive, "alien" ideas that would corrupt the minds of Jewish students and lead to heresy. Then, as now, the debates about the composition of the curriculum was a political matter, reflecting communal struggles, class tensions, and personal agendas. In the main, the debate on happiness (and in turn on the composition of Jewish education) was part of a larger issue—the desired degree of interaction between Judaism and non-Jewish civilizations.

7

The Kabbalistic Prescription for Happiness

As the Maimonidean Controversy was raging, another program for the interpretation of rabbinic Judaism came to the fore—kabbalah. Literally, *kabbalah* means "received tradition," but the term is used specifically to denote mystico-theurgic speculations and practices that constituted a distinct intellectual strand in medieval Judaism. While the roots of kabbalah go far back to the Second Temple period, it became a self-conscious program for the interpretation of Judaism only in the late twelfth century, appearing first in Provence, the hotbed of the Maimonidean Controversy, from where it spread to Spain. There, it flourished during the thirteenth century in several schools that did not agree among them about its precise meaning. The most important text of Spanish kabbalah was *Sefer ha-Zohar* (The Book of Enlightenment), composed during the third phase of the Maimonidean Controversy.

In this chapter, I present the *Zohar* as an alternative to the philosophic conception of happiness and, in turn, to the philosophers' approach to religious life. I argue that the homilies of the *Zohar* intended to dramatize the life of the holy men of Judaism, the rabbinic sages who appeared as its protagonists. Putting them "on stage," so to speak, enabled the *Zohar* to demonstrate the nature and meaning of the holy life of Judaism, whose core was Torah study. For the *Zohar*, the Torah contained mysteries not only about the structure of the world and its governance by God, but also about the personality of God and the dynamic of His inner life. The philosophers, the *Zohar* maintained, were correct in their belief that the key to the perfect life lies in the acquisition of virtues, but these virtues can be acquired only when the student of Torah cleaves to the *sefirot*, the attributes that reveal God's essence. It is through the cleaving to God (*devequt*) that the inherent holiness of the human soul is protected from the contamination of the body and assured eternal life in heaven.

While kabbalah is the most profound restatement of the Jewish myth, it was also deeply indebted to medieval Jewish Aristotelianism. Kabbalah itself, we should note, exhibited the tension between logos and mythos.

Moshe Idel has distinguished between two main strands within it: "theosophic kabbalah," whose main exponent was the *Zohar*, and "mystical kabbalah," or "prophetic kabbalah," whose main exponent was Abraham Abulafia.[1] Whereas the *Zohar* developed the sacred narrative of rabbinic Judaism as an alternative to Maimonides, Abulafia articulated his mystical speculations as a development of Maimonides' epistemology and cosmology. In Chapter Nine we will see how both types of kabbalah were intertwined in the discourse on happiness in the fifteenth and sixteenth centuries. In this chapter we focus on the *Zohar* as the paradigmatic exponent of the kabbalistic prescription for happiness.

Kabbalah as an Alternative to Philosophy

Kabbalah, I concur with Idel,[2] emerged in the late twelfth century precisely as an attempt to curb the spread of Maimonidean rationalism, which the kabbalists regarded as a deviation from the authentic Jewish tradition. This is not to say, however, that Jewish Aristotelianism and kabbalah should be viewed simplistically as diametrically opposed programs. Kabbalists in Spain were well-educated Jewish intellectuals who understood rationalist philosophy to various degrees and shared many of the metaphysical, cosmological, and psychological assumptions of the philosophers. Indeed, without knowledge of medieval philosophy it is very difficult to make sense of medieval kabbalah. Concomitantly, without close attention to the intricate interplay between philosophy and kabbalah in the post-Maimonidean era, it is impossible to understand the evolution of Jewish intellectual history.[3] While kabbalah did not become a serious cultural alternative to Maimonideanism until the sixteenth century, already in the thirteenth it proposed a full-fledged theory of religious perfection that could challenge the philosophic outlook.

Like the Aristotelian philosophers, the kabbalists claimed to possess an esoteric knowledge that could be transmitted only to the worthy few and was not available to ordinary Jews. In fact, in terms of content and intended audience the kabbalists were even more radical and restrictive than the rationalist philosophers. Whereas the philosophers claimed to prove that God exists and to know how He manages the created world, the kabbalists claimed to know no less than the essence of God—precisely the knowledge that the Maimonidean philosophers believed was beyond the domain of human comprehension.[4] According to the kabbalists, the hidden secrets of the Torah, its supernal mysteries, pertain not to the laws of nature by which God governs the world, but to God's personal identity, to the rhythm of God's inner life. It is this spiritual knowledge that is both necessary and sufficient for the attainment of the religious perfection in this world that, according to kabbalah, would in turn facilitate experiencing the delight of the world to come. Such knowledge, needless to say, is very difficult to attain and only those who are morally, intellectually, and spiritually perfect can fathom it. Ordinary Jews remain ignorant of it as much as they are ignorant of the abstract metaphysical knowledge of the philosophers. However, as we shall see below, the *Zohar* would challenge some of the social conventions that maintained a gap between the elite and the masses, for sometimes those who were supposed to be ordinary Jews turned out to be spiritually very gifted.

Knowledge of God's essence, according to theosophic kabbalah, is not simply an epistemic matter. It is not knowledge *about* God, but knowledge *of* God—an understanding of the Other that emerges only in an intimate, love relationship. This is a non-discursive, non-theoretical, intuitive, experiential knowledge possible only in the intimacy of the relationship between the kabbalist (and by extension, Israel) with God. The more intimate the kabbalist is with God, the wholly, holy Other, the more he can know God as the kabbalist knows himself; conversely, the more the kabbalist understands himself, the more intimate can be his relationship with God. It is a kind of knowledge that the Bible reserves for sexual intimacy when it says (Gen. 4:1) that "Adam knew his wife, Eve." This, according to kabbalah is precisely the meaning of the covenant, the eternal love affair between God and Israel. Accordingly, the intimacy of the relationship between God and Israel is expressed in erotic and sexual categories, the highest ones available to human beings for expressing intimacy and the merging of identities.

The love relationship between God and Israel is also the context for the development of the ideal virtues that lead to wisdom. In Chapter One we presented Aristotle's teaching on virtue friendship as interaction between equals in which the friend becomes the mirror of the self. In Chapter Three we showed how rabbinic Judaism absorbed that notion in its discussion of the ideal character traits of the rabbinic sage, who is a true friend (or lover) of God. In this chapter, we will see how theosophic kabbalah extended the meaning of the love relationship between God and Israel by providing a "thick description," so to speak, of the two lovers—God and Israel—as well as of their dynamic interaction, namely, the life of Torah. Because God and Israel mirror each other according to kabbalah,[5] and the Torah is the context of their love relationship, the *Zohar* could sum up this dynamic interrelationship in the famous statement: "The Holy One, blessed be He, Torah and Israel are one."[6] The entire Zoharic corpus can be seen as an elaboration of this statement.

This dynamic intertwining of God, Israel, and Torah will yield a different notion of human perfection than that of the rationalist philosophers. For the Aristotelians, God is a perfect Being, the ultimate reality that is singular, unique, incorporeal, static, and self-absorbed. As an intellect *in actu*, God is engaged in the most perfect activity: self-contemplation. God eternally thinks itself and that activity is causative, bringing about the world. For human beings, who possess the capacity to reason, to seek perfection means to actualize intellectual potential to the fullest extent possible. The ultimate expression of human intellectual perfection, then, is when men are engaged in the contemplation of abstract, necessary truths—namely, when they contemplate God. The philosopher who strives to be perfect like God does have some relationship with God, but it is a relationship of imitation, and it is non-personal.[7]

In contrast, for the kabbalists to become humanly perfect means to enter a personal, intimate relationship with the divine—even to the point of partaking or participating in the inner rhythm of God's life, as one would with a true lover. However, any relationship, especially one of love, is a dynamic process; it changes constantly in response to what the partners do. Accordingly, kabbalah could articulate the notion (audacious and absurd from the perspective of the Maimonideans) that God (at least the revealed aspect of God) is not immutable (as the philosophers held), but is constantly changing in the context of the interaction with non-divine existents, both human and non-human. Kabbalah went even further to claim that God (or more precisely, the revealed aspect of God) is in a state of imperfection, imbalance, and disharmony. Beginning with the first sin of Adam, the divine reality became unbalanced, which is described in kabbalah as a separation between the masculine and feminine aspects of the androgynous male deity.[8] From the perspective of kabbalah, then, not only mankind is in need of perfection but also God, and the task of perfecting God depends on the human agent, or, more precisely on the (male) members of the Jewish people. They alone can reestablish the initial equilibrium of the deity that was and is constantly disrupted by human actions.

The task of perfecting God is awesome, but it is not an exercise in futility. God revealed himself to Israel in the Torah, and it is precisely through this self-revelation that Israel obtains the prescriptions for perfecting both men and God, namely the commandments.[9] The pursuit of perfection, therefore, is understood more ambitiously in kabbalah than it is in Jewish

Aristotelianism. The process involves not only the improvement of the human self through the cultivation of virtues and the acquisition of wisdom, but the improvement or perfection of God, and, thereby of the relationship between Israel and God. In this relational model, as Israel is engaged in the task of perfecting itself by following the prescriptions of Torah, it brings about perfection in God, which, in turn, benefits the human individual, the society, and the cosmos. Such perfection is what the Jewish tradition, according to kabbalah, meant when it envisioned the final redemption (*ge'ulah*). For the kabbalists, then, the pursuit of perfection means engagement in a redemptive activity.[10]

Kabbalah and the Elaboration of the Rabbinic Conception of God

Space limitations prevent me from exploring the history of kabbalah and its relationship to other intellectual aspects of medieval Jewish culture, such as the teachings of Hasidei Ashkenaz (German Pietists) in the late twelfth and thirteenth centuries. What is relevant to our study is that by the late twelfth century the personalist, anthropomorphic conception of God, characteristic of rabbinic midrash, was reinstated in an anonymous midrash called *Sefer ha-Bahir* (The Book of Brightness), which attributed itself to R. Nehunya ben Ha-Qanah, one of the heroes of the Heikhalot and Merkabah tradition.[11] This fragmentary opaque text was apparently composed in a Middle Eastern setting sometime between the eighth and eleventh centuries and received its final editing in Provence during the late twelfth century.

In style, the *Bahir* appears to be a rabbinic midrash on the Torah. However, instead of the verse-centered, free flowing, non-metaphysical homilies of rabbinic midrash, the *Bahir* presupposed a well-developed theosophy about a multi-layered divine reality. Building upon the motifs of the ancient mystical tradition it did not elaborate on the magnitude of God's body, but rather on the attributes of God's personality, namely, the aspects of God's soul. Referred to by many names such as "kings," "sounds," "branches," and "children," the divine attributes are primarily known as *sefirot*, the term coined by *Sefer Yetzirah*. In the *Bahir*, however, the sefirot were understood not only as the principles through which God's power is manifested in the physical universe, but also as the ten dynamic stages through which the divine personality is made manifest.

The *Bahir* retained the anthropomorphic conception of God by arranging the ten sefirot in the form of a human body. The terrestrial human being was thus believed to mirror the divine anthropos and to be structured like Him.[12] Concomitantly, the makeup of the human personality was believed to mirror the divine Gestalt. The human being is indeed created in the image of God, possessing both body and soul. So presented, this view entails God's sexuality. On the basis of rabbinic homilies that echoed the Platonic myth of creation, the *Bahir* imaged God as an androgen. The upper nine sefirot constitute the male principle, and the last, the tenth, the female.

What had been merely hinted in ancient Jewish esoterica was made explicit in the *Bahir*, where God is truly a living reality, and the mystery of the divine is a creative energy that gives rise to life. Since life entails procreation, the energy that pulsates through the Godhead is sexual in nature, and the processes within the Godhead are governed by the rhythm of sexuality—penetration and withdrawal, union and separation. The constant flux of the sefirotic realm reflects both the ever-changing nature of the human psyche and bodily processes and the changes in God's relationship with the created world. In particular, the supernal drama reflects both the intimacy and the vicissitudes of the eternal love between God and Israel.

Referred to primarily as *Shekhinah*, the *Bahir* imaged the divine female as queen, bride, sister, daughter, wife, matron, mother, earth, sea, moon, field, orchard, and a host of related feminine symbols. She represents the relational dimensions of the deity and its receptive quality. The Shekhinah is the face that God shows to the created world, especially to Israel. As a liminal boundary between the Godhead and the extra-deical reality, she is both the entry gate into the Godhead and the channel through which divine efflux is transmitted to the created universe.

Her relationship with the masculine forces of the Godhead is unstable, affected by human deeds. Human sins empower the domain of evil (the reification of profane forces) and induce discord in the supernal world, represented by the sundering of the male and female aspects of the deity. In contrast, righteous conduct—through the performance of the commandments—reunites the masculine and feminine aspects of the bisexual Godhead, restoring it to its primordial harmony. In turn, the repairing of the Godhead results in an abundance of the divine efflux to the created universe, the sign of redeemed reality. In this way, the *Bahir* insinuated the intrinsic connection between theosophy, theurgy, and eschatology that Spanish kabbalah would develop later.

Most importantly, the *Bahir* articulated a new understanding of Torah when it identified the Shekhinah with the Torah that God gave to Israel in an everlasting marriage. Reifying midrashic literary tropes, the *Bahir* hypostatized the Torah as a mythological person that has come down to earth. This motif was undoubtedly linked to the personification of Torah/Wisdom as female in ancient Judaism and to the Gnostic myth of Sophia, although the details of the *Bahir*'s conception of Torah are not entirely clear. In some passages it links the Torah with the tenth sefirah, *Malkhut*, without differentiating between the Written and Oral Torah. In others the Shekhinah is the supernal manifestation of the Oral Torah, and *Tiferet* (the sefirah that symbolizes the male power) is viewed as the symbol of the Written Torah.[13] Both are viewed as the unfolding of the Primordial Torah (*torah qedumah*), which the *Bahir* identified with God's wisdom, the second sefirah, *Ḥokhmah*. In the theosophy of the *Bahir*, God's self-disclosure through the ten sefirot is a twofold process in which God's word and God's world came into being.

By making revelation and creation internal processes within the Godhead, the *Bahir* articulated the central hermeneutic principle of theosophic kabbalah. The Bible is a symbolic text that speaks exoterically of mundane things and esoterically of supernal events within the divine *pleroma*. Since the biblical text pertains to events within the Godhead, and since God is presumed to be the author of the Bible, the sacred text can be said to be God's autobiography. Most importantly, God's personal life lends organic unity to the biblical text; all portions and verses of the text are intrinsically linked to one another, like the branches and twigs of a tree or the limbs, tissues, and blood vessels of the human body.[14] The Torah is literally "The tree of life," as the Jewish liturgy asserts, functioning as the immediate cause of Israel's flourishing. Furthermore, precisely because the revealed text makes manifest God's dynamic inner life, the Bible must be read through multiple, simultaneously correct interpretations.

Kabbalah in the Context of the Maimonidean Controversy

It is not clear who edited, studied, and circulated the *Bahir*, and whether these people were located in Provence or in Christian Spain.[15] They were clearly committed, whoever they were, to the anthropomorphic conception of God characteristic of rabbinic Judaism (both exoteric and esoteric). However, after the Almohad persecution of 1148–1150, refugees from Andalusia introduced the rationalist tradition to Provençal Jewry by translating the classics of Andalusian Jewish philosophy into Hebrew. This philosophic conception of God articulated by Saadia Gaon, Solomon ibn Gabirol, Abraham ibn Daud, Bahya ibn Paqudah, Abraham ibn Ezra, and, above all,

Maimonides, was a far cry from the personalist conception of God to which the early kabbalists were committed.

The first critic of Maimonides' *Mishneh Torah*, R. Abraham ben David of Posquières, the author of the glosses on the Code, was also the leader of a group of people who regarded themselves as *ba`alei ha-kabbalah* ("masters of the tradition"). These early exponents of kabbalah were known to cultivate an ascetic, contemplative life, culminating in ecstatic experiences.[16] Attributed to communication with the prophet Elijah—the symbol of the Jewish tradition—these revelations presumed to make known secrets about God. Thus, the Provençal advocates of kabbalah were engaged in the paradoxical activity of publicizing what was taken to be a secret tradition about God and about the way Jews can relate to Him. Why did they do it? Most likely because they were alarmed by the spread of Maimonidean rationalism and wished to protect the tradition from what they regarded as a disturbing deviation. The cultivation of philosophy, in its Aristotelian form, could result in grave religious errors; hence, esoteric traditions carefully transmitted in private had to be made known to a larger audience.

The kabbalists' claim that they were in possession of a received oral tradition that constituted the true, albeit, esoteric meaning of divine revelation makes sense only in the context of the rabbinic myth of dual Torah; it cannot be verified historically. However, the claim need not be dismissed as incredible and unbelievable. Jewish traditional learning did prize the oral mode of teaching, emphasized the merit of memorization and retention, and was transmitted from master to disciple often within distinct kinship patterns. It is plausible that the written phase of kabbalah came after a long period of oral activity, in which the meaning of key biblical texts was transmitted within this tradition.[17] These texts functioned as a reference system—whether or not actual texts were present and whether they were transmitted orally or through some form of abbreviated writing that functioned as mnemonic devices (*rashei peraqim*).

Exegesis, however, involves interpretation, and the kabbalists' textual transmission must have involved some creative innovation, notwithstanding the claim that it merely preserved received teachings. The innovation was even evident once kabbalah shifted from an oral to a written mode of transmission. With Isaac the Blind (known in the euphemistic epithet "Sagi Nahor"), the son of R. Abraham ben David, kabbalah became a literary, creative tradition. The mental energy that was invested in memorization of the received teachings could now be invested in free activity by the imagination. Writing also contributed to the dissemination of kabbalah, for in principle anyone who wished to study it could avail himself of written texts. Although its study during the late twelfth century and throughout the thirteenth remained the activity of tiny groups of scholars, the fact that there were different versions of "*the* kabbalah" indicates the tradition was by no means monolithic. Creative activity based on human imagination, rather than a mere reception of a prefabricated tradition, facilitated its growth.

During the Maimonidean controversies of the thirteenth century, in various urban centers in Catalonia (e.g., Gerona, Barcelona) and in Castile (Toledo, Burgos, Soria, Guadaljara), distinctive kabbalistic teachings were expressed in literary genres formerly in the rabbinic domain. Spanish kabbalists in Catalonia and Castile composed commentaries on the Bible, commentaries on talmudic homilies, commentaries on ancient mystical texts of the Heikhalot and Merkabah corpus and on *Sefer Yetzirah*,. They also produced lists of symbolic codes, systematic expositions of the commandments, speculations on the Hebrew alphabet and Torah cantillation, and manuals for the attainment of ecstatic mystical experiences. By means of exegetical activity, Spanish kabbalah consolidated a distinctive worldview that was rooted in, but elaborated and expanded, the motifs and ideas of rabbinic Judaism.

The exegetical, nonsystematic nature of kabbalistic style was integrally related to the self-perception of kabbalah as an authentic interpretation of the Jewish sacred tradition. Indeed, the ideas of kabbalah about God, the created world, Israel, the problem of evil, and the life of Torah and mitzvot were to be gleaned from the very interpretation of sacred texts, rather than from systematic theorization. Moreover, the views of kabbalah were intrinsically linked to the Hebrew language, which is divine and cannot be translated into any other language.[18] In continuity with the views of ancient Jewish esoterica, the kabbalists maintained that Hebrew is not a conventional language in which signifiers have arbitrary meaning, but that the letters of its Hebrew alphabet are the very building blocks of the created world. Knowledge of the divine language and its various permutations thus leads to knowledge of reality. For the kabbalists, then, the interpretation of Scripture was an act of penetrating not just the mysteries of the universe, but, no less, the mysteries of God. From this perspective, kabbalists could argue that the philosophical interpretation of Scripture was but an imposition of external modes of thought unto the Jewish sacred texts, an eisegesis rather than an exegesis, since the abstract proposition of the philosophy did not originate from the Hebrew.

Various formulations of "the kabbalah" came into being during the thirteenth century, associated with specific geographic locations. Some, like the kabbalists in Gerona, had a strong philosophical bent and their metaphysical leaning was characteristically Neoplatonic. Others, such as the kabbalists in Burgos and Toledo, were more preoccupied with the reality of evil and issues typical of Gnostic thinking. Still others, such as the anonymous people who produced the *Sefer Ha-Iyyun* (The Book of Contemplation) and its cognate literature, were interested in visualization of God. All these trends, as well as ancient Jewish esoterica and German pietism, were finally consolidated into one coherent outlook by the powerful creation of Spanish Kabbalah—Sefer ha-Zohar. It is there, especially in its main section, that we find the most comprehensive alternative to the philosophic conception of happiness.

THE *ZOHAR*

The Literary Structure

To be able to see the *Zohar* as a discourse on happiness, we need to examine its literary structure. On the surface it appears to be an ancient rabbinic midrash on the Pentateuch, written in Aramaic.[19] While it is arranged in accordance with the sequence of the Torah's weekly portions, the *Zohar* is not a linear commentary on the Pentateuch, in which the meaning of each verse or certain verses is explicated, but a series of elaborate and intricate homilies that merely take their point of departure from the verses of the given Torah portion. With unparalleled spiritual energy, creative imagination, and subtle artistry, it interweaves biblical, rabbinic, pietistic, philosophic, and kabbalistic motifs into a colorful fabric, which it presents as the true, hidden meaning of the divinely revealed, authoritative Jewish tradition.

What makes the Zoharic homilies unique is the fact that they are presented as live conversations between rabbinic sages as they are strolling in the Land of Israel.[20] The specifics of the conversations change from one scene to the next, but the context of the conversation remains the same—the act of Torah study in which the hidden meanings of the Torah are disclosed. By dramatizing the activity of rabbinic learning, the *Zohar* illustrates how Torah study should be conducted and what happens to Jews when it is done properly. The *Zohar*, I suggest, was a didactic drama that created literary or fictitious exempla from the lives of Jewish holy men, its protagonists. Thus, instead of theorizing about the components of the ideal life, as did the rationalist philosophers, the *Zohar* allows the holy men of Judaism to speak to each other and to the reader directly.

The *Zohar*'s dramatization of the ideal way of life should be understood against the cultural context of thirteenth-century Europe. That century was the culmination of monumental changes that took place in church dogma and religious instruction since the seventh century. During this period of geographical expansion of Christianity and conversion of new peoples, Christian theologians expanded and systematized their various doctrines, refined the confessional system, and reformed the monasteries. These changes required constant teaching materials, giving rise to the homiletic narratives of the exempla collections.

An exemplum was a story about the life of saints that was set within the context of a sermon to be delivered to both clerical and lay audiences. Because it made Christian theology vivid and palpable, accessible to listeners and readers of varied educational levels, it served "a central role in the revitalization of the art of preaching."[21] By the thirteenth century, edited collections of exempla were used first for the instruction of monastic novices and later as an effective tool in the teaching of lay audiences. These pious narratives were used in the Church campaigns against the various heresies, especially the Albigensians in Languedoc, in support of the Crusades against the Muslims, and most commonly, against the archenemy of Christianity—the Jews—who remained the pernicious, ever-present "Other" within Christian society. The primary task of the sermon story was to illustrate, as Joan Gregg has put it, "why and how to carry out the precepts crucial to the irrevocable disposition of their souls: whether to salvation with God, Christ, the angels, and the saints, or the eternal torments of damnation in hell with Satan and his devils, unchaste women, Jews and other sinners."[22]

It is within this setting that we can understand the homiletic narratives of the *Zohar*, which tells stories about the activities of virtuous holy men, presumably the ancient rabbinic sages, in order to illustrate to Jews the ideal way of life so as to merit eternal salvation.[23] A failure to imitate the ideal way of life will result in the victory of the demonic powers of the Sitra Ahra (the "Other Side")—the Jewish version of the medieval belief in the Devil. More than any other medieval text, the *Zohar* provided a vivid description of the domain of evil and its perpetual struggle against God and the forces of holiness and purity. The exempla of the *Zohar* could thus teach readers and listeners how to deal with evil and respond to its invidious temptations. In its sermonic stories, it preached the components of the ideal way of life, instructing Jews how to attain happiness.

In thirteenth-century Europe, the exemplary tales were not just limited to sermons. In the streets of burgeoning European towns, exempla of the lives of saints were dramatized for laity whose life of commerce necessitated a higher level of education than the life on the rural manor. One main form of inculcating Christian values was the dramatization of ideal Christian life on stage. The most important story, of course, was the passion narrative of Jesus' suffering and death on the cross, but there were endless other morality plays, which were put on stage in public spaces in order to teach the values and life style of the ideal Christian believer.[24] To eliminate the contaminating presence of Jews from the holy space, the Fourth Lateran Council forbade them to be in the streets on Christian holy days. Since these public events were often occasions for physical attacks on Jews, the legislation might have offered relative protection to Jews in medieval towns.[25] However, it is important to remember that animosity toward Jews was fuelled not only by the charge that they killed Christ (as if this were not enough), but also by negative representation of them in contemporary sermons and didactic drama.[26]

By dramatizing the lives of Jewish saints, the *Zohar* created a Jewish counter-drama to the one that permeated Christian culture of the day. The difference is that in the *Zohar* the stage upon which the drama of the Jewish saints was enacted is not the streets of a medieval city, but the private imagination of the reader/spectator. The world of the kabbalist works verbally and abstractly rather than spatially and physically.[27] Either by listening to the sermon stories of the *Zohar* or by reading them, the mind of the reader or listener provides the stage upon which the *dramatis personae* of the *Zohar* perform their incredible deeds, visit otherworldly terrains, and preach their profound sermons about the Torah.

If this conjecture is correct, then the *Zohar* provided Jews with a store of new rabbinic exempla, and the virtuous lives presented in them were an instrument of salvation. If the reader/listeners wished to become perfect in this world and attain eternal life, they had to emulate the life style of the *Zoharic* heroes. In this regard the *Zohar* is a didactic drama that carries a polemical message: there is only one proper Jewish activity in the world—the study of Torah, and there is only one proper way to study—the way presented by the *Zohar*.

The dramatic structure makes clear what the *Zohar* expects of the reader. Like all dramatic texts, it does not view him as a remote observer but as an active participant who will identify emotionally with the *dramatis personae*, empathetically share their adventures, imitate their exemplary behavior, and internalize their doctrinal teachings. In other words, because of this experience, the reader is supposed to behave and think differently, that is, to reorient his life in accordance with the direction provided by the *Zohar*.

The setting of the rabbinic conversations is also quite unusual. Whereas the mishnaic and talmudic rabbis and their Gaonic and medieval heirs studied within the walls of the rabbinic academy, the *Zohar* sets many of its dialogues outdoors.²⁸ In their travels, the protagonists undergo many adventures that often involve unexpected encounters with individuals who are not supposed to be learned in Torah, such as a young boy (*yanuqa*), a very old man (Rav Hamnuna Sava), or a poor, presumably unlearned muledriver (*taya'a*). To the surprise of the sages, these individuals turn out to possess deep knowledge of the Torah and impressive spiritual abilities. The incorporation of surprise as a literary device intends to maintain the interest of the reader in the unfolding drama as well as to ridicule the social conventions of the day. True knowledge of Torah is to be found in unexpected places and has little to do with social status in the Jewish community or even formal membership in the rabbinic class. Ironically, those who are conventionally presumed to possess knowledge of Torah turn out to be fools who lack the understanding of its deep mysteries.

Itinerant Preaching Scholars

We can only speculate as to why the *Zohar* chose to present its protagonists as itinerant scholars who gain wisdom as they travel. One possible explanation is that the *Zohar* attempted to imitate and dramatize information gleaned from talmudic literature about the rabbis. The talmudic corpus is replete with stories about ancient sages who travel within the Land of Israel or to faraway places as emissaries of the patriarchs. The greatest such traveler was Rabbi Judah ha-Nasi, the redactor of the Mishnah, who was accompanied on his extensive travels by his rabbinic court, thereby asserting his authority as the official representative of the Jews to the Romans. It is very likely that the *Zohar* chose the itinerant model in order to imitate the talmudic stories, thereby making the adventures more credible.

Another, not mutually exclusive, conjecture is that the *Zohar* chose the itinerant life as imitation and possible satire of the *maqamah* genre popular among the Jews in thirteenth-century Spain. The hero of these rhymed prose narratives experiences all sorts of funny mishaps, from which he is supposed to learn the truth about himself, human society, and the human condition.²⁹ Thus the genre was used to entertain the Jewish audience as well as to promote certain social ideals. Philosophers such as Shem Tov Falaquera and Yehudah Alharizi, who popularized Maimonidean philosophy, used the *maqamah* genre extensively to disseminate their philosophical outlook and educational program. The trope of the itinerant scholar who acquires wisdom through travel provided the structure of Falaquera's *Sefer ha-Mevaqesh* (The Book of the Seeker, composed in 1265), which we mentioned in the previous chapter. Perhaps the *Zohar* used the motif to reject and even poke fun at the search for wisdom in *Sefer ha-Mevaqesh*. As such, the literary structure of the *Zohar* itself constitutes an argument that true wisdom is not to be pursued individually through tutorship with experts in various arts and sciences, but in a group of like-minded scholars seeking to penetrate the mysteries of Scripture.

Finally, for me, the most plausible explanation for the itinerant traveler motif is the Christian environment in which the *Zohar* itself was composed. The thirteenth century saw the flowering of the mendicant preaching orders, primarily the Dominicans and the Franciscans, who preached in town and countryside, bound by the ideal of voluntary poverty and principled opposition to collective and private ownership.[30] Although the lay ministry of the new orders conflicted with the professional standards of the medieval Church, the enormous success of the orders in teaching urban populations garnered them the official support of the Papacy. The Dominicans in particular were itinerant preachers who produced a large body of didactic literature, technical aids for the teacher, and "collections of exempla, moralizing anecdotes, drawn from the lives of saints or from the more workaday world, that a preacher could use to touch his audience in the quick of their experience."[31] The preaching of the begging friars stimulated the development of religious moral drama and miracle plays as much as they energized the religious life of the laity by dramatizing the scriptural narrative. According to John W. Harris, the mendicant preachers

> constituted a kind of mobile priesthood, zealously devoted to propagating the faith among all orders of the society. [T]hey were responsible for creating an atmosphere of urgency and lively spiritual concern, and for 'dramatizing' scriptural and moral matters in all sorts of ways, both visual and verbal, to make them more immediate for people. [T]he preachers used all sorts of devices in their sermons which were useful pointers for dramatists—moral allegories and parables, lively descriptions of everyday life, and, particularly, "exempla'" or "examples'" which were popular stories with moral emphasis, stories that could be sensational or comic, fantastical, or strongly grounded in everyday life, but which were, above all vivid and memorable.[32]

In the second half of the thirteenth century, the Jews were very familiar with the "Black Friars" (the Dominicans) and the "Gray Friars" (the

Franciscans): the Jews were forced to listen to their sermons in the synagogue—one of the main outcomes of the Barcelona debate between Nahmanides and the apostate Pablo Christiani in 1263, which ended with a political victory for the Dominicans at the expense of Jewish influence at the court. The friars were given permission to preach to Jews so as to bring about their desired conversion, thus curtailing the long accepted principle of Jewish religious autonomy.[33]

That the friar preachers were seen as the best living exponents of the Gospel is not irrelevant to the presentation of the protagonists of the *Zohar*, which expresses profound hatred for Christianity and even equates gentiles (Christians) with the forces of Evil (the Sitra Aḥra). Such hostility toward the persecuting majority, however, does not negate Christian influences, as Liebes was the first to note.[34] Some of the deepest teachings of the *Zohar* make sense only as Jewish variants of or as responses to Christian religious beliefs. That the *Zohar* chose to present the holy men of Judaism as itinerant scholar-preachers who exemplified the ideal way of life could have been a response to the successful evangelization of the urban laity by the mendicant orders of its own day. Indeed, as we will make clear in the next chapter, since happiness pertains to the eternal salvation of the soul, that theme also undergirded the interreligious confrontation between Judaism and Christianity, from the thirteenth century onward.

Saints' Travels to the Other World

The sages' travels in the *Zohar* are not limited to the terrestrial realm. In many homilies the landscape changes from the earthly domain to the otherworldly spheres when the protagonists undergo ecstatic experiences and their souls ascend to the heavens. In their tours of the celestial domains, the protagonists not only get a glimpse of the afterlife, but also encounter the immortal souls of the righteous ones, represented as biblical or rabbinic figures. In other words, the protagonists of the *Zohar* get a sense of what constitutes the blissful state of immortal life; they actually arrive at the heavens, the very destiny to which the philosophers only aspire.[35]

The Zoharic depiction of heavenly ascents clearly built upon the motifs of the Heikhalot and Merkabah literature, even though the cosmology of the *Zohar* was quite different, since it was shaped by the conventions of medieval Neoplatonized-Aristotelianism. Yet the *Zohar* shared the assumption of the ancient Jewish texts that the one who reaches religious perfection is able to ascend to the heavenly sphere and remain alive, since he possesses privileged, esoteric knowledge. Conversely, the knowledge and spiritual energy gathered in the ecstatic experience can transform life on earth. In this regard, too, the *Zohar* may be seen against its medieval context, which produced rich visionary literature, replete with descriptions of otherworldly visits.[36] As Aron Gurevitch explains, "Visions and dreams were by no means attributed to the order of the illusory; they were rather the intrusions of a higher reality into daily life by which one could penetrate the secrets of the Other World and catch a glimpse of the future." [37] Gurevitch adds insightfully that "in contrast to the otherworldly regions in which travelers of antiquity or heroes of chivalric romances in an Icelandic saga sojourned, the Other World of the visions represents a picture, distinctively transposed onto the screen of theology, of the interior life of a man craving salvation and overcome by fear of posthumous punishments."[38] The same, I suggest, applies to the visitations of heavenly realms in the *Zohar*.

The Exemplary Way of Studying Torah

The *Zohar* presents itself as a series of revelations of secret knowledge. It opens access to hidden mysteries pertaining to the nature of God, the structure of the universe, the place of man in the order of things, the purpose of human life, the problem of evil, the relations between Israel and the nations, and the dynamics of the eternal covenant between God and Israel. It discloses that which is ordinarily concealed, either because of the way things are or because of human cognitive and volitional limitations. The revelation of secrets is an empowering, transformative act; those who receive them are changed by the received knowledge (the literal meaning of *kabbalah*). Indeed, the recipients of the secrets are blessed (literally speaking) by the divine power or energy inherent in the secrets. The knowledge empowers them with psychological and spiritual growth (i.e., the acquisition of higher epistemic functions of the soul as well as a higher degree of holiness), the ability to change the material world (i.e., to perform miracles),[39] and even the ability to affect God (i.e., to engage in theurgy).[40] Ultimately the possession of secrets enables their possessor to engage in redemptive activity.

According to the *Zohar*, the reception of secrets produces overwhelmingly intense joy (*ḥedvata*), expressed outwardly in uncontrollable crying, although not all cases of crying in the *Zohar* manifest such joy.[41] The joyous crying functions as a powerful release, which comes after the arduous efforts, anguish, anticipation, and anxiety involved in the process of penetrating the mysteries of the Torah. (By extension, the release is also experienced by the reader, who patiently follows the unfolding of the *Zohar's* secrets). Thus in contrast to the rationalist philosophers, for whom learning was a cerebral and ponderous intellectual activity, predicated on self-control and the extirpation of emotions, the crying and other expressions of extreme joy (for example, hugging) make the *Zohar* a highly emotional text that portrays Torah study as an activity that involves enthusiasm, passion, emotion, sound, bodily movements, and physical contact, all of which culminate in a spiritual release when the secrets are revealed and received.

Torah study in the *Zohar* is also presented as an erotic activity that must be undertaken jointly by people who love each other. Moreover, it increases intimacy among the learners, reflecting the intimacy between God and the kabbalist student of Torah.[42] Like its rabbinic and pre-Zoharic sources, the *Zohar* images the Torah as a female.[43] As noted above, the spiritual energy that is stored in the Torah, according to kabbalah, has creative and procreative powers; it literally brings things into existence. The mystery of the Godhead is thus the mystery of life, which means sexual activity and procreation; the cathartic experience is portrayed in sexual language—crying is analogous to sexual orgasm. Not only do the protagonists experience the joyful release of sexual energies in themselves: the exegetical activity of the *Zohar's* protagonists is itself believed to unify the male and female aspects of the Godhead and to unite the earthly (male) kabbalist to the female of God (the Shekhinah). Therefore, the act of Torah study must be undertaken with utmost purity. Hence only circumcised Jewish males can engage in it.[44]

The love of Torah, the pillar of rabbinic religious ethics, was given a more precise and daring meaning in the *Zohar*. To love the Torah and to be devoted exclusively to its study is the only way to enter a personal relationship with God, or, more precisely, with the face that God shows to Israel—namely, the Shekhinah. The devotion to Torah/Shekhinah by male kabbalists who manifested their love to each other while studying Torah begs for interpretation. We presume (we have little factual knowledge) that in accordance with Jewish law, all students of kabbalah were married males. Moreover, the *Zohar* speaks at great length about heterosexual marriage as the ideal context for a man to find his perfection, and there is no doubt that the *Zohar* regarded celibacy as well as childless marriages the gravest sin.[45] However, heterosexual marriage did not logically exclude (let alone actually eliminate) homoerotic feelings among male students of Torah. Nor does the Zoharic insistence on the duality of the feminine and masculine aspects of the deity mean that the *Zohar* saw the two sexes as totally separate.

As Elliot Wolfson has convincingly shown, the *Zohar* (very much like its rationalist coreligionists and other medieval texts) presupposed a one-sex theory: the female is an incomplete extension of the male and not a separate sex.[46] The ideal sexual situation is not a parity between the male and the female (as contemporary feminists would have it), but an inclusion or containment of the female into the male. This becomes most evident in the Zoharic symbolism of the Shekhinah, where the main theme is the Diadem (*atarah*), the very term that Jews reserve for the corona of the circumcised penis. Thus, the dynamic of concealment or disclosure, closure and openness, separation and union—in short, the rhythm of life itself—is focused in the most concentrated form on the mystery of the circumcised penis, to which the *Zohar* devotes many homilies. This obsession may reflect not just the particular sense of inadequacy of the main editor of the Zoharic corpus, Moses de Leon, but the deepest logic of the Zoharic outlook. Sexuality is at the core of the Zoharic conception of perfection.

The notion that learning has an erotic dimension, of course, was not the invention of the *Zohar;* it was recognized long before by Plato and accepted by almost all ancient Hellenistic philosophical schools and their Jewish counterparts, the rabbis. Yet in the context of the Maimonidean controversy, the Zoharic emphasis on the erotic dimension of learning might have had an additional polemical tinge against the Jewish rationalists. The pursuit of wisdom in the *Zohar* is presented as a creative, productive activity, where, literally, speaking gives birth to new life—i.e. it bears "fruits" or "children" both in the human world and in the supernal world.[47] In the human world the study of kabbalah (as depicted in the *Zohar*) must result in the birth of children, whereas in the divine world, it leads to the union of Shekhinah and her husband, *Tiferet*, and to the birth of souls. The study of philosophy, by contrast, has no parallel creative results; it is a barren activity that does not perpetuate Jewish life.[48]

The Paradigmatic Saint: R. Shimon bar Yohai

At the center-stage of the Zoharic drama stands R. Shimon bar Yohai, the second-century sage who reputedly hid for twelve years during the Hadrianic persecution. Referred to as "the Holy Luminary" (*butzina qadisha*),[49] R. Shimon is depicted in the *Zohar* as an unusually gifted spiritual figure whose mystical knowledge and exegetical activities carry messianic import. In the rabbinic tradition, he was not an outstanding legal authority; his minority position never determined halakhah. But the experience of hiding from the Romans made R. Shimon the appropriate character for the

Zoharic drama about concealment and revelation of the Torah's mysteries. Not only did he protect the Torah and save it from falling into oblivion; the very study of Torah in secret saved the rabbinic sage and his son from perishing during the period of hiding. Thus, as much as R. Shimon's experience dramatizes what happens when the secrets of the Torah become known, it also can serve as a good example for the readers of the *Zohar* of the kind of devotion the Torah requires.

The emergence of R. Shimon from hiding and the revelations of Torah's secrets are presented in the *Zohar* as redemptive activities that herald the coming of the messiah, as Yehudah Liebes has shown.[50] And the depiction of R. Shimon bar Yohai is hagiography par-excellence: when he engages in Torah study, the population of the supernal world stands and listens.[51] R. Shimon can communicate with animals, spirits of the dead, and angels. He can even abort the work of the angel of death. His profound knowledge of the mysteries of Torah benefits Israel directly, since he can struggle against the forces of evil and even change the course of divine providence.[52] Without R. Shimon, his generation would have been greatly diminished, since his wisdom and leadership are foundational to the well-being of society. Finally, in his death, R. Shimon heralds the messianic age as he unites with the Shekhinah and brings about the desired union between the masculine and feminine aspects of God.[53]

The Zohar *as an Alternative to the* Guide of The Perplexed

The literary structure of the *Zohar*, Liebes has convincingly argued, reflects the actual circumstances of its composition.[54] Its dramatization of the ideal life may tell us how it was composed, and, by implication, *why* it was composed. Although it was most probably the product of a group effort rather than the creation of a single author, Liebes conjectures that Moses de Leon, the Spanish kabbalist most associated with its composition,, wrote or redacted the main part of it, and his uniquely creative mind and literary style gave the corpus its distinct power.

Liebes identified other contributors as Bahya ben Asher, R. Joseph ben Shalom Ashkenazi ha-Arokh, R. David ben Yehuda he-Hasid, R. Joseph of Hamadan, and R. Joseph Gikatilla. If Liebes is correct, which is very likely, the kabbalistic fraternity that produced the *Zohar* was quite international, including Jewish mystics from Spain, Germany, and Persia. In thirteenth-century Europe, such group efforts were not implausible, since students and established scholars traveled long distances to the newly established centers of learning in order to acquire wisdom from known masters.

The spiritual leader of the *Zohar* project, Liebes has also proposed, might have been the kabbalist R. Todros ben Joseph Halevi Abulafia, the historical personality that was fictionalized in the character of R. Shimon bar Yohai. This conjecture also seems reasonable if we recall that the son of the famous kabbalist Joseph ben Todros was a friend of Moses de Leon and the recipient of a first copy of the *Zohar*.[55] A member of the distinguished Abulafia family of Jewish courtiers, Todros ben Joseph Abulafia was influential in the court of Alfonso X (1252–81) "the Wise," the famous patron of the arts and sciences who granted him extensive land holdings and sent him on diplomatic missions.[56] Furthermore, Todros' own kabbalistic commentary on Psalm 19—the very Psalm we discussed in Chapter Two as the key link between Torah, wisdom, and creation—used citations from *Midrash Ha-Ne'elam*, the oldest stratum of the Zoharic corpus. That Todros was also the nephew of R. Meir Halevi Abulafia (Ramah), the main instigator of the first debate of the Maimonidean controversies and a central actor in the second controversy, lends further support to the notion that the composition and dissemination of the *Zohar* should be understood in the context of the debate on the Maimonidean legacy.

With all this in mind, it is not too far-fetched to propose that the *Zohar* was written to function as *the* guide for the perplexed Jews of its generation, the spiritual guidance perceived as missing in Maimonides' *Guide of the Perplexed*. There is an intriguing parallelism between Maimonides' *Guide* and the *Zohar*. Both regarded the Torah as esoteric text, whose mysteries (*sitrei torah*) require decoding; and both present themselves as necessary for that decoding. Both presuppose the tension between the hidden (*nistar*) and the revealed (*nigleh*) in reality, in the human being, and in the Torah. Both set up intentional obstacles (as intentional contradictions in the *Guide* or riddles in the *Zohar*) and invite readers to solve their own mysteries as a precondition for the understanding of the Torah's mysteries. Finally, both regard the act of fathoming the meaning of Torah as the primary activity for the attainment of happiness. Just as the philosophic reader of the *Guide* needed to solve its intentional contradictions in order to grasp the hidden philosophic truths of the Torah, so must the kabbalistic reader of the *Zohar* decode its symbolic language in order to uncover those concealed truths. That the *Zohar* was to be the guide to Jewish life can become clearer once we present it as a discourse on happiness.

THE ZOHAR AS A DISCOURSE ON HAPPINESS

The Ethical Teachings of the Zohar

Instead of theorizing *about* happiness, the *Zohar* illustrates in a dramatic narrative what happens when Jews actually live the holy life and attain perfection through the kabbalistic study of Torah. Rhetorically and emotionally, this Zoharic dramatization is a much more persuasive way of telling Jews how they ought to live. Behind the dramatic structure, however, lies a full-fledged ethical theory about the nature of man, the composition of body and soul, the relationship between *theoria* and *praxis*, and the ultimate end of human life. Like all other ethical theories, the Zoharic approach includes a wide range of assumptions about God, the universe, and the place of man in the order of things. However, if modern readers seek to find a systematic exposition of this ethical theory, whose core is the meaning of human happiness, they may fail to find it. Such was the case with Isaiah Tishby, whose magisterial *Mishnat Ha-Zohar* (The Wisdom of the Zohar) is the best thematic presentation of the work. Tishby, of course, was well aware of the dramatic structure of the *Zohar* and appropriately chose to begin his presentation by discussing its *dramatis personae*. However, because he wished to glean from the narrative a set of doctrines, which he proceeded to arrange into a consistent, speculative system, he missed the degree to which the *Zohar* was a dramatization of the well-lived life. In so doing, Tishby followed the tendency of his teacher, Gershom Scholem, who, as Moshe Idel has argued, tended to highlight the doctrinal aspects of Kabbalah over and above its experiential dimension. For example, Tishby opens the section on "Morality" saying:

> An examination of the Zohar from the point of view of its ethical content produces a negative result. The subject occupies only a very minor place whichever part of the Zohar one looks at. Not only are the passages dealing with morality, whether personal or social, very few in number, but those which do exist are mostly brief and sketchy and lack that creative, original, and energetic spirit that characterizes the Zohar when it deals with other topics.[57]

The alleged paucity of interest in ethics is surprising, Tishby summarizes, given the presence of "comprehensive Jewish moral literature" in the Middle Ages. In comparison to Saadia Gaon, Solomon ibn Gabirol, Bahya ibn

Paquda, and Maimonides, according to Tishby, the *Zohar* presented no ethical theory.

Tishby came to this erroneous judgment not only because of his methodology, but also because he defined "ethical theory" too narrowly, and because he failed to understand that ethical reflections in the Middle Ages were always focused upon the features of the well-lived life. The entire *Zohar*, I contend, can be read as a dramatization of an ethical theory about the intrinsically good life, and the Zoharic style of presentation is in part an implicit polemic against the systematic discourses of the rationalist philosophers. Ethical theory in Judaism, as the *Zohar* implies, can be articulated homiletically only by working with the literary motifs of the biblical and rabbinic sources rather than with the abstract categories of Greek philosophers.

Expressions of Happiness in the Zohar

That the *Zohar* is profoundly concerned with the ideally happy life is evident in its linguistic continuity with rabbinic views of well-being. As we discussed in Chapter Two, the Hebrew word that comes closest to the English "happiness" is the verbal form *ashrei* ("happy is/are"). With this formula begins the first hymn of the Book of Psalms, which presents the well-lived life as the exclusive preoccupation with Torah. Psalm 1 makes it clear that the study of God's Torah and the observance of its commandments constitute the intrinsically good life, whose practitioner enjoys divine blessings. The early rabbis spelled out the meaning of that life by absorbing the Greco-Roman ethics of virtue into the Judaic ethics of obligation, and in numerous rabbinic homilies, the formula *ashrei* functions to advocate a certain idea or social ideal. The rabbinic conception of happiness is articulated most succinctly in the liturgy, which all Jews, regardless of their degree of learning, shared in their daily prayer. In it the rabbis carefully selected Psalms that included the *ashrei* formula, embedded *ashrei* verses from other Psalms (as in the introduction to Psalm 145 in which the formula is missing[58]), and coined new *ashrei* statements that spell out the rabbinic perspective on happiness just as the daily morning service explicitly linked the life of Torah to the attainment of happiness, as the following passage shows:

> Therefore, it is our duty to give thanks to thee, to praise and glorify thee, to bless and hallow Thy name, and to offer many thanksgivings to thee. Happy are we! How good is our destiny, how pleasant our lot, how beautiful our heritage! Happy are we who, early and late,

morning and evening, twice every day proclaim: Hear O Israel, the Lord is our God, the Lord is One.[59]

Ashrei in the Zohar

In the artificial Aramaic of the *Zohar* the phrase "happy is/are" is rendered as *zaka'ah ihu/zaka'in inon,* or "happy is the portion of he/those" (*zaka'ah ḥelqeih/zaka'ah ḥelqehon*).[60] These phrases and their variations appear numerous times throughout the Zoharic corpus, either as exhortations to the reader to behave or to think in a certain way, or as affirmations that the protagonists of the *Zohar* have already achieved the ideal state of well-being or perfection because they live in accord with its recommendations. Here are a few examples from among the hundred utterances of this kind:

> Happy is Israel (*zaka'in inon Yisrael*), the portion of God, blessed be He, who guarantees them and protects them, as it is said [Ps. 144:] "Happy is the people who have it so; happy is the people whose God is the Lord" [*Zohar* I:48b].
>
> Happy are the righteous ones [*zaka'in inon zaddiqaya*] who walk the straight path; they are truly righteous and their sons are righteous in the world, and about them it was said [Proverbs 2:21] "the upright will inhabit the earth" [*Zohar* I: 55a].
>
> Happy is he [*zaka'ah ihu man*] who belittles himself in this world; how great and mighty [he will be] in that [other] world [*hahu alma*] [i.e., the world to come] [*Zohar* I:122b].
>
> Happy are Israel that God, blessed be He, called them "human"[*adam*], as it is said [Ezekiel 34], "For you, my flock, flock that I tend, are men" . . . What is the reason for calling them "men'" ? Because it is said, [Deut. 4:4] "You who held fast [*deveqim*] to the Lord, your God [are alive today]." "You" and not other nations of idolaters [*ovdei kokhavim u-mazalot*], and therefore you are called "human'" [*adam*] and the idolaters, "gentiles," are not called "human" [*Zohar* II:86b].
>
> Happy is the portion of he who is sanctified [*zaka'ah ḥulqei deman*] in this holiness and knows this secret [*Zohar* II:89a].
>
> Happy is the portion of he who merits her [*zakhei bah*] [i.e., the Torah]; the one who meritoriously [receives] the Torah [*man de-zakhei be-oraita*], [meritoriously] receives the holy name of God, blessed be He [*Zohar* II: 90b].

Happy are Israel [*zaka'in inon Yisrael*] that in every place they are found, God, Blessed be He, is found with them, and God, blessed be He, exists among them and is glorified by them, as it is said [Isaiah 49:3] "Israel in whom I glory." Even more so because Israel perfects the faith [*ashlim de-mehmanuta*] in the world, and Israel is the perfection of the holy name [*Zohar* III 7b].

Happy are the righteous ones [*zaka'in inon zaddiqaya*], who are entirely holy [*dekulhu qadishin*] and exist in holiness [*ve-ashtakkhu bi-qedushah*] before the holy king, and the holy spirit [*ruah qadisha*] is bestowed upon them (*sharya alayhu*) in this world and in the world to come [*Zohar* III: 55b].

Happy are the righteous ones (*zaka'in inon zaddiqaya*) who sanctify the holy king [*Zohar* III: 77a].

Happy are the righteous ones (*zakka'in inon zaddiqaya*) in this world and in the world to come that God, blessed be He, desires their glory (*ba'ei bi-yeqarehon*) and reveals to them the supernal secrets of His holy name, that He did not reveal to the holy ones [*Zohar* III: 78b].

Happy are the righteous ones [*zaka'in inon zaddiqaya*] that many supernal mysteries are reserved for them in that [other] world [*ha-hu alma*] that God, blessed be He, delights in them in those worlds, as we interpreted . . . [*Zohar* III:79b].

Happy are Israel who cleave to God, blessed be He, they and not the nations of idolaters, and for this reason they cleave as one to each other [*iddabqu ke-hada da be-da*] [*Zohar* III:82a].

Interestingly, the Aramaic phrase *zaka'ah ihu/zaka'in inon* contains an ambiguity that does not exist in the Hebrew word *ashrei*. In talmudic literature (Hebrew and Aramaic) the word *zakai* means one who is clear, guiltless, righteous, deserving, or worthy. The Aramaic phrase, much more than its Hebrew equivalent, captures the causal link between righteousness or worthiness and the well-lived life. Moreover, the Aramaic term *zaka'ah* also evokes the Hebrew word *zekhut*, meaning "merit," which is the basis of rabbinic theodicy, where the righteous person is the one whose good deeds function as credits (Hebrew: *zekhuyot*, Aramaic: *zakhvan*) against his sins (Hebrew: *hovot*, Aramaic: *hayvei*) in the divine accounting system. Thus, when the *Zohar* uses the formula "*zaka'ah ihu,*" the reader immediately grasps that those who follow the teachings of the *Zohar* are the righteous ones whose good deeds function as credits.

The opposite of "happy is/are" is the exclamation beginning "Woe to" (in

Aramaic, *vei leih*). The *Zohar* uses this formula either to lament the sad spiritual condition prevalent in its own day (for example in *Zohar* III:6a), or to warn against certain undesirable ideas, postures, or deeds that the *Zohar* finds antithetical to the holy life. If the *ashrei* formula is an exhortation intended to motivate the reader in a certain direction, the exclamation "Woe to" should be viewed not simply as a neutral description of those who behave contrary to the ideal, but also as a kind of curse against those who do not heed the advice or recommendations of the *Zohar*. This use makes sense if we recall that in biblical and rabbinic usage the *ashrei* formula overlaps the word *barukh* (i.e., "blessed is").

As noted in Chapter Two, biblical scholars dispute the precise range of the formula *ashrei*. Some say it pertains only to human affairs, whereas *barukh* concerns divine-human relations. The *Zohar*, however, makes it clear that such a distinction cannot be maintained; the righteous enjoy well-lived lives because they receive the divine blessing (*berakhah*). When it says "Woe to," it denounces those who do not do what is necessary to attain the divine blessing and declares them opponents of the ideal way of life.

In the *Zohar* (and in theosophic kabbalah in general), the divine blessing is understood as a spiritual energy that sustains and nourishes all existents.[61] In the sefirotic hierarchy, "blessing" (*berakhah*) is the lowest sefirah, the gate through which the divine energy, or efflux, is communicated to extra-divine reality.[62] Thus the kabbalist who possesses knowledge of the Torah's mysteries unites with the Shekhinah and directly draws the divine, spiritual blessing from her. When the *Zohar* uses the phrase *zaka'ah ihu/zaka'in inon*, it can often be translated as "blessed is/blessed are," which means that the ones who possess the secrets revealed in the *Zohar* are endowed with the spiritual energy of God (*shefa*). The divine blessing that overflows from the Godhead to the human recipient is divine grace (*ḥesed*), which originates specifically in the fourth sefirah, *ḥesed*, but whose ultimate source is the divine origin, the *ein sof*.[63]

Torah Study as the Source of Happiness

Most commonly the *Zohar* uses the phrase "happy is . . ." in association with Torah study. The Torah itself is considered to be the source of the well-lived life in this world and the blissful life of the world to come. For example:

> Happy is the portion of Israel from above the nations of the idolaters [*ovdei kokhavim u-mazalot*], because God, blessed be He, created the

world only for the sake of Israel so that they will receive the Torah on Mt. Sinai [*Zohar* III: 7a].

Happy are the righteous ones who study Torah and know the concealed mysteries of the supernal world [*Zohar* III:10a].

Happy is the portion of the righteous ones in this world and in the world to come, because they know the ways of the Torah and they walk the path of truth (*oraḥ qeshot*) [*Zohar* III: 27a].[64]

Happy is the portion of the righteous ones who study Torah, especially in a time that the king desires the words of Torah. Come and see the mystery of the covenant [*raza de-milah*]. The Shekhinah [*kenesset Yisrael*] does not stand before the king except through the Torah, and as long as Israel on earth studies Torah, Kenesset Yisrael [i.e., the Shekhinah] stays with them [*Zohar* III: 22a].[65]

Happy are those who study Torah [*zaka'in inon de-mishtadlei*] because they are in a higher rank above all [*Zohar* III:35a].

Happy are the righteous one who walk the path of truth in this world and in the world to come [*Zohar* III:51b].

Happy is the portion of the man [*zakaah ḥelqei de-bar-nash*] who studies Torah [in order] to know the ways of the Holy One, Blessed be He, because he who studies Torah, it is as if he studies His Name itself [*Zohar* III: 76a].

In short, the common refrain "Happy are those who study Torah" lends the *Zohar* its relentless, polemical, and didactic tone. What the *Zohar* has in mind is not the conventional study of the Torah—both Written and Oral—as defined by the halakhic authorities of its day, but the study whose goal is to fathom and disclose its esoteric meaning, the secrets of the divine life concealed in the Torah.[66] The Aramaic word for "study," *eshtadel*—connotes "exertion" or "devotion to making an effort." Thus the Torah study that the *Zohar* presents as ideal involves knowledge, total devotion, and proper intention to encounter God and participate in the rhythm of divine life about which the Torah speaks. The kabbalistic study of Torah is to be distinct from the halakhic and the philosophical approaches to the life of Torah.

The Torah and Human Flourishing

The causal link between the devotion to Torah and happiness is expressed in many ways in the Zohar. The imagery of Psalm 1, which depicts the righteous man as a "tree planted by a water," pervades the text. The following citation (from *Zohar* III:200b) makes the point very clearly:

> How happy is the lot of man who is continually preoccupied with the Torah. What does Scripture say about the man who studies it? "His delight is in the Torah of the Lord, and in his Torah does he meditate day and night, and he shall be like a tree" [Ps. 1:2–3]. What is the connection between one and the other? Whoever studies the Torah day and night will not be like a shriveled tree, but "like a tree planted by streams of water." Just as a tree has roots, bark, pith, branches, leaves, flowers and fruit—these seven parts amounting to seven [times] ten, to seventy—so the words of the Torah have literal meaning, homiletic meaning, speculative allusions, *gematriot*, hidden mysteries, ineffable mysteries, one above the other, unfit and fit, unclean and clean, forbidden and permitted. The branches spread out from here on every side. He shall be like a veritable tree; and if not, then he is not a master of wisdom."[67]

The organic imagery of Psalm 1, the *Zohar* is saying, aptly depicts not only the righteous man who studies the Torah, but the Torah itself. The righteous man is so well rooted and nourished because the Torah itself is a living organism, whose organic complexity and unity is best captured by the symbol of the tree. The righteous man who studies Torah experiences the joy of the well-lived life and (as the rest of the homily makes clear) can withstand the presence of evil in the world. The very act of Torah study sustains not only the student of Torah (the kabbalist who knows how to study it) but the entire society, the world, and finally God.

Another homily (from the *Zohar* III:53b) elaborates on the key phrase in rabbinic Judaism that links Torah study and happiness. We have already noted that Proverbs 3:18—"She is the tree of life to those who take hold of it, and those who support her are happy"—originally had cosmic wisdom (*ḥokhmah*) as its subject, but in the rabbinic liturgy the subject of the sentence was the Torah. By the time the liturgy was put together, the equation of Torah and Wisdom was fully in place. By the Middle Ages all Jews took this identification for granted and uttered it in the course of the synagogue service each time they returned the Torah to the ark. The traditional Jew whose life was shaped by daily prayer took it for granted that Torah/wisdom is the "tree of life."

The *Zohar*'s explication of the verse reveals how traditional metaphors turned into theosophic symbols, pertaining to the inner life of God, whose knowledge yields happiness. In the Zoharic interpretation, the Torah is literally a source of life because it contains divine life. Consequently, those who take hold of the Torah receive spiritual vitality that enables them to flourish, live the happy life in this world, and experience eternal life after death. The *Zohar* states:

> R. Yehudah opened with words of Torah saying: [Proverbs 3:18]: "It is a tree of life to those who take hold of it, and those who support her are happy". "A tree of life"—this is the Torah which is the supernal, great and mighty tree. Why is [the tree called] Torah? It is called Torah because it enlightens and discloses that which was concealed and unknown. [The Torah is called] "tree of life," because all life of the supernal world (*ḥayim dil`ela*) is included in her, and comes forth from her. "To those who take hold of her," [means that she is life] to those who hold her [*de-aḥadin bah*], because the one who holds the Torah becomes united with everything, below and above. "And those who support her are happy"—these are the people who fill up [*metilin melai*] the pockets of the scholars, as we explained above. "And those who support her" are blessed that faithful prophets come from them. "Happy"—do not read it as *me'ushar*, but *me-rosho* [meaning: 'from its head'], [because] they support the Torah from head/beginning [*me-rosho*] to its end [*ve-`ad sofo*]. *Me-rosho*—that means the beginning of everything, as it is said [Proverbs 8:23]: "at the beginning at the origin of the earth"; and "beginning" is wisdom [*ḥokhmah*]. Because wisdom is the beginning of every body [*gufa*], and a body extends, by virtue of it [*etpashet bei*], until its end [*siyuma*] at the six extremities. And (as for) "her adherents," it is said [Song of Songs 5:15] "His legs are like marble pillars." These are the ones who fill up the pockets of the sages; they support the Torah from the beginning to the end of the body; all faith [*mehmanuta*] depends on it, and they are supported and blessed with children that will be seen as faithful prophets.

This homily is a typical example of the symbolically packed language of the *Zohar*. To decode it one must be familiar with a large body of associations, many of which are taken for granted by any Jew who lives in the matrix of rabbinic Judaism and whose worldview is textured by the language of Scripture and rabbinic texts. For example, the association of Torah and light (in Hebrew *or*) requires no explanation for a traditional Jew, and it enables the

Zohar to speak about the tree of life, the Torah, as enlightening. Other statements make sense only if one is familiar with the technical, symbolic code of theosophic kabbalah and its underlying theoretical assumptions. Thus, wisdom (*hokhmah*) is a specific reference to the second sefirah of the divine realm, which in Kabbalah is also called "Beginning," because it is the paradigm of all existents. Finally, the homily makes sense only to those who know both Hebrew and Aramaic: the *Zohar* exploits the similarities and overlapping terms of these related Semitic languages, without losing their distinctiveness.

To explicate the meaning of biblical verses means to expose or disclose the secret (*raza*) concealed in the Torah. The disclosure of secrets makes available the spiritual energy, or light, inherent in the Torah, so that the exegetical activity itself sheds light on what was earlier unknown (*setim*), or metaphorically was "in the dark." Thus, the revelation of the Torah's secrets, which constitutes the content of the *Zohar*, enlightens those who are fortunate enough to receive them.[68]

The enlightenment about which the *Zohar* speaks is quite different from the one proposed by the philosophers. Instead of cognizing intelligibles that are culled from observation of nature, the *Zohar* claims that enlightenment comes only from fathoming those mysteries of the Torah that pertain to the inner life of the Godhead. And because the *Zohar*'s esoteric doctrines pertain to God and not to the created or emanated universe, the kabbalists felt themselves to be spiritually superior to the rationalist philosophers.

Encoded in the Torah are the mysteries of life itself: the energy or power that brings everything into existence and sustains it thereafter. We recall that for Maimonides the hidden meaning of the Torah encompasses the abstract principles, the general laws by which God governs the created universe. The enlightened, rationalist philosopher (the *maskil*) who cognizes the intelligibles is the one who understands how the universe manifests divine providential care. The *Zohar* implicitly and polemically claims to go deeper than the philosophers: it talks not just about the laws of nature but about the most foundational mystery of all, life itself. The tree of life is the symbolic expression of that mystery.

In Zoharic theosophy the tree is viewed both as the totality of the divine pleroma—the entire sefirotic system, or better still, the sefirotic ecosystem.[69] More specifically, the tree of life is associated with the central sefirah—Tiferet—the male principle that is also the symbol of the written Torah. When the liturgy asserts that the Torah is a "tree of life," then, it means that the Torah is the source of all life—hence appropriately associated with the male principle—so that those who take hold of the Torah are literally nourished and sustained by its vitality and creative power.

The sefirotic realm is multifaceted and multilayered, a dynamic system of forces that are interlinked, mutually affecting each other. The tree symbolism conveys, moreover, that the sefirotic realm, the divine reality that is hidden in the Torah, has many aspects, but all of them are organically linked. The *Zohar* explores the organic unity of the Torah by exploiting the ambiguity between Hebrew and Aramaic. The original verse states that those who take hold of the Torah/wisdom (*la-mahaziqim bah*) benefit from its vitality. The Zohar then interprets the act of "taking hold" as the act of "uniting with" or "bringing union to" the sefirotic realm. It can make this jump because in Hebrew there is another verb that means "to take hold"—*le-ehoz*. However, the *Zohar* changes the last letter of the stem, the letter *zayin*, to the letter *dalet*, to form the Aramaic equivalent of "to take hold." With this change of letters, the *Zohar* brings another Hebrew word into the homily, the word *ehad* and its related verbal forms. "To take hold of the Torah" thus means in this passage not only to cognize its internal, underlying unity, but also to engage in an act that itself brings about unity. This is the act of Torah study that unifies the male and female aspects of the Godhead.

Through this subtle word play, the *Zohar* actually expresses one of the main differences between the rationalist philosophers and the theosophic kabbalists' conception of the meaning of the monotheistic faith. For Maimonides and his followers, it meant to assert that God is radically simple (i.e., no division of composition is possible in God) and radically singular. In this interpretation, the radical oneness of God entails that nothing can be said of God's essence and that there can be no relationship with the deity.[70] The *Zohar* disputes Maimonides' radical negative theology. It claims, instead, that the oneness of God entails integrating the various forces of the Godhead, and the unity of God is radically different from the unity of anything else. Indeed, the *Zohar* calls the sefirotic realm "*alma de-yihuda*" (the realm of unity) in contradistinction to the differentiation that marks everything else ("*alma de-peruda*"). However, the unity of the divine realm is rich rather than simple, and the goal of the monotheistic kabbalist is to grasp the full unity despite its complexity.

The most creative expression of the link between happiness and the study of Torah is captured by the anagrams *me'ushar* (meaning, "happy") and *me-rosho* (meaning, "from its beginning"). In the *Zohar* "beginning" is one of the symbols of the second sefirah, *Hokhmah* (wisdom), the singularity out of which comes forth the process of differentiation and individuation, resulting in the world that we know. The passage asserts that the wisdom of the Torah makes one happy because it comes from the very source of all existence, from the second sefirah. Though the sefirotic realm has different aspects, each revealing a specific facet of infinite divine reality, the entire system manifests organic unity: one vital force pulsates through it, "from beginning to end" (*me-rosho ve-ad sofo*). The tree or the human body, the two main symbols of the sefirotic realm, manifest that organic unity and vitality.

The *Zohar* imperceptibly shifts from the tree symbolism to the symbolism of the divine anthropos, the primordial man (*adam qadma'ah*), when it presents the process of universal physical and human history as an extension of vitality from the head, the literal meaning of "*me-rosho*" to its end (*ve-ad sofo*). "End" (or in Aramaic *siyuma*) is used in the *Zohar* as a symbol of the male genitals of the divine anthropos, which it identifies with the sefirah *Yesod* (Foundation). This shift is evident in the proof-text from the Song of Songs. The rabbis already understood the male lover of the biblical poem as a reference to God, which the ancient Jewish mystics elaborated upon in their speculations about the body of God. Proper knowledge of the mysteries of the Torah, then, pertains to knowledge of who God truly is. This is the true faith (*mehemanuta*) that the kabbalists alone possess. And on the basis of that faith, the kabbalists, or more precisely the *Zohar*, will redeem Israel, the cosmos, and ultimately even God.

Underlying the dramatic narrative, the symbolic language, the literary associations, and the puns and wordplay, the *Zohar* articulates a very clear message—the esoteric teachings of the Torah pertain to the divine self, to the "master," the Holy One, blessed be He. Knowledge of these mysteries is possible only to those who possess the correct knowledge about the nature of human beings as a composition of body and soul, and about the structure of the world, both terrestrial and supernal. This kind of knowledge prepares the knower to encounter the divine personality. The attainment of the supernal knowledge is also the precondition for the afterlife. The mysteries of Torah are salvific.

Torah, Perfection and Peace

A final support of our argument is the interpretation, in *Zohar* II: 31a, of the verses from Proverbs 3 that Jews recite each time they return the Torah to the ark at the conclusion of Torah reading.

> He (R. Ḥezkeyah) opened and said: (Proverbs 3:17) "Her ways are pleasant ways, and all her paths, peaceful." "Her ways are pleasant ways"—these are the paths of the Torah, so that he who walks by the path of the Torah of God, blessed be He, the pleasantness of the Shekhinah (*ne'imuta de-Shekhinah*) is bestowed upon him (*ashrei alei*), so that it will never depart from him. "And all her paths are peaceful"—that all the paths of the Torah are peace (*shalom*), meaning, peace to him above and peace to him below; peace to him in this world, (and) peace to him in the world to come.

The homily continues to explore the meaning of the "pleasantness" or "bliss" (*ne'imu*) that is bestowed on the one who studies Torah properly. The "pleasantness" is depicted as numerous lights [*butzinin*] that spring from the third sefirah *Binah* (whose symbol is "the world to come"), and spread in all directions. This infinite light is the goodness (*tivu*) that enables its recipients—the members of the covenant—to experience the blissful life of peace and perfection in the world to come. By contrast, those who are sinful end in Gehenna and do not benefit from the blissful life of the world to come.

The homily is based on the fact that in Hebrew and in Aramaic the word for "perfect" (*shalem*) has the same root as the word for peace (Hebrew: *shalom*, Aramaic: *shelama*).[71] This perfection (*shelimu*) is presented in the *Zohar* as a flow of uninterrupted spiritual energy that springs forth from the source and pervades the sefirotic world without obstacle or blemish. The righteous man who has become perfect cleaves to the Shekhinah and through her absorbs the abundance of divine blessing (*berakhah*), or better still, divine grace (*ḥesed*). At this moment of mystical union all things become one; the sefirot unite with each other, and the human is united with God. In short, it is only the study of Torah according to its secret meaning that opens up the sefirotic realm and facilitates the reception of spiritual energy that enlightens and enlivens the recipients in this world and secures the afterlife in the world to come.

Happiness and the Problem of Evil

If we need any more proof that the *Zohar* can be read as an elaborate discourse on happiness, we can find it in the numerous Zoharic homilies that juxtapose two ways of being in the world, the "way of the righteous" and its antithesis, "the way of the wicked."[72] In the Wisdom literature of the Bible, expressed most succinctly by Psalm 1, the two ways are presented together in order to pose a clear existential choice for the reader. Rabbinic Judaism elaborated upon the meaning of the ideal way of life by spelling out its legal and ethical content and by promising that the righteous will reap the rewards of their good conduct in the remote future of the world to come. This was a partial solution to the ancient problem posed by the Book of Job: Why do the wicked prosper and the righteous suffer?

Because of their approach to the problem of evil, medieval Jewish philosophers did not need to elaborate on the specific differences between the two patterns of life. In a metaphysical schema of Neoplatonized Aristotelianism, there was no room to talk about the reality of evil: the philosophers identified *being* with good. Evil, therefore, was not an existing thing; it was only a privation, the absence of the good, metaphysically identified with prime matter.[73] All forms of imperfection in the mundane world were thus ascribed to matter, but matter in and of itself did not exist because it was nothing.

As we saw in Chapter One, in the hierarchical, emanationist ontology of medieval Neoplatonized Aristotelianism, the lower a thing is in the chain of being the more corporeal it is, and thus necessarily more evil, more distant from the source of being. In human terms, then, the corporeal body was viewed as the source of evil, the seat of desires and temptations that led one away from the good by enticing him to pursue apparent goods. To overcome evil, the philosophers advised control of bodily desires by the rational soul, which can orient a person towards the real good. The philosophic life thus consisted of the acquisition of virtues that facilitated engagement in the pursuit of wisdom, culminating in the perfection of the intellect. This denial of the reality of evil explains why the philosophers had relatively little to say about the "way of the wicked," focusing instead on the efforts to attain intellectual perfection.

The *Zohar* took a very different approach. Reviving old Gnostic motifs, it posited a dualism of good and evil, albeit with important qualifications that attempted to accommodate traditional Jewish theodicy.[74] The *Zohar* recognizes the existence of a separate domain—the Sitra Aḥra (the "other side")—which is structured like the domain of the good but has a lower and derivative ontological status. Utilizing prevailing popular beliefs about the demonic forces that operate in the world, the *Zohar* provides a rich description of the demonic realm, its rulers—the arch-demon, Samael, and his female consort, Lilith—and its inhabitants of evil spirits and harmful male and female demons. In the Zoharic worldview, at every level of reality including God's, there is a relentless struggle between good and evil.

The *Zohar* is by no means consistent on the origin of evil and advances several rationales to explain it, some structural and other teleological. In some homilies evil originates in the imbalance between the divine attributes of lovingkindness (*ḥesed*) and its antithesis, judgment (*gevurah*), which led to the "spillover" of negative energy, giving rise to a separate realm of evil. In other homilies, evil was created by God for the sake of the human. In these cases the existence of evil serves as a test for humans, allowing them, or more precisely, Israel, to gain credit through the very effort to overcome it. Yet the dominant explanation of the origin of evil is that it was but a potentiality within God, and it was the human primordial sin of Adam that actualized that potential, giving rise to a separate realm. The primordial sin produced the separation between the male and female aspects of the Godhead—a sin known in kabbalah as *qitzutz ba-neti`ot* ("cutting down the shoots")[75]— resulting in an imperfect and out-of-balance Godhead. Since human agency is the direct cause of evil, human beings, or more precisely Israel, also have the exclusive responsibility to perfect the imperfect, to repair the broken deity.

Indeed, in the human world the struggle between the good and evil and the imperfection of the Godhead are experienced most acutely by Israel. Individually, Jews experience the imbalance as an internal psychological tension between the corporeal body and the incorporeal soul. The corporeal body itself is viewed as the seat of the evil inclination (*yitzra bisha*), which seduces one to sin and transgress. Sinners thus further empower evil and perpetuate its existence. The human task, then, is to place the body under the control of the soul—an act that will lead one to observe the commandments of Torah. The evil desires and actions of the body can thus be purified and the observer of the Torah's prescription sanctified. Collectively, the struggle between good and evil is manifested in the status of the nation of Israel; when evil has the upper hand, Israel is in exile, controlled by gentiles. The suffering of Israel collectively and individually reflects the fact that the deity itself is out of balance and its masculine and feminine aspects sundered apart. When Israel is in exile, the Shekhinah itself is controlled by Samael and is unable to reconnect with her husband, *Tiferet*.[76] The deity itself is in a state of imperfection, requiring the help of the human agent, namely the kabbalist.

In recognizing the reality of evil, the *Zohar* severely limits the omnipotence of God. Yet God, according to theosophic kabbalah, is by no means utterly powerless. Both God's power and God's benevolence are made known in the act of creation as well as in the act of divine self-revelation.

The Torah, which God revealed to himself, contains in it the energy that gives rise to life, and that power sustains life, thereby serving as the only antidote for the atrocity and havoc of the evil forces. Containing no less than the essence of God, the revealed Torah has in it the spiritual remedies for the misery and afflictions Israel suffers because of the Sitra Aḥra, but only those who possess the spiritual power of the Torah can subdue the demonic forces.[77] The commandments of the Torah are the prescriptions that help curb the seductive temptations of evil inclination, thereby diminishing the power of evil in the world and its grip over the Shekhinah. By observing the commandments of the Torah, the righteous man can release her from her imprisonment by Samael, restoring her to her husband *Tiferet* and re-establishing the original unity of the masculine and feminine aspects of the Godhead.[78] This re-pairing of God will result historically in the political redemption of Israel from the control of the gentiles, but it was the mending of God that preoccupied the imagination and concern of the *Zohar*.

Acknowledging the reality of evil enables the *Zohar* to elaborate upon the juxtaposition, common in biblical and rabbinic sources, between the "way of the righteous" and its antithesis, "the way of the wicked," common in biblical and rabbinic sources. Whereas the righteous live the sacred life of Torah in accordance with the teachings of kabbalah, the wicked follow the temptations of their evil impulse, resulting in sin and the transgression of God's Torah. Whereas the righteous focus on the study of Torah and benefit from its spiritual vitality, the wicked are mired in the illusory life of the corporeal world and pursue the pleasures of the body. Whereas the righteous cling to the Shekhinah and receive from her the spiritual energy that makes them holy, the wicked forsake God's way and attach themselves to the demonic forces of the Sitra Aḥra, wreaking havoc in the world. Finally, whereas the virtuous will experience the bliss of eternal life, the wicked sinners, who often prosper in this world, will suffer the punishments of hell. The clear distinction between the two paths makes the existential choice for Jews clear cut; only the life of Torah, as explicated by kabbalah, constitutes the well-lived life in this world, and guarantees immortality in the afterlife. To choose between the "way of the righteous" and the "way of the wicked" is to choose between good and evil.

How to become a Righteous Person

What are the components of the "way of the righteous" that constitute the well-lived life? To begin with, the righteous must, according to the *Zohar*, live within the strictures of halakhah. This takes for granted that halakhah defines the outer limits of the upright, righteous life for Jews: its 365 positive commandments and 248 negative commandments determine what is right and wrong, what is permitted and what is forbidden.[79] Yet the commandments are much more than mere instructions to guide human conduct. They are themselves divine holy entities: their external "body" parallels the parts of the human body, whereas their internal "soul" is linked to aspects of the divine anthropos, namely to the sefirotic realm. Created in the image of God, the human, or more precisely the Jewish male, is viewed as a microcosm of the divine anthropos and as such his 365 sinews and 248 body parts mirror the divine anthropos.[80] By performing a particular commandment one is literally linked to an aspect of God. Thus the meaning of each commandment is to be found in the "intention" (*kavanah*) that links the performer to a particular locus in the sefirotic world, to a specific aspect of God. A proper performance of a given commandment, according to theosophic kabbalah, thus involves not only doing something with the limbs of the physical body but also accompanying the act with proper mental activity. The combination of action and cognition, of performance and thought, not only transforms the performer, making him holy. It also creates a spiritual energy that acts as a lever, so to speak, to elevate the human performer to the divine realm, cleaving to the Shekhinah.

The spiritual energy created by the performance of the commandments is itself a powerful tool in the struggle of the righteous person against the forces of evil. It is presumed to disarm those forces from their power, denying evil its vitality and sustenance. Conversely, the properly performed commandment strengthens the powers of holiness and purity, enabling the kabbalist to release the Shekhinah from her imprisonment by the archdemon, Samael, and to restore her to the rightful husband, *Tiferet*. In restoring the balance between good and evil in the world, the kabbalist perfects divine reality itself, the very reality that became imperfect on account of human sins. Through the commandments, the male worshipper is presumed to integrate himself into the rhythm of God's inner life and draw further spiritual energy from the divine source to which he now cleaves. In the symbolic language of kabbalah, through cleaving to the Shekhinah the performer receives the vital, spiritual energy from the upper nine sefirot of the divine anthropos, transmitted through the genitals of the divine anthropos, *Yesod*.

Those who follow the "way of the righteous" taught by kabbalah possess the esoteric knowledge of the inner meaning of each and every mitzvah and accordingly perform it correctly. Presumably, all those Jews lacking knowledge of kabbalah are engaged in either a low level of divine worship or, worse, idolatrous practices. By insisting that the mitzvot have an esoteric, hidden, symbolic dimension, the *Zohar* (and theosophic kabbalah in general) proposed its version of the "rationales of the commandments" to replace the Maimonidean one. Maimonides held that those rationales are accessible to human reason, that the commandments were a divine response to the degree of intellectual perfection of Israel at the time of the reception of the Torah, that the commandments facilitate the cultivation of virtues, and that they establish the just society in which one can engage in philosophic activity so as to attain the ultimate end of human life. By contrast, the *Zohar* insists that the commandments are holy acts whose performance produces holiness in the performer and in the world and even increases the holiness of the Godhead, bringing about the re-union of the masculine and feminine aspects of God. In this regard, performance of the commandments was to be done not only "for the sake of humans" (*le-tzorekh hedyot*) but also for the sake of the supernal, i.e., God (*le-tzorekh gavoha*).[81] The ultimate end of the "way of the righteous" is the perfection of God, which is the responsibility of the human.

KABBALISTIC VIRTUES

Rejection of Maimonides' Ethics of Moderation

A life devoted entirely to the worship of God requires certain mental dispositions. The group that produced the Zoharic corpus was clearly familiar with Maimonides' ethical teachings and his doctrine of the virtues as the mean between two vices, one an excess and the other a deficiency. However, in the main part of the *Zohar* that notion is absent and, I believe, intentionally so. It seems to me that the *Zohar* implicitly rejects the Maimonidean doctrine of the mean and instead defines desirable character traits in terms of clinging to the sefirot, the character traits of the ideal personality—God.

Acquiring the virtues through imitation (*mimesis*) was indeed part of the Aristotelian theory of how a child should be educated. Because he depersonalized God, however, Maimonides de-emphasized imitation of the divine. In contrast, the Zohar could highlight the mimetic aspect of virtue cultivation, precisely because it restored the personalist conception of God characteristic of rabbinic Judaism. To imitate God, so as to be holy as God is holy, one must not observe how the natural world is governed by God (the "ways" of God). Instead, one focuses on the traits of the divine personality, symbolized in each of the sefirot. It is through the study of the Torah that the kabbalist can fathom the various aspects of the divine personality and become like them, through clinging to the Shekhinah. From this "Gate" the righteous man of kabbalah receives the spiritual energy of the sefirot and thereby acquires divine character traits, becoming holy, as God is holy. Herein lies a major difference between the kabbalistic and Aristotelian approaches to the moral life: for the Greeks, the gods cannot be supposed to have moral virtues.

Acquiring the virtues through mimesis of the sefirot leaves little room for moderation or prudence. The holy men of the *Zohar* epitomize supererogatory conduct, especially in regard to Torah study and to sexual purity. Their preoccupation with the latter in particular suggests certain ascetic tendencies not so different from Maimonides' suspicion of bodily pleasures. Instead of the Maimonidean-Aristotelian idea of a mean between two vices, however, the *Zohar* advances the ideal of an equilibrium between the opposing forces of good and evil, light and darkness, purity and impurity, and male and female. As Elliot Wolfson has shown, the ideal balance of forces does not entail the extirpation of the negative aspect, but rather the proper containment of the negative in the positive, by which equilibrium is re-established. Psychologically speaking, it means that the cultivation of virtue can be undertaken only if one accepts the presence of the evil inclination, and learns how to transform it from within in order to employ it in the service of God.

The virtuous personality thus emerges through a supreme attempt to cling to God, which can be accomplished only if one develops those character traits that enable the religious personality to stand in a love relationship with the divine. For this reason, the *Zohar* reiterates ideas that we found earlier in Bahya ibn Pakuda and predicates happiness (the well-lived life) on the acquisition of humility. Thus, the *Zohar* I: 122b states: "Happy is the man who belittles himself in this world. How great and exalted he will be in the next."[82] *Zohar* III: 90b–91a depicts the humble person as a "broken vessel" who is fit to receive the divine overflow.[83] That individual reaches perfection by breaking his pride [*ga'avata*], which the *Zohar* associates with preoccupation with the body and bodily pleasures, especially sexual pleasures. The "broken vessel" metaphor is also associated with a poor person who is in want or one who suffers pain and illness.

The emphasis on poverty as a mark of humility can be construed as a critique of the Jewish courtier class who are proud of their worldly success. Such intimations permeate the *Ra'aya Mehemna* and the *Tiqquney Zohar*, and clearly suggest the displeasure of this anonymous kabbalist with the social stratification of that day.[84] The emphasis on suffering and illness as the mark of humility captures the ascetic ethos promulgated at the time by

Hasidei Ashkenaz among Jews and by various religious orders in the majority society. That the *Zohar* chose a verse from Isaiah 53 to represent the secret of humility may be read as an attempt to rebut Christian readings of that famous chapter.[85]

No less important, and in accord with the teachings of Bahya, the *Zohar* praises the righteous person who possesses complete trust in God. It states (I: 142 a):

> "Happy is the man whose strength is in you, in whose heart is the highway" [Ps. 84:6]. Happy is the man who relies on the Holy One, blessed be He, and puts his strength in Him. . . . A man should not rely [on God] to such an extent as to say, "The Holy One, blessed be He, will deliver me, or he will do such and such for me." However, let him place his strength in the Holy One, blessed be He, [trusting] that He will help him if he strives to fulfill the commandments of the Torah and walk in the way of truth; for when a man strives to purify himself, he certainly receives help. He can rely on the Holy One, blessed be He, to help him, if he relies on Him alone, and does not place his strength elsewhere. Therefore Scripture says that his "strength is in you." "In whose heart are the highways" means that he directs his heart correctly, so that it harbors no alien thoughts. His heart is like a highway that always leads directly to its appointed destination[86] (*Zohar* I:142a).

Trust in God entails rejection of pride and self-reliance. Indeed, the *Zohar* considers pride a major means by which the Sitra Aḥra operates and leads one to sin. Likewise, it denounces anger as a serious vice that separates one from the source of holiness and allows the Sitra Aḥra to take hold of him. However, it recognizes that anger employed in the service of Torah study does have a positive function: it leads the scholar of Torah to be zealous in the worship of God. Whether the denunciation of pride and anger has a more specific social dimension—such as a critique of the courtier class or a rejection of specific members of the circles who were prone to anger—is difficult to ascertain, but it is not implausible.

The Centrality of Sexuality

Humility and trust in God both require self-control, which in the *Zohar* applies primarily to sexual temptations. The *Zohar* speaks endlessly against those who commit sexual transgressions "such as emission of semen for no purpose (i.e., through masturbation, onanism, etc.), sexual relations with the 'forbidden decrees,' adultery, and intercourse with gentile women."[87] This preoccupation with sexual misconduct is directly related to the *Zohar's* association of religious perfection with holiness and purity.

The covenant between God and Israel is neither an abstract idea nor merely a political arrangement. It is, according to the *Zohar*, the arrangement that sustains the world: through it the divine energy is transmitted to the corporeal world. The covenant is sealed in the circumcised penis in the body of the male Jew, who can attain perfection only if he manages his sexual affairs in purity, as defined by Jewish law and interpreted by the *Zohar*. The sign of circumcision is the bodily locus of the divine presence as much as it is the vehicle through which the Jewish male can aspire to envision God, to unite with God, and to bring about the reunification of the male and female aspects of God.

Typical examples of this Zoharic theme include:

- Secrets of the divine mystery are revealed through the holy seal, which is the sign of the covenant of circumcision. "It is taught: Wherever a man is marked with the sacred mark of this sign he can see from it the Holy One, blessed be He; from it literally. . . . And it is written concerning this, "And from my flesh shall I see God" [Job 19:26], this is the perfection of all: "from my flesh" literally—from this actual sign.[88]
- He who is false to the holy covenant sealed in a man's flesh is false, as it were, to the name of the Holy One, blessed be He. He who is false to the seal of the king is false to the king. He has no portion in the God of Israel, except through the power of deep repentance.[89]
- Come and see. Those who do not maintain the holy covenant cause a separation between Israel and their father who is in heaven. Such a man is like one who bows down to another god, for he is false to the sign of the holy covenant.[90]
- When a man is false to the covenant of circumcision, YHVH and Shade leave him, and Satan, who is "another god," dwells with him. The serpent takes the place of YHVH within, and a deadly poison takes the place of Shade without.[91]

It is by virtue of purity that the righteous man can imitate God and integrate himself into the rhythm of divine life. If for the philosophers the righteous man was called to imitate God by developing his intellect, in the *Zohar* the righteous man is called to imitate all aspects of the divine personality, as revealed in the ten sefirot. The sefirotic world, however, is a unity rather than a composition of independent qualities, and its unity is expressed by the divine efflux from the upper sefirot to the sefirah *Yesod* ("Foundation"), whose symbol is the Zodiac. In the paradigm of the divine anthropos, this sefirah functions as the male genitals, through which the divine creative energy pours into the Shekhinah, and from her it is bestowed on the earthly Zodiac who sustains the world and hence can be appropriately called a "pillar" of the world. According to the *Zohar*, R. Shimon bar Yohai was the "pillar" of his generation, serving as the ultimate paradigm for all Jewish males.

The righteous man in the *Zohar*, who is aligned with the divine Zodiac, sefirah *Yesod*, is a spiritually transformed individual. By cleaving to the divine potencies, he becomes super-human, drawing the divine spiritual energy into his own body and sanctifying himself.[92] The righteous man acts as a channel for the divine spiritual energy, transmitting the received overflow to the earthly reality. Empowered with divine energy, he can transform the mundane world around him by dispensing power to those who need it or by using it himself to subdue the forces of evil. In so acting, he is engaged in redemptive activity. At death the soul of the righteous man will join the angels in the seventh palace of the heavenly realm and there enjoy the bliss of eternal life. The paradigmatic righteous man who accomplished all these feats, according to the *Zohar*, is of course R. Shimon bar Yohai. As Y. Liebes has shown, the most esoteric segments of the *Zohar* pertain to his departure from the mundane world and his unification with the Shekhinah.

"The Way of Truth"

With this in mind it is understandable why the *Zohar*, and prior theosophic kabbalists, presented the "way of the righteous" as "the way of truth" (*oraḥ qeshot*). The latter term, I believe, has an implicit polemical tinge directed against the claims of the Maimonideans, who reckoned the truths of philosophy to have salvific and redemptive powers. "The way of truth" pertains not to knowledge that God exists and that God manages the universe justly and wisely, but to the very essence of God, which the kabbalists believed is sealed and concealed in the Torah. Since the "mysteries of Torah" are thus the mystery of God's essence, and since a name expresses the essence of a thing, the *Zohar* and other kabbalists could claim that Torah comprises numerous permutations of the Divine Name. Maimonides rightly held that knowledge of the true mysteries of the Torah was essential for proper interaction with God, but he was wrong in identifying these mysteries.

Moreover, "the way of truth," which the righteous man must walk, is not merely theoretical. Rather, the "mysteries of the Torah" constitute the inner meaning of the commandments that the kabbalist must know in order to observe the prescriptions of Jewish law properly. In the *Zohar* specific commandments, or aspects of a given commandment, are linked to a particular sefirah, which serves as the divine destination of the commandment. While performing a given commandment bodily, the kabbalist must accompany the physical act with a particular "mental intention" (*kavanah*), a thought that directs the deed toward its divine destiny. Together the mental and the physical aspects of the commandments sanctify and spiritualize the performer of the commandments. In the "way of truth" there is no tension between the theoretical and practical aspects of divine worship.

PERFECTION, PURIFICATION, AND SALVATION: KABBALISTIC ANTHROPOLOGY

Human Nature and the Soul

The kabbalistic alternative to Aristotelian philosophy could tempt one to conclude that kabbalah is mythos par excellence. While kabbalah indeed reestablished the sacred narrative of Judaism and the personalist conception of God, it also developed its speculative exposition of rabbinic Judaism by employing many philosophic categories. We see it most clearly in kabbalistic anthropology and its understanding of the career of the human soul, its relationship to the body, and its afterlife.

The Zoharic conception of human perfection shares some assumptions with Maimonides, while articulating a quite different theory of the human soul.[93] The theory is not presented in the discursive style of the philosophers, but through the dramatic homilies on the verses of the Torah. So, what the *Zohar* presents as the inner, esoteric meaning of biblical verses adds up to an elaborate story about the human soul—its origin, its descent into the corporeal world, its interaction with the body, its task during one's lifetime, and finally its career after the death of the corporeal body. This is an elaborate myth in the same way that Maimonides (and Plato, his source) understood myth—that is, as a narrative that presents truths not known by any other means. The myth of the human soul constitutes the Zoharic view of human nature or happiness.

The myth of the soul in the *Zohar* resembles the one in Plato's *Republic* (614c–620d). Although familiarity with the Platonic dialogue is not implausible by the time of the *Zohar*,[94] the composers of the *Zohar* did not have to be familiar with this text directly. Plato's dualism of body and soul, as we noted in Chapter Three, was absorbed into rabbinic Judaism, and elements of the Platonic doctrine were elaborated in the eleventh and twelfth centuries in the works of Neoplatonic Jewish philosophers who derived their inspiration from Muslim philosophic and Sufi sources. Most of the components of the Zoharic doctrine of the soul—that the soul is an incorporeal substance that pre-exists the body and unites with the body temporarily for the duration of one's life; that the soul's entry to the corporeal world is a decline in ontological status; that the body is the prison of the soul from which it seeks to extricate itself through doing good acts and acquiring wisdom; that the soul must control the body, or else it will lose its initial divinity; finally, that the righteous soul returns to the divine source—can be found in other traditions, be they rabbinic midrashim, Platonism, Neoplatonism, Gnosticism, Sufism, Muslim philosophy, Jewish secular poetry, or early Kabbalah. The *Zohar* fused them all with remarkable creativity into a reasonably coherent story—notwithstanding inconsistencies of details—that provided the anthropological basis of its conception of happiness.

In the *Zohar* the term "soul" (*nishmeta*) is used to refer both to the soul in contradistinction to the body and to the highest function of the human soul, the cognitive and spiritual power by which persons can interact with God, as opposed to the lower functions of the soul, which are related more closely to the body. This makes it difficult to sort out the details of the theory, even though its gist is quite clear. In general, it is the highest function of the soul that identifies what is most distinctive about human beings, in total agreement with Maimonides and his followers. However, when the *Zohar* speaks about the human soul as a divine substance, it has in mind specifically the soul of but one group of people—Israel. For the *Zohar* the souls of non-Jews are of a different and lower ontological status. It unabashedly states that the souls of gentiles originate not from the sefirot, but from a lower rung in the hierarchical cosmology (the realm of the angels, which the philosophers called "separate intellects") and unambiguously equates the souls of gentiles with the domain of evil. The *Zohar* thus posits a qualitative difference between Jews and non-Jews that in today's parlance will be considered "racist" or minimally, "ethnocentric." It follows that when the *Zohar* speaks about creation in the image of God and about the attainment of perfection it has in mind Jews only.

With respect to the Jewish people, as we already suggested, the ideal perfection can be attained only by males. They alone can acquire the most holy aspect of the soul, because only they possess the organ by which human beings can truly imitate God, the circumcised penis. As the philosophers regarded females as incomplete males and hence excluded them from the pursuit of philosophic wisdom, so the *Zohar* excluded them from the pursuit of perfection because of their defective nature. However, whereas the Aristotelian philosophers focused on the defective reasoning faculty of women, the *Zohar* locates the female inferiority in the sexual organ. Lacking a circumcised penis, the vehicle that enables the male kabbalists to penetrate the mysteries of the Torah and benefit from its abundant energy, the Jewish female has to remain external to the process of Torah study. At best, women can serve only as facilitators of Torah study by male kabbalists and as necessary partners in procreation. At worst, women can lure the kabbalist away from Torah study, and can hinder the procreation of children by refusing to engage in sex or by not following the sexual prescriptions of Jewish law. On her own, the Jewish female cannot strive for, let alone achieve, the ideal perfection. The exclusion of earthly women, however, does not prevent the *Zohar* from depicting encounters with the souls of deceased women in paradise (mostly biblical characters),[95] or from delving into the mysteries of the feminine aspect of God. The elevated status of the heavenly female, the Shekhinah, so it seems to me, came at the expense of the actual social status of the earthly females to whom male kabbalists were married.[96] In short, human nature in the *Zohar* pertains exclusively to Jewish males.

The Nature of the Soul

Maimonides, we recall, followed Aristotle in viewing the soul as the form *of* the human body. The soul is the organizational principle of the body that gives it life and sustains all its functions. A human being is thus an indissoluble unity of body and soul; in the corporeal world a body cannot live without a soul; a soul cannot exist apart from a body. The *Zohar*, on the other hand, which follows Platonic psychology, considers the human soul to be an incorporeal, eternal substance that pre-exists the body. In principle it can and does exist independent of the body prior to its descent to the corporeal world, and, if a person manages his affairs correctly throughout life, it will be able to be liberated from the body at death.

The incorporeality and pre-existence of the soul are in kabbalah the marks of the soul's divinity, or intrinsic holiness. The human soul literally comes from God, originating in the sefirotic realm itself. Since God is life and the source of all living things, it should not be surprising that the *Zohar* depicts the coming to be of the soul in terms of impregnation, conception, and birth.[97] In the sefirotic realm these "biological" processes are noncorporeal and atemporal; they are part of the mystery of unity within multiplicity characteristic of the interaction between the various aspects of the Godhead. While the *Zohar* describes the birth of the soul in various ways, the most common one is the result of intercourse between the divine "father" (*Tiferet*) and the Shekhinah, the divine "lower mother." The souls of Israel are thus literally the "children" of God, who stands with them in a very special relationship, precisely as rabbinic midrash states when it names Israel as "children of God" (*banim la-maqom*).

The various stages of coming into being—impregnation, conception, and birthing—are also understood as a process of individuation. In the beginning of the process, the human soul is an undifferentiated unity (identified with *ḥokhmah*). As the process continues (which is expressed by descending in the emanation of the sefirot), the soul receives its individual characteristics.

As a product of a divine intercourse, it is not surprising that the human soul is constelled in the sefirotic paradigm. The paradigm of the divine anthropos itself, however, attests the familiarity of the *Zohar* with the psychological doctrines of the philosophers. Like them the *Zohar* distinguishes between distinctive functions of the soul—the nutritive, the appetitive, and the rational—but refers to them in the Hebrew terms *nefesh*, *ruaḥ*, and *neshamah* respectively. The *nefesh* is responsible for all the physiological activities that sustain the human body; the *ruaḥ* is the faculty of the desirous and emotional functions of the soul that link the mental and the physiological aspects of a human being; and the *neshamah* is that aspect of the human that facilitates clinging to God. These various functions are associated with particular sefirot. Not entirely consistent, the dominant view in the *Zohar* is that the *neshamah* is linked to *Binah* (or sometimes *Ḥokhmah*), *ruaḥ* is associated with *Tiferet*, and the *nefesh* originates from *Malkhut*.

As much as the functions of the human soul are linked to specific sefirot, so does the structure of the divine anthropos reflect the intellectual, emotional, and physiological aspects of human beings. The first three sefirot—*Keter*, *Ḥokhmah* and *Binah*, are the head, signifying mental functions. *Ḥesed* and *Gevurah* constitute the upper arms of the divine anthropos and are associated with the opposing emotional dispositions that are balanced by the middle one—*Tiferet*—which is the torso of the male deity. *Nezeḥ* and *Hod* are the legs of the primordial man, symbolizing moral qualities that are closely related to the physiological functions of the body. Between them is

Yesod, the end of the male torso and the male sex organ, through which the creative and procreative energy of God is transmitted to the *Malkhut*, the female receptacle. To attain its perfection, the human soul will have to descend into the corporeal world and be united with a particular human body. Without a body the soul remains imperfect.

The Descent of the Soul

The fully individuated human soul pre-exists in a special domain prior to its descent into the corporeal world. The *Zohar* usually locates the souls in the Upper Garden of Eden, which is located within the region of the *Malkhut*. During its life in the supernal world, souls enjoy a delightful time because they are not encumbered by corporeality and are protected from the pollution of the forces of evil. In its paradisiac pre-existence, the soul enjoys a playful pleasure (*sha`ashu`a*) with her divine "father," a pleasure that has clear erotic overtones.[98] Having such a blissful time, it is not surprising that it refuses to descend into the corporeal world to assume its appointed tasks of conditioning and governing the body. One of the most elaborate narratives in the *Zohar* depicts the separation anxieties of the soul and her pleading with her divine father to allow her to stay longer. Alas, she (like any good, obedient daughter in a patriarchal society) has to do her father's bidding, and, despite her reluctance, descends into a human body, as a daughter would enter the household of the man to whom she is given in marriage by her father. Not all souls, however, successfully weather the descent into the corporeal world. The very balance of power between the forces of good and evil in the world at the time of the soul's entrance into the body determine her career on earth. The *Zohar* (II: 95b) fictionalizes this cosmic condition in the metaphor of the scale (*tiqla*) that weighs the relative balance between the merits and sins of humans. If sins are more numerous than merits in the world, the souls are snatched by the Sitra Aḥra and enter into the world in a defective form, albeit without losing their initial holiness. In this manner the *Zohar* creatively attempts to solve some of the problems of traditional Jewish theodicy (for example: Why do innocent children die?) and account for the dispositional differences among human beings.

Another version of this idea is that the souls who go through the cosmic scale when evil governs the world are more prone to suffering. This is the explanation that the *Zohar* (II 96a-b) presents for the suffering of Job. However, in some homilies the *Zohar* addresses the problem of evil by stating that some souls on their own accord attach themselves to the Sitra Aḥra prior to entering the world—which is presented as an explanation of the existence of stubbornly vicious people.[99]

The journey of the soul into the body is understood as a decline in ontological status. The holy soul experiences the descent into the corporeal world as a punishment, an imprisonment, from which it will have to extricate itself by following its own wisdom and gaining control over the passions and appetites of the corporeal body. Despite the fundamental ontological difference between the soul and the body, the divine decree to send the soul to earth seems an exercise in cruelty. The *Zohar* employs the rabbinic explanation that the presence of the soul in the body enables the soul to perfect itself by accumulating merits through doing what is right and good. Human life, then, is not a futile struggle between the incorporeal soul and the corporeal body, but an opportunity for the soul to do good—that is, to purify the body through the performance of commandments and acts of lovingkindness. Whether one chooses to do the good—and hence accomplish the task assigned to the soul and merit a return to her source—remains in the hands of each person.

Soul-Body Relations

The soul and the body are closely interdependent. If the soul governs the body, then the individual is directed properly toward the knowledge of God and the performance of the commandments. However, if the body has the upper hand over the holy soul, the person is doomed to fall prey to the forces of the Sitra Aḥra. The human body is a corporeal entity, made out of the elements of earth, air, water, and fire.[100] Without a soul the human body not only lacks life; it also lacks the ability to fend off the forces of evil.

Many homilies in the *Zohar* pertain to the relationship between the body and the soul. Tishby has isolated three distinct strands in those relations:. One view considers the corporeal body to be inherently evil, and thus associates it with the demonic powers of the Sitra Aḥra. A second view considers the body an imperfect vessel that requires purification and spiritualization. The third view regards the body as a holy vessel that enables the human being to become like God.[101] Tishby shows how these notions of the human body result in three different ethical programs. The first leads to asceticism; the second articulates an ethical theory whose goal is the spiritualization of the body; and the third regards all natural functions as holy activities that connect man to God.

The Zoharic perspective may be more coherent than Tishby assumed if the three views are seen as stages of one program for spiritual development whose ultimate end is integration of the human into the rhythm of the divine. In the early stages, the corporeal body functions as an obstacle to proper divine worship. At this point it is indeed in the possession of the forces of evil, leading to sinful behavior. However, as the individual progresses spiritually, by virtue of following the regimen of the commandments, he learns how to spiritualize the corporeal and to make the body itself into a vehicle for attaining religious perfection. Some Jewish males who are successful in their program of spiritualization reach the state in which the body itself is a holy vessel that can cleave directly to the holy body (*gufa qadisha*) of the divine anthropos.

If the various attitudes toward the body are viewed as progressive stages in the program toward ideal human perfection, the Zoharic program can be seen to parallel the gradual attainment of epistemic perfection discussed by the philosophers. In both programs the corporeal body requires conditioning and control by the soul if one is to reach perfection, and in both there is some tension between the soul and the body. The difference between the two approaches is that according to the philosophers the body itself cannot be made incorporeal; the conditioning of the body means suppression or stilling of physiological functions to the minimum, without causing death. In the kabbalistic program the corporeal body of Israel can become spiritualized: it is literally made holy by the performance of the holy commandments.

The Zoharic conception of the mitzvot is thus the key to its program of sanctification, a process in which the corporeal can be made to be more refined—that is, less corporeal. Such a notion makes sense only in a schema that recognizes degrees of being and in which "corporeality" and "spirituality" are relative terms. These ideas make no sense in a strict Aristotelian ontology, but the Aristotelianism of the Jewish philosophers in the Middle Ages was anything but strict; it was suffused with many Neoplatonic themes.

ETERNAL SALVATION

Problems with Maimonides' Conception of Life after Death

If the *via perfectionis* is so demanding—physically, morally, intellectually and spiritually—why should one desire to walk it? In the premodern period the answer was quite clear: perfection in this life was the prerequisite for surviving death and attaining the bliss of immortal life. At stake in the debates about human perfection, among Jews or between Jews and non-Jews, was the eternal salvation of the individual. To a modern reader this may seem quaint, but in the premodern period the promise of a blissful life in heaven and the fear of the punishment in Gehenna were the main incentives for adhering to the life of Torah. Life in this world was thus a preparation for everlasting life in the next, a life devoid of corporeality, evil, and imperfection.

The Maimonidean Controversy of the thirteenth century was in part an attempt to address this concept. Maimonides predicated survival after death on the attainment of intellectual perfection, equating it with the "world to come," which he explained was a state of the individually perfected intellect rather than a phase in the linear history of the Jewish people. He also distinguished the "world to come" from the messianic age. How this relates to the collective Jewish destiny was understood by Maimonides in strict naturalistic terms. The messianic age, as we saw in Chapter Five, has no apocalyptic or supernatural qualities and is characterized by the effortless attainment of intellectual perfection in the best social reality possible for mankind.

Maimonides' conception appears to conflict with the traditional Jewish doctrine of retribution. For one thing he predicated entry into the "world to come" on cognition of intelligibles rather than on deeds, which were at best a means to the attainment of intellectual contemplation. Second, intellectual perfection is, by definition, non-personal. Whatever survives the death of one person is identical to what survives the death of another. The traditional belief that individuals are rewarded and punished for what they themselves do is thus annulled. Third, the Maimonidean conception of the afterlife in the "world to come" cannot be given any specific content. Description is, in this case, the product of the imagination, a physiologically bound faculty that is transcended when one reaches intellectual perfection. In principle, then, there can be no meaningful description of the state of intellectual perfection; it can only be stated or postulated. Finally, if human life is to be devoted primarily to self-perfection in order to attain the immortality of the rational soul, why is there a need to believe in the resurrection of the dead? That primary belief of rabbinic Judaism appears to be superfluous in the Maimonidean system. For these reasons, among others, the Maimonidean position aroused significant opposition, even though it did affirm life after death. Therefore, the kabbalists of the thirteenth century, most notably Nahmanides, found it necessary to articulate an alternative to Maimonides' view in order to preserve and protect what they considered to be the authentic Jewish tradition.

The Zohar as a Traditionalist Response to Maimonides

The *Zohar* differs from Maimonides in some important respects. First, in the Zoharic view, the very fact of the afterlife is not a theoretical problem. The *Zohar* (not entirely consistently) speaks about the soul as an individuated entity even before her association with the particular body. Hence, when the body dies, the individual soul survives the event: its very existence as a separate substance does not depend on the body itself. What matters in the *Zohar* is not that the soul survives, but what kind of life the soul will experience after the death of the body.

Second, the final assessment of the quality of one's life includes not only intellectual perfection but the entire gamut of human actions throughout life. The afterlife is not only dependent upon what one has learned during a lifetime, but upon what one has done throughout one's lifetime. The career of the soul after the death of the body depends on the balance between the merits and sins that one has accrued throughout life. The actual deeds, and not only the thoughts or intentions, determine what will happen after death, because human perfection in the *Zohar* pertains to holiness, and not just to the content of one's thought. If one lived a holy life, the soul returns to her divine source, but if one lived a sinful life, the soul is destined to go to hell. Moreover, a soul that did not perfect itself during a lifetime will have to come back to corporeality once more and accomplish the appointed task, namely, regain its perfection.[102]

Third, precisely because the *Zohar* regarded the imagination as a valid source of supra-rational knowledge, it could provide the reader/listener/spectator with a rich description of what happens to the soul immediately before the moment of death, the few days thereafter, and even the first year after death, during which its status is settled. The ecstatic, visionary narratives of the *Zohar* provide detailed descriptions of the various palaces in the heavenly domain and the blissful pleasure of the souls of the righteous as they resume their intimate, incestuous relationship with their "father" in heaven. Conversely, information about the Sitra Aḥra provided awareness of the suffering in Gehenna—and addressed readers' deepest human fears and anxieties about death in a manner that was much more existentially meaningful than the dim description of the world to come provided by the rationalist philosophers. The rich description of the first year after death was based on motifs in rabbinic literature, combined with medieval folk beliefs. The Zoharic treatment of death gave rise to rituals surrounding death, some of which are practiced to this day.[103]

Fourth, the *Zohar* differs from Maimonides with regard to the ultimate goal of the *via perfectionis*—not only the purification of the individual soul and its return to the divine source, but the perfection of God, namely, the restoration of the initial harmony in the sefirotic realm, which had been destroyed by the primordial sin of Adam and Eve. The *theurgic* end of kabbalah would dictate its position on the *eschatological* end.

Events in the apocalyptic *eschaton* described within the body of the *Zohar* do not inspire much interest: the *Zohar* focuses more on the attainment of perfection in the present through the performance of Jewish rituals that bring about the perfection of the Godhead. The messianic end, then, is a by-product of the successful restoration of the Godhead to its harmonious condition prior to the primordial sin.[104] The later parts of the *Zohar*—the *idrot* (assemblies)—focus on the activities of R. Shimeon bar Yohai, who is able to accomplish precisely that feat, thereby sustaining the present generation and heralding the final messianic age. Yet, the messianic age itself is not described in significant detail. It is the spiritual activity of a few perfect men who can bring about the perfection of the deity and, as a result, the perfection of the present. Whether one should draw from it optimistic conclusions about the *via perfectionis* for Jews, or rather read the *Zohar* as an admission that perfection is no more a possibility for kabbalah than it was for Maimonides, remains an open question for the reader.

Summary

The Zoharic perspective illustrates the complexity of the logos/mythos dynamics within the discourse on happiness. The *Zohar* elaborated the meaning of the rabbinic myth about the love relationship between God and Israel, and it did so in a complex narrative, hermeneutical narrative rather than in philosophical propositions. As much as the *Zohar* presented itself as an alternative to Maimonidean philosophy, the conceptual framework of kabbalah was itself rooted in the ontology, cosmology, and psychology of medieval Jewish Aristotelianism, itself suffused with many Neoplatonic themes. Kabbalah highlighted the Neoplatonic dimensions while presenting a highly particularistic, ethnocentric conception of happiness that placed the values of holiness and purity at the center of kabbalistic performance of the mitzvot.

The Zoharic conception of happiness consists of the following claims: True human well-being is reserved for Jews only. They alone are the recipients of the one and only divine revelation. They alone have access to the hidden mysteries of the Torah, and therefore to the mysteries of God and the created universe. They alone are truly created in the image of God, possessing a holy soul that can return to its origin and reunite with its divine maker. They alone can live a holy life that protects the initial holiness of the soul and perfects it by observing the laws of the Torah. Finally, they alone can attain the bliss of immortality and enjoy eternal life in heaven in the company of God. This powerful and highly ethnocentric message is indeed an ethical theory, but it is presented through dramatic narratives and homilies, rather than through general, abstract arguments.

Despite all the differences between theosophic kabbalah and the Maimonidean position it sought to replace, kabbalah too should be viewed as a variant of a scholarly ethos. The struggle for perfection took place in an interior life that required enormous self-control. Furthermore, it was directed only to the few who were worthy of it, and it privileged the esoteric over the exoteric. For the kabbalists, human well-being was predicated on knowledge and virtue no less than for the rationalist philosophers, and the kabbalists made the connection between the two metaphysically important by claiming that only the righteous man can bring about the perfection of God.

The teachings of kabbalah were known to only a few thinkers, at least until after the expulsion from Spain. However, even before the expulsion, it began to influence the way a larger group of Jewish thinkers in Spain viewed the world. Kabbalah eventually fused into Jewish Aristotelian philosophy during the fifteenth and sixteenth centuries, changing the discourse on happiness. But in the fourteenth century, the claim that the ultimate end of life was to be found in the bliss of immortality—a view accepted by both philosophers and kabbalists—became the focal point of the Jewish-Christian confrontation.

8

Intellectual Perfection and Jewish-Christian Rivalry

As we have seen, the ultimate end of human life and the way to attain it were the core issues of the Maimonidean Controversies of the thirteenth century. They were also the issues that fueled the emergence of kabbalah as a conceptual alternative to rationalist philosophy. Yet despite the passionate debates engendered, Jewish rationalist philosophers and the kabbalists agreed that ultimate happiness pertained primarily to the well-being of the individual soul, that the final end of human life could be attained only in the afterlife, and that the world to come was a state of being of the immortal soul rather than a post-historical phase. In other words, all—philosophers and kabbalists alike—were preoccupied with personal salvation.

This notion might surprise those who believe that personal salvation characterizes Christianity rather than Judaism. In the Middle Ages, however, Jews ferociously debated what it took to enter the world to come and what this state consisted of. Did performance of the mitzvot alone bring immortality of the soul, or did one need to possess certain knowledge in order to attain it? If knowledge was a precondition for personal salvation, what did such knowledge consist of and was it available to all Jews or just to the wise among them? These were hotly contested issues, but all Jews took for granted that they were better disposed to experience personal immortality because their lives were organized by the Torah.

This calculation, however, was the bone of contention between Judaism and Christianity, a rival monotheistic religion that disputed with Judaism the correct meaning of the Bible and regarded its own Scriptures, beliefs, and practices as the exclusive path to personal salvation. The intra-religious debates about the kind of knowledge necessary for the attainment of happiness were thus inseparable from the inter-religious confrontation between Judaism and Christianity.

By looking at the discourse on happiness during the fourteenth century, this chapter will shed light on the connection between internal Jewish debates and those involving Christians. To do so, I will juxtapose the works of two luminaries of fourteenth-century Jewish philosophy: Levi ben Gershom

(Gersonides) (1288–1344), and Hasdai Crescas (1340–1410/11). We will also consider the exchange between a Jewish rationalist, Isaac Polleqar (first half of the fourteenth century), and a Jewish intellectual who converted to Christianity, Abner of Burgos (alias Alfonso de Valladolid) (c. 1270–1340). Whereas Gersonides, the ultimate Jewish Aristotelian, was boldly optimistic about philosophy and science and regarded them as an antidote to Christianity, Crescas was convinced that the philosophic conception of happiness was responsible for the mass apostasy of Iberian Jews to Christianity in 1391.

Gersonides' boldness reflected his own intellectual brilliance and scientific expertise. His mastery of philosophy, astronomy, and astrology also reflected the total absorption of the Aristotelian corpus by Jewish thinkers due to the translations of the commentaries on Aristotle by ibn Rushd (Averroes in Latin). Crescas, however, would argue that this philosophic self-confidence was misplaced: the philosophy of Aristotle was anything but certain. In fact, because many of its physical theories were mistaken, logically contradictory, or unproven, Crescas was able to subject Aristotle's philosophy and the views of his Jewish followers, Maimonides and Gersonides, to a scathing critique. In place of knowledge of God, Crescas located happiness in the love of God. Happiness, he held, pertains to the holiness of the soul and to the joy one derives in the actual performance of the commandments. Moreover, some of Crescas' views about the meaning of faith and its relationship to knowledge were derived from Christian scholastic sources that became known to him through the works of the convert Abner of Burgos, who compelled Jewish intellectuals to reconsider their views about the meaning of faith and its relationship to rational choice and to natural determinism.

THE RIVALRY BETWEEN JUDAISM AND CHRISTIANITY

In medieval Europe, the Jews constituted a permanent "alienated minority," to use the apt title of Kenneth Stow's recent work.[1] The Christian civilization that emerged from the ruins of the Roman Empire had allowed Jews to live by their own laws, although the rivalry of the fourth century produced intense verbal hostility toward them, especially in areas where Judaism was quite attractive to the pagan population.[2] Theologically Jews were regarded as the "witness people," a term coined by St. Augustine.[3] Because ancient Israel was the recipient of God's initial revelation, the first "witness people" of God, Jews must not be killed or molested. At the same time, however, because they refused to acknowledge the messiahship of Jesus Christ and his salvific ministry—and worse, because they committed the most horrible crime of deicide—the Jews lost their status as the chosen people and had to be kept inferior and subordinate to the True Israel—i.e., the Church. Theologically, their social inferiority and subordination should attest to the election of Christianity. The official papal policy that translated this theology into practice asserted that the Jews must not be forced to convert to Christianity, but instead should be brought to the salvific truth through persuasion and peaceful means that make clear the spiritual superiority of Christianity.

From the fifth to the eighth centuries, the number of Jews in northwest Europe (i.e. France and Germany) was exceedingly small, and most communities who were there in the late Roman empire did not survive the breakdown of Roman civilization and the rise of feudalism. It was not until the ninth century that Jewish presence could be documented with some certainty. Carolingian monarchs invited individual Jews to settle in Germany, and their presence was legally guaranteed by charters that defined their privileges and their obligations.[4] The charters ensured the safety of the Jews, granted them permission to live in accordance with their religious laws, and regulated their economic activities. Those activities were the primary reason European rulers invited Jews to settle in their territory. With the re-emergence of towns in the ninth and tenth centuries, Jewish commercial activity was an asset to the burgeoning new economy that emerged alongside the manorial system.

Given first to individuals and their families and then to Jews of entire regions, the charters established the dependence of the Jews on the ruling power (imperial, monarchic, or papal).[5] However, from the very start the fact that Jewish presence was linked to economic utility meant that their status was rather precarious; when Jews were no longer deemed an asset to a given ruler, he revoked their privileges.

The situation of benign toleration of Jews in the Christian West began to deteriorate in the late eleventh century. A series of monastic and papal reforms invigorated the religious life of Western Europe, improved the quality of the secular priesthood, strengthened the power of the papal monarchy, and raised the level of general education of the populace. Christian ideals and ethical mores were now applicable not only to monks and nuns in cloistered monasteries but to all classes and social ranks. The increase in European population (due to a combination of climatic changes and technological advances in food production) and the re-emergence of towns turned the Christian West into a more self-confident and militant society by the end of the eleventh century. Under the leadership of the papal monarchy, Europe launched the crusading movement with the express intent of liberating the Holy Land from the control of infidels. While the Crusades ultimately failed to accomplish their intended goal, they profoundly transformed the Christian West.

For Jews the First Crusade spelled a major turning point for the worse.[6] Viewed as the infidel within, the Jews in several towns on the Rhine Valley were physically attacked and forced to convert to Christianity. Many Jews were killed and many chose suicide, though it is difficult to establish precise numbers. While the First Crusade did not put a halt to Jewish life, and might have even stimulated Jewish intellectual life, the traumatic events of Jewish martyrdom became seared into Jewish memory. The religious frenzy of the crusader movement widened the gap between Jews and Christians. As Christians increasingly viewed the Jews with suspicion and hostility, the Jews linked commitment to Judaism with willingness to sacrifice one's life for the sanctification of God's name. Despite this devotion to their faith, conversion of Jews to the dominant religion did occur throughout the Middle Ages.

During the twelfth century, Jewish presence in the Christian, Latin West became more precarious, even though physical attacks on Jews were more sporadic. Although church authorities reiterated the rights of the Jews to be physically protected[7] and secular rulers protected those Jews under their jurisdiction because they served as a source of valuable income, money lending, the economic activity so hateful to Christians, became more and more a Jewish occupation. Even though it provided the necessary fuel for the economy of burgeoning urban centers.[8] Jewish money lending itself further accentuated the negative perception of the Jews in Christian society. From 1144 on, Jews had to sustain not only sporadic attacks on their lives and property, but also blood libels that accused them of killing Christians and using their blood for religious rituals.[9] Gradually but consistently the dehumanization and demonization of the Jews took hold in the popular imagination, which led to the perception of them as the manifestation of the anti-Christ, the eternal enemy of Christianity. The perceived need to protect the Christian majority from them led Pope Innocent III, in the Fourth Lateran Council of 1215, to impose the wearing of a yellow circle on the outer garment to distinguish Jews from their neighbors. After 1236 the Jews were legally regarded as "the serfs of the chamber," a political servitude, or collective slavery, that manifested their inferior theological status.[10]

Ironically, popular animosity toward Jews went hand in hand with the spread of education among the urban population. The mendicant orders, as noted in the previous chapter, were heavily involved in the struggle against heresy within Christian society, and their growing intellectual sophistication was used to heighten the rivalry between the two monotheistic religions. As the scholastic movement spread throughout Europe and transformed the structure of universities, Jews had to face staged public debates in which Scripture and rabbinic Judaism were put on trial and (as expected) found guilty. The debates were conducted by members of mendicant orders—especially the Dominicans, who had staffed the tribunals of the Papal Inquisition since 1236. However, the debates were always instigated by recent Jewish converts to Christianity. Apparently feeling a psychological need to legitimize their newly chosen identity and to prove themselves as worthy Christians, these zealous converts posed a serious threat to Jews for the duration of the Middle Ages and well into the modern period.

In 1240, as noted in Chapter Six, Nicholas Donin's accusations that the Oral Torah contained blasphemies against Christianity put the Talmud on trial in Paris. When found guilty as charged, copies of it were confiscated throughout France and publicly burned.[11] In 1263 in Barcelona the accusations of Pablo Christiani that the Talmud in fact teaches ideas that confirm the truth of Christianity led to a serious corrosion of Jewish religious autonomy in Spain and to the forced departure of Nahmanides.[12] In both cases scholastic education, which actually benefited from collaboration between Jewish and Christian scholars, was put to use in the anti-Jewish persecutions.

Throughout the eleventh and twelfth centuries Jews and Christians engaged in debates about their religious differences, each using the Bible to prove its own claims.[13] In the twelfth century, Jewish disputants generally felt secure in their ability to prove the intellectual and spiritual superiority of Judaism and to puncture the arguments of their opponents through better mastery and understanding of the biblical text itself.[14] However, by the thirteenth century such a posture became less tenable: the Jewish apostates who pleaded the case of Christianity to their former coreligionists were themselves steeped in the Jewish tradition. Armed with the scholastic method of argumentation, Christianity could no longer be dismissed as intellectually inferior. In fact, the thriving talmudic scholarship of the twelfth century was used as an argument against the Jews: Jews, it was said, were now committed to the Talmud rather than to the Bible.[15] Judaism of the thirteenth century was no longer continuous with its biblical ancestry. Jews themselves, so the argument went, had jeopardized their place within Christendom, and the majority no longer had an obligation to protect them.

The secular rulers of Europe would carry out the implications of this theological view by expelling Jews from their domain, even though the immediate reasons for such decisions had to do with politics and economics more than with theology.[16] The first general expulsion took place in 1290, when the Jews were ordered to leave England. Throughout the fourteenth century, a series of local, regional, and general expulsions ensued in France and Germany as Jews became pawns in political struggles between emperors and popes, monarchs and landed aristocracy, and between rival principalities. If this were not enough, Jews also had to contend with additional hostility occasioned by the Black Death of 1348–50, when Jews were accused of poisoning the water supplies of Europe and hence responsible for the bubonic plague that decimated a third of Europe's population.

Given these realities and the constant decline of Jewish status in the Latin West, continued allegiance to Judaism required a firm conviction of its spiritual superiority—a conviction that could be supported only if one believed that Judaism was the exclusive path to the eternal afterlife. Without such conviction, loyalty to Judaism was very difficult indeed. The Jewish philosopher who remained convinced that Judaism is true had to get involved in the inter-religious debate and use his intellectual skills and rhetorical talent in the service of the polemical defense of Judaism.[17] *It is no coincidence that during the fourteenth century the focus of the philosophical discourse on happiness was the afterlife of the individual soul.*

The fourteenth century ended with an unprecedented event that indicated a new balance of power between the two rival religions: forced mass conversion to Christianity wrought havoc on the Jewish communities in Spain, although it did not exterminate Jewish life.[18] The disturbances began on June 4, 1391 when mobs attacked the Jewish quarter of Seville. From there the riots spread to other communities in Andalusia, then to other parts of Castile, Aragon-Catalonia, and Navarre. As synagogues were converted into churches, Jews were faced with the impossible choice: conversion or death. Entire congregations that had practiced and promoted Jewish life for centuries were decimated, and Jewish social institutions were in ruins. The precise scope of the destruction is difficult to estimate, but the impact of these events was shocking: the first collective conversion of Jews to Christianity.

The emerging class of New Christians, *conversos* (or, as they were known derogatorily, *marranos*) would pose numerous legal, theological, and administrative problems for the beleaguered communities of openly professing Jews. Since many converted under duress (*anusim*), the question was whether they were still considered to be legally Jewish in accordance with

Jewish law. Was there a halakhic difference between those who converted under duress and those who did so voluntarily? What was the legal status of the children of forced converts, and what happened if they wished to marry a professing Jew? How many generations had to pass before a convert was no longer considered a Jew? These were some of the problems that engaged Jewish halakhists during the fifteenth century, as evidenced by the rich responsa literature of the time.[19]

After the traumatic events of 1391, Jewish intellectuals were compelled to ponder their conduct and cultural orientation. According to the premises of traditional Jewish theodicy, these events could not have been a manifestation of God's providential care for his people Israel. It had to be interpreted as a punishment for Jewish transgressions and religious disobedience. However, who was to blame? Since the study of philosophy and its related sciences characterized Judeo-Hispanic culture, any self-examination led to a debate on the status of the so-called foreign wisdoms (*hokhmot hitzoniyot*). Once again Maimonideanism and the *paideia* of the rationalist philosophers were put on the defensive as the cause of the Jews' failure to uphold their faith. The most substantive critique of Maimonidean philosophy and its philosophic conception of happiness came from Hasdai Crescas, the rabbi of Saragossa, himself a brilliant philosopher. Crescas' critique will make sense to us if we understand the philosophic boldness of Gersonides, the most rigorous Jewish Aristotelian in the Middle Ages.

GERSONIDES: HAPPINESS AS SCIENTIFIC KNOWLEDGE

Gersonides' Literary Activity[20]

Very little is known about Gersonides' life except that he lived in Provence, made a living from money lending, and perhaps practiced medicine. It was his mastery of the sciences of astronomy and astrology that brought him to the attention of the papal court in Avignon, where he was employed for a while, and several of his treatises were translated into Latin.[21] It is possible that because of his contacts with church officials Gersonides pleaded on behalf of his coreligionists, but there is no indication that he was involved in public disputations with Christian scholars. Gersonides wrote his philosophical texts in Hebrew, and there is no clear evidence that he mastered Latin; communication with Christian scholars at the court was thus conducted in the vernacular. The style of Gersonides' philosophical writings, the problems that concerned him, and some of his views have strong parallels in the scholastic philosophy of his day.[22] It thus makes sense to situate

Gersonides in his Christian cultural setting, even though his literary context was still framed by the Judeo-Arabic philosophic tradition.

Gersonides was instrumental in the absorption into Judaism of Aristotelian philosophy, which was now studied through the commentaries of ibn Rushd. The commentaries provided Jewish philosophers access not only to Aristotle's text, but also to its Hellenistic commentators (especially Alexander of Aphrodisias and Themistius) and to other Muslim philosophers (especially al-Farabi, ibn Sina, and al-Ghazali, whose views ibn Rushd considers and often rejects). By writing a super-commentary on Ibn Rushd's commentaries and weighing the pros and cons of each philosophical position,[23] a Jewish philosopher could become a "professional" philosopher, mastering the intricacies of a given philosophic-scientific discipline, even though he had no institutional setting in which to practice philosophy.

Mastering Aristotle through ibn Rushd was no easy matter. First of all, Ibn Rushd changed his views over time,[24] and the Jewish philosopher who ascribed to him a certain view was either not aware of the changes or presupposed that he could harmonize them. Second, what Jewish thinkers attributed to Aristotle or Ibn Rushd depended on the specific texts they had access to. The position a given Jewish scholar ascribed to his earlier sources could be incomplete or even mistaken. Third, manuscripts were reproduced by fallible copyists who inadvertently introduced mistakes in the transmission of the received text, no matter how accurate they wished to be. Despite these serious limitations, the discourse on happiness during the fourteenth century became more technically philosophical, as Jewish philosophers focused on the details of the cognitive process by which man can attain perfection of the intellect.

Gersonides mastered the various disciplines of Aristotelian philosophy and science by composing super-commentaries on Ibn Rushd's commentaries.[25] By summarizing the views of Ibn Rushd and his sources and subjecting them to careful, minute analysis, Gersonides painstakingly articulated his own position, endorsing, modifying, or rejecting the views of his predecessors. His knowledge of Jewish philosophy was derived primarily from Maimonides' *Guide*, but Gersonides significantly departed from the great master on many issues. The dialectical procedure of examining arguments was very similar to the scholastic method of reasoning, even though it lacked the formal structure of the scholastic *questiones* or the *quodlibetales*. Gersonides' rather cumbersome style of writing (which may appear tedious to the modern reader) reflected his relentless commitment to the pursuit of truth by which one attains the bliss of eternal life.

For Gersonides, as for all medieval Jewish philosophers, mastery of Aristotelian science and philosophy was not simply an academic activity, but a religious endeavor of the highest order. Because God is truth, knowledge of truth approximates God and fulfills the commandment to imitate God.[26] Gersonides' crowning achievement was the composition of a work of comprehensive philosophical theology—*Milḥamot Ha-Shem* (*The Wars of the Lord*)—written between 1317 and 1325. In this tightly argued text Gersonides articulates his views on the stock issues of medieval philosophy: the origin of the universe, the existence and attributes of God, divine knowledge and human freedom, the immortality of the soul, the relationship between prophecy and philosophy, the nature of miracles, and the meaning of the Torah's commandments.

The *Wars* is a technical text written for trained philosophers who were familiar with Gersonides' super-commentaries on Ibn Rushd. Like all philosophers in his day and beforehand, Gersonides privileged the wise man over others and believed that only the one who devotes his life to the pursuit of truth is engaged in the activity that makes humans both distinct from other animals and most like God. A person who rejects the pursuit of truth both alienates himself from God and forfeits the ability to experience the ultimate joy available to humans, the eternal life of the intellect. However, contrary to Maimonides, who held that philosophy should be hidden from the masses, lest they commit religious and philosophical errors, Gersonides believed philosophy and science should be taught openly, systematically, and as clearly as possible because making the truth accessible to all enables some to approximate the ultimate felicity. Thus in order to disseminate the truths of philosophy to a broad Jewish audience, he composed philosophical commentaries on Scriptures.[27]

In principle, Gersonides believed, there can be no conflict between what is true in Scripture and what is true in philosophy, since truth is one and undivided. Although truth can be taught through various rhetorical procedures to fit the intellectual level of the student, it is not the case that a proposition can be declared to be true in one domain and untrue in another.[28] His version of the so-called Double Truth theory—which was erroneously ascribed to Ibn Rushd by the opponents of scholastic masters known as the "Latin Averroists"—was never endorsed either by Gersonides or by Ibn Rushd. The task of the philosopher, then, is to make the truths of Scripture manifest and accessible to all Jews by explicating the philosophical meaning of the biblical text.

According to Gersonides, the Bible is a philosophic-scientific text that teaches the truth about the universe in a manner accessible on some level even to those not trained in philosophy. The biblical story of creation, for example, explains the coming-to-be of the universe in total agreement with Aristotelian cosmology and physics.[29] In this way his philosophical exegesis of Scripture rejected philosophical esotericism, enabling his Jewish readers to understand these truths and thereby to have a greater chance of perfecting their intellects.[30]

His philosophy is the best example of the "intellectualist," or "exclusivist" reading of Aristotle's view of *eudaimonia* discussed in Chapter One. Accordingly, human well-being is predicated on the possession of true knowledge, and it is only the perfected intellect that can survive the death of the body. Gersonides insisted that only a certain kind of human knowledge—the knowledge of God—constitutes the perfection of the intellect and hence its immortality. However, is such knowledge possible for embodied human beings? Gersonides gave a qualified "yes," thereby departing from the agnosticism of Maimonides, with whom he differed on this crucial point: Gersonides had a different view of the relationship between God and the created universe.

God and the Created Universe

Maimonides, we recall, insisted that knowledge of God's essence is inaccessible to human beings: an unbridgeable ontological gap separates God from everything else in the universe. Of God's essence we can only have negative knowledge; we can know what God is not, but never what God is. The only positive knowledge human beings can have of God is knowledge of his actions in the universe, a knowledge that can be gleaned through empirical observation of the world of corporeal nature. Physics is the science that provides demonstrative knowledge about God's management of the world and exemplifies His attributes of mercy, justice, and lovingkindness. However, according to Maimonides, the science of physics can yield valid knowledge only about the sublunar world that is composed of four elements in their numerous combinations. About the supra-lunar world of the celestial bodies and the separate intelligences that move them, humans cannot have demonstrative knowledge. And if that is so, even more so they cannot know God.

To understand how Gersonides differed from Maimonides, we need a little more information about the connection between cosmology and astronomy. Maimonides' picture of the world was a mixture of Aristotelian, Ptolemaic, and Neoplatonic elements. It was a hierarchical schema in which the corporeal world emanated indirectly from the first cause, or God, through a series of noncorporeal intermediaries, the ten intelligences, or separate intellects. These were considered the efficient causes of the motions of the celestial bodies—the diurnal sphere, the five visible planets, the sun and the moon—though the motion was non-corporeal. The intelligences moved the stars by virtue of the "desire" that the latter, possessing a soul, "felt" toward the former. The intelligences themselves came into being in a process of nontemporal, successive emanation that terminated with the last, the tenth intelligence, which governs the affairs of the sublunar world. This semi-divine intelligence was given the name "Active Intellect" (or for the Latin, the "Agent Intellect" [*intellectus agens*]), the term that Aristotle used to explain how human beings acquire knowledge.

Maimonides accepted the general outline of this hierarchical cosmology, but critiqued certain aspects of it. He understood correctly that because the process of emanation is necessary and eternal, it conflicts with the Jewish belief that the universe was created by God in a voluntary act. The universe did not come into being out of necessity, but out of a divine will that could not be fathomed or predicted through the knowledge of astronomy. For Maimonides, then, even astronomy (let alone the science of physics, which pertains to the sub-lunar world) was an inadequate way to perfect the human intellect so as to come to know God. Because Maimonides insisted on the limitations of human knowledge, he was fixed upon the figure of Moses and the uniqueness and excellence of his prophecy. It was Mosaic prophecy that charted the way to intellectual perfection, despite human cognitive limitations.

Gersonides was much more optimistic about the possibility of human knowledge of God, and he modified many elements in the astronomy, cosmology, and ontology of the inherited Maimonidean system.[31] As a loyal Aristotelian, Gersonides envisioned the universe as a hierarchy of substances linked to each other by virtue of emanation (*shefa*). He held that the separate Intelligences are movers of celestial bodies, and that the corporeal sublunar world is composed of four elements—water, air, fire, and earth. However, Gersonides adopted some of the modifications of Ibn Rushd's astronomy and introduced others of his own, which lay the foundation for his own understanding of the relationship between God and the world.[32]

According to Ibn Rushd, the first cause of the universe, God, does not transcend the universe, but is part of the comprehensive system of causes that link all existents. For him, the first mover, that is, the Intelligence that moves the outermost sphere (the sphere of the fixed stars), is also itself the first cause of the universe, namely God. However, instead of talking about the emanation of the intelligences from each other, Ibn Rushd (in the *Long Commentary on the Metaphysics*) explained the relationship between the Intelligences and God as follows:

> each incorporeal intelligence . . . eternally turns its mental gaze upon the unitary first cause, and the conception of the first cause which each thereby receives lends it the measure of perfection befitting its rank in the cosmic hierarchy.[33]

The last intelligence is the Active Intellect, of which Aristotle spoke in the *De Anima* as the efficient cause of human intellect. The Active Intellect possesses the unified pattern of the sublunar world.

Gersonides rejected Ibn Rushd's notion that God is the mover of the outermost celestial sphere. He was determined to document and understand the actual motions of the stars rather than merely construct hypothetical, mathematical models that could predict what the motions of the stars should be.[34] For this purpose he designed an instrument—known as the *baculus Jacob*—that enabled astronomers to measure more accurately the distance between stars and their relative height. His empirical astronomical observations had a religious purpose; they were intended to produce a deeper understanding of how the universe created by God actually works.[35] On the basis of his observations, Gersonides' account of motions in the celestial region differed significantly from the account of ibn Rushd. The novelty of Gersonides' astronomy was the claim that the celestial bodies were not so radically different from the corporeal bodies in the sublunar world, because both worlds were created from the same stuff—"formless matter" (*geshem bilti shomer temunato*).[36]

Unlike Maimonides, who maintained that the origin of the universe was obscure, Gersonides was convinced that we can have some idea about it: God created the universe out of "formless matter" in an act of divine will.[37] As Norbert Samuelson explains, the act of creation itself did not occur in time; it has no beginning and no end, and it brings into existence a world of becoming of things composed of matter and form. Prime matter, however, is not a thing; it has no form that defines it, or puts a limit on it. In this regard, the created world is one that is and is not at the same time.[38] The biblical narrative of creation conveys these deep truths in the form of a true story, a myth, delineating the corporeal and noncorporeal aspects of divine creation.[39] The former includes the sublunar world of material, concrete particulars as well as the supra-lunar celestial regions; the latter consists of God, the formal aspect of the universe, and the sole principle of what is. In this regard, God is the intellect or mind of the universe.

Gersonides' doctrine of creation had profound ramifications for all aspects of his philosophy. First, he reduces the ontological gap between the sub-lunar and the supra-lunar world. The corporeal aspect of the universe consists of objects in the sublunar world that are made from the four elements as well as celestial bodies that are made from the fifth element, ether. To understand the structure of the universe means to have demonstrative knowledge (that is, scientific, theoretical knowledge) of both the sub-lunar and supra-lunar realms, knowledge that belongs to the scientific disciplines of physics and astronomy, respectively. Knowledge of astronomy, then, is necessary for the attainment of human intellectual perfection, contrary to Maimonides' rejection of that science.[40]

Second, the fact that the celestial bodies are ultimately made from "formless matter" indicates that the motions of the stars are not necessary and perfect, as Aristotle and the Muslim Aristotelians thought. On the contrary, even they exhibit a certain degree of imperfection and contingency. That contingency, in turn, imposes a limit on God's knowledge, which for Gersonides follows from the very perfection of God. God cannot know that which, in principle, is unknowable. The corporeal, and hence, contingent aspect of the universe remains unknowable to God. God knows only the formal, intelligible order of reality (*siddur ha-muskal asher be-nafsho*), which exists in God in a super-eminent way.[41]

Third, the claim that God created the universe from "formless matter" places a limit on God's omnipotence, for changes in concrete particulars emerge without direct divine intervention (for example, the sickness or death of a particular body), and contingent events, which result from human free choice, are neither known to God in their particularity nor governed by God. This is not to say that God does not know individuals or contingent events at all, but rather that God does not know them insofar as they are determined by matter. As Samuelson succinctly put it, God "can know what an individual is, but he cannot know one individual as distinct from another individual."[42]

Gersonides' doctrine of creation led him to reformulate the relationship between God and the separate intelligences. Contrary to Maimonides and his Muslim sources (who posited a hierarchical succession of separate intelligences one from the other), Gersonides claimed that intelligences proceed not from each other but directly from God. As H. Davidson puts it, each primary intelligence acquires its character from the partial thought, unique to itself, which it has of the first cause; and the character that the intelligence thereby obtains adapts it for governing its particular sphere.[43]

The notion that all of the separate intelligences come from God, but that each has individuality, despite the fact that each is devoid of matter, functions as the foundation of Gersonides' novel ontology, influencing every aspect of his philosophy.

Gersonides was the first Jewish philosopher to differentiate among "individuals" (*ishim*), "particulars" (*peratim*), and "universals" (*kollelim*). Particulars are material individuals that have extension and can be known through the senses. The corporeal world (both celestial and sub-lunar) is comprised of particulars. However, there are also individuals that have no extension or dimensions. They exist as numbers do: individual, non-material entities that are individuated not through matter but through form.[44] Gersonides was on the way to developing a theory of individual essences, even though he fell short of the comprehensive theory proposed by his scholastic contemporary, Duns Scotus.[45]

The full implications of the claim that the separate intelligences are non-material individuals will become clearer when we talk about the human material intellect and its implications for individual immortality. For now we need to explore further the relationship between God and the world by focusing on the Active Intellect.

THE ACTIVE INTELLECT AND HUMAN KNOWLEDGE

The Ambiguity of the Term "Active Intellect"

For all medieval Jewish Aristotelians the point of contact, so to speak, between the sublunar and the supra-lunar realms was the Active Intellect. In that hierarchical universe, the Active Intellect linked the question of how the universe is structured to the question of how the universe can be known, and, in turn, to the question how the human intellect attains its perfection. In the *De Anima* 3:5 (430a 13, 17–18), Aristotle left for posterity very enigmatic comments about human intellection. While distinguishing between the "passive" and "active" aspects of human intellection, Aristotle described the "Active Intellect" both as a cognitive function that is "present in the soul," as well as the "actuality" of the soul, which is "separate" from matter. Making sense of these obscure comments has given rise to an ongoing analysis of Aristotle's position that lasts to our own day.

Al-Farabi, ibn Sina, ibn Rushd, and Maimonides, who followed them, understood the "active intellect" of Aristotle's *De Anima* to be a transcendent substance and identified it with the tenth and last separate intelligence that emanates from the First Cause. Maimonides and his Muslim sources discussed the role of the Active Intellect in two main contexts: a) the production of natural forms, and b) the production of knowledge in humans. In general, the Active Intellect was the incorporeal source of natural forms that emanated from it on a certain "blend" (*mezeg*) of material elements. The same transcendent entity was also the efficient cause of cognition by which the human rational potential (known as the "material intellect" or "hylic intellect") is actualized. Maimonides spoke vaguely about the "overflow" or "emanation" that issues from the Active Intellect on the human intellect. However, he did not fully explain exactly how that actualization takes place, though his Muslim predecessors did.

Gersonides' Analysis of the Active Intellect

Following in the footsteps of Maimonides, Gersonides said much more about the Active Intellect and its operation. Through an exhaustive analysis of the views of his predecessors, he fashioned his own position about the Active Intellect as the source of natural forms in the sublunar world and as the source of human cognition. In regard to the natural forms, Gersonides concluded that the Active Intellect is the incorporeal agent of all living things, and that it is precisely what Plato and the Platonists who followed him meant when they spoke about the World Soul.[46] However, Gersonides went further than his predecessors by emphasizing that the incorporeal agent responsible for the generation of living things is also the agent that imposed purposive orderliness on the corporeal world, both supra-lunar and sublunar. The Active Intellect is the intelligible pattern of all corporeal existents (*siddur ha-muskalot yoshram ve-sidram*). As such, it possesses a "wisdom and perfection" that is exhibited throughout the universe.

As the intelligible pattern of the sublunar world, the Active Intellect knows the forms of particular things in the sublunar world as well as in the supra-lunar region of the celestial bodies. Indeed, the Active Intellect is the "giver of forms" for corporeal things in both regions.[47] As the originator of all corporeal forms, the Active Intellect knows them like an artisan who possesses the knowledge of a building before he is about to build it.[48] Likewise, the Active Intellect also knows the essences of everything that exists in the corporeal world (both supra-lunar and sublunar) as well as the operation that follows from them. The Active Intellect has perfect knowledge of the pattern of all corporeal things in the universe. All lower perfections in the corporeal world are found in the Active Intellect in a more refined, unified, perfect way.

Since the Active Intellect was created directly by God, whatever the Active Intellect knows is also known by God, but in an even more perfect and unified manner. God is the perfection and the final end of the universe as a whole. Furthermore, the knowledge that constitutes the separate intelligences, including the Active Intellect, is God's own self-knowledge.[49] By knowing Himself, God knows everything that is knowable—namely, the intelligent plan of the universe—in the most perfect manner possible.

As indicated above, according to Gersonides, God cannot know that which is unknowable—namely, particulars qua particulars.[50] Nor can God know future contingents, because that aspect of reality originates in "formless matter." However, such "unknowing" is not a limitation in God; in fact, it manifests God's perfect knowledge. We will return to this point below when we discuss Gersonides' position on determinism and choice. For now let us reiterate that Gersonides' world view is a unified hierarchy in which God functions as the soul of the entire universe, and the Active Intellect functions as the soul of the corporeal world. In such a system there is no room for a radical separation between physics and metaphysics, since the former pertains to the corporeal aspect of the world that consists of both sublunar and supra-lunar domains. In a continuous, hierarchical, internally linked universe, the corporeal and the non-corporeal aspects of reality are two aspects of the same reality, just viewed from different perspectives.[51] In making scientific knowledge bear directly on the human ultimate felicity, Gersonides differed from Maimonides.

The doctrine of the Active Intellect, then, can be viewed as a medieval reformulation of the ancient belief in cosmic Wisdom, going all the way back to the Egyptian conception of *maat*, and it is reminiscent of Philo's doctrine of Logos.[52] Since cosmic wisdom is the cause of human wisdom, however that is explained, it is understandable that medieval Aristotelianism made the Active Intellect the source of human knowledge. Medieval Aristotelian cosmology can be seen as an adaptation of the notion of cosmic wisdom to Aristotelian cosmology, astronomy, and psychology of the day.

Gersonides' Account of Human Knowledge

The Views of Gersonides' Predecessors

Like all Jewish Aristotelianism, Gersonides posited that human knowledge involves some interaction, contact, or communication with the Active Intellect.

How, according to Gersonides, does the Active Intellect produce knowledge in human beings? To answer this question we need first to understand Gersonides' view on the nature of the human rational soul. In a typical scholastic fashion he considers the strengths and weaknesses of each view and then develops his own out of what he takes to be true in the positions at his disposal. Gersonides reduces the available positions to four basic views:[53]

a) Alexander of Aphrodisias held that the human soul is not a substance, but only a passive potentiality to receive knowledge.

b) Themistius regarded the human soul as an incorporeal, eternal substance.

c) Ibn Rushd maintained that the human material intellect is identical with the Agent Intellect, and is, therefore, the same in all human beings.

d) The view of the "moderns" is that the "material intellect is generated essentially, but not from something else."

The Questions to be Resolved

Gersonides' laborious examination of these views revolves around the following major questions: a) Is the human intellect a substance or a disposition? b) Is the human intellect changed through the process of cognizing intelligibles? c) Does the cognition of intelligible forms, which are universal, entail the loss of the individuality of the human material intellect? d) Is the product of the cognitive process—the "acquired intellect"—individual or not? These questions were not of mere speculative importance; they had serious religious ramifications because, for the Aristotelian philosophers, survival after death is predicated on cognition.

If the human intellect is only a disposition to know (the view of Alexander), then it becomes a substance only through the cognitive process. However, if a new substance emerges through intellection, how can it be said to be the same material intellect? Whatever results in the process of intellection, "the acquired intellect" is not the same as the material intellect. It amounts to saying that the human material intellect does not survive, which is the same as denying individual immortality.

If, however, one claims that the human intellect is by definition an immaterial, eternal substance (the view of Themistius and its variant in the view of the "moderns"), individuality is assured, but then the process of cognition seems irrelevant to the pursuit of immortality. The individual, nonmaterial intellect will survive the death of the body regardless of what one cognizes during one's lifetime. If so, there is no reason to be concerned with the arduous process of cognizing intelligibles.

If one takes the view that the material intellect is in fact the Active Intellect as instantiated in a given human soul (the view of Ibn Rushd), then one compromises the personal identity of the human intellect, and in so doing undermines belief in individual immortality. The entire process of cognition is understood as a deliberate attempt to get rid of the personal markers of the human intellect, and to seek absorption into the universal Active Intellect. The more one cognizes the intelligible forms in the mind of the Active Intellect, the more universal and impersonal one's intellect becomes, thus negating the individuality of the acquired intellect.

Gersonides' Solution

Gersonides' solution to these problems is rooted in his ontological distinction between "individuals" and "particulars," and his claim that there are individual entities that are non-material. According to his view of the human intellect, the human rational soul, the "material intellect," is an individual, non-material substance that has a disposition to receive intelligibles. The human individual, material intellect is instantiated in a human particular (namely a corporeal human being), and the disposition to know will be actualized only when the human intellect cognizes intelligible forms. The intelligible forms are universals that inhere in particular things. They become accessible to the human intellect indirectly first through sense perception, and then directly when the particular and material aspects of sense perception are "stripped away." The intelligible form that is now known by the human material intellect is universal in the sense that it can be instantiated by many, but it is also individual in the sense that it is one and not many.

The intelligible form that the human intellect cognizes exists extra-mentally in material particulars, and, after being cognized, it exists as well in the mind of the human knower. However, the intelligible form, as we noted earlier, exists also in the mind of the Active Intellect as part of the intelligible order of the universe, as well as in the mind of God. In fact, ontologically speaking, the intelligible form exists first in the mind of God and the Active Intellect prior to its existence in material things.[54] It follows that to cognize an intelligible form means to know what is in the mind of the Active Intellect and even in the mind of God. How is that possible?

The Emanated Acquired Intellect

In the writings of ibn Sina, which Gersonides knew through the mediation of ibn Rushd, the Active Intellect was said to "illumine" particular things, thereby making them accessible to the human intellect. The Active Intellect thus turned particulars into "intelligibles," or mental concepts. Some of the statements in Gersonides suggest that he was familiar with this doctrine and perhaps even endorsed it. There are indeed passages where he employed the emanationist schema and said that the Active Intellect emanates on the material intellect or that the "material intellect . . . receive[s] the emanation (*shefa*) of the Active Intellect" with the aid of "sense perception."[55] The "acquired intellect" that results in the process of intellection can therefore be described as "emanated." The highest state of the human intellect is thus known as an "emanated acquired intellect" (*sekhel niqneh ne'etzal*).

Gersonides explains the process of intellectual cognition as one of "abstraction" of intelligible forms from impressions caused by extra-mental objects. The senses have perceptions of extra-mental objects, which are internal impressions stored in the imagination. The Active Intellect "strips away" the materiality of the imaginative forms, thereby "exposing" the universal intelligible that inheres in particular things extra-mentally. To possess knowledge—namely, to reach the state of "acquired intellect"—the human material intellect must possess the intelligible forms that exist primarily in the mind of the Active Intellect and secondarily in material particulars. This "acquired intellect" survives the death of the body, and it is to this state that humans should aspire if they wish to experience immortality.[56]

The contact between the human intellect and the Active Intellect, however, does not entail the disintegration of the material intellect or its loss of individual identity. That doctrine was proposed by ibn Rushd and was taken up by younger contemporaries of Gersonides, especially Moses Narboni (d. 1362).[57] Gersonides emphatically rejected ibn Rushd's notion that the human material intellect is one and the same with the Active Intellect and that the human material intellect disintegrates into the Active Intellect. Like other scholastic teachers, such as Thomas Aquinas,[58] Gersonides rejected ibn Rushd's epistemology. Debating with ibn Rushd on the basis of different texts,[59] the Christian and Jewish philosophers defended the belief in personal immortality. For Gersonides the acquired intellect is an incorporeal, individual substance that cannot "unite with" the Active Intellect. But he uses unitive language to depict the contact between the human acquired intellect and the semi-divine Active Intellect, i.e., *devequt*. This is the same language used by the kabbalists to depict the ultimate end of human life. It would seem, then, that Gersonides posits a form of rational mysticism. Yet he shuns the full implication of unitive language by saying that "total conjunction" (*devequt bi-shlemut*) is attained only "somewhat" (*be-ofen mah*), because of the material foundation of human knowledge; conjunction is only epistemological and not ontological.[60]

In his Commentary on Genesis: 1 Gersonides speaks about the conjunction between the human intellect and the Active Intellect in less guarded language. The Garden of Eden narrative is a parable about the ultimate end of human life. "True happiness" (*hatzlaha amitit*), Gersonides says, is the cognition (*hasagah*) of the intelligible order in the mind of the Active Intellect (*nimus ha-nimtza'ot yoshram ve-sidram*), to the extent it is accessible to humans (*kefi mah she'efshar lo*). Such knowledge is the ultimate pleasure available to humans (*takhlit ha-ta`anug ha'efshari*), an experience so intense that it has "no relationship to bodily pleasures," differing from the bliss of immortality only in degree but not in kind.[61] In the language of the Torah myth, this powerful bliss is conveyed in the word "Eden," which refers to the Active Intellect. The narrative of the Garden of Eden is about the ideal that all humans must strive to attain. The Tree of Life in the Garden is the "intelligible order of reality [*siddur ha-muskal asher la-nimtz'ot*], which the human mind can potentially comprehend [*she ha-sekhel ha-enoshi kohiyi al hasgatam*]"; eating from the Tree of Life yields "eternal life" (*hayyim nitzhiyyim*). Immediately thereafter Gersonides evokes the key verse of the discourse on happiness—Proverbs 13:8—reminding the reader that "Tree of Life" is the crucial metaphor for Torah in Judaism. Indeed, he asserts that "the comprehension of the Torah [*hasagat ha-Torah*] is a tree of life to those who adhere to it." Put differently, those who devote their lives to the acquisition of knowledge will gain the knowledge of the "Tree of Life," i.e., the conjunction with the Active Intellect, by which humans can attain eternal life. In the *Wars*, Gersonides states the same thing straightforwardly: the goal of human life is to become a philosopher-scientist "for human happiness is achieved when a man knows reality as much as he can." (*Wars*, Introduction, p. 96). By grasping the intelligible order of reality, albeit imperfectly, the philosopher-scientist experiences the ultimate pleasure in life, tasting of the bliss of the world to come.

Because Gersonides was more optimistic than Maimonides about the possibility of attaining intellectual perfection in this world, he rejected Maimonides' negative theology. Ontologically prior to the universe and the cause of the universe, the creator is the perfection of the universe. Qua perfection, God is not totally unrelated to everything else, because what God knows perfectly and supremely comes into existence imperfectly and subordinately in the corporeal universe created out of "formless matter." Ordinary language, therefore, is not absolutely equivocal with respect to God, and neither is it totally inadequate. Ordinary language can say something positive and meaningful about God, because God is the most refined and perfect form of the intelligible order of the universe. Ordinary language is equivocal in a particular manner that Aristotle called *pros en* equivocation.[62] What is knowable about the corporeal world is knowable because it exists first in God in the most perfect way. It is appropriate, therefore, to speak about God in positive language and to claim some knowledge about the way God relates to the universe. In short, the ultimate end of human life is the knowledge of God, to the extent that God is knowable by human beings. Given the impediments of the corporeal body and the mistaken choices that people make, such knowledge is difficult to attain but it is not in principle impossible.

The Individuated Immortality of the Human Rational Soul

Gersonides' examination of human knowledge was meant to prove that the perfection of the intellect does not destroy its individuality. Human beings differ from one another in their natural disposition to pursue knowledge and in their commitment to philosophic wisdom. While they cognize intelligible forms that are universal, the process of intellection does not erase distinctions between individuals. Each human intellect retains its individual identity throughout the process and reaches its distinct level of perfection, depending on the kind of life a person lives. Needless to say, the one who devotes himself to the acquisition of intelligibles is more perfect than a person who pursues bodily pleasures. The chance of survival is much higher for the former. Furthermore, even two persons who are committed to the acquisition of scientific-philosophic knowledge will still differ from one another, since the *content* of their knowledge is unique to them.

According to Gersonides, then, the religious belief in individual immortality taught by Judaism is consistent with the philosophic claim that only perfection of the intellect yields immortality. The only wise way to live, then, is to be solely devoted to the pursuit of truth through which one cognizes the intelligibles, and only in this way does a person have a chance to survive the disintegration of the body. Hence there can be no conflict between what philosophy establishes as true and what the Jewish tradition teaches in regard to the immortality of the personal soul.

As Gersonides and his contemporaries worked out the details of the cognitive process that leads to perfection of the intellect, new problems arose concerning the relationship between philosophical knowledge and religious faith. If ultimate human felicity is identified with the knowledge of God, does that knowledge constitute religious faith, or is faith a distinctive cognitive state? Does religious faith require any voluntary choice, or does it consist of beliefs that one is compelled to hold because one knows certain facts? Finally, if human beings experience the afterlife because of what they know and believe, do actions matter at all in its attainment? How is the claim that intellectual perfection is the ultimate felicity to be reconciled with traditional Jewish belief in divine retribution? Gersonides addressed these questions, and he regarded philosophy as the best polemics against Christianity.

Providence, Causal Determinism, and Rational Choice

General and Individual Providence

Gersonides' intellectualist vision of human perfection contains the following claims: a) Human perfection consists only in the perfection of the human intellect. b) The perfect man is the wise man who expands his "acquired intellect." c) The perfected intellect enjoys the bliss of eternal life.

To Gersonides, the life in pursuit of scientific, theoretical knowledge will benefit a person even before he dies. The wise man who lives in accordance with reason can be saved from the accidental misfortunes and mishaps of the corporeal world, which are due to material, natural factors because he can predict future events. To live rationally is to live in accordance with the intelligible order of the universe to the fullest extent possible for humans. The life in accordance with reason manifests the presence of divine providential care in the life of corporeal particular human beings.

Like Maimonides, Gersonides differentiates between "general providence" (*hashgahah kelalit*) and "individual providence" (*hashgahah peratit*). The regularity and orderliness of the universe that is evident in nature exhibits the purposefulness of "general providence." As stated above, God does not know corporeal particulars as such, but only the degree to which they participate in the intelligible order of reality. Human beings who are endowed with reason are the only corporeal creatures who benefit from "individual providence." However, because God only knows corporeal particulars to the extent that they participate in the intelligible order of the universe, "individual providence" is extended only to those who are intellectually perfect. Divine providential care, then, is commensurate with the intellectual perfection of the individual human intellect. Gersonides is no less an elitist than Maimonides.

Voluntary Action and Astral Determinism

The life of reason, says Gersonides, in accordance with Aristotle, is the source of human freedom from material conditioning. Like other Jewish Aristotelians in the thirteenth and fourteenth centuries, Gersonides had no notion of a free will (*ratzon ḥofshi*): for him (following Aristotle) the will is a "rational appetite" that desires what is apprehended by reason to be good. All choice (*beḥirah*) is thus a rational activity caused by the intellect, which makes its judgments on the basis of knowledge of extra-mental reality. In Gersonides' Aristotelian theory of knowledge, to know means to know the causes of things, which is to know why things are the way they are. Because everything has a cause that is accessible to the human intellect, everything is explicable. The causes of the corporeal dimension of reality are known to the Active Intellect, and the causes of the universe as a whole are identical with God's knowledge of himself. Human participation in the knowledge of the Active Intellect provides at least partial knowledge of the corporeal aspect of the universe, and, by extension, partial knowledge of God.

The teleological causality that pervades the universe indicates that everything is determined by its causes. A deterministic view of the world raises serious questions with regard to human action and moral responsibility. Are we compelled to act because of certain external causes, or is human voluntary action independent of the hierarchical system of causes? Since all causes are ultimately known by God, does God's foreknowledge preordain how humans are going to act? If humans are compelled to act because of the existence of certain causes, can they be morally responsible?

Soft Determinism

I conjecture that these questions were at the forefront of Jewish concern in the fourteenth century in response to the intensification of the Jewish-Christian polemics. After the traumas of 1391 and the mass conversion of Iberian Jews to Christianity, the last question in particular—regarding determinism and choice—would become very troubling indeed. The tense confrontation between Judaism and Christianity brought the debate about this question to the forefront of Jewish philosophy from the second third of the fourteenth century on.

Gersonides posited a "soft" form of determinism that reconciles causal determinism with human voluntary action.[63] On the one hand, everything in the universe is determined by its causes and can be explained through them, since to know something means to know its causes. In Gersonides' cosmology the natural causes that determine how the corporeal world operates and how humans will act are the celestial bodies. Gersonides was an expert practitioner of astrology, a scientific discipline that employed knowledge of astronomy in order to explain the natural tendencies of human beings and to prognosticate future events in human affairs. The position of the stars at the time of one's birth determines one's natural disposition or temperament (*mezeg*), which in turn affects how one tends by nature to act and even to think. Astral determinism, according to Gersonides, is part of the comprehensive causality that pervades everything in the world.

It appears that everything is necessitated by its causes. If so, can human beings act independently and voluntarily? Gersonides answers in the affirmative. The source of human voluntary action is the intellect, which moves a person toward that which the intellect considers to be good. Because the intellect is the efficient cause of human action, it can establish human independence from material causality. How? When human beings act solely in accord with their natural, material disposition, they subordinate themselves to astral determinism.[64] However, if they are aware of the stars and their influences but choose to act against their natural inclinations, they are free from astral determinism. Like Aristotle, then, Gersonides held that the less one is conditioned by matter (in this case by the material forces of the astral constellations), the less determined are one's actions.[65]

Rational choice, says Gersonides, is an expression of the presence of individual providence in the life of particular people. Because he maintained that the universe was created from "formless matter," and because in Aristotelian philosophy matter is inherently evil, he acknowledged the imperfection of the corporeal world. Thus various forms of evil in human life such as suffering, pain, poverty, disease, loss, and ultimately death, are all expressions of the material dimension of reality. However, the "necessity of evil," so to speak, can be mitigated somewhat through reason, since it enables people to choose against their natural tendencies and direct their efforts to a knowledge of the universe that culminates in the knowledge of God. The fools who devote themselves solely to the pursuit of sensual pleasures and the accumulation of possessions will find their lives cut short by misfortunes that arise necessarily from matter. By contrast, the chance to experience the true and everlasting delight of the afterlife lies in the choice to cognize intelligibles through the study of science, which is the preoccupation of the philosopher.

Voluntary Choice and Divine Foreknowledge

If astral determinism is consistent with voluntary choice, so is God's foreknowledge.[66] We already indicated that according to Gersonides, God does not know particulars qua particulars, but only to the extent that particulars participate in the intelligible order of the universe. This means that God does not have foreknowledge of future contingent events. This is not a limitation but an expression of the exalted and sublime nature of God, who "only knows His essence, and in His knowledge of Himself, He knows everything which exists insofar as it possesses a universal nature."[67] However, Gersonides' view entails God's ignorance of Israel as a particular group of people in time; nor can God be involved directly in the affairs of the people by performing miracles that negate the general order of creation.

Like Maimonides, Gersonides rejected the notion that miracles are events that contradict either the laws of logic or the laws of nature. All miracles have natural, rational explanations: they involve God's activity through natural causes and are limited by what is logically possible. Miracles themselves manifest the stability and regularity of the natural order because the orders (*siddurim*) that dictate that such and such will happen are "programmed" into God's creation.[68] The agent of miracles is not a human being but the Active Intellect that possesses knowledge of the pattern of the corporeal universe (*Wars* V, 6. 2.10). Gersonides' naturalistic approach to miracles illustrates what Amos Funkenstein characterized as "dogmatic rationalism." "A rationalist," says Funkenstein, "is a thinker who refuses to be surprised; nothing seems to him mysterious."[69] Even chance and contingency, which Gersonides ascribes to matter, are ultimately explicable.

PROPHECY, PHILOSOPHY, AND THE TORAH OF MOSES

The Challenge of Optimistic Rationalism to Revealed Scripture

Gersonides' optimistic rationalism may seem to pose a challenge to a religious tradition based on revealed Scriptures. If science and philosophy can bring one to attain the ultimate felicity of human life, the perfection of the intellect, why is there a need for divine revelation? At least for the philosophically inclined few who can perfect their intellect, the revealed tradition is of little use, since the truth necessary and sufficient for perfection can be attained without the divine assistance. The more successful one is as a philosopher-scientist, the less one has to glean truth from the teachings of the Torah and the rabbinic tradition that interprets it. Indeed, in the fifteenth century Gersonides became the symbol of rigorous rationalism and its resulting thoroughgoing naturalism in the interpretation of Scripture. His views were severely criticized by other Aristotelian thinkers and his commentary on the Pentateuch was put under a ban by Judah Messer Leon in Italy.[70] The details of the critique need not concern us here, but it is important to note that the perception of Gersonides as the "arch-rationalist" who undermines the integrity of traditional Judaism was due not to his denial of the uniqueness of the Torah of Moses, its immutability, or its function in the attainment of human perfection, but to the fact that he was open and straightforward about the primacy of philosophy in the worship of God.

Gersonides was no less an intellectual elitist than Maimonides, and the readers he had in mind when he composed his philosophical texts were those who were already familiar with "the mathematical sciences, the natural sciences, and metaphysics" (*Wars*, Introduction, 92). But unlike his predecessors, Gersonides did not believe that philosophy was harmful to the masses. On the contrary, in his view the primary task of the scientist-philosopher was to propagate scientific knowledge and to do his best to raise the philosophic level of his community so that more people would be able to attain the ultimate felicity and experience the bliss of immortal life. Gersonides, therefore, discredited philosophical esotericism, even though he continued to assert the superiority of the few who knew truth over the many who remained ignorant of it.

The knower of truth has an obligation to impart it to those who do not possess it. In so doing, he imitates God.[71] However, he should be aware that reception of truth varies in degree, due to material impediments. People differ from one another in their natural capacity to know and in their devotion to the pursuit of truth. Hence the teaching of truth must involve rhetorical strategies and adopt the most appropriate ones. Gersonides' philosophical commentaries on ibn Rushd were directed to the "professional" students of philosophy and its related sciences, while his philosophical theology was directed to a broader audience of Jewish intelligentsia, and his biblical commentaries, perhaps with the exception of the commentary on Song of Songs,[72] were addressed to all Jews. Though these avenues of communicating truth differed greatly from one another, the content of what Gersonides sought to teach was fundamentally the same, because in his view truth is one and undivided.

Gersonides' Naturalist Account of Prophecy

The congruence between revealed Judaism and philosophy rests on the phenomenon of prophecy. Maimonides, and before him Saadia Gaon and Abraham ibn Daud, followed the cue of Muslim philosophers when they interpreted prophecy as a natural, cognitive phenomenon. For Maimonides, the prophet is a philosophically trained person whose intellect can receive the overflow from the Active Intellect. However, unlike the philosopher, the prophet is also endowed with a well-developed power of imagination. The overflow from the Active Intellect is thus "translated" into figurative images that the prophet conveys when he communicates abstract truths in the form of parables.

Gersonides adopted Maimonides' naturalist and cognitive approach to the phenomenon of prophecy. For him too prophecy is "a natural outcome of the human urge to perfect itself,"[73] and "the prophet is necessarily a philosopher."[74] However, Gersonides' understanding of prophetic activity differed from Maimonides' in three main respects. First, Gersonides presented prophets as "super-philosophers" who obtained theoretical knowledge with greater ease than philosophers, drawing conclusions from premises faster and in a less laborious manner. This is not to say that prophetic knowledge is "intuitive," if by the latter we mean non-discursive knowledge. Rather, prophetic knowledge employs the same procedures, but does so with greater excellence and speed.

Second, for Gersonides, the prophets, contrary to Maimonides, are not engaged in the propagation of theoretical knowledge through figurative speech, as Maimonides held, because prophets are not distinguished from philosophers by virtue of their imagination. Rather, what distinguishes them is their ability to predict future chance events, an ability that arises from the prophet's scientific-philosophic excellence. In this regard, they are closer to dreamers and diviners than to philosophers, contrary to Maimonides' views. Because the prophet apprehends the knowledge of a deterministic system of causes, he can warn about impending evil and direct people toward the objectively good. In this manner, "prophecy is part of the mechanism of providence," as Robert Eisen succinctly put it.[75] Prophetic predictions of future events can save people from mishaps, enable them to better their ways, and direct their lives toward the good.

Third, counter to Maimonides, prophets are not statesmen who are engaged in the political task of legislating laws, as Maimonides believed. Only one prophet—Moses—was a legislator, and his activity was unique and unrepeatable. All philosopher-prophets before and after Moses were engaged not in legislative activity, but in predicting future events. Not even the messiah, who will also be a philosopher-prophet, will be able to undo or supersede the legislative activity of Moses.[76] However, the messiah will perform more awesome miracles than did Moses, the greatest of which will be the resurrection of the dead.[77] Gersonides considered resurrection as a fundamental biblical principle (*pinot ha-torah*), perhaps in order to avoid potential charges like the one leveled against Maimonides.

Gersonides' De-Politization of Maimonides' Conception of Prophecy[78]

Gersonides, at least in the *Wars*, seems to de-politicize the phenomenon of prophecy by divorcing it from human governance. It is his most radical departure from Maimonides' conception of prophecy and can be accounted for on both philosophical and historical grounds.

According to Maimonides, the highest form of knowledge available to human beings is the knowledge of God's governance of the universe through natural intermediaries. For him, when one possesses such exalted knowledge, one necessarily acts in imitation of God's action, governing other people through legislative activity that exemplifies God's attributes of action. For Gersonides, by contrast, we can know not only how God governs the world. We can also have some positive knowledge, albeit dim and imperfect, of God's essence, in whom all things exist in a super-eminent and perfect way. To possess some knowledge of God, therefore, does not lead to action in the political sphere, but to thinking of the intelligible order of the universe. In God thinking is creative; it results in the emanation of the intelligences. Likewise the theoretical knowledge of the scientist-philosopher-prophet imparts knowledge to others through information about future events. The ordinary scientist-philosophers who are not prophets have to disseminate their knowledge to others by teaching them science and philosophy, thereby making it possible for others to reach intellectual perfection and enjoy the immortality of the intellect.[79]

Historically, Gersonides' de-emphasis of the political role of the prophets makes sense in the context of the encounter with Christianity, as Menachem Kellner tentatively suggested.[80] Kellner proposed that it was Gersonides' familiarity with Christian culture itself that led him to focus on spiritual perfection rather than on temporal perfection. While this is a plausible explanation, I believe it applies more to Jewish philosophers in the fifteenth century than to Gersonides. It seems to me, though it is a conjecture on my part, that Gersonides' depolitization of prophecy has more to do with his awareness of the political powerlessness of the Jews in his own day. Whereas Maimonides functioned as the *rais al-Yahud* in Fatimid Egypt and was involved in halakhic legal activity as well as management of communal affairs, Gersonides held no official position in the community and witnessed the growing curtailment of Jewish autonomy in Christian Europe. His mature life was punctuated by the expulsion of Jews from France in 1306, and again in 1322, and the eruption of large-scale anti-Jewish disturbances in Provence in 1331 and 1340. Given Jewish vulnerability and powerlessness, it makes little sense to speak about prophet-philosophers as statesmen who were engaged in legislation.

The Uniqueness of Moses and the Torah

The exception, of course, was the prophet Moses, who gave Israel the Torah, the only law that can bring mankind to the attainment of ultimate felicity. What makes the Torah of Moses unique is not the unprecedented intellectual perfection of Moses, as Maimonides labored to prove, but that Moses was singularly concerned with the attainment of human perfection.

Gersonides agreed with Maimonides that the prophet Moses was superior to all other prophets. He could prophesy when he was awake, at any time he pleased, without fear and trembling, and without any admixture of the imagination. Gersonides states:

> Someone who is concerned only with human perfection will give information that concerns this perfection and the things that are conducive to its attainment insofar as they lead to this end. It would seem that in Moses (may he rest in peace) all these elements were conjoined: he was perfect in intellect, he could easily isolate [this faculty], and he devoted all his attention to human perfection only. Therefore, among all the prophets, his prophetic illumination was uniquely concerned with this perfection. Indeed, the combined presence in one man of all three factors in the highest degree possible is extremely difficult: therefore, the Torah says, "Never again will there arise in Israel a prophet like Moses."[81]

The Torah that Moses gave to Israel is a set of directives that "thoroughly guides those who observe it to true felicity [*hatzlaḥa amitit*]."[82] That true felicity is the immortality of the perfected intellect, but it can be attained only by those who acquire the moral virtues that the Torah itself teaches. To make that clear Gersonides composed his extensive commentary on the Pentateuch.

The Torah of Moses perfects the life of those who live by it for three reasons. First, the commandments of the Torah train one to achieve moral and intellectual virtues that are necessary for human perfection. Second, the narratives of the Torah pertain to the organization of the ideal social order. Third, these same narratives provide theoretical information about the structure of reality (*siddur ha-nimtzaot*).

In his commentaries on the Pentateuch, Gersonides sums up the ethical and philosophical "advantages" (*to`aliyot*) that are taught by each Torah portion. The exposition either contextualizes the ancient text in time and place—thus making it possible for the reader to treat the ancient personae as concrete models for emulation—or the exposition clarifies what is obscure in the biblical text in light of the sciences, especially physics and astronomy. Everything in the Torah, from the sacrificial cult to the genealogies of the patriarchs, serves the ultimate function of instructing Israel how to attain their moral and ultimately intellectual perfection.

Although the Torah and philosophic-scientific knowledge are identical, there is a need for both because in some cases the Torah's presentation of profound truths is more succinct and easily accessible. Thus the narrative of creation conveys in a graphic manner deep philosophical truths about the generation of the corporeal world—truths that are difficult to apprehend. The Torah also can furnish "valuable clues to solve philosophy's most difficult problems."[83] Importantly, Gersonides never uses biblical texts as propositions in his philosophical discourse, which is established independent of Torah. It is only because he claims to possess scientific and philosophic truth that he can prove the verity of the Torah. In the rationalist outlook of Gersonides not only the world is mystery-free: so is the Torah of Moses.

Gersonides' presentation of the Torah as a guide for human perfection might have had an anti-Christian polemical intent. If Jews possessed the best guide for human perfection and had access to the most advanced science of their day (manifested by Gersonides' own scientific activity), why would Jews be interested in conversion? Indeed, not only did a commitment to the pursuit of scientific truth per se not provide the incentive to convert to Christianity: it could have conceivably functioned as a deterrent to the temptation. As long as the Jewish religious philosopher was convinced that Judaism was true and that the Torah established the social order most conducive to the attainment of ultimate felicity, he could resist the temptation to convert. If the Jewish intellectual began to doubt the assumptions of

Jewish religious intellectualism, conversion to the majority religion would become a real option. Otherwise, conversion was attributable to profound fear and the determination to survive, as well as the desire to improve one's economic conditions and social status.

INTELLECTUAL PERFECTION, DETERMINISM, AND CHOICE

Rationalism in Defense of Judaism

We can illustrate how polemics with Christianity changed the Jewish discourse on happiness during the fourteenth century by looking at another contemporary of Gersonides. Isaac Polleqar (or Pulgar) was a Jewish religious thinker in Spain who sought to persuade Jews not to convert by arguing that Judaism alone leads to perfection of the intellect, and therefore to the survival of the individual soul. Polleqar is the author of *Ezer ha-Dat* (The Support of the Faith), a semi-philosophical text written to strengthen the faith of Jews against despair and skepticism from within as well as Christian polemics from without.[84] Although the book treats issues of theoretical import, it is not a technical philosophical treatise, but a rhetorical text that makes its case by personifying various ideological positions. In a rhymed prose similar to that of Shem Tov Falaquera's works, Polleqar gives expression to views that were debated within the Jewish community.

The Debate of Isaac Polleqar with Abner of Burgos

While the audience of Polleqar's work was the struggling Jewish community in Spain, *Ezer ha-Dat* was specifically written to address the position of a particular individual—Abner of Burgos (d. 1346).[85] For twenty-five years this scribe and bookbinder for the infanta Blanca, granddaughter of Alfonso X and senora of the Monasterio de las Huelgas of Burgos, was tormented with doubts about Judaism as the sole path for salvation. About 1320 he finally converted to Christianity, changing his name to Alfonso de Valladolid, but he continued to write in Hebrew to his former colleagues, and then supervised the translation of his works into Castilian. Abner not only actively missionized to Jews; he also composed a work to train "relatively unlettered priests engaged in proselytizing to Jews."[86] He rationalized his conversion in a treatise on messianism, which he sent to Polleqar. Polleqar responded in a treatise that Abner dubbed as *Iggeret ha-Ḥarafot* (Epistle of Blasphemies), to which Abner replied in a treatise entitled *Teshuvot la-Meḥaref* (Refutation of the Blasphemer).[87] This fascinating exchange is a mine of information about the issues of concern to Jewish intellectuals in the first half of the fourteenth century. What matters to us is that Abner's critique of Judaism was directed against the very premises of the philosophic conception of happiness that equated perfection of the intellect with the life in accordance with the Torah of Moses.

Polleqar represented the approach to human happiness articulated by Maimonides, according to which life in the ideal political regime is necessary for the attainment of intellectual perfection. He states:

> [L]aw and convention are absolutely necessary for orderly human behavior . . . because we are endowed with a rational soul, we are obliged to accept those tenets whose truth had been logically established. However, the human being in his youth—and indeed, in the case of most people throughout life—has neither the leisure nor the disposition to learn these tenets through the study of their sources, namely the exact sciences. Therefore, the founder of the divinely revealed faith found it necessary to incorporate into it all those fundamental truths without which the human being cannot achieve perfection and to make them part of tradition, so that a man would not remain throughout his entire lifetime until he dies, ignorant of them.[88]

Abner, however, considered this view to be a "serious error" because it presupposed that religious beliefs are cognitions. Against Polleqar, Abner claimed that

> precisely because man possesses a rational soul he does not have to accept any traditional belief; for that which one learns from tradition, whatever the reasons for it, can be called knowledge only in a homonymous sense, and in accepting it he is not functioning as an active thinker.[89]

Abner then charged that Jews remain Jewish not because Judaism consists of rational knowledge but because Jews are *habituated* to hold certain beliefs about the superiority of the tradition. While some of these beliefs may be true opinions, many have nothing to do with knowledge. Indeed the "Jews accept the rabbinic interpretation of the biblical precepts even when it is not logically tenable, as in the case of the dietary laws, some of the laws of injury and damages, and others."[90] Knowledge of the Torah has nothing to do with knowledge of the structure of the universe, but with reasons for the performance of the commandments. The knowledge established by Torah is but "specialized lore" and not the comprehensive knowledge of all existents. According to Abner, even if one accepts that the Torah teaches knowledge, it cannot possibly qualify as the comprehensive knowledge that is supposed to secure the immortality of the soul according to the religious rationalists.

The Distinction Between Knowledge and True Opinion

Abner challenged the premises of medieval Jewish philosophy that reduced religious faith to cognition. For Maimonides, holding or not holding a certain view was a cognitive issue—namely, it expressed the degree of perfection of one's intellect. After Maimonides Jewish philosophers who became intimately familiar with the commentaries of Ibn Rushd on the Aristotelian corpus introduced the distinction between *knowledge* and *true opinion*. To know x is to understand why x is what it is, and how it cannot be otherwise. A true opinion is of a lower epistemic level because it lacks the certainty of knowledge. However, immortality of the intellect is possible only for those who come to know God. Then what about the traditional believer who merely holds traditional beliefs on the grounds of the authority of the tradition? According to the philosophers, such a believer cannot possibly attain intellectual perfection. Thus even if the uneducated multitude hold true opinions about God, they are unable to attain immortal life. Judaism, therefore, cannot be a salvific faith to all Jews.

The Distinction between Rational Knowledge and Faith

Jewish philosophers insisted on the rationality of Judaism in order to prove its spiritual superiority over Christianity. However, Abner challenged his conversation partner to differentiate between faith and rational knowledge. He argued that the highest expression of faith is the love of God, but the love of God is *not* commensurate with the degree of intellectual perfection.

> Man's love of God is not identical with his comprehension of the secrets of all creation and his reflection upon it with his intelligence, as Maimonides asserted (Guide III: 51), but those intellectual pursuits have as their purpose the love of God which is identical with obeying him and walking in his ways (Baer, *Jews in Christian Spain*, I: 342).

The intellectual pursuits of the philosophers, charged Abner, do not lead to the love of God or to affirmation of traditional Jewish beliefs. Indeed, philosophical knowledge "which consists mostly of doubts and controversial opinions, denies the miracles and divine wonders, creatio ex nihilo, resurrection, divine providence and retribution" (Baer, ibid). Furthermore, the philosophers are "free thinkers who make light of the Torah and of the commandments to a greater extent than other people."[91] By contrast, Abner holds that the love of God "stems from acceptance of principles of faith" rather than from "comprehension of the secrets of all creation" (Baer, ibid). Abner wanted Polleqar to admit that Judaism is a set of dogmas that is "confirmed by tradition and implied in biblical verses." The rivalry between Judaism and Christianity was thus a rivalry between two sets of dogmas, neither of which contained knowledge of the structure of the universe.

A Rivalry of Dogmas

Abner spent much of his intellectual acumen disputing the Jewish readings of biblical verses and arguing for the validity of a Christological reading of the Bible. As a Christian he argued that only the belief in the "triune nature of the Divinity," which, the messiah teaches, "holds forth the promise of rewards in the world to come."[92]

That Judaism has dogmas, of course, was one of Maimonides' most revolutionary innovations when he formulated the Thirteen Principles of Faith.[93] However, in the thirteenth and fourteenth centuries, Jewish rationalists had relatively little to say about the dogmas of Judaism, precisely because they understood the ultimate end of human life in terms of the knowledge of God. The intellectualization of Judaism meant that if the dogmas were rationally demonstrable, they would be assimilated into rational knowledge, i.e., into philosophy; however, if dogmas were not demonstrable, they would be mere pedagogic devices to help the masses to achieve proper worship. The more scientific Jewish philosophy became in the early fourteenth century, the less room there was to define Judaism as a set of religious dogmas. Philosophy and religion converged into one science—the divine science of metaphysics. The intensification of Jewish-Christian polemics, however, in the fourteenth century, as illustrated by the exchange between Abner of Burgos and Isaac Polleqar, compelled Jewish philosophers to reconsider their approach. By the turn of the fifteenth century, as Kellner has shown, Jewish philosophers were heavily engaged in reformulating the dogmas of Judaism.

By the second third of the fourteenth century and thereafter, Jewish philosophers became more actively involved in the defense of Judaism, marshalling their knowledge of Aristotelian philosophy to prove that Christianity is an irrational religion—its God commits what is logically impossible—and that the dogmas of Judaism, which serve as the foundation of the Torah, are rational. The rationality of Judaism, which Maimonides established most consistently, provided the rationale against conversion to Christianity.

Mosaic Prophecy

Though Abner's critique of Judaism would compel Jewish philosophers to reconsider many of their views, his immediate conversation partner, Isaac Polleqar, was not persuaded by his arguments and continued to endorse the Maimonidean rationalist interpretation of Judaism. For Polleqar, Judaism was the sole path to individual salvation because the Torah is the most perfect law, and its perfection, in turn, resides in the singularity of Moses' prophecy. The prophet Moses was the most perfect human being

> whose soul was withdrawn, detached from its matter and despising it. [The soul of Moses] changed the laws of nature and performed the well-known miracles in the same way as the separate forms change matter at their will; Moses prophesied whenever he wished to do so . . . and all this because he was always conjoined to the spiritual [beings] and had become divine, perfect.

By living the moral life, as dictated by the commandments of the Torah, a Jew can purify his soul from association with matter, enabling him to become a "polished mirror" (*Ezer ha-Dat*, p. 42) that reflects the intelligible order of the sub-lunar world.[94] Since this is not a technical philosophical treatise, it is difficult to determine what Polleqar's position was on the nature of the human soul, but it seems reasonable to assume that his views were very similar to those of Moses Narboni.

Polleqar's defense of Maimonidean rationalism, we should note, was presented in contradistinction to the views of the "pseudo-philosophers" (*mitpalsefim*) that he depicted as "undisciplined youngsters" (*ne'arim bilti meyusarim*) who are "heretics [and] cursed fools" (*koferim, ha-sekhalim ha-arurim*). According to Polleqar, as soon as these youngsters study logic, they raise questions about the validity and authority of the received tradition[95] (*Ezer ha-Dat*, p. 42). Polleqar's "philosophers" are indeterminate, but his comments make it reasonable to assume that the "professionalization" of Jewish philosophy, as a result of the absorption of Aristotelian logic, gave rise to skepticism about many traditional claims.

The Maimonidean Controversy, then, did not end with the ban on the study of philosophy in 1306; it continued to simmer throughout the next century and beyond. In the fourteenth century, however, the controversy looked very similar to the debates between the members of the theology faculty and the masters of the liberal arts at the University of Paris during the 1270s,[96] though the Jews did not experience these debates in the context of formal institutions. Regardless, the mastery of Aristotelian sciences by the early fourteenth century may have brought about challenges to many traditional beliefs and Jewish traditions. Polleqar's semi-philosophical work is an attempt to address those challenges.

Determinism and Choice: Intellect and Will

A major aspect of the internal controversies in the fourteenth century concerned the question of determinism and choice. The Jewish rationalists, as noted above, followed Aristotle in claiming that voluntary acts are motivations to do what the intellect judges to be good. Prior to Abner, Jewish Aristotelian philosophers did not recognize the will as a distinct psychic function independent of the intellect, and therefore they spoke only of "voluntary choice" and not "free will." Abner, by contrast, was steeped in the scholasticism of his day,[97] and he distinguished between the operation of the intellect and the will and proposed a new position in terms of the tension between determinism and choice. Charles Manekin summarizes Abner's position as follows:

> Abner defined a voluntary agent as one who can, by his nature, equally perform one of two alternatives, that is, one who is not constrained by his nature, or by virtue of himself, to perform just one alternative. But that agent has no control over what he does or refrains from doing. What causes him to pursue one alternative and not the other is a combination of the motivating stimulus (sense images, cognition, or "intelligible imagination"), which stretches back in a causal chain to the movement of the spheres, and the imaginative faculty; this conjunction yields a new asset which Abner calls the "complete will." So actions are voluntary insofar as they are the product of a will, but completely determined insofar as the will is part of a rigid causal

chain. If there are various outcomes, it is only because the will can be determined in various ways.[98]

Causal determinism and human deliberation, then, are compatible. However, most fourteenth-century Jewish rationalists rejected Abner's psychological approach to the problem and remained committed to the intellectualism of the Maimonidean tradition. Abner's position, however, did influence Hasdai Crescas, who was the main critic of Maimonides and Gersonides and of the philosophic conception of happiness.

Hasdai Crescas' Critique of and Alternative to Maimonideanism

An Overview of Crescas' Endeavor

From the perspective of technical philosophy, Hasdai Crescas was perhaps the most original Jewish philosopher in the Middle Ages; his only equal was Gersonides. Crescas was born to an old Jewish family in Barcelona in 1340 and his Jewish education was supervised by Nissim Gerondi (c. 1310–1375), a learned halakhist and moralist who was very familiar with the Maimonidean tradition but did not endorse its radical intellectualism. Already in 1367 Crescas emerged as a communal authority in Barcelona, and when he moved to Saragossa, the capital of Aragon, he was appointed Chief Rabbi by King John II. In 1383 he negotiated the renewal of the privileges of the Jews of Aragon, and during the riots of 1391, in which he lost his only son, he hired a militia to defend the Jews. Thereafter, Crescas supervised the effort to rebuild Jewish communal life in Spain.[99]

Crescas' conviction that philosophy was the catalyst for the moral and spiritual bankruptcy of Spanish Jewry was also voiced by rabbinic orators such as Shlomo Alami in Portugal, who had but a superficial exposure to philosophic literature.[100] The view was also held by people, such as Shem Tov ibn Shem Tov, who were themselves steeped in the Maimonidean tradition, but who forsook philosophy to embrace kabbalah.[101] Though kabbalah would become a credible substitute for Maimonideanism only after 1492, ibn Shem Tov's response to the crisis of 1391 anticipated that shift.

Viewing Maimonides' intellectualism as the direct cause of Iberian Jewry's spiritual breakdown, Crescas set out to liberate rabbinic Judaism from the clutches of Aristotelian philosophy. While he was inspired by a similar attempt undertaken during the twelfth century by Judah Halevi, the way Crescas went about it was informed by challenges to Aristotle's natural philosophy during the fourteenth century, especially in Merton College at Oxford University and the College of Navarre at the University of Paris.[102]

In Oxford the critics of Aristotle focused on his theories of motion, developing new mathematics and new physical theories to account for the motion of projectiles. In Paris, the critique was directed against Aristotle's notions of space, time, void, and causality.

Crescas' access to the so-called new physics was most likely derived from Nicole Oresme, as several scholars have noted.[103] Since Oresme taught at the College of Navarre at the University of Paris from 1348 to 1362, it is possible that Crescas either heard about his teachings from his students in Navarre or had access to copies of his works.[104] Between the Kingdom of Navarre and the Kingdom of Aragon there were many commercial and cultural ties that made Crescas' access to Oresme imaginable. For example, Crescas' own work was exported to Christian scholars; a long excerpt from Crescas' *Or Ha-Shem* (Light of the Lord) was translated into Latin by Gianfrancesco Pico della Mirandola in his *Examen Vanitatis Doctrina Gentium* (1520). It would influence Christian thinkers during the sixteenth and seventeenth centuries.[105]

Crescas' main composition, *Light of the Lord*, was completed in 1410, but it was in the making for several years beforehand. Warren Harvey has shown that Crescas revised the text several times between 1405 and 1410 but that the final version preserved earlier versions.[106] As a result, the final text contains contradictory positions that can be reconciled only if one assumes that Crescas changed his views over time. This assumption is further supported by comparing his *Light* with his earlier "Sermon on Passover,"[107] which dealt with theological matters such as the epistemic status of faith, the freedom of will, perfection of the intellect, miracles, and prophecy, as well as legal aspects of the Passover holiday. Crescas was aware of the tensions between the views he expressed earlier, in the "Sermon," and his more mature position in the *Light*. He tried to smooth out the differences, but he was not entirely successful.

It is difficult to summarize Crescas' views: not only did he change them over time, but his thought was primarily critical and not systematic or constructive. Furthermore, his critique proceeded on several fronts, at the same time using the very categories he criticized. With reference to Aristotle, Crescas' critique was directed against his physics and cosmology, but it was carried out by using Aristotelian logic. Similarly, while he was critical of both Maimonides' theory of intellectual perfection and his attempt to articulate the dogmas of Judaism, Crescas himself continued to speak about the human soul in terms of Aristotelian psychology. Furthermore, Crescas affirmed a dogmatic approach to Judaism, even though he presented a view of Jewish dogmas that differed significantly from his predecessors.[108]

Crescas himself was involved in anti-Christian polemics and battled the influential proselytizing of Abner of Burgos. His *Bittul Iqqarey ha-Notzrim (Refutation of the Christian Principles)* was written in the Catalan vernacular, although the only extant version is the Hebrew translation by Joseph ibn Shem Tov from 1451.[109] Crescas' views in this document on the meaning of faith and the problem of determinism and choice suggest the influence of Abner as well as familiarity with the positions of Christian scholastics such as Thomas Aquinas and Duns Scotus.[110]

None of this should diminish the stature of Crescas' thought: all conversations involve to some degree the adoption and adaptation of the views held by the conversation partner. Crescas' originality lies in his ability to rethink the fundamental assumptions of the Aristotelian worldview, and to challenge the conventions of Jewish rationalist culture in order to revive what he considered to be the authentic meaning of Jewish life.

CRESCAS' CRITIQUE OF THE ARISTOTELIAN-MAIMONIDEAN PARADIGM

Critique of Aristotle's Physics

Crescas mounted a two-pronged attack on Aristotelian philosophy. First, he attempted to undermine the validity of Aristotle's philosophy by disproving Aristotle's physics. Second, Crescas refuted Maimonides' political theory, especially the conception of ultimate human happiness.

Crescas rejected Aristotle's picture of the universe as a self-contained hierarchy of beings in which each entity tends towards its own natural place. His goal here was not to construct an alternative outlook, but only to disprove the claims that all Aristotelian philosophers took for granted. By refuting the scientific foundations of Jewish philosophy, Crescas believed he could convince his contemporaries to renounce their loyalty to the Aristotelian-Maimonidean paradigm, which he believed contributed to the spiritual decline of Spanish Jewry.

Crescas' attempted refutation of Aristotle's physics and cosmology cannot be reproduced here in detail. Some of his major conclusions include the following claims: The infinite can exist *in actu*; the infinite can be an incorporeal extension; the vacuum does exist as an incorporeal continuous magnitude; space is an "infinite magnitude" (*godel bilti ba'al takhlit*) and would exist even if there were no physical objects in the universe; the place of a thing is the interval or the vacuum of the distance that is occupied by the thing; an infinite number of proper places is possible; time too is separate from physical objects: it exists "in the soul," and is not the "number of motion or rest of physical objects," as Aristotle defined it; time is infinite, and is eternal in the past and in the future; a plurality of worlds is logically possible; there can be an infinite series of causes; the motion of the spheres can be explained without assuming that they are animate beings endowed with will. As Colette Sirat summarizes, "infinity of space, infinity of time, infinity of causal series, because God is infinite—this is Crescas' central intuition."[111] To some extent this insight was inspired by the kabbalistic conception of the *Ein Sof*, as W. Harvey has noted.[112]

Critique of Maimonides' Views: The Impossibility of the Acquired Intellect

Having refuted the principles of Aristotle's physics, which Maimonides summarized in the *Guide* under 25 premises, Crescas directed his attack against Maimonides' intellectualism and his view of ultimate felicity. Crescas ascribed to Maimonides a strong reading of the "exclusive" interpretation of happiness, according to which man's ultimate felicity resides in one activity only—contemplation of God by the acquired intellect. Crescas charged that this ideal of happiness is subversive to Judaism because it denies personal immortality and ignores the intrinsic value accorded by the rabbinic tradition to performance of the commandments. Moreover, it is philosophically unsound because the doctrine of the acquired intellect is self-contradictory.[113]

In the *Light of the Lord* II:6, Crescas presented his alternative understanding of man's ultimate felicity. Accepting Aristotelian teleology (at least for the sake of the argument), he set out to determine the ultimate purpose of the law "inductively" (*derekh ha-ḥipus*). He showed that it secures four perfections: (1) perfection of moral qualities (*shelemut ha-middot*), 2) perfection of opinions (*shelemut ha-de`ot*), (3) bodily well-being, or happiness (*hatzlaḥot gufaniyot*), and (4) the well-being of the soul (*hatzlaḥot nafshiyot*). On the surface the list appears to resemble Maimonides' four perfections, but in fact Crescas' position was a direct assault on Maimonides' contemplative ideal of happiness.

Crescas agreed that the ultimate end of human life requires the attainment of certain perfections—perfection of the body, perfection of moral qualities, and perfection of opinions. He further conceded that these three perfections are hierarchically ordered, so that bodily and moral perfections are subordinate to perfection of opinions. However, he sharply disagreed with Maimonides (and the Jewish Aristotelians) about the "perfection of opinions." Whereas Maimonides held that cognition of intelligibles is the source of eternal perdurance, Crescas severed the connections between cognition and eternal happiness. By so doing, he indirectly argued against Christianity by claiming that salvation does not depend on holding certain views, least of all the doctrines of the Church.[114] In chapter nine of his *Bittul Iqqarey ha-Notzrim*, Crescas made the point explicit. The chapter considers Christian arguments against the eternality of the Torah and its salvific power and refutes them one by one.

To prove that perfection of opinions does not lead to eternal life, Crescas proceeded to refute the concept of an acquired intellect.[115] First, the notion is self-contradictory because an acquired intellect is both the form of a man and a substance separate from that man. Second, according to this concept, a man is truly human only through becoming an intellectual substance *in actu*. However, since such a substance is different from the man "in species," a man is most human when he becomes a non-man, which is self-contradictory. Third, the notion that the intellect becomes a substance through its objects of cognition is absurd because it requires that "the individuals of all species would be one in number."

Finally, when Maimonides' concept of the acquired intellect is viewed in relation to his negative theology, it would follow that transcendence through conjunction with a separate intelligence is impossible since human beings have only negative knowledge of incorporeal beings. Therefore the acquired intellect cannot be the part of man that survives death.[116] Hence if perfection of opinion does not lead to personal immortality, it must belong to temporal, or bodily, happiness. Crescas concludes that the doctrine of the acquired intellect is both philosophically unsound and religiously heretical.

CRESCAS' MOVE FROM INTELLECTUALISM TO VOLUNTARISM

The Intellectualism of Aristotelianism: Maimonides and Gersonides

After 1391 Jewish philosophers had a harder time endorsing Maimonidean intellectualism wholeheartedly. How could a Jewish rationalist account for the mass conversion of Jews to Christianity? If one is to approach this event on the basis of Maimonides' intellectualism, he would have to conclude that the Jews became convinced that Christianity is intellectually and spiritually superior to Judaism. Conversely, a strict intellectualist position could not account for the fact that many Jews still remained loyal to their tradition, despite the mass conversion. It appears that intellectual assent to certain propositions was not the only way to account for human conduct; other factors had to be taken into consideration as well—most importantly, the human will. The new historical situation, I believe, brought a shift from the exclusive focus on the intellect (in God and in humans) to a new focus on the will (in both God and humans).[117]

Whereas Maimonides and all the Aristotelians thereafter conceptualized God as a pure intellect, Crescas viewed Him primarily as a lover who "possesses passion, will, joy, and love and all with infinite power."[118] According to Crescas, God is not an intellect that thinks itself eternally, but a personal, infinite, dynamic, and free entity whose "will is his essence." The infinite divine goodness is expressed when God willingly decides to emanate existents and sustain them as a "divine gift of love."

Whereas Maimonides, we recall, held that we cannot have positive knowledge of God's essence, Gersonides argued that some positive knowledge of God's essence is possible. Gersonides, therefore, did attribute joy and love to God, but he understood these terms in the context of God's perfect cognition. Like Aristotle, Gersonides regarded intellection as the most pleasurable, delightful, and glorious of activities: it is devoid of materiality, it is eternal, and it is effortless. Because God is the most perfect intellect, ultimate joy belongs to God. Gersonides was even willing to speak about God's love of the world in terms of passion, and he explained the love of the subject (God) for the object (world) in the context of his explanation of creation. As the creator of the world "God worked six days and on the seventh day" God passionately loved his work which he had made, that is, the intelligible of his work, which is the *nomos* of existing things, their order, and their organization.[119]

In his Commentary on I Chronicles:16, Gersonides enumerates "the foundations of the law and of faith (*pinnot atzumot mi-pinnot ha-Torah ve-ha-emunah*)." The fourth foundational principle is

> that the ultimate happiness and delight is God's, may He be blessed, and so it behooves every human being to connect with this wondrous joy, as far as he can, and one attains this when one intellectually cognizes and knows God, may He be blessed, in accordance with one's ability.[120]

In other words, for Gersonides the ultimate delight is cognitive.

Crescas' Critique of Gersonides' Conception of Divine Love

Fully familiar with Gersonides' works, Crescas thought that Gersonides' views on love and joy were self-contradictory and thus unacceptable.

Crescas agreed with Aristotle and the Aristotelians that joy and love are passions, and that passions cannot be attributed to God. If joy and love are to be attributed to Him, He has to be understood not as a pure intellect but as an active *will*. Crescas defines will as "nothing but the love of the one who wills for that which he wills" (III:1:5). And love for him is "nothing but the pleasure of the will" (*ein . . . zulat arevut ha-ratzon*).[121] Crescas could dissociate intellection and love because he emphasized God as an active agent who brings everything into existence, namely, as a creator.

As the creator, God is not a being that can possess passions. Instead, "God is the true agent of all existent things by intention and will." God's love has no direct object (as Gersonides depicted it), but it is the rejoicing that God experiences when He "causes His good to overflow into his created beings."[122] We can now see the connection between Crescas' critique of Aristotle's physics and his rejection of Maimonidean intellectualism. God's creative activity is itself an expression of joy and love, which stem from His own essence. As creator, God is not so much the most perfect knower (or intellect) but the most perfect lover.[123] God's love expresses God's essence, goodness, and benevolence. God's love of the universe is not the love of a subject for an object, but an essential property of God's own perfection.

> Inasmuch as it is known that God, may He be blessed, is the source and foundation of all perfections, and in virtue of His perfection, which is His essence, He loves the good, as may be seen from His actions in bringing into existence the entire universe, sustaining it perpetually, and continuously creating it anew, and all by means of His simple will, it must necessarily be that the love of the good is an essential property of perfection. It follows from this that the greater the perfection [of the lover] the greater will be the love and the pleasure in the desire.[124]

Because God's love is perfect and infinite, His creative activity is not limited to but one world; nor is God's love limited to the temporal creation of the world at a particular moment in time. Rather, God's infinite love requires the creation of an infinite number of worlds, and is manifested in the "perpetual creation" of our world, precisely as the rabbinic morning prayer states in gratitude for God who "in his goodness creates daily."[125] God eternally and perpetually wills the world into existence out of His infinite divine goodness. In so doing, God's love (the expression of His will) not only sustains the world, it also functions as the perfection of natural things.

Divine Providence Reconsidered

By claiming that God's love is the cosmic principle that sustains all existence, Crescas in effect reformulated the philosophic doctrine of providence in a manner that expresses the personalist conception of God in rabbinic Judaism. For Crescas, the infinite universe is held together by the abundance of infinite, divine love that regulates both the cosmic order and human affairs. This worldview was expressed most beautifully in the religious poetry of Judah Halevi in the twelfth century. Like Halevi in his philosophical critique of medieval Aristotelianism, Crescas insisted that God, rather than a series of incorporeal intermediaries, is the causal explanation of the universe. This notion could be traced to the ancient Greek philosopher Empedocles and was later adopted by Judah Abrabanel (Leone Ebreo), one of the major Jewish exponents of humanism at the turn of the sixteenth century.

Ultimate Felicity

Crescas' emphasis on love as a cosmic principle transformed his understanding of human happiness. If God is a lover par excellence, to imitate God so as to be perfect involves not the contemplation of eternal intelligibles but the love of God. Crescas proceeds to replace the Maimonidean view of ultimate felicity with a non-intellectualist interpretation of human love that focuses on the willingness of the individual to be committed to God. The primacy of love as an activity of the will is presented, however, in the context of the traditional Judeo-Muslim discourse on happiness, which focuses on the intellect rather than on the will.

Crescas agreed with Maimonides and his followers that the ultimate end of human life and the ultimate purpose of the law is the happiness of the soul. However, whereas Maimonides and the Jewish Aristotelians viewed the soul as an insubstantial form of the body, Crescas defined it as a "spiritual substance, disposed to intellectual cognition."[126] Crescas' definition is very close to that of Themistius, which is found also in ibn Sina and to some extent in Aquinas: as an incorporeal substance, the soul is self-subsistent and hence capable of immortality. Man's ultimate felicity consists of a kind of life that is commensurate with the nature of the soul as an incorporeal substance; hence it is evident that its happiness does not belong to life in this world (where the soul is commingled with the body), but to the afterlife (once the soul is separated from the body). This happiness of the soul is predicated not on cognitive activity but on the ability of the will to freely choose the good.

The Love of God and Individual Immortality

It is the love for God, said Crescas, that leads to the eternal life of the individual soul. Human love for God, however, is reflected not in the contemplation of intelligibles but in the actual performance of the commandments. Thus his view of the law varied greatly from that of Maimonides. For Crescas, the Torah is the direct expression of divine will. It is "the product of a voluntary action from the commander, who is the initiator of the action to the commanded, the receiver of the action." The infinitely good God wants His creatures to attain happiness; therefore He disclosed His will by giving them the Torah. To choose to do good is ultimately to choose to do God's will as expressed in the commandments. The one who chooses God and loves God truly hearkens "unto Him with exceeding alacrity to fulfill His commandments, and with great vigilance not to transgress His prohibitions, with joy and goodness of the heart."[127] The more diligent one is in the performance of divine commandments, the greater the happiness and joy one finds in this world. Shifting the focus from the intellect to the will and severing the connection between cognitive activity and pleasure, Crescas maintained that perfection is in love, and pleasure is in the act of willing.

The Will and the Performance of Commandments

Crescas' emphasis on the performance of the commandments was directed against both the Jewish Aristotelians and against Christianity. Unlike Maimonides who followed Aristotle in subordinating action to thought, Crescas insisted that action is intrinsic to the attainment of happiness of the soul. The Torah does not merely establish the political order in which the intellectually gifted few can attain perfection; it defines the very activities that enable the soul to retain its essential incorporeality—that is, its holiness.

By highlighting the importance of actual performance of the mitzvot, Crescas obliterated the Maimonidean hierarchy between the philosophers and the multitude: performance of the commandments is obligatory for all Jews, regardless of whether they hold perfect opinions or not.

Moreover, Crescas' emphasis on actual performance of the commandments has a clear anti-Christian import as well. The road to the personal immortality of the soul lies not in holding certain views, but in the performance of specific commandments that only Israel received directly from God. Only those who observe the divine commandments—Israel—can be saved. "True love and service" for God will be rewarded by "adhesion [*devequt*] unto the radiance of His indwelling."[128]

Love for God, said Crescas, is "an essential property of perfection,"[129] and "the greater the love between God, may He be blessed, and man, the greater and stronger will be the adhesion.[130] Perfect happiness, then, is the conjunction of the separated soul with God in the afterlife. This infinite delight constitutes the "world to come" as Crescas understood it. However, while this spiritual delight pertained only to the afterlife, the very enjoyment and vigorous pleasure yearned for by the righteous ones lead them to delight and take pleasure in this life, even while their souls are still conjoined to matter.

CRESCAS' MORAL-RELIGIOUS PHILOSOPHY

Crescas' Voluntarism

Crescas' conception of God as lover reaffirms the rabbinic personalist and non-intellectualist understanding of the deity as much as it resonates with elements in theosophic kabbalah. Because God is understood to be an active will rather than an intellect, and because humans are created in the image of God, Crescas would also have new things to say about the operation of the human will in the attainment of human perfection. For this reason it is appropriate to designate Crescas' position as "voluntarism" in contradistinction to the intellectualism of the Maimonidean tradition. However, "voluntarism" does not mean that Crescas believed that one is free to *act* capriciously or arbitrarily, or to *believe* whatever one wishes. To understand the meaning of Crescas' "voluntarism," we need to explore his views on the main issue debated among Jewish philosophers in the fourteenth century—the relationship between causal determinism and human choice.

Crescas discussed the operation of the human will in two distinct contexts—acts of will with respect to *belief* and with respect to *action*. In terms of beliefs, Crescas' rejected the entire Maimonidean enterprise of defining those beliefs, i.e., the dogmas of Judaism that all Jews *must* believe in order to attain immortal life. According to Crescas, not only are Jews *not* commanded to believe that God exists (the existence of God is conspicuously missing from Crescas' list of true beliefs that constitute the foundations of Judaism), but *Jews are not commanded to believe anything*. Crescas argues that assent or denial of a given proposition is *not* a matter of choice or will. Believing or not believing is *not* a volitional act, because all *true* beliefs are *compelled* upon the believer, either because of logical demonstration or because of empirical facts. The believer does not have a choice whether to believe or not to believe, because belief is a matter of correspondence between a certain cognitive content and an objective reality. The evidence itself (logical or empirical) "forces" itself on the believer.[131] The belief in Sinaitic revelation is one example of a compelling belief the evidence for which is (presumably) historical. There are other true beliefs, such as the dogmas of Judaism; reason can demonstrate them, but Jews are compelled to believe in them as well.[132]

Yitzhak Baer was the first modern scholar to argue that Crescas developed his position on these issues by wrestling with the views of Abner of Burgos, through whom Crescas became familiar with scholastic authors—especially Thomas Aquinas and Duns Scotus—whose views left traces in Crescas' own formulation. Aviezer Ravitzky has shown that Crescas was familiar with Aquinas' analysis of faith as a special epistemological category situated between opinion and knowledge. For Aquinas, faith is distinguished from knowledge in that it is not cognitively compelling. The gap between the subjectively strong conviction of the believer and objectively weak proof is bridged by divine grace, which moves the will to assent to true propositions that limited human reason cannot demonstrate.[133]

The Relation between Will and Cognition

In contrast to Aquinas, however, Crescas rejected the notion that the will moves the intellect in the realm of cognitive activity; belief is not a voluntary act. For Crescas, divine grace is found not in the internal conviction of the believer, but in the objective miraculous history of the people of Israel. However, he acknowledged a tension between the emotional posture of the believer and objective reality. In this regard, Ravitzky argues plausibly, Crescas' view was close to that of Duns Scotus, who also distinguished between the content of belief and the effort of the believer to assent to certain beliefs. Scotus spoke about *delectio*, which comes as a result of the volitional act, and Crescas spoke about "the delight of the will" (*arevut ha-ratzon*). For Crescas, too, the will does not motivate the believer to hold certain convictions, but to *feel joy* in celebrating certain views. The will is thus the emotional energy that enables believers to deepen their orientation toward God. As Seymour Feldman has put it, "The believer is free in regard to the emotional stance toward 'binding' beliefs, namely, joy or regret."[134]

The Relation between Will and Divine Providence

Precisely because beliefs are not voluntary, Crescas rejects the connection between holding certain, true beliefs and gaining the reward of the afterlife, which characterized the position of all rationalists. Reward and punishment in Judaism are appropriate only for volitional acts, and, because holding certain beliefs is not voluntary, God does not reward or punish individuals for their beliefs. Rather, reward is commensurate, as Charles Manekin put it, with "the attitude of joy and pleasure that one takes toward one's belief as well as the diligence that one displays in confirming their truths."[135]

Crescas does not explain with sufficient clarity how the human will operates, and it appears that his views underwent change over time.[136] Ravitzky showed that earlier in his career (reflected in the "Sermon on Passover" and in the early version of the *Light*) Crescas held that reward is given to the *inner* decision to do the good rather than to the external action. Reward and punishment follow necessarily from a certain mental posture—the decision of the will to do the good. Later in his career (i.e., in the later stratum of the *Light*), Crescas attempted to distinguish between a cause that compels the believer to hold a certain view that is not accompanied with an awareness or consciousness of freedom on one hand, and a cause that is accompanied with such awareness. In Crescas' later teachings, one is compelled to choose the good, namely God, and is rewarded for this choice by the joy of cleaving to God.

In matters of action, however, the status of the will is quite different: the will is free to *act or not to act*. Crescas apparently adopted Abner's position that an act is free if it is motivated by the will, even if this will and this act are subject to a causal chain that is itself necessary. The act is free if the agent does not *feel* compelled to do it. As Seymour Feldman has put it, Crescas asserted "both that the human will is free and that all events, including human behavior, are governed by strict causal laws."[137] Feldman explains that Crescas, as did Abner before him, distinguished between "an act that is compelled and an act that is merely caused." In the former, the act is externally brought about without the agent's consent; in the latter the "origin" of the act is the agent's desire, wish, or motive."[138] An act can thus be both caused (as far as its origin is concerned) and voluntary. A free, voluntary act is recognized by the "feeling of joy which expresses the personality of the agent." Accordingly, reward and punishment are meted out for the choice itself, and not for the deed that follows from that act.[139]

Although Crescas was a philosopher of the first order, he shifted the focus of religious life from *contemplating truths* to *choosing to do the right thing*. The choice expresses the choice of God, which is the choice of the good. It is this choice that involves a "desire and joy" to seek intimacy with God. For

Crescas, the religious life is about *commitment* to God, the very commitment that many Jews failed to make in 1391 and thereafter.

Between Crescas and Maimonides

Crescas' alternative to Maimonides and Gersonides compelled subsequent philosophers to choose between two distinctive philosophies of Judaism. What was at stake was not only the legitimacy of rationalism within Jewish traditional society, but also the survival of the whole medieval conceptual framework that Maimonides' philosophy represented. Crescas' refutation of Aristotelianism was devastating, but because it was too original, most Jewish philosophers in the first half of the fifteenth century were not ready to accept it. Because Crescas' critique was derived from a theoretical analysis of Aristotle's own premises and employed the tools of Aristotelian logic, Jewish philosophers interpreted it as internal criticism of Aristotle rather than as a dismantling of the Aristotelian worldview. Moreover, Crescas did not (and could not) offer a full-fledged cosmological alternative to the Aristotelian one he had debunked. To back up his claims against Aristotle, he would have needed the kind of new scientific data that would be supplied in the sixteenth century by Galileo, Newton, and other astronomers and physicists. In this sense, one can agree with Ravitzky that Crescas "came too late in one respect and too early in another respect."[140]

By the same token, most Sephardic intellectuals of the time were unprepared to accept Crescas' assault on Maimonideanism, the cultural program that had given the Iberian Jewish aristocracy its distinct identity. To give up the Maimonidean legacy was to commit cultural suicide. It is not surprising, therefore, that Crescas' own students (Joseph Albo, Matityahu ha-Yitzhari, Zehariya ha-Levi, and Abraham Shalom) and others scholars (e.g., Simon ben Zemah Duran, Isaac Arama, and Isaac Abravanel) did not adopt Crescas' innovative views on free will and determinism, the primacy of the human will, and the compulsory dimensions of faith.[141] Nor did fifteenth-century thinkers endorse Crescas' attempt to sever the link between intellectual perfection and human felicity, between Torah and philosophic wisdom. They continued to defend the Maimonidean intellectualist approach to human happiness and to claim that the final good consists of the knowledge of God. This is not to say that Crescas' thought had no impact whatsoever. Some elements of his critique of Maimonides were accepted by the very scholars who remained loyal to Maimonides. Iberian scholars during the fifteenth and sixteenth centuries agreed with Crescas' claims that perfection of the soul cannot be attained merely through cognitive activity in this world but only in the afterlife, that the final good consists in cleaving to God and not only in knowledge of God's governance in the world, and that only a revelation from God directs man to the ultimate felicity. Charting a middle course between Maimonides and Crescas, these philosophers offered a new reconciliation of Aristotelianism and rabbinic Judaism and a new perspective on man's ultimate felicity. Indeed, these changes in Jewish Aristotelianism made possible the gradual transition from philosophy to kabbalah by the early seventeenth century.

SUMMARY

In the fourteenth century the discourse on happiness changed as a result of the intense confrontation of Judaism with Christianity. Maimonides' view of happiness was given a strict intellectualist reading that reflected the growing self-confidence of the philosophers. It was argued that ultimate felicity consists of the perfection of the human intellect alone and that cognitive perfection entails mastering all there is to know, including having some positive knowledge of God. The moral virtues that are cultivated in the political sphere are at best a means to an end; the moral life itself does not constitute the immortality of the intellect. Perfection of the intellect was explained in the context of Aristotle's theory of knowledge, which was now better understood through the commentaries of ibn Rushd.

The radical intellectualist understanding of happiness went hand in hand with a growing confidence in the ability of the human mind to know the intelligible order of the universe, and with a growing interest in the processes of the natural world that were assumed to be determined by the celestial spheres. The more Jewish thinkers trusted their ability to know how the sub-lunar world works, the more they approached Scriptures as a scientific-philosophic text that was amenable to rational explication. Since the philosophers relinquished esotericism and believed that the deep meanings of the Torah were explicable by human rational knowledge, they could be easily accused of disrespect for the received tradition.

These accusations pertained to the core of the identification between Torah and Wisdom that underlies the discourse on happiness. If the Torah says exactly what is known through rational knowledge, then why is philosophy necessary? At least the intellectually perfect philosopher appears to have little need to consult the Torah, since its philosophic meaning is totally known by natural means. Furthermore, if the Torah is a figurative expression of philosophic truths for the sake of the nonphilosophical masses, then it appears to be subordinate to philosophy. Finally, if the Torah is a store of scientific knowledge that leads either to intellectual perfection or to manipulation of natural processes (as endorsed by the advocates of astrology and astral magic), then it only has instrumental value. However one looks at it, the more intellectually rigorous and consistent Jewish rationalists became in the fourteenth century, the more problematic became the identification of Torah with scientific wisdom.

The philosophic conception of happiness was reconsidered in the wake of the crisis of 1391 and the mass conversion of Jews to Christianity. In the aftermath of these events, Crescas identified genuine difficulties in the cognitive theories that underscored the radical version of Jewish rationalism in the fourteenth century. If happiness means the perfection of the intellect and its immortality, attaining immortality becomes either too trivial, making the life of Torah irrelevant to perfection, or humanly impossible, making the pursuit of wisdom an exercise in futility. In the fifteenth century Jewish philosophers addressed these challenges by retreating from the boldness of the fourteenth century and asserting the qualitative difference between the supra-rational and salvific knowledge of the Torah and the human knowledge about the operation of the natural world. They ascribed this view to Maimonides in order to defend him against Crecas' critique and to affirm the commitment to Aristotelian philosophy and its cultural program. Interestingly, the conservative interpretation of Aristotelian philosophy among Jewish thinkers paralleled the views of the Christian theologian Thomas Aquinas.

9

Religious Perfection and the Interplay of Philosophy and Kabbalah

With the gradual demise of medieval Jewish Aristotelianism and the emergence of kabbalah to become the dominant exposition of rabbinic Judaism during the seventeenth and eighteenth centuries, the premodern discourse on happiness ended. This final chapter of our story, then, traces the transformation of the concept during the fifteenth and sixteenth centuries. It is the most fascinating period in our study, but also the most puzzling: the interplay of philosophy and kabbalah appears to be full of contradictory trends.

In the fifteenth and sixteenth centuries, Jewish intellectuals in Spain, Italy, and the Ottoman Empire continued to reason about human happiness in terms of Aristotelian ethics. They even gained a better command of the ancient text by composing new Hebrew translations and commentaries. The mastery of the *Ethics* by Jewish intellectuals matched the popularity of the text among Christian academics, noblemen, and courtiers, and manifested Jewish interest in scholastic and humanist texts. Jewish thinkers, however, were increasingly aware of the limitations of human reason and insisted that philosophic knowledge alone is not sufficient to lead one to eternal life. Human reason must be complemented and perfected by supra-rational truths that can be known only through revelation. Mastery of vast philosophical literature, then, went hand in hand with awareness of the limits of philosophy.

Another source of apparent contradiction was that trained Aristotelian philosophers also had a positive attitude toward kabbalah. It would gradually be viewed as an integral part of the divinely revealed tradition and the *Zohar* would be accepted as an authentic, authoritative rabbinic midrash. Since the philosophers subordinated philosophic knowledge to the revealed tradition, they either adopted kabbalistic themes, especially in regard to the human soul, its origin and destiny, or gave kabbalah a philosophical exposition. Kabbalah, however, was rooted in Platonic and Neoplatonic ontology and psychology. Thus while the discourse on happiness was framed within the conceptual vocabulary of medieval Aristotelianism, it was also suffused with Platonic and Neoplatonic themes as well as with kabbalistic motifs.

Third, Jewish thinkers became more familiar with Christian authors, referring to them directly and treating them with respect. At the same time, however, Jewish thinkers espoused highly ethnocentric views, according to which Jews were ontologically superior to non-Jews. The Jewish soul was now claimed to be literally a divine substance, and the life of Torah was geared to protecting and enhancing its holiness. The ultimate end of human life was framed in religious terms as a mystical absorption of the holy soul into the divine source. And the happiest life—the bliss of immortality—was reserved for Jews alone, not only because their life of Torah was the best social order, but because their souls were of inherently higher quality. Thus openness to European culture went hand in hand with an assertion of Jewish spiritual uniqueness.

Fourth, in the fifteenth and sixteenth centuries, philosophy was no longer an esoteric subject taught to the elite few and hidden from the masses. Instead, larger segments of the educated public cultivated its study and had access to philosophical texts from printed editions. Although the texts to be printed were carefully chosen, privileging theological treatises over technical discourses, philosophic literature became a household commodity for the literate public. Furthermore, philosophy was routinely used in public preaching in the synagogue, for exposition of sacred texts, and in the shaping the moral training of youth. But as philosophy became more widely accepted, it also lost its intellectual rigor as well as its naturalist edge. With the exception of ethics, Jewish philosophy in the last phase of the premodern period was engaged in consolidation, systematization, and summation of ideas that were in place centuries before. By and large, the creative impetus in Judaism was now to be found not in philosophy but in kabbalah and its hermeneutics of Jewish sacred texts. And by the end of the sixteenth century philosophy was fully subordinated to theology and to biblical exegesis.

These seeming contradictions make more sense if we keep in mind the historical conditions of the Jews during the fifteenth and sixteenth centuries. The dubious fruits of mass conversion—the emergence of a distinct class of New Christians—were a constant source of tension between the Christian society and its Jewish minority. The *conversos* posed numerous legal, economic, and theological problems for professing Jews, and curtailing contacts between them and *conversos* was the main reason for the expulsion of the Jews from Spain in 1492. The decree of expulsion was extended to the dominions of the Spanish Crown in Sicily (1493) and in the Kingdom of Naples (1510). With other expulsions, from Provence (1494) and from Portugal (1497)—the latter after a brutal forced conversion—Western Europe was practically devoid of professing Jews. The expulsions spelled displacement, humiliation, loss of possessions, dangerous travel, harassment, abuse, captivity, starvation, diseases, rape of women, breakup of families, and death.[1] They did not, however, curtail Jewish culture, and paradoxically may even have contributed to its creative growth during the sixteenth century. Similarly the expulsions did not sever Jewish ties with *conversos*: throughout the sixteenth century these converts left Iberia and returned to the Jewish fold in Italy, the Ottoman Empire, and the Netherlands. As the university-educated ex-*conversos* integrated themselves into established Jewish communities, they introduced their new coreligionists to European culture. But, in turn, this development came with greater intrusion of the Inquisition into Jewish affairs, renewed conversionary pressures on Jews, censorship of Jewish books, and formal public debates. In Italy after 1555 the Church and the secular authorities instituted a harsh policy of residential segregation, restriction on Jewish economic activities, and repression of Jewish culture.

The last phase of the discourse on happiness manifested the Jewish response to this harsh historical reality. The more Jews were excluded, marginalized, and persecuted by the Christian society, the more they defined their happiness in religious terms that emphasized the qualitative difference between Jews and non-Jews. The sense of Jewish spiritual superiority, however, was entirely compatible with growing openness toward European culture. For Iberian Jews, who were very proud of their Spanish culture and their aristocratic lineage, the conversation with the beloved homeland continued after the expulsion, especially in the Ottoman Empire, where the Jews enjoyed legal protection as *dhimmis* and were free from the persecutions of the Inquisition. For the Jews in Italy, the dazzling achievements of Renaissance culture shaped Jewish cultural sensibilities and initiated new forms of Jewish creativity, even as Jews were forced to live in ghettos. In Italy in particular, contacts between Jewish and Christian scholars intensified: the humanists were deeply interested in the study of Hebrew and had profound respect for kabbalah, which they believed taught the deepest truths of Christianity. If Jews were to curtail the temptation to convert, they had to assert Jewish spiritual superiority.

We can shed further light on the last phase of the discourse on happiness by examining three scholars who are known today only to specialists in medieval Jewish thought. I refer to two Iberian scholars—Joseph ben Shem Tov ibn Shem Tov (ca. 1400—ca.1460), Moses ben Baruch Almosnino (ca.

1515–ca. 1580), and an Italian scholar, Yohanan ben Isaac Alemanno (1433/34–1504). Ibn Shem Tov and Almosnino composed commentaries on the entire *Ethics,* illustrating how the work continued to shape Jewish moral philosophy. Their commentaries provided the categories for describing desirable conduct in worldly affairs and enabled Jews to reflect systematically about the ultimate end of human life. Both ibn Shem Tov and Almosnino manifested continuity with medieval scholasticism as well as openness to Renaissance humanism. Alemanno illustrates the same cultural syncretism, but his contribution is to be found not in a commentary on the *Ethics* but in a biography of King Solomon in which he analyzed the virtues and knowledge of the ideal man who actually attained religious perfection in this world. Alemmano shows how the religious naturalism of the fourteenth century, with its preoccupation with astrology and astral magic, led to intellectual mysticism within the paradigm of kabbalah. In their own distinctive ways, all three authors shed light on the gradual transition from medieval Aristotelianism to kabbalah and on the eventual transformation and demise of the philosophic discourse on happiness.

Joseph ibn Shem Tov: The Hierarchy of Torah and Philosophic Wisdom

The name of Joseph ben Shem Tov ibn Shem Tov is known today to but a handful of Jewish scholars who specialize in Hispano-Judaic culture.[2] Yet in his own day, ibn Shem Tov was a high level Jewish functionary in the courts of the Castilian kings John II (who imposed residential segregation on Jews) and Enrique IV, whom ibn Shem Tov served as a physician and auditor of accounts. In this capacity he represented the Crown in attempts to suppress anti-Jewish riots in 1452 and was involved in formal debates with Christian scholars. In 1455 he lost his position at the court, due to a court intrigue in which *conversos* were involved. The rest of his life was devoted to writing and preaching to fellow Jews, and nothing is known about him after 1460.

As a typical representative of the Jewish courtier class in Spain, Joseph ibn Shem Tov's literary harvest shows loyalty to rabbinic Judaism as well as to Aristotelian philosophy. He composed biblical and talmudic commentaries, homilies, anti-Christian polemics, a commentary on Maimonides' *Guide of the Perplexed,* super-commentaries on ibn Rushd, and commentaries on Aristotle. Most important to our discussion, ibn Shem Tov composed the first full-length Hebrew commentary on the *Ethics* of Aristotle. His major theological work, *Kevod Elohim,* is his most systematic attempt to show that Aristotle's *Nicomachean Ethics* is compatible with rabbinic Judaism, as long as philosophy is understood in its proper place, as subordinate to supernatural, divine revelation.

The Ethics among Jews and Christian: A Comparison

Ibn Shem Tov's interest in the *Ethics* reflects a change in the status of the text among Jewish intellectuals. In Chapter Six we noted that the work became available in Hebrew when Samuel ben Judah translated Averroes' *Middle Commentary on the Ethics* in the 1320s. As the knowledge of Arabic waned among Sephardic and Provençal scholars, that Hebrew translation became increasingly difficult to use because of its cumbersome style. We also noted that the science of ethics was regarded as a branch of practical philosophy. As such, it was marginal to Jewish philosophic interests, which focused on the theoretical sciences of physics and metaphysics. Preoccupation with nature (in which the science of astrology had a prominent place) further diminished interest in Aristotle's *Ethics* among Jewish thinkers during the second half of the fourteenth century.

A reverse process, however, was taking place in the Christian academic community, where scholars had been getting a firm hold on the *Ethics* since the second half of the thirteenth century.[3] In 1246–47 the entire *Ethics* became available in a Latin translation by Robert Grosseteste, which became the standard version used in Latin commentaries. Albert the Great composed two commentaries on the work (in 1248–52 and again between 1263 and 1267) and Albert's student, Thomas Aquinas, composed his own commentary on it, either during 1271–72 while teaching in Paris, or in 1265 while still in Orvieto, Italy.[4] Aquinas showed how Aristotle's conception of happiness could be framed inside a Christian theological perspective. Although several elements of that philosophic conception were included in the list of propositions condemned by Stephen Tempier, the Bishop of Paris, the *Ethics* was never banned. In 1335 it became a required text for the Dominicans in Provence, and in 1366 it was required for the M.A. degree at the University of Paris. In the 1330s new commentaries were composed, the most famous of which were by Walter Burley (1275–1343) and Jean Buridan (c. 1295–1356), whose general tendency was philosophical rather than theological. In the 1370s the *Ethics* was translated into French by Nicole Oresme for King Charles V. It was generally regarded as a guide to proper conduct for the noble class.

Given the popularity of the *Ethics*, Jewish courtiers found it necessary at the turn of the fifteenth century to translate it anew. The task was completed in 1405 by R. Meir Alguades, the Chief Rabbi of Castilian Jewry and personal physician to several Castilian kings.[5] Alguades, however, consulted not the Arabic original of Averroes' *Middle Commentary* but the Latin translation by Hermann the German, composed in 1240.[6] He used Samuel ben

Judah's original translation as a starting point, and attempted to improve it—sometimes in accordance with the Latin, and sometimes in accordance with his own stylistic sense. The result was a mixture of two textual traditions of the *Ethics*, one Arabic and the other Latin.[7]

Alguades' new Hebrew translation was not the only attempt to render ibn Rushd's *Middle Commentary* anew. An anonymous translator/compiler also composed a super-commentary on ibn Rushd's text. In the introduction to that text, the anonymous author included a brief summary of the major aspects of the *Ethics*. Lawrence Berman has noted that this summary was merely an extract from al-Farabi's "Introduction" to his own, no longer extant *Commentary on the Ethics*. Moreover, whoever produced the new revision of ibn Rushd's *Middle Commentary* ascribed the summary not to al-Farabi but to Thomas Aquinas![8] The anonymous author regarded Aquinas as merely one among many authoritative commentators on the work of ibn Rushd, and had no qualms about incorporating selections from Aquinas' *Commentary* into his own super-commentary on ibn Rushd's *Middle Commentary*. In other words, in fifteenth-century Spain there was a hybrid text of Aristotle's *Ethics* that fused elements from ibn Rushd, al-Farabi, and Aquinas. That syncretist text existed only in Hebrew and was available primarily, if not exclusively, to Jews. Thus, the history of the reception of the *Ethics* itself reflects the transition of Iberian Jewry from the cultural orbit of Islam to that of Christendom.

By the early fifteenth century humanism began to take shape and with it the realization that the medieval translations of the *Ethics* were flawed. The humanists produced new translations of the work as well as commentaries comparing Aristotle's analysis of human well-being with post-Aristotelian moral philosophies, especially with Stoicism and Epicureanism. In 1416–17 Leonardo Bruni of Arezzo (1374–1444) completed his translation, which was but a revision of Grosseteste's translation,[9] and in 1457 John Argyropolus (1410–1487) translated it yet again, this time from the Greek original.[10]

Ibn Shem Tov's interest in the *Ethics* was sparked during his service at the court of King Enrique IV. According to his own testimony, the work was often discussed at the court as a guide to right conduct.[11] As a Jewish courtier he had to take part in the discussion, but to his chagrin he "found no commentary by the sages of our Torah, the pious, saintly ones, may their memory be blessed."[12] In other words, he lamented that he could not rely on any authoritative Jewish commentary of the *Ethics*. To fill this lacuna he composed *Kevod Elohim* in 1442, which was a summary of the *Ethics* with a short commentary.[13] Given the differences between Latin and Arabic textual traditions of the *Ethics*,[14] ibn Shem Tov decided to paraphrase the main points of Book X of the *Ethics* and explore their implications for Judaism in a separate work. Thirteen years later, after studying Alguades' Hebrew translation of Averroes' *Middle Commentary* and some Latin commentaries on the *Ethics*, ibn Shem Tov composed another work, a detailed, linear commentary on the entire *Ethics*. This text became a standard source for knowledge of the *Ethics* among Jews throughout the fifteenth and sixteenth centuries. Ibn Shem Tov also composed "a very short commentary" and a summary of the major points of the *Ethics*.[15]

One reason ibn Shem Tov was so interested in the *Ethics* was to ensure that fellow Jews would "catch up" with their Christian counterparts.[16] If the *Ethics* was the main text that shaped moral discourse, Jews had to be familiar with it, especially the Jews who were still involved in public life. A second, very plausible reason is that in the *Ethics* ibn Shem Tov found a description of the educated nobleman who is involved in politics—a person not unlike himself. Like the authors of the *adab* literature in Islam, who were interested in the *Ethics* because it showed how to wed wisdom and politics, ibn Shem Tov could appreciate the relevance of the *Ethics* to his own life at the court. The *adab* culture, as we have shown in Chapter Four, was fully absorbed by Jewish courtiers from the eleventh century on. However, by 1440 the Jewish courtier class lost much of its luster and actual political power. The return to Aristotle's *Ethics* could therefore provide the remaining Jewish courtiers with an ideological justification for their privileged self-perception.

The support for this conjecture comes from ibn Shem Tov's treatment of Aristotle's virtue of magnanimity and his depiction of the "great-souled man" (*gedol ha-nefesh*) as the nobleman who possesses appropriate self-worth and receives honors without discomfort.[17] As we have seen in this study, Aristotle's virtue of high-mindedness stands in marked opposition to the rabbinic emphasis on humility as the primary virtue of the righteous person.[18] In his *Commentary on the Ethics*, however, ibn Shem Tov was not in the least concerned with this contradiction. The examples that he adduces to illustrate magnanimity are all connected to activities within the Jewish communities, such as philanthropy on a large scale and providing funds for the building of synagogues and schools.[19] Moreover, ibn Shem Tov turns to the remote past of the rabbinic period and presents rabbinic personalities—most notably, Judah the Patriarch—as the epitome of the Jewish great-souled man, the wise nobleman who was deeply involved in politics.[20]

Ibn Shem Tov's treatment of Judah the Patriarch as a historical figure was derived from the Josippon, a tenth-century Jewish reworking of Josephus that was translated into Castilian in the 1450s and was of great interest to intellectuals of *converso* descent. That ibn Shem Tov portrayed the rabbinic sage in this manner, I believe, suggests the influence of civic humanism, which began to spread in Spain after the conquest of Naples in 1443 and with the rigorous support of King Alfonso V. That ibn Shem Tov composed a manual on Hebrew rhetoric, *Ein ha-Qore* (The Eye of the Reader) may also suggest his awareness of the Renaissance cult of rhetoric.[21]

A third reason for ibn Shem Tov's interest in the *Ethics* is that he understood its implications for Jewish religious life. If the *Ethics* is to be read as a recommendation for the social-moral life, what about the life of philosophic contemplation? If philosophic contemplation leads to happiness, as Aristotle stated in Book X of the *Ethics*, what is the function of a divinely revealed Torah? Ibn Shem Tov resolved this seeming conflict in *Kevod Elohim* by arguing that Aristotle spoke only about temporal, imperfect happiness in this world, which is not the ultimate end of human life. The ultimate felicity, or perfect happiness, is to be found only in the afterlife and is only attainable by following the Torah. This rather conservative interpretation of Aristotle is a retreat from the bold optimism of Jewish philosophy of the fourteenth century. Ibn Shem Tov would ascribe his views to Maimonides and thus defend him against the accusation of Crescas. We should note, however, that ibn Shem Tov's conservative reading of Aristotle is very similar to the way Thomas Aquinas was able to frame the same philosophy within the context of Christian theology.

Kevod Elohim *and Aquinas*

There is a remarkable affinity between *Kevod Elohim* and Aquinas' analysis of human felicity in the *Summa Contra Gentiles* Book III: 16–55 and the *Summa Theologica* I-II, q. 1–22. Given ibn Shem Tov's unambiguous reference to the Latin commentaries on the *Ethics*, of which Aquinas' was the most prominent, it stands to reason that he consulted Aquinas' *Commentary on the Ethics* as well.[22] Ibn Shem Tov's access to the writings of the "Angelic Doctor" is not at all surprising, given his knowledge of Latin, his daily contacts with Dominican scholars in the court, the proliferation of Aquinas' works in fifteenth-century Spain, the missionary activities of the Dominicans, and ibn Shem Tov's own interest in refuting Christianity.[23]

Creation Theology and Human Perfection

Kevod Elohim is a theological treatise that moves within the framework of revealed truth, where a supernatural order of knowledge and action exists beyond the natural order that is perfected by it. This is why ibn Shem Tov began his commentary on the *Ethics* with exegesis of Isaiah 43:7: "Everyone who bears my name, all whom I have created, whom I have formed, whom I have made for my glory." This is no mere rhetorical embellishment but an expression of ibn Shem Tov's underlying theology of creation. In contrast to Maimonides, who was notoriously ambiguous about the origins of the world, ibn Shem Tov was loud and clear—God created the world *ex nihilo*.

The relationship between the creator and the created universe is analogous to the relationship between the artist and his art. God brought the universe into existence according to an intelligible design that pre-exists in Him in a super-eminent, unified, and perfect manner. We presented this analogy in the previous chapter with regard to Gersonides. Ibn Shem Tov, like other philosophers in the fifteenth century, was very familiar with the Provençal thinker, but, unlike Gersonides, ibn Shem Tov explicitly identified the intelligible order of the universe with the esoteric, primordial Torah that pre-exists in the divine mind as an exemplar of the created universe.[24] This was not unique to ibn Shem Tov; other Jewish theologians of his generation did the same.[25] But it was this connective that enabled ibn Shem Tov and other Jewish theologians to argue that knowledge of Torah completes and perfects knowledge of the created world. By the same token it was this link that enabled Aristotelian-trained philosophers to absorb kabbalah into the conceptual framework of medieval Aristotelianism.

The ontological gap between the creator and the created is bridged by virtue of participation, a metaphysical doctrine that was characteristic of Platonism and Neoplatonism but endorsed by medieval Aristotelians such as Thomas Aquinas and Gersonides. "Being" is an equivocal term of a *pros hen* type equivocity. As Aristotle taught in the *Metaphysics* (Book IV: 3 1003a 33–34, b 6–9), "All that 'is' is related to one central point, one definite kind of thing, and is not said to 'be' by mere ambiguity." It is by virtue of this reference to one primary instance of being that all other things are said to be and fall under one science, metaphysics. For ibn Shem Tov, God, of course, is that one starting point, and things are said *to be* to the extent that they participate in the divine being. All created things depend existentially on God, and they are ordered hierarchically in accordance with their degree of participation in the divine being. Therefore, created things approach God according to their nature, namely, according to their ontological status in the hierarchy of beings.

The unified notion of being has its corollary in a unified notion of good. Like "being," "good" is an equivocal term—all good things refer to one primary good, God. God is not only the highest Good. God is also the cause of goodness in all good things. Things are good to the extent that they participate in divine goodness. The good (as both Aristotle and Aquinas taught) is that thing toward which everything is aimed; therefore God must be the ultimate good of all things.

Ibn Shem Tov's claims in the first two pages of *Kevod Elohim* read like a loose paraphrase on Aquinas' *Summa Contra Gentiles* III: 18–25, though the Hebrew text lacks the lucidity and order of the Christian source. Both philosophers assert that God is the end of all things, that all things imitate divine goodness, that all things tend to become like God inasmuch as God is their cause, that things are ordered to their ends in various ways according to their ontological status, and that intellectual substances approach God through knowledge. Human beings are sentient beings. It means that man approaches God through the perfection of his intellect.

Ibn Shem Tov perpetuated the intellectualism of Aristotle and all his medieval followers who saw the intellect as the defining mark of humanity. Human happiness does not consist of pleasures of the body, nor is it derived from gaining honors, possessing wealth, or having any goods of the body such as health, beauty, and strength.[26] Because reason alone makes us what we are, happiness cannot lie in virtue alone, since it is the effect of reason. And since happiness has to do with knowledge, ultimate human happiness must be the knowledge of the most perfect being, namely, God. Ibn Shem Tov thus is in accord with Aquinas that all sentient beings desire to know God as their ultimate end.[27] Thus, the ultimate felicity for men cannot be the activity of practical reason, which involves human emotions and action, but only the knowledge of God through the activity of theoretical reason.[28]

To know God, however, is not simply to know that God exists, but to know the essence of God. Maimonides' negative theology made it impossible for men to possess such knowledge, and he held that only God's actions in the world are accessible to human knowledge. A more positive approach to the possibility of human knowledge of God's essence emerges in a philosophy that presupposes the doctrine of participation and the doctrine of analogy. But two questions remain: first, Does human philosophical knowledge lead to perfect happiness? and second, Can this knowledge be attained while human beings live the embodied life of this world? Aquinas answered both questions in the negative. Philosophic knowledge is insufficient for attaining ultimate felicity. The bliss of eternal life, which Aquinas defined as the vision of God's essence, is experienced only in the afterlife and can be attained only as a result of God's grace through Christ and the revealed dogmas of the Christian Church. As Anthony J. Celanno explains, according to Aquinas "the immutable beatitude that a Christian awaits at death must be considered as more perfect than the ideal described by Aristotle in the *Nicomachean Ethics*."[29] Aquinas thus distinguished between imperfect and perfect happiness. Perfect happiness, he insists, lies beyond human earthly existence, because human beings cannot experience anything in perpetuity. Even the most permanent of all human activities, the contemplation of truth, cannot be undertaken without interruption. Human bodily needs—such as fatigue, hunger, and the need for sleep—always interfere with intellectual activity, thereby preventing humans from attaining perfect happiness in this life. Because true and perpetual blessedness is divine, it can be attained only in the afterlife, when the human soul is liberated from the imperfection of this life. Moreover, perfect beatitude is not the result of human endeavor, but of a divine, supernatural grace.

Ibn Shem Tov approached Aristotle similarly to Aquinas, except that he moved strictly within the parameters of Judaism. Ibn Shem Tov did not find Aristotle's view a challenge to his religious beliefs. What Aristotle said about human happiness (both its practical and theoretical aspects) pertained merely to temporal life in this world because as a pagan, he did not have access to the revelation of the Scripture. Jews should consult Aristotle if they wish to know how to conduct themselves in this world, especially if they wish to hold their position in the court. He was correct to state that human happiness does not lie in the acquisition of wealth, power, honor, fame, or bodily pleasures, as most people assume, but in an activity in accordance with virtue.[30] He was also correct when he subordinated the moral virtues to the intellectual ones, and when he placed speculative reason above practical reason. Most importantly, Aristotle was right when he emphasized that only the knowledge of God constitutes ultimate happiness. Through the contemplation of God man lives not only human life, but "the divine life which is the most happy."[31] Of course, ibn Shem Tov defended Aristotle, because he interpreted him tendentiously.

Happiness as Perfection of the Intellect

Ibn Shem Tov upheld the intellectualism characteristic of Aristotelian philosophy. In the corporeal, created world, the human species is the peak of creation. Formed in the image of God, we possess a unique power—reason, which not only distinguishes us from all other animals, but enables us to come closest to God. On this point there is full agreement between Aristotle and the Torah; both teach that man is a rational animal, and that reason is his characteristic activity. Especially because ibn Shem Tov upheld the primacy of the intellect, he went on to defend Aristotle against his Jewish detractors, such as Hasdai Crescas.

Ibn Shem Tov ascribed to Aristotle the "exclusive" interpretation of happiness. However, unlike Crescas, who found this conception of human life to be subversive to Judaism, ibn Shem Tov saw it as compatible with it. Ibn Shem Tov ascribed to Aristotle the view that the intellect is not only "the most divine power in us," but literally a divine power that resides in man (*ha-koaḥ ha-elohi asher ba-adam*).[32] The intellect, or the rational soul, is a created intelligible form, ontologically akin to, though lower than, the separate intelligences.[33] As an intelligible form, the rational soul gives unity to the individual while being capable of existence independent of the body.

Ibn Shem Tov's view of the mind-body relationship is close to that of Aquinas, who taught that "the human soul is neither a separate form, nor a form in body, but a created intelligible form which exists by the presence of God."[34] Thus, both ibn Shem Tov and Aquinas, in accord with Aristotle's philosophical anthropology, walked the fine line between insisting on the unity of the human psycho-physical complex, on the one hand, and acknowledging the substantial incorporeality of the rational soul on the other. The benefit of this position is obvious; both could remain loyal to Aristotelian psychology while showing that Aristotle's view is compatible with the belief in personal immortality. It is easy to see how this position would place ibn Shem Tov between Maimonides and Crescas.

The ontological affinity between the human intellect and the separate intelligences dictates that human happiness consists in cognition of incorporeal substances. As an incorporeal substance the human intellect has a natural proclivity toward the realm of the separate intelligences. The rational soul desires to return to its origin in order to enjoy the excellence that properly belongs to incorporeal substances, that is, contemplation of things eternal. It follows that perfection of the human intellect, and hence of man, is to be attained by participating in the activity of the separate intelligences. Ibn Shem Tov stated,

> When we understand the perfection proper to the separate intelligences, we will know the true happiness (*osher*) of man inasmuch as man is happy. We must realize that the divine human intellect comes

from the separate intelligences and that man partakes in their perfection.... The essence of happiness is when man is likened to that perfection in the separate intelligences out of which his rational soul was carved [*nehzevah*].³⁵

In short, through cognition of incorporeal substances the human intellect approximates that which is truly incorporeal, perfect, self-sufficient and happy—God.³⁶

The Superiority of Torah Over Philosophy

Ibn Shem Tov, like Maimonides and Aquinas before him, highlighted the intrinsic limitations of knowledge derived from sense perception of created things.³⁷ Philosophy is an arduous procedure, available only to the very few. It lacks certainty, it is prone to mistakes and controversies, and it is inherently related to matter.³⁸ In the fourteenth century Jewish philosophers such as Gersonides and Narboni believed it was possible for human beings to overcome these limitations and achieve intellectual perfection in this life. Ibn Shem Tov, by contrast, held that these limitations dictate that philosophy alone does not provide the knowledge of God and that it must be complemented by divinely revealed knowledge.

For ibn Shem Tov, only knowledge that comes from God can direct man to the immortal life of the individual soul. In His infinite divine grace, God revealed the Torah to Israel at Sinai, making known to man truths that exceed the ken of natural knowledge. More precisely, revelation makes known to man the intelligible order of reality that exists in God in the most perfect, supernatural manner.³⁹ Therefore, the revealed Torah completes and perfects natural human reason as grace completes and perfects nature.

With Maimonides and the Jewish Aristotelians, ibn Shem Tov distinguished between the esoteric and exoteric dimensions of the Torah. However, while Maimonides and Gersonides identified the esoteric dimension with the natural truths of physics and metaphysics, ibn Shem Tov identified it with the supra-natural truths of divine revelation that cannot be exhausted by human reason. Put differently, ibn Shem Tov identified the Torah with God himself, exactly as did the kabbalists. For ibn Shem Tov, then, the Torah is divine, not because it can be shown that it perfects body and soul (as Maimonides had asserted) but, because it comes from God. By the same token, the Torah is not merely the constitution of the most virtuous regime, but the ideal exemplar of the universe, according to which the universe was created. As such, the Torah pre-existed in the divine mind in a super-eminent, perfect manner. The Torah alone is salvific; it "brings about the ultimate perfection, namely survival after death with its delight that surpasses anything else."[40] If follows that the highest cognitive activity that brings man to God is not the knowledge of philosophy, but the knowledge of Torah.[41]

> Perfect contemplation [*ha-iyyun ha-shalem*] is not the cultivation of the wisdom of Aristotle, but the contemplation of God, which is above the natural, created and fanciful inquiry which is the road of philosophy. Indeed [this contemplation] is the contemplation of the mysteries of existence [*sitrei ha-mezi'ah*] which are the mysteries of the Torah [*sitrei torah*].[42]

We can situate Ibn Shem Tov's depiction of happiness as a compromise between the views of Maimonides and those of Crescas. With Maimonides, ibn Shem Tov held that ultimate felicity is comprised of cognitive activity, i.e., knowledge of God, and that such knowledge is the highest expression of human love for God. Yet, with Crescas, ibn Shem Tov used unitive language to describe the final good for man. The ultimate end of human life is the cleaving (*devequt*) of the individual rational soul to God. He describes this intimate relationship in terms of the reciprocal love between the creator and the created, of the most perfect and the imperfect.

> The felicitous man is the chosen one, most beloved by God, blessed be He, because love is commensurate with closeness and likeness, and when man actualizes his intellect and contemplates the divine intellect that is in him, he comes close to God and is likened to God in the most perfect way possible. Therefore, he is so beloved by God and God's love is commensurate with closeness.[43]

Precisely because the Torah is a supernatural knowledge that comes from God, those who contemplate it and follow its commandments can attain perfection even outside the social-political context. Citing ibn Bajja's *Regimen of the Solitary* as his authoritative source, ibn Shem Tov claimed that truly felicitous men seek God not in the midst of society, but in the solitude of deserts and caves.[44] Continuing the trend of de-politicizing human perfection, ibn Shem Tov regarded the life of the reclusive philosopher-mystic as the ideal for holy men.

Ibn Shem Tov's high regard for solitude might reflect despair with human political affairs and a desire to find consolation in intellectual activity apart from society.[45] Not surprisingly, he names R. Shimon bar Yohai (as we recall, the rabbi who was also the presumed author of the *Zohar*) and the prophet Elijah as models of felicitous men (*me'usharim*) who achieved perfection in solitude and seclusion. These two exemplary figures of the Jewish mystical tradition are presented as wise men who reached adhesion with God through contemplation of the mysterious realities taught by Torah rather than by the philosophy of Aristotle.

Two Orders of Happiness and Jewish Particularism

We may conclude that ibn Shem Tov, like Aquinas before him, distinguished between two orders of happiness—an imperfect, natural, and temporal happiness, and a perfect, supernatural and eternal happiness. The two orders correspond to the distinctions between the natural and the supernatural, between philosophy and revealed knowledge, between conventional law and divine law, and between reason and faith. Whereas imperfect happiness pertains to all human beings who pursue moral and intellectual virtues in accordance with the philosophy of Aristotle, perfect happiness pertains to the recipient of the one and only divine law, the Torah. It follows that only Jews can attain perfect happiness; all others can at best achieve imperfect happiness.

Ibn Shem Tov found support for this claim in the *Ethics* itself. Exactly as did Aquinas before him, ibn Shem Tov argued that Aristotle did not speak about the immortality of the personal rational soul because that doctrine can be known only through a divine revelation that Aristotle did not receive.[46] Therefore, the *Ethics* poses no threat to the integrity of Jewish religious society: it speaks only of imperfect happiness and, on the contrary, Jews who follow the ideal of happiness in the *Ethics* will find themselves better prepared to pursue true happiness. The threat to Jewish society comes only from those pernicious interpreters of Aristotle (ibn Shem Tov cites Gersonides as an example) who reduced the ideal of human perfection to cognition of any intelligible, rather than to the knowledge of God.[47] Jews alone can reach salvation, since they alone received revelation from God.

Ibn Shem Tov goes even further. As much as the supernatural, divine Torah is superior to all other natural pursuits, so is Israel superior to all other nations, and the Israelites superior to all other human beings. The term "man" then is an equivocal term that applies primarily to Jews and only secondarily to non-Jews. Whereas the non-Jew belongs to the realm of nature, Israel belongs to the supernatural realm governed directly by God.[48] This idea, which will become paramount in Jewish theology during the sixteenth century, can be traced back to Gersonides' analysis of causal determinism and human choice. The relationship between Jews and non-Jews is hierarchical; as man is the peak of creation, so are the Jews the peak of humanity. This is, of course, not a new idea. It was articulated most forcefully by Judah Halevi and elaborated in kabbalah.

Ibn Shem Tov's blatant ethnocentrism was the ultimate polemical response to Christian pressure. Christianity need be neither tempting nor threatening to Jews because it too belongs to the realm of nature. A Jew who converts to Christianity forfeits the chance for salvation. At best, non-Jews may attain imperfect happiness in this world. Ibn Shem Tov was fully cognizant that this claim could not be proven philosophically and had to be affirmed by a voluntary act of faith that distinguishes believers from non-believers. In the final analysis, while salvation is cognitive, it is faith, the voluntary assent of the will to revealed truths that determines whether one will be saved.[49]

Philosophy and revealed knowledge differ with regard to the way each approaches the truth. The tension between philosophy and Judaism can thus be resolved by positing a hierarchical relationship between human knowledge and divinely revealed knowledge. The revealed Torah itself makes known supra-rational, undemonstrable truths, whereas philosophy makes known scientific knowledge of the created world culled from sense data. Whereas philosophy proceeds from the effect to the cause, revealed knowledge proceeds from the cause to the effect; whereas philosophy is prone to error and mistakes, revealed knowledge is certain and complete; whereas philosophy encompasses knowledge extracted from sensible, created things, revealed knowledge pertains to the uncreated realm of God. However, philosophical and revealed truths do not conflict with each other. With regard to some truths—such as the claims that God exists, that God is one, and that God knows particulars, there is an overlap between philosophy and revealed knowledge. Other, supernatural, theological truths that are beyond the domain of natural human reason complete and perfect natural human reason as grace completes and perfects nature.

If *Kevod Elohim* is understood as proposed here, its polemical intent becomes clear. This text was written first against Jews who opposed philosophy altogether and claimed that it was subversive to Judaism. To them ibn Shem Tov intended to show that Aristotle does not challenge Torah, but rather contributes to proper religious worship. Educated Jews should continue to study philosophy and follow the recommendations of the *Ethics* as far as worldly life is concerned. Second, ibn Shem Tov wrote *Kevod Elohim* against radical Jewish rationalists who reduced Judaism to a set of demonstrative propositions and who identified the good life exclusively with cognition of intelligibles. To them he attempted to show that while philosophy prepares mankind to attain the supreme good, philosophic wisdom does not constitute ultimate felicity. Third, ibn Shem Tov wrote *Kevod Elohim* to persuade Jews who were tempted to convert to Christianity that Judaism is the exclusive road to personal salvation and immortal life.

The hierarchy between the revealed Torah and philosophy was endorsed by other Jewish thinkers in the fifteenth century such as Joseph Albo, Abraham Rimoch, Abraham Shalom, Abraham Bibago, Joel ibn Shuaib, Joseph Hayyun, Isaac Arama, and Isaac Abravanel. The conservative tendencies of these thinkers most likely reflect close political and cultural interaction with their Christian neighbors, who were also theologically conservative. It is best to see these thinkers as philosophical theologians who harmonized their religious beliefs and the truth-claims of philosophy in a way that enabled them to legitimize the study of philosophy—while at the same time proving the superiority of Judaism over Christianity and philosophy. It was also this paradigm that enabled trained Aristotelian philosophers to be well-disposed toward kabbalah and to view it as an integral part of divinely revealed tradition.

The Ethics *After ibn Shem Tov*

Ibn Shem Tov was not alone in focusing attention on Aristotle's *Ethics*. Bernard Septimus has already noted that it had been quoted by a number of fifteenth-century Spanish Jewish thinkers.[50] Though the *Ethics* was known to Jewish thinkers in the fourteenth century, it became of primary interest to quite a few in the fifteenth.

Based on the translation of Meir Alguades, ibn Shem Tov's commentary on the *Ethics* became the standard resource for Jewish intellectuals who studied it. Arama used it extensively and adopted ibn Shem Tov's views, but with some modifications. In his analysis of Arama's references to the *Ethics*, Septimus showed that, like ibn Shem Tov and Aquinas, Arama also distinguished between two orders of happiness—temporal and transcendent. For Arama, as Septimus put it,

> the divine subsumes the natural and builds upon it. Because he considered cultivation of natural excellence an integral part of the Torah,

the *Ethics* became, for him, an important instrument of biblical and aggadic interpretation.[51]

With great respect for the practical reasoning of the *Ethics*, Arama attempted to show that the moral teachings of the Torah were compatible with it. Whether the Torah is "this-worldly" rather than "other-worldly" was one of the bones of contention in Jewish-Christian polemics. Arama was involved in various exchanges of that nature, and he reports a debate with a Christian preacher in which he used the practical reasoning of the Torah as a claim for its superiority over the Christian doctrine of grace.

In short, however one would interpret Aristotle's *Ethics*, it is clear that in the fifteenth century that text attracted a lot of attention by Jewish and Christian intellectuals. Whether they viewed it as a repository of practical wisdom, useful especially for the ruling classes, as a text that showed the compatibility of rational knowledge and religious faith, or as evidence to be used in Jewish-Christian debates, the centrality of the *Ethics* illustrates the widespread focus on the discourse on happiness during the fifteenth century.

In the second half of that century, the paradigm taken over from Aquinas was adopted by professing Jewish theologians. The hierarchical relationship between "the path of investigation" and "the path of faith" paralleled the distinction between the natural and supernatural orders of reality. This notion permeates the writings of Isaac Abravanel and was shared by his contemporaries Arama, Abraham Bibago, and Abraham Shalom. According to these thinkers, Israel (both collectively and individually) belongs simultaneously to the natural and supernatural orders. As created human beings, the Jews fall under the laws of nature (*teva*), whose regularity and stability manifest God's wisdom and general providential care for the created universe. On this level, all events can be known scientifically, especially by employing the science of astrology, which was at the time an integral part of natural philosophy.[52] Yet Israel also benefits from a special, direct, particular providence that transcends natural determinism and is not transparent to human reason. God's revelation at Sinai was a miraculous event, expressing God's free will and intervention in nature. As such, the revelation from God was not predicated on a perfection of the natural human intellect, and it encompassed all of Israel, regardless of its degree of intellectual perfection. With the giving of the Torah, Israel was governed directly by the will of God. Israel's affairs, therefore, manifested the believers' faith in God and their willingness to observe the Torah's commandments.

YOHANAN ALEMANNO: KNOWLEDGE OF NATURE AND THE MYSTICAL UNION WITH GOD

Alemanno in the Context of Renaissance Humanism

Whereas ibn Shem Tov paved the way for the transition from Aristotelianism to kabbalah by positing a hierarchical relationship between philosophy and revealed knowledge, Yohanan Alemanno arrived at the same end by developing the religious naturalism of the fourteenth century to its logical conclusion. For Alemanno a mystical union between the human soul and God was attainable in this life by outstanding individuals who actually mastered all knowledge and possessed all the virtues—moral, intellectual, and religious. Alemanno claimed that at least one such individual existed—the biblical King Solomon—and he composed *Shir ha-Ma`alot asher li-Shelomo* (The Song of Solomon's Virtues) which was an introduction to his commentary on the Song of Songs. The *Song of Solomon's Virtues* is a "how-to" book, a practical guide for the attainment of human perfection in this life. In this regard, Alemanno reflected the perpetuation of the philosophical optimism of the fourteenth century, but in his case the final end was framed as a mystical conjunction between the human intellect and the central sefirah of the divine pleroma, rather than with the Active Intellect. Alemanno developed his ideas on the basis of the "prophetic kabbalah" of Abraham Abulafia (1240–ca. 1290), which was an idiosyncratic development of Maimonideanism.[53]

Yohanan Alemanno was one of the most creative minds of Jewish philosophy in Renaissance Italy: his vast knowledge was deeply valued by Renaissance humanists.[54] We know very little about his life except that he was born in France in 1433 and settled in Florence in 1454, where like other humanists he enjoyed the patronage of the Jewish banker Yehiel da Pisa. Alemanno studied with Judah ben Yehiel Messer Leon in Padua and later in Mantua and received a doctorate degree from him. That Judah Messer Leon was empowered to grant a doctorate degree to Jewish students was unique and reflected his outstanding status in Italy. Alemanno returned to Florence in 1488 and remained there perhaps until 1497, when the Jews were expelled from the city. Alemanno had no official position in the Jewish community and was not interested in the cultivation of virtues for the sake of governing. He was much closer to the outlook of the philosophers-scientists of the fourteenth century, who sought to fathom the secrets of nature only in order to achieve perfection in one's lifetime. Alemanno contributed directly to Renaissance humanism when he introduced a student of his—the most illustrious humanist, Pico della Mirandola—to the mysteries of kabbalah.

The Humanist Discourse on Human Happiness

The humanists were obsessed with the meaning and purpose of human life, perhaps because they did not belong to any existing social institutions or, more personally, because of the precariousness of the tumultuous politics of Italian city-states in the fifteenth century.[55] The humanist discourse on happiness treated the following themes: Can happiness be attained in this life? Is virtue as important an ingredient of happiness as are good health and sufficient means? Is nobility acquired or inherited? Can the humanist be truly noble if he lacks wealth and social standing? What are the virtues of the truly noble? And finally, does nobility necessitate involvement in public life?

The basic insecurity of the humanists led them to adopt Stoic themes and postures toward the vicissitudes of life. The humanist discourse on happiness has a noticeable pessimistic strain and "snobbish aloofness," as Charles Trinkaus put it,[56] even when it is expressed by people who were successful in politics and quite wealthy. The Stoics' emphasis on virtue as the only good, their rejection of external goods, and the counsel of apathy were easily combined with Christian values and postures. For example, for Caluccio Salutati (1331–1406), an early humanist who was also the Chancellor of the Republic of Venice,

> virtue was conceived as being the means to eternal felicity in the next life, and in this sense was otherworldly. It also came to be considered as a means to happiness in this world. Virtue, however was defined as the pursuit of knowledge and beauty of form. Thus the ideal life was the humanist one, dedicated to studies.[57]

The humanist emphasis on the value of education was no less elitist than the approach to education of medieval scholastics. "The wise and eloquent men stand higher above other men than man through the possession of reason stands above the animal." Virtue and learning were the only criteria of a man's worth. "The true sign of nobility was the obligation of virtue, which meant devotion to studies."[58]

While humanists reflected on the meaning of human life in light of ancient pagan sources, they did so as practicing Christians with various degrees of personal commitment. As Christians, they believed that the world was created by God, so when they reflected on the place of man in the order of creation, they accepted the biblical belief that man was created in the image of God. For the medieval scholastics, like Aquinas, "created by God" meant to be endowed with an intellect. The humanists, in contrast, highlighted the centrality of the human will and the freedom of men to determine the quality of their own lives.

For example, Gianozzo Manetti (1396–1459), Florence's ambassador to Naples, claimed that the world was created by an omnipotent God not for the sake of God: rather, souls and all other animate life forms were created for the sake of man. Man's excellence derives from the fact that he seems to be the ultimate end or purpose of the created world. Man was created both out of the free will of God and out of necessity: God's quality of goodness required the charity of the act of creation. Man is free to find the supreme end for himself, but it has to be the contemplation and service of God.

The most famous reflection on human excellence by humanists was articulated by the aforementioned Pico della Mirandola (1463–1494), who derived his judgment about man's greatness from the manner of his creation. According to Pico's rereading of the biblical myth of creation, God

> decided to create man and to set him at large in the world with no particular position of his own but with the great gift of the power to occupy whatever position he willed. . . . In this power of choosing freely what position to occupy in the universe is the basis of man's dignity.[59]

Man can degenerate to a lower level and lose his dignity, or he can realize a mystical unity with God. Human freedom to choose is thus ultimately subordinated to the need to choose God, lest one lose human dignity. The multiple potentialities of human beings place a higher moral responsibility on them to live well so as to achieve union with God.

The humanist preoccupation with the meaning of human life inspired a close look at human emotions, attitudes, moods, and sensibilities—in short, at the *psychological life of men*. Humanist psychology became more attuned to the dynamics of inner life, and more honest about human passions such as avarice, fear, lust, envy, pride, and ambition. Humanist discourses on happiness thus considered humans beings as they actually behave rather than the human species as an abstract category.

In the context of their reflections on the human condition, the humanists paid attention to the interaction between the soul and the body, and to the role that the body plays in the acquisition of virtues. Some humanists highlighted the irresolvable conflict between body and soul. Others emphasized the possible harmony between the material and the spiritual dimensions. Still others called for the complete domination of the soul over the body. These positions were supported in each case by a re-reading of an ancient text—Gnostic, Stoic, Epicurean, Platonic, and Aristotelian—to reflect the specific preference of the Renaissance interpreter.

KING SOLOMON: A PORTRAIT OF THE IDEALLY VIRTUOUS MAN

The Song of Solomon's Virtues

Yohanan Alemanno exemplifies the Jewish humanist who embraced the new cultural sensibilities and involved himself in the expansion of the discourse on happiness, the fusion of medieval Aristotelianism and kabbalah, and a fresh reading of biblical and rabbinic sources. His *Song of Solomon's Virtues* was composed as the introduction to his commentary on the Song of Songs entitled *Ḥesheq Shelomo* (The Desire of Solomon). Alemanno composed it at the request of Pico della Mirandola in 1488–89,[60] three years after Pico presented to the Pope his famous *900 Theses,* in which he attempted to defend his syncretistic *prisca theologica*, which presumably culminated in Christianity. It was befitting to write about the perfection of King Solomon in a commentary on the Song of Songs not only because the biblical king is its putative author, but also because in the Middle Ages Jewish and Christian thinkers alike interpreted the text as a reference to the individual human soul. The love song pertained not to the collective relationship between God and Israel, as rabbinic Judaism understood it, but to the individual progression of the soul, culminating in a mystical union with the Active Intellect or with Christ. As we noted in Chapter Eight, Gersonides also composed a commentary on the Song of Songs and showed how philosophic knowledge leads to immortality of the intellect. At the end of the fifteenth century Pico della Mirandola was interested in the Song of Songs for the same reason: as a guide to the attainment of intellectual perfection in this life. Though Pico's innovative rendering of Christianity was not well received by Church authorities (he was condemned to heresy and imprisoned in France), he did not give up his aspiration to possess comprehensive knowledge of all things, which he believed was expressed parabolically in the Song of Songs. In order to achieve this goal he hired Yohanan Alemanno to teach him, thereby displacing his previous Jewish teacher, Elijah Delmedigo, who had instructed him in Aristotelian natural philosophy. Alemanno translated into Latin for Pico the commentary of Narboni on ibn Tufayl's *Ḥai ibn Yaqzan*[61] and composed his own commentary on the Song of Songs to help Pico better grasp the meaning of the allegorical text.

While the *Song of Solomon's Virtues* was composed at the request of a Christian humanist, its audience was a Jewish one. Alemanno was aware, as was his teacher Judah Messer Leon, that Pico's positive valuation of kabbalah had missionary intent. Indeed, Pico was quite successful in this regard: a significant number of Jews did convert to Christianity, having in mind the fusion of Christianity with Platonism that Pico represented. The most famous of these converts were Flavius Mithridates and Paulus Ricius, who translated rabbinic and kabbalistic texts into Latin for Pico and forged others in an attempt to prove that the inner teaching of Judaism (as Pico and his associates believed) was in full accord with the truth of Christianity.[62]

Alemanno composed the *Song of Solomon's Virtues* to present a Jewish alternative to Renaissance Platonism. He believed that a proper exposition of Solomon's successful attainment of perfection would inspire other Jews to follow the rigorous, but not impossible, program to achieve perfection within the borders of Jewish life. As a biography of an illustrious historical persona, it was also in accord with the humanist attempt to draw lessons from history. While the text is written in a prose style, the title indicates that for Alemanno it was in fact a "poem" (*shir*). Arthur Lesley has shown that Alemanno's title makes sense against Aristotle's definition of poetry as

> a logical, "instrumental" art, [that] dealt with imaginative representation of reality; the poetic genre of panegyric, the prescriptions for which became assimilated to those for epideictic rhetoric, was a tool of the political division of practical art.[63]

More specifically, the "poem" that Alemanno composed, though lacking meter and rhyme, fits Aristotle's definition of "tragedy" as "a poetic praise of virtues which were illustrated by reference to the life of a historical personage."[64] To instruct Jews of his time how to attain perfection *in this life*, Alemanno composed the detailed analysis of King Solomon's virtues and achievements, culminating in conjunction with God, or more precisely, *Tiferet*, the sixth sefirah and center of the ten sefirot that emanated from God.

On the Classification of the Virtues and the Sciences

Combining Aristotle's analysis of the virtues in the *Nicomachean Ethics* with post-Aristotelian treatment of the Roman rhetoricians, especially Cicero, Alemanno proposed an elaborate analysis of human virtues and the requisite knowledge that enables one to acquire the virtues. The virtues, the arts, and the sciences are all arranged in an architectonic order from the lowest to the highest.[65] This structure comprises a "ladder of perfections," which Solomon himself ascended and which the reader is invited to imitate. An unusually rich description of all aspects of human life, the work captures the richness of the term *ma'alot* in Hebrew as virtues, excellences, ranks, and steps. The one who follows the detailed recipe for perfection provided by Alemanno will presumably experience it in this life, as did King Solomon.

The acquisition of human excellence is predicated on the possession of knowledge. Alemanno was familiar with the various classifications of the sciences proposed earlier by Muslim and Jewish philosophers such as al-Farabi and Shem Tov Falaquera. In continuity with his predecessors, Alemanno articulated a very comprehensive program of study incumbent on Jewish students in the small Jewish communities of north central Italy.[66] By the age of twenty, they were to be trained in Hebrew language, the vernacular, Bible, Mishnah, and Talmud, as well as logic, grammar, rhetoric, arithmetic, geometry, and astronomy. Thereafter they needed to study physics, metaphysics, medicine, political philosophy, alchemy, theology, kabbalah, and magic.[67] The very comprehensive nature of Alemanno's proposed curriculum is not novel; what is innovative is the claim that an educated Jew must be conversant in kabbalah, alchemy, and astral medicine, in addition to philosophy and traditional Jewish learning. Alemanno's ambitious curriculum exemplifies the complete fusion of all forms of knowledge, human and divine, characteristic of the Renaissance scholar.[68]

The perfect man possesses the entire architectonic list of human perfections—namely, virtues, arts, and sciences. Alemanno's organization of these accomplishments indicates how a skillful rhetorician could combine Platonic, Aristotelian, and Ciceronian moral discourses into a coherent scheme. He classifies all human perfections, or goods, into two main classes—physical and spiritual. The physical goods are further subdivided into "internal physical goods" and "external physical goods." The former class includes beauty, health, strength, and long life, and the latter includes honor, noble ancestry, companions, and supporters. The spiritual goods too are subdivided into "internal spiritual goods" and "external spiritual goods." The first class includes the four cardinal virtues of the

Platonic list—intelligence, self control, fortitude, and justice—and each is further subdivided to encompass a full listing of all intellectual and moral virtues. Thus, under the virtue of "intelligence," Alemanno distinguishes between "right thinking" and "right understanding." "Right thinking" for him means art (*techne*), which is subdivided into "productive," "theoretical," "mathematical," and "musical," and each of these is further subdivided to encompass a whole range of human activities. "Right understanding" is subdivided into political science, natural sciences, theoretical wisdom, and intuitive knowledge, and each of these classes is further subdivided to encompass all the sciences known to man. Under the second cardinal virtue of "self control," or temperance, Alemanno enumerates self-restraint, decorous action, discretion in spending, moderation of necessities, generosity, cleanliness, contentment with one's lot, satisfaction with the happiness of others, munificence, sociality, congeniality, pride in accomplishments, shame, and humility. Under the cardinal virtue of "fortitude" he includes endurance, diligence, pride in achievements, honoring of virtue, magnificence, high mindedness (greatness of soul), expansion of the soul, and determination. Finally, under "justice" he includes a "right will," harmony between faculties of the soul, and ascent toward God.

Having achieved all the "internal spiritual goods," one is equipped to attain "external spiritual goods." These are depicted as objective factors that are bestowed upon an individual who is prepared to receive these objective goods, or "influences." The first objective good is bestowed at birth and pertains to the spiritual elevation of the parent at the time of conception; then there is attention paid to a person by contemporaries, divine assurance of good fortune, divine guidance, and finally, the ultimate goodness and felicity.

All of these human activities, arts, sciences, and character traits are claimed to have been part of Solomon's personality and life achievement. Indeed, the monarch's name, *shelomo*, signifies his perfection, *shelemut* in Hebrew.[69] The proof for this idealized portrait of King Solomon is rhetorical rather than philosophic. Alemanno's view of Solomon is based not only on the account of his life in the Bible,[70] but also on the very teachings of Proverbs, Ecclesiastes, and Song of Songs that the Jewish tradition ascribed to the king, as well as on rabbinic aggadot, rabbinic exempla, folk tales, and narratives about ancient heroic figures in non-Jewish sources. By fusing diverse literary modalities (exegetical, historical, and scientific-philosophical) and diverse literary sources (biblical, rabbinic, Hellenistic, Muslim, and Jewish), Alemanno teaches by example what it means to be a wise and virtuous man who has experienced perfection in this life. The purpose of the treatise, then, is not to supply decisive proof that King Solomon was a great man, but to illustrate to Jewish readers of the time that by emulating such a Solomon they could attain perfection in this life and immortality in the next.

What did Alemanno mean when he claimed that the virtuous man who acquires the proper dispositions and possesses all requisite knowledge attains conjunction with God? Jewish Aristotelians prior to Alemanno understood perfection to mean a union between the human intellect and the Active Intellect. This conjunction, which Crescas found so objectionable, was for Alemanno not the highest rank of perfection, because the Active Intellect was *not* God. In the Neoplatonized-Aristotelian cosmological scheme, the Active Intellect was only the intelligence that governed the affairs of the sub-lunar world. Above it, however, other separate intelligences moved the planets, and still above them, the realm of the ten sefirot, according to kabbalah, emanated from God. Conjunction with God, which is the final good of human life, must mean a mystical union with the sefirot, or more particularly, with the central sefirah, *Tiferet* ("Beauty"). Even conjunction with the Shekhinah, which the kabbalists identified with the tenth and lowest sefirah, cannot count as the ultimate perfection, because she is but the gate into the sefirotic realm. The perfected man who possesses all virtues and knowledge is able to receive the overflow from the *Ein Sof* and the upper sefirot that are gathered in *Tiferet* and experience a total mystical union with God.

Mystical Union and Controversy

Clearly, in Alemanno the mystical union with God, as understood by kabbalah, is the highest end of human life, the ultimate felicity. The revival of Platonism in fifteenth-century Italy facilitated the growing popularity of kabbalah among Renaissance intellectuals, Jews and non-Jews alike. From the very start of its dissemination in Italy, kabbalah was perceived as a speculative science whose mastery yielded control of nature on the one hand and the attainment of a mystical union with God on the other. The works of Abraham Abulafia and Menachem Recanati, the anonymously written *Ma'arekhet ha-Elohut* (The Constellation of the Godhead) and the commentary of Reuben Zarfati were the major sources for knowledge of kabbalah in Italy from the late thirteenth century until the last quarter of the fifteenth.[71] The *Zohar*, however, was relatively unknown in Italy until the end of the fifteenth century.[72] Viewed as a type of speculative lore, kabbalah was studied autodidactically from extant texts without the supervision of authoritative mentors. The absence of authoritative traditions, as Moshe Idel has shown, facilitated a degree of hermeneutic freedom that was not common in Spain. A scholar interested in kabbalah could rely on his own reasoning powers and knowledge of general philosophy to interpret kabbalistic texts and articulate his own peculiar reading. This activity, in turn, further enhanced the image of kabbalah as an ancient, theoretical science with a universal appeal rather than as a set of practices for the proper observance of Jewish law. Therefore, in Italy many Christian humanists viewed it as an integral part of universal, ancient wisdom and desired to study it from Jewish masters.

By the middle of the sixteenth century the *Zohar* became an authoritative, venerated text for Italian kabbalists, both Jewish and Christian. Five years after the Talmud was consigned to the flames and Jewish works were subject to severe censorship, the *Zohar* was printed in 1558 and 1559 by two Christian publishing houses—an event surrounded by vehement controversy.[73] Nonetheless, Alemanno's brand of philosophical kabbalah did not disappear. His works were preserved by scholars such as Mordekhai Rossillo and ben Elijah Menachem Halfan. They also inspired other scholars in Italy to harmonize philosophy, kabbalah, science, and magic.

Alemanno understood the mystical union with God in accord with his spiritual mentor, Abraham Abulafia, rather than along the lines of the *Zohar*. Like Abulafia, Alemanno envisioned that mystical union as prophecy. However, the language that Alemanno used to portray this lofty mental state was colored by Plato's characterization of "divine madness," the ecstatic state that culminates in the erotic pursuit of wisdom. In that paranormal state, the human soul loses any taint of the corporeality it got from its association with the body, and is able to become one with the form of the Good. For Alemanno, as for Plato, the energy that fuels the human drive to unite with *Tiferet* ("Beauty") is a passionate, erotic desire (*ḥesheq*). King Solomon not only best exemplified the erotic spirituality that leads to the mystical union with God; he also expressed it most perfectly in the Song of Songs. It is thus befitting that the title of Alemanno's book was *Ḥesheq Shelomo* (The Desire of Solomon).

Within the Jewish tradition that is based on divine revelation in sacred Scriptures, however, Alemanno's mystical vision of the final good for human beings is quite problematic. Of what use is the Torah in a system that considers union with God as a real possibility for this life? Does the mystic who attains conjunction with God know only the inner meaning of the revealed

Torah? Or does he know what is beyond the confines of the revealed Torah? Can there be, in principle, anyone who is superior in knowledge to Moses? The same objections that were raised against the prophetic kabbalah of Abraham Abulafia and the intellectualist mysticism of philosophers such as Moses Narboni could be raised against Alemanno. It seems that he was fully aware of the connection between mysticism and the scent of heresy.

The Torah of Moses vs. the Wisdom of Solomon

As a professing Jew, Alemanno did not (and could not) deny the superiority of the Torah over all other sources of knowledge, including the accomplishments of mystics. Thus although he asserted that King Solomon was perfect—more perfect than Adam, the patriarchs, Joseph, and David—he was not flawless. Moses was the only flawless human being, and, therefore, his Torah is the most perfect revelation. Nevertheless, contrary to the Maimonidean philosophers, who elaborated on the primacy and uniqueness of Moses, in Alemanno's manual for the attainment of human perfection, Moses is a marginal figure.

The Torah of Moses is indeed the most perfect law, but observance of the Torah per se is not the ultimate end of human life. The felicity of mystical union with God is the end. The means is the Torah observance elaborated by a broad range of knowledge of arts and sciences (including magic and astrology).

Alemanno's syncretism and magical approach to the Torah made him a favorite mentor of Renaissance humanists such as Pico, Pico's nephew Alberto Pio, and Johannes Reuchlin, but it enraged the Aristotelian philosopher Elijah Delmedigo. Alemanno's philosophic-magical interpretation of kabbalah also did not find favor in the eyes of the Sephardic kabbalists who began to settle in Italy during the last decade of the fifteenth century. These kabbalists brought with them the authoritative texts of the *Zohar* and its theosophic-theurgic outlook, which differed markedly from the philosophical kabbalah of Alemanno. Already in 1490, the kabbalist Isaac Mar-Ḥayim, who briefly sojourned in Italy on his way to the Land of Israel, complained to Isaac da Pisa that Alemanno misinterpreted the doctrine of sefirot: he regarded them as instruments (*kelim*) of divine activity rather than as the essence (*atzmut*) of God.[74] Moreover, in 1493 another Sephardic exile who settled in Italy, Judah ben Jacob Hayyat, went even further to specify which texts constituted authentic and authoritative kabbalah and which texts were not and should not be studied.[75] The latter category included the harmonization of philosophy and kabbalah by Abraham Abulafia, Isaac ibn Latif, Samuel ibn Motot, and Yohanan Alemanno.

Language and the Mastery of Nature

Alemanno's optimism about the possibility of a mystical union with God and his proto-experimental approach to nature was closely related to his conception of language. Along with other Renaissance Neoplatonic thinkers (e.g., Cornelius Agrippa), he made a sharp distinction between natural, human languages, in which words signify things through the mediation of concepts, and divine languages, in which words express the essence of things.[76] The words of a divine language possess an innate creative power: they are composed from the elementary particles of nature—the sacred letters of the divine name. Needless to say, Alemanno regarded Hebrew as the one and only divine language, whose letters are the "building blocks" of the created universe. This magical conception of the Hebrew language goes back to the origins of kabbalah and received its philosophical formulation in the teachings of Abraham Abulafia.[77]

For Alemanno (who was an ardent student of Abulafia's writings), the mastery of nature and the mystical union with God were thus possible through the manipulation of language. Whoever possesses the knowledge of the supernal, esoteric Torah can tap into, so to speak, the spiritual energy of the Godhead and channel the divine efflux to the corporeal world, either into his own body or into material objects. Through self-spiritualization, the magician-philosopher may control natural substances, prognosticate future events, heal the physically and mentally afflicted, attain a temporary union with God in this life, and enjoy the bliss of immortality in the afterlife. That outlook made Alemanno attractive to sixteenth-century Jewish scientist-philosophers such as Abraham Yagel, who was attuned to new, non-Aristotelian conceptions of nature.[78] It was Alemanno's particular fusion of philosophy and kabbalah that facilitated the reception of Lurianic kabbalah in Italy during the late sixteenth century as a type of speculative wisdom about God, the world, and humanity.

Alemanno was a real maverick whose creative but eclectic mind absorbed all forms of knowledge while opening new ways of interpreting Judaism. Directly, his ideas influenced relatively few Jewish intellectuals, though the most important one was Judah Abrabanel (Leone Ebreo). But the fusion of rabbinic Judaism, Aristotelian philosophy, kabbalah, and Renaissance humanism was not unique to him. We will discover this same fusion in Moses

Almosnino, a scion of a rich aristocratic Iberian family that was exiled to the Ottoman Empire and settled in Salonika after the expulsion from Spain. With him the medieval philosophic discourse on happiness flowered for the last time and then wilted, supplanted by the kabbalistic version of the link between virtue, knowledge, and well-being.

MOSES ALMOSNINO: HAPPINESS AS A PURSUIT OF HOLINESS

Moses ben Baruch Almosnino was a teacher, judge, and communal leader in Salonika in the second and third quarters of the sixteenth century.[79] In sixteenth-century Salonika, the Jewish community was a thriving intellectual and cultural center due to the determination of Iberian exiles to preserve their culture and bring it to new heights.[80] Almosnino received an excellent halakhic education along with superior instruction in philosophy and science, which he received from the ex-*converso* Aaron Afiya. Almosnino mastered both Latin and Turkish and perhaps even Greek and was familiar with a large number of scholastic works. As a communal leader, he was concerned about the reintegration of ex-*conversos* into the Jewish fold, the tensions that erupted between various immigrant groups, and the social unrest due to growing class stratification. At first the Jewish community of Salonika thrived economically: it was required to provide clothes for the Ottoman army, which, in turn, stimulated the Jewish textile industry. However, in the early 1560s the Ottoman government required Jews to provide meat rather than clothes, which was a major economic setback for the community. For two years (1566–68) a delegation from Salonika, including Almosnino, negotiated with the authorities and attempted to restore the status quo.

As a leader who represented the Jewish community to the government, Almosnino was deeply concerned with proper conduct. His main sources of moral training were the Torah and Aristotle's *Nicomachean Ethics*, which he studied with the help of scholastic and humanist commentaries, and rabbinic exempla. Almosnino composed yet another commentary on the *Ethics* in 1558, entitled *Penei Mosheh* (The Countenance of Moses).[81] He consulted two Hebrew commentaries written in the fifteenth century: that of Joseph ibn Shem Tov,[82] which we discussed above, and that of Baruch ibn Yaish, composed in the 1480s.[83] Ibn Yaish's commentary was based on two new fifteenth-century translations of the *Ethics* by the humanists in Italy mentioned above: the translation of Leonardo Bruni from the version of Robert Grosseteste and from the Greek original by the Byzantine humanist scholar, John (Ioannes) Argyropoulos in 1457. In Almosnino's day, the *Ethics* was translated into French by Philippe Le Plessis, who improved on

Nicole Oresme's fourteenth-century translation, and into Italian by Bernardo Segni (1504–58), who dedicated it to Cosimo I (d. 1574).[84]

As a good humanist, Almosnino devoted much effort to determining the correct text of Aristotle's *Ethics*. But the main contribution of his commentary is not so much his philological observations but the degree to which he anchored the *Ethics* on the Bible and rabbinic literature yet at the same time drew heavily on scholastic commentaries on the work. Indeed, Almosnino often refers to the commentaries on the *Ethics* by Eustratius,[85] Albert the Great, Thomas Aquinas,[86] Geraldus Odonis,[87] Jean Buridan,[88] Walter Burley,[39] Faber Stapulensis Jacobus (Jacques Lefevre d'Etaples),[90] and Agostino Nifo.[91] The range of this list indicates the degree to which a Jewish intellectual in the sixteenth century was aware of the scholastic tradition. It is also evidence of the continued interest in Aristotle's work during that period. During the 1540s and 1550s both Italian and French humanists composed new commentaries on this celebrated text. Thus the Benedictine scholar Joachim Perion—an avowed Ciceronian—translated the *Ethics* in 1540, provoking much criticism from other humanists and leading to a new translation, published in Venice in 1558 and later in Paris, by the French humanist Denys Lambin.[92]

Preoccupation with Religious Perfection

Almosnino's concern with the *Ethics* was not merely academic. The work provided the theoretical vocabulary for the analysis of virtue and knowledge in the pursuit of religious perfection, the main topic that, after the expulsion, preoccupied the Sephardic exiles in the Ottoman Empire to the point of obsession, a response to their personal and collective tragedies. Reflections on the ultimate felicity, or beatitude, appear in their sermons and compositions devoted to systematic theology, and they loom large in their biblical commentaries, especially those on Proverbs, Psalms, and Ecclesiastes.[93] The Sephardic exiles instituted the custom of reading from the Psalter during the winter months and from Proverbs and Tractate Avot every Sabbath between Passover and Shavu'ot (Feast of Weeks). It was believed that by so doing the individual would attain moral perfection, reaching the high degree of self-purification necessary for the reenactment on Shavu'ot of the Sinaitic theophany.

Besides these readings, no less crucial for the moral training of the exiles was the *study* of Tractate Avot of the Mishnah. The Sephardim brought with them this long-standing tradition inaugurated by Maimonides, which fused rabbinic moral values distilled in Tractate Avot with Aristotelian ethics.[94]

Almosnino's detailed study of the *Ethics* was to prepare him to do his main educational work, preaching and teaching the meaning of divinely revealed tradition. Throughout his theological and homiletical writings, he referred to the *Ethics* and took for granted that moral perfection for Jews could not come except through familiarity with its vocabulary.[95] Numerous references to and citations from the *Ethics* are to be found in the works of his contemporaries as well.[96] As mentioned, his philosophical commentary on the *Ethics* is replete with references to Scripture and rabbinic sources. The moral teachings of King David and King Solomon—recorded in Psalms, Proverbs, and Ecclesiastes and interpreted by the rabbinic sages—were in complete accord with the moral wisdom of Aristotle, Seneca, and Cicero. Thus Almosnino, like Yohanan Alemanno, presented King Solomon as the embodiment of the Renaissance ideal *homo universalis* and the wisest of all ancient sages[97] and claimed that the religious poetry of King David was favorably compared to Greek and Roman poetry.[98] The very attempt to prove that the Bible equaled the aesthetic, moral, and intellectual achievements of the ancients necessitated a rereading of Scripture against this background of humanist culture. Thus Almosnino inspired a distinct discourse of moral philosophy that fused Jewish, Aristotelian, Platonic, and Stoic elements.[99] In the ancient Jewish sources he rediscovered the humanist emphasis on the dignity and worth of the human personality, the primacy of the human will, and the striving for personal immortality through cultivation of moral virtues. As much as their intense suffering made Iberian Jews receptive to the humanist emphasis on human emotions and passions, so did the Bible provide them with evidence that the virtuous man who lives by the Torah is able to transcend the limitations of this world.[100]

Almosnino explicitly expounded upon the full educational and religious merit of the *Ethics* in a practical manual for good conduct that he composed in Spanish with a Hebrew introduction for the instruction of his nephew. The title of the text—*Regimiento de la vida y tratado de los suenyos*, known in Hebrew as *Sefer Hanhagat ha-Ḥayyim* (The Book of Management of Life)[101]—indicates how Almosnino understood his educational goal. In his view, moral, intellectual, and religious training, which lead to human well-being, must begin at a young age. The disciplined acquisition of virtues liberates the soul from its corporeal conditioning, restoring it to its heavenly abode. Almonino's preoccupation with the *Ethics* was thus an integral part of his moral philosophy, whose goal was to lead Jews to religious perfection.

A New Moral Philosophy: Aristotelianism, Kabbalah, and Biblical Exegesis

Almosnino's moral philosophy fuses Aristotelian philosophy and kabbalah. His position on the nature of the human soul and the ultimate end of human life reveal the impact on him of the zoharic perspective. Although he was not a creative kabbalist, Almosnino took at face value that Shimon bar Yohai wrote the *Zohar*, which he viewed as a rabbinic midrash. Because it contained a sacred supra-rational knowledge that was qualitatively superior to demonstrative philosophy,[102] Almosnino had to harmonize Jewish Aristotelianism with the views of the *Zohar*. This could be done because of the changes that Jewish philosophy underwent in the fifteenth century under Joseph ibn Shem Tov.

In the following section I outline the main components of Almosnino's moral philosophy, which have been culled from his homiletical and philosophic works. The purpose of his moral inquiry was not to solve metaethical problems, but to guide the Jewish public toward the attainment of human perfection. In a society of immigrants ravaged by communal and interpersonal disputes and subjected to diverse interpretations of moral values, Almosnino's philosophical commentaries filled an important civic function: they molded the inchoate Jewish masses into a genuine community seeking to attain spiritual perfection. Though the philosophic moral discourse reflected a dialogue with non-Jewish systems of thought, its overall tenor was highly ethnocentric. It was the dignity of Israel (rather than the dignity of Man), the personal immortality of Jews (rather than the survival of non-Jews), and the divine perfection of Torah that concerned the Jewish scholars in the Ottoman Empire. In short, the discourse on the ultimate end of human life provided answers to Jewish perplexity after the expulsion from Iberia.

Psychological Dualism

The Aristotelian conception of happiness presupposed a certain view of human nature, or more precisely, a psychological theory that explained the relationship between the mental and the physical aspects of the human species. Almosnino fused Aristotelian and Platonic psychological theories. When he spoke about the human species at large, he employed Aristotelian theories: the soul is the form *of* the body, the organizational principle of the physical and the mental functions of the human organism.[103] But when he reflected on the soul-body nexus in the case of Jews, he adopted the Platonic two-substance theory: the soul is a form *in* a body.

The "Platonization" of the Aristotelian tradition is understandable, given the dissemination of kabbalah (whose doctrines presupposed Platonic ontology and psychology), the resurgence of Jewish and Muslim Neoplatonic philosophy, and the blossoming of Renaissance Platonism. But beyond the circumstances of culture lay the realization that Platonic doctrines were more compatible with the traditional Jewish beliefs in personal immortality and divine retribution than Aristotle's views were. By applying Platonic psychology exclusively to Jews, Almosnino rationalized continued allegiance to Judaism: Jews alone can enjoy the bliss of immortality because their souls are by nature made of a pre-existent and eternal substance.

Under the sway of kabbalah, Almosnino held that the souls of Jews are literally divine; they are a part of the divine essence, or a "particle of God" (*ḥeleq mimenu*). Israel's soul "was carved from under the Throne of Glory" (*kise ha-kavod*) and was "infused" (*mushpa`at*) into the human body by God.[104] As a divine substance, the soul of Israel is pre-existent, holy, and eternal. Prior to its descent into the body, the soul resides in a special realm (*olam ha-neshamot*) to which she will return after the demise of the body, provided she had perfected herself on earth.[105] Precisely because the Jewish soul is literally a divine spark, Israel alone can be said to have been created in the image of God. Therefore, whenever Scripture uses the word "man" (*adam*), it refers exclusively to Israel rather than to the human species at large.[106]

Whereas the soul of Israel is a pre-existent, holy substance, the human soul is but "an incorporeal substance with a propensity for intellection (*etzem ruḥani mukhan el haskalah*).[107] The human soul is "generated" (*mithavah*) in the realm of the Separate Intelligences (*sekhalim nifradim*) and requires an association with the body in order to actualize its potential for intellection. By abstracting intelligibles from perception of sensible things, the human soul can perfect itself. It can acquire moral and intellectual virtues, culminating in philosophical wisdom, as Aristotle teaches. But precisely because the post-expulsion philosophers believed that the "way of investigation" (*derekh ha-ḥaqirah*) is inherently imperfect, they claimed that philosophic wisdom can at best constitute earthly happiness; it falls short of ensuring the survival of the individual soul.[108] Lacking a divine soul and devoid of the grace of divine revelation, gentiles are barred from the afterlife.

The pursuit of perfection or happiness varies for Jews and non-Jews. Because Israel received a revelation from God, Jews need not rely on the imperfect "path of investigation." Instead they walk in "the path of faith" (*derekh ha-emunah*), which makes known the true beliefs and just actions necessary for perfection in this world, as well as the supra-rational and supra-natural knowledge necessary for transcendent happiness.[109] The two paths differ from each other not only regarding content and ultimate end, but also in terms of epistemic procedure. Whereas the "path of investigation" consists of abstracting intelligible universals from perception of sensible particulars, the "path of faith" consists of "recollection" (*hizakhrut*) of truths that the divine soul possessed prior to its descent into the body, precisely as Plato had taught. The full significance of this view will become apparent below. For now suffice it to say that according to Moses Almosnino the absolute verity and certitude of the "path of faith" entail that a Jewish child who has just learned to read Torah and can understand its literal meaning is wiser and closer to the attainment of immortal life than a non-Jewish adult who studied philosophy all his life.[110]

Body and Soul

The acquisition of knowledge is a mental activity that requires the mediation of the body. Since the souls of Jews are literally a divine substance, they experience a very acute conflict between the spiritual soul and the corporeal body. The corporeal body naturally seeks sensuous pleasures (derived primarily from food and sex) and seduces the soul to pursue apparent goods such as wealth and honor. The sense appetite (*ha-ko'ah ha-margish*) is the power of sensation and perception and the appetitive part (*ha-ko'ah ha-mitorer*) is the location of all desires and passions that become aroused as a result of the information provided by the senses. Both powers are bodily-dependent and as such are the source of the human tendency to sin. Therefore, the body and the physically-related functions of the soul function as a "partition" or "dividing barrier" (*mehitzah; masakh mavdil*) between the spiritual soul and her divine origin—alienating the soul from God.[111] If left to satisfy its own desires, the body could hinder the return of the soul to the supernal world. The task of the soul, therefore, is to gain control over the body and spiritualize it through the acquisition of virtues, directing it toward the attainment of the ultimate end of life—the love of God.

Ideally, says Moses Almosnino, there should be "peace between the matter and the form" of man (*shelom ha-homer ve-ha-tzurah*).[112] Such peace indicates the attainment of mental health. Yet this inner balance is not the harmonious co-existence of two equal partners but a hierarchical relationship in which the soul dominates the body. The perfect man (*ha-shalem*), says Almosnino, "subdues and subordinates the corporeal part (*ha-ḥeleq ha-ḥomri*) to the rational part (*ha-ḥeleq ha-sikhli*). When one subdues (*yashpil*) the material [principle] and elevates (*yinase*) the formal [principle], one removes himself from all inequities (*peḥituyot*) and ascends in the ladder of perfections." [113] A failure of the soul to control the body manifests a mental sickness that requires healing (*refu'ah*) no less than physical sickness.[114] As recipients of divine revelation, Israel already possesses the best and only true medication for the sickness of body and soul—the divine Torah.[115] Those who cling to the Torah through study and performance of its commandments attain the desired inner balance and experience happiness in this world and immortality in the next.

Even though God revealed the path that enables the soul to regain her spirituality, the process itself is painful, suffused with misery and anguish. The soul experiences her temporary association with the body not merely as a form of imprisonment (as Plato taught) but rather as a dangerous exile.[116] Desperately the soul seeks to liberate herself from the body and regain her initial spirituality and holiness. No one understood the yearnings of the soul and her anguish better than King David, whose celebrated Psalms express the profound truths of the human condition in a poetic language. Those who penetrate the meaning of the Psalms could gain a deeper understanding of the ultimate end of human life and focus on its attainment.[117] The Sephardim, as we noted above, instituted the ritualized study of the Psalms (along with Proverbs, Ecclesiastes, and Tractate Avot) as part of a rigorous program of ethico-religious training. By virtue of that program, the soul of the believer could "polish and purify" (*le-zakekh u-lemareq*) herself from the contaminating influences of the body,[118] preparing the believer to encounter God during the reenactment of Sinaitic theophany on the festival of Shavu'ot.

Perfection and Self-Purification

Almosnino understood pain and suffering positively as a cathartic means for self-purification. Adversity and pain cleanse the body from its natural inclination to pursue physical pleasure, and the soul from the polluting influences of the body.[119] Yet Almosnino was no ascetic. Unlike the kabbalists of Safed, he did not institute practices that mortify the body in order to gain a higher level of spirituality. As a member of a wealthy family, he enjoyed material comforts and endorsed Aristotle's claim that human perfection requires the presence of certain external goods as well as human association.[120] But Almosnino repeatedly exhorted his audience to accept suffering "*be-sever panim yafot*," i.e., with a positive attitude and even with joy (*simḥah*).[121] This acceptance of adversity reflects the impact of Stoic attitudes (derived primarily from the writings of Cicero and Seneca) at least as much as it suggests the impact of Bahya ibn Paquda's ascetic teachings or contemporary kabbalah. According to Almosnino, the acceptance of suffering indicates that the soul has already neutralized the passions of the body and has reached the desired control over the body.[122] Those who perfect themselves through clinging to the Torah can release the soul from its embodied conditioning while they are still alive. They can attain communion with God (*devequt*) in this world.[123]

Not unlike Abraham Abulafia and Yohanan Alemanno, Almosnino advocated a nonpolitical, individualistic interpretation of the messianic ideal.[124] The redemption (*ge'ulah*) to which the Jews aspire is not the ingathering of the exiles in the Land of Israel but the freedom (*ḥerut*) of the individual soul from its exile in the body.[125] This is true freedom from the travails of Time and from the determinism of natural causality (*ma'arakhah*).[126] By psychologizing the historical experience of exile, Almosnino took the sting out of the bite of history and articulated a hopeful message: redemption is within the reach of each and every Jew in this life despite of the vicissitudes of Time.

Human Perfection and Hermeneutics

It is here that psychology, ethics, moral training, and hermeneutics converge in the discourse on happiness. Almosnino viewed the pursuit of happiness (both earthly and transcendent) as a fundamental Jewish activity, i.e., midrash. One can become perfect only through the hermeneutic act of interpretation, which unveils the inner, esoteric meaning of the sacred text. This idea can be traced to Maimonides, as I suggested in Chapter Five. But if for Maimonides the inner meaning of the Torah consisted of abstract, philosophic truths of physics and metaphysics, for Almosnino its esoteric core was the essence of the Divine Self. The revealed Torah is not only the most perfect law, whose observance assures perfection of body and soul, but a sacred medium through which the human self and the divine Self can encounter one another. In Almosnino's words, "the Torah is the 'intermediary' (*emtza'i*)" through which Israel can communicate with God by doing God's Will.[127]

Almosnino believed that the esoteric Torah is the essence of God, comprised of infinite permutations of the Divine Name. Since the soul of Israel is also "carved" from the essence of God, it follows that God, the supernal Torah, and the souls of Israel are one and the same, precisely as the *Zohar* teaches. This is why the study of the Torah and the acquisition of knowledge are two sides of the same endeavor, two aspects of the process of self-knowledge. The pursuit of perfection consists of two parallel acts: removing the veil of corporeality from the believer and from the Torah, respectively. In the human believer the veil of corporeality is the body; in the revealed Torah, it consists of the figurative expressions that enclose the esoteric, divine truth in metaphors, narratives, and laws.[128] The attainment of union between the divine and the human requires that the believer spiritualize himself through the study of Torah and the performance of its laws. The better Jews understand themselves and purify themselves, the deeper they can penetrate the infinite mysteries of the Torah that paradoxically both conceal and reveal the Divine Self.

The conceptual vocabulary lighting the path to perfection was articulated by the philosophers and especially by Aristotle's *Ethics*. Maimonides, of course, was the first to argue that the eudaimonian ethics of Aristotle was consistent (though not entirely identical) with the moral and religious ideals of the rabbis. On the level of *praxis* there was no significant conflict. This is the argument in Almosnino's commentary on the *Ethics*, *Penei Mosheh*. He shows that the anecdotes on rabbinic sages in talmudic aggadot and their moral aphorisms in Tractate Avot verify Aristotle's moral philosophy and, conversely, that a correct interpretation of biblical and rabbinic texts illuminates the obscure or disputed points in Aristotle's *Ethics*. By so reading Aristotle, Almosnino in fact invested the science of ethics with a religious import: whoever acquires the virtues in accord with Aristotle's moral philosophy and the teachings of the rabbis could attain the desired level of spirituality and encounter God in the verses of the revealed text. Whether or not one in fact devotes one's life to the Torah depends largely on the will, which freely decides whether to follow divine commands or not.

The Interplay of the Will and the Intellect

The Maimonidean tradition, as this book makes clear, put a premium on the intellect. In accord with Aristotle, Maimonides conceptualized God as a perfect intellect that is absorbed in eternal self-contemplation and insisted that creation in the image of God refers to the rational potential of man. Maimonides further depersonalized God by denying Him any volition and desire. Because God is absolutely perfect, there is neither want nor desire in

Him. God wills only to the extent that He knows Himself. In contrast to God, created human beings are endowed with a free will and are responsible for their choice. Despite his reaffirmation of rabbinic belief in human freedom, Maimonides, no less than Aristotle, reduced volition to the cognitive activity of practical reason. Human beings desire only that which their intellect judges to be good (whether this good is real or apparent). Thus a given choice is good if it promotes human happiness, and it is bad if it leads man to pursue apparent goods. When one chooses badly it is a failure of the intellect rather than the weakness of the will.

The bitter confrontation between Judaism and Christianity and the mass apostasy of the Iberian Jews compelled Jewish Aristotelians such as Almosnino to reconsider the Maimonidean approach to human choice and pay closer attention to the role that the will plays in human conduct. Especially after 1391 a Jewish philosopher could no longer explain why some Jews remained loyal to Judaism while others converted to Christianity, either under duress or voluntarily. A mere conviction of the intellect was not enough to account for the new historical situation. The trauma of the expulsions further underscored these problems because in 1492 the choice to profess Judaism was clearly not the most rational course of action. It was instead a voluntary act of faith that expressed the believer's love of God and the willingness to suffer pain in the sanctification of God's name (*qiddush ha-shem*). As Almosnino turned to look more closely at the role of the will in the pursuit of human perfection, he resorted to the rich scholastic literature on the subject, gleaning from it subtle distinction and sophisticated arguments.[129]

The works of Almosnino (especially the commentary on the *Ethics*, *Penei Mosheh*) illustrate the shift from intellectualism to voluntarism during the sixteenth century.[130] By this I do not mean to say that Almosnino denied the teleological and intellectualist perimeters of Maimonideanism. To do so would undermine his entire study of philosophy as well as his conception of Torah and his own cultural identity. Instead, by agreeing with Crescas that God is the supremely good Will, that the pursuit of human perfection depends on the perfection of both the intellect and the will, and that the ultimate end of human life is a combination of both the knowledge and the love of God, Almosnino's works suggest a certain softening of Maimonidean intellectualism.

Almosnino's voluntarism is evident in his conception of God. He shared the premises of the Maimonidean tradition that God is the First Cause of the universe, the Necessary Being whose essence is identical with

His existence. But instead of dwelling on the unity of essence and existence in God, Almosnino talked about the goodness of the Divine Will: "The Divine Will is the Good that is desired for its own sake and that is not subject to change."[131] In accordance with this personalist conception of God, Almosnino reinterpreted Maimonides' teachings on divine attributes.

Maimonides stated that the "Ways" that God revealed to Moses are the attributes of action. While the Torah speaks of these attributes in interpersonal terms (e.g., lovingkindness and justice), in truth, these attributes of divine action are revealed in the realm of nature. God's love for His creatures is manifested in the regularity of nature and the knowability of its laws. The better one understands the laws of nature (i.e., through the study of physics and metaphysics), the more one avoids mishaps and errors, thereby appearing to enjoy a special favor from God. Similarly, Maimonides interpreted miracles naturalistically: they do not manifest supernatural divine intervention in nature, but the preprogrammed exceptions to natural laws, built into nature at creation.

Almosnino departed from Maimonides' and Gersonides' intellectualist naturalism when he stated that the "Ways" are the perfect character traits (*middot*) of the supremely good Divine Self.[132] The hidden core of the divine Torah, therefore, does not consist of the fixed laws by which God governs the universe, but the infinite, dynamic perfections of God that the kabbalists call sefirot. Human perfection is possible because God revealed His perfections to Israel in the Torah. By doing so, He enabled those who love him to imitate Him and attain happiness in this world and immortal life in the next. Those who freely cling to God's Torah and love God unconditionally—the love of the noble for its own sake[133]—become like God and enjoy earthly as well as transcendent happiness. Such love, however, manifests the perfection of the will that, for Almosnino, is a distinct power within the faculties of the soul.

Human excellence (*ma'alat ha-adam*), says Almosnino, lies in the freedom of the will to determine whether to be as happy as God or as unhappy as beasts.[134] The human will is by nature rational and free. It is rational because it acts in accordance with information provided by the intellect, but it is free because it can either will the known object, will against it, or not will it at all.[135] The will is superior to the intellect not only because the known object cannot compel the will in any way, but also because the will is free to act or not to act. The intellect's freedom is more limited than the freedom of the will because the intellect is bound by the teleological structure of the universe. Hence the freedom of the intellect is limited only to doing something for its own sake rather than for the sake of something else.[136]

In the hierarchy of the soul, the will belongs to the appetitive power. Located between reason and the sense appetite, the will carries out the soul's task of taming or subduing the natural inclinations of the body. The freedom of the will entails not only ignoring the information provided by the intellect but freely choosing to pursue evil, an idea that both Aristotle and Maimonides would have found self-contradictory. The human desire to sin is neither uncommon nor merely a result of mistaken judgment by the intellect. Rather, it reflects the imperfection of the will, or the sickness of the will.

Finally, the freedom of the will is evident even within the act of cognition. The human intellect does not engage in cognitive activity at all times. What moves it to do so is a command by the will to cognize this or that object. Moreover, the acquisition of knowledge is a free activity, lacking either compulsion or necessity. Even logical thought, as in syllogisms, can be derailed by the will. And after the intellect has acquired a certain piece of knowledge, it is the will that determines whether the intellect will reflect it. The act of mental concentration (*hitbodedut*) is therefore not solely the domain of the perfect intellect but a contemplative act that requires the involvement of the will as well.[137] Almosnino summarizes the arguments in favor of the primacy of the will by saying that the intellect acts as a "counselor" (*yo`etz*) to the will. But the will is free to either accept or ignore the information provided by the intellect, exactly as a king can either accept or reject the advice of his ministers.[138]

The upshot of Almosnino's analysis of the interplay of the will and the intellect is that human happiness requires the perfection of both.[139] Wisdom (*ḥokhmah*) is the perfection of the intellect, and love is the perfection of the will. Almosnino therefore concludes that the ultimate end of human life consists of "contemplation [of God] combined with love" (*iyyun be-tzeruf ahavah*).[140] Unlike Maimonides, who thought that the love of God was an intellectual activity that reflected the perfection of theoretical reason, Almosnino and his contemporaries viewed love as the perfection of the will and, therefore, the perfection of practical reason. The love of God thus belongs to the realm of *praxis* (*ma`aseh*) rather than *theoria* (*iyyun*).

The Love of God and the Primacy of Praxis

The Aristotelian tradition (and indeed Greek and Hellenistic moral philosophy in general) emphasized the intrinsic link between intellectual perfection and moral goodness. The wise man must be morally good by habitually practicing just acts toward other persons. Conversely, moral goodness exhibited in the social sphere presupposes knowledge about the Supreme Good. The thrust of Aristotelian ethics was to develop the moral personality while living intelligently by curbing desires and practicing virtuous acts toward other persons, governed by a worthwhile end, i.e., happiness. Aristotle posited the faculty of practical reason (*phronesis*) as the middle ground between the theoretical and the moral life.

According to Aristotle, the man of practical reason (*phronimos*) deliberates with a view not merely to particular goals but to the good life in general, with a view to the best, and with a view to happiness. Concomitantly, the prudent man is concerned not only with universals, such as the good life in general but also with particular actions in concrete situations. By perfecting practical reason one can act "just right" in concrete situations. That is, one can act according to the rule of the mean, doing the right amount of good, at the right time, in the right manner, toward the right object, and for the right reason. Moral training thus involves the discovery of the mean between two extreme vices: overindulgence on the one hand and abstinence on the other. But moral goodness arises not through mere following of abstract rules, but through habitual practice and cumulative experience in interpersonal relations.

Maimonides incorporated these ideas into his analysis of Jewish Law when he attempted to show that the Torah perfects body and soul. Yet he had relatively little interest in practical reason per se because he invested the moral life with an instrumental value only. Moral perfection is but the means to the attainment of a higher perfection, i.e., theoretical wisdom that culminates in the knowledge of God. Moreover, Maimonides' own analysis of halakhah (the *praxis* of Judaism) rendered the discussion of practical reason almost unnecessary. The one who lives by halakhah (as interpreted by Maimonides) was to attain perfection of body and soul.

Moses Almosnino took a different approach to the cultivation of moral virtues. For him, the moral life is not only a means to an end but the very core of religious life in this world. The moral life that is guided by practical reason is informed by the values of the religious tradition. By imitating divine perfections revealed in the Torah, the devotee can acquire the moral virtues and attain the necessary self-spiritualization that leads to *devequt* in this world and eternal life after death. Moreover, for Almosnino the moral life of action is the very arena where one manifests the perfection of the will and the total devotion to God. Hence, the highest virtue in this life is not the intellectual virtue of philosophical wisdom but rather the virtue of prudence. Such an approach is closer to the Christian understanding of the moral life than to Maimonides'.

Borrowing from Buridan's commentary on the *Ethics*, Almosnino posited prudence (*tevunah*) as the supreme virtue, the most important of the four cardinal virtues.[141] The man of practical reason (*ha-navon*) is the wise man who has acquired all moral virtues,[142] especially prudence.[143] The prudent man is religiously perfect because he lives by the divine commands of the Torah. The prohibitions of the Torah (*mitzvot lo ta'aseh*) enable the good man to subdue the passions of the body and steer away from sin, and the positive commandments of the Torah (*mitzvot aseh*) facilitate the acquisition of moral virtues through habitual practice of good deeds. The man who acquires prudence knows how to distinguish between real and apparent goods. He realizes that bodily pleasures, wealth, honor, glory, and fame do not constitute true happiness even though a certain modicum of external goods is necessary for the performance of good deeds toward others (for example, charity).

The perfection of practical reason encompasses the perfection of the will, i.e., the love of the good for its own sake. Since the Supreme Good is the Divine Will, the prudent man who knows "divine things" is also the one who unconditionally loves God. Maimonides was indeed correct, says Almosnino, in teaching that the more one knows God the more one loves God. But Almosnino reinterprets the meaning of the love of God. Love is not the perfection of theoretical intellect but rather the perfection of the will, the inner dimension of *praxis* (*ma'aseh penimi*).[144] The man of prudence is therefore the one who diligently performs the mitzvot not because they are instrumental to the theoretical knowledge of God but because they have an intrinsic value as the expression of God's Will. In short, the felicitous man (*ha-me'ushar*) who has acquired the virtue of prudence is the human ideal about whom King David sang in the Psalms, that King Solomon praised in Ecclesiastes and Proverbs, and that the Tannaim portrayed in Tractate Avot.

The love of God is the ultimate end (*ha-takhlit ha-aharon*) of human life.[145] The love of God is the love of the honorable that enables the human will to resist the passions. In any perfect virtue there is a love of the honorable that leads to right reasoning and right choice and connects it to the other virtues. With each choice of every virtue the love of God is reinforced. Hence, it is through love of God that one attains the perfection of all virtues in this world and for which one is rewarded with eternal life. The love of God is everlasting and inexhaustible because it is an unconditional love.[146] Almosnino agrees with Maimonides and all those who followed him that the love of God is commensurate with knowledge. But for Almosnino the love of God is not a communication between two perfect intellects that share the identity of universals, but rather the love of the infinite "details of the beloved" (*pirtei ha-davar ha-ne'ehav*).[147] Only a perfect will that can discern the infinite variations of particulars can love God, the most perfect Will, unconditionally. Therefore, those who unconditionally love the Torah, the manifestation of God's infinite love, love God and enjoy everlasting salvation.

Love of God yields the blissful union of the separated soul with God. The perfected soul that removed from herself the vestiges of corporeality embraces God in a mystical union (*hithabrut, hitahadut*) in which the known, the knower, and the act of knowing are one and the same, as Maimonides taught in the *Guide* I:68. Transcending material limitations, the separated soul of Israel becomes one with God and the supernal Torah as she was before her descent into the body. Enjoying an incomparable spiritual delight (*ta'anug*), the soul finds her final repose and completion, whose religious symbol is the Sabbath.[148]

Almosnino's message is thus clear: those Jews who devote themselves to God and His Torah could experience the bliss of immortality despite the continuation of political exile and the continual waiting for the messiah. Almosnino did not ignore the traditional hope for the coming of the messiah but he depoliticized it by spiritualizing its meaning. The messianic age is not a historical period of the ingathering of Jews in the Land of Israel but the total transformation of human existence from corporeality to spirituality. In the Messianic Age, all Jews will envision the "the face of the Shekhinah" during their lifetimes because their bodies will no longer be material entities.[149]

The bliss of personal immortality is reserved for perfect Jews. Surprisingly, however, the community of the perfect now include both men and women. In a remarkable departure from the Maimonidean tradition, Almosnino and other cohorts held that women *could* enter the world to come even though the female intellect is naturally imperfect.[150] Precisely because ultimate felicity does not depend on philosophical wisdom—but rather on faith, the perfection of the will, and the actual performance of mitzvot—women can also enjoy the bliss of immortality. Even though post-expulsion thinkers continued to regard women (whose task was to facilitate the perfection of their husbands), as intellectually inferior to men, they did agree that as religious devotees women were equal to men.[151]

SUMMARY

During the fifteenth and sixteenth centuries the Jewish discourse on happiness underwent significant changes in response to traumatic events in Jewish history (the persecution of 1391, the mass conversion of Jews to Christianity, and the expulsions), as well as to growing Jewish familiarity with Christian scholasticism and Renaissance humanism. In the context of the discourse on happiness, predicated on greater familiarity with the original text by Aristotle, Jewish intellectuals articulated a vision of religious perfection that reaffirmed the spiritual superiority of Judaism. Ibn Shem Tov provided a conservative interpretation of Maimonides and Aristotle that recognized the inherent limitations of human reason and therefore claimed that it fails to provide the knowledge necessary for individual salvation and personal immortality. Only divine grace can reveal salvific knowledge. Yohanan Alemanno, by contrast, continued to perpetuate the religious naturalism of the fourteenth century but envisioned the ultimate end of human life as a mystical union with the central sefirah of the Godhead. And Moses Almosnino asserted that ultimate happiness depends on faith, the free operation of the will, and actual performance of the revealed Law.

By the end of the sixteenth century the fusion of Aristotle and Judaism was complete, but the more Jews became familiar with the text of the *Ethics*, the more they used their textual knowledge to assert religious traditional values. By the end of the Middle Ages, Jewish philosophers returned to a personalist conception of God; they endorsed the dualism of body and soul; they paid greater attention to the noncognitive dimension of human personality; they highlighted the importance of the will in human conduct; they recognized the religious value of moral action through the performance of mitzvot; they diminished the importance of theoretical wisdom and focused instead on the role of practical reason in religious life; they posited the love of God as the ultimate end of life and envisioned ultimate felicity as a mystical union with Him. As a result of these changes in the conception of happiness, the very scholars who studied philosophy also paved the way for the emergence of kabbalah as the dominant interpretation of Judaism.

Postscript

This book has traced the evolution of the discourse on happiness in Judaism from antiquity to the seventeenth century. Though its scope is broad, it was not intended to be a definitive study that exhausts all the issues under consideration. On the contrary, it was written with the hope that other scholars would supply additional information and correct, modify, or challenge specific claims made herein. More importantly, I intended it to be an invitation to all academic and general readers to reflect on their own views of human happiness in light of the views expounded in this book.

I chose to write about happiness for three reasons. First, reconstructing the discourse on happiness was a good way to tell the story of premodern Jewish philosophy, a story that is known today to but a small group of academic specialists. By focusing on that discourse, I have shown how Jewish intellectuals framed their attitudes toward life and death, individual and society, body and soul, good and evil, male and female, Jews and non-Jews, religion and philosophy. The discourse on happiness could be so comprehensive in its scope because to answer its main question—"What sort of person ought I to be in order to flourish as a human being?"—Jewish thinkers had to take a stand on the nature of humanity, the place of human beings in the order of things, the purpose of human life, the way human beings learn about the world, and the role of knowledge in making us distinct from other animals. Because reflections on these issues were predicated on a host of metaphysical, cosmological, psychological, and ethical questions, the discourse on happiness captures the complexity and dynamic evolution of Jewish religious thought in the premodern period.

Second, I chose this specific theme in order to correct the contemporary misperception that Judaism is not interested in the question of human happiness. Not only were Jewish thinkers over the centuries preoccupied with the concept; traditional Judaism has understood itself to be *the* best path to the attainment of happiness. In fact, I argued that one of the major reasons for the survival of Jewish life was the conviction that Judaism was the sole path to human well-being. Precisely because Jews passionately adhered to that belief, they could resist the pressure to convert to the majority religion and were able to withstand the hostility and animosity directed against them. This Jewish self-perception makes sense only if we realize that happiness does not mean "having fun," "feeling good at a given moment," or "experiencing pleasant bodily sensations." Likewise, happiness in traditional Judaism was not equated with possessions, wealth, power, or fame. Rather, *it was understood to mean human flourishing, an objective standard that*

organizes all activities into a meaningful pattern for the duration of one's life.
The happy life is a life in which what is objectively good for human beings is attained when they conduct themselves in a particular manner and undertake those activities that promote their objective good. Traditional Judaism has viewed itself as the best pattern of life because it best accords with the objective facts of human existence.

And third, I wanted to explore the discourse on happiness to shed light on the dialectical relationship between the universal and the particular dimensions of Judaism. The Jewish people today is a house divided, especially for those who live in the State of Israel. A deep cleavage between secular and religious Jews threatens to tear asunder the fabric of Israeli society, with no consensus in sight. This book was written with the conviction that a clear understanding of the Jewish past is useful and indeed necessary to Jewish self-understanding in the present. Although we have shown that controversy about the meaning of Judaism has been a constant feature of the Jewish experience, the premodern history of the Jewish philosophical tradition indicates that there need not be a contradiction between religious commitment and devotion to scientific truth, between faith in God and full participation in worldly affairs, between taking Judaism seriously and seeking to be happy.

In reconstructing that history I have pursued several themes, which at first glance may appear unrelated. I showed that Jewish thinkers shared an objectivist approach to happiness and that Judaism understood itself as the best path to the happy life. Tracing the reception of the *Nicomachean Ethics* among Jews, I argued that the Jewish approach to happiness had much in common with Aristotle's views. Since both Jews and Greek philosophers agreed that happiness is predicated on the cultivation of virtues and the attainment of knowledge, we disclosed the connection between virtue and knowledge in Jewish ethics. Contrary to contemporary ethical theories, which tend to pit ethics of virtue against ethics of duty, I showed that in Judaism there is no necessary tension between the two. The reason for this is to be found in the fact that already in the Bible, the Torah of God (and hence the source of all duties) is identified with the Wisdom of God (whose pursuit is itself virtue).

The identification of Torah and Wisdom was at the core of the Jewish conception of happiness, demanding that Jews pursue wisdom as part of their loyalty to God. As Jews encountered philosophy and its related sciences in medieval Islam, they expanded the category of "wisdom" and devised a new course of study for the education of the virtuous person. These changes provoked debates about the curriculum—the Maimonidean Controversies, which were inseparable from the rise of kabbalah as an alternative to rationalist philosophy. I presented the teachings of the *Zohar* as a prescription for happiness and analyzed how its own anthropology was indebted to philosophical categories. Both philosophy and kabbalah agreed that the ultimate end of life pertained to the soul and that it could be experienced most fully only in the afterlife. In the late Middle Ages, kabbalah and rationalist philosophy were not mutually exclusive programs for the attainment of happiness, but instead closely influenced one another.

Focus on the salvation of the soul was also the bone of contention between Jews and Christians and the cause of much of Jewish suffering in the late Middle Ages. Thus the debate on happiness also shaped the interaction between Judaism and Christianity, even though Jewish intellectuals expressed themselves in terms borrowed from their cultural environment, through conversation with medieval scholasticism and Renaissance humanism. Lastly, I showed how the fusion of philosophy and kabbalah led to the demise of philosophy and the rise of kabbalah as the official interpretation of rabbinic Judaism, but without explaining why this happened. Such an explanation would require writing yet another book.

The Medieval Legacy

The previous chapter brought the story of the discourse on happiness to about 1580, but reflections about happiness continued to engage Jewish thinkers in the centuries that followed, particularly in the ethical (Musar) literature of the late sixteenth and seventeenth centuries, written mostly under the spell of kabbalah and transformed in Hasidism of the eighteenth century.[1] The early modern ethical literature perpetuated many of the elements of the medieval worldview. The discourse was exegetical rather than conceptual and philosophic, and its goal was the purification of the soul and the creation of a holy community. The assumption that human well-being is predicated on the link of virtue and knowledge remained intact, but knowledge pertained not to the laws by which God manages the physical world but to God's personal character traits, symbolized in the sefirot. Thus virtues were to be cultivated through cleaving to the sefirot, rather than through following the mean between excess and deficiency.

Tomer Devorah (The Palm Tree of Deborah) by Moses ben Jacob Cordovero (1522–1572) was the kabbalistic ethical manual that spelled out in detail the principal of *imitato Dei*—the connection between the theoretical knowledge of the sefirotic structure and the acquisition of virtues, postulated by the *Zohar*.[2] Each virtue is here connected to a particular sefirah, exemplifying a particular attribute of God. In descending order from the uppermost sefirah, Keter, to the lowest, Malkhut, Cordovero explained how the imitation of a particular sefirah resulted in the cultivation of a desirable virtue leading to a particular behavior. To be perfect, as God is perfect, a kabbalist had to fathom the character traits and ideal modes of conduct of the divine personality and make them his own. Thus the religiously perfect Jew could acquire the Godly virtues of humility, lovingkindness, and compassion, and devote his life to the exclusive study of Torah, a life of perfect purity.

The kabbalistic speculations about God's personal traits were no less abstract than the philosophic speculations about God's ways, construed as the laws of nature. The difference between the two lay in the fact that the kabbalists highlighted the interpersonal relationship between God and Israel. That relationship was construed on the basis of the rich tapestry of examples in biblical and rabbinic sources, and its homiletical elaborations could be connected to ordinary experience. Thus Cordovero not only explained how the sefirot were linked to particular character traits, but also composed specific rules for conduct (*hanhagot*) that provided spiritual leadership to a mystical fraternity of his disciples and associates.[3] Those ethical rules insisted that one must conduct himself in humility and lowliness of spirit, never insult others, be indifferent to insults directed at him, never be prone to anger, and be charitable. Other rules regulated purity of body and purity of speech and promoted fasting and other ascetic practices, all of which were intended to create a holy way of life.

Cordovero's *Tomer Devorah* was influential among both Sephardi and Ashkenazi kabbalists. The text was summarized in *Ḥesed Le-Abraham* (Grace to Abraham) by a Moroccan kabbalist, Abraham ben Mordecai Azulai (c. 1570–1643), who settled in the Land of Israel. It was further developed in *Shenei Luḥot ha-Berit* (The Two Tablets of the Covenant) by R. Isaiah ben Abraham Halevi Horowitz (ca. 1565–1630). Born in Prague and educated in Poland, Horowitz too moved to the Land of Israel, where he functioned as the Rabbi of the Ashkenazic community. Convinced that the time was ripe for the public disclosure of the esoteric teachings of the Zohar as a preparation for the imminent redemption, he created a unique fusion of halakhah, midrash, and kabbalah to chart the path of the religiously perfect life. Drawing on both philosophic and kabbalistic sources, he advised how one could cleave to God and sublimate negative feelings while pursuing normal physical and economic activities. For the one who wished for eternal life, Horowitz defined the ideal path: association with righteous people; preoccupation with repentance, and performance of the commandments "with the animation of the heart and with joy." Generations of Jews in Central and Eastern Europe based their lives on the ethical program of this influential book (known by the acronym of *Shelah*), which perpetuated the kabbalistic ethical spirituality of Moses Cordovero. Although the religious tenor and hermeneutical practices of these early modern texts were indebted more to kabbalah than to rationalist philosophy, they can be seen as an extension and transformation of the medieval discourse on happiness.

In the seventeenth century, medieval Jewish Aristotelianism was no longer a creative intellectual program—in part because of the dissolution of the Aristotelian worldview in the seventeenth century and the rise of new scientific models to explain the relationship between God and nature and the place of human beings in the order of things. Jewish thinkers would continue to use Aristotelian philosophical terminology well into the eighteenth century, but how to live rightly as a Jew was determined by kabbalah and halakhah, and how to think about the world was dictated by alternative philosophies of nature, such as Atomism or Platonism. Nonetheless, the major challenge to the medieval discourse on happiness was dealt not by kabbalah or by alternative philosophies of nature, but by Baruch Spinoza, who severed the identification of Torah and Wisdom—an identification that had served as the foundation of the discourse since antiquity.

A child of *converso* parents who had settled in Amsterdam, where they returned to Judaism, Spinoza began to express views that challenged the notion that the Torah is a philosophic text. His skepticism was directed against the traditional Jewish understanding of God and of Torah. Spinoza denied that God is a wholly spiritual and intellectual being. Rather, He is the one and only substance that exists; all other existents are but modes of God. In the monistic worldview of Spinoza, both extension and thought are modes of God. In such a view God is not the creator of nature: God *is* nature, conceived in its totality. Given this conception, there is little sense in talking about the imitation of God as the ultimate end of human life. Between the divine and the human there is no longer a gap; humans are but one of the infinite modes of God.

More detrimental to the discourse on happiness was Spinoza's critique of the Bible.[4] For him the biblical text was not a Torah in the sense of revealed, divine instruction, but a human document that expresses the political situations of an ancient people, Israel. Furthermore, it is not a philosophic-scientific text whose teachings lead to the attainment of happiness. In contrast to Maimonides and his followers, Spinoza claimed that prophecy, the agency that received the divine revelation, was not a cognitive phenomenon: the Bible teaches nothing philosophical. It has much to say about morality and the politics of the theocratic state, but these insights have little to do with knowledge of God, or nature, or the ultimate end of human life. Moreover, the ritual laws of the Bible are not the laws of nature: they belong to the realm of politics and not philosophy or science. Thus the biblical text itself is no key to the mysteries of the universe or to intimate relationship with God. And the intellectual love of God is not a salvation of the individual soul but "the highest possible contentment of the mind." With Spinoza, then, we return to a modified Stoic understanding of human nature.

All human beings possess a drive for self-preservation and their goal is "to maximize their pleasure and utility."[5] As material entities they are creatures of passions, to which they can easily become enslaved. The emotions cannot be extirpated, but they can be transformed through cognitive activity. The more we understand them, the more we can understand our place in the world and chart the right course of action. Spinoza, then, continued the therapeutic understanding of reason. According to him, liberation is recognizing human finite limitations, and it has nothing to do with the Bible, a text that pertains to politics rather than to knowledge. Because Spinoza openly challenged the claim that the Torah has a cognitive content relevant to human intellectual perfection, his views were considered heretical, and the Jewish community of Amsterdam excommunicated him in 1656. His separation of revelation and reason paved the way for a modern Jewish philosophy and with it to secular understandings of human happiness.

The medieval discourse on happiness resurfaced in the late eighteenth century as part of the new Jewish attempt to rethink Judaism in light of modern philosophy. Adopting the ideals of the Enlightenment, several scholars felt that something was missing in traditional Judaism because it did not cultivate "human knowledge." This lacuna, they felt, was the reason for the lack of social graces in Jews—which in turn contributed to their discrimination by the host culture. If Jews were to be granted equal civil rights and integrate into European culture, Jews and Judaism must change from within. To accomplish this goal, the *maskilim,* proponents of Jewish Enlightenment (*Haskalah*), turned to their medieval past and published the works of their medieval predecessors, reconsidering once more the nexus of Torah and Wisdom.

To show that commitment to Judaism is totally compatible with openness toward contemporary philosophy and science, in 1790 Isaac Satanow (1732–1804) printed a new translation of and commentary on Aristotle's *Ethics*—which once again was used to facilitate a conversation between Jews and the surrounding culture.[6] The new Hebrew translation was based on that of Meir Alguades, and Satanow was familiar as well with the commentaries of Joseph ibn Shem Tov and Moses Almosnino. Satanow, however, realized that these medieval texts needed to be made current if they were to appeal to modern readers. Reading Aristotle "inclusively," this Jewish advocate of Haskalah sought to convince his Jewish readers that involvement in worldly affairs and the cultivation of desirable character traits was necessary if Jews wished to be emancipated. Satanow also composed *Mishlei Assaf* (The Proverbs of Assaf) imitating the biblical Book of Proverbs, in praise of wisdom and the wise and promoting the interest in the sciences.

Though Aristotle was again available in a Hebrew version, however, Aristotelian virtue ethics failed to mold modern Jewish thought during the nineteenth century. By then Aristotelianism was totally discredited as a scientific explanation of the world, and its virtue ethics was replaced with the rule-centered moral philosophies of Immanuel Kant and the Utilitarians. Since Jewish law is also about rules and obligations, Judaism had to be rethought in terms of Kantian philosophy—a task accomplished most fully by Hermann Cohen. On a more popular level, however, the Utilitarian understanding of happiness shaped the way the general educated Jewish public understood its meaning during the nineteenth century. It was this conception that Samson Raphael Hirsch, the founder of Neo-Orthodoxy, probably had in mind when he claimed that traditional Judaism has nothing to do with happiness. In his *The Nineteen Letters on Judaism*, he berates the fictitious addressee of the treatise, Benjamin, saying: "You measure the value of Judaism by a standard of the purpose of human existence, which you find to be happiness and perfection. I could ask: Is it so sure that happiness and perfection constitute the goal and objective of man's existence?"[7] Hirsch's critique of his enlightened interlocutor is not surprising: the premodern paradigm that linked Wisdom and Torah was no longer considered philosophically or religiously valid. In the nineteenth and twentieth centuries, Jews articulated a plethora of religious responses to the challenges of modernity—Reform, Conservative, Orthodox, Ultra-Orthodox, and Hasidic—as well as several secular ones—Zionist, Socialist, and Humanist—all of which wrestle with the meaning of human well-being and the boundaries of Judaism. Alas, as fascinating as these modern developments are, we will have to discuss them in another book.

Final Reflections

Happiness in Premodern Judaism has amassed a lot of information, but all academic exercises have to face a simple question: "So what?" Let me respond by stressing some of the implications of our study for modern Judaism and conclude with reflections upon what I find personally meaningful in the premodern approach to happiness.

For Jewish readers, I hope that the encounter with the Jewish philosophic past may lead to a rethinking of the nature of Judaism. The material presented in this book makes it clear that Judaism is not a monolithic tradition, but a highly variegated religious civilization that has long harbored diverse voices, intellectual programs, and ideological agendas. These diverse elements were often in conflict with each other, generating an ongoing internal debate that has made Jewish civilization extremely dynamic, perhaps even restless. Those conflicts were fueled by the constant interaction of Judaism with the surrounding cultures, with Jews adapting and adopting their influences to fit a distinctly Jewish way of looking at the world. Through the conversation with its cultural neighbors, Judaism was continually transformed and enriched. Thus any attempt to examine Jewish culture without consideration of its interaction with other modes of thought will fail to grasp its true historical trajectory. In other words, the history of Judaism can be told only when Jews are studied in their interaction with non-Jews.

What gave the rich and multi-vocal Jewish tradition its internal unity was a religious factor, namely, the Jewish commitment to sacred Scriptures, the Torah. Believed to be divinely revealed, the Torah was the link between God and Israel. The interpretation of the sacred text, then, was the overarching theme that provided structure to Jewish intellectual life and brought together Jews who held very different views or lived by very different customs. As long as Jews believed the Torah was the prescription for the happy life, they could sustain their sense of spiritual superiority over other religious traditions and withstand the persecutions to which they were subjected for their refusal to convert.

Given the profoundly religious nature of Jewish civilization, it is very doubtful that a strict secular understanding of Judaism, based solely on ethnicity is either historically true or existentially viable. Judaism is not to be identified merely with the events that constitute the history of one ethnic group, the Jews, even though the Jewish people is the carrier of the story of Judaism. Rather, the story of Judaism is the story of the relationship of one group of people to God. The medium of that relationship is the Torah and the way of life that flows from it. The material presented in this book spells out an argument that all Jews need to wrestle with: qua Jews, it is impossible to live well, or experience happiness, outside the perimeters of Torah. Jews may disagree about the meaning of "Torah" and its implications, but for Jews there can be no reflections about happiness without it.

The centrality of Torah in Jewish life, however, need not be construed in a parochial and exclusionary manner. On the contrary, the discourse on happiness presented in this book explores the dialectical relationship between the universalistic and particularistic aspects of Judaism. By focusing on one strand within Jewish thought—the strand that began with the Wisdom stratum of the Bible and ended with Spinoza—I wish to inspire all Jewish readers to reflect about the place of philosophy in Judaism. "Wisdom" is the Jewish category that refers to the pursuit of truth accessible to all human beings by virtue of their being rational. Under that rubric, Jews have acquired knowledge about the world and about God from a variety of sources and traditions. The pursuit of truth, the pursuit that constitutes the love of wisdom—that is, philosophy—transcends ethnic or cultural boundaries. Indeed, the Jewish Wisdom tradition presented herein shows that to love God Jews must be willing to examine all truth claims; if found to be true, these claims are part of Judaism, because what is true is Jewish. Philosophical activity, therefore, is inherently Jewish.

This conclusion is particularly relevant for Jews who feel alienated from Judaism because they presume it to be unenlightened and intellectually backward. To these readers, who are to be found especially in the secular academy, this book shows that Judaism is intellectually rich, that thinking and the pursuit of truth are integral to being Jewish, and that Jewish intellectuals have pondered the deepest questions about the world and about human existence since ancient times. Especially during the Middle Ages, Jewish thinkers were very knowledgeable about the latest scientific theories and were often at the forefront of the intellectual currents of their time. Put differently, Judaism has always had an "Enlightenment" strand in it; the modern epoch known by that name was but a variation on an existing tradition, not a totally new innovation. By tracing Judaism's long premodern discourse on happiness, I hope to convince the alienated to regard Judaism as an intellectual challenge worthy of their undertaking.

I hope this encounter with the Jewish past will serve as an inspiration for non-Jewish readers, too, to rethink the main questions posed by the ancient Greek philosophers. Just as the premodern Jewish thinkers presented particularistic answers to these universal questions, so too will contemporary readers approach them from within their own cultural and religious locations. And for all readers, Jews and non-Jews alike, I hope this book has convinced them that as far as human happiness is concerned, the ancient and medieval philosophers had some deep and useful insights, even though some of their philosophical assumptions were mistaken.

For me, the premodern discourse on happiness is meaningful because the ancient and medieval thinkers approached the question of happiness in terms of an *objective* pattern of life based on fundamental truths about human beings. For us, too, the answer to the question "How can we flourish as human beings?" requires that we develop a philosophy that takes into consideration objective truths about our species. These truths, of course, are by no means as simple as talking about "human nature." Nor can they be reduced to but one activity, thinking. But the more we know about ourselves, the more we can understand what we share with other animals, where we differ, where humans excel, and where they are limited. To experience well-being as humans, then, requires us to understand what all humans share as much as we must take into consideration diversity among humans. The contemporary preoccupation with "difference" and "identity politics" has made it easy to forget our commonalities. The desire to be happy is perhaps the most universal of human desires, giving rise to a discourse that can, in turn, cut across cultural and ethnic boundaries.

Many will disagree and argue that people across cultures interpret the truths of the human condition very differently and organize their images of reality into widely divergent stories or myths. While this may be true, I still maintain that those who have reflected about human happiness share a certain understanding about how to live rightly. Regardless of their religious beliefs, ethnic affiliation, or philosophic training, they all advocate self-control, self-discipline, temperance, and moderation. Lives governed by impulses, cravings, strong passions, or lusts usually end in disaster either to the individual or to the society. A life of self-control presupposes delay of gratification, ability to plan for future results, and patience. These qualities are not possible for young children, who have short attention spans and require that their biological desires be met sooner rather than later. Immediate gratification, then, is a childish tendency that can be overcome only through conscious training and intentional frustration of desires.

The well-lived life is thus not a characteristic of children or childish adults. It is a life-long process that requires thought, effort, practice, dedication, and determination. It does not come easily or automatically, but only through conscious wrestling and reflection. For this reason, there is no contradiction between living a happy life (as the premoderns understood it) and feeling occasional doubt, sadness, aggravation, or displeasure. These are temporary mental states that can disappear when the particular circumstances that gave rise to them are gone, or when we frame in proper perspective either the feelings and the mood or the circumstances that gave rise to them. The well-lived life, then, is not a life free of negative feelings or events, but a life in which these imperfections are properly understood and, therefore, better coped with.

Finally, the premoderns were right to hold that human well-being pertains to *who we are* rather than to *what we own* or *how other people perceive us*. Thus I regard the premodern focus on excellence of character to be a healthy departure from the relentless pursuit of material goods, wealth, power, and celebrity that characterizes much of our rather childish culture. I believe that many of our social ills (e.g., violence, theft, lying, exploitation, abuse, and injustice) are due to actions of people with insufficiently developed or deformed characters no less than to external economic and social circumstances. This is not to say that virtue alone is the panacea for all our moral dilemmas, but the ongoing effort to acquire the virtues that constitute a good character is a noble goal for us, individually and collectively. Even though I did not provide philosophical arguments in favor of virtue ethics, I hope the issues discussed will be found to be worthy of further study on both historical and philosophical grounds. I trust I have made the ancient and medieval texts somewhat more accessible and hope that they will enable contemporary readers to ask the right questions about happiness, and perhaps even affirm the connection between virtue, knowledge, and well-being.

Notes

Notes to the Preface

1. The philosophical literature on happiness is very large and cannot be cited here. A useful overview of the literature until the early 1980s is offered by Douglas den Uyl and Tibor R. Machman, "Recent Work on the Concept of Happiness," *American Philosophical Quarterly* 20 (2) (1983): 115–35. A useful analysis of the concept of happiness is provided by V. J. McGill, *The Idea of Happiness* (New York: Frederick A. Praeger, 1967); Wladyslaw Tatarkiewicz, *Analysis of Happiness* (The Hague: Martinus Nijhoff, 1976); Elizabeth Telfer, *Happiness* (New York: St. Martin Press, 1980).

2. The revival was launched by the British philosopher Elizabeth Anscombe, who called for the replacement of rule-centered moral theories, such as Kantianism and Utilitarianism, with ancient virtue ethics. She argued that both modern theories are flawed because they presuppose a legislative model that is, in turn, grounded in theistic assumptions that the secular world could no longer endorse. For Anscombe the return to ancient Greek virtue ethics must be a secular answer to the moral predicament of the modern world. See G.E.M. Anscombe, "Modern Moral Philosophy," *Philosophy* 33 (1958): 1–59. For an overview of the revival of virtue ethics see Arthur Flemming, "Reviving the Virtues," *Ethics* 40 (1980): 587–95; Marcia Baron, "Varieties of Ethics of Virtue," *American Philosophical Quarterly* 22 (1985): 47–53; Gregory Trianosky, "What is Virtue Ethics All About," *American Philosophical Quarterly* 27 (4) (1990): 335–44; Roger Crisp (ed.), *How Should One Live: Essays on the Virtues* (Oxford: Clarendon Press, 1996); John Kekes, *Moral Wisdom and Good Lives* (Ithaca: Cornell University Press, 1995); Daniel Statman (ed.), *Virtue Ethics: A Critical Reader* (Washington DC: Georgetown University Press, 1997), 42–55.

3. Julia Annas, *The Morality of Happiness* (Oxford: Oxford University Press, 1993) is the most prominent example of this scholarship.

4. For an overview of the differences between these two types of ethical theories see Michael Slote, *From Morality to Virtue* (New York: Oxford University Press, 1992); Roger Crisp, "Modern Philosophy and the Virtues," in Roger Crisp (ed.) *How Should One Live*, 1–16; Schenk David, "Recasting the Ethics of Virtue/Ethics of Duty Debate," *Journal of Religious Ethics* 4 (1976): 269–86; Marcia Baron, "The Ethics of Duty/Ethics of Virtue Debate and Its Relevance to Educational Theory," *Educational Theory* 2 (1985): 135–49; David Clowney, "Virtue, Rules and the Foundation of Ethics," *Philosophia* 20 (1984): 49–68.

5. Two semi-academic books, which represent the current revival of virtue ethics, received a lot of public attention and were on the best-seller list of the New York Times: William Bennet (ed.), *The Book of Virtues: A Treasure of Great Moral Stories*

(New York: Simon and Schuster, 1993) and Andre Comte-Sponville, *A Small Treatise on the Great Virtues: The Uses of Philosophy in Everyday Life* (New York: Metropolitan Books, 2001). The first indicates the attempt by a conservative political theorist and policy maker in the Reagan administration to introduce the discourse of virtues to contemporary Americans in order to combat what he considers undesirable in American secular, popular culture. The second, written originally in French for a philosophically educated reading public in France, contains philosophical reflections on the essential virtues anchored in classical philosophy but refracted through Kantian ethics. The Jewish analogue of these books is Eugene B. Borowitz and Frances Weinman Schwartz, *The Jewish Moral Virtues* (Philadelphia: Jewish Publication Society, 1999), although to my knowledge this book has received very little public attention. It was recently reviewed by Elliot Dorff along with two other books on Jewish ethics in *AJS Review* 26 (no.1) (2002): 198–202.

6. See Robert Louden, "Virtue Ethics and Anti-Theory," *Philosophia* 20 (1984): 93–114; Stanley G. Clark, "Anti-Theory in Ethics," *American Philosophical Review* 24 (1987): 237–44.

Notes to Chapter 1

1. For an excellent treatment of this point, see Lawrence J. Hatab, *Myth and Philosophy: A Contest of Truths* (La Salle, IL: Open Court, 1990). The discussion of the next three paragraphs is based on that book. While I follow Hatab's exposition, there is no consensus on this issue among scholars of Greek philosophy. On the status of this debate, consult Richard Buxton (ed.) *From Myth to Reason?: Studies in the Development of Greek Thought* (New York: Oxford University Press, 1999).

2. Since the Enlightenment, the logos/mythos dichotomy has been central to Western consciousness. See Hans-Georg Gadamer, *Truth and Method*, revised by Joel Weinsheimer and Donald G. Marshall (New York: Crossroad Publishing, 1989), 273–74.

3. Joseph M. Bryant, *Moral Codes and Social Structure in Ancient Greece: A Sociology of Greek Ethics from Homer to the Epicureans and Stoics* (Albany: State University of New York Press, 1998), 170.

4. For overview of the Sophists, consult W.K.C. Guthrie, *The Sophists* (Cambridge: Cambridge University Press, 1971); George B. Kerferd, *The Sophistic Movement* (Cambridge: Cambridge University Press, 1981); Henri I. Marrou, *A History of Education in Antiquity*, trans. George Lamb (New York: Sheed and Ward, 19567), 46–60.

5. Guthrie, *The Sophists*, 50.

6. Bryant, *Moral Codes*, 28.

7. Ibid. 189.

8. Ibid. 30.

9. Alasdaire MacIntyre, *A Short History of Ethics* (New York: Macmillan Publishing Co., 1966), 14.

10. Gorgias (472 c-d).
11. Bryant, *Moral Codes,* 188.
12. Ibid. 189.
13. This sentence requires some qualification: 1) not every view stated in Plato's dialogues expresses his own position and 2) Plato's thought developed over time. The view of the soul as a fallen spirit is expressed in the middle dialogues *Gorgias, Phaedo, Phaedrus,* and *Republic.*
14. For a review of the pertinent literature, consult Kent F. Moors, *Platonic Myth: An Introductory Study* (Washington, DC: University Press of America, 1981), 1–24.
15. Stephen Halliwell, *The Poetics of Aristotle: Translation and Commentary* (Chapel Hill: The University of North Carolina Press, 1987), 79.
16. Stephen Halliwell, *Aristotle's Poetics* (Chapel Hill: University of North Carolina Press, 1986), 25.
17. The word *mythos* in Greek carries a range of meanings, including speech, story, report, narrative, myth, fable, and fiction. The translation of *mythos* as "plot-structure" was coined by Stephen Halliwell, *Aristotle's Poetics*, 24, and will be used herein for the same reasons he cites.
18. Ibid. 25.
19. Aristotle, *The Nicomachean Ethics,* trans. W.D. David Ross, rev. J.L. Ackrill and J.O Urmson (Oxford and New York: Oxford University Press, 1980). All citations from Aristotle are from this edition. An earlier version of this revised translation by J.O. Urmson alone is included in *The Complete Works of Aristotle,* ed. Jonathan Barnes (Princeton: Princeton University Press, 1984), vol. 2.
20. The secondary literature on Aristotle's conception of happiness is extensive and cannot be reproduced here in full. Some of the recent works consulted for this study include the following: Sarah Broadie, *Ethics with Aristotle* (Oxford: Oxford University Press, 1991); Richard Kraut, *Aristotle on the Human Good* (Princeton: Princeton University Press, 1989); Amelie Oksenberg Rorty, ed., *Essays on Aristotle's Ethics* (Berkeley: University of California Press, 1980); John M. Cooper, *Reason and Human Good in Aristotle* (Indianapolis: Hackett, 1986); Julia Annas, *The Morality of Happiness* (Oxford: Oxford University Press, 1993); Nancy Sherman, *The Fabric of Character: Aristotle's Theory of Virtue* (Oxford: Clarendon Press, 1989); W. F. R. Hardie, *Aristotle's Ethical Theory,* 2nd ed. (Oxford: Clarendon Press, 1980). For an extensive bibliography on Aristotle's ethical theories consult Jonathan Barnes (ed.), *The Cambridge Companion to Aristotle* (Cambridge: Cambridge University Press, 1995), 357–72. For a convenient summary of the structure of the *Nicomachean Ethics* consult J. L. Ackrill (trans.) *Aristotle's Ethics* (London: Faber and Faber, 1973), 13–34.
21. *Physics* II:1 192b 22–23. In *Metaphysics* V:4 Aristotle provides a more subtle definition of "nature," distinguishing the following meanings: 1) "the genesis of growing things"; 2) "the immanent part of growing things, from which its growth first proceeds"; 3) "The source from which the primary movement in each natural

object is present in it in virtue of its own essence"; 4) "the primary material of which any natural object consists or out of which it is made"; 5) "the essence of natural objects"; 6) "every essence in general has come to be called a 'nature', because the nature of a thing is one kind of essence." These nuances will not be considered in our discussion.

22. Sir David William Ross, *Aristotle* (London: Methuen, 1977 [1923]), 68.

23. R. G. Collingwood, *The Idea of Nature* (Oxford: Clarendon Press, 1957), 82.

24. For an analysis of this central notion in Aristotle's philosophy consult George A. Blair, *Energia and Entelechia: "Act" in Aristotle* (Ottawa: University of Ottawa Press, 1992).

25. Thomas Nagle, "Aristotle on Eudaimonia," in *Essays on Aristotle's Ethics*, ed. Amelie O. Rorty (Berkeley: University of California Press, 1980), 8.

26. The medical model of philosophy is essential to the Greek conception of the good life. See Martha Nussbaum, *The Therapy of Desire: Theory and Practice in Hellenistic Ethics* (Princeton: Princeton University Press, 1994), esp. 13–101; Joseph Owens, "Aristotelian Ethics, Medicine, and the Changing Nature of Man" in his *Aristotle: The Collected Papers of Joseph Owens*, ed. John R. Catan (Albany: State University of New York Press, 1981), 169–80.

27. For analysis of Aristotle's refutation of Plato's conception of the good, see Ivor Leclerc, "The Metaphysics of the Good," in *The Good Life and Its Pursuit*, ed. Jude P. Dougherty (New York: Paragon House, 1984), 51–76; Hellmut Flashar, "The Critique of Plato's Theory of Ideas in Aristotle's Ethics," in *Articles on Aristotle*, vol. 2, *Ethics and Politics*, ed. Jonathan Barnes, Malcolm Schofield, and Richard Sorabji (London: Duckworth, 1977), 1–24.

28. For an analysis of the trans-categorical nature of "being" and "one," see J. L. Ackrill, "Aristotle on "Good' and the Categories," in *Articles on Aristotle*, vol. 2.

29. I owe this term to Joseph Owens, "The KALON in Aristotelian Ethics," in Dominic J. O'Meara (ed.), *Studies in Aristotle*, (Washington: Catholic University of America Press, 1981), 262.

30. See Kraut, *Aristotle on the Human Good*, 200.

31. See Annas, *Morality of Happiness*, 32–3.

32. See Kraut, *Aristotle on the Human Good*, 205. We should note that the word *teleion* translated here as "final" is rendered in Urmson's other translation as "complete." Much of the ambiguity in Aristotle's analysis of happiness is based on the difference between these two words.

33. Some scholars, e.g., Terence H. Irwin and Richard Kraut, translate *teleion* as "most perfect," and their analysis is based on the nuanced connotation of that word. See Terence H. Irwin, *Translation of Aristotle, Nicomachean Ethics* (Indianapolis: Hacket, 1985). For a recent analysis see Thomas Hurka, *Perfectionism* (Oxford: Oxford University Press, 1993). Hurka is a contemporary Neo-Aristotelian who wishes to reinstate virtue ethics but without its grand teleological moorings.

34. J.L. Ackrill is the most important exponent of this reading. See J.L. Ackrill,

"Aristotle on Eudaimonia," in *Essays on Aristotle's Ethics*, 15–33. Ackrill's position is carefully analyzed by Kraut, in order to be rejected, in his *Aristotle on the Human Good*, 230–37.

35. I consider Richard Kraut the most important exponent of the "exclusive," or "dominant" interpretation. His views will be discussed further below.

36. Annas, *Morality of Happiness*, 40.

37. See Kraut, *Aristotle on the Human Good*, 294–300.

38. The Greek prefix *eu* means "good" and *daimon* means "spirit." *Eudaimonia* thus means the possession of a good *daimon*. In colloquial usage *eudaimon* was the equivalent of "lucky," even when some powers were thought to be responsible for the luck. For Plato, the *daimon* is the *nous* in each of us, the direct creation of the Demiurge. To look after this *daimon*, that is, to devote oneself to knowledge, is to pursue true *eudaimonia*. For Aristotle a *daimon* is a spirit, a god in a more literal sense. The *daimon* is something somewhat distinct from the individual, a sort of helmsman. To pursue *eudaimonia* is to actualize our best and wisest aspect.

39. William J. Prior, *Virtue and Knowledge: An Introduction to Ancient Greek Ethics* (London and New York, Routledge, 1991), 150.

40. On the debate concerning the proper translation of *eudaimonia* see Kraut, *Aristotle on the Human Good*, 3.

41. Annas, *Morality of Happiness*, 41, and Sherman, *The Fabric of Character*, 9.

42. The distinction between activity or actuality (*energeia*) and movement or process (*kinesis*) is crucial to the Aristotelian analysis of the good life. While both terms are fulfillment or realizations (*entelecheia*), actuality is wholly complete, whereas movement occupies a stretch of time. Examples of *energeia* are seeing, knowing, and being pleased. Examples of *kinesis* are building, curing, working at sculpture. See Abraham Edel, *Aristotle and His Philosophy* (Chapel Hill: University of North Carolina Press, 1982), 84. As much as one cannot be partially seeing, so one cannot be partially flourishing. *Eudaimonia*, therefore, must be an activity and not a process or a movement.

43. In recent decades ethical theories rooted in the notion of human nature have been under sustained attack. At the forefront stand feminist theorists who argue that theories of human nature are androcentric, identifying the universal human with but half of the human species, namely, men. For an overview of feminist critique of Aristotle, consult Cynthia A. Freeland, ed., *Feminist Interpretations of Aristotle* (University Park: The Pennsylvania State University Press, 1993); Arlene Saxonhouse, "Aristotle: Defective Males, Hierarchy, and the Limits of Politics," in *Feminist Interpretations and Political Theory*, ed. Mary Lyndon Shanley and Carol Pateman (University Park: The Pennsylvania State University Press, 1991), 32–52; Lynda Lange, "Woman is Not a Rational Animal: On Aristotle's Biology of Reproduction," in *Discovering Reality*, ed. Sandra Harding and Merrill B. Hintikka (Dordrecht, Holland: D. Reidel Publishing Company, 1983), 1–15. Indeed, Aristotle and the Hellenistic and medieval scholars who followed in his footsteps regarded the female as an incomplete male and did not take her into consideration when

they reflected about human nature. To avoid an anachronism, I will remain loyal to the Aristotelian texts at my disposal and will use the male gender to talk about human nature and the well-being of the human species. I see no good reason to impose my own feminist sensibilities on the ancient and medieval sources. To do so would distort their meaning. The discourse on happiness indeed has a gendered aspect: happiness is reserved for men only. As interesting as this theme is, it will not be treated in this book in any detail because of space considerations.

44. The Hellenistic commentators and their medieval successors all took for granted that Aristotle's psychology in the *De Anima* underscores his analysis of the good life in the *Nicomachean Ethics*. Contemporary scholars of Aristotle disagree among them on this point. Some scholars, such as Nagel and Irwin, take for granted the internal unity of the Aristotelian corpus and highlight the interdependence of the *Ethics* and the *De Anima*. By contrast Arthur Hyman argues that Aristotle did not construct an "all embracing philosophic system" and that his ethical and psychological views must be studied separately. See Arthur Hyman, "Aristotle's Theory of the Intellect and Its Interpretation by Averroes," in *Studies in Aristotle*, ed. Dominic J. O'Meara (Washington, DC: Catholic University of America Press, 1981), 161–91. Hyman appears to be a lone voice in contemporary scholarship on Aristotle. The dominant trend today is to read the *Ethics* not only in light of the *De Anima* but also in light of the *Rhetoric*, the *Poetics*, and the *Politics*. See, for example, Victorino Tejera, *Modes of Greek Thought* (New York: Appleton-Century-Croft, 1971); Cynthia A. Freeland, "Aristotle's Poetics in Relation to the Ethical Treatises," in *Aristotle's Philosophical Development: Problems and Prospects*, ed. William Wians (Lanham, MD: Roman & Littlefield, 1996), 327–45; J. Donald Monan, *Moral Knowledge and its Methodology in Aristotle* (Oxford: Clarendon Press, 1968); W. W. Fortenbau, "Aristotle's Distinction Between Moral Virtue and Practical Wisdom," in *Essays in Ancient Greek Philosophy* vol. iv, *Aristotle's Ethics*, ed. John P. Anton and Anthony Preus (Albany: State University of New York Press, 1991), 97–106; Terence H. Irwin, "The Metaphysical and Psychological Basis of Aristotle's Ethics," in *Essays on Aristotle's Ethics*, ed. Amelie Oksenberg Rorty (Berkeley, University of California Press, 1980) 35–53; idem, "First Principles in Aristotle's Ethics," in *Midwest Studies in Philosophy*, vol. 3, *Studies in Ethical Theory*, Peter A. French, Theodore E. Uehling Jr., Howard K. Wettstein, eds. (Morris, MN: The University of Minnesota Press, 1978), 252–72.

45. For a recent discussion of Aristotle's psychological theories, consult Martha C. Nussbaum and Amelie Oksenberg Rorty (eds.), *Essays on Aristotle's De Anima* (Oxford: Clarendon Press, 1992).

46. Irwin, "The Metaphysical and Psychological Basis," 41.

47. See Edel, *Aristotle*, 144.

48. Irwin, "The Metaphysical and Psychological Basis," 44–45.

49. *Rhetoric* I:1 1355a 15–17: "Men have sufficient instinct for what is true, and usually do arrive at the truth. Hence the man who makes a good guess at truth is likely to make a good guess at probabilities."

50. Sherman, *Fabric of Character*, 1.
51. See Prior, *Virtue and Knowledge*, 155.
52. See Schofield, "Aristotle on the Imagination," 247–77.
53. On the primacy of self-mastery in the formation of character and its connection to freedom, see Andreas Eshte, "Character, Virtue and Freedom," *Philosophy* 57 (1982): 495–513, and the bibliography cited there.
54. See Sherman, *Fabric of Character*, 44–50.
55. L.A. Kosman, "Being Properly Affected: Virtues and Feelings in Aristotle's Ethics," in *Essays on Aristotle's Ethics*, (Berkeley: University of California Press, 1980), 105.
56. This point is raised against Kant's critique of Aristotle. See Annas, *Morality of Happiness*, 52, 57; Sherman, *Fabric of Character*, 176–83; Richard Sorabji, "Aristotle on the Role of the Intellect in Virtue, in *Essays on Aristotle's Ethics*, (Berkeley: University of California Press, 1980), 216.
57. Annas, *Morality of Happiness*, 59.
58. On the analogy of virtues to skills see Annas, *Morality of Happiness*, 67–73.
59. The distinction between action (*praxis*) and production (*poeisis*) operates throughout all of Aristotle's philosophy. It is analogous to the distinction between activity (*energeia*) and movement (*kinesis*) discussed above. In general, Aristotle considered action to be superior to production, because the former does not involve the process of coming into being (*genesis*), but is the attainment of the desired state of being. In Aristotelian metaphysics, being is superior to becoming. See Michael J. White, "Aristotle's Concept of Theoria and the Energia-Kinesis Distinction," *Journal of the History of Philosophy* 18 (1980): 253–63.
60. This point is well taken by Steven D. Hudson, *Human Character and Morality* (London: Routledge and Kegan Paul, 1985), 43–87.
61. On the formation of character within a moral/religious tradition, see Stanley Hauerwas, *A Community of Character: Towards a Constructive Social Ethics* (Notre Dame: University of Notre Dame Press, 1981); idem, *Character and the Christian Life: A Study in Theological Ethics* (San Antonio: Trinity University Press, 1975); MacIntyre, *After Virtue*: A Study in Moral Theory (Notre Dame: University of Notre Dame Press, 1984); idem, *Whose Justice? Whose Rationality (Notre Dame: Notre Dame University Press, 1988)* To some extent, the present study can be seen as a Jewish counterpart to the approach endorsed by Hauerwas and MacIntyre. Put differently, this book covers the Jewish material that MacIntyre left out in his discussion of Western moral philosophy. However, unlike MacIntyre, who highlights the differences between diverse moral discourses, I highlight what they share in common.
62. The term "just right" is indebted to Edel, *Aristotle and His Philosophy*, 270.
63. J. O. Urmson, "Aristotle's Doctrine of the Mean," in *Essays on Aristotle's Ethics*, 162.
64. On the Platonic analysis of the four cardinal virtues, see Terence H. Irwin,

Plato's Moral Theory: The Early and Middle Dialogues (Oxford: Clarendon Press, 1977), 195–204.

65. A standard account of the virtues can be found in Ross, *Aristotle,* 202–21.

66. The literature on practical wisdom in Aristotle is extensive. The following discussion of practical reason is especially indebted to Sorabji, "Aristotle on the Role of Intellect in Virtue," in *Essays on Aristotle's Ethics,* 201–20; Sherman, *Fabric of Character,* 56–117; Broadie, *Ethics with Aristotle,* 179–265; Norman O. Dahl, *Practical Reason, Aristotle, Weakness of the Will* (Minneapolis: University of Minnesota Press, 1984); J. L. Ackrill, "Aristotle on Action," in *Essays on Aristotle's Ethics,* 93–101; Hardie, *Aristotle's Ethical Theory.*

67. See Sherman, *Fabric of Character,* 25–26; 43–44.

68. On the distinction between voluntary and involuntary acts, see A. W. Price, *Love and Friendship in Plato and Aristotle* (Oxford: Clarendon Press, 1989), 105–6.

69. Ibid., 107.

70. On the unity of virtue in Aristotle's philosophy and the elaboration of this doctrine in Hellenistic philosophy see Annas, *Morality of Happiness,* 73–84; Sherman, *Fabric of Character,* 105–6.

71. See Eugene Garver, "Aristotle on Virtue and Pleasure," in *The Greeks and the Good Life,* ed. David J. Depew (Fullerton: California State University, 1980), 157–76.

72. For a detailed analysis of Aristotle's conception of pleasure, see J. C. B. Gosling and C. C. W. Taylor, *The Greeks on Pleasure* (New York: Clarendon Press, 1982), 193–317.

73. *Akrasia* is commonly translated as "weakness of the will," but, as Amelie O. Rorty notes, this is a misleading translation because Aristotle did not recognize the will as a separate psychic function. See Amelie O. Rorty, "*Akrasia* and Pleasure: *Nicomachean Ethics* Book 7," in *Essays on Aristotle's Ethics,* 282, n.1. Indeed, that notion was introduced after Aristotle through the Stoics. Precisely because there is no will in the Aristotelian psychological scheme, the case of a person who recognizes the good but fails to act accordingly is a serious problem, which Aristotle failed to solve. For additional discussion of Aristotle's treatment of *akrasia* see Anthony Kenny, *Aristotle's Theory of the Will* (New Haven: Yale University Press, 1979); Richard Robinson, "Aristotle on *Akrasia,*" in *Articles on Aristotle* vol. 2, *Ethics and Politics,* ed. Jonathan Barnes, Malcolm Schofield, and Richard Sorabji (London: Duckworth, 1977), 79–91.

74. For analysis of Aristotle's understanding of friendship see Irving Singer, *The Nature of Love* (Chicago: The University of Chicago Press, 1966) vol. 1, 88–110; W. W. Fortenbaugh, "Aristotle's Analysis of Friendship: Function and Analogy, Resemblance and Focal Meaning," *Phronesis* 20 (1975): 51–62; A. W. Price, *Love and Friendship in Plato and Aristotle,* 103–61; Kraut, *Aristotle on the Human Good,* 131–54; Sherman, *Fabric of Character,* 128–51; Annas, *Morality of Happiness,* 249–62; John Cooper, "Aristotle on Friendship," in *Essays on Aristotle's Ethics,* 301–40.

75. This point is made by Singer, *The Nature of Love*, 90.

76. See Marcia L. Homiak, "Virtue and Self-Love in Aristotle's Ethics," *Canadian Journal of Philosophy* 11 (4) (1981): 633–51; John Benson, "Making Friends: Aristotle's Doctrine of the Friend as Another Self," in *Polis and Politics: Essays in Greek Moral and Political Philosophy* (Aldershot: Avebury, 1990), 50–68.

77. Price, *Love and Friendship*, 121.

78. For further clarification of this point, consult Joseph Owens, "Aristotelian Soul as Cognitive of Sensibles, Intelligibles, and Self," in his *Aristotle: The Collected Papers of Joseph Owens*, ed. John R. Catan (Albany: State University of New York Press, 1981), 81–98.

79. Jonathan Lear, *Aristotle: The Desire to Understand* (Cambridge: Cambridge University Press, 1988), 297. Herein lies the substantive difference between the Judaic and Greek views of happiness discussed in this book. We must not, however, exaggerate the difference, since medieval Jewish philosophical theology depersonalized God and, conversely, late Greek philosophical theology had a relational dimension, as in the return of the soul to its origin.

80. Hardie noted that in I:7, Aristotle first thought of happiness as an "inclusive" end, but toward the end of the chapter he committed himself to the "dominant" or "exclusive" conception. See W. F. R. Hardie, "The Final Good in Aristotle's Ethics," *Philosophy* (1965): 277–95; reprinted in *Aristotle: A Collection of Critical Essays*, ed. Julius M. F. Moravcsik (Garden City, NY: Anchor Books, 1967), 297–322. For further discussion of the two possible readings of Aristotle, see Daniel T. Devereux, "Aristotle on the Essence of Happiness," in *Studies in Aristotle*, ed. Dominic J. O'Meara (Washington: Catholic University of America Press, 1981), 247–60; Carlo Natali, *The Wisdom of Aristotle*, trans. Gerald Parks (Albany: State University of New York, 2001), 111–81.

81. John Kekes, "Happiness," *Mind* XCI (1982): 358–76.

82. Stephen S. White, "Is Aristotelian Happiness a Good Life or the Best Life," *Oxford Studies in Ancient Philosophy* 8 (1990): 103–44.

83. Anthony Kenny, *The Aristotelian Ethics: A Study of the Relationship between the Eudemian and Nicomachean Ethics of Aristotle* (Oxford: Clarendon Press, 1978). Kenny has shown that there are significant differences between the two works by Aristotle, even when the same terminology is used. Our study focuses only on the *Nicomachean Ethics* because it was this text rather than the *Eudemian Ethics* that was known to Jews in the Middle Ages.

84. Robert Heinaman, "Eudaimonia and Self-Sufficiency in the Nicomachean Ethics," *Phronesis* 33 (1988): 31–53.

85. For an analysis see Deborah K. W. Modrak, "Aristotle's Theory of Knowledge and Feminist Epistemology," in *Feminist Interpretations of Aristotle* ed. Cynthia A. Freeland (University Park: The Pennsylvania State University Press, 1998), 93–117.

86. Kraut, *Aristotle on the Human Good*, 172.

87. See Kathleen V. Wilkes, "The Good Man and the Good for Man in Aristotle's *Ethics*," in *Essays on Aristotle*, 341–57.

88. A typical example of such attempt is the reading of Amelie O. Rorty, "The Place of Contemplation in Aristotle's Nicomachean Ethics," in *Essays in Aristotle*, 377–94.

89. For an overview of Hellenistic Ethics and its reliance on the ethical theories of Socrates, Plato and Aristotle, see Anthony A. Long, "Hellenistic Ethics and Philosophical Power," in *Hellenistic History and Culture* ed. Peter Green (Berkeley: University of California Press, 1993), 143–67; F. H. Sandbach, *Aristotle and the Stoics*, Supplementary Volume no. 10 (Cambridge: The Cambridge Philological Society, 1985); Martha C. Nussbaum, *The Therapy of Desire: Theory and Practice in Hellenistic Ethics* (Princeton: Princeton University Press, 1994), chaps. 8–13; Terence H. Irwin, "Stoic and Aristotelian Conceptions of Happiness," in *The Norms of Nature: Studies in Hellenistic Ethics* ed. Malcolm Schofield and Gisela Striker (Cambridge: Cambridge University Press, 1986), 205–44. For primary sources of Hellenistic philosophy consult Anthony A. Long and David N. Sedley, *The Hellenistic Philosophers*, 2 vols.(Cambridge: Cambridge University Press, 1987).

90. Bryant, *Moral Codes*, 303.

91. Ibid. 304.

92. Ibid. 370.

93. Ibid. 404.

94. Gisela Striker, *Essays on Hellenistic Epistemology and Ethics* (Cambridge: Cambridge University Press, 1996), 185.

95. Bryant, *Moral Codes*, 406.

96. Ibid. 409.

97. Ibid. 411.

98. In Mishnah Sanhedrin X:1 the term Apikoros is a reference to a man who refuses to believe in life after death. In commenting on Numbers 15:31 the Sifre (Num. 112) says: "For the word of the Lord he has despised, this is the Sadducee; and his commandment he has broken, this, the Apikoros." In the Tosefta (Sanhedrin, ed. Zuckermandel, xiii, 5, p. 43), the Apikorsim, along with the Minim, the apostates, and the informers are said to be "punished in hell forever." The talmudic rabbis of the third and fourth centuries either did not know the precise meaning of the term, or extended it intentionally to mean "a person who insulted a rabbi," or who speaks of rabbis disrespectfully (BT Sanhedrin 99b,100a). In the Jerusalem Talmud (Sanhedrin X, 27d), Korah is portrayed as a type of Apikoros who ridicules the Law.

99. Ibid., 416.

100. For an overview of Stoic philosophy consult John M. Rist, *Human Value: A Study in Ancient Philosophical Ethics* (Leiden: E.J. Brill, 1982); idem (ed.), *The Stoics* (Berkeley: University of California Press, 1978); Gisela Striker, "Following Nature: A Study in Stoic Ethics," in *Essays on Hellenistic Epistemology and Ethics*,

221–80; Margaret E. Reesor, *The Nature of Man in Early Stoic Philosophy* (New York: St. Martin's Press, 1989).

101. Bryant, *Moral Codes,* 432.

102. Ibid. 433.

Notes to Chapter 2

1. Stephen A. Geller, "Nature's Answer: Meaning of the Book of Job in Its Intellectual Context," in *Judaism and Ecology: Created World and Revealed Word,* ed. Hava Tirosh-Samuelson (Cambridge, Mass.: Harvard University Press, 2002), 109–32.

2. The scholarship about the Wisdom tradition of the ancient Near East is voluminous. An excellent resource of recent scholarship and extensive bibliography is John G. Gammie and Leo G. Perdue, eds., *The Sage in Israel and the Ancient Near East* (Winona Lake, Ind.: Eisenbrauns, 1990).

3. The Egyptian and Mesopotamian backgrounds of biblical wisdom have long been noted by biblical scholars. For an overview of the issues, consult James L. Crenshaw, "Studies in Ancient Israelite Wisdom: Prolegomenon," in *Studies in Ancient Israelite Wisdom* (New York: Ktav, 1976), 1–59 and the extensive bibliography cited therein.

4. James L. Crenshaw, *Old Testament Wisdom: An Introduction* (Atlanta: John Knox Press, 1981), 28.

5. For a recent overview of Wisdom literature in the Bible and the main disputed questions, consult Ronald E. Clements, "Wisdom" in *It is Written: Essays in Honor of Barnabas Lindras* ed. D. A. Carson and H. G. M. Williamson (Cambridge: Cambridge University Press, 1988), 67–83; James L. Crenshaw, "Wisdom Literature: Biblical Books," in his *Urgent Advice and Probing Questions: Collected Writings on Old Testament Wisdom* (Macon GA: Mercer University Press, 1995), 1–13 and "The Wisdom Literature," ibid. 14–44. On the diverse meanings and usages of the term "ḥokhmah" ("wisdom") in the Bible, consult Georg Fohrer, "Sophia" in *Studies in Ancient Israelite Wisdom,* ed. James L. Crenshaw (New York: Ktav, 1976), 63–83.

6. On the "Solomonic Enlightenment," see Crenshaw, "Prolegomenon," 16–20; R. B. Y. Scott, "Solomon and the Beginning of Wisdom in Israel," in *Vetus Testamentum* Supplement 3 (1955): 262–79. Reprinted in *Studies in Ancient Israelite Wisdom,* ed. James L. Crenshaw (New York: Ktav, 1976), 84–101; Roger N. Whybray, "The Sage in the Israelite Royal Court," in *The Sage in Israel,* 133–39; idem, "The Social World of the Wisdom Writers," in *The World of Ancient Israel: Sociological, Anthropological, and Political Perspectives* ed. Ronald E. Clements (Cambridge: Cambridge University Press, 1989), 227–50.

7. Whether biblical wisdom originated in an oral folk tradition or in the work of teachers in schools is a highly disputed question among biblical scholars. For an overview consult G. I. Davies, "Were There Schools in Ancient Israel?" in *Wisdom in Ancient Israel: Essays in Honor of J. A. Emerton* ed. John Day, Robert Gordon, and

H. G. M. Williamson (Cambridge: Cambridge University Press, 1995), 199–211 and the literature reviewed therein; James L. Crenshaw, "Education in Ancient Israel," *Journal of Biblical Literature* 104 (1985): 601–15; Menachem Haran, "On the Diffusion of Literacy and Schools in Ancient Israel," in *Congress Volume, Jerusalem 1986,* ed. J. A. Emerton (*Vetus Testamentum* Supplement, 40) (Leiden: Brill, 1988), 81–95.

8. Walter A. Bruegemann, "The Social Significance of Solomon as a Patron of Wisdom," in *The Sage in Israel,* 117–32.

9. R. B. Y. Scott, *The Way of Wisdom in the Old Testament* (New York: Malcolm, 1971), 23–47.

10. See W. Lee Humphreys, "The Motif of the Wise Courtier in the Book of Proverbs," in *Israelite Wisdom: Theological and Literary Essays in Honor of Samuel Terrien* ed. John G. Gammie et al. (Atlanta: Scholars Press, 1978), 177–89.

11. The origin of this notion is the Egyptian concept of *Maat,* which stands both for the cosmic order and for the order in human life. For an analysis of this central concept in Egyptian religion, see Henri Frankfort, *Ancient Egyptian Religion* (New York: Columbia University Press, 1961), passim; David P. Silverman, ed. *Ancient Egypt* (New York: Oxford University Press, 1997); Roger N. Whybray, *Wisdom in Proverbs: The Concept of Wisdom in Proverbs 1–9* (Naperville, IL.: Alec R. Allenson, 1965), 53–54.

12. Crenshaw, *Old Testament Wisdom,* 20.

13. That character formation through education is the primary concern of Wisdom literature and that character is the foundation for the right attitude to life is well stated by Ronald E. Clements, "Wisdom and Old Testament Theology," in *Wisdom in Ancient Israel: Essays in Honor of J. A. Emerton* ed. John Day, Robert Gordon, and H. G. M. Williamson (Cambridge: Cambridge University Press, 1995), 281.

14. For an analysis of the juxtaposition between the wise and the fool in the Book of Proverbs see Claus Westermann, *Roots of Wisdom: The Oldest Proverbs of Israel and Other People* (Louisville: Westminster John Knox Press, 1995), 38–84.

15. On the post-exilic dating of biblical Wisdom books (Psalms, Job, Proverbs, and Ecclesiastes), see Brevard S. Childs, *Introduction to the Old Testament as Scripture* (Philadelphia: Fortress Press, 1979), 504–59; 580–89.

16. See Moshe Weinfeld, *Deuteronomy and the Deuteronomic School* (Winona Lake, IN: Eisenbrauns, 1992), 244–319, esp. 189; Joseph Blenkinsopp, *Wisdom and Law in the Old Testament: The Ordering of Life in Israel and Early Judaism,* (Oxford: Oxford University Press, 1995), 86; Andre Lamaire, "The Sage in School and Temple," in *The Sage in Israel,* (Winona Lake, IN: Eisenbrauns, 1990), 165–81. Lamaire notes that while the Wisdom tradition was not anti-cultic, "the wisdom teacher was not involved in the details of cultic rituals and sacrifices, whereas in the priestly school, the student had to learn the specific features of rituals, feasts, rules pertaining to clean and unclean, and temple maintenance" (178).

17. Clements, "Wisdom and Old Testament Theology," 274.

18. Childs, *Introduction to the Old Testament as Scripture,* 558.

19. On the dating of the final version of the Book of Psalms, see Gerald H. Wilson, *The Editing of the Hebrew Psalter*, Society of Biblical Literature Dissertation Series 76 (Chico CA: Scholars Press, 1985); idem, "The Shape of the Book of Psalms," *Interpretation* 46 (1992): 129–42; William L. Holladay, *The Psalms through Three Thousand Years: Prayerbook of a Cloud of Witnesses* (Minneapolis: Fortress Press, 1993), 67–80.

20. See Ronald E. Murphy, "A Consideration of the Classification 'Wisdom Psalms,'" in J. A. Emerton et al (eds.), *Congress Volume, Bonn 1962* (*Vetus Testamentum* Supplement, 9) (Leiden: Brill, 1963), 156–67. Reprinted in *Studies in Ancient Israelite Wisdom*, ed. James L. Crenshaw (New York: Ktav, 1976), 456–67; Roger N. Whybray, "The Wisdom Psalms," in *Wisdom in Ancient Israel: Essays in Honour of J.A. Emerton* (Cambridge: Cambridge University Press, 1995), 152–60.

21. For an overview of the scholarly debates about the relationship between "Wisdom Psalms" and "Torah Psalms," the dating of the Book of Psalms, as well as *the Sitz im Leben* of the various genres of Psalms, see Norman Whybray, *Reading the Psalms as a Book, Journal of the Study of the Old Testament,* Supplement Series 222 (1996), 15–35; James L. Mays, "The Place of the Torah-Psalms in the Psalter," *Journal of Biblical Literature* 106 (1987): 3–12.

22. Gerhard von Rad, *Wisdom in Israel,* trans. James D. Martin (Valley Forge, PA: Trinity Press International, 1972); Herman Gunkel, *The Psalms: A Form-Critical Introduction,* trans. Thomas M. Horner (Philadelphia: Fortress Press, 1967); Sigmund Mowinckel, *The Psalms in Israel's Worship* 2 vols. (Oxford: Basil Blackwell, 1962 [Oslo. 1951]); Herman L. Jansen, *Die spatjudische Psalmdichtung* (Oslo, 1937).

23. See Leo G. Perdue, *Wisdom and Cult: A Critical Analysis of the Views of Cult in the Wisdom Literature of Israel and the Ancient Near East,* Society of Biblical Literature Dissertation Series 30 (Missoula, MT: Scholars Press, 1977).

24. See Avi Hurvitz, *Wisdom Language in Biblical Psalmody* [Hebrew] (Jerusalem: The Magnes Press, 1991), 17–31. Hurvitz surveys and criticizes the main approaches to the analysis of the Wisdom Psalms.

25. However, as Hurvitz notes, not all Psalms with the formula *ashrei* can be considered "Wisdom Psalms."

26. See Waldemar Janzen, "'Asre' in the Old Testament," *Harvard Theological Review* 57 (1965): 215–26.

27. *Theological Dictionary of the Old Testament,* ed. G. Johannes Botterweck and Helmer Ringgren, trans. John T. Willis (Grand Rapids, MI.: Berdmans, 1974), 445.

28. Janzen, "'Asre' in the Old Testament," 216.

29. Nahum Sarna, *On the Book of Psalms: Exploring the Prayers of Ancient Israel,* (New York: Schocken, 1993), 29. It may be relevant that the Hebrew noun *osher* appears only once in the Bible, though it is commonly used in medieval Jewish philosophy. The verbal formula *ashrei* captures the Israelite approach to happiness as a state of being that emerges from a certain pattern of life.

30. Sarna, *On the Book of Psalms,* 30. Sarna's statement should be read as an

agreement with Waldemar Janzen, who argued that *ashrei* "is a word expressive of envious desire." Janzen, "Asre in the Old Testament," 225. Sarna, 29.

31. See Sarna, *On The Book of Psalms*, 224, n. 106.

32. For a survey and analysis see Christopher W. Mitchell, *The Meaning of BRK "To Bless" in the Old Testament* (Atlanta: Scholars Press, 1983).

33. Mowinckel, *The Psalms in Israel's Worship*, 3.

34. Ibid. 4.

35. Hans-Joachim Kraus, *Psalms 1–59: A Commentary*, trans. Hilton C. Oswald (Minneapolis: Augsburg, 1988), 115.

36. Sarna, *On the Book of Psalms*, 30. This wording seems to conflict with Sarna's own suggestion, cited above, according to which the term *ashrei* expresses the envy of the observer.

37. Much has been written on the presumed differences between Hebrew and Greek mentalities, or worldviews. A typical example is Thorleif Boman, *Hebrew Thought Compared with Greek* (New York: Norton, 1970). It is the contention of this book that despite its distinctiveness, the Hebraic/Judaic perspective should always be understood against the cultural milieu of a given period. This claim is true during the Greco-Roman period as well as during the Middle Ages.

38. Sarna, *On the Book of Psalms*, 32–36.

39. Childs, *Introduction to the Old Testament as Scripture*, 513.

40. On the meaning of the word *yehegh* (meditate) in relationship to speech, see Sarna, *On the Book of Psalms*, 38. Sarna notes that in the Bible the heart is "the organ of speech" so that the oral teaching of God's Torah expresses the intentionality of the speaker. Interestingly, the word *higayon* also comes from the stem h-g-h and it is this word that the rabbis used to denote a kind of study that should be prohibited to Jews. Whether *higayon* means "rhetoric," as some scholars believe, or all forms of Greek-influenced studies, will be discussed in the next chapter.

41. It is reasonable to ponder whether the prophets included women in their vision of Israel as a community. To my knowledge, there is no indication that prophetic oracles were intended for males only or that the commandments of the Torah pertained to men alone. Even though biblical law recognizes differences between men and women in regard to specific bodily functions and ritual obligations, the Torah was given to all of Israel and obedience to God's revelation is not gender specific. The very fact that women functioned as prophets in biblical Israel indicates an inclusive understanding of the prophecy. It is only in the Hellenistic period under the influence of Greek cultural paradigms that women were excluded from Torah study and negative statements about women's intellectual powers were voiced. For an overview of women's status in biblical society consult Tikvah Frymer-Kensky, "The Bible and Women's Studies," in *Feminist Perspectives on Jewish Studies*, ed. Lynn Davidman and Shelly Tenenbaum (New Haven: Yale University Press, 1994), 16–39.

42. See Geo Widengren, *The King and the Tree of Life in Ancient Near Eastern Religion* (Uppsala: A.B. Lundequistska Bokhandelm, 1951).

43. The verb *p-r-ḥ* "to flourish" also occurs in Prov. 11:28 and 14:11 with reference to the respective fates of the righteous and the wicked. In Ps. 92 the verb *p-r-ḥ-* is used with reference to the righteous. The statement of v. 13 that the righteous will flourish like a palm tree is reminiscent of Ps. 1:3, which states that those who delight in the Law are like trees that prosper and do not wither.

44. In Ezekiel 17: 9–10 the verb *tz-l-ḥ-* is used in the sense of "thriving vine." In medieval texts the term *hatzlaḥah* will be the Hebrew equivalent of the Arabic *sa'adah*, which was the translation of the Greek *Eudaimonia*.

45. Sarna, *On the Book of Psalms*, 33.

46. Perdue, *Wisdom and Cult*, 119; For commentaries on Psalms 19 and 119, I consulted Whybray, *Reading the Psalms as a Book*, 42–47; J. Clinton McCann, *A Theological Introduction to the Book of Psalms: The Psalms as Torah* (Nashville: Abingdon Press, 1993), 28–40; Mitchell Dahood, *The Anchor Bible, Psalms I, 1–50: Introduction, Translation and Notes* (Garden City: Doubleday, 1965), 120–23; idem. *The Anchor Bible, Psalms III, 101–150: Introduction, Translation, and Notes* (Garden City: Doubleday, 1970), 161–93; Walter Bruegemann, *The Message of the Psalms* (Minneapolis: Augsburg, 1984), 39–40.

47. Bruegemann, *The Message of the Psalms*, 40.

48. Clements, "Wisdom and Old Testament Theology," 284.

49. In a penetrating study, Yochanan Muffs showed that the Hebrew word *tob* (meaning "good"), like its Akkadian cognate "tub," has a volitional aspect and that it connotes "joy." This insight will be very instructive to the evolution for the discourse on happiness discussed in this book. See Yochanan Muffs "Joy and Love as Metaphorical Expressions of Willingness and Spontaneity in Cuneiform Ancient Hebrew and Related Literatures," in *Christianity, Judaism and Other Greco-Roman Cults: Studies for Morton Smith at Sixty* ed. Jacob Neusner (Leiden: E.J. Brill, 1975), 1–36, esp. 6, n. 14; reprinted in his *Love and Joy: Law, Language and Religion in Ancient Israel* (New York: Jewish Theological Seminary, 1992), 121–64.

50. Perdue, *Wisdom and Cult*, 278.

51. For an extensive analysis of the term *ḥesed* see Nelson Glueck, *Ḥesed in the Bible*, trans. Alfred Gottschalk (Cincinnati: Hebrew Union College Press, 1967).

52. Sarna, *The Book of Psalms*, 71.

53. In the next chapter we will see how the adjective *gibbor* ("mighty" or "powerful") will be given a new interpretation during the rabbinic period. True might and heroic conduct would be understood not in terms taken from the battlefield but in terms of internal, psychological strength.

54. For analysis of biblical creation theology, see Jon D. Levenson, *Creation and the Problem of Evil: The Jewish Drama of Divine Omnipotence* (New York: Harper & Row, 1988). Whereas many Christian theologians agree that the Bible contains a full-fledged theology, Jewish scholars of the Bible have been much more reticent to treat the Bible as a theological text. See Jon D. Levenson, "Why Jews Are Not Interested in Biblical Theology," in *Judaic Perspectives on Ancient Israel*, ed. Jacob

Neusner, Baruch A. Levine, and Ernest S. Freirichs (Philadelphia: Fortress Press, 1987), 281–307.

55. Clements, "Wisdom and Old Testament Theology," 271.

56. This is not to say that the Bible shares Aristotle's conception of nature as originate source of motion and rest in things that change. The Bible instead speaks about the "ways" of creatures established by God rather than by their intrinsic nature. Even though Aristotle's teleology is immanent, it is possible to interpret him to mean, as did medieval philosophers, that the universe has God as its *telos*.

57. We already noted above (n. 9) that this idea was indebted to the concept of *Maat* of ancient Egyptian religion. It is important to keep in mind that during the Hellenistic period, when the biblical texts received their final form, *Maat* was identified with the great Egyptian goddess Isis, whose cult was extremely popular throughout the Mediterranean world. This was especially the case in the Ptolemaic empire to which Judah belonged during the third century B.C.E. See Blenkinsopp, *Wisdom and Law in the Old Testament*, 161. We will return to this point below when we discuss the Wisdom of Ben Sira.

58. Hans-Jurgen Hermisson, "Observations on the Creation Theology in Wisdom," in *Israelite Wisdom*, ed. John G. Gammie et al. (New York: Scholars Press, 1978), 44.

59. Clements, "Wisdom and Old Testament Theology," 281.

60. See Shaye J. D. Cohen, *From the Maccabees to the Mishnah* (Philadelphia: Fortress Press, 1987), 37–38; 45.

61. For information on Greek cities in Palestine, consult Menachem Stern, "Judaism and Hellenism in Palestine during the Third and Second Centuries B.C.E.," [Hebrew] in *Acculturation and Assimilation: Continuity and Change in the Cultures of Israel and the Nations*, eds. Yosef Kaplan and Menahem Stern (Jerusalem: The Zalman Shazar Center for Jewish History, 1989), 41–60. Reprinted in Menachem Stern, *Studies in Jewish History: The Second Temple Period*, ed. Moshe Amit, Isaiah Gafni, Moshe David Herr (Jerusalem: Yad Izhaq ben-Zvi, 1991), 3–21.

62. The term "Second Sophistic" was coined by Philostratus in *Vitae Sophistarum* to distinguish the Sophists of his generation (second century B.C.E.) from those of the fifth and early fourth centuries. The standard study of this cultural phenomenon is G. W. Bowersock, *Greek Sophists in the Roman Empire* (Oxford: Clarendon Press, 1969). For further analysis consult Graham Anderson, "The Second Sophistic: Some Problems of Perspective," in D. A. Russell, ed. *Antonine Literature* (Oxford: Clarendon Press, 1990); Robert A. Kaster, *Guardians of Language: The Grammarians and Society in Late Antiquity* (Berkeley: University of California Press, 1988).

63. Menahem Stern, "Yahadut ve-Yavnut be-Eretz Yisrael," in *Studies in Jewish History*, 14.

64. The literature on this topic is very extensive. For two diametrically opposed perspectives contrast the views of Martin Hengel, *Judaism and Hellenism*, trans. John Bowden (Minneapolis: Fortress Press, 1974) and Louis H. Feldman, "How

Much Hellenism in Jewish Palestine," *Hebrew Union College Annual* 57 (1986): 83–111.

65. Ben Sira 38:24–39:11 provides the most extensive description of the ideal scribe. Whether or not Ben Sira was a scribe who was also a priest is disputed by scholars. See Anthony Saldarini, *Pharisees, Scribes and Sadduccees in Palestinian Society* (Wilmington: Michael Glazier, 1988), 256. Saldarini concludes, "It is very likely that he was associated with the governing class either as a teacher or some kind of official."

66. The degree to which Ben Sira responded to the Hellenistic challenge is a highly disputed issue. For an overview of the various scholarly positions, consult Burton L. Mack and Roland E. Murphy, "Wisdom Literature," in *Early Judaism and its Modern Interpreters* (Philadelphia: Fortress Press, 1986), 374–77. Our formulation follows Martin Hengel, "The Interpenetration of Judaism and Hellenism in the Pre-Maccabean Period," in *The Cambridge History of Judaism*, ed. W. D. Davies and Louis Finkelstein, vol. 2 (Cambridge: Cambridge University Press, 1989), 225.

67. For information about the history of the text of Ben Sira, consult M. Gilbert, "Wisdom Literature," in *Jewish Writings of the Second Temple Period* (Assen: Van Gorcum and Philadelphia: Fortress Press, 1984), 290–301; for an analysis of the structure and themes of Ben Sira in light of contemporary social theories, see Harold Van Broekhoven, "A New Social Model for Discerning Wisdom: The Case of Sirach and Pseudo Solomon," in *New Perspectives on Ancient Judaism*, vol. 5, ed. Paul V. M. Flesher (University Presses of America, 1990), 14–28.

68. See John J. Gammie, "The Sage in Sirach," in *The Sage in Israel*, 355–72, esp. 372.

69. See Robert Gordis, "The Social Background of Wisdom Literature," *Hebrew Union College Annual* 18 (1943–44): 77–118. Reprinted in *Poets, Prophets, and Sages: Essays in Biblical Interpretation* (Bloomington, IN: Indiana University Press, 1971, 160–97.

70. Hengel, *Judaism and Hellenism*, 147–49; Jack T. Sanders, *Ben Sira and Demotic Wisdom* (Chico CA: Scholars Press, 1983), 29–30.

71. On the personification of wisdom as female in Wisdom literature, especially the Book of Proverbs, see Claudia Camp, *Wisdom and the Feminine in the Book of Proverbs* (Sheffield: Almond Press, 1985); idem "Woman Wisdom as Root Metaphor: A Theological Consideration," in K. G. Hoglund et al., eds., *The Listening Heart: Essays in Wisdom and Psalms Presented to Roland E. Murphy* (*Journal for the Study of the Old Testament*, Supplement 58; Sheffield: Journal for the Study of the Old Testament Press, 1987), 55–76; Athalya Brenner, "Some Observations on the Figurations of Woman in Wisdom Literature," in *On Prophets' Visions and the Wisdom of the Sages: Essays in Honour of R. Norman Whybray on his Seventieth Birthday*, ed. Heather A. McKay and David J. A. Clines (*Journal for the Study of the Old Testament* Supplement 162) (Sheffield: 1993), 192–208. For a detailed study of Ben Sira's feminization of wisdom, consult Warren C. Trenchard, *Ben Sira's Views of*

Women: A Literary Analysis, Brown Judaic Series 38 (Chico CA: Scholars Press, 1982).

72. Reginald Eldred Witt, *Isis in the Ancient World* (Baltimore: Johns Hopkins University, 1997).

73. The Lady Wisdom construct was also prevalent in the Apocalyptic tradition preserved by the sectarians in Qumran. See Torleif Elgvin, "Wisdom in Qumran," in *Judaism in Late Antiquity,* ed. Alan J. Avery-Peck, Jacob Neusner and Bruce D. Chilton, pt. 5 vol. 2 (Leiden/Boston/Koln, 2001), 147–69.

74. A. A. Wieder, "Ben Sira and the Praise of Wine," *Jewish Quarterly Review* 61 (1970–71): 155–66.

75. Jack Sanders, "Ben Sira's Ethics of Caution," *Hebrew Union College Annual* 50 (1979): 73–106.

76. Gordis, "The Social Background of Wisdom Literature," 110.

77. Sanders, "Ben Sira's Ethics of Caution," 83–86.

78. For an overview of Jewish literature in Greek, see Nicholas De Lange, *Apocrypha: Jewish Literature in the Hellenistic Age* (New York: Viking Press, 1978); John J. Collins, *Between Athens and Jerusalem: Jewish Identity in the Hellenistic Diaspora* (New York: Crossroad, 1986); George W. E. Nickelsburg, *Jewish Literature Between the Bible and the Mishnah* (Philadelphia: Fortress Press, 1981); Lawrence M. Wills, *The Jewish Novel in the Ancient World* (Ithaca, NY: Cornell University Press, 1995).

79. Hengel, "The Interpenetration of Judaism and Hellenism," 201. An English translation of the fragments of Aristobulus' philosophy in the writings of Eusebius is available in Adela Yarboro Collins, "Aristobulus: A New Translation and Introduction," in *Old Testament Pseudepigrapha,* vol. 2, ed. James H. Charlesworth (Garden City, NY: Doubleday & Company, 1985), 831–42.

80. An excellent analysis of his allegorical method as a tool in cultural transformation is offered by David Dawson, *Allegorical Readers and Cultural Revision in Ancient Alexandria* (Berkeley: University of California Press, 1992), 74–81.

81. Elias J. Bickerman, *The Jews in the Greek Age* (Cambridge: Harvard University Press, 1988), 228.

82. Collins, *Between Athens and Jerusalem,* 177.

83. Bickerman, *The Jews in the Greek Age,* 228.

84. The ambivalent attitude of Greek authors toward Jews is well documented by Menahem Stern, *Greek and Latin Authors on Jews and Judaism,* vol. 1 (Jerusalem, 1974).

85. Though I focused on Aristotle's interpretation of the "mean," it should be noted that the doctrine itself was well known in Greece prior to Aristotle. It permeated the Greek medical tradition in the concept of *krasis,* meaning, due proportion. Plato discusses the doctrine of the mean in *Protagoras* 346d, *Republic* 10: 602d; *Timaeus* 36a, and *Laws* 3:691c; 3:679b; 701e; 5:728e ff; and 7:792d. I thank the anonymous reader of the manuscript for this point and for the references.

86. An exhortatory discourse is a particular form of speech that "attempts to prove itself to be just, lawful, expedient, honorable, pleasant and practicable." See

David Winston, trans. and ed. *The Wisdom of Solomon: The Anchor Bible* (Garden City, NY: Doubleday, 1979), 18.

87. Winston, *The Wisdom of Solomon*, 34.

88. David Winston, "The Sage as Mystic in the Wisdom of Solomon," in *The Sage in Israel*, 384.

89. Scholarship on Philo now constitutes a distinct sub-field in classical studies. For bibliography, consult Roberto Radice and David T. Runia, *Philo of Alexandria: An Annotated Bibliography 1937–1986* (Leiden: Vigiliae Christianae Supplements 8, 1988; 1992). We relied heavily on Harry A. Wolfson, *Philo: Foundations of Religious Philosophy in Judaism, Christianity and Islam* (Cambridge: Harvard University Press, 1947), Ronald Williamson, *Jews in the Hellenistic World: Philo* (Cambridge: Cambridge University Press, 1989) and David Winston, "Philo's Ethical Theory," *Aufstieg und Niedergang der romischen Welt* II (Berlin and New York: Walter de Gruyter, 1984), 372–416.

90. Alan Mendelson, *Secular Education in Philo of Alexandria* (Cincinnati: Hebrew Union College Press, 1982).

91. The extent of Philo's mastery of Greek philosophy is evident to any reader of his voluminous work. To date the best philosophical exposition of Philo's thought and its Greek sources remains Harry Wolfson's *Philo*. However, whether or not Philo can be considered a philosopher is itself debated among Philonic scholars. For a negative answer to this question and a review of the existing literature, consult Robert M. Berchman, "Philo and Philosophy," in *Judaism in Late Antiquity*, ed. Alan J. Avery-Peck and Jacob Neusner, pt. 3, vol. 3 (Leiden, Boston, Koln: Brill, 2000), 49–70. I do not share Berchman's conclusions.

92. See Jean Laporte, "Philo and the Tradition of Biblical Wisdom," in *Aspects of Wisdom in Judaism and Early Christianity*, ed. Robert Wilken (Notre Dame: University of Notre Dame Press, 1975), 103–41, esp. 131–35.

93. All citations are from *The Works of Philo Complete and Unabridged*, trans. C.D. Yonge (Peabody MA: Hendrickson, 1993). This updated edition of Yonge's 1854 translation matches it with the twelve-volume edition of the Loeb Classical Library (Cambridge, MA: Harvard University Press, 1929–1953) which, in turn, was based on the standard major edition of the Greek text of Philo by L. Cohn and P. Wendland, *Philonis Alexandrini opera quae supersunt* (7 vols. In 8; Berlin, 1896–1930). I chose to use the revised Yonge translation, even though this translation is less felicitous than the authoritative version of Loeb Classical Library, because the former is now readily available in one volume.

94. Williamson, *Jews in the Hellenistic World*, 104.

95. On that debate in Philonic scholarship consult Ellen Birnbaum, *The Place of Judaism in Philo's Thought: Israel, Jews and the Proselytes* (Atlanta: Scholars Press, 1996), 85–86.

96. On the difference between the Stoics and the Aristotelians on this point and Philo's use of his sources, see David Winston, "Philo's Ethical Theory," 402–4.

97. This book was a philosophical discourse written by a Jew who was

profoundly influenced by Greek philosophical thought. The goal of the book was to show that fidelity to the Law is the best way to fulfill the Greek idea of virtue and its main theme was reason's control over the passions. The anonymous author attempts to show that "the cardinal virtues self-control, courage, justice, and temperance, indeed the very essence of Greek wisdom, are subsumed under the Law or obedience to it." H. Anderson, trans., "4 Maccabees," in *The Old Testament Pseudepigrapha,* 538. On the date (ca. 40 C.E.) and place of origin (Antioch) of *IV Maccabess* and its debt to Plato, see Moses Hadas, *The Third and Fourth Books of Maccabees* (New York: Ktav, 1953), 95–118.

98. Williamson, *Jews in the Hellenistic World,* 203.

99. Wolfson, *Philo,* 274.

100. Williamson, *Jews in the Hellenistic World,* 205.

101. Ibid. 204.

102. Wolfson, *Philo,* 180.

103. See Helen North, *Sophrosyne: Self Knowledge and Self-Restraints in Greek Literature* (Ithaca: Cornell University Press, 1966), 324–5.

104. Wolfson, *Philo,* 203.

105. Ibid. 216.

106. The term "faith" (*pistis*) is used by Philo to denote the following: a) pledge, security, or proof; b) faithfulness in the execution of a charge or a duty; c) trust), d) conviction. See Dennis R. Lindsay, *Josephus and Faith: Pistis and Pistenein as Faith Terminology in the Writings of Flavious Josephus and in the New Testament* (Leiden/New York/Koln: E.J. Brill, 1993), 56. The most prominent use of the term is the religious meaning of faith in God and indeed, for Philo, faith in God is the goal of life. For recent literature on Philo's conception of faith, see David M. Hay, "Pistis as 'Ground for Faith' in Hellenized Judaism and Paul," *Journal of Biblical Literature* (108) (3) (1989): 461–76; idem. "The Psychology of Faith in Hellenistic Judaism," in *Aufstieg und Niedergang der romischen Welt* II (Berlin: DeGruyter, 1987), ed. Wolfgang Haase, 881–925.

107. Winston, "Philo's Ethical Theory," 395.

108. Williamson, *Jews in the Hellenistic World,* 211.

109. Ibid. 164.

110. Winston, "Philo's Ethical Theory," 381.

111. Dawson, *Allegorical Readers and Cultural Revision,* 86.

112. For further discussion of the Mosaic authorship of the Torah according to Philo consult Dawson, *Allegorical Readers,* 110–13; Williamson, *Jews in the Hellenistic World,* 163.

113. Dawson, *Allegorical Readers,* 87.

114. Ibid. 98.

115. Ibid. 108.

116. There is no discrepancy between the claim that Philo adopted Aristotle's ethics of virtue and the claim that the Law makes possible the attainment of the Stoic ideal. The "mean" is for everyone, the ordinary as well as the exceptionally

wise, such as Moses, because the "mean" makes everyone a better person. In practice, however, only a few actually live by the mean. This point was well understood by Steven Schwarzschild, "Moral Radicalism and 'Middlingness' in the Ethics of Maimonides," in his *The Pursuit of the Ideal: Jewish Writings of Steven Schwarzschild*, ed. Menachem Kellner (Albany: State University of New York Press, 1990), 137–60.

117. According to Wolfson, Philo's speaking against desire is analogous to the rabbinic railing against *yetzer ha-ra`*.

118. See David T. Runia, *Philo in Early Christian Literature: A Survey* (Assen: Van Gorcum; Minneapolis: Fortress Press, 1993).

119. Williamson, *Jews in the Hellenistic World*, 213.

120. For a short overview of the disputed issues and an argument for seeing Philo as part of the socio-cultural world that produced rabbinic Judaism, see Naomi Cohen, "Philo and Midrash," *Judaism* 44, 2 (1985): 196–207.

Notes to Chapter 3

1. For a succinct overview of the historical context for the rise of rabbinic Judaism, consult Isaiah M. Gafni, "The Historical Background," in *The Literature of the Sages*, pt. 1, ed. Shmuel Safrai (Assen/Maastrict: Van Gorcum; Philadelphia: Fortress Press, 1987), 1–34.

2. On the causes and development of the Great War, consult Martin Goodman, *The Ruling Class of Judea: The Origins of the Jewish Revolt Against Rome A.D. 66–70* (Cambridge: Cambridge University Press, 1987); Aryeh Kasher, ed., *The Great Jewish Revolt: Factors and Circumstances Leading to its Outbreak* [Hebrew] (Jerusalem: The Zalman Shazar Center, 1983).

3. The literature on Jewish sectarianism in the late Second Temple period is extensive. A very accessible summary is provided by Shaye J. D. Cohen, *From the Maccabees to the Mishnah* (Philadelphia: Westminster Press, 1987), 143–73. For an overview of the methodological difficulties that beset the modern attempt to reconstruct the sectarian landscape, consult Shaye J. D. Cohen, "The Political and Social History of the Jews in the Greco-Roman Antiquity: the State of the Question," in *Early Judaism and its Modern Interpreters* ed. Robert A. Kraft and George W. E. Nickelsburg (Philadelphia: Fortress Press; Atlanta: Scholars Press, 1986), 33–56. The major views among modern scholars concerning the various sects are analyzed by Gary G. Porton, "Diversity in Postbiblical Judaism," ibid. 57–80.

4. See Cohen, "The Significance of Yavneh: Pharisees, Rabbis and the End of Jewish Sectarianism," *Hebrew Union College Annual* 55 (1984): 32. To what extent the rabbinic documents preserved the actual statements of the Pharisees or instead ascribed their own innovations to the Pharisees need not concern us here.

5. For an overview of the rabbinic movement and its social significance in second-century Palestine, see Shaye J. D. Cohen, "The Place of the Rabbis in Jewish Society of the Second Century," in *The Galilee in Late Antiquity*, ed. Lee I. Levine

(New York: The Jewish Theological Seminary, 1992), 157–73. Cohen emphasizes the difference in status of the rabbinic sages in the second century (the Tannaim) and their heirs, the Amoraim, of the subsequent centuries. Whereas the Amoraim administered Jewish self-government in Palestine and Babylonia, the Tannaim "were neither agents of the state nor communal leaders . . . the rabbis did not control the religious and civil life of second-century Palestinian Jewry." Ibid, 164. For an overview of modern scholarship on the rabbinic movement and rabbinic literature, consult Anthony J. Saldarini, "Reconstruction of Rabbinic Judaism," in *Early Judaism and its Modern Interpreters*, ed. Robert A. Kraft and George W. E. Nickelsburg (Philadelphia: Fortress Press; Atlanta: Scholars Press, 1986), 437–77.

6. On the establishment of the rabbinic movement in Babylonia, consult Jacob Neusner, *A History of the Jews in Babylonia*, 5 vols. (Leiden: E. J. Brill, 1965–1970) vol. 4, 279–402; David Goodblatt, *Rabbinic Instruction in Sassanian Babylonia* (Leiden: E. J. Brill, 1975); Gafni, "The Historical Background," 27–33.

7. On the organization of the philosophical schools in the Greco-Roman world, see R. Alan Culpepper, *The Johannine School: An Evaluation of the Johannine-School Hypothesis Based on an Investigation of the Nature of Ancient Schools*, SBLDS 26 (Chico, CA: Scholars Press, 1975), 258–59; Henri Marrou, *A History of Education in Antiquity* (New York: Mentor, 1964). The similarities and differences between the rabbinic academies and their Greco-Roman counterparts have long been debated. I follow the view of Shaye J. D. Cohen, according to whom "the organization and procedures of the patriarchal school in the second century were modeled on those of the Athenian philosophical schools. Of all the rabbis, the ones who unquestionably were the most Hellenized, who had the best Greek education, and who were most acquainted with the world around them, were the patriarch, his associates and the patriarchal house." Shaye J. D. Cohen, "Scholars and Patriarchs," *Proceedings of the American Academy of Jewish Research* 84 (1981): 83.

8. See Martin Goodman, *State and Society in Roman Galilee AD 132–212* (Totowa N.J.: Rowman and Allenheld, 1982), 74; Saldarini, Anthony, *Scholastic Rabbinism: A Literary Study of the Fathers According to Rabbi Nathan* (Atlanta: Scholars Press, 1982), 55. In this regard the rabbinic sage can be viewed as a continuation of the earlier ideal of the Jewish *sophos* discussed in the previous chapter. The notion that the rabbinic sage was the heir of the wise men of the late Second Temple period is to be distinguished from the rabbis' deliberate attempt to present themselves as the bearers of an uninterrupted "chain of tradition" that transmitted the divine Torah from Sinai to their own time.

9. Lee I. Levine, *The Rabbinic Class of Roman Palestine in Late Antiquity* (Jerusalem: Yad Itzhak Ben Zvi, 1989), 67.

10. Rabbinic literature is replete with expressions of disdain towards the so-called *am ha-aretz* (literally, "the people of the land"). The precise social make-up of these non-rabbinic segments of the Jewish society in Palestine is disputed. See Aharon Oppenheimer, *The Am Ha-Aretz: A Study in the Social History of the Jewish People in the Hellenistic-Roman Period* (Leiden: E.J. Brill, 1977). For rabbinic

attitudes toward the "*am ha-aretz*," see Levine, *The Rabbinic Class*, 112–17; Cohen, "The Place of the Rabbi," 165.

11. See Levine, *The Rabbinic Class*, 55–59.

12. On the relationship between masters and disciples, known in rabbinic literature as *shimush hakhamim* (serving the sages), see Levine, *The Rabbinic Class*, 59–61.

13. See William S. Green, "Story Telling and Holy Men: The Case of Ancient Judaism," in *Take Judaism for Example: Studies Toward the Comparison of Religions*, ed. Jacob Neusner (Chicago: University of Chicago, 1983), 39.

14. On the rabbinic use of biblical narrative in the depiction of the sages, see Shmuel Safrai, "Tales of the Sages in the Palestinian Tradition and the Babylonia Talmud," in Joseph Heinemann and Dov Noy, eds. *Studies in Aggadah and Folk Lore* (Jerusalem: Magnes Press, 1971), 209–32.

15. On the study of Torah as the vehicle for character formation in rabbinic Judaism, see Louis Finkelstein, "The Ethics of the Pharisees," in *Social Responsibility in an Age of Revolution* (New York: The Jewish Theological Seminary, 1971), 59.

16. See Lewis E. Newman, "Ethics as Law, Law as Religion: Reflections on the Problem of Law and Ethics in Judaism," in *Contemporary Jewish Ethics and Morality: A Reader* ed. Elliot N. Dorff and Louis E. Newman (New York: Oxford University Press, 1995), 79–93; idem, *Past Imperatives: Studies in the History and Theory of Jewish Ethics* (Albany: State University of New York Press, 1998).

17. The size of the rabbinic movement is still disputed. For the period of Yavneh (from 80 C.E. to the Bar Kokhba Revolt in 132–135 C.E.) the Mishnah mentions 54 figures. An additional 29 names are mentioned for the period after the failed rebellion of Bar Kochba. Additional names can be gleaned from the rabbinic corpora, but the number roughly includes about 100 names. The number of Amoraim, the sages who were active from the third to the sixth century, is larger, but scholars dispute the size of the movement. The maximalist account has a total of 3,400 for Palestinian and Babylonian sages. The minimalist account "lists a total of 761 Amoraim, of whom 367 lived in Palestine and 394 in Babylonia." See Levine, *The Rabbinic Class*, 66.

18. On the alliance between the Patriarchs and the rabbinic class in Palestine, see Goodman, *State and Society*, 111–18. On the links between the Babylonian exilarchs and the rabbinic movement, see Gafni, *The Jews of Babylonia in the Talmudic Era: A Social and Cultural History* [Hebrew] (The Zalman Shazar Center: Jerusalem, 1990), 94–109.

19. On the rabbis as holy men endowed with supernatural powers, see Jacob Neusner, *There We Sat Down: Talmudic Judaism in the Making* (New York: Ktav, 1978), 79–86.

20. By contrast, Jacob Neusner holds that "The Mishnah, seen whole, presents a profoundly philosophical system, one that employs numerous cases to make a single general point." See Jacob Neusner, "The Mishnah's Philosophical Method: The Judaism of Hierarchical Classification in Greco Roman Context," in *From*

Literature to Theology in Formative Judaism: Three Preliminary Studies (Atlanta: Scholars Press, 1989), 23. Neusner goes as far as to claim that the Mishnah should be read as *a statement of a philosophy*, that "the method of the Mishnah is like that of Aristotle; the message, congruent with that of Neoplatonism." See also Neusner, *Judaism as Philosophy: The Method and Message of the Mishnah* (Baltimore and London: The Johns Hopkins University Press, 1999), x-xi. Neusner presents the Mishnah as a philosophical document because he understands the term "philosophical" to mean "a rational classification." To my knowledge, few other scholars have adopted the view that the Mishnah is a philosophical text or that its method is like Aristotle's syllogistic reasoning. However, long before Neusner, Judah Goldin presented the academy of Yohanan ben Zakkai in Yavneh as the context for philosophical speculations. See Judah Goldin, "A Philosophical Session in a Tannaite Academy," in *Essays in Greco-Roman and Related Talmudic Literature* ed. Henry A. Fischel (New York: Ktav, 1977), 366–86. Goldin concludes by saying, "Living in the Hellenistic-Roman world, the Tannaim could not remain unaffected by that world. It is not simply a matter of loan words; it is something much more profound. Not only did the Palestinian sages appropriate the terminology for some hermeneutic rules from the Hellenistic rhetors, but inside the *bet ha-midrash*, the rabbinic academy, apparently one did take up from time to time philosophical questions, and one did attempt to answer these questions in the current philosophical idiom. Study of the Law, of course, remained paramount. But along with such activity went an awareness, at least in the school of Johanan ben Zakkai, of the subject and style popular in intellectual circles generally." Ibid. 385.

21. Saul Lieberman, "How Much Greek in Jewish Palestine," in *Essays in Greco-Roman and Related Talmudic Literature,* ed. Henry Fischel (New York: Ktav, 1977), 325. Originally appeared in *Biblical and Other Studies* ed. Alexander Altmann (Cambridge: Harvard University Press, 1963), 123–41.

22. That Epicureanism was taken to signify "deviant" behavior was noted by Henry Fischel in "Epicureanism," *Encyclopedia Judaica* (Jerusalem: Keter; New York: MacMillan, 1971). Epicureanism might have been the likely background to the rabbinic narrative of the "four who entered paradise" in Hagigah 14b. The *pardes* (literally, "orchard") could have been a reference to Epicurus' "Garden" (i.e., his philosophical school), since "it fits Akiva's past, Ben Azzai's celibacy and many Epicurean sayings, Elisha ben Abuya's heterodoxy, and Ben Zoma's Gnosticism." Ibid. 817. For a more extensive discussion of Epicurean and Cynic influences on rabbinic thought consult Henry Fischel, *Rabbinic Literature and Greco-Roman Philosophy: A Study of Epicurean and Rhetorica in Early Midrashic Writings* (Leiden: Brill, 1973). That Epicureanism was the background for the traditions about Elisha ben Abuya is also suggested by Judah Liebes, *The Sins of Elisha: The Four Who Entered Paradise and the Nature of Talmudic Mysticism* [Hebrew] (Jerusalem: Aqadamon, 1990).

23. Scholars of the rabbinic corpus dispute the degree to which rabbinic sages mastered the Greek language. The studies of Saul Lieberman have proven that the

rabbinic corpus is replete with Greek words and concepts, but that does not prove that the rabbis were able to avail themselves of Greek philosophical treatises. Indeed, it was Lieberman who noted that philosophical terminology is conspicuously absent from the rabbinic corpus. However, it seems to me that Henry Fischel was right to note that familiarity with Greek philosophical teachings did not necessarily require mastery of Greek philosophical literature. The rabbis could have been informed about it through the display of philosophical brilliance in the public domain (e.g., the market place) and from informal communications with Greek and Roman teachers and orators. Greco-Roman rhetorical literature itself, which was popularized in a variety of literary forms (such as the oration, diatribe, essay, symposium, epistle, biography, and political fable) served as a source of knowledge about philosophers and their ethical values. I, therefore, agree with Fischel, who argues that the sages "could gain their insight into Hellenism from the popularized form of rhetoric (which was the usual medium of the Greco-Roman writer-scholar-administrator class too)." Henry Fischel, "Story and History: Observations on Greco-Roman Rhetoric and Pharisaism," in *American Oriental Society, Middle West Branch, Semi Centennial Volume*, ed. Denis Sinor (Bloomington IN: Indiana University Press, 1969), 59–88. Reprinted in *Essays in Greco-Roman and Related Talmudic Literature*, ed. Henry Fischel (New York: Ktav, 1977), 443–72. The quote is from p. 449 [65].

24. On the presence of Greek philosophers and orators in Palestine from the second century B.C.E. to the end of the sixth century C.E., see Joseph Geiger, "Athens in Syria: Greek Intellectuals of Gadara," [Hebrew] *Cathedra* 35 (1985): 3–16; idem, "Greek Intellectuals of Ascalon," [Hebrew] *Cathedra* 60 (1991): 5–16; "Greek Orators in Palestine," *Cathedra* (1992): 47–56; Yaron Dan, "Cultured Liberal Professionals in the Cities of Eretz Israel in the Byzantine Period" [Hebrew], *Cathedra* 8 (1978): 95–122; idem. *Urban Life in Eretz Israel in Late Antiquity* [Hebrew] (Jerusalem: Yad Itzhaq Ben Zvi, 1984), 118–83.

25. On Antiochus of Ascalon and his philosophy, see Jonathan Barnes, "Antiochus of Ascalon," in *Philosophia Togata: Essays on Philosophy and Roman Society*, edited by Miriam Griffin and Jonathan Barnes (Oxford: Clarendon Press, 1989), 51–96.

26. On the Second Sophistic, see the literature cited in Chapter Two.

27. In addition to the studies by Fischel cited above, consult also Elimelekh Epshtain Halevi (Hallewi), *Sha`are Ha-Aggada* (On the Nature of the Aggadah)(Tel Aviv: Armony, 1963); idem. *Olamah shel ha-Aggada* (The World of the Aggadah) (Tel Aviv: Dvir, 1972). Even if Halevi was too keen on detecting parallels between rabbinic sources and Greco-Roman literature, the gist of his argument seems to me to be a cogent one.

28. See Steven D. Fraade, "The Early Rabbinic Sage," in *The Sage in Israel*, 417–36.

29. Fischel, "Story and History," 461 [77].

30. The evolutionary approach to the Mishnah is characteristic of Israeli

scholarship. For example, Abraham Goldberg, "The Mishnah—A Study Book of Halakha," in *The Literature of the Sages* Pt. 1, 211–59. By contrast, Jacob Neusner (and many of his students) has presented the Mishnah as a revolutionary and innovative departure from earlier activities by the sages. For Neusner, the Mishnah did not reflect existing religious reality but attempted to shape it. See Jacob Neusner, *Judaism: The Evidence of the Mishnah* (Chicago: University of Chicago Press, 1981). A very useful survey of the methodological difficulties in studying the Mishnah and its cognate literature, the Tosefta and the Jerusalem and Babylonian Talmuds, is available in Alan J. Avery-Peck, "The Mishnah, Tosefta, and the Talmuds: The Problem of Text and Context," in *Judaism of Late Antiquity* (Leiden: E. J. Brill, 1995), 173–216.

31. See Jack Lightstone, "Problems and New Perspectives in the Study of Early Rabbinic Ethics," *Journal of Religious Ethics* 9 (1981): 199–209.

32. William Scott Green, "What's in a Name—The Problematic of Rabbinic "Biography," in William S. Green, ed. *Approaches to Ancient Judaism: Theory and Practice*, Brown Judaic Studies 1 (Missoula, MT: Scholars Press, 1978), 77–96.

33. This is the main claim of Shaye J. D. Cohen's essay, "The Significance of Yavneh," cited in n. 3 above.

34. Jacob Neusner, "Defining Rabbinic Literature and its Principal Parts," in *Judaism in Late Antiquity*, ed. Jacob Neusner, pt. 1 (Leiden: Brill, 1995), 119.

35. Ibid. 132.

36. For analysis of Max Kadushin's approach to rabbinic Judaism, consult Peter Ochs (ed.), *Understanding the Rabbinic Mind: Essays on the Hermeneutics of Max Kadushin* (Atlanta: Scholars Press, 1990); Theodore Steinberg, "Max Kadushin: An Appreciation," *Conservative Judaism* 35, 4 (1982): 3–16. Kadushin's "organic" or "organismic" approach is very similar to that of Isaac Heinemann in *Darkhey Ha-Aggadah* (The Ways of the Aggadah) (Jerusalem, 1949), though Heinemann lacked Kadushin's indebtedness to Whitehead's process philosophy. The presentation below endorses Kadushin's assumptions that rabbinic thought "is not a system in which each concept occupies a place in a definite hierarchical order. The conceptual terms are only connotative and suggestive, and connotations, of course, are not propositions; hence they cannot be connected in a diagrammatic fashion." Max Kadushin, *A Conceptual Approach to the Mekilta* (New York: The Jewish Theological Seminary of America, 1969), 16–17.

37. See M. Bialik Lerner, "The Tractate Avot," in *The Literature of the Sages*, pt. 1, 263–81. The final editing of Tractate Avot is most likely mid-third century and it contains many aphorisms attributed to sages of the late second-century Mishnah.

38. *The Fathers According to Rabbi Nathan* is an exposition, revision, and supplement of Tractate Avot. It was written and edited sometimes between 250–600 C.E. and was based on an earlier form of Tractate Avot than the one edited by Judah the Patriarch. The text is extant in two versions, which scholars denote as ARN A and ARN B. Version A of *Avot de Rabbi Nathan* was printed in the *editio princeps* of the Babylonian Talmud (Venice, 1550) along with the "minor" or "supplementary"

tractates of the Talmud. During the Middle Ages a few scholars were also familiar with Version B. The two versions were published in parallel columns by Solomon Schechter, *Aboth de Rabi Nathan* (Vienna, 1887; reprinted with corrections New York, 1967). ARN A is available in an English translation by Judah Goldin: *The Fathers According to Rabbi Nathan* (New Haven: Yale University Press, 1955). Another translation of ARN A is by Jacob Neusner, *The Fathers According to Rabbi Nathan: An Analytical Translation and Explanation* (Atlanta: Scholars Press, 1986). ARN B is available in the English translation of Anthony J. Saldarini, *The Fathers According to Rabbi Nathan (Abot de Rabbi Nathan): Version B* (Leiden: Brill, 1975). For a comparison of the different orientation of the two versions consult Judah Goldin, "The Two Versions of Abot de Rabbi Nathan," *Hebrew Union College Annual* 19 (1945–6): 97–120; idem. "The Third Chapter of Abot de Rabbi Nathan," *Harvard Theological Review* 58 (1965): 365–86. For a recent detailed analysis of the various versions consult Menahem Kister, *Studies in Avot de-Rabbi Nathan: Text, Redaction and Interpretation* (Jerusalem: Yad Itzhak Ben Zvi, 1998). For our purposes the differences between the two versions are not crucial. For thematic analysis of the text, see Saldarini, *Scholastic Rabbinism*, 1982. For analysis of the rhetorical modalities of *Avot de Rabbi Nathan* consult Jacob Neusner, *Judaism and Story: The Evidence of the Fathers According to Rabbi Nathan* (Chicago and London: University of Chicago Press, 1992); idem, "Abot deRabbi Nathan (The Fathers According to Rabbi Nathan)," in his *Introduction to Rabbinic Literature* (New York: Doubleday, 1994), 591–608.

39. The two talmudic tractates bearing this title are independent compositions that were geared to shape the ethics and moral conduct of the rabbinic sages, although any Jew who wished to imitate them was encouraged to do so. On the composition of these two texts, see M. Bialik Lerner, "The External Tractate," in *The Literature of the Sages*, pt. 1, 379–87.

40. The date and place of composition of the *Tana debe Eliyahu* (The Lore of the School of Elijah) cannot be ascertained. It is safe to say, however, that this collection of ethical teachings did not receive its final form before the ninth century and that it reflects the outlook of earlier talmudic sages in both Palestine and Babylonia. The English translation is by William G. Braude and Israel J. Kapstein, *Tanna Debe Eliyahu: The Lore of the School of Elijah* (Philadelphia: The Jewish Publication Society, 1981). For overview of the themes in this Midrashic compilation, see Max Kadushin, *The Theology of Seder Eliyahu: A Study in Rabbinic Judaism* (New York: Bloch, 1932).

41. For a close reading of this Psalm, consult Reuven Kimelman, "Psalm 145: Theme Structure, and Impact," *Journal of Biblical Literature* 113,1 (1994): 37–58; Adele Berlin, "The Rheotric of Psalm 145," in *Biblical and Related Studies Presented to Samuel Iwry*, ed. Ann Kort and Scott Morschauser (Winona Lake, IN: Eisenbrauns, 1985), 17–22.

42. Bereshit Rabbah 1:1; Midrash Tehilim 90:12.

43. For the various positions in this debate, consult Newman, "Ethics as Law, Law as Religion," 79–93 and the literature cited there.

44. Max Kadushin, *Organic Thinking: A Study in Rabbinic Thought* (New York: Bloch, 1976 [1938]), 117–18; idem. *Worship and Ethics: A Study in Rabbinic Judaism* (Evanston: Northwestern University Press, 1964), 39–57.

45. Kadushin, *Organic Thinking*, 126.

46. The English word "diet" comes from the Greek word *diatia*, meaning "way of living" or "mode of life." Ancient and medieval philosophers took it for granted that to preserve health and achieve longevity required knowledge of how to regulate one's life so that one would remain in balance with nature. As Martin Goodman noted, the rabbis were "as Greek philosophers [who] were expected to teach practical ethics as physicians of souls rather than impractical theorizers." Goodman, *State and Society*, 74.

47. Goldin (trans.), *The Fathers According To Rabbi Nathan*, 32.

48. Ibid. 24.

49. Ibid. 50.

50. See Sifre Deut. # 45 (Finkelstein ed.) 103; BT Erubin 55a; BT Yoma 71 a; BT Qiddushin 30b; BT Avodah Zarah 19b; Leviticus Rabba # 16 (Margulies ed.), 349–50.

51. Kadushin, *Organic Thinking*, 45. The following notes indicate a heavy reliance on Kadushin rather than on the rabbinic sources—*Seder Eliyahu Rabba* and *Seder Eliyahu Zuta*—for three reasons. First, Kadushin successfully captured the dynamic nature of rabbinic ethical discourse, which cannot not be grasped immediately by citing isolated rabbinic texts. Second, Kadushin used the edition of M. Friedmann (Wien, 1902), which is not easily accessible today. Third, by referring to Kadushin's own work, rather than to the rabbinic texts themselves, one illustrates to the reader how "value concepts" function in rabbinic thought. For his notion of "value-concepts," consult Max Kadushin, *The Rabbinic Mind* (New York: Bloch Publishing Company, 1972), 35–58.

52. Kadushin, *Organic Thinking*, 52.

53. Ibid. 53.

54. Ibid. 55.

55. The erotic dimension of Torah study is explored by David Biale, *Eros and the Jews: From Biblical Israel to Contemporary America* (New York: Basic Books, 1992), 46–48; Daniel Boyarin, *Carnal Israel: Reading Sex in Talmudic Culture* (Berkeley: University of California Press, 1993), 63–76.

56. Kadushin, *Organic Thinking*, 44.

57. The discourse in BT Abodah Zarah 18a indicates that the rabbis used Ps. 1 as the point of departure for reflections on the connection between happiness and Torah. See also Henry Fischel, "The Transformation of Wisdom in the World of Midrash," *Aspects of Wisdom in Judaism and Early Christianity*, ed. Robert Wilken (Notre Dame: University of Notre Dame Press, 1975), 67–101.

58. Goldin (trans.), *Fathers According to Rabbi Nathan*, 75–76.

59. I thus suggest reading the pronouncement of Avot 1:6 ("Provide yourself

with a teacher; get yourself a companion") in light of Aristotle's analysis of friendship discussed in the previous chapter.

60. See Solomon Schimmel, "Free Will, Guilt and Self Control in Rabbinic Judaism and Contemporary Psychology," *Judaism* 26 (1976): 418–29.

61. These are explored in Solomon Schimmel, *The Seven Deadly Sins: Jewish, Christians and Classical Reflections on Human Nature* (New York: The Free Press, 1992).

62. For an overview of rabbinic anthropology, consult Ephraim E. Urbach, *The Sages: Their Concepts and Beliefs* (Jerusalem: Magnes Press, 1975), 214–54; George Foot Moore, *Judaism in the First Centuries of the Christian Era: The Age of the Tannaim* (Cambridge: Harvard University Press, 1927–30), vol. 1, 445–59; Nissan Rubin, "From Monism to Dualism: Relations between the Body and Soul in Talmudic Thought," *Da`at* 23 (1989): 33–64. This essay is incorporated into his recent work, *The End of Life: Rites of Burial and Mourning in the Talmud and Midrash* (in Hebrew) (Hakibbutz Hameuchad, 1997), 54–75.

63. See Urbach, *The Sages*, 471–83.

64. Goldin (trans.), *Fathers According to Rabbi Nathan*, 172.

65. For example, BT Menahot 44a. I thank Dan Ben Amos for directing me to this source.

66. Moore, *Judaism*, Vol.1, 491.

67. Goldin (trans.), *Fathers According to Rabbi Nathan*, 85.

68. BT Eruvin 5a; Sifre Deut. # 4; B Qiddushin 30b.

69. Urbach, *The Sages*, 475.

70. David Winston, "Free Will," in Arthur A. Cohen and Paul Mendes-Flohr, eds., *Contemporary Jewish Religious Thought: Original Essays on Critical Concepts, Movements, and Beliefs* (New York: The Free Press, 1972), 270. To my knowledge there is no systematic analysis of the operation of the human will in rabbinic sources. For an attempt to articulate the Mishnaic theory on human intention, see Howard Eilberg-Schwartz, *The Human Will in Judaism: The Mishnah's Philosophy of Intention* (Atlanta: Scholars Press, 1986). For a critical review of this attempt consult Louis Jacobs, *Journal of Jewish Studies* 39 (1988): 279–81.

71. The famous maxim in Avot 3:19 (*ha-kol tzafui ve-ha-rashut netunah*) captures the rabbinic ambiguity on the subject.

72. *Avot de Rabbi Nathan*, chap. 14.

73. Braude and Kapstein (trans.) *Tanna Debe Eliyahu*, 144; 228.

74. Walter S. Wurzburger, *Ethics of Responsibility: Pluralistic Approaches to Covenantal Ethics* (Philadelphia: The Jewish Publication Society, 1994).

75. Kadushin, *Organic Thinking*, 115.

76. Ibid., 93.

77. Ibid., 51.

78. Ibid., 91.

79. For a fuller analysis of the virtue of *megalopsychia*, see W.F.R. Hardie, "Magnanimity" in Aristotle's Ethics," *Phronesis* 78 (1978): 63–79.

80. For a recent analysis see Ronald Green, "Jewish Ethics and the Virtue of Humility," *Journal of Religious Ethics* 1 (1) (1973): 53–63. Cf., Daniel M. Nelson, "The Virtue of Humility in Judaism: A Critique of Rationalist Hermeneutics," *Journal of Religious Ethics* 13 (1985): 298–313.

81. For the rabbis, "creation in the image of God" pertained to the entire human psycho-physical complex. See Urbach, *The Sages*, 226.

82. David Stern, "*Imitatio Hominis:* Anthropomorphism and the Character of God," *Prooftext* 11 (1991): 152.

83. Kadushin, *Organic Thinking*, 142; The notion of *imitatio Dei* was distinctively Jewish. BT Shabbat 113b; Sotah 14a. For analysis of this concept consult Schechter, *Aspects of Rabbinic Theology*, 199ff.

84. See Steven Fraade, "Ascetical Aspects of Ancient Judaism," in *Jewish Spirituality: From the Bible through the Middle Ages* (New York: Crossroad, 1986), pt. 1, 270.

85. On the so-called "First Hasidim" (*hasidim rishonim*), see Shmuel Safrai, "Teaching of Pietists in Mishnaic Literature," *Journal of Jewish Studies* 16 (1965): 15–33.

86. Kadushin, *Organic Thinking*, 54.

87. See Saul J. Berman, "Lifnim Mishurat Hadin," *Journal of Jewish Studies* 26 1–2 (1975): 86–104; 28 (2) (1977): 181–93; Louis E. Newman, "Law, Virtue and Supererogation in the Halakhah: The Problem of 'Lifnim Mishurat Hadin' Reconsidered," *Journal of Jewish Studies* 40 (1) (1989): 61–88; Eugene B. Borowitz, "The Authority of the Ethical Impulse in Halakha," in *Studies in Jewish Philosophy*, ed. Norbert M. Samuelson (Lanham: University Press of America, 1987), 489–505.

88. Kadushin, *Organic Thinking*, 54.

89. Goldin (trans.), *Fathers According to Rabbi Nathan*, 20.

90. Kadushin, *Organic Thinking*, 55.

91. Ibid. 56.

92. See Oliver Leaman, *Evil and Suffering in Jewish Philosophy* (Cambridge: Cambridge University Press, 1995).

93. The rabbinic treatment of this theme is analyzed by David Kraemer, *Responses to Suffering in Classical Rabbinic Literature* (New York and Oxford: Oxford University Press, 1995).

94. See Gary Anderson, "The Expression of Joy as a Halakhic Problem in Rabbinic Sources," *Jewish Quarterly Review* 80 (3–4)(1990): 212–52. Anderson has shown that in the Amoraic period the commandment to rejoice was "understood to include the obligation to study Torah. At the same time that Torah study became on occasion for rejoicing it also became an activity that was proscribed for mourners." For a more elaborate treatment of joy in Israelite religion, see idem. *A Time to Mourn and a Time to Dance: The Expression of Grief and Joy in Israelite Religion* (University Park, PA: The Pennsylvania State University, 1991).

95. Braude and Kapstein (trans.), *Tana Debe Eliyahu*, 206. Cf. ibid. 49: "Blessed be the Preserver of the world, blessed be He whose joy on account of Israel is ever

great: as Israel obeys the Torah in this world and rejoices in it, so, in return, Torah rejoices in them for ever, as it said, "The 'mother' of children [In Israel] rejoices. Hence and thereafter He finds His joy in us;" Ibid. 13. "Each and every man will rejoice in his absorption of Torah and his understanding of it"; ibid. 209: "Because of a man's presence in a synagogue or a house of study, joy is renewed for him every day without fail."

96. Kadushin, *Organic Thinking*, 43.

97. Braude and Kapstein, trans., *Tana debe Eliyahu*, 314.

98. Kadushin, *Organic Thinking*, 44.

99. The rabbinic speculations about the remote future included diverse concepts such as "Garden of Eden" "Sheol," "Gehenna," "World-to-Come," "End of Days," "Messianic Age," and "Resurrection of the Dead." For overview of these interweaving themes in rabbinic thought consult Moore, *Judaism*, vol. 2, 287–395; Simchah Paull Raphael, *Jewish Views of the Afterlife* (Northvale NJ: Jason Aronson, 1994), 117–62; Neil Gillman, *The Death of Death: Resurrection and Immortality in Jewish Thought* (Woodstock VT: Jewish Lights Publishing, 1997), 113–42.

100. For an anthropological analysis of rabbinic burial and mourning rituals, see Rubin, *The End of Life*, 114–89.

101. Zoroastrianism is a likely source for the doctrine of resurrection in Judaism. On resurrection of the dead in Zoroastrianism, see *The Encyclopedia of Religion*, editor in chief, Mircea Eliade (New York: Macmillan, 1987), vol. 15, 579–91.

102. See Saul Lieberman, *Yevanim ve-Yavnut be-Eretz Israel: Meḥaqarim be-Orḥot Ḥayim be-Eretz Yisrael bi-Tequfat ha-Mishnah ve-ha-Talmud* (Jerusalem: Mosad Bialik, 1962), 52–59, esp. 55.

Notes to Chapter 4

1. On the legal status of the Jews in Islam, see Mark R. Cohen, *Under Crescent and Cross: The Jews in the Middle Ages* (Princeton: Princeton University Press, 1994), 52–74.

2. Ibid. 70–71.

3. On the economic diversification of the Jewish community in medieval Islam, see ibid, 88–103 and the extensive literature cited there.

4. Whether Saadia Gaon should be labeled a philosopher or a theologian is a disputed question that requires some clarification. In medieval Islam there was a formal distinction between scholastic theology (Kalam) and philosophy (Falsafa): the former used philosophic material in order to defend the rationality of the received tradition, whereas the latter used reason to discover and articulate the truth. However, it is a mistake to make the two discourses mutually exclusive or antagonistic to each other. First, for Aristotle "theology," namely, discourse about God, was another name for metaphysics, the highest of all philosophical sciences. Second, Kalam theologians dealt with the questions of concern to the philosophers, such as origin of the universe and destiny of human life. Not coincidentally, modern surveys of the history of

Islamic philosophy all include discussion of Kalam theology. And third, when Saadia (and other Jewish philosophers) defended the rationality of rabbinic Judaism, they did so on the basis of a *philosophical* claim that Judaism is truth. Therefore, I think it is justified to call Saadia Gaon a philosopher.

5. On their contribution to the Aristotelian tradition, see Robert W. Sharples, "The School of Alexander?" in *Aristotle Transformed: The Ancient Commentators and their Influence*, ed. Richard Sorabji (Ithaca: Cornell University Press, 1990), 83–111; Henry J. Blumenthal, "Themistius: The Last Peripatetic Commentator on Aristotle?" in *Aristotle Transformed*, 113–23; idem, *Aristotle and Neoplatonism in Late Antiquity: Interpretations of the De Anima* (Ithaca: Cornell University Press, 1996).

6. The relevant primary sources on the classification of the sciences are available in Franz Rosenthal, *The Classical Heritage in Islam*, trans. Emile and Jenny Marmorstein (London and New York: Routledge, 1975), 52–73. The formal classifications of the science reflected the Islamic penchant for encyclopedic activity, itself a continuation of Alexandrian Hellenism. See Francis E. Peters, *Aristotle and the Arabs* (New York: New York University Press, 1968), 104–20; *The Cambridge History of Islam*, vol. 2b, 507–603.

7. To date the most comprehensive study of *Kalam* remains Harry A. Wolfson, *The Philosophy of the Kalam* (Cambridge: Harvard University Press, 1976). Very useful are the entries "Kalam," "Mu'atazilah," in *Encyclopedia of Religion*, ed. Mircea Eliade (New York: Macmillan, 1987); M. Abdel Haleem, "Early Kalam," in *History of Islamic Philosophy*, pt. 1, 71–88.

8. For an overview of Atomism in Islamic philosophy, see Shlomo Pines, *Studies in Islamic Atomism*, trans. Michael Schwarts, ed. Tzvi Langermann (Jerusalem: Magnes Press, 1997).

9. This is the target of the experiences that gave rise to the speculations that constitute the Heikhalot and Merkabah literature. We will return to this literature in Chapter Seven below. The visualization of the Throne of Glory is discussed in great detail by Elliot R. Wolfson, *Through a Speculum that Shines: Vision and Imagination in Medieval Jewish Mysticism* (Princeton: Princeton University Press, 1994), 74–124.

10. A good overview of this genre is available in Joseph Dan, "The Religious Experience of the Merkavah," in *Jewish Spirituality: From the Bible through the Middle Ages*, ed. Arthur Green (New York: Crossroad, 1986), 289–307.

11. "Shi`ur Qomah" is in fact the name of a literary tradition that existed in various recensions until their consolidation about the ninth or tenth centuries. See Martin S. Cohen, *The Shiur Qomah: Texts and Recensions* (Tubingen: J.C.B. Mohr, 1985), 5.

12. See Moshe Idel, "Infinities of Torah in Kabbalah," in *Midrash and Literature*, ed. Geoffrey H. Hartman and Sanford Budick (New Haven: Yale University Press, 1986), 144–45.

13. See Zvi Ankori, *The Karaites in Byzantium* (New York: Columbia University Press, 1959).

14. On Saadia's campaign against the Palestinian Gaonate and his rise to power, see Henry Malter, *Saadia Gaon: His Life and Works* (Philadelphia: The Jewish Publication Society, 1921), 69–134; Robert Brody, *The Geonim of Babylonia and the Shaping of Medieval Jewish Culture* (New Haven: Yale University Press, 1998), 235–48.

15. The Arabic text in Arabic characters was published by S. Landauer (Leiden, 1880). The same text in Hebrew characters with a modern Hebrew translation was published by Joseph Kafih (Jerusalem, 1970). The standard Hebrew translation was done by Judah ibn Tibbon in 1161. It was first printed in Constantinople, 1562. Our reference will be to the English translation by Samuel Rosenblatt, *The Book of Beliefs and Opinions* (New Haven: Yale University Press, 1948). For an overview of Saadia's philosophy consult Colette Sirat, *A History of Jewish Philosophy in the Middle Ages* (Cambridge: Cambridge University Press, 1985), 18–37; Brody, *The Geonim of Babylonia*, 289–91.

16. According to Joseph Dan, the Tenth Treatise was the first "secular-eudaimonistic" ethics in Judaism. Taking 'secular' (in Hebrew, *ḥiloni*) to be antithetical to 'religious,' Dan claims that even though Saadia adduces biblical and rabbinic prooftexts, these are no more than "additional ornamentations" to his non-religious philosophical views, advancing a utilitarian ethics. See Joseph Dan, *Hebrew Ethical and Homiletical Literature (The Middle Ages and Early Modern Period)* [Hebrew] (Jerusalem: Keter, 1975), 20. Therefore, Dan considers the Tenth Treatise to be in conflict with the religious outlook advocated by the rest of the book.

17. Eliezer Schweid, "The Ethical-Religious Doctrine of Saadia Gaon," [Hebrew] *Jerusalem Studies in Jewish Thought* 3 (1982): 15–31.

18. Ibid. 31.

19. Al-Farabi's commentary on the *Nicomachean Ethics* did not survive, but reports about its content abound in later works by ibn Bajja, ibn Rushd, and ibn Tufayl. Apparently the gist of the commentary was that there is no happiness except political happiness. In other words, al-Farabi followed the "inclusive" reading of Aristotle. See Miriam Galston, "The Theoretical and Practical Dimensions of Happiness as Portrayed in the Political Treatises of al-Farabi," in *The Political Aspects of Islamic Philosophy: Essays in Honor of Mushin S. Mahdi*, ed. Charles E. Butterworth (Cambridge, Mass.: Harvard University Press, 1992), 95–151.

20. Marshall G.S. Hodgson, *The Ventures of Islam: Conscience and History in a World Civilization*, vol. 1, 451. On the translations of the *Nicomachean Ethics* into Arabic, see Hans Daiber, "Political Philosophy," *The History of Islamic Philosophy* pt. 2, ed. Seyyed Hossein Nasr and Oliver Leaman (London and New York: Routlege, 1996), 842–43; A.J. Arberry, "The Nicomachean Ethics in Arabic," *Bulletin of the School of Oriental and African Studies* 17 (1955): 1–9.

21. On philosophical ethics in Islam, see Majid Fakhry, *Ethical Theories in Islam* (Leiden: E.J. Brill, 1991); George F. Hourani, *Reason and Tradition in Islamic Ethics*

(Cambridge: Cambridge University Press, 1985); Dwight M. Donaldson, *Studies in Muslim Ethics* (London: S.P.C.K., 1953).

22. Fakhry, *Ethical Theories*, 74. For an English translation of this text see Arthur J. Arberry (ed.), *The Spiritual Physic of Razes* (London: John Murray, 1950).

23. Ibid. p. 102; Cf. Donaldson, *Muslim Ethics*, 119–20.

24. The Arabic version, *Kitab al-Akhlaq li-Jalinus* was edited by P. Kraus in *The Bulletin of the Faculty of Arts of Egyptian University* 5 (1) (1937): 1–51; English translation by J.N. Mattock in *Islamic Philosophy and Classical Tradition: Essays Presented by his Friends and Pupils to Richard Walzer on His Seventieth Birthday*, ed. S.M. Stern, Albert Hourani and Vivian Brown (Columbia SC: University of South Carolina Press, 1973), 235–60. On this text see F. Klein-Franke, "The Arabic Version of Galen's Peri Ethon," *Jerusalem Studies in Arabic and Islam* 1 (1979): 125–50.

25. Plotinus discussed the cultivation of virtues in the *Enneads* 1.2.19. He understood the goal of human life to be the imitation of God and his ethical theory is an interesting fusion of elements from Plato and Aristotle. Plotinus distinguished between the "practical virtues," which emerge in social interaction and improve the quality of life but which fail to lead to the imitation of God, and the "purifying virtues," which release people from corporeality and lead to pure contemplation, the ultimate end of human life. On Islamic Neoplatonism see Majid Fakhry, *A History of Islamic Philosophy*, 2nd ed. (New York: Columbia University Press, 1983), 107–62.

26. Sirat, *The History of Jewish Philosophy in the Middle Ages*, 31.

27. See Herbert Davidson, "Saadia's List of Theories on the Soul," in *Jewish Medieval and Renaissance Studies*, ed. Alexander Altmann (Cambridge: Harvard University Press, 1967), 75–94.

28. The significance of the fact that vision was the main metaphor for knowledge is discussed and critiqued by Richard Rorty, *Philosophy and the Mirror of Nature* (Princeton: Princeton University Press, 1979).

29. On the ascetic tendencies of Karaism, see Brody, *The Geonim of Babylonia*, 95–96.

30. See Norbert M. Samuelson, "Saadia and the Logic of Religious Authority," *Judaism* (1971): 460–66.

31. See Harry A. Wolfson, "The Kalam Problem of Non-Existence and Saadia's Second Theory of Creation," *Jewish Quarterly Review* 36 (1945–46): 371–91; idem. "The Meaning of Ex-Nihilo in the Church Fathers, Arabic and Jewish Philosophy, and St. Thomas," in *Studies in the History of Philosophy and Religion*, Vol. 1, 207–21.

32. See Herbert Davidson, "John Philoponus as a Source of Medieval Islamic and Jewish Proofs of Creation," *Journal of the American Oriental Society* 85 (1969): 358–91. For an analysis of John Philoponus' position see Seymour Feldman, "Philoponus on the Metaphysics of Creation," in *A Straight Path: Studies in Medieval Philosophy and Culture, Essays in Honor of Arthur Hyman*, ed. J. Hackett, M.

S. Hyman, R. J. Long and C. Manekin (Washington: Catholic University Press, 1988), 74–85.

33. See Daniel J. Lasker, "The Destiny of Man in Karaite Philosophy" [Hebrew], *Daat* 12 (1994): 5–14.

34. See Bernard S. Bachrach, *Early Medieval Jewish Policy in Western Europe* (Minneapolis: University of Minnesota Press, 1977), 3–26.

35. The so-called royal alliance between the Jews and Spanish monarchs is well analyzed by Salo Baron, *Social and Religious History of the Jews*, vol. 10 (New York: Columbia University Press, 1965), 118–219.

36. For overview of *adab* literature see Hodgson, *The Venture of Islam*, vol. 1, 444–72.

37. See Rosenthal, *The Classical Heritage in Islam*, 24–51.

38. See Raymond P. Scheindlin, *Wine, Women, Death: Medieval Hebrew Poems on the Good Life* (Philadelphia: The Jewish Publication Society, 1986), 1–17.

39. On the military campaigns of Samuel ibn Naghrella, see Jefim Schirmann, *The History of Hebrew Poetry in Muslim Spain* [Hebrew], ed. Ezra Fleischer (Jerusalem: The Magnes Press, 1995), 193–97.

40. See Ross Brann, *The Compunctious Poet: Cultural Ambiguity and Hebrew Poetry in Muslim Spain* (Baltimore and London: The Johns Hopkins University Press, 1991), 23–58.

41. For surveys of this literature, see Ezra Fleischer, *Hebrew Liturgical Poetry in the Middle Ages* [in Hebrew] (Jerusalem: Keter, 1975); Raymond P. Scheindlin, *The Ghazelle: Medieval Hebrew Poems on God, Israel and the Soul* (Philadelphia: Jewish Publication Society, 1991), 3–51.

42. For a thematic study of the genres of Hebrew secular poetry, consult Israel Levin, *The Embroidered Coat: The Genres of Hebrew Secular Poetry in Spain* [Hebrew], 3 vols. (Tel Aviv: Hakibbutz Hameucad, 1985); Arie Schippers, *Arabic Tradition and Hebrew Innovation: Arabic Themes in Hebrew Andalusian Poetry.* 2nd ed. (Amsterdam: University of Amsterdam Press, 1988).

43. This reading conflicts with the approach of Eddy M. Zemach and Tovah Rosen-Moked, *A Sophisticated Work* [Hebrew] (Jerusalem: Keter, 1983), 108.

44. Scheindlin, *Wine, Women, and Death*, 26.

45. On these collections of sententious aphorisms and its *adab* sources, see Israel Levin, *The Embroidered Coat*, vol. 3, 28–59.

46. See ibid. 48–52.

47. The Hebrew translation by Judah ibn Tibbon is available with an English translation by B. H. Ascher (London, 1859).

48. On ibn Gabirol's metaphysics, see Jacques Schlanger, *La philosophie de Salomon ibn Gabirol : Etude d'un neoplatonisme* (Leiden: E. J. Brill, 1968); John M. Dillon, "Solomon ibn Gabirol's Doctrine of Intelligible Matter," in *Neoplatonism and Jewish Thought*, ed. Lenn E. Goodman (Albany: State University of New York Press, 1992), 43–59.

49. The Arabic original was translated into Hebrew with an English translation

by Steven Wise (New York: 1902). The Hebrew translation was published in Constantinople 1550. I used the Lineville edition (1807) reprinted in Jerusalem, 1967.

50. This translation, along with other philosophic-scientific works in Arabic, was occasioned by the destruction of Andalusian Jewry in 1148–1150 due to the persecution of the Almohades. We will discuss this development in Chapter Six. The English citations will be from Stephen S. Wise (trans.), *The Improvement of the Moral Qualities* (New York, 1902).

51. The title indicates that Gabirol's work should be seen in the context of what the Muslim philosophers named "the science of character" (*ilm al-akhlaq*). Among Muslim philosophers, al-Ghazzali made the most systematic examination of the connection between right conduct and purification of the soul as means to a harmonious relation with God and the attainment of everlasting joy. See, M. A. Sherif, *Ghazali's Theory of Virtue* (Albany: Statue University of New York Press, 1974); George F. Hourani, "Ghazali on Ethics of Action," in his *Reason and Tradition in Islamic Ethics* (Cambridge: Cambridge University Press, 1985), 135–66.

52. Joseph Dan, *Ethical and Homiletical Literature*, 22–25.

53. Yehudah Alharizi's Hebrew translation of Hunayin ibn Yishaq's *Adab al Falasifah* was published in Abraham Loewenthal (Frankfurt, 1896).

54. See Richard Waltzer, "New Light on Galen's Moral Philosophy," in his *Greek into Arabic* (Cambridge: Harvard University Press, 1962), 142–63.

55. Fakhry, *A History of Islamic Philosophy*, 174.

56. The Islamicate civilization of the Middle Ages perpetuated the Greek and Hellenistic link between the well-being of the body and the well-being of the soul. Not coincidentally, Jewish and Muslim philosophers derived their livelihood quite often from the practice of medicine.

57. This arrangement too reflects Pythagorean principles: the negative and the positive correspondence to the principles of "odd" and "even."

58. In great measure this was due to the fact that the philosophy involved was Neoplatonism, the most religiously and mystically oriented of the traditional schools of thought. The tension between rabbinic Judaism and philosophy was felt more acutely once Jewish thinkers became familiar with Aristotle's philosophy

59. Herbert Davidson, "The Study of Philosophy as a Religious Obligation," in *Religion in a Religious Age,* ed. Solomon D. Goitein, (Cambridge, MA: Association for Jewish Studies, 1974), 53–69.

60. The Arabic original was published by A. S. Yahuda (Leiden, 1912). The Hebrew translation of Judah ibn Tibbon was published in Naples in 1489. Moses Hayim Hyamson published a Hebrew-English edition. The quotations herein will be from Menahem Mansoor (trans.), *The Book of Directions of the Duties of the Heart* (London: Routledge & Kegan Paul, 1973).

61. On the dating of Bahya's life and the relevant scholarly literature, see Menahem Mansoor, "Translator's Introduction," in *Duties of the Heart*, 1–2.

62. See Bezalel Safran, "Bahya ibn Paquda's Attitude toward the Courtier Class,"

in *Studies in Medieval Jewish History and Literature*, ed. Isadore Twersky (Cambridge: Harvard University Press, 1979), 154–96.

63. On Bahya's Sufi sources see Alan Lazaroff, "Bahya's Asceticism against its Rabbinic and Islamic Background," *Journal of Jewish Studies* 21 (1970): 29–66. For a more thorough and comprehensive treatment of the impact of Sufism on Bahya's generation, see Paul B. Fenton, "Judaism and Sufism," in *History of Islamic Philosophy*, pt. 1, 755–68; Diana Lobel, *Between Mysticism and Philosophy: Sufi Language and Religious Experience in Judah Halevi's Kuzari* (Albany: State University of New York, 2000), 4, 25, 182–83, n. 11 and the literature cited therein.

64. The Brethren of Purity initiated its members into the life of philosophy culminating in the knowledge of God. Their fifty-two epistles, which constituted a kind of philosophico-scientific encyclopedia, embodied a peculiar blend of Neo-Pythagorean and Neoplatonic ideas. For an overview see Ian Richard Netton, "The Brethren of Purity (Ikhwan al Safa')" in *History of Islamic Philosophy* vol. 1, 222–30 and the literature cited there; Fakhry, *A History of Islamic Philosophy*, 166–81. The relevant section about the classification of the sciences from the *Epistles of the Brethren of Purity* is available in Franz Rosenthal, *The Classical Heritage in Islam* (London and New York: Routledge, 1992), 55–58.

65. This classification corresponds to Saadia's distinction between "rational" and "ceremonial."

66. The Brethren of Purity differentiated between the "real one" and "figurative oneness." The real one is "that which has no parts, is indivisible, and because of this indivisibility is one." The figurative oneness, by contrast, refers to any sum of things, such as one man, or one horse. See *Rasa'il Ikhwan al-safa'* (Beirut: n.p., 1957), vol. 1, 49.

67. This claim is clearly indebted to the Islamic prohibition of any form of association between created beings and God.

68. This text is referred to in modern scholarship as "the Pseudo-Bahya." On this text see Tamar Rudavsky, "Medieval Jewish Neoplatonism" in *History of Jewish Philosophy*, 162–64.

69. Bahya's work deeply influenced Abraham Maimonides, the son of Maimonides. See Samuel Rosenblatt (ed.), *The High Ways to Perfection of Abraham Maimonides* (New York: AMS Press, 1966), 42. In the fifteenth century, Bahya's *Duties of the Heart* was one of the first books to be printed in the Ottoman Empire, indicating its popularity among Sephardic exiles.

70. For a critical edition, English translation and analytic essays, consult Norbert M. Samuelson *The Exalted Faith: Abraham ibn Daud* (Rutherford/Madison/Teaneck: Fairleigh Dickinson University, 1986). For a summary of the Third Treatise, where ibn Daud echoes Aristotle's *Nicomachean Ethics*, see 256–59.

71. See Amira Eran, *From Simple Faith to Sublime Faith* [Hebrew], (Tel Aviv: Hakibbutz Hameuchad, 1998), 272–91.

Notes to Chapter 5

1. See P. M. Holt, Ann K. S. Lambton, and Bernard Lewis (eds.), *The Cambridge History of Islam* (Cambridge: Cambridge University Press, 1970), vol. 2b, 785.

2. See Abu Hamid Muhammad al-Ghazzali, *The Alchemy of Happiness*, trans. Claud Field; revised and annotated by Alton L. Daniel (Armonk, NY and London: M. E. Sharpe, 1991).

3. In his political philosophy, al-Farabi largely followed Plato's political theories. Although al-Farabi devoted some attention to ethical issues such as the nature of practical wisdom, the moral virtues, and deliberation, most of his interest was the ideal state and its ruler and the relationship between philosophy and religion in the ideal state. For an overview of al-Farabi's political theory, consult Deborah L. Black, "Al-Farabi," in *History of Islamic Philosophy*, vol. 1, 178–97. On the indebtedness of Maimonides to al-Farabi, see Lawrence V. Berman, "Maimonides the Disciple of Alfarabi," *Israel Oriental Studies* 4 (1974): 154–78; idem, "The Political Interpretation of the Maxim: The Purpose of Philosophy is the Imitation of God," *Studia Islamica* 15 (1961): 53–61.

4. On the scholarly debate concerning Maimonides' official position and an argument against ascribing him the title "Rais al-Yahud," see Jacob Lavinger, "Was Maimonides 'Rais al-Yahud' in Egypt?" in *Studies in Maimonides*, ed. Isadore Twersky (Cambridge, MA: Harvard University Press, 1990), 83–93.

5. The interpretation of Maimonides is inseparable from the contemporary debate about the meaning of Judaism. On the link between Maimonidean scholarship and contemporary Jewish self-perceptions, see Arthur Hyman, "Interpreting Maimonides," *Gesher* 5 (1976): 46–58; Warren Z. Harvey, "The Return of Maimonideanism," *Journal of Jewish Social Studies* 42 (1980): 249–68; Menachem M. Kellner, "Reading Rambam: Approaches to the Interpretation of Maimonides," *Jewish History* 5 (1991): 73–93; Marvin Fox, "The Many-Sided Maimonides," in his *Interpreting Maimonides: Studies in Methodology, Metaphysics and Moral Philosophy* (Chicago and London: The University of Chicago Press, 1990), 3–25.

6. For an overview of recent studies on Maimonides' view of human perfection see Ehud Benor, "Perspectives on Maimonides," *Religious Studies Review* 20 (3)(1994): 189–95.

7. Maimonides' intentional esotericism has been the focus of extensive scholarship that was largely indebted to Leo Strauss. See Leo Strauss, "The Literary Character of the Guide of the Perplexed," in *Essays on Maimonides, An Octocentennial Volume*, ed. Salo W. Baron (New York: Columbia University Press, 1941), 37–91; reprinted in *Maimonides: A Collection of Critical Essays*, ed. Joseph A. Buijs (Notre Dame: University of Notre Dame Press, 1988), 30–58; idem. "How to Begin to Study the Guide," in Moses Maimonides, *The Guide of the Perplexed*, trans. Shlomo Pines (Chicago: The University of Chicago Press, 1963), x–lvi. All citations will be from this edition. For an overview of Leo Strauss' reading of Maimonides in the

larger context of his political theory consult Kenneth Hart Green, "Editor's Introduction: Leo Strauss as a Modern Jewish Thinker," in *Leo Strauss, Jewish Philosophy and the Crisis of Modernity: Essays and Lectures in Modern Jewish Thought* (Albany, NY: State University of New York Press, 1997), 1–84. On the history of the esoteric approach to Maimonides see Aviezer Ravitzky, "Sitrei Torah shel Moreh ha-Nevukhim: Ha-Parshanut be-Dorotav v-be-Doroteinu," *Al Da'at ha-Maqom: Meḥqarim ba-hagut ha-Yehudit ve-Toldoteha* (Jerusalem: Keter, 1991), 142–81; idem, "Samuel ibn Tibbon and the Esoteric Character of the *Guide of the Perplexed*," *AJS Review* 6 (1981): 87–123; idem. "The Secrets of the Guide of the Perplexed: Between the Thirteenth and the Twentieth Centuries" [Hebrew], *Jerusalem Studies in Jewish Thought* 5 (1986): 23–70. For a critique of this way of reading Maimonides' philosophy, see Marvin Fox, "The Esoteric Method," in his *Interpreting Maimonides*, 47–66.

8. *Guide*, "Introduction with Respect to this Treatise," 17–18.

9. Ibid. 15.

10. See Shlomo Pines, "Translators' Introduction: The Philosophic Sources of the Guide of the Perplexed," in *The Guide of the Perplexed*, lvii–cxxxiv.

11. Maimonides' conception of human perfection has been the topic of many studies. In particular, consult Erwin I. J. Rosenthal, "The Concept of 'Eudaimonia' in Medieval Islamic and Jewish Philosophy," in his *Studia Semitica*, vol. 2: Islamic Themes (Cambridge: Cambridge University Press, 1971), 127–44; Norman Roth, "Attaining 'Happiness' (*Eudaimonia*) in Medieval Muslim and Jewish Philosophy," *Centerpoint* 4 (1981): 21–32; Menachem M. Kellner, *Maimonides on Human Perfection* (Atlanta: Scholars Press, 1990); Lawrence V. Berman, "The Ethical Views of Maimonides within the Context of Islamicate Civilization," in *Perspectives on Maimonides: Philosophical and Historical Studies*, ed. Joel L. Kraemer (Oxford: Oxford University Press for the Littman Library, 1991), 13–32; Howard Kreisel, *Maimonides' Political Thought: Studies in Ethics, Law and the Human Ideal* (Albany, NY: State University of New York Press, 1999).

12. The history of the discourse on happiness in medieval Jewish philosophy illustrates Maimonides' vacillation between these two possible readings of Aristotle. Generally speaking, in the thirteenth and fourteenth centuries the "exclusive" reading of Maimonides dominated the Maimonidean tradition, while in the fifteenth and sixteenth centuries the "inclusive" reading was more common. Whether a given thinker opposes or endorses Aristotle's moral philosophy, and in turn, Maimonides' ethics, depends (among other factors) on which of these views of human happiness the thinker ascribes to his authoritative sources. The discourse on happiness is thus an ideal case for charting the reception of Aristotle and Maimonides in late medieval Jewish thought more than it helps to determine their "true" position.

13. On the status of the *Nicomachean Ethics* in Islam, see Charles E. Butterworth, "Ethics in Medieval Islamic Philosophy," *Journal of Religious Ethics* 11 (2)(1983): 224–39.

14. See Miriam Galston, *Politics and Excellence: The Political Philosophy of Alfarabi* (Princeton: Princeton University Press, 1990), 55–94.

15. On ibn Bajja's political theory, see Erwin I. J. Rosenthal, "The Place of Politics in the Philosophy of ibn Bajja," in his *Studia Semitica*, vol. 2 (Cambridge: Cambridge University Press, 1971), 35–39; Pines, "The Literary Sources of the Guide," ciii-cviii. On the indebtedness of Maimonides to ibn Bajja, consult Lawrence Berman, "Ibn Bajja and Maimonides: A Chapter in the History of Political Philosophy" (Ph.D. diss., Hebrew University of Jerusalem, 1959).

16. See Alexander Altmann, "Ibn Bajja on Man's Ultimate Felicity," in *Harry Austryn Wolfson Jubilee Volume* (Jerusalem: American Academy for Jewish Research, 1965), I, 47–87, reprinted in *Studies in Religious Philosophy and Mysticism* (Ithaca: Cornell University Press, 1969), 15–24.

17. Maimonides' relationship to ibn Sina is a riddle not yet solved. Most recently, Alfred Ivry has suggested that Maimonides' ambiguous attitude toward ibn Sina reflects his uneasiness with Neoplatonism. On the one hand, Maimonides was attracted to Neoplatonism, but on the other hand he thought it to be philosophically "inadequate." See Alfred Ivry, "Maimonides and Neoplatonism: Challenge and Response," in *Neoplatonism and Jewish Thought*, ed. Lenn E. Goodman (Albany, NY: State University of New York Press, 1992), 137–56. For a documentation of Maimonides' direct borrowing from ibn Sina, consult Herbert Davidson, *Alfarabi, Avicenna, and Averroes, on Intellect: Their Cosmologies, Theories of the Active Intellect, and Theories of the Human Intellect* (New York and Oxford: Oxford University Press, 1992), passim.

It seems to me fruitful to explore the following avenue: Maimonides' reticence to cite ibn Sina might lie in the fact that the Persian thinker held a non-Orthodox position on the question of bodily resurrection. Ibn Sina's denial of bodily resurrection was attacked by Alghazali and was well known to Maimonides, who likewise held a non-Orthodox view on this matter. It stands to reason that Maimonides thought it prudent to minimize his overt reliance on ibn Sina in order to protect himself on a very sensitive issue, for which he was indeed attacked, as we shall see in the following chapter.

18. For a recent discussion of this letter consult Steven Harvey, "Did Maimonides' Letter to Samuel ibn Tibbon Determine which Philosophers would be Studied by Later Jewish Thinkers," *Jewish Quarterly Review* 83 (1992): 51–70.

19. Aristotle, *Ethics* X:4 1174a 14-b9; *Metaphysics* IX:6 1048b 18–36. The Aristotelian distinction between activity (*energia*) and process (*kinesis*) is discussed in our Chapter One and in Kraut, *Aristotle on the Human Good*, 68.

20. According to this functionalist definition, a myth is neither true nor false. Rather it is a narrative that either has or does not have the power to evoke a meaningful response. See Elliot Deutch, "Truth and Mythology," in *Myths and Fictions*, ed. Shlomo Biderman and Ben-Ami Scharfstein (Leiden: E.J. Brill, 1993), 41–50.

21. See Kenneth Seeskin, *Maimonides: A Guide for Today's Perplexed* (West Orange, NJ: Behrman House, 1991), 22. "Demythologizing," as is well known, was

the core of Rudolph Bultmann's hermeneutics of the New Testament. He undertook to show that what was regarded as reliable history was not so, but rather a myth in the sense of pre-scientific assertions. To get to the historical kernel behind the myth, Bultmann proposed to demythologize the mythic framework of the New Testament and extract the divine message addressed to people of a post-mythic age. It is justified to say that Maimonides "demythologized" rabbinic Judaism because, like Bultmann, he attempted to extract the philosophic truth (or message) from biblical and rabbinic narratives. He did so in part by pointing out that certain texts, which are not usually recognized as parables, are truly so.

22. On ibn Sina's philosophical novel, see Peter Heath, *Allegory and Philosophy in Avicenna (Ibn Sina)* (Philadelphia: University of Pennsylvania Press, 1992). Avicenna's impact on this genre in Jewish philosophy is explored by Aaron Hughes, "Philosophy's Mythos: Aesthetics, the Imagination, and the Philosophical Novel in Medieval Jewish and Islamic Thought" (Ph.D. diss., Indiana University, 2000).

23. I call all four narratives "myths" although I admit that they are not identical in form: (1) and (4) are technically philosophical parables, namely, they are narratives with an internal philosophical meaning; (2) is a retelling of a historical narrative but without a clear correspondence between the external and internal levels of the story, and (3) is not presented as a story but is a constructed portrayal of Moses that emerges from numerous statements in Maimonides' writings. Nonetheless, I think that all four are not only "myths" in the functionalist sense of interpretative schemas that provide meaning and articulate norms of conduct, but also in the sense that they teach philosophic truths that cannot be apprehended except through a story.

24. Strauss expressed this point most succinctly when he spoke about the *Guide* as the "Torah for the perplexed." Strauss, "How to Begin to Study the *Guide*," xliii.

25. This position is compatible, though not identical, with Howard Kreisel's argument that Maimonides' conception of *imitatio Dei* reflects his metaphysics. See Howard Kreisel, "*Imitatio Dei* in Maimonides' Guide of the Perplexed," *AJS Review* 19 (2) (1994): 169–211; reprinted in his *Maimonides' Political Thought*, 125–58. Going beyond Kreisel, I wish to expose the close link between metaphysics, psychology, epistemology, ethics, and rhetoric in Maimonides' thought.

26. Leo Strauss' framing of the so-called conflict between "Athens and Jerusalem" is best explored by the essays in *Leo Strauss and Judaism: Jerusalem and Athens Critically Revisited*, ed. David Novak (Lanham, Md.: Rowman & Littlefield, 1996).

27. Maimonides was indeed concerned that the misunderstanding of philosophy by the uneducated masses could be harmful and even lead to idolatry. See *Guide*, I: 17. The "conspiratorial" reading of the *Guide* was Leo Strauss' legacy to contemporary readings of Maimonides. Such a reading, not unrelated to Strauss' own biography as a Jewish refugee from Germany, may be called "political" esotericism and it comes at the expense of the "philosophical" esotericism that this article wishes to highlight. For a recent review of the negative impact of Strauss' reading of

Maimonides on modern scholarship and recent attempts to go beyond it consult Norbert M. Samuelson, "Maimonidean Scholarship at the End of the Century," *AJS Review* 26, 1 (2002): 93–107.

28. For Maimonides, the rabbinic injunction against teaching *Ma`aseh Bereshit* and *Ma`aseh Merkabah* in public (*Mishnah Ḥagiga* 2:1) consists exclusively of a prohibition on teaching of physics and metaphysics respectively.

29. An excellent summary is provided in Alfred L. Ivry, "The Logical and Scientific Premises of Maimonides' Thought," in *Perspectives on Jewish Thought and Mysticism*, ed. Alfred L. Ivry, Elliot R. Wolfson, and Allan Arkush (Amsterdam: Harwood Academic Publishers, 1998), 63–98.

30. See Alexander Altmann, "Essence and Existence in Maimonides," *Bulletin of the John Rylands Library* 35 (1953): 294–315; reprinted in his *Studies in Religious Philosophy and Mysticism* (Ithaca: Cornell University Press 1969), 108–27. For a critique of Altmann's analysis see Ivry, "Maimonides and Neoplatonism, 143–46.

31. See Y. Tzvi Langerman, "Maimonides' Repudiation of Astrology," *Maimonidean Studies* 2 (1991): 123–58. In this regard Maimonides' critique was part of a larger challenge raised in the twelfth century among philosophers of the Muslim West. See A. I. Sabra, "The Andalusian Revolt against Ptolemaic Astronomy: Averroes and al-Bitruji," in *Transformation and Tradition in the Sciences: Essays in Honor of I. Bernard Cohen* (Cambridge: Cambridge University Press, 1984), 133–53.

32. See *Guide* III: 8, 430. On Maimonides' conception of matter, consult Idit Dobbs-Weinstein, "Matter as Creature and Matter as the Source of Evil: Maimonides and Aquinas," in *Neoplatonism and Jewish Thought*, ed. Lenn E. Goodman (Albany: State University of New York Press, 1992), 217–35.

33. Lenn E. Goodman, "Maimonides Naturalism" in *Neoplatonism and Jewish Thought*, 165.

34. *Guide* III: 8, 430–31.

35. See Lenn E. Goodman, *Avicenna* (London: Routledge, 1992), 49–122.

36. Maimonides' *Guide* itself includes both positions. In the Guide I:72, II:1, II:4 one finds references to ibn Sina's position, but there are two other passages in which Maimonides is closer to Averroes' view. For further discussion see Pines, "Translator's Introduction," cxiv-cxvi. I somewhat oversimplify Maimonides' position by presenting him as a more consistent follower of Avicenna's view.

37. According to this ontology, "to exist," "to be" and "to be real" are not identical. "To exist" means to be material whereas "to be" means to be actualized. Thus, trees exist but numbers do not, but numbers can be said to be because they are actualized in sets. God, in whom there is no distinction of matter and form, is. But God does not exist in the same way that a tree exists. As for what is real, God is the most real of things. Because God is the standard of reality, the more material a thing is, the less real it is, even though it exists and is actualized.

38. See Sara Klein-Braslavy, *Maimonides' Interpretation of the Adam Stories in Genesis: A Study of Maimonides' Anthropology* [Hebrew], (Jerusalem: Reuben Mass,

1986); idem. *Maimonides' Interpretation of the Story of Creation* (in Hebrew), (Jerusalem: Reuben Mass, 1987).

39. Moses Maimonides, *Mishneh Torah, The Book of Knowledge*, trans. Moses Hayim Hymson (Jerusalem and New York, 1981), 39a. This translation is inexact and does not correspond to philosophical terminology.

40. Ibid. 39b.

41. Medieval Jewish philosophers had knowledge of Alexander's commentary on Aristotle's *De Anima* and his *De Intellectu* (On the Intellect) as well as of Themistius' commentary on the *De Anima*. However, these Hellenistic sources were known through the references to them in Arabic philosophic sources, especially in the works of al-Farabi and ibn Rushd (Averroes). The theological implications of their psychological theories would be sorted out in the fourteenth century in the works of Levi Ben Gershom (Gersonides) (1288–1344), which will be discussed in Chapter Eight.

42. *Guide* I: 70; 72.

43. Davidson, *Alfarabi, Avicenna and Averroes on Intellect*, 200.

44. Davidson, *Alfarabi, Avicenna, and Averroes*, 12; Fazlur Rahman, *Prophecy in Islam* (London: George Allen and Unwin, 1958), 11–20, esp. 14, 20.

45. It is easy to see how the doctrine of the Active Intellect is a transformation of the Logos doctrine that goes back to Philo.

46. *Guide* III: 8. For a closer analysis of this citation and its relation to ibn Sina's philosophy, see Davidson, *Alfarabi, Avicenna and Averroes on Intellect*, 201.

47. The best way to make sense of the "overflow" from the Active Intellect is suggested by Norbert M. Samuelson's analogy. The overflow is like a "radio station which is transmitting from a very great distance." While the radio transmits to all, only some receive the signal, even though these individuals are unknown to the radio station. "On this analogy the Active Intellect is the distant, strong station, the weaker but closer stations are the senses, and the individual listeners are respectively prophets, seers, and dreamers. Their radios are their intellects." Norbert M. Samuelson, *Gersonides' on God's Knowledge* (Toronto: Pontifical Institute of Mediaeval Studies, 1977), 285–86.

48. *Guide*, I: 71.

49. *Mishneh Torah*, Hilkhot Yesodei ha-Torah 4:8.

50. Ibid. 7:1

51. I refer here to the prophecy of all prophets, not to Mosaic prophecy, which is *sui generis*.

52. *Guide* III: 54, 635. In *De Anima* III:5, Aristotle was notoriously ambiguous about the connection between knowledge and immortality. Since in his theory of knowledge cognized universals are *in* the mind that cognizes them, they are said to be identified with the content of one's mind.

53. *Guide* III: 27.

54. The limitations of even Moses' knowledge are reiterated in the *Guide* I: 72; II: 4; III: 9; *Mishneh Torah*, Hilkhot Yesodei ha-Torah, 2:5–8.

55. Goodman, "Maimonides Naturalism," 161. Maimonides' rather positive attitude toward mimesis, especially linguistic mimesis, is thus rooted in the productive nature of God's thoughts.

56. This is the basis for the so-called political interpretation of Maimonides' conception of happiness championed by Lawrence Berman and critiqued by Menachem Kellner. See Berman, "The Political Interpretation of the Maxim," 53–61; Kellner, *Maimonides on Human Perfection*, 47–53.

57. *Guide* III: 53; 54. This reading is shared by Daniel H. Frank, "The End of the Guide: Maimonides on the Best Life for Man," *Judaism* 34 (1985): 485–95. For a full exposition of this point see Howard Kreisel's article cited in n. 25 above.

58. *Guide* I: 2, 24–25.

59. On this point see Lawrence V. Berman, "On the Fall of Man," *AJS Review* 5 (1980): 1–15.

60. Following Maimonides' own instruction, this interpretation is based on combining Maimonides' statements in several places in the *Guide*. However, I cannot explain why *eve* is conspicuously missing from the account of Guide 1:2. Such omission means that *adam*'s change of priorities was not based on the temptations of matter, represented by *eve*, but on *adam*'s own free choice, triggered by the appetitive faculty and the imaginative faculty working together.

61. Maimonides' ascription of this view to Plato is based on the *Timaeus* 50d, where Plato compares the role of limiting form to the father and the role of indefinite matter to the mother. Aristotle followed suit, as we have already noted, in *Metaphysics* I:6 998 1–10. That Maimonides conflated the views of Plato and Aristotle was understandable, because his major Muslim philosophical source, al-Farabi, had held that Aristotle simply elaborated the views of his teacher Plato.

62. Maimonides' fascinating use of gender categories required a separate study. For now compare the close reading by Sara Klein-Braslavy in *Maimonides' Interpretation of the Adam Stories, passim* with Susan E. Shapiro, "A Matter of Discipline: Reading for Gender in Jewish Philosophy," in *Judaism Since Gender*, ed. Miriam Peskowitz and Laura Levitt (New York and London: Routledge, 1997), 158–73. The latter is a feminist reading whereas the former is not. For a comprehensive analysis of Maimonides' view on women, consult Abraham Melamed, "Maimonides on Women: Formless Matter or Potential Prophet," in *Perspectives on Jewish Thought and Mysticism*, ed. Alfred L. Ivry, Elliot R. Wolfson and Allan Arkush (Amsterdam: Harwood Academic Publishers, 1999), 99–134. Space limitations compel me to eliminate the consideration of the gender aspect of the discourse on happiness from this study. I will take it up in a separate study focusing on medieval philosophical commentaries on Proverbs.

63. To say that the post-lapsarian Adam stands for the human condition does not mean that the activities of Adam apply to each and every human.

64. *Guide* II: 40, 389.

65. *Guide* III: 27, 510.

66. Maimonides then distinguishes between the "well-being" of the soul (*tiqqun*)

and its "ultimate perfection" (*shelemut*). The purpose of the Law as a whole is the latter. See Miriam Galston, "The Purpose of the Law According to Maimonides," *Jewish Quarterly Review* 69 (1978–79): 27–51.

67. The most explicit statement appears in the Introduction to Tractate Avot of the Mishnah (the so-called Eight Chapters): IV. See Raymond L. Weiss and Charles Butterworth, *Ethical Writings of Maimonides (Moses ben Maimon)* (New York: Dover, 1975), 70.

68. Maimonides' health instructions about the amount of food necessary for humans are very much in line with the view of "caloric restriction" that shapes many health diets, be it in ancient days or in our own time.

69. *Guide* III: 27, 511.

70. See Shlomo Pines, "The Limitations of Human Knowledge according to Al-Farabi, Ibn Bajja, and Maimonides," in *Studies in Medieval Jewish History and Literature*, ed. Isadore Twersky (Cambridge: Harvard University Press, 1979), 82–109.

71. This narrative is most developed in the *Guide* I: 36; II: 13; 39; III: 29; 37; 49. Cf., *Mishneh Torah*, Hilkhot Avodah Zarah, chap. 1. For a discussion of the myth, consult Salo W. Baron, "The Historical Outlook of Maimonides," in *History and Jewish Historians,* compiled by Arthur Hertzberg and Leon A. Feldman (Philadelphia: The Jewish Publication Society, 1964), 109–63, esp. 114–20; Amos Funkenstein, "The Historical and Messianic Conception of Maimonides," in *Perceptions of Jewish History: From Antiquity to the Present* (in Hebrew) (Tel Aviv: Am Oved, 1991), 103–56, esp. 29–36; idem. "Maimonides' Political Theory and Realistic Messianism," in *Perceptions of Jewish History* (Berkeley: University of California Press, 1993), 141–43.

72. The *Sabi'un* are mentioned in the Koran II:62; V:69; XXII:17 in the company of Believers, the Jews, and the Christians with whom they share the title of "people of the Book" (*ahal al-Kitab*). Modern scholarship has exposed the ambiguity of the term. While the Sabians were a Gnostic sect, the term denotes both Christian and pagan groups. Thus, on the one hand, the term denotes a Judeo-Christian sect, akin to the Ebionites, Elchasaites, and the Mandeans, who were known for their baptismal practices. On the other hand, it refers to a pagan Greco-Roman sect from the region of Haran who had a developed astrological religion with strong Platonic tendencies. For the most current review of research on the Sabians, consult "Sabia" in *The Encyclopedia of Islam*, New Edition, ed. C. E. Bosworth (et al) (Leiden: E. J. Brill, 1994): vol. 8, 675–78, and the bibliography cited there. For further discussion of the Sabians in Islamic culture, see Jane Dammen McAuliffe, "Exegetical Identification of the Sabi'un," *Muslim World* 74 (1984): 95–106; Christopher Buck, "The Identity of the Sabi'un: An Historical Quest," *Muslim World* 74 (1984): 172–86. For an overview of Islamic historiography see Claude Cahen, "History and the Historians," in *Religion, Learning and Science in the 'Abbasid Period,* M. J. L. Young et al, eds., (Cambridge: Cambridge University Press, 1990), 188–233.

73. *Guide* III: 29, 515.

74. To realize that Maimonides' retelling of the Sabian story is a polemic against the Quran, one needs to look at the actual references. The first two are the same: "Believers, Jews, Christians and Sabi'un—whoever believes in Allah and the Last Day and does what is right—shall be rewarded by their Lord; they have nothing to fear or regret." The third citation is slightly different: "As for true believers, the Jews, the Sabi'un, the Christians, the Magians, and the Pagans, Allah will judge them on the Day of Resurrection. He bears witness to all things." Precisely because the Quran made no qualitative distinction between Jews, Sabians, and Christians, Maimonides insisted that the Sabians (and the Christians) represent a lower level of epistemic perfection than the Jews. A different interpretation is offered by Ivry, "Maimonides and Neoplatonism," 140. According to Ivry the "Sabians" of Maimonides were "Aristotle and his ilk, Maimonides' closest allies philosophically."

75. It is safe to say that Maimonides believed that God created the universe, even though the precise meaning of the term "create" is still a matter of scholarly dispute. For an analysis of the current contemporary debate and an attempt to resolve it, see Norbert M. Samuelson, "Maimonides' Doctrine of Creation," *Harvard Theological Review* 84:3 (1991): 249–71.

Maimonides' puzzling views on the origins of the universe are not surprising. Precisely because his point of departure is the historically located knower, he believed that the origins of the universe, in principle, could not be demonstrated philosophically. The origin of the universe must remain a myth in the Platonic sense of "a likely story." All one can do is provide rational arguments in support of the belief in creation, arguments that Maimonides thought are superior to the counter arguments in favor of the eternity of the universe. Yet these arguments do not constitute demonstrative proofs.

76. *Guide* I; 36, 63; II: 39; III: 39. *Mishneh Torah*, Hilkhot Avodah Zarah, 1:3.

77. *Guide* II: 11. For a detailed discussion consult Lawrence Kaplan, "Maimonides on the Singularity of the Jewish People," *Da`at* 15 (1985): v-xxvii.

78. *Guide* I:71; II:11.

79. Book III 412 b–IV 421c.

80. Funkenstein, "The Historical and Messianic Conception of Maimonides," 131.

81. Three times in the *Guide* Maimonides calls Moses "the master of all wise men." The portrayal of Moses as a philosopher is most forceful in the *Commentary on the Mishnah*, Sanhedrin X (Pereq Ḥeleq). In *Guide* II: 32–48, Maimonides discusses Moses' political actions as a communicator of God's message and a giver of the law. For a comprehensive discussion of this portrayal, consult Kalman P. Bland, "Moses and the Law According to Maimonides," in *Mystics, Philosophers and Politicians: Essays in Jewish Intellectual History in Honor of Alexander Altmann*, ed. Y. Reinharz (Durham, NC: Duke University Press, 1982), 49–66.

82. See ibid. 49–66, esp. 53.

83. In the rungs of prophecy listed in *Guide* II: 45, Moses is mentioned on the lowest rung, along with judges, whereas Abraham is listed on the four highest

rungs. By stating that Moses is both the "master of all prophets" as well as the lowest on the list, Maimonides did not contradict himself. Rather he attempted to suggest that in a profound sense Moses was *not* a prophet, because imagination was not involved in the reception of his divine emanation. I owe this point to Aryeh L. Motzkin in an unpublished paper, "Maimonides on the Imagination," delivered at Indiana University on March 25, 1993. It is important to note that the imagination was absolutely absent from Mosaic apprehension of the truth, but not from the communication of the Torah to Israel.

84. This premise undergirded the exegetical approach of the Maimonidean tradition. Funkenstein called it "the maximalist interpretation" of the principle *dibrah Torah bi-leshon benei adam*, and its result was that the Torah was viewed as a scientific text that relates to the way things are. To study nature one must interpret the Torah. The most consistent exponent of Maimonides' exegetical principle was Gersonides. See Amos Funkenstein, *Theology and the Scientific Imagination: From the Middle Ages to the Seventeenth Century* (Princeton: University of Princeton, 1986), 213–19; idem. *Perceptions of Jewish History*, 124–30.

85. The ambiguity about the human condition cannot be removed. In relation to other animals, with whom human beings share bodily powers, the distinguishing mark is the rational capacity. But in relation to the Separate Intelligences and God, with whom humans share reasoning activities, corporeal embodiment is the distinguishing mark. In Maimonides' portrayal, Moses is a superior human being because he reached intellectual perfection, but Moses is not divine or a semi-divine entity; Moses still has a human body.

86. This is the essence of Maimonides' critique of the Kalam theologians in the *Guide* I: 73. Maimonides, who presupposes the existence of immutable nature, including human nature, argued that these theologians do not distinguish between the intellect and the imagination, and so they blur the distinction between the way things are and the constructs of human imagination. Maimonides closely followed Aristotle's theory of the imagination already discussed in Chapter One.

87. Alfred Ivry, "Neoplatonic Currents in Maimonides Thought," in *Perspectives on Maimonides: Philosophical and Historical Studies,* ed. Joel L. Kraemer (Oxford: The Oxford University Press for the Littman Library, 1991), 135.

88. On the basis of this principle, Maimonides can argue in the *Guide* III: 33 that even though the Torah "speaks in the language of human beings" it contains "mysteries" and "secrets" that are accessible to the intellect.

89. See Stephen D. Benin, "The 'Cunning of God' and Divine Accommodation," *The Journal of History of Ideas* 45 (1984): 179–92.

90. For further information on the ancient and medieval understanding of "diet" as a mode of life or way of living see Harold J. Cook, "The New Philosophy and Medicine in Seventeenth-Century England," in *Reappraisals of the Scientific Revolution,* ed. David C. Lindberg and Robert S. Westman (Cambridge: Cambridge University Press, 1990), 407. Like the rabbis and their Hellenistic sources, Maimonides

presupposed the causal connection between physical and mental well-being and argued that the Torah is the most perfect "diet," because it secures both.

91. For a detailed discussion, see Raymond L. Weiss, *Maimonides' Ethics: The Encounter of Philosophic and Religious Morality* (Chicago and London: The University of Chicago Press, 1991).

92. This formulation is in direct conflict with Marvin Fox's view, according to which Maimonides held that "Man *qua* man is incorporeal." See Fox, *Interpreting Maimonides*, 169. In the *Guide* I: 1, Maimonides indeed equated the "image of God" in which *man* was created with an incorporeal form. However, in the temporal-spatial order no such form does actually exist, because human beings as we know them are a composite of form and matter.

93. Maimonides, *Commentary on the Mishnah*, Introduction to Tractate Avot ("Eight Chapters"), chap. 1. Modern scholars of Maimonides have tended to focus either on his theory of knowledge (i.e., the operation of the rational soul) or on his ethics (i.e., the acquisition of moral virtues and the formation of good character) which correspond to theoretical life and practical life, respectively. Relatively little attention, however, has been given to the connection between these two aspects and Maimonides' rhetoric and hermeneutical theory.

94. I suspect that many readers may find this point objectionable, because it goes against our belief that sick or handicapped people can be happy. That belief, however, is based on the notion that happiness is a subjective feeling, a mood, or an attitude. Maimonides' view of happiness, by contrast, has little to do with emotional contentment and much more to do with the well-functioning of the organism in accordance to its *telos*. Viewed from this perspective, Maimonides' position is more reasonable, since it is clear that, all other factors being equal, a sick person does not enjoy the same quality of life as a healthy person.

95. See Elinor Lieber, "The Medical Works of Maimonides: A Reappraisal," in *Moses Maimonides: Physician, Scientist and Philosopher*, ed. Fred Rosner and Samuel S. Kottek (Northvale, NJ: Jason Aronson, 1993), 13–24; Samuel S. Kottek, "Maimonides on the Perfect Physician," ibid, 25–32, and the sources cited there.

96. *Ethical Writings of Maimonides* (New York: Dover Publications, 1975), 35.

97. Eight Chapters: IV; *Ethical Writings of Maimonides*, 67.

98. For other interpretations of Maimonides' relations to Aristotle's doctrine of the mean, see Steven Schwarzschild, "Moral Radicalism and 'Middlingness' in the Ethics of Maimonides," *Studies in Medieval Culture* 11 (1977): 65–94, reprinted in *The Pursuit of the Ideal: Jewish Writings of Steven Schwarzschild*, ed. Menachem Kellner (Albany: State University of New York Press, 1990), 137–60; Herbert Davidson, "The Middle Way in Maimonides' Ethics," *Proceedings of American Academy of Jewish Research* 54 (1987): 31–72; Daniel H. Frank "Humility as a Virtue: A Maimonidean Critique of Aristotle's Ethics," in *Moses Maimonides and His Time*, ed. Eric Ormsby (Washington D.C.: The Catholic University of America Press, 1989), 88–99; idem, "Anger as a Vice: A Maimonidean Critique of Aristotle's Ethics," *History of Philosophy Quarterly* 7 (1990): 269–81; Marvin Fox, "The Doctrine of the

Mean in Aristotle and Maimonides: A Comparative Study," *Studies in Jewish Religious and Intellectual History Presented to Alexander Altmann on the Occasion of His Seventieth Birthday*, ed. Siegfried Stein and Raphael Loewe (University, Ala.: University of Alabama Press, 1979), reprinted in his *Interpreting Maimonides*, 93–123.

99. Howard Kreisel, "The Practical Intellect in the Philosophy of Maimonides," *Hebrew Union College Annual* 59 (1988): 189–215, reprinted in his *Maimonides' Political Thought*, 63–92.

100. Maimonides' anti-apocalyptical posture is but another expression of his opposition to a supernatural interpretation of miracles. Miracles are not the disruption of nature by a supernatural intervention, but, as Norbert Samuelson put it, "an event that uniquely verifies that the laws of nature are expressions of divine will." See Samuelson, "Maimonides' Doctrine of Creation," 265.

101. For an excellent analysis of Maimonides' messianic vision consult Aviezer Ravitzky, "'To the Utmost Human Capacity': Maimonides on the Days of the Messiah," in *Perspectives on Maimonides: Philosophical and Historical Studies,* ed. Joel L. Kraemer (Oxford: Oxford University Press, 1991), 221–56.

102. *Mishneh Torah*, Hilkhot Teshuvah 9:2.

103. Hilkhot Melakhim 12:4

104. Ralph Lerner already noticed the significance of the fact that Maimonides invented the myth of the king's palace. See Lerner, "The Governance of the Solitary," in *Perspectives on Maimonides*, 35.

105. *Guide* III: 51. For a close reading of this myth consult Kellner, *Maimonides on Human Perfection*, 13–39. Other discussions are offered by Ravitzky, "'To the Utmost Human Capacity'," 245–50; Steven Harvey, "Maimonides in the Sultan's Palace," in *Perspectives on Maimonides*, 47–75; Ralph Lerner, "Maimonides' Governance of the Solitary," 33–46; Hannah Kasher, "The Parable of the King's Palace in *The Guide of the Perplexed* as a Directive to the Student" [Hebrew], *AJS Review* 14 (1989): 1–19; Howard Kreisel, "Intellectual Perfection and the Role of the Law in the Philosophy of Maimonides," in *From Ancient Israel to Modern Judaism: Intellect in Quest of Understanding; Essays in Honor of Marvin Fox*, ed. Jacob Neusner, Ernest S. Freirichs, Nahum Sarna (Atlanta: Scholars Press, 1989), 25–46, esp. 29–30. The essay is included in his *Maimonides' Political Thought*,189–224.

106. *Guide*, III: 51.

107. *Mishneh Torah*, Hilkhot Teshuvah, 10:6

108. According to this interpretation, unless one is a halakhic Jew, one cannot experience happiness as fully as possible. It follows that qua philosopher, for example, Aristotle experienced a higher level of well-being than others who lacked philosophic knowledge, but as a pagan, Aristotle's flourishing was deficient because he did not live by the Torah of Moses. This rather particularistic reading of Maimonides will most likely be rejected by those who regard Maimonides as the epitome of universalism in Judaism.

109. The Stoic resonance of Sufi material known to Maimonides was already

noticed by Raymond L. Weiss, *Maimonides Ethics: The Encounter of Philosophic and Religious Morality* (Chicago: University of Chicago, 1991), 46–48.

110. Among contemporary readers of Maimonides, the one who understood this principle best was the late Marvin Fox. He presented his commentary on the *Guide* I: 1–2 as a prolegomena to the ideal commentary on the *Guide*, using "Rashi as his [i.e., Fox's] model," *Interpreting Maimonides*, 153. This, I believe, is precisely how Maimonides wished to have been read. A similar approach is shared by Jose Faur, *Homo Mysticus: A Guide to Maimonides' Guide for the Perplexed* (Syracuse, NY: Syracuse University Press, 1999). For a recent assessment of Faur, consult Samuelson, "Maimonides Scholarship," 96–98.

Notes to Chapter 6

1. For a detailed account of the *Reconquista*, consult Joseph F. O'Callaghan, *A History of Medieval Spain* (Ithaca and London: Cornell University Press, 1975), 191–357. For the impact of the reconquest on Jewish life see Yitzhaq Baer, *The History of the Jews in Christian Spain* (Philadelphia: The Jewish Publication Society of America, 1978), trans. Louis Schoffman, vol. 1, 39–185.

2. These events are analyzed in detail in Hugh Kennedy, *Muslim Spain and Portugal: A Political History of al-Andalus* (London and New York: Longman, 1996).

3. Jane S. Gerber, *The Jews of Spain: A History of the Sephardic Experience* (New York: Free Press, 1992), 93.

4. Several charters from Spain are available in an English translation in Robert Chazan, *Church, State and Jew in the Middle Ages* (New York: Behrman House, 1980), 69–75.

5. The social patterns analyzed by Yom Tov Assis for the Jews of Aragon are applicable to other parts of Spain. See Yom Tov Assis, *The Golden Age of Aragonese Jewry: Community and Society in the Crown of Aragon, 1213–1327* (London and Portland: Oxford University Press for The Littman Library of Jewish Civilization, 1997), 67–196.

6. See Yom Tov Assis, "The Jews in the Kingdom of Aragon and the Regions under its Control" [Hebrew], in *Moreshet Sepharad: The Sephardi Legacy* [Hebrew], ed. Haim Beinart (Jerusalem: The Magnes Press, 1992), 61–67.

7. On a basis of a passage from Hillel of Verona's *Tagmulei ha-Nefesh* (The Rewards of the Soul) Marc Saperstein has adduced some evidence that in Spain in the mid-thirteenth century "philosophical studies occurred in a setting of a school . . . [where] instruction was led by a master, called *rav* and a number of students were present." See Marc Saperstein, "The Social and Cultural Context: Thirteenth to Fifteenth Centuries," in *History of Jewish Philosophy*, ed. Daniel H. Frank and Oliver Leaman (London and New York: Routledge, 1997), 304. In the late fourteenth and fifteenth centuries, the study of philosophy penetrated the curriculum of some Yeshivot in Castile. Ibid. 305–6. This information, however, does not alter the judgment that the study of philosophy for Jews was largely a private matter.

8. This was apparently the case of Levi ben Abraham ben Hayyim of Villefranche de Conflent, a major proponent of rationalist philosophy who featured prominently during the last phase of the Maimonidean Controversy in Provence. On this scholar and his role in the Maimonidean Controversy, see Abraham S. Halkin, "Why was Levi ben Hayyim Hounded," *Proceedings of the American Academy for Jewish Research* 34 (1966): 65–76. We shall return to him below.

9. The social utility of philosophical studies is made clear in the ethical will of Judah ibn Tibbon. The Hebrew text and English translation are published in Israel Abraham, ed. *Hebrew Ethical Wills* (Philadelphia: The Jewish Publication Society of America, 1976), 50–92.

10. The most important of these pseudo-Aristotelian works was a text that circulated under the title *The Theology of Aristotle*. Written originally in Arabic, it was, in fact, a paraphrase from Plotinus' *Enneads*. Because it was ascribed to Aristotle, this text contributed to the medieval fusion of Aristotelianism and Neoplatonism in medieval Jewish philosophy. On the place of the *Theology of Aristotle* in medieval Jewish philosophy see Paul Fenton, "The Arabic and Hebrew Versions of the *Theology of Aristotle*," in *Pseudo-Aristotle in the Middle Ages,* ed. Jill Kraye, W. Ryan, and Charles Schmitt (London: Warburg Institute Surveys and Texts XI, 1986), 241–64.

11. To date the most comprehensive study of the translations of Arabic philosophical and scientific texts into Hebrew remains Moritz Steinschneider, *Die Hebraischen Ubersetuzngen des Mittlealters und die Juden als Dolmetscher* (Berlin: Kommisionsverlag des Bibliographischen Bureaus, 1893). A new English translation and updating of this valuable research tool been undertaken by Charles Manekin and Tzvi Langerman. For some new information on these translations, consult Mauro Zonta, *La filosophia antica nel Medioevo ebraico: Le traduzioni ebraiche medievali dei testi filosofici antichi* (Brescia, 1996).

12. For an analysis of the re-reading of the biblical creation narrative in light of Aristotelian physics, see Sara Klein-Braslavy, *Maimonides' Interpretation of the Story of Creation* (Jerusalem: Reuben Mass, 1987).

13. To date there is no systematic and comprehensive overview of this philosophic material, even though much has been written about individual texts or authors. The most useful overview of medieval Jewish philosophy is Colette Sirat, *A History of Jewish Philosophy in the Middle Ages* (Cambridge: Cambridge University Press, 1985). A more detailed overview of individual thinkers and or trends in medieval Jewish philosophy is provided by the relevant essays in Daniel H. Frank and Oliver Leaman, eds., *History of Jewish Philosophy* (London and New York: Routledge, 1997) and the updated bibliography cited therein.

14. For an overview of these super-commentaries see Ruth Glasner, "Levi Ben Gershom and the Study of Ibn Rushd in the Fourteenth Century: Historical Reconstruction," *Jewish Quarterly Review* 86 (1995): 51–90; Alfred Ivry, "Ibn Rushd in Light of His Jewish Translators and Readers" [Hebrew], in *Tribute to Sara: Studies in Jewish Philosophy and Kabbalah Presented to Sara O. Heller Wilensky,* ed.

Moshe Idel, Devorah Dimant, and Shalom Rosenberg (Jerusalem: Magnes Press, 1994), 334–46.

15. Harry A. Wolfson, "The Classification of the Sciences in Medieval Jewish Philosophy," in *Studies in the History of Philosophy and Religion*, ed. Isadore Twersky and George H. Williams (Cambridge MA: Harvard University Press, 1973), 493–550.

16. For information about these philosophical encyclopedia texts, consult Steven Harvey, ed., *The Medieval Hebrew Encyclopedias of Science and Philosophy* (Dordrecht: Kluwer Academic Publishers, 2000).

17. Saperstein, "The Social and Cultural Context," 301.

18. For overview of the dissemination of philosophy from the pulpit and sample texts, see Marc Saperstein, *Jewish Preaching: 1200–1800; An Anthology* (New Haven: Yale University Press, 1989); idem, "Sermons as Evidence for the Popularization of Philosophy in Fifteenth-Century Spain," in his *"Your Voice Like a Ram's Horn": Themes and Texts in Traditional Jewish Preaching* (Cincinnati: Hebrew Union College Press, 1996), 75–87.

19. *Sefer ha-Mevaqesh* (Amsterdam, 1772). Part 1 was translated into English by M. Herschel Levine, *Falaquera's Book of the Seeker* (New York: Yeshiva University Press, 1976).

20. The Hebrew text, an English translation, and a discussion of this text in its proper socio-cultural context are provided by Steven Harvey, *Falaquera's Epistle of the Debate: An Introduction to Jewish Philosophy* (Cambridge, MA and London: Harvard University Press, 1987).

21. For a comprehensive study of his life and works, see Raphael Jospe, *Torah and Sophia: The Life and Thought of Shem Tov ibn Falaquera* (Cincinnati: Hebrew Union College Press, 1988).

22. On the portrayal of King Solomon by Maimonides see Sara Klein-Braslavy, "King Solomon and Metaphysical Esotericism according to Maimonides," *Maimonidean Studies* 1 (1990): 57–86; idem, *King Solomon and Philosophical Esotericism in the Thought of Maimonides* (Jerusalem: The Magnes Press, 1996), esp. 109–63. On the claim that philosophy originated with the Jews and was stolen by the Greeks consult Norman Roth, "The Theft of Philosophy by the Greek from the Jews," *Classical Folia* 2 (1978): 53–67.

23. Scholars debate whether al-Farabi or al-Ghazai were Falaquera's immediate sources. According to R. Jospe, Alghazali was the immediate source, but according to Israel Efros, *Reshit Ḥokhmah* was "a complete and literal translation of Alfarabi's *Ihsa al Ulum.*" See Jospe, *Torah and Sophia*, 40; Israel Efros, "Palquera's Reshit Ḥokmah and Alfarabi's Ihsa' al ʿulum," *Jewish Quarterly Review* 25 (1934–5): 227–35.

24. The order of the works in Aristotle's Organon is different from the order in contemporary editions and translations (e.g., the *Topics* follows the *Analytics*).

25. Harry A. Wolfson, "The Classification of the Sciences," 528.

26. See Jospe, *Torah and Sophia*, 39.

27. For an overview of Aristotle's *Politics* and its departure from Plato's political theory, consult C. C. W. Taylor, "Politics," in *The Cambridge Companion to Aristotle* ed. Jonathan Barnes (Cambridge: Cambridge University Press, 1995), 233–58, and the secondary literature cited in 372–79.

28. Ibn Rushd's commentary on Plato's *Republic* is available in two English translations. E. I. J. Rosenthal, trans., *Averroes' Commentary on Plato's Republic* (Cambridge: Cambridge University Press, 1969); Ralph Lerner, trans., *Averroes on Plato's Republic* (Ithaca and London: Cornell University Press, 1974). For an analysis of this text, see Charles E. Butterworth, "Ethics and Classical Islamic Philosophy: A Study of Averroes' Commentary on Plato's Republic," in *Ethics in Islam*, ed. Richard G. Hovannisian (Malibu, CA: Udena Publications, 1985), 17–45; ibn Rushd's *Middle Commentary* on Aristotle's *Ethics* was translated into Hebrew by Samuel ben Judah of Marseilles in the 1320s and will be discussed below.

29. See Steven Harvey, "The Sources of the Quotations from Aristotle's *Ethics* in the *Guide of the Perplexed* and the *Guide to the Guide*," in *Joseph Baruch Sermoneta Memorial Volume,* ed. Aviezer Ravitzky (*Jerusalem Studies in Jewish Thought* 15) (Jerusalem, 1998), 87–102.

30. Lawrence V. Berman, "Greek into Hebrew: Samuel ben Judah of Marseilles, Fourteenth-Century Philosopher and Translator," in *Jewish Medieval and Renaissance Studies* ed. Alexander Altmann (Cambridge: Harvard University Press, 1967), 289–320.

31. See Basil Herring, *Joseph Kaspi's Gevia` Kesef: A Study in Medieval Jewish Philosophic Bible Commentary* (New York: Ktav, 1983), 18.

32. On the life of ibn Kaspi see ibid. 8–10. For an overview of ibn Kaspi's intellectual activity, see Isadore Twersky, "Joseph ibn Kaspi: Portrait of a Medieval Jewish Intellectual," in *Studies in Medieval Jewish History and Literature* ed. Isadore Twersky (Cambridge: Harvard University Press, 1979), 231–57.

33. This was the case, even though medieval Jewish philosophers wrote extensively on political theory, which, according to the Aristotelian classification of the sciences, included ethics. For an overview of political theory in medieval Jewish philosophy consult Abraham Melamed, "Medieval and Renaissance Jewish Political Philosophy," in *History of Jewish Philosophy* ed. Daniel H. Frank and Oliver Leaman (London and New York: Routledge, 1997), 415–49.

34. See Harvey, *Falaquera's Epistle of the Debate*, 104.

35. Ibid. 105.

36. A typical example of the expressed disdain of the philosopher to the masses is to be found in the works of Joseph ibn Kaspi. See Herring, *Joseph ibn Kaspi's Gevia` Kesef*, 12.

37. On Falquera's defense of esotericism, see Jospe, *Torah and Sophia*, 78–92.

38. The literature on the Maimonidean Controversy is quite extensive and the various accounts enumerate the distinct phases slightly differently. For general overviews of the Maimonidean Controversy, see the essays by Idit Dobbs-Weinstein and Marc Saperstein in *History of Jewish Philosophy*. Excerpts for the relevant

primary sources are available in Benzion Dinur, *Israel in the Diaspora: A Documentary History of the Jewish People* (In Hebrew), vol. 2, book 4 (Jerusalem: Bialik Institute, 1969). A useful historical overview is provided in Hayim Hillel Ben Sasson, *Trial and Achievement: Currents in Jewish History* (Jerusalem: Ktav, 1974) 230–42. The social foundation of the debate on philosophy, which dispels some of the prevalent misconceptions in modern historiography, is laid out by Saperstein, "The Social and Cultural Context," 294–330.

39. Idit Dobbs-Weinstein, "The Maimonidean Controversy," in *History of Jewish Philosophy*, 335.

40. On the debate in the East see Sarah Stroumsa, *The Beginnings of the Maimonidean Controversy in the East: Yosef ibn Shimon's Silencing Epistle Concerning the Resurrection of the Dead* [Hebrew] (Jerusalem: Ben Zevi Institute, 1999).

41. For English translation and discussion see, "The Essay on Resurrection," in *Crisis and Leadership: Epistles of Maimonides* (Philadelphia: Jewish Publication Society of America, 1985), 211–45 (text) and 246–92 (analysis). For an earlier translation see Fred Rosner, *Moses Maimonides' Treatise on Resurrection* (New York: Ktav, 1982). For an analysis of the Treatise on Resurrection in Islamic cultural context, see Joshua Finkel, "Maimonides' Treatise on Resurrection: A Comparative Study," in *Essays on Maimonides* ed. Salo W. Baron (New York: AMS Press, 1941), 93–121.

42. See Bernard D. Septimus, *Hispano Jewish Culture in Transition: The Career and Controversies of Ramah* (Cambridge: Harvard University Press, 1982).

43. Ibid. 44.

44. Ibid. 43.

45. Ibid. 73.

46. Ibid. 45.

47. Ibid. 54.

48. Ibid. 58.

49. See Dov Rappel, "Greek Wisdom—Rhetoric" [Hebrew], *Jerusalem Studies in Jewish Thought* 2(3) (1982/83): 317–22.

50. The events and disputed issues of this controversy are discussed in detail by Daniel J. Silver, *Maimonidean Criticism and the Maimonidean Controversy 1180–1240* (Leiden: Brill, 1965); Joseph Schatzmiller, "Li-Temunat ha-Maḥloqet ha-Rishona al Kitvei ha-Rambam," *Zion* 34 (1979): 126–44; Azriel Shohat, "Concerning the First Controversy on the Writings of Maimonides," [Hebrew] *Zion* 36 (1971): 27–60.

51. See Shatzmiller, "Li-Temunat ha-Maḥloqet," 128–29.

52. Ibid. 128.

53. Septimus, *Hispano-Jewish Society*, 64.

54. The activities of David Kimhi in the controversy are detailed by Frank Ephraim Talmage, *David Kimhi: The Man and the Commentaries* (Cambridge: Harvard University Press, 1979), 27–53; idem. "David Kimhi and the Rationalist Tradition," *Hebrew Union College Annual* 18 (1968): 213–35; idem. "David Kimhi and the Rationalist Tradition II: Literary Sources," in *Studies on Jewish Bibliography,*

History and Literature in Honor of I. Edward Kiev, ed. Charles Berlin (New York, Ktav, 1972), 453–78.

55. See Bernard Septimus, "A Struggle for Public Control in Barcelona during the Debate on Maimonides' Works" [Hebrew], *Tarbiz* 42 (1972–73): 389–400.

56. The great grandfather of Jonah apparently married a concubine because his first wife was childless. The validity of the second marriage was challenged. See Silver, *Maimonidean Criticism*, 173.

57. For a most nuanced presentation of Nahmanides' involvement in the Maimonidean Controversy, see Shohat, "The First Controversy," 39–40. For a penetrating analysis of Nahmanides as a transition figure in Jewish culture, and the link between his role in the Maimonidean Controversy and his involvement in Jewish-Christian debate in 1263 in Barcelona, consult Bernard Septimus, "'Open Rebuke and Concealed Love': Nahmanides and the Andalusian Tradition," in *Rabbi Moses Nahmanides (Ramban): Explorations in His Religious and Literary Virtuosity*, ed. Isadore Twersky (Cambridge: Harvard University Press, 1983), 11–34. Septimus also discusses Nahmanides' involvement in the Maimonidean Controversy in his *Hispano-Jewish Culture*, passim.

58. On the kabbalist associates of Nahmanides, see Gershom Scholem, *Origins of the Kabbalah*, trans. Alan Arkush (Philadelphia: Jewish Publications Society, 1987), 393–414. For an analysis of Nahmanides' precise understanding of kabbalah, consult Moshe Idel, "We Have No Kabbalistic Tradition on This," in *Rabbi Moses Nahmanides*, 51–73; and Bezalel Safran, "Rabbi Azriel and Nahmanides: Two Views of the Fall of Men," ibid. 75–106.

59. See Bernard Septimus, "Piety and Power in Thirteenth Century Catalonia," in *Studies in Medieval Jewish History and Literature*, ed. Isadore Twersky (Cambridge: Harvard University Press, 1979), 197–232.

60. Septimus, "Open Rebuke and Concealed Love," 14.

61. Ibid. 24, n. 45.

62. For further analysis of Maimonides consult Alvin J. Reines, "Maimonides Concept of Miracles," *Hebrew Union College Annual* 45 (1974): 243–85; Howard Kreisel, "Miracles in Medieval Jewish Philosophy," *Jewish Quarterly Review* 75, no. 2 (1984): 99–133. Despite their differences, these authors agree with each other in their conclusions.

63. See *Guide* II:6, 13, 19, 21, 25.

64. Guide II: 29. As Kreisel explains, Maimonides distinguished between two types of exceptional events in nature: those that are "possible in nature" and those that are "impossible in nature." The debate between Aristotle and Maimonides pertains to the limit of the "possible." In contrast to Aristotle and his medieval followers, Maimonides held that some miracles are "impossible in nature," namely, there are no natural causes that account for them. An example is the changing of the rod into a serpent.

65. This is the view that Maimonides ascribes to R. Jonathan and R. Jeremiah in the Guide II:29 (Pines ed., p. 345). Since certain views which Maimonides cites

under his own name are in harmony with this conception of miracles, it is reasonable to conclude that this position is indeed his own. See *Guide* II:19.

66. For example, the ability of God to withhold prophecy from one who is in all respects worthy of it, reflecting the divine ability to suspend the laws of nature (*Guide* II:32).

67. Moses ben Nahman, Commentary on Exodus 13:16 (in standard editions of Miqraot Gedolot); Moses ben Nahman "'Nahmanides,' Torat ha-Shem Temimah," in *Kitvei Rabenu Moshe ben Nahman* ed. Hayim Dov Schevel (Jerusalem: Mosad ha-Rav Kook, 1973), 153. It is intriguing to suggest that Nahmanides' title of that sermon was meant as a polemic against Maimonides' understanding of the Torah's perfection that we presented in the previous chapter. For an analysis of Nahmanides' view of miracles, see David Berger, "Miracles and the Natural Order," in *Rabbi Moses Nahmanides (Ramban)*, 107–28.

68. "Torat ha-Shem Temimah," 155.

69. The implications of the Barcelona debate for the evolution of the discourse on happiness will be discussed in Chapter Eight.

70. Chayim Henoch, *Nachmanides Philosopher and Mystic: The Religious Thought of Nachmanides from His Exegesis of the Mitzvot* [Hebrew] (Jerusalem: Torah La-`am Publications, 1978), 90–95.

71. See Silver, *Maimonidean Criticism*, 182–98; James H. Lehmann, "Polemic and Satire in the Poetry of the Maimonidean Controversy," *Prooftexts* 1 (1981): 133–51. The author attempts to decode the postures of Meshulam Da Pierra within the literary conventions of satire.

72. Lehmann, "Polemic and Satire," 142–48.

73. On the bans of 1210 and 1215, see Michael Haren, *Medieval Thought: The Western Intellectual Tradition from Antiquity to the Thirteenth Century* (Toronto and Buffalo: University of Toronto Press, 1985), 147–48; on the condemnation of 1277, ibid. 207–11; Norman Kretzmann (ed. et al), *The Cambridge History of Later Medieval Philosophy* (Cambridge: Cambridge University Press, 1982), 537–39; John Marenbon, *Later Medieval Philosophy (1150–1350): An Introduction* (London and New York: Routledge, 1987), chaps. 3 and 4, *passim*.

74. Jeremy Cohen, *The Friars and the Jews: The Evolution of Medieval Anti-Judaism* (Ithaca and London: Cornell University Press, 1982), 52.

75. David Kimhi accused Solomon ben Abraham of Montpellier of bringing Maimonides' works to the inspection by the Christian clergy, but the evidence for it is by no means certain. D. Silver conjectures plausibly that a Jewish convert to Christianity who was aware of the cultural wars in both camps brought the works of Maimonides to the attention of the Christian authority.

76. Cohen, *The Friars and the Jews*, 52–60.

77. Ibid. 58. In 1239 Pope Gregory IX issued a series of bulls ordering European rulers to submit the Talmud to ecclesiastical authorities for inspection. The decrees were implemented only in France by King Louis IX. For a general overview of the Church's attitudes toward the Talmud during the thirteenth century, see Jeremy

Cohen, *Living Letters of the Law: Ideas of the Jew in Medieval Christianity* (Berkeley: University of California Press, 1999), 317–63.

78. Excerpted in Septimus, *Hispano-Jewish Society*, 92.

79. *Nasi* (literally, "prince") was a hereditary title of Jewish leaders in Provence during the Middle Ages. The title is a vestige of the independent Jewish principality in Provence in the early Middle Ages, even though by the thirteenth century the title had no political import. See Arthur J. Zuckerman, *A Jewish Princedom in Feudal France 768–900* (New York: Columbia University Press, 1965).

80. Ibid. 81.

81. Ben Sasson, "The Maimonidean Controversy," in his *Trial and Achievements*, 238.

82. On Abraham Maimonides (1186–1237) see Fenton, "Judaism and Sufism," 755–68; Solomon D. Goitein, "Abraham Maimonides and his Pietist Circle," in *Jewish Medieval and Renaissance Studies* (Cambridge: Harvard University Press), 145–64.

83. Joseph Sermoneta, "The Glosses of R. Moses ben Solomon of Salerno and Nicholas of Giovinazzo on the *Guide of the Perplexed*" [Hebrew], *Iyyun* 20 (1969): 212–40.

84. See Aviezer Ravitzky, "The Thought of R. Zerahiah ben Isaac ben Shealtiel Hen and the Maimonidean-Tibbonian Philosophy in the Thirteenth Century" (Ph.D. diss., Hebrew University of Jerusalem, 1977); Sirat, *A History of Medieval Jewish Philosophy*, 267–69.

85. For exposition of Abulafia's idiosyncratic reading of Maimonides, consult Moshe Idel, *Studies in Ecstatic Kabbalah* (Albany: State University of New York Press, 1988), 1–31; idem. *Messianic Mystics* (New Haven: Yale University Press, 1998), 58–100. I am fully aware that by excluding Abraham Abulafia from our analysis, the story of Jewish reflections on happiness remains incomplete. His importance, however, will be recognized in Chapter Nine when we discuss the contribution of Yohanan Alemanno to the discourse on happiness.

86. Excerpts from the relevant documents are in Ben Zion Dinur, *Israel in the Diaspora* [Hebrew] (Tel Aviv: Dvir, 1969), vol. 4, 225–37.

87. See Joseph Sermoneta (ed.), *Hillel ben Shemu'el of Verona: Sefer Tagmulei ha-Nefesh (The Book of the Rewards of the Soul)* (Jerusalem: Israeli Academy of Sciences and Humanities, 1981).

88. Sermoneta's critical notes demonstrate that the scholastic style of Hillel's work and many of his specific arguments were directly indebted to Aquinas' debate against several masters of arts at the University of Paris, such as Siger of Brabant, who defended the Averroist position on the afterlife. See Ralph McInerny, *Aquinas Against the Averroists: On There Being Only One Intellect* (West Lafayette: Purdue University Press, 1993).

89. Ibid. 162–63; 168.

90. Ibid. 206.

91. The critical remarks of Meir Ben Simon of Narbonne are excerpted in Scholem, *Origins of Kabbalah*, 54–55, 196.

92. Little is known about the motivation of Nicholas Donin's conversion to Christianity. According to one rather vague reference in the response of R. Yehiel of Paris, Donin had contacts with Karaites. It is plausible that critique of rabbinic Judaism, which paved the way to his conversion, was influenced by Karaite rationalism. For an English translation of the Hebrew and Latin accounts of the disputation in Paris in 1240, see Hyam Maccoby, *Judaism on Trial: Jewish-Christian Disputations in the Middle Ages* (London: The Littman Library of Jewish Civilization, 1993 [1982]), 153–62, 163–67.

93. This change in Christian view took place during the twelfth century. See Jeremy Cohen, "Reconceptualizing Jewish Disbelief in the Twelfth Century," in his *Living Letters of the Law: Ideas of the Jew in Medieval Christianity* (Berkeley: University of California Press, 1999), 147–66.

94. A detailed account of this debate is provided in Robert Chazan, *Barcelona and Beyond: The Disputation of 1263 and Its Aftermath* (Berkeley: University of California Press, 1992). As in the case of Nicholas Donin, very little is known about the activities of Pablo Christiani prior to the Barcelona disputation. Robert Chazan attempted to reconstruct it on the basis of a letter by Jacob ben Elijah de Lattes, who probably was Pablo's teacher prior to his conversion. Chazan concludes that Pablo came from a pious, aristocratic, learned family in Provence and that his conversion related to "internal stresses within the Jewish community." See Chazan, *ibid.* 25–26. Like Donin, Pablo Christiani attacked the irrational material in the Talmud, though the latter was not the core of Donin's campaign. Even if philosophical rationalism paved the way to the conversion of Nicholas Donin and Pablo Christiani, I doubt that we can draw general conclusions about the causal connection between Jewish rationalism and conversion to Christianity, even though this charge will be raised in the late fourteenth century, as we shall see in Chapter Eight.

95. Marc Saperstein, "The Conflict over the Rashba's *Ḥerem* on Philosophical Study: A Political Perspective," *Jewish History* 1 (2) (1986): 27.

96. See Joseph Shatzmiller, "Bein Abba Mari la-Rashba—Ha-Masa U-Mattan she-Qadam La-Ḥerem Be-Barcelona," in *Meḥaqarim be-Toledot am-Israel ve-Eretz Yisrael* 3 (Haifa: Haifa University Press, 1985), 121–37.

97. Saperstein, "The Conflict," 29.

98. See William Chester Jordan, *The French Monarchy and the Jews: From Philip Augustus to the Last Capetians* (Philadelphia: University of Pennsylvania Press, 1989), passim.

99. See Amos Funkenstein, "Basic Types of Christian Anti-Jewish Polemics in the Twelfth Century," *Viator* 2 (1971): 373–82.

100. On the expulsion of the Jews in 1306 see Sophia Menasche, "Faith, Myth and Politics: The Stereotype of the Jews and their Expulsion from England and France," *Jewish Quarterly Review* 75 (1985): 351–74.

101. The collection was published in Pressburg in 1838 and reissued in New

York in 1958 in a new edition by Haim Zalman Dimitrovsky, ed., *Teshuvot ha-Rashba*, pt. 1 vols. 1–2 (Jerusalem: Mosad ha-Rav Kook, 1990). My references are to the Pressburg edition.

102. See Joseph Shatzmiller, "In Search of the Book of Figures—Medicine and Astrology in Montpellier at the Turn of the Fourteenth Century," *Association of Jewish Studies Review* 7/8 (1982/93): 383–407; Dov Schwartz, "The Debate on Astral Magic in Provence" [Hebrew], *Zion* 58 (2) (1993): 141–74.

103. See Maimonides, "Letter on Astrology," in Ralph Lerner and Muhsin Mahdi, eds., *Medieval Political Philosophy: A Sourcebook* (Ithaca: Cornell University Press, 1968), 227–36. For analysis of Maimonides' position, consult Ralph Lerner, "Maimonides' Letter on Astrology," *History of Religions* (1968): 143–58; Y. Tzvi Largermann, "Maimonides' Repudiation of Astrology," *Maimonidean Studies* 2 (1991): 123–58.

104. We cannot do justice here to Halevi's subtle position. In general, he was not committed to the pursuit of intellectual perfection associated with the teachings of the Brethren of Purity, nor to the prognostication of future events or the performance of miracles based on intellectual attainments. Even when he compared performance of the commandments with theurgy, they have no necessary efficacy in producing the desired results. See *Kuzari* I:77–79, III: 53, 65 for relevant discussion of these issues. While Halevi's position was quite different from ibn Ezra's, for the sake of our discussion these differences are not crucial. My point is that in the writings of Halevi and ibn Ezra later Jewish philosophers found a non-Aristotelian conception of nature (Neoplatonic or Neopythagorean), which was hospitable to astrology.

105. Schwartz, *Astral Magic*, 24.

106. For detailed analysis of Abraham ibn Ezra's use of astrology, consult Shlomo Sela, *Astrology and Exegesis in Abraham ibn Ezra's Thought* [Hebrew] (Ramat Gan: University of Bar Ilan Press, 1999). The numerous studies of Dov Schwartz have examined in detail the contribution of the super-commentaries on ibn Ezra to fourteenth-century Jewish philosophy in Provence and Spain. A full bibliography of Schwartz's studies is available in his *Astral Magic*, 359–61.

107. Dov Schwartz, "The Debate about Astral Magic in Provence in the Fourteenth Century" [Hebrew] *Zion* 58 (1983): 141–74; idem, *Astral Magic*, 191–261.

108. Moses Narboni, a loyal Averroist, equated human perfection with the perfection of the intellect and adopted the view that the human intellect is a disposition to cognize intelligibles that are predicated on an eternal substance, namely, the Active Intellect. Narboni's position is discussed in more detail in Chapter Eight, n. 57. For an overview of Nissim of Marseille's rationalism consult Howard Kreisel, "Some Observations on Ma`ase Nissim by R. Nissim of Marseilles," in Alfred L. Ivry, Elliot R. Wolfson and Allan Arkush, eds. *Perspectives on Jewish Thought and Mysticism* (Amsterdam: Harwood Academic Publishers, 1998), 201–22; Howard

Kreisel, ed. *Perush La-Torah le-Rabbi Nissim ben Moshe Mi-Marsei* (Jeruslaem: Meqitzey Nirdamim, 2000), 1–52.

109. Gad Freudenthal, "Holiness and Defilement: The Ambivalent Perception of Philosophy by Its Opponents in the Early Fourteenth Century," *Micrologus* 9 (2001) (*Gli Ebrei e le Science*). *The Jews and the Sciences* (Florence: Sismel/Edizioni del Galluzo, 2001): 169–93. I thank Prof. Freudenthal for sharing the manuscript of this essay with me before it appeared in print.

110. The main example of the subtle attitude toward Maimonides among halakhists in Provence is R. Menahem Ha-Meiri. See Moshe Halbertal, *Between Torah and Wisdom: Rabbi Menachem ha-Meiri and the Maimonidean Halakhists in Provence* (Jerusalem: Magnes Press, 2000).

111. The notion of the "other within" is central to the postmodern critique and interpretative strategies. For an overview of the manner in which Otherness has been operating in Jewish consciousness and in perception of Jews, consult Laurence J. Silberstein, "Others Within and Others Without: Rethinking Jewish Identity and Culture," in *The Other in Jewish Thought and History: Constructions of Jewish Culture and Identity* (New York: New York University Press, 1994), 1–34.

112. The phrase was based on the description of the seductive woman in Proverbs 5 and it connotes illicit sexual interaction with a non-Jewish woman. That the traditionalists used negative gender imagery to depict philosophic wisdom requires no explanation, but that philosophers too have done so, suggests a certain decline in the status of Wisdom that requires further study.

113. *Minhat Qenaot*, 21, 66, 81. The identification of philosophy with Hagar goes back to Philo.

114. *Minhat Qenaot*, Letter # 24.

115. *Minhat Qenaot*, 41, 50, 51, 72, 74, 77.

116. *Minhat Qenaot*, 86.

117. The annotated text is available in Abraham S. Halkin, ed. *After Maimonides: An Anthology of Writings by His Critics, Defenders and Commentators* [Hebrew] (Jerusalem: The Zalman Shazar Center, 1979), 39–52. The text is discussed by Abraham S. Halkin, "Yedaiah Bedersi's Apology," in *Jewish Medieval and Renaissance Studies* ed. Alexander Altmann (Cambridge: Harvard University Press, 1967), 165–84.

118. Halkin, *After Maimonides*, 167.

119. Individual Jews in Spain, of course, continued to be involved in the study of the sciences, especially astronomy, for the following three centuries. See Y. Tzvi Langermann, "Science in the Jewish Communities of the Iberian Peninsula," in his *The Jews and the Sciences in the Middle Age* (Aldershot: Ashgate/Variorum, 1999), 1–54; Bernard Goldstein, "Scientific Traditions in Late Medieval Communities," in Gilbert Dahan, ed. *Les Juifs au regard de l'histoire: Melanges en l'honneur de Bernard Blumenkranz* (Paris: Picard, 1985), 235–47; idem. "The Hebrew Astronomical Tradition: New Sources," *Isis* 72 (1981): 237–52. Goldstein documents the continued interest of Jews in astronomy in the late fifteenth century and after the expulsion

from Spain in the newly established communities of Turkey, Africa, Palestine, and the Balkans. Although Goldstein established that philosophic-scientific interest among Sephardic Jews continued well into the sixteenth century, a claim to which we add further support in Chapter Nine, the Maimonidean Controversy did signal a certain unease about the natural sciences and philosophy in traditional Jewish society, especially among Ashkenazi Jews.

Notes to Chapter 7

1. See Moshe Idel, *Kabbalah: New Perspectives* (New Haven and London: Yale University Press, 1988) and the review essay by Hava Tirosh-Rothschild, "Continuity and Revision in the Study of Kabbalah," *AJS Review* 18 (1991): 161–92. While this classification is helpful, it should not be taken too rigidly. For a critique of this typology and a different reading of Abraham Abulafia's Kabbalah see Elliot Wolfson, *Abraham Abulafia, Kabbalist and Prophet: Hermeneutics, Theosophy and Theurgy* (Los Angeles: Cherub Press, 2000).

2. See Idel, *Kabbalah: New Perspectives*, 251. This view is a return to the position of Heinrich Graetz, which was rejected by Gershom Scholem.

3. For an overview of the relationship between philosophy and kabbalah in Jewish thought of the Late Middle Ages consult Hava Tirosh-Rothschild, "Jewish Philosophy on the Eve of Modernity," in *History of Jewish Philosophy*, ed. Daniel H. Frank and Oliver Leaman, (London and New York: Routledge, 1997), 499–573; Elliot Wolfson, "Jewish Mysticism: A Philosophical Overview," ibid. 450–98 and the bibliography cited in these essays.

4. Kabbalists debated among themselves whether the essence of God is manifested in the sefirot, or whether these are spiritual entities that emanate from God's essence and that function as the instruments of divine activity. For a succinct and very accessible presentation of the "essentialist" and "instrumentalist" positions in kabbalah, consult David S. Ariel, *The Mystic Quest: An Introduction to Jewish Mysticism* (New York: Schocken, 1992), 68–88. For a technical analysis of these issues, see Moshe Idel, "Between the Views of Sefirot as Essence and Instruments in the Renaissance Period" [Hebrew], *Italia* 3 (1982): 89–111; idem. "Divine Attributes and Sefirot in Jewish Theology" [Hebrew], in *Studies in Jewish Thought*, ed. Sara O. Heller Willensky and Moshe Idel (Jerusalem: Magnes Press, 1989), 87–111.

5. In this respect, as well as in many others, kabbalah betrays its similarity to Platonism.

6. *Zohar* III: 73a is the origin of the phrase.

7. This understanding of God explains why Maimonides (*Guide* I: 58) emphatically denied that God could be understood in relational attributes.

8. The phrase "androgynous male deity" was coined by Elliot Wolfson and explicated in his many studies. He argued persuasively that kabbalah, like rabbinic Judaism in general, conceptualized God as a male deity, even though it speaks in great detail about the feminine dimension of God. The divine female, the Shekhinah, is

not a separate entity, but an extension of the male God that will be fully included in the male in the redemptive future. See, for example, Elliot R. Wolfson, "Woman—The Feminine as Other in Theosophic Kabbalah: Some Philosophical Observations on the Divine Androgyne," in *The Other in Jewish Thought and History: Constructions of Jewish Culture and Identity*, ed. Laurence J. Silberstein and Robert L. Cohen (New York: New York University Press, 1994), 166–204 and his collection of essays *Circle in the Square: Studies in the Use of Gender in Kabbalistic Symbolism* (Albany: State University of New York Press, 1995).

9. This notion is not a kabbalistic innovation. Rather it is central to rabbinic Judaism and was articulated theoretically by Judah Halevi as argued in the Kuzari II:34; II:50.

10. See Moshe Idel, "Types of Redemptive Activities in the Middle Ages" [Hebrew], in *Messianism and Eschatology*, ed. Zvi Baras (Jerusalem: Magnes Press, 1984), 253–79.

11. To date the best analysis of *Sefer ha-Bahir* remains Gershom Scholem, *Ursprung und Anfange der Kabbalah*, translated into English as *Origins of the Kabbalah*, ed. R. J. Z. Werblowsky and trans. Allan Arkush (Philadelphia: Jewish Publication Society, 1987), 35–198.

12. The anthropomorphic conception of God in the Bahir received its full elaboration in the Zohar. For an excellent exposition of it consult Pinchas Giller, *Reading the Zohar: The Sacred Text of the Kabbalah* (Oxford: Oxford University Press, 2001), 105–38.

13. See Wolfson, "Female Imaging of the Torah," 1–28, esp. 9–14.

14. The organic unity of the Torah in kabbalah is explored by Gershom Scholem, "The Meaning of the Torah," in his *On Kabbalah and Its Symbolism* (New York: Schocken Books, 1965), 32–86.

15. The dominant view among scholars of kabbalah is that the text was edited in Provence. See Havivah Pedaya, "The Provençal Stratum in the Redaction of Sefer ha-Bahir" [Hebrew], *Jerusalem Studies in Jewish Thought* 9 (1990) (Pines Jubilee Volume): 139–64.

16. On the kabbalists in Provence see Scholem, *Origins of the Kabbalah*, 199–334. A useful collection of a small number of texts in an English translation is available in *The Early Kabbalah*, ed. Joseph Dan, trans. Ronald C. Kiener (New York: Paulist Press, 1986).

17. Much work has been done on situating the kabbalistic notion of orality in the context of the Jewish understanding of Oral Torah and the oral nature of legal transmission in rabbinic Judaism. More work is needed to locate kabbalistic oral teachings in the larger context of orality in the Middle Ages. For an overview of orality in medieval culture, consult D. H. Green, "Orality and Reading: The Status of Research in Medieval Studies," *Speculum* 65 (1990): 267–80.

18. This is not to say that one should avoid writing about kabbalah in languages other than Hebrew. Yet it is true that much of the power of kabbalistic hermeneutics is lost in translation because the kabbalistic claim is based on the numerical

values of Hebrew letters, and because the very act of translation conflicts with the kabbalists' own proprietary claims upon the Hebrew language.

19. The Aramaic of the *Zohar* is largely artificial. For a general description of the *Zohar*'s language, consult Scholem, *Major Trends,* 163–66. A first step toward a detailed understanding of the peculiar Aramaic of the *Zohar* is Yehudah Liebes, "Sections of the Zohar Lexicon" [Hebrew] (Ph.D. diss., Hebrew University, 1976).

20. Yehudah Liebes was the first to show that the literary structure of the Zohar is the key to the interpretation of its message. See Yehudah Liebes, "The Messiah of the Zohar" [Hebrew], in *The Messianic Idea in Jewish Thought: Festschrift in Honor of the Eightieth Birthday of Gershom Scholem* (Jerusalem: Israel Academy of Sciences and Humanities, 1982), 87–215. An English translation is "The Messiah of the Zohar," in Yehudah Liebes, *Studies in the Zohar*, trans. Arnold Schwartz, Stephanie Nakache, Peninah Peli (Albany: State University of New York, 1993), 1–84. Further contributions to the literary features of the Zoharic story-telling were made by Michal Oron. See Michal Oron, "Me-Omanut ha-Derush shel Ba`al Ha-Zohar," *Jerusalem Studies in Jewish Thought* 8 (1989): 299–310; idem, "Simeni ke-Ḥotam al Libekh: Iyyunim ba-Poetiqah shel Ba`al ha-Zohar be-Parashat Mishpatim," in *Masuot: Studies in Kabbalistic Literature and Jewish Philosophy in Memory of Prof. Ephraim Gottlieb,* ed. Michal Oron and Amos Goldreich (Jerusalem: Bialik Institute, 1994), 1–24. In the following discussion I propose that instead of thinking about the *Zohar* simply as a text to be read, we should view it as a didactic drama—namely a dramatic interaction between protagonists intended to inculcate a certain teaching.

21. Joan Young Gregg, *Devils, Women and Jews: Reflections of the Other in Medieval Sermon Stories* (Albany NY: State University of New York Press, 1997), 3.

22. Gregg, *Devils, Women and Jews*, 13.

23. The main Jewish source of exempla is *Sefer Ḥasidim,* which includes about four hundred exemplary stories with a clear didactic point. Other collections of didactic stories in the Middle Ages are *Midrash Aseret ha-Diberot* (The Midrash of the Ten Commandments) and *Ḥibbur Yafeh min ha-Yeshuah* by R. Nissim of Qayrouan, both of which were the product of a Muslim environment. On the exemplum in medieval Jewish literature, see Eli Yassif, *The Hebrew Folktale: History, Genre, Meaning* [Hebrew] (Jerusalem: The Bialik Institute, 1994), 310–24.

24. For an overview of these dramatic presentations in medieval culture, see Clifford Davidson, ed., *The Saint Play in Medieval Europe* (Kalamazoo, MI: Medieval Institute Publications, 1986).

25. On anti-Jewish violence during Holy days, see David Nirenberg, *Communities of Violence: Persecution of Minorities in the Middle Ages* (Princeton: Princeton University Press, 1996), 202 ff.

26. On the perceptions of Jews in medieval sermonic literature and didactic drama see Gregg, *Devils, Women and Jews,* 171–235; Ivan G. Marcus, "Images of the Jews in the Exempla of Caesarius of Heisterbach," in *From Witness to Witchcraft: Jews and Judaism in Medieval Christian Thought,* ed. Jeremy Cohen (Wiesbaden:

Harrassowitz Verlag, 1996), 247–56; Stephen Spector, "Anti-Semitism and the English Mystery Plays," in *The Drama of the Middle Ages,* ed. Clifford Davidson, C. J. Gianakaris, and John H. Stroupe (New York: AMS Press, 1982), 328–41. The changes in medieval popular literature reflect similar transformation in the theological literature since the twelfth century. On the changes in the perception of the Jews in twelfth-century theology, consult Robert Chazan, "The Deteriorating Image of the Jews—Twelfth and Thirteenth Centuries," in *Christendom and its Discontents: Exclusion, Persecution, and Rebellion, 1000–1500,* ed. Scott L. Waugh and Peter D. Diehl (Cambridge: Cambridge University Press, 1996), 220–23.

27. The term "imaginal world" was coined by Henry Corbin for his analysis of ibn-Sina's poetic philosophy. See Henry Corbin, *Avicenna and the Visionary Recital,* trans. Willard R. Trask (Princeton: Princeton University Press, 1960). Elliot R. Wolfson employed Corbin's term for the role of the imagination in kabbalistic visualization of God. See Wolfson, *Through the Speculum that Shines,* passim, and my review of this work in the *Journal of Religion* 76 (1996): 506–9. There I proposed that "the mystics subverted the prohibition on graven images by visualizing God not in space but through symbolic language, to which the kabbalists among them assigned symbolic colors. Thus instead of narrating the religious myth on stained-glass windows to be gazed at by the public eye, the Jewish mystics projected their colorful visions of God onto the private screens of their imagination and communicated its meaning to the public through exegesis of canonic text."

28. The Holy Land is the setting for the outdoor excursions of the holy men of the *Zohar.* While the author(s) of the *Zohar* had some literary information about its geography and topography from talmudic literature, it is evident that the actual land was unknown; hence the various mistakes in locations or improbable travels. See Scholem, *Major Trends,* 168–69; Tishby, *Wisdom of the Zohar,* 1: 63–64.

29. For an overview of the Hebrew *maqamah* literature see Pagis, *Change and Tradition,* 199–244. On the representation of women in this genre see Tovah Rosen "Sexual Politics in a Medieval Hebrew Marriage Debate," *Exemplaria* 12 (1) (2000): 157–84.

30. For a useful overview of these orders consult Lester K. Little, *Religious Poverty and the Profit Economy in Medieval Europe* (Ithaca: Cornell University Press, 1978), 146–69.

31. C. H. Lawrence, *Medieval Monasticism: Forms of Religious Life in Western Europe in the Middle Ages,* 2nd ed. (London and New York: Longman, 1984), 257.

32. John Wesley Harris, *Medieval Theater in Context: An Introduction* (London and New York: Routledge, 1992), 88–89.

33. On the Barcelona debate and its aftermath in terms of the power relations between the Jews and the Dominican Order in Spain, see Martin Cohen, "Reflections on the Text and Context of the Disputation of Barcelona," *Hebrew Union College Annual* 35 (1964): 157–92; Robert Chazan, "The Barcelona 'Disputation' of 1263: Christian Missionizing and Jewish Response," *Speculum* 52 (1977): 824–42; idem. *Barcelona and Beyond,* 80–99.

34. See Yehudah Liebes, "Christian Influences in the Zohar" [Hebrew], *Jerusalem Studies in Jewish Thought* 2 (1983): 43–74; English translation in his *Studies in the Zohar*, 139–61. Elliot R. Wolfson too has stressed the indebtedness of kabbalah to Christianity. For example, see his "The Tree is All: Jewish-Christian Roots of a Kabbalistic Symbol in *Sefer ha-Bahir*," *Journal of Jewish Thought and Philosophy* 3 (1993): 31–76.

35. *Zohar* III: 161b–174a is a discrete literary unit known as "Rav Mativta" (the Head of the Academy). It includes the description of the ascents to heaven by R. Shimon and his circle to whom the head of the heavenly academy reveals deep mysteries, especially about the world to come. Similarly, *Zohar* I: 41a–45b includes a description of the seven palaces in the celestial Garden of Eden, where the souls of the righteous ascend either during prayer or after the death of the body. Most of this material is available in an English translation in Tishby, *Wisdom of the Zohar*, 2: 597–614. The literary depiction of these ascent experiences, I maintain, may be viewed as indirect polemics against the philosophers: the spiritual knowledge of the kabbalist, revealed in the Zohar, facilitates his transport to heaven, where deeper mysteries are revealed. For this reason, the *Ra`aya Mehemna* and the *Tiqqunei Zohar* are presented as live conversations between R. Shimon Bar Yohai, Moses, and the prophet Elijah in heaven. See Liebes, "The Messiah of the Zohar," 104.

36. See Aron Gurevich, *Medieval Popular Culture: Problems of Belief and Perception,* trans. Janos M. Bak and Paul A. Hollingsworth (Cambridge: Cambridge University Press, 1988), 123.

37. Ibid. 124.

38. Ibid. 125.

39. The causal connection between possession of knowledge and the ability to change mundane reality was the corner of the philosophic analysis of prophecy during the Middle Ages. See Aviezer Ravitzky, "The Anthropological Theory of Miracles," [Hebrew] in his *Crescas' Sermon on the Passover and Studies in His Philosophy* (Jerusalem: Israel Academy of Sciences and Humanities, 1988), 69–110.

40. While I formally distinguish among mysticism, magic, and theurgy, it is important to note that in kabbalistic literature (especially of the sixteenth century) this distinction was blurred. It was the privileged, experiential knowledge of the kabbalists that brought about unification with God (i.e., mysticism), a transformation of the mundane world (i.e., magic), and changes in the internal dynamics of the divine world (i.e., theurgy).

41. Joyous weeping after arduous work that leads to revelation of secrets can be found in the "Sava de-Mishpatim," II 74 b–79b and several other examples, but it is by no means the only way the Zohar refers to weeping. On weeping as a technique to attain a mystical experience, see Idel, *Kabbalah: New Perspectives*, 77–88.

42. This point is elaborated in Yehudah Liebes, "Eros in the Zohar" [Hebrew], *Alpayyim* (1995): 67–119; idem. "The Messiah of the Zohar" [Hebrew], 157–65. The very presence of love among the members of the kabbalistic fraternity is itself

taken to be a sign of the dawn of the messianic era ushered in by the activities of R. Shimon bar Yohai.

43. See Elliot R. Wolfson, "Female Imaging of the Torah: From Literary Metaphor to Religious Symbol," in his *Circle in the Square: Studies in the Use of Gender in Kabbalistic Symbolism* (Albany: State University of New York Press, 1995), 1–28.

44. The point is elaborated in Elliot R. Wolfson, "Circumcision, Vision of God, and Textual Interpretation: From Midrashic Trope to Mystical Symbol," *History of Religion* 27 (1987): 189–215; reprinted in his *Circle in the Square*, 29–48. The exclusion of women from the obligation to perform certain time-bound commandments is cited in the *Zohar* I: 126–a as the general proof that "the Torah was given to men alone . . . since women are exempt from the commandments of the Torah."

45. See Tishby, *Wisdom of the Zohar*, 3:1361–63. *Zohar Ḥadash Huqqat* 50c states: "When a man marries he cleaves to the Shekhinah . . . because he then dwells in the shelter of the consort and perfects himself on the pattern of the upper world." And the passage continues to reason: ". . . Because with regard to the Shekhinah all the females in the world exist by virtue of her mystery. If a man has a wife [the Shekhinah] dwells with him, but if he has no wife, she does not dwell with him" (translated in Tishby, *Wisdom of the Zohar*, 3: 1357). The *Zohar* III: 7b specifically equates human perfection with heterosexual activity that leads to the birth of children: "When is a man called perfect, on the model of the world above? When he has intercourse with his wife in unity, joy and common desire, and there emerge from him and from his wife a son and a daughter. . . . He is then complete in the world below on the model of the supernal holy name, and the supernal holy name is proclaimed over him." Tishby, *Wisdom of the Zohar* 3:1361. Similarly *Zohar* III: 16b states: "That one is so called only when they are in one union. Woe is to those sinful [men] who cause separation above; happy are the righteous who sustain the life above; and happy are the repentant ones who return to their [proper] place." For this reason we may understand why the *Zohar* insists that the mysteries of the Torah must not be revealed to unmarried [Jewish] men. Zohar I: 309a; III: 141a. See Liebes, "The Messiah of the Zohar" [Hebrew], 200.

46. A one-sex theory follows from Aristotle's notion that the woman is a "mutilated male" and the claim that "the male semen produces the form and impetus from which an embryo grows and the female womb contributes only the material nourishment." See Maryanne Cline Horowitz, "Aristotle and Women," *Journal of the History of Biology* 9 (2) (1976): 185. On Aristotle's influence on the medieval conception of women see Vern L. Bullough, "Medieval Medical and Scientific Views of Women," *Viator* 4 (1973): 485–501. A fuller treatment of medical theories on sex differentiation is Joan Cadden, *Meanings of Sex Difference in the Middle Ages: Medicine, Science, and Culture* (Cambridge: Cambridge University Press, 1993).

47. In the symbolic language of the *Zohar*, "to procreate" is referred to as "to make fruit" (for example, Tiqqunei Zohar, Tiqqun 43, 82b).

48. The *Zohar* does not actually say that, but I think it is a reasonable deduction from the general polemics of the *Zohar*. I would even take this conjecture further and say that since childlessness is characteristic of celibate Christianity, the *Zohar*'s association of kabbalistic study and fertility (both literal and symbolic) could be read as a campaign both against rationalist philosophy and against Christianity. The study of philosophy by Jews is similar to the useless speculations of Christian monks. That is to say, it is a barren activity that neither results in the birth of children nor brings about entry into the world to come.

49. In *Zohar* 156a, R. Shimon bar Yohai is referred to as "The Light of the World" (*butzina de-khol ar'aa*). I find it very intriguing that the phrase "the Light of the World" was precisely the phrase used to refer to Jesus in Christian liturgy. Indeed, the Easter Vigil was a dramatic enactment intended to illustrate how the "Light of the World" was brought low when Christ had assumed perishable flesh in order to save humanity. See Harris, *The Medieval Theater*, 29. I do not think it is too far fetched to suggest that the *Zohar*'s reference to Rabbi Shimon bar Yohai was intended to be a Jewish rebuttal to Christian messianic claims. Indeed, I am inclined to think that the *Zohar* becomes more intelligible if read in the Christian cultural context of the thirteenth century and the exacerbation of the Jewish-Christian confrontation.

50. In the "The Messiah of the *Zohar*," Liebes has shown conclusively that the Idra Rabba (*Zohar* III: 127b–145) and Idra Zuta (*Zohar* III: 187b–297b) are literary units with strong messianic import. The first unit depicts the assembly of scholars around R. Shimon for the expressed purpose of revealing secrets that will usher in the final redemption, and the second unit depicts the death of R. Shimon bar Yohai, who reached the highest spiritual goal of unification with the Shekhinah. The redemptive import of the Zohar was understood by the anonymous author of the *Tiqqunei Zohar* and the *Ra`aya Mehemna*, who imitated the style of the *Zohar* because he was convinced that its spiritual message had to be disseminated. By the mid-sixteenth century, especially after the printing of the *Zohar*, the book was venerated as a text that possesses occult powers to heal, to alleviate suffering, and to help people in need. On the perception of the *Zohar* as an energetic text, consult Boaz Huss, "Sefer ha-Zohar as a Canonical, Sacred and Holy Text: Changing Perspectives of the Book of Splendor between the Thirteenth and Eighteenth Centuries," *Journal of Jewish Thought and Philosophy* 7 (1998): 257–307.

51. *Zohar* II: 14a–15a. *Wisdom of the Zohar*, vol. 1, 151.

52. *Zohar Ḥadash*, Parashat Va-Yera, 26b; *Wisdom of the Zohar*, vol. 1, 146.

53. For analysis of the messianic implications of the unification of the male and female aspects of God, see Idel, *Messianic Mystics*, 103–109.

54. Yehuda Liebes, "How was the Zohar Written" [Hebrew], *Jerusalem Studies in Jewish Thought* 8 (1989)1–71; English translation in his *Studies of the Zohar*, 85–138.

55. On this kabbalist, see Michael Kushnir-Oron, ed., *Shaar ha-Razim; Abulafia*

Todros ben Joseph [Hebrew] (Jerusalem: Bialik Institute 1989), 13–36 and the secondary literature cited there.

56. On the Jewish policies of Alfonso X, see Dwayne E. Carpenter, *Alfonso X and the Jews: An Edition of and Commentary on Siete Partidas 7.24 "De Los judios"* (Berkeley: University of California Press, 1986) (*Modern Philology* vol. 115).

57. Tishby, *Mishnah ha-Zohar* 2: 581; idem. *Wisdom of the Zohar*, 3: 1329.

58. The so-called Ashrei Psalm (145), which has two verses from Ps. 84:5 and 144:15.

59. *Daily Prayer Book*, trans. Philip Birnbaum (New York: Hebrew Publishing Company, 1949), 26.

60. I have no doubt that the Aramaic phrase "*zaka'ah ihu/zaka'in inon*" was intended as the equivalent of *ashrei*, and, therefore, should be translated as "happy is/are." Nonetheless, it is important to note that the root *z-kh-h* also connotes "worth," so that the phrase could be translated as "worthy is/are." The connotations of the Aramaic expression are discussed further below.

61. The notion of a divine energy that sustains all levels of existence is not the invention of the kabbalists; it was an integral part of medieval cosmology, which Jewish philosophers associated with divine providence. In theosophic kabbalah the spiritual efflux was given a "biological" interpretation because the divine energy is believed to give rise to life (literally and symbolically).

62. The most succinct exposition of the linking of "blessing" (*berakhah*), the tenth sefirah, Malkhut, and spiritual efflux (expressed in the symbol of a pool of water, *bereikhah*) is articulated in Joseph Gikatilla's *Sha`arei Orah* (Gates of Light). An English translation is available in Avi Weinstein, *Gates of Light* (New York: Harper Collins Publishers, 1994), 16–18.

63. The Zoharic conception of divine grace, or divine spiritual energy, is related to the prevailing medieval belief that the brain is the origin of the sperm. Again, a "biological" understanding of divine grace, I would dare to suggest, may be viewed as a denunciation of the Christian "spiritual" understanding of divine grace.

64. The term "path of truth" to refer to kabbalah was coined by Nahmanides. Its full significance in the context of the Zoharic conception of human well-being will become clear below.

65. On the identification of the Shekhinah and *Kenesset Yisrael* in kabbalah, see Gershom Scholem, "Shekhinah: The Feminine Element in Divinity," in his *On the Mystical Shape of the Godhead*, 140–96, esp. 145–46.

66. A detailed analysis of the Zoharic conception of Torah and the act of Torah study is provided in Tishby, *Wisdom of the Zohar*, 3: 1077–1121.

67. Tishby, *Wisdom of the Zohar*, 1: 144.

68. The association between Zohar and enlightenment (as in *Zohar* II: 23a) was derived from the verse in Daniel 12:3 "Those who are wise will shine like the brightness of the sky." For this reason it is quite appropriate to render *Sefer ha-Zohar* as "The Book of Enlightenment," as did Daniel C. Matt, trans., *Zohar: The Book of Enlightenment* (Ramsey, NJ: Paulist Press, 1983). That title highlights the anti-

philosophical import of the work: true enlightenment belongs to the kabbalists who possess the mysteries of the deity.

69. In contemporary environmentalist discourse "ecosystem" expresses the dynamic interdependence of all components in a given environment. I find this term an apt one for capturing the way kabbalists thought about the divine world.

70. Maimonides, of course, affirmed attributes of action (such as merciful or gracious), which tells us much about God's governance of the world, but he insists that God's nature remains unknowable.

71. The term *shalom* in the Bible captured "an all around, comprehensive sense of welfare, facilitating and supporting life." It connoted wholeness, integrity, perfection, well-being. See Walter Homolka and Albert H. Friedlander, *The Gate to Perfection: The Idea of Peace in Jewish Thought* (Providence: Berghahn Books, 1994), 5.

72. For analysis of the "two paths," the two ways of being in the world, and the references in the *Zohar*, see Tishby, *Mishnat ha-Zohar*, 2: 658–702; idem. *Wisdom of the Zohar*, 3: 1407–97.

73. We should note, however, that according to Maimonides, evil as a privation is not more unreal than illness, ignorance, poverty, darkness, and cold are unreal. These are all evil because they are particular kinds of deprivations (i.e., the deprivation of health, knowledge, the means of subsistence, light, and heat). See Maimonides, *Guide* III:10.

74. The Zoharic conception of evil is explained most fully in Tishby, *Wisdom of the Zohar*, 2: 447–546.

75. The origin of this term is the talmudic story of the "four sages who entered the orchard" in Hagigah 14a. In that story, R. Elisha ben Abuyah is depicted as a sinner who entered "the orchard" and "cut down the shoots," an experience that resulted in his apostasy. In all likelihood the passage refers to skepticism about monotheism and his affirmation of two divine powers. In kabbalah, the sin of Elisha ben Abuyah was the prototype of the mistaken tendency to isolate the Sefirot and to deny their dynamic unity. This indeed was the sin of Adam according to the *Zohar* (e.g., *Zohar* I: 12 a-b; 35b–36a, 221 a-b). For an analysis of the rabbinic traditions about Elisha ben Abuyah, see Yehudah Liebes, *The Sin of Elisha, The Four Who Entered Paradise and the Nature of Talmudic Mysticism,* 2nd ed. [Hebrew] (Jerusalem: Aqadamon, 1990). For a discussion of the primordial sin of Adam, see Tishby, *Mishnat ha-Zohar* 1: 222; *Wisdom of the Zohar*, 1: 373–76.

76. See, for example, Zohar II: 79a.

77. This belief that the *Zohar* contains spiritual energy was the basis of the claim that the study of the *Zohar* fulfills theurgic and messianic functions. On this notion and the emergence of the *Zohar* as a sacred text, see Boaz Huss, "Sefer Ha-Zohar as a Canonical, Sacred, and Holy Text," 290–94.

78. The depiction of the righteous man as a liberator of the Shekhinah bears intriguing similarities to motifs in the tale of the prince who releases sleeping beauty from the enchantment of evil spells.

79. On the interplay between halakhah and kabbalah in the *Zohar*, see Jacob Katz, *Halakhah and Kabbalah: Studies in the History of Jewish Religion, its Various Faces and Social Relevance* [Hebrew] (Jerusalem: Magnes Press, 1984), 34–51.

80. For example, see *Zohar* II: 162a; III: 152a. On the parallelism of human body parts, the Sefirot, and the mitzvot in kabbalah, see Moshe Halamish, *Introduction to the Kabbalah,* trans. Ruth Bar-Ilan and Ora Wiskind-Elper (Albany: State University of New York Press, 1999), 249.

81. The dual functions of the commandments in kabbalah indicate that it is both theocentric and anthropocentric. That the commandments are performed "for the sake of God" was articulated by Nahmanides in his *Commentary on the Pentateuch* on Ex. 29:46.

82. Tishby, *Wisdom of the Zohar*, 3: 1337.

83. Ibid. 3: 1331.

84. On the social critique in the *Zohar*, see Baer, *The History of the Jews of Christian Spain*, 1: 261–81. While Baer's analysis has been accepted by both Scholem and Tishby, the general tendency in contemporary scholarship was to be more skeptical about Baer's conclusions. However, my attempt to read the Zoharic material as exemplary literature is in accord with Baer's attempt to present the mystics of the *Zohar* against the background of the Spiritual Franciscans of the day.

85. On the centrality of Isaiah 53 in medieval Jewish-Christian polemics, see E. I. J. Rosenthal, "Anti-Christian Polemics in Medieval Bible Commentaries," *Journal of Jewish Studies* 11 (1960): 115–35; Ana Sapir Abulafia, "Jewish-Christian Disputations and the Twelfth-Century Renaissance," *Journal of Medieval History* 15 (1989): 105–25; Ora Limor and Guy G. Stroumsa, *Contra Iudaeos: Ancient and Medieval Polemics Between Christians and Jews* (Tubingen: J. C. B. Mohr, 1996); David Berger, "Mission to the Jews and Jewish-Christian Cultural Contacts in the Polemical Literature of the High Middle Ages," *American Historical Review* 91 (1986): 576–91.

86. Tishby, *Wisdom of the Zohar*, 3: 1339.

87. Ibid. 3: 1356

88. *Zohar* I: 94a; Tishby, ibid. 3: 1364.

89. Ibid. 3: 1365.

90. Ibid.

91. Ibid.

92. The practice of "drawing spiritual energy" from the supernal world to the mundane world was not limited to kabbalah. It was shared by Jewish philosophers of the late thirteenth century and throughout the fourteenth century, especially those who were more Neoplatonically inclined and who were deeply interested in astrology and astral magic. We will discuss these thinkers in the next chapter.

93. For an overview of the Zoharic doctrine of the soul, see Tishby, *Wisdom of the Zohar*, 3: 677–807. Kabbalistic anthropological doctrine, as Tishby has shown, not only presupposes detailed knowledge of Aristotelian and Platonic psychology, it also uses philosophic terminology extensively, while transforming its meaning.

94. Averroes' commentary on Plato's *Republic* was already available in a Hebrew translation when the *Zohar* was composed, although in and of itself this fact is not crucial to explaining the Platonic nature of kabbalistic anthropology and psychology. The Platonic myth of the soul was presupposed by and incorporated into the philosophy of Jewish Neoplatonic thinkers such as Abraham bar Hiyya and Abraham ibn Ezra. It is more likely that these Jewish thinkers served as the source for the *Zohar*.

95. *Zohar* III: 167b (part of the Rav Matta unit) depicts the encounter with the souls of Batya, the daughter of Pharoah, Serah, the daughter of Asher, Jochebed, the mother of Moses, and Deborah, the Judge. Why these four women are singled out for mention requires a separate study. For our purposes, it is interesting to note that the *Zohar* did envision the souls of women as part of the heavenly population of souls. In this regard the *Zohar* is more egalitarian than the philosophic literature of its day.

96. I made this point already in "Continuity and Revision in the Study of Kabbalah." On the contribution of kabbalah to Jewish sexual mores, consult Moshe Idel, "Sexual Metaphor and Praxis in Kabbalah," in *The Jewish Family: Metaphor and Memory,* ed. David Kraemer (New York: Oxford University Press, 1989), 197–213. The social marginalization of women as a result of Kabbalah is highlighted by Elliot R. Wolfson in his "Woman—The Feminine as Other in Theosophic Kabbalah," 169 where he states: "nowhere in kabbalistic literature, as far I am aware, do we hear of a tendency to harmonize or equalize the social roles of men and women."

97. *Zohar* II: 12a; III: 174b.

98. *Zohar* I: 67b. The incestual connotations of kabbalistic theosophy were already noted by Raphael Patai, *The Hebrew Goddess* (Detroit: Wayne State University Press, 1967), 123–24. The notion that the divine father derives from the human soul is an extension of that idea, since the human soul is associated with Malkhut, the Daughter of God.

99. *Zohar* III: 61a-b.

100. *Zohar* III: 170a describes the creation of the human body from the four elements.

101. Tishby, *Wisdom of the Zohar* 3: 761–70.

102. On the doctrine of *gilgul* in kabbalah, consult Gershom Scholem, "Gilgul: The Transmigration of Souls," in his *On the Mystical Shape of the Godhead,* 197–225; Halamish, *Introduction to the Kabbalah,* 230–45.

103. On kabbalistic rituals of death, see Gershom Scholem, "Tradition and Creation in the Rituals of the Kabbalists," in his *On Kabbalah and Its Symbolism,* 118–57, esp. 155–56. A very useful overview of kabbalistic anthropology, conception of death, and particularly death rituals is available in Simcha Paull Raphael, *Jewish Views of the Afterlife* (Northvale, NJ: Jason Aronson, 1994).

104. Idel, *Messianic Mystics,* 107.

Notes to Chapter 8

1. Kenneth R. Stow, *Alienated Minority: The Jews of Medieval Latin Europe* (Cambridge: Harvard University Press, 1992).

2. The most poignant example of this trend is the six sermons of John Chrysostom, the bishop of Antioch, delivered in 386–87. Robert Wilken has demonstrated conclusively that Chrysostom's profound hostility toward Jews and Judaism is a response to the Judaizing practices in his own community. See Robert Wilken, *John Chrysostom and the Jews: Rhetoric and Reality in the Late Fourth Century* (Berkeley: University of California Press, 1983).

3. For an analysis of the Augustinian doctrine of toleration see Cohen, *The Living Letters of the Law*, 19–71.

4. For a discussion of the Carolingian charters see Stow, *Alienated Minority*, 59–64; Cohen, *Under Crescent and Cross*, 43–45; and Robert Chazan, *Medieval Stereotypes and Modern Antisemitism* (Berkeley: University of California Press, 1997).

5. A sample of later local and general charters is available in Robert Chazan, *Church, State, and Jew in the Middle Ages* (New York: Behrman House, 1980), 57–93.

6. For an overview of the events of the First Crusade and their significance in Jewish history, see Robert Chazan, *European Jewry and the First Crusade* (Berkeley: University of California Press, 1987). Although the First Crusade was not a watershed in Jewish history, it indicated the future deterioration of Jewish status in the Latin West. For an overview of the persecution of Jews in the First Crusade from the perspective of a non-Jewish medievalist, see Jonathan Riley-Smith, "The First Crusade and the Persecution of the Jews," *Studies in Church History* 21 (1984): 51–72.

7. This tendency was illustrated during the First Crusade in the actions of Bishop John of Speyer, who offered the Jews actual protection behind the fortified walls of his castle. While not all bishops acted likewise, the senior clergy was generally protective of the Jews during the persecution of the First Crusade. That persecution led St. Bernard of Clairvaux to explicitly defend the Jews during the Second Crusade in 1146. Though scholars still debate his motives, Jeremy Cohen's suggestion appears most reasonable. The Abbot of Cluny was motivated not by religious tolerance per se but by his concern for the ultimate goal of the Crusade: the salvation of Christian individual souls and the salvation of Christendom. Attacks on Jews seemed to derail that goal. See Cohen, *Living Letters of the Law*, 221–45; David Berger, "The Attitude of St. Bernard of Clairvaux toward the Jews," *Proceedings of the American Academy for Jewish Research* 40 (1972): 89–108.

8. The role of Jews in the nascent European urban economy as merchants and moneylenders is summarized in Cohen, *Under Crescent and Cross*, 82–88.

9. For analysis of the first accusation of ritual murder in Norwich, England (1144), its psychological roots, and its aftermath in Jewish-Christian relations

during the Middle Ages consult Gavin Langmuir, *Toward a Definition of Antisemitism* (Los Angeles: University of California Press, 1990), 209–98.

10. The notion that the Jews are the private property of the chamber was first articulated in the charter that Emperor Frederick I (Barbarosa) issued for the Jews of Worms in 1157. That the Jews are the "serfs of the royal chamber" was legally stated in the charter that Frederick II issued for all Jews of the Holy Roman Empire. Jewish "serfdom" to the royal power entailed both a relative measure of protection as well as social inferiority and powerlessness. See, Cohen, *Under Crescent and Cross*, 45–46.

11. The details of the Church's campaign against the Talmud and rabbinic literature during the thirteenth century are in Cohen, *Living Letters of the Law*, 317–63 and in the scholarly literature cited there.

12. For analysis of this confrontation, a comparative study of the Latin and Jewish reports, and the significance of the events in Jewish history, consult Robert Chazan, *Barcelona and Beyond: the Disputation of 1263 and Its Aftermath* (Berkeley: University of California Press, 1992).

13. For overviews of Jewish-Christian polemical strategies, see Funkenstein, "Basic Types of Christian Anti-Jewish Polemics," 373–82; Berger, "Mission to the Jews," 576–91.

14. On the Jewish self-confidence and aggressiveness toward Christian disputants prior to and during the twelfth century, see David Berger, *The Jewish Christian Debate in the High Middle Ages: A Critical Edition of the Nizzahon Vetus* (Philadelphia: Jewish Publication Society of America, 1979), 3–37, esp. 22.

15. This accusation was first articulated by the Jewish apostate Nicholas Donin during the 1230s. It was based on the (factually accurate) assessment of the immensely creative talmudic scholarship in Franco-German Jewry during the twelfth century. On Nicholas Donin's campaign against rabbinic Judaism, see Cohen, *Friars and the Jews*, 60–76.

16. For an overview of the expulsions of Jews from the Latin West, see Stow, *Alienated Minority*, 281–308.

17. The use of philosophical reasoning to buttress Judaism in its polemical confrontation with Christianity began with the very rise of medieval Jewish philosophy in the tenth century. Rationalist arguments were employed specifically against Christianity in *Milḥamot ha-Shem* (The Wars of the Lord) by Jacob ben Reuben written in 1170. A systematic, philosophical refutation of Christianity, however, belonged to the fourteenth and fifteenth centuries in response to the marked decline in Jewish status. For an overview of anti-Christian philosophical polemics see Daniel J. Lasker, *Jewish Philosophical Polemics against Christianity in the Middle Ages* (New York: Ktav, 1977).

18. The events of 1391 are discussed in Isaac Baer, *Jews in Christian Spain*, vol. 2: 95–169; Jaume Riera Sans, "Los tumultos contra las Juderias de la corona de Aragon de 1391," *Cuaderons de historia*, 8 (1977): 213–25; Philippe Wolfe, "The 1391 Pogrom in Spain: Social Crisis or Not," *Past and Present* 50 (1971): 4–18;

Emilio Mitre Fernandez, *Los judios de Castilla en tiempo de Entique III. El pogrom de 1391* (Valladolid, 1994)

19. These are reconstructed by B. Netanyahu, *The Marranos of Spain: From the Late 14th to the Early 16th Century*, 3rd ed. updated and expanded (Ithaca: Cornell University Press, 1999). Netanyahu's work has been a subject of considerable criticism. For a detailed critique of it, see Allan Harris Cutler and Helen Elmquist Cutler, "The Netanyahu Thesis on the Marranos: A New Ethnic Approach to the Origins of the Spanish Inquisition," in their *The Jew as Ally of the Muslim: Medieval Roots of Anti-Semitism* (Notre Dame, IN: University of Notre Dame Press, 1986), 205–48.

20. Scholars of Jewish philosophy have devoted considerable attention to Gersonides in the last three decades. Two collections of essays reflect the main contributors to this scholarship: Gilbert Dahan (ed.) *Gersonide en son temps* (Louvain-Paris: E. Peeters, 1991) and Gad Freudenthal, ed., *Studies on Gersonides: A Fourteenth-Century Jewish Philosopher-Scientist* (Leiden: E. J. Brill, 1992). For overviews of Gersonides' life, works, main philosophical positions, and scholarly bibliography consult Gad Freudenthal, "Gersonides: Levi ben Gershom," in *History of Islamic Philosophy*, pt. 1, ed. Seyyed Hossein Nasr and Oliver Leaman (London and New York: Routledge, 1996), 739–54; Seymour Feldman, "Levi ben Gershom (Gersonides)," in *History of Jewish Philosophy*, ed. Daniel H. Frank and Oliver Leaman, (London: Routledge, 1997), 379–98; idem (ed.), "Introduction," in *Levi ben Gershom (Gersonides): The Wars of the Lord*, vol. 1. (Philadelphia: Jewish Publication Society, 1984), 3–54.

21. Gersonides' contribution to astronomical computation and observation is analyzed by Bernard Goldstein, *The Astronomy of Levi ben Gerson* (New York and Berlin: Springer-Verlag, 1985).

22. Historians of medieval Jewish philosophy debate the degree to which Gersonides was informed of scholasticism. Shlomo Pines argued that Gersonides was aware of the major issues that concerned the scholastic masters of his day, especially in Avignon, because his views *parallel* theirs. See Shlomo Pines, "Scholasticism after Thomas Aquinas and the Philosophy of Hasdai Crescas and His Predecessors," [Hebrew] *Beyn Maḥshevet Yisrael le-Maḥshevet ha-Amim*, 182–84. English translation in his *Studies in the History of Jewish Thought*, ed. Warren Zev Harvey and Moshe Idel (Jerusalem: Magnes Press, 1997), 489–589; Idem, "Some Views Put Forward by the 14th Century Jewish Philosopher, Isaac Polgar, and Some Parallel Views Expressed by Spinoza" [Hebrew], *Studies in Jewish Mysticism, Philosophy and Ethical Literature Presented to Isaiah Tishby On his Seventh-fifth Birthday* (Jerusalem: Magnes Press, 1986), 447–57. Pines' evidence for scholastic influence was based on the assumption that similar views entail using the same texts, rather than on citations of individual Christian sources. By contrast, Charles Touati and Seymour Feldman have argued that Gersonides did not know Latin and that his philosophy was formulated strictly within the Judeo-Arabic philosophical tradition, known to him only in Hebrew. See Seymour Feldman, ed., "Introduction," 47. The structure

of this chapter indicates that my view is closer to that of Pines, especially as stated in "Scholasticism after Thomas Aquinas," n. 98. Even though Gersonides does not mention any Christian scholastic by name, it is reasonable to assume that he, like other Jewish contemporaries, had some contact with Christian men of science. After all, the Jewish philosopher-scientist visited the Papal Court of Avignon and it is unreasonable to assume that he was totally ignorant of the intellectual activity around him. However, as Norbert Samuelson suggested to me, it is plausible that Gersonides did not have a high opinion of contemporary scholastic masters: he regarded the Judeo-Arabic philosophic tradition to be intellectually superior to Latin scholasticism. Therefore, Gersonides found no need to cite scholastic authors by name. Even though he shared their style of argumentation and the philosophical problems of the day, he did not consider them authoritative. In favor of this interpretation, we can cite the fact that chapters from the *Wars of the Lord* dealing with the astronomical device, which Gersonides had invented (to be discussed below), were translated in 1342 for Pope Clemens VI from Hebrew into Latin. In any case, my claim that Gersonides' view of happiness should be situated in the context of the intensifying rivalry with Christianity is independent of whether or not he cited Christian authors. He lived in a Christian society and was fully aware of its culture. He was also aware of Jewish suffering during the expulsion of the Jews from France (1306) and the persecution of the so-called Shepherds Crusade (1321–22).

23. We should note that when a Jewish philosopher ascribed a certain view to ibn Rushd, he might also be summarizing a view that ibn Rushd discussed either in the commentaries or one of his other works and which ibn Rushd may or may not endorse. In the fourteenth century summarizing and quoting accurately were not to be taken for granted, so a view ascribed to ibn Rushd may not necessarily be his own.

24. This has been demonstrated conclusively by Herbert Davidson in regard to ibn Rushd's psychological and epistemological doctrines. See Davidson, *Alfarabi, Avicenna, and Averroes, on Intellect*, 220–356.

25. Gersonides' super-commentaries on ibn Rushd are listed in Feldman, "Introduction," 27–30. Ruth Glasner has shown, contra Steinschneider, that Gersonides was the first Jewish philosopher to write super-commentaries on Averroes and that he was the central figure in a scholarly group in southern Spain who composed super-commentaries on Averroes. The texts that Steinshcneider dated to the thirteenth century in fact belonged to the fourteenth century. See Ruth Glasner, "Levi ben Gersohm and the Study of Ibn Rushd in the Fourteenth Century," *Jewish Quarterly Review* 86 (1995): 51–90.

26. See Menachem Kellner, "Gersonides on Imitatio Dei and the Dissemination of Scientific Knowledge," *Jewish Quarterly Review* 85 (3–4) (1995): 275–96. While I do not endorse some of Kellner's conclusions, as we shall see below, the essay is extremely helpful in presenting Gersonides' views.

27. Even though the declared audience of the Torah commentaries was the learned Jew, rather than the ignorant masses (*hamon ha-mitlamdim*), the very choice

of the exegetical mode indicates that Gersonides believed that philosophy, at least in principle, could and should be taught in the synagogue to all Jews. This is precisely what happened in Italy during the fifteenth century, where Gersonides' Commentary on the Pentateuch became quite popular, to the chagrin of Judah Messer Leon, who attempted to ban it. For an overview of Gersonides' philosophical biblical commentaries see Amos Funkenstein, "Gersonides' Biblical Commentary: Science History and Providence (or: The Importance of Being Boring)," in *Studies on Gersonides*, 305–15. For the first comprehensive study that relates Gersonides' philosophical views and his biblical exegesis, see Charles Touati, *La pensee philosophique et theologique de Gersonide* (Paris: Le Editions de Minuit, 1973). For a detailed analysis of Gersonides' conception of providence as reflected in his biblical commentaries, which was not discussed by Touati, consult Robert Eisen, *Gersonides on Providence, Covenant, and the Chosen People: A Study in Medieval Jewish Philosophy and Biblical Commentary* (Albany: State University of New York Press, 1995).

28. This position was ascribed to the Latin Averroists. Gersonides could be regarded as a "Jewish Averroist" in the sense that he developed his views through conversation with Averroes, even though he did not agree with him on most of the important issues. However, Gersonides' successors such as Isaac Poleqar, Isaac Albalag, and Moses Narboni could be viewed as "Jewish Averroists" with justification, even though they did not hold the specific doctrines advocated by the Latin Averroists such as Boetius of Dacia and Siger of Brabant. For a short, accessible summary of their views, consult Frederick Copelston, *A History of Philosophy* (Garden City: Image Books, 1985 [1962], vol. 2, 435–41.

29. Gersonides' philosophical exposition of the biblical creation narrative is explained by Norbert M. Samuelson, "The Role of Elements and Matter in Gersonides' Cosmogony," in *Gersonide en son temps*, 199–233.

30. The dissemination of truth as a political commitment of the philosopher is discussed by Menachem Kellner, "Politics and Perfection: Gersonides vs. Maimonides," *Jewish Political Studies Review* 6:1–2 (1994): 49–82.

31. Book Five of the *Wars* contains the description of the celestial realm and Book Six deals with the Creation of the World. For very useful synopses of Gersonides' views and an English translation of these books consult Seymour Feldman, trans. and ed. *Levi ben Gershom (Gersonides): The Wars of the Lord*, vol. 3 (Philadelphia: The Jewish Publication Society/New York: The Jewish Theological Seminary of America, 1999). Synopsis of Book Five, 5–25; Synopsis of Book Six, 193–211.

32. On Gersonides' modifications of ibn Rushd, see Herbert A. Davidson, "Gersonides on the Material and Active Intellects," in *Studies on Gersonides*, 195–265, esp. 212. Ibn Rushd changed his views about whether emanation was a genuinely Aristotelian notion in a central work such as the *Metaphysics*. In his *Epitome of the Metaphysics*, ibn Rushd treated emanation as genuinely Aristotelian. A few years later, after 1179, ibn Rushd rejected that idea, but retained some of the traditional language, as a kind of a "dead metaphor." By the time he wrote the *Long Commentary on the Metaphysics*, he dispensed with even the metaphorical usage. See Barry S.

Kogan, *Averroes and the Metaphysics of Causation* (Albany: State University of New York Press, 1985), 253–54; idem. "Averroes and the Theory of Emanation," *Mediaeval Studies* 43 (1981): 384–404. It is intriguing to ask why Gersonides, who was such a close reader of Averroes, did not notice that Averroes changed his mind. One answer could be that Gersonides did not have access to all of Averroes' works, but that issue is still a matter of conjecture among Gersonides' scholars. Another answer could be that even if Gersonides had access to all of ibn Rushd's works, the medieval notion of authority prevented Gersonides from subjecting his sources to historical criticism. Whatever it is, the matter requires further reflection.

33. Davidson, "Gersonides on the Material and Active Intellects, 210. See also Herbert Davidson, "Averroes on the Active Intellect as a Cause of Existence," *Viator* 18 (1987): 198–99.

34. See Gad Freudenthal, "Human Felicity and Astronomy in Gersonides' Revolt against Ptolemy" [Hebrew], *Daat* 22 (1989): 64.

35. Gersonides built another version of the instrument designed to measure the perceived size of the stars, but that instrument (which combined the first with the *camera obscura*) did not become nearly as popular as the *baculus Jacob*. See ibid. 69.

36. See Samuelson, "Elements and Matter," 213. For a more elaborate discussion of this foundational concept in Gersonides' philosophy, see Jacob J. Staub, *The Creation of the World According to Gersonides* (Brown Judaic Series, 24) (Chico: Scholars Press, 1982). Gersonides' position on formless matter is much closer to Plato's position in the *Timaeus* than to Aristotle's views. See Seymour Feldman, "Platonic Themes in Gersonides' Cosmology," in *Salo Wittmayer Baron Jubilee Volume* ed. Saul Lieberman and Arthur Hyman (Jerusalem: American Academy for Jewish Research, 1975), 383–405.

37. Samuelson, "Elements and Matter," 216.

38. Ibid.

39. In this regard, as N. Samuelson has argued, the creation narrative in the Bible functions as a myth precisely as does the creation narrative in Plato's *Timaeus* and as do various theories such as the "Big Bang Theory" in contemporary physics. See Norbert M. Samuelson, *Judaism and the Doctrine of Creation* (Cambridge: Cambridge University Press, 1994).

40. This point is developed by Gad Freudenthal, "Human Felicity and Astronomy" cited in n. 33 above.

41. Gersonides, *The Wars of the Lord*, bk. V, pt. 3, chap. 8, 162: "The First Cause, [however], apprehends the law, order and rightness of the sub-lunar world in so far as it is a unified system."

42. Norbert Samuelson, "Gersonides' Account of God's Knowledge of Particulars," *Journal of the History of Philosophy* 10 (1972): 416.

43. Davidson, "Material and Active Intellects," 213. In the *Wars*, bk. V, pt. 3, chap. 7, 155, Gersonides explains the difference between how the cause knows of the effects that proceed from it and how the effects know of their cause. He concludes: "the effect apprehends its cause only insofar as it recognizes that it is itself an

effect and that its existence is from another; whereas [what] the cause, in so far as it knows itself, knows of its effect is more perfect than the existence that the effect [itself] possesses." The Intelligences depend on the First Cause as a formal cause then rather than as an efficient cause.

44. For further discussion consult Tamar Rudavsky, "Individuals and Individuation in the Thought of Gersonides," in *Gersonide en son temps*, 185–97. The issue will be central to Maimonides' analysis of divine knowledge.

45. The metaphysics of individual essences is the hallmark of Duns Scotus' philosophy, which attempts to solve problems in Aristotle's ambiguous legacy. Gersonides' position is not so far from Scotus', but there is no way to prove that he had access to the teachings of the Franciscan master. One possible source of Gersonides could have been Yeda`aya Bedersi, since he articulated a position remarkably close to that of Scotus. See Shlomo Pines, "Individual Forms in the Thought of Yedaya Bedersi" [Hebrew], in his *Bein Mahshevet Yisrael*, 263–76. Duns Scotus' position on individual forms is an attempt to overcome a problem in Aristotle's legacy, which al-Ghazali had already spotted. Aristotle's notion that the separate intelligences are separate species with but one member is not merely a cosmological theory, but an epistemological problem. How can the human mind know immaterial substances such as the separate intelligences if matter is the principle of individuation and if knowledge is only of the universal? Duns Scotus and other scholastic masters struggled with the problem of universals and attempted to solve it by positing "individual forms." Hence, I find Pines' claim that "there are no ties between Aristotle's theory and that of Duns Scotus" rather odd. See Pines, "Scholasticism after Thomas Aquinas" [Hebrew], 181; English version, 493.

46. See H.J. Blumenthal, "Platonism in Late Antiquity," in his *Soul and Intellect: Studies in Plotinus and Later Neoplatonism* (Aldershot: Ashgate/Variorum, 1993), 1–27.

47. Gersonides, *The Wars of the Lord*, bk. 1, chap. 7, ed. and trans. Seymour Feldman (Philadelphia: The Jewish Publication Society, 1984), 165–69.

48. While this was a common analogy, it is possible that the immediate source of Gersonides is Averroes in *Sefer ha-Ḥush ve-ha-Muḥash*, which is the Hebrew version of ibn Rushd's Epitome of Aristotle's *De Sensu et Sensibili*. This was the first unit in the Greek editions of Aristotle's *Parva Naturalia*. Maimonides also used this analogy in the *Guide* III: 19.

49. See Sara Klein-Braslavy, "Gersonides on Determinism, Contingency, Choice and Foreknowledge" [Hebrew], *Da`at* 22 (1989): 39.

50. For a more nuanced reading of Gersonides' views on God's knowledge, see Charles Manekin, "On the Limited-Omniscience Interpretation: Gersonides' Theory of Divine Knowledge," in *Perspectives on Jewish Thought and Mysticism*, 135–70. Interestingly, Gersonides' subtle position on God's knowledge was well understood in the late Middle Ages, for example, by David ben Judah Messer Leon, but later generations have missed his point. See Hava Tirosh-Rothschild, *Between Worlds:*

The Life and Thought of R. David ben Judah Messer Leon (State University of New York Press, 1991), 220–22.

51. For this reason I find it difficult to accept Menachem Kellner's portrayal of Gersonides' view of ultimate felicity. According to Kellner, the novelty of Gersonides lies in the claim that knowledge of physics alone is sufficient for intellectual perfection. However, since to know how the world is structured (i.e., the subject of the science of physics) requires understanding of the relationship between God and the world (i.e., the subject of metaphysics), the two sciences are closely related. It seems to me that what is novel in Gersonides' philosophy is not the claim that "only" physics leads to ultimate felicity, but the claim that correct knowledge of physics *necessarily* leads to the knowledge of God.

52. See also Feldman, ed. and trans., *Wars of the Lord*, vol. 3, "The Synopsis of Book Five," 24–25.

53. See Rudavsky, "Individuals and Individuation," 189.

54. In this regard it is difficult to accept Tamar Rudavsky's claim that Gersonides was not a realist. Rather, as Seymour Feldman has noted, Gersonides' metaphysical position is a modified version of Platonic realism, characteristic of Jewish medieval Aristotelianism.

55. See Davidson, "Material and Active Intellects," 243.

56. See ibid. 248.

57. See Alfred Ivry, ed., *Moses of Narbonne Ma'amar Bi-Shelemut Ha-Nefesh (Treatise on the Perfection of the Soul)* (Jerusalem: Israel Academy of Sciences and Humanities, 1977). Idem, "Moses of Narbonne's 'Treatise on the Perfection of the Soul': A Methodological and Conceptual Analysis," *Jewish Quarterly Review* 57 (1966): 271–97. This work was based on the Hebrew translation of Averroes' *Middle Commentary on Aristotle's De Anima* done in the thirteenth century by Shem Tov ben Isaac of Tortosa. Conceptually there is little novelty in Narboni, except in two respects. First, for Narboni conjunction between the human intellect and the Active Intellect can take place in this world, while the rational soul is still embodied. Thus Narboni was more radical than earlier Aristotelians. Second, Narboni is an early example of a Jewish intellectual who attempted to read kabbalah philosophically. He identified Shi`ur Qomah (the Measurements of God's Body), of which the kabbalists spoke, with the pattern of the sub-lunar world, known to the Active Intellect and to the philosopher who achieves conjunction with it. For analysis of the first point consult Kalman P. Bland, ed. and trans., *The Epistle on the Possibility of Conjunction with the Active Intellect by ibn Rushd with the Commentary of Moses Narboni* (New York: Jewish Theological Seminary, 1982). For the second point see Alexander Altmann, ed. and trans., "Iggeret Shiur Qomah, Moses Narboni's Epistle on Shiur Qomah," in his *Jewish Medieval and Renaissance Studies* (Cambridge Mass.: Harvard University Press, 1967), 225–88.

58. See Ralph McInerny, *Aquinas Against the Averroists: On There Being Only One Intellect* (West Lafayette, IN: Purdue University Press, 1993).

59. The doctrine of the unicity of the material intellect, against which Aquinas

railed, was not known to Gersonides. This doctrine was mentioned in the *Long Commentary on the De Anima* of ibn Rushd, which became available in Hebrew only in the fifteenth century. In the *Long Commentary*, ibn Rushd adopted a position that is very similar to that of Themistius. As Davidson explains, ibn Rushd "construes the human material intellect as a single incorporeal eternal substance, which occupies the lowest rank within the incorporeal hierarchy and hence stands immediately below the active intellect." Davidson, "Gersonides on the Material and Active Intellects," 198.

60. See Seymour Feldman, "Gersonides on the Possibility of Conjunction with the Agent Intellect," *AJS Review* 3 (1978):119. For a different conclusion that affirms the mystical import of Gersonides' views see Georges Vajda, *L'amore de Dieu dans la theologie juive du moyen age* (Paris, 1957), 251–52. How a given scholar reads Gersonides reflects the scholar's comfort or discomfort with kabbalah as well as the training of the historian. Vajda appreciated the similarities between philosophy and kabbalah and highlighted the mystical possibilities of Gersonides' theory of knowledge: he regarded "intellectual mysticism" to be characteristic of medieval Islamic culture in which Gersonides was steeped. Feldman, by contrast, who sees a qualitative difference between rationalist philosophy and the irrational mysticism of kabbalah presents Gersonides as one who defended philosophy "against the encroachment of mysticism."

61. The same point is made in *Wars* I:13: "This pleasure is not comparable to other pleasures and has no relation to them at all. All the more so will the pleasure be greater after death; for then all knowledge that we have acquired in life will be continuously contemplated and all the things in our minds will be apprehended simultaneously, since after death the obstacle that prevents this [kind of cognition], i.e., matter, will have disappeared" (Feldman [Trans.] vol. 1, 224).

62. What Aristotle called *pros en* equivocation is termed in Gersonides' Hebrew works as *qedimah ve-ihur*, namely "predicates that refer primarily to God in a perfect sense and secondarily or derivatively to anything else in a less perfect sense." See Norbert M. Samuelson, *Gersonides on God's Knowledge* (Toronto: Pontifical Institute of Mediaeval Studies, 1977), 31.

63. I use the term "soft determinism" to capture two claims: (a) that all things are determined and (b) that determinism is compatible with moral responsibility. That, I believe, is Gersonides' position.

64. I rely here on Sara Klein-Braslavy, "Gersonides on Determinism, Contingency, Choice and Foreknowledge" [Hebrew], *Da'at* 22 (1989): 18.

65. Of course this does not solve the problem; it only moves it one step back because we can ask Gersonides what are the causes that enable one person to be more or less conditioned by matter than another person.

66. The discussion is indebted to Charles H. Manekin, "Hebrew Philosophy in the Fourteenth and Fifteenth Centuries: Overview," in *History of Jewish Philosophy*, 369–72.

67. *Wars* III:1. See Samuelson, "God's Knowledge of Particulars," 411.

68. Feldman, "Levi ben Gershom," 394. For further discussion of Gersonides' view consult Howard Kreisel, "Miracles in Medieval Jewish Philosophy," *Jewish Quarterly Review* 75 (1984): 106–14.

69. Funkenstein, "Gersonides' Biblical commentary," in *Studies on Gersonides*, 314.

70. On the ban that Judah Messer Leon imposed on Gersonides' Commentary on the Pentateuch see Hava Tirosh-Rothschild, *Between Worlds: The Life and Thought of R. David ben Judah Messer Leon* (Albany: State University of New York Press, 1991), 27.

71. See Gersonides' Introduction to the *Wars*. Feldman, trans., *Wars of the Lord*, vol. 1, 97; 100.

72. Menachem Kellner proposes that the addressee of the Song of Songs Commentary is the philosophically trained person rather than the ordinary Jew. See Menachem Kellner, "Gersonides on the Song of Song and the Nature of Science," *The Journal of Jewish Thought and Philosophy* 4 (1994): 1–21; idem. "Translator's Introduction," in *Commentary on Song of Songs: Levi ben Gershom (Gersonides)*, trans. Menachem Kellner (New Haven and London: Yale University Press, 1998), xxiii.

73. Kellner, "Politics and Perfection," 67

74. Ibid. 66.

75. Eisen, *Gersonides on Providence*, 74.

76. Ibid. 80.

77. For a description of the Messianic Age according to Gersonides consult Eisen, *Gersonides on Providence*, 147–55.

78. I am aware that the matter requires further discussion since in his biblical commentaries Gersonides does assign a political role to the prophets.

79. Kellner, "Politics and Perfection," 69. Since Gersonides himself was actively engaged in prognostication of future events, there is room to wonder if he considered himself to be a prophet.

80. Kellner, "Politics and Perfection," 73–74.

81. Excerpted in Eisen, *Gersonides on Providence*, 77–78.

82. Ibid. 85.

83. Ibid. 93.

84. On Isaac Polleqar, his *Ezer ha-Dat* and his polemics with Abner of Burgos see Yitzhaq Baer, *The Jews in Christian Spain*, vol. 1, 331–54; Sirat, *History of Jewish Philosophy*, 315–22; Charles H. Manekin, "Hebrew Philosophy in the Fourteenth and Fifteenth Centuries: An Overview," in *History of Jewish Philosophy*, 366–69.

85. On this famous Jewish apostate and his works see Baer, *Jews in Christian Spain*, vol. 1, 327–54; Norman Roth, *Conversos, Inquisition, and the Expulsion of the Jews from Spain* (University of Wisconsin Press, 1995), 190–92; Sirat, *A History of Jewish Philosophy*, 308–17; Shoshana Gershenzon, "A Tale of Two Midrashim: The Legacy of Abner of Burgos," in *Approaches to Judaism in Medieval Times*, vol. 3

(Atlanta: Scholars Press, 1988), 133–45; idem, "The View of Maimonides as a Determinist in *Sefer Minḥat Qenaot* of Abner of Burgos," in *Proceedings of the Ninth World Congress of Jewish Studies* (Jerusalem: Magnes Press, 1986), 93–100. Excerpts from the Hebrew writings of Abner of Burgos were published by Judah Rosenthal in his *Studies and Sources* [Hebrew] (Jerusalem: Reuben Mass, 1967), 324–67.

86. See Dwayne E. Carpenter (ed.) *Text and Concordance of Libro de las tres creencia* (Madison: Hispanic Seminary of Medieval Studies, 1994), 11. This popular text was written for Christian clergy unfamiliar with Semitic languages, and Abner even included a Spanish translation for those priests whose Latin was insufficient. Abner's attacks on Judaism were most influential among educated clergymen and large excerpts from his works were incorporated in the widely diffused *Fortalitium fidei* by Alfonso de Espina, a Franciscan monk who was the confessor to King Enrique IV.

87. For analysis of this text consult Shoshana Gershenzon, "A Study of *Teshuvot la-Meharef* of Abner of Burgos," Ph.D. Diss., Jewish Theological Seminary, 1984.

88. Excerpted in Baer, *Jews in Christian Spain*, vol. 1, 336.

89. Ibid. 337.

90. Ibid. 343.

91. Ibid. 342. This view was accepted by Baer as a statement of facts.

92. Ibid. 346–47.

93. For an analysis of Maimonides' Thirteen Principles and the place of Jewish dogmatic reflection in medieval Jewish philosophy consult Menachem Kellner, *Dogma in Medieval Jewish Thought: From Maimonides to Abrabanel* (Oxford: Oxford University Press, 1986).

94. *Ezer ha-Dat* (The Support of Faith) ed. with an English Introduction by George S. Belasco (London: J. Jacobs, 1970), 42.

95. Isaac Polleqar, *Ezer ha-Dat*, ibid.

96. On these confrontations consult Michael Haren, *Medieval Thought: The Western Intellectual Tradition from Antiquity to the Thirteenth Century*, 2nd ed. (Toronto: University of Toronto Press, 1992) 194–211.

97. On the depth and sophistication of Abner's scholasticism see Shoshana Gershenzon and Dwayne Carpenter.

98. Charles H. Manekin, "Hebrew Philosophy in the Fourteenth and Fifteenth Centuries," 367.

99. Crescas helped the immigration of Jews from Aragon and Castile and their resettlement in Comtat Venaissin, the Kingdom of Navarre, and perhaps even the Land of Israel. On Crescas' diplomatic activities see Baer, *Jews in Christian Spain*, vol. 2, 120–30 and Yom Tov Assis, "Rabbi Hasdai Crescas' Plans for the Rehabilitation of Spanish Jewry after the 1391 Massacres" [Hebrew], *Proceedings of the Tenth World Congress of Jewish Studies* Division B (Jerusalem, 1990), vol. 1, 145–48.

100. See Shlomo Alami, *Iggeret Musar*, ed Abraham Haberman (Jerusalem: Meqorot, 1945). For a discussion of Alami's position see Netanyahu, *Marranos of Spain*, 1999 [1965], 103–6.

101. On Shem Tov ibn Shem Tov, the author of *Sefer ha-Emunot* (The Book of Beliefs), and his critique of philosophy see Ephraim Gottlieb, *Studies in the Kabbalists Literature* [Hebrew], ed. Joseph Hacker (Tel Aviv: Chaim Rosenberg School for Jewish Studies, 1976), 347–56.

102. On the challenges to Aristotle's philosophy of nature see David C. Lindberg, *The Beginnings of Western Science: The European Scientific Tradition in Philosophical, Religious and Institutional Context, 600 B.C. to A.D. 1450* (Chicago and London: University of Chicago Press, 1992), 295.

103. See Warren Zev Harvey, *Physics and Metaphysics in Hasdai Crescas* (Amsterdam: J. C. Gieben, 1998), 23–30.

104. Ibid. 24.

105. Ibid. 4.

106. Ibid. 20.

107. See Aviezer Ravitzky, *Crescas' Sermon on the Passover and Studies in his Philosophy* (Israel Academy of Sciences and Humanities) Jerusalem, 1988), 16.

108. See Kellner, *Dogma in Medieval Jewish Thought*, 108–39.

109. The text was published by Daniel J. Lasker (Ramat Gan: University of Bar Ilan Press, 1990) and in an English translation, *The Refutation of the Christian Principles by Hasdai Crescas* (Albany: Statue University of New York Press, 1992). For a short discussion of the text in the context of Crescas' legacy see idem, "Hasdai Crescas," in *History of Jewish Philosophy*, 400–402.

110. Shlomo Pines, "Scholasticism after Thomas Aquinas and the Teachings of Hasdai Crescas and His Predecessors," trans. Alfred Ivry, in *Studies in the History of Jewish Thought by Shlomo Pines*, edited by Warren Zev Harvey and Moshe Idel, vol. 5, 489–589.

111. Sirat, *History of Jewish Philosophy in the Middle Ages*, 362.

112. Warren Zev Harvey, "Kabbalistic Elements in Crescas' *Light of the Lord*" [Hebrew], *Jerusalem Studies in Jewish Thought* 2 (1982/3): 75–109.

113. For the details of Crescas' critique see Warren Zev Harvey, "Hasdai Crescas' Critique of the Theory of the Acquired Intellect" (Ph.D. diss., Columbia University, 1973), esp. 28–63; idem. "R. Hasdai Crescas and his Critique of Philosophical Happiness" [Hebrew], *Proceedings of the Sixth World Congress of Jewish Studies,* vol. 3 (Jerusalem: World Union of Jewish Studies, 1977), 143–49.

114. The anti-Christian import of Crescas critique of philosophic happiness is evident in his *Sefer Bittul Iqqarey ha-Notzrim*. Lasker (ed.), 41, 84.

115. Crescas' critique of the acquired intellect must not be seen in isolation. As we noted in the previous chapter, similar attacks against the epistemological doctrines of Averroes and ibn Bajja were articulated by Christian scholastics, especially by Thomas Aquinas in the late thirteenth century. See Thomas Aquinas, *Summa contra Gentiles III*: 42–45, trans. Vernon J. Bourke (Notre Dame: University of Notre Dame, 1975), 138–54; *On the Unity of the Intellect Against the Averroists,* trans. Beatrice H. Sedler (Milwaukee, WI: Marquette University Press, 1968).

116. Harvey, "Crescas' Critique of the Theory of Acquired Intellect," 51–52.

117. A similar shift took place in Christian ethics. See Bonnie Kent, *Virtues of the Will: The Transformation of Ethics in the Late Thirteenth Century* (Washington, DC: The Catholic University of America, 1995).

118. Harvey, *Physics and Metaphysics*, 100.

119. Ibid. 104.

120. Ibid. 102.

121. *Light* II: 6; Harvey, *Physics and Metaphysics*, 105.

122. Harvey, *Physics and Metaphysics*, 107; *Light* I: 5; 3

123. *Light* II: 6:1.

124. Harvey, *Physics and Metaphysic*, 111.

125. On this theme see Seymour Feldman, "The Theory of Eternal Creation in Hasdai Crescas and Some of His Predecessors," *Viator* 11 (1980): 289–320.

126. *Light of the Lord* II, 6, 1; III:2, 1. That the soul is an incorporeal substance was held by both Avicenna and Judah ha-Levi, Crescas' most likely sources. See Herbert Davidson, "The Active Intellect in the Cuzari and Halevi's Theory of Causality," *Revue des Etudes Juives* 131 (1972): 363–65.

127. Crescas, *Light*, II, 6, 1; English translation by Harvey, "Crescas' Critique of the Theory of the Acquired Intellect," 441.

128. *Light*, III: 5, 4.

129. *Light*, II, 6, 1. English translation, Harvey, "Crescas' Critique," 454.

130. Ibid. 458.

131. *Light*, II: 5,5.

132. See Seymour Feldman, "A Debate Concerning Determinism in Late Medieval Jewish Philosophy," *Proceedings of the American Academy for Jewish Research* 51 (1984): 15–54, esp. 35.

133. Ravitzky, *Crescas' Sermon*, 49–53.

134. Feldman, "A Debate Concerning Determinism in Late Medieval Jewish Philosophy," 36.

135. Manekin, "Philosophy in the Fourteenth and Fifteenth Centuries," 356.

136. See Aviezer Ravitzky, "The Development of R. Hasdai Crescas' Views on the Problem of Freedom of the Will" [Hebrew], *Tarbiz* 51 (1982): 444–67. The chronology of Crescas' views, however, was challenged by Warren Zev Harvey in his review of Ravitzky, *Derashat ha-Pessaḥ le-Rab Ḥasdai Crescas*, in *Tarbiz* 58 (1989): 531–35.

137. Crescas' doctrine of the will has attracted considerable scholarly attention. Several attempts were made to pinpoint the literary sources that influenced Crescas. J. Guttmann highlighted the indebtedness of Crescas to Muslim Aristotelians, especially to Averroes. Y. Baer, on the other hand, showed that Crescas developed his views in the posthumous debate with the apostate Abner of Burgos, but that in the debate Crescas himself adopted some of the views of the Christian scholastics whom he attempted to refute. S. Pines agreed with Baer that Crescas' views must be understood against the background of Christian scholasticism, but he suggested that in some key doctrines Crescas followed Duns Scotus rather than Thomas

Aquinas. Contrary to Baer and Pines, S. Feldman sided with Guttmann saying that Crescas' theory of the will should be located within the Hebrew Arabic philosophic tradition, but Feldman cited Avicenna rather than Averroes as Crescas' immediate source. In contrast to Feldman, A. Ravitzky supported Baer and Pines when he showed that Crescas was familiar with works of Aquinas and Duns Scotus but that Crescas often articulated a Jewish response to them.

138. Feldman, "A Debate Concerning Determinism," 27.

139. Crescas here attempts to refute the determinism of Abner of Burgos, who taught that reward and punishment follow necessarily from the act itself. See Yitzhaq Baer, "Minḥat Qenaot by Abner of Burgos and its Influence on Hasdai Crescas" [Hebrew] *Tarbiz* 11 (1950): 193; Ravitzky, *Crescas' Sermon,* 40–41.

140. Ravitzky, *Crescas' Sermon,* 13.

141. See Feldman, "A Debate Concerning Determinism," 37–53 and Ravitzky, *Crescas' Sermon,* 15.

Notes to Chapter 9

1. On the expulsion experience, its impact on Jewish culture, and the scholarly debate about the significance of the expulsion in Jewish culture, see Hava Tirosh-Samuelson, "The Ultimate End of Human Life in Postexpulsion Philosophic Literature" in *Crisis and Creativity in the Sephardic World 1391–1648* ed. Benjamin R. Gampel (New York: Columbia University Press, 1997),

2. For the biography and literary activity of Joseph ibn Shem Tov consult Shaul Regev, "Theology and Rational Mysticism in the Writings of R. Joseph ben Shem Tov," Ph.D. Dissertation [in Hebrew] Hebrew University, 1983. A full bibliography of Regev's work about ibn Shem Tov is available in my "Jewish Philosophy on the Eve of Modernity" (see chap.7, n.3).

3. See Georg Wieland, "The Reception and Interpretation of Aristotle's Ethic," in *The Cambridge History of Later Medieval Philosophy: From the Rediscovery of Aristotle to the Disintegration of Scholasticism 1100–1600,* ed. Norman Kretzmann, Anthony Kenny, and Jan Pinborg (Cambridge: Cambridge University Press, 1982), 657–72.

4. Vernon J. Bourke, "The Nicomachean Ethics and Thomas Aquinas," in *St. Thomas Aquinas 1274–1974: Commemorative Studies* (Toronto: Pontifical Institute of Medieval Studies, 1974), 239–59.

5. The text is extant in several manuscripts. In MS Oxford-Bodleian Poc 17 (Neubauer 1427), fol. 3v, Meir ben Solomon Alguades states that he translated the *Ethics* at the request of Don Samuel Labi of Aragon, a member of the famous de la Cabelleria family of Jewish courtiers. While it is true that this patron of the arts subsidized the translation of many works, I do not believe that interest in the *Ethics* was a coincidence. Rather, I suggest that the Jewish courtiers in Spain found in the *Ethics* an ideological justification for their own aristocratic self-perception. Bolstering the image of the Jewish courtier was particularly necessary during the fifteenth

century when this social group experienced real loss of power. Aristotle's "inclusive" portrayal of happiness in particular must have been very appealing to these courtiers because it justified their worldly and intellectual pursuits. On Meir Alguades' life and political career see Baer, *Jews in Christian Spain*, vol. 2, passim. Alguades' Introduction to the translation was published by Lawrence Berman in *Shlomo Pines Jubilee Volume*, vol. 1 (*Jerusalem Studies in Jewish Thought* 8) (Jerusalem, Magnes Press, 1990): 147–68.

6. Alguades specifically states that he studied the *Ethics* with Christian teachers and that he could not get much help from the Hebrew translations of the Arabic version. Ibid. fol. 2a.

7. Lawrence V. Berman, "Ibn Rushd's Middle Commentary on the Nicomachean Ethics in Medieval Hebrew Literature," in *Multiple Averroes,* ed. Jean Jolivet (Paris: Les Belles Lettres, 1978), 301.

8. Berman, "Ibn Rushd's Middle Commentary," 300–302.

9. Leonardo Bruni, the famous humanist and chancellor of Florence, composed a new translation of the *Ethics* in 1416–17. The translation was no more than a revision of Grosetteste's translation but it became a great success. Bruni's translation reflected the role of moral philosophy in the *studia humanitatis,* the humanist ideal of eloquence, and Renaissance rereading of Aristotle on the basis of textual analysis. Bruni also wrote a short introduction to the *Ethics* entitled *Isagogicon moralis philosphiae.* Moses Almosnino refers to Bruni's translation in his commentary on the *Ethics,* entitled *Penei Mosheh,* fol. 14b.

10. John Argryropoulos translated the *Ethics* from Greek into Latin in 1457. In *Penei Mosheh* fol. 31b Almosnino states that Argryropolous's translation is considered to be the best translation of the *Ethics* in Latin. For a detailed reconstruction of Argryropolous academic activities and influence in Florence, see Arthur Field, *The Origins of the Platonic Academy of Florence* (Princeton: Princeton University Press, 1988), 107–26.

11. Ibn Shem Tov's report was factually correct. See A. Pagdon, "The Diffusion of Aristotle's Moral Philosophy in Spain, ca. 1400–ca. 1600," *Traditio* 21 (1975): 287–313.

12. *Kevod Elohim*, 3a.

13. In his Commentary on the *Ethics* written in 1455, MS Oxford-Bodleian, Michael 404 (= Neubauer, 1431, fol. 1v), ibn Shem Tov specifically states that he had written *Kevod Elohim* thirteen years earlier, i.e., in 1442. During those thirteen years, ibn Shem Tov gained a better understanding of the *Ethics* by consulting the Latin commentaries on the work, a practice that he says was common among Jewish intellectuals who had mastered Latin. Cooperman, *In Iberia and Beyond,* 88.

14. *Kevod Elohim,* 4b.

15. See Regev, "Theology and Rationalist Mysticism," 37. The total number of ibn Shem Tov's compositions related to the *Ethics* is four, but it was *Kevod Elohim* and the long commentary that were the most influential. I believe that the other two texts were composed by ibn Shem Tov for didactic purposes.

16. In the introduction to his *Commentary on Aristotle's Ethics*, MS. Oxford-Bodleiana 1432 (Michael 404), fol. 1b, Ibn Shem Tov states that he often engaged in public discussions with "the greatest of Christian scholars" (*gedolei ḥakhmei ha-notzrim*) in the presence of "kings and counselors" (*melakhim ve-yo`atzei aretz*) and that these scholars helped him to understand "the principles of this book and its mysteries" (*shorashav ve-ta`alumotav*).

17. In the *Commentary on the Ethics*, fol. 44a, Joseph ibn Shem Tov discusses the "great-souled man" of Aristotle (in Hebrew, *gedol ha-nefesh* or *gedol ha-lev*). A detailed discussion of this fascinating issue cannot be undertaken here. I will devote a separate study to it.

18. A quick perusal of ibn Shem Tov's commentary and the popular moralistic treatise *Sefer Ma'alot ha-Middot* (The Book Praises of Virtues) by Yehiel Anav will illustrate the degree to which the worldly ideal of the "great-souled man" differed from the traditional Jewish view of the virtuous person.

19. Ibn Shem Tov, *Commentary on the Ethics,* book IV, chaps. 4–7, fols. 79a–83b.

20. Ibn Shem Tov, *Commentary on the Ethics*, fol. 82b.

21. On *Ein ha-Qore,* see Regev, "Theology and Rationalist Mysticism," 15–18. On the use of sermons as a medium for the popularization of philosophy in fifteenth-century Spain, see Saperstein, *Your Voice Like a Ram's Horn*, 75–87. A sermon of ibn Shem Tov is available in an English translation in Saperstein, 167–79. Although neither Regev nor Saperstein suggest the humanist context of ibn Shem Tov's rhetorical theory and practice, I believe that it is fruitful to explore this connection. For an overview of humanism in Spain see O. Di Camillo, "Humanism in Spain," in *Renaissance Humanism*, edited by A. Rabil (Philadelphia: University of Pennsylvania Press, 1988), vol. 2, 55–108. Interestingly, as this essay shows, the *converso* Alonso de Cartagena criticized the new translation of the *Ethics* by Leonardo Bruni.

22. *Kevod Elohim*, 2b. Cf. Aquinas, *SCG*, III: 25,4.

23. Ibn Shem Tov's interest in anti-Christian polemics is evident from his translation of Crescas' *Reutations of Christian Dogmas*, and from Ibn Shem Tov's commentary on Profiat Duran's *Do Not Be Like Unto Your Fathers*. However, we should note that the Jewish-Christian encounter in fifteenth-century Spain was not entirely repressive. Some scholarly debates were carried out in a friendly atmosphere, and there is evidence that Jews were genuinely attracted to Christian preaching and were able to appreciate them on their own merit. See Heller-Wilensky, *The Philosophy of Isaac Arama*, 27, n. 31.

24. In the commentary on Genesis: I quoted in the previous chapter, Gersonides himself was not far from equating the intelligible order of reality in the mind of the Active Intellect with the philosophic meaning of the Torah.

25. See Bracha Sack, "R. Joseph Taitazak's Commentaries," in *Shlomo Pines Jubilee Volume,* vol. 1, edited by M. Idel, E. Schweid, and W. Z. Harvey (Jerusalem Studies in Jewish Thought 7), 341–55.

26. ST, I-II, q. 11, a. 1–6.
27. SCG, book III, chap. 25.
28. ST, I-II q. 3. a. 5.
29. Anthony J. Celanno, "The Concept of Worldly Beatitude in the Writings of Thomas Aquinas," *Journal of the History of Philosophy* 25 (2) (1987): 222.
30. The same view is expressed in Abraham Bibago, *Derekh Emunah*, 41b.
31. Ibn Shem Tov, *Kevod Elohim*, 11b–12a.
32. *Kevod Elohim*, 8b.
33. The same view was shared by Joseph Albo, *Sefer ha-Iqqarim (The Book of Principles)* I:24 and by Abraham Bibago, *Derekeh Emunah*, 45a.
34. Pegis, "St. Thomas and the Nicomachean Ethics," 8. For a detailed discussion of Aquinas' definition of the soul and his opposition to other psychological theories see Anton C. Pegis, "Some Reflections on *Summa Contra Gentiles* II, 56," in *An Etienne Gilson Tribute* (Milwaukee: The Marquette University Press, 1959), 169–88.
35. *Kevod Elohim*. 8b. Cf. Aquinas SCG, III: 25, 8.
36. Cf., *Kevod Elohim*, 8b and ST, I-II, q. 3, a. 2, reply.
37. *Kevod Elohim*, 19b–20a. The same skeptical approach toward natural human reason was shared by Albo, *Sefer ha-Iqqarim*, III: 28; Abraham Bibago, *Derekh Emunah*, 42a; 45b; Shimon ben Zemach Duran, *Magen Avot* (Livorno, 1785), 2b; Abraham Shalom, *Neveh Shalom* (Venice: 1525), 68b; Isaac Arama, *Hazut Qashah* (Warsaw: 1911), 8.
38. In emphasizing the intrinsic limits of natural philosophy, fifteenth-century thinkers followed Thomas Aquinas. Cf. Aquinas, SCG I: 1–8.
39. This conception of the Torah was prevalent among Sephardic thinkers in the fifteenth and sixteenth centuries. For further exposition of this view see Tirosh-Rothschild, *Between Worlds*, 209–10.
40. *Kevod Elohim*, 20b.
41. Ibid. 23a-b.
42. Ibid. 20a.
43. Ibid. 14b.
44. Ibid. 13b.
45. The association of human perfection and seclusion from human affairs appeared in the writings of other fifteenth-century Jewish thinkers, such as Abraham Rimoch, and reflected their despair and desire to flee from worldly affairs. See Frank Talmage, "Trauma at Tortosa: The Testimony of Abraham Rimoch," *Mediaeval Studies* 47 (1985): 379–415, esp. 389–92.
46. Cf., *Kevod Elohim* 16a and Aquinas, *Commentary on Aristotle's Ethics*, bk. I, lec. 9, no. 113.
47. Ibn Shem Tov's critique does not do justice to Gersonides' subtle views, but he does represent the perception of Gersonides by more conservative Jewish thinkers in the fifteenth century. This tendency is well captured by Herbert A. Davidson, "Medieval Jewish Philosophy in the Sixteenth Century," in *Jewish*

Thought in the Sixteenth Century, ed. Bernard Dov Cooperman (Cambridge: Harvard University Press, 1983), 106–14.

48. *Kevod Elohim,* 21a-b.

49. A similar position was expressed by Joseph Albo, *Sefer Ha-Iqqarim,* I:21, and Abraham Bibago, *Derkeh Emunah,* 49b, 50a, 50b.

50. Bernard Septimus, "Isaac Arama and the *Ethics,*" in *Jews and Conversos at the Time of the Expulsion,"* ed. Yom Tov Assis and Yosef Kaplan (Jerusalem: The Zalman Shazar Center for Jewish History, 1999), English Section, 12.

51. Ibid. 23.

52. On Abravanel's use of astrology see Shaul Regev, "Messianism and Astrology in the Thought of R. Isaac Abrabanel" [Hebrew], *Asufot* 1 (1987): 169–87.

53. Alemanno's fusion of philosophy and kabbalah still awaits systematic analysis. For now the best treatment is Moshe Idel, "The Magical and Neoplatonic Interpretations of the Kabbalah in the Renaissance," *Jewish Thought in the Sixteenth Century,* ed. Bernard Dov Cooperman (Cambridge: Harvard University Press, 1983), 186–242; reprinted in *Essential Papers on Jewish Culture in Renaissance and Baroque Italy,* ed. David B. Ruderman (New York: New York University Press, 1987) 107–69; "The Anthropology of Yochanan Alemanno: Sources and Influences," *Annali di storia dell'esegesi* 7 (1) (1990): 93–111.

54. The following discussion of Alemanno is based on Arthur Lesley, *The Song of Solomon's Ascents* by Yohanan Alemanno: Love and Human Perfection according to a Jewish Colleague of Giovani Pico," Ph.D. Diss., University of California Berkeley, 1976.

55. The theme is treated in detail by Charles Trinkaus' *Adversity's Noblemen* (New York: Octagon Books, 1965). The information in the following three paragraphs is based on that study.

56. Trinkaus, *Adversity's Noblemen,* 57.

57. Ibid. 58.

58. Ibid. 60.

59. Ibid. 55.

60. See Lesley, "The Song of Solomon's Ascent," 4; 12–13.

61. Ibn Tufayl's work was attractive to fourteenth-century philosophers such as Moses Narboni, who wrote a commentary on it, because it depicted the philosophical enlightenment of an individual who grew up alone on a remote island. The attainment of philosophic perfection in this world, notwithstanding injustice and suffering, is possible. For an analysis of Ibn Tufayl's intellectual mysticism, see Lawrence I. Conrad, T*he World of Ibn Tufayl: Interdisciplinary Perspectives on Hayy ibn Yaqzan* (Leiden, New York, Koln: E. J. Brill, 1996).

62. On Flavius Mithridates and Paulus Ricci, see David Ruderman, *The World of a Renaissance Jew*: *The Life and Thought of Abraham ben Mordecai Farissol* (Cincinnati: Hebrew Union College Press, 1984), passim.

63. Lesley, "Song of Solomon's Ascents," 52.

64. Ibid. 52.

65. Ibid. 80–83.

66. Moshe Idel, "The Study Program of Rabbi Yohanan Alemanno" [Hebrew], *Tarbiz* 48 (1979): 303–30.

67. Lesley, "Songs of Solomon's Ascents," 63.

68. David ben Judah Messer Leon is a primary example of the "hakham kolel" (literally, the "comprehensive scholar") in the fifteenth and sixteenth centuries. See Hava Tirosh-Rothschild, *Between Worlds*, 34–54.

69. Lesley, "Songs of Solomon's Ascents," 85.

70. I Kings 1–11; I Chronicles 22:5–23:1 and 28:5–28:9; II Chronicles 1–9.

71. The dissemination of kabbalah in Italy is analyzed by Moshe Idel, "Major Currents in Italian Kabbalah between 1560–1660," in *Essential Papers on Jewish Culture in Renaissance and Baroque Italy*, 345–72; idem, "Religion, Thought and Attitudes," 123–39; Roberto Bonfil, *The Rabbinate in Renaissance Italy* [Hebrew] (Jerusalem: Magnes, 1979), 179–90. English translation, *Rabbis and Jewish Communities in Renaissance Italy*, trans. J. Chipman (Oxford: Oxford University Press, 1990), 280–298.

72. The importance of this fact is elaborated in great detail by Moshe Idel, "Encounters between Spanish and Italian Kabbalists in the Generation of the Expulsion," *Crisis and Creativity in the Sephardic World 1391–1648*, 189–222.

73. The printing of *Sefer ha-Zohar* was surrounded by a heated controversy within the Jewish community. See IsaiahTishby, "The Controversy about Sefer ha-Zohar in Sixteenth-Century Italy" [Hebrew], in *Studies in Kabbalah and Its Branches: Researches and Sources* (Jerusalem: Magnes Press, 1982), vol. 1, 79–130. First published 1976.

74. On the correspondence of Isaac Mar Hayim and Isaac of Pisa and the debate on the nature of Sefirot see Idel, "Between the Views," 89–111.

75. What constitutes the "true Kabbalah" (*qabbalah amittit*) was a subject of constant dispute among the kabbalists themselves ever since kabbalah emerged in the late twelfth century. The debate was heated in fifteenth-century Italy because of the encounter between Sephardic and Italian kabbalists after the expulsion from Spain and the rise of Christian kabbalah. For an instructive list of definitions of "true kabbalah," see J. S. Penkover, "New Considerations Concerning *Sefer Massoreth ha-Massoret* by Elia Levita" [Hebrew], *Italia* 3 (1989): 7–73.

76. Brian Vickers, "Analogy Versus Identity: The Rejection of Occult Symbolism, 1580–1680," in his *Occult and Scientific Mentalities in the Renaissance* (Cambridge: Cambridge University Press, 1984), 95–153, esp. 105–109.

77. On Abulafia's conception of language see Moshe Idel, *Language, Torah, and Hermeneutics in Abraham Abulafia* (Albany: State University of New York Press, 1989), 1–28. On the origins of this approach to the Hebrew language, consult idem. *Golem: Jewish Magical and Mystical Traditions on the Artificial Anthropoid* (Albany: State University of New York Press, 1990).

78. On Yagel's indebtedness to Alemanno, see David B. Ruderman, *Kabbalah,*

Magic and Science: The Cultural Universe of a Sixteenth-Century Jewish Physician (Cambridge: Harvard University Press, 1988), passim.

79. For an excellent new biography of Almosnino, consult Meir Zvi Bnaya, *Mosheh Almosnino of Salonika: His Life and Work* (Ramat Aviv: Tel Aviv University, 1996). In addition to the commentary on the Ethics the following works of Almosnino will be cited: *Ma'ametz Koah* (Venice, 1532); *Pirqei Mosheh* (Salonika, 1563 reprinted Jerusalem: Machon Torah Shelemah, 1970); *Tefilah le-Mosheh* (Salonika, 1563); *Yedei Moshe* (Jerusalem: Machon le-Ḥeqer Yahadut Saloniqi, 1986).

80. For a detailed exposition of this cultural renewal, see my essay cited in n. 1 above.

81. Almosnino's commentary on the *Ethics* is extant in a single manuscript, MS Oxford-Bodleian Michael 409 (Nuebauer 1435). The extant manuscript is incomplete. It consists of Almosnino's commentary on books I, II and X of the *Ethics*, but reference therein and in other extant works by Almosnino indicate that the original commentary covered all ten books of the *Ethics*. While modern scholars have known about this manuscript, no one has, to my knowledge, studied it in depth.

82. Joseph Ibn Shem Tov's commentary is cited in almost every other page of *Penei Mosheh*. However, Almosnino often debates with Ibn Shem Tov's rendering of Aristotle's original text or his understanding of Aristotle's original intent because Almosnino consulted other translations and commentaries on the *Ethics*. The translation of the *Ethics* by Alguades with the commentary of Joseph Ibn Shem Tov was also cited by Solomon Almoli (*Sha`ar Adonai he-Ḥadash* pp. 20a-b). Ibn Shem Tov's commentary was the major source for the knowledge of the *Ethics* among Sephardic scholars in Salonika during the sixteenth century.

83. About 1485 Baruch ibn Yaish composed a new translation and commentary on the *Ethics* that relied on both Bruni's and Argryropoulos' translations. The translation is extant in three manuscripts. MS Paris Heb. 1001; 1002; 1003, that have not been studied so far. It is very possible that the translation was occasioned by the first printed edition of Aristotle's *Organon* with the *Ethics* in 1483, edited by Nicoletto Vernia.

One intriguing question about this text concerns its place of composition. In the colophon of MS. Paris Heb. 1001 we read as follows: "I, Samuel bar Solomon of Tortosa, translated this text (*he`etaqtiv*) and wrote down what I heard from my master, R. Baruch ibn Yaish, may God bless and sustain him. And I completed it (*vehishlamtiv*) in the town of Benevento in the year [5]285." The statement is somewhat ambiguous. It is not clear if both master and student were together in Benevento, Italy (where both the translation and commentary on the *Ethics* were done), or whether Samuel bar Solomon studied with Baruch ibn Yaish in Spain (perhaps in Tortosa) and only completed the writing of the commentary in Benevento, Italy. Given the spread of Italian humanism in Spain during the 1480s, it is not inconceivable that ibn Yaish had access to the translations of Bruni and Argyropoulos already in Spain. If so, more attention should be given to the impact of humanism on Sephardic Jewish thought prior to the expulsion from Spain, especially given the role of *conversos* in the dissemination of humanist scholarship in Spain. And if ibn Yaish's translation and commentary were produced entirely in Italy, it would support the claim (expressed by Arthur Lesley and other scholars, myself included) that there were Jewish humanists in Italy already in the 1480s. See Hava Tirosh-Rothschild, "In Defense of Jewish Humanism," *Jewish History* 3 (1988): 31–57.

Almosnino considered ibn Yaish's translation superior to the one produced by Meir Alguades. He therefore referred to it quite often and debated with Joseph ibn Shem Tov on the basis of ibn Yaish's rendering of the text. For example, fols. 14b, 31b, 33b–34a, 41b, 71a, 103b.

84. See Ullrich Langer, "Aristotle Commentary and Ethical Behaviour: Bernado Segni on Friendship between Unequals," in *Philosophy in the Sixteenth and Seventeenth Centuries: Conversations with Aristotle*, ed. Constance Blackwell and Sachiko Kusukawa (Aldershot: Ashgate, 1999), 107–25.

85. Eustratius was a twelfth-century Byzantine commentator whose commentary on Aristotle's *Ethics* was suffused with Platonic and Neoplatonic themes. Almosnino refers to this commentary in *Penei Mosheh,* fol. 105v, but it is not clear whether he had access to the original or whether he knew it through commentaries of the late Christian scholastics, especially Walter Burley and John Buridan.

86. *Penei Mosheh,* fol. 40b.

87. Gerald Odo (or Geraldus Ododins) was the Minister General of the Dominican Order in the first decades of the fourteenth century. Almosnino refers to him as "*odo ha-komer*" in *Penei Mosheh* fol. 24r, where he states that he consulted his commentary on the *Ethics.* The commentary is entitled *Expositio in Aristotelis Ethicam* and was published in 1500 in Venice. On the manuscripts of this text, see Charles H. Lohr, "Medieval Latin Aristotle's Commentaries: Authors G-I," *Traditio* 24 (1968): 149–245, esp. 163–64. Odo's views were incorporated into Jean Buridan's commentary on the *Ethics* from which Almosnino copied extensively. On Buridan's indebtedness to Odo see James J. Walsh, "Some Relationships between Gerald Odo's and John Buridan's Commentaries on Aristotle's 'Ethics,'" *Franciscan Studies* 35 (1975): 237–75.

88. Jean Buridan, the French philosopher and scientist, studied philosophy at Paris with William Ockham and remained there as a member of the arts faculty and twice as its rector. His *Commentary on the Ethics (Questiones super decem libros Ethicorum Aristotelis ad Nicomachum)* was published in Paris in 1489 and again in 1513. Buridan viewed the science of ethics as practical science in the strong sense of the word. For Buridan ethics is the productive science of goodness. Identifying the knowledge of ethics with prudence, Buridan regarded ethics to be closely related to rhetoric, which he called the *logica moralis*. In accordance with the Ockhamist demarcation between reason and faith, Buridan sharply distinguished between theology and ethics. Theology is the only science that directs human action toward its eternal goal; through revelation, theology grasps this goal "in detail." Ethics, on the other hand, concerns goodness in this world alone. The science of ethics pertains to

the free man, a theme Buridan culled from his consultation of Seneca's moral philosophy and whose *Letters to Lucilius* were frequently cited in Buridan's commentary on the *Ethics*.

Buridan's approach to ethics inspired several fifteenth-century Italian humanists as much as it recommended itself to Moses Almosnino. In *Penei Mosheh*, Almosnino cites Buridan's work in fols. 32v, 105v–106v, 146r–151v and follows Buridan's position on the interplay between the will and the intellect in the road to happiness. Buridan's influence accounts in part for the frequent references to Seneca as well as the nexus between rationality, virtue, and freedom in the writings of Almosnino and his younger contemporary Solomon ben Isaac Halevi.

89. Almosnino refers to "Burleo" in his commentary in *Penei Mosheh*, fol. 105v. Walter Burley, the liberal arts professor at Merton College, Oxford, composed his *Expositio Gualteri Burley super decem libros Ethicorum Aristotelis* between 1333–1345. For a discussion of Burley's moral philosophy, see G. Gomes, "Foundations of Ethics in Walter Burleigh's *Commentary on Aristotle's Nicomachean Ethics*" (Ph.D. diss., Columbia University, 1973).

90. In *Penei Mosheh*, fol. 40v Almosnino refers to commentary on the *Ethics* by "*fabro he-hacham.*" This is the famous French humanist Faber Stapulensis Jacobus (1460–1536), whose commentary on the *Ethics* illustrates the so-called "humanist Aristotelianism" in which humanist philological methods were used to reinterpret the Aristotelian text in order to show that it is compatible with the teachings of the early Church, especially St. Paul's. Lefevre edited patristic texts and launched a major research program on the Bible. He wrote commentaries on the Psalms, the Epistles of Paul, and the Gospels, along with commentaries on Aristotle and works on mathematics. Lefevre's "reform" of Aristotelianism was occasioned by his encounter with Italian humanists during the early 1480s. For a general overview of Lefevre d'Etaples' intellectual and literary activities, see Eugene F. Rice, ed., *The Prefatory Epistles of Jacques Lefevre d'Etaples and Related Texts* (New York: Columbia University Press, 1972), xi–xxv, and for bibliographical information about his commentary on Aristotle, consult 548; Gerhard Kessler, "Introducing Aristotle to the Sixteenth Century: The Lefevre Enterprise," in *Philosophy in the Sixteenth and Seventeenth Centuries*, 1–21.

91. Moses Almosnino mentions specifically Nifo's *Commentary on Aristotle's Physics* in *Penei Moshe*, fol. 144a. Agostino Nifo (1469/70–1538) was a student of Nicoletto Vernia at the University of Padua during the 1490s. Nifo succeeded to Vernia's chair after his death in 1499 and became involved in the famous controversy on the immortality of the soul occasioned by the publication of Pietro Pomponazzi's *De Immortalitate animae* (1516). Although Nifo began his career as a convinced Averroist who supported the doctrine of the unity of the intellect, he changed his views in his *De Intellectu* (1497), in which he attacked Averroes and Alexander for denying personal immortality. Nifo did not write a commentary on the *Ethics* but discussed the problem of human happiness in his *De immortalite animae*, written to refute Pompanazzi's *Tractatus de immortalite animae*. For an excel-

lent study of the academic controversy on the nature of the human soul and the end of human life, see Martin L. Pine, *Pietro Pomponazzi: Radical Philosopher of the Renaissance* (Padua: Editrice Antenore, 1986) and the bibliography cited there. The academic debates in Italian academe were well known to Jewish scholars in Italy such as Obadia Sforno, Abraham de Balmes, and Jacob Mantino. Jewish scholars were intimately involved with the translation and publication of Aristotelian-Averroean corpora during the early decades of the sixteenth century. See Edward Kranz, "Editions of the Latin Aristotle Accompanied with the Commentaries of Averroes," in *Philosophy and Humanism: Renaissance Essays in Honor of Paul Oscar Kristeller*, ed. Edward P. Mahoney (New York: Columbia University Press, 1976), 116–28. On Nifo's direct influence on Obadia Sforno see Reuben Bonfil, "The Doctrine of the Soul and Holiness in the Teachings of Obadia Sforno" [Hebrew], *Eshel Beer Sheva* 1 (1976): 200–257.

The academic controversy on the nature of the soul and the immortality of the personal soul reverberates in the writings of Jewish philosophers in Salonika during the second half of the sixteenth century.

92. See John O'Brien, "Translation, Philology and Polemics in Denys Lambin's *Nicomachean Ethics* of 1558," *Renaissance Studies* vol. 3 (no. 3) (1989): 267–89.

93. On the moral training of Sephardic Jews in the Ottoman Empire consult Joseph Hacker, "Intellectual Activity of the Jews of the Ottoman Empire during the Sixteenth and Seventeenth Centuries," in *Jewish Thought in the Seventeenth Century* (Cambridge: Harvard University Press, 1987), 111–12, n. 34. The institutionalization of moral training reflects a community obsessed with the pursuit of moral perfection.

94. Relevant commentaries on Tractate Avot include Isaac Abravanel, *Nahalat Abot* (New York, 1953), Moses Almosnino, *Pirqei Mosheh* (first printing Salonika, 1563; Jerusalem: Machon Torah Shlemah, 1970); Solomon ben Isaac Halevi, *Lev Avot* (Salonika, 1565).

95. On the basis of the *Ethics* III:6–V:9, Almosnino discusses the moral virtues: courage, temperance, liberality, magnificence, magnanimity, humility, patience, affability, truth, and friendliness. The inclusion of humility is an interesting departure from the original discussion of Aristotle. It indicates how much Aristotle was transformed in the late Middle Ages by centuries of religious interpretations.

96. The numerous references to the *Ethics* are no surprise, given the status of this text in the writings of fifteenth century thinkers in Spain. Isaac Arama's *Aqedat Yitzhaq*, in particular, was extremely popular among the exiles, and its attitude toward the *Ethics* was shared by other Sephardic intellectuals.

97. See, for example, Almosnino, *Yedei Mosheh*, 248. Almosnino joined Alemanno in reading the Bible as a biography of virtuous men. On this trend in Renaissance Jewish writings see Arthur Lesley, "Hebrew Humanism in Italy: The Case of Biography," *Prooftext* 2 (1982): 163–77.

98. Beginning with Petrarch, Renaissance Jewish thinkers exalted the poetic excellence of King David as matching that of the Greek and Roman poets. See James

L. Kugel, *The Idea of Biblical Poetry: Parallelism and Its History* (New Haven and London: Yale University Press, 1981), 212–18. Thus, while the Jewish preoccupation with the Psalms was primarily for their ethical content, indirectly, they also insisted on the Jewishness of the greatest poet.

99. Moses Almosnino refers to "*kat ha-istoicos*" (i.e., the Stoics) in *Penei Mosheh* fol. 144a but he mentions Cicero and Seneca by name a good number of times. See Almosnino, *Tefillah le-Mosheh,* 9b; 23b–24a; idem, *Pirqei Mosheh,* 235; *Penei Mosheh,* fol. 14v, 16v, 32v, 129v. It was the impact of Stoicism that accounts for the thematic novelty in the philosophic discourse on happiness in the post-expulsion period. Two elements in particular—the association of happiness with freedom (*ḥerut*) and the central role of suffering in the acquisition of moral virtue—reflect the indebtedness of Jewish scholars to Stoicism. So far scholars of Jewish ethics in the sixteenth century have tended to focus on the ethical literature of Safed, Italy, and Eastern Europe, leaving unexplored the moral philosophy discussed in this paper. See Dan, *Hebrew Ethical and Homiletical Literature,* 175–229; Mordecai Pachter, "The Homiletical and Ethical Literature of Safed's Scholars in the Sixteenth Century and its Major Ideas" (Ph.D. diss., Hebrew University 1976).

100. See Almosnino, *Penei Mosheh,* fol. 172b; *Yedei Mosheh,* 85.

101. This text was printed in Salonika in 1564. It is written in Spanish with a Hebrew summary of the chapters' contents. A Hebrew translation of a few pages from the introduction is available in Simha Assaf, ed., *Meqorot le-Toledot ha-Ḥinnukh* (Tel Aviv: Dvir, 1954), vol. 3, 11–14. Prof. John Zemke has prepared a critical edition of the text to be published soon by the Arizona Center of Medieval and Renaissance Studies at Arizona State University. His introduction includes a detailed chronology of Almosnino's life and a summary of the Hebrew introduction. I thank the center for allowing me to consult this edition prior to publication.

102. In *Lev Avot,* 59b Solomon ben Isaac Halevi states that "*Sefer ha-Zohar* was composed one thousand and two hundred years ago." The emphasis on the antiquity of the *Zohar* reflects both Halevi's attempt to refute charges that it was but a medieval innovation (expressed, for example, by Judah Messer Leon) as well as the impact of humanist historiography.

103. In accordance with the Aristotelian tradition, Almosnino understood the duality of matter and form in genderized categories: form (*tzurah*) relates to matter (*ḥomer*) as the male relates to the female respectively. See, for example, Almosnino, *Tefilah le-Mosheh,* 26a, 35a. Almosnino and other contemporaries departed from the rationalist tradition by placing more emphasis on the human will. In turn, this led them to include women in the community of those who can attain personal immortality even though their intellect could never reach perfection.

104. Almosnino, *Tefilah le-Mosheh,* 10b; *Pirqei Mosheh,* 70; *Penei Mosheh,* fols. 47r, 96r. The notion that the soul is "carved" from under the Seat of Glory is *Tiqqunei Zohar,* Tiqqun 22, 65b.

105. See Almosnino, *Tefilah le-Mosheh,* 23b, 34b. The descent of the soul into the body serves a moral purpose: by performing good deeds and acquiring the

knowledge of truths, the soul spiritualizes the body and cleanses herself from the negative impact of the body. The reward for perfection is commensurate with the degree of perfection.

106. Almosnino, *Pirqei Mosheh*, 4; *Penei Mosheh*, fol. 47r.

107. This was Hasdai Crescas' definition of the soul in *Or Adonai* III, 2, 1, which pre-expulsion Sephardic scholars accepted at large. That the soul is an incorporeal substance was held by both Avicenna and Judah Halevi, Crescas' most obvious sources. For a recent analysis of Avicenna's psychology see Goodman, *Avicenna*, 149–83 and the bibliography cited there. For Halevi's conception of the human soul, see Davidson, "The Active Intellect in the *Kuzari*," 363–65. Crescas' definition of the soul was commonly accepted by fifteenth-century scholars in Iberia.

108. Almosnino, *Ma'ametz Koaḥ*, 51b.

109. Almosnino's position is reminiscent of Abraham Bibago's as spelled out in *Derekh Emunah* (Constantinople, 1522).

110. Almosnino, *Tefilah le-Mosheh*, 41 b.

111. Almosnino, *Tefilah le-Mosheh*, 12a. Almosnino perpetuated the Maimonidean notion that the acquisition of moral and intellectual virtues removes the barriers that separate the human and the divine. But if Maimonides viewed the body as a barrier to intellection of abstract truths, Almosnino viewed it as a barrier that prevents the mystical union with God.

112. Almosnino, *Tefilah le-Mosheh*, 26b; *Pirqei Mosheh*, 22.

113. Almosnino, *Pirqei Mosheh*, 70.

114. Already Aristotle (*Ethics* 1138b 30) posited ethics as a science for the healing of the soul as much as medicine is the knowledge necessary for the healing of the body. Maimonides Judaized this view when he attempted to show that the Torah provides the best cure for physical as well as mental illnesses. This view was shared by all subsequent Jewish philosophers who understood the interdependence of physical and mental health.

115. See Almosnino, *Pirqei Mosheh*, 4, 98.

116. Almosnino, *Tefilah le-Mosheh*, 9b.

117. Almosnino's interpretation of Psalm 42 in *Tefilah le-Mosheh* 11a-b is a typical example of this psychological reading of the Psalms, which recaptured the personal mood of these hymns. In contrast to earlier political interpretation of this Psalm, Almosnino interprets its central verse ("As a hind longs for the running streams, so I long for you, my God") as a metaphor for the yearning of the soul to free herself from exile in the body.

118. Almosnino, *Pirqei Mosheh*, 114; *Tefilah le-Mosheh*, 7b.

119. See Almosnino, *Tefilah le-Mosheh*, 33a-b; 34a.

120. Almosnino, *Penei Mosheh*, fol. 20v.

121. See, for example, *Tefilah le-Mosheh*, 23b; 24a-b, 33a-b; *Pirqei Mosheh*, 235; *Penei Mosheh*, fol. 172v.

122. In *Tefilah le-Mosheh*, 23b, Almosnino adopts the notion that the virtue of patience (*savlanut*) is one of the prerequisites for happiness, an idea that is not

found in the teaching of Aristotle and is quite close to Stoic teachings on equanimity. The doctrine of equanimity, of course, was not the monopoly of the Stoics. It was commonly taught by the Sufis and entered Jewish philosophy and kabbalah through the influential teachings of al-Ghazali. See Moshe Idel, "Hitbodedut as Concentration in Ecstatic Kabbalah," in his *Studies in Ecstatic Kabbalah* (Albany: SUNY Press, 1988), 103–69.

123. Almosnino, *Tefilah le-Mosheh*, 51b.

124. On Abulafia's psychological interpretation of the messianic idea see Idel, "Patterns of Redemptive Activity," 275–78.

125. The notion that rationality is the source of human freedom was of course the hallmark of Greek philosophy, especially in Stoic philosophy. See Shlomo Pines, "The Historical Evolution of a Certain Concept of Freedom," in *Between Theory and Practice: Essays in Honour of Nathan Rotenstreich,* ed. Yirmiyahu Yovel and Paul Mendes-Flohr (Jerusalem: Magnes Press, 1984), 254–55.

126. In accord with Abraham ibn Ezra and the Jewish Neoplatonists of the late fourteenth century and in contrast to Maimonides, post-expulsion thinkers took the science of astrology very seriously as a scientific tool for the understanding of natural causality. However, the entire gist of the discourse on happiness was to show that Israel can transcend nature because it is endowed with a divine soul and has received the grace of divine revelation. Jews who live by the Torah do not fall under natural determinism since they are governed by God directly. See, for example, Almosnino, *Tefilah le-Mosheh*, 54b.

A major source for the knowledge of astral determinism in sixteenth-century Salonika was Shem Tov ibn Shaprut's *Even Bohan*. On this text and its contribution to the study of astrology in Iberia, see Dov Schwartz, "The Theology of Shem Tov ibn Shaprut," in *The Life and Thought of Shem Tov ibn Shaprut* by Norman E. Frimer and Dov Schwartz (Jerusalem: Machon Ben Tzvi and the Hebrew University, 1992), 139–48.

127. Almosnino, *Tefilah le-Mosheh*, 48a, 51b.

128. Ibid. 36a.

129. It is safe to say that during the fifteenth century Maimonidean philosophers were open to the intellectualism of Thomas Aquinas for the same reason that they defended Maimonides against Crescas. In the sixteenth century, however, when Jewish scholars were more ready to incorporate Crescas' critique of Maimonides, they turned to Duns Scotus and the Franciscan theologians who highlighted the centrality of the will in the pursuit of perfection. The scholarship on Aquinas' intellectualism and Scotus' voluntarism is voluminous. For a short summary, consult Patrick Lee, "The Relation between Intellect and Will in Free Choice according to Aquinas and Scotus," *The Thomist* 49 (1985): 321–42.

130. The most extensive analysis of the interplay between the intellect and the will is in *Penei Mosheh,* book X, chap. 8. Almosnino presented a short popular summary of that philosophical discourse in his *Tefilah le-Mosheh*, 57b.

131. Almosnino, *Pirqei Mosheh*, 37. For the scholastic background of this

viewpoint, consult Bonnie Kent, "The Good Will according to Geraldus Odonis, Duns Scotus, and William of Ockham," *Franciscan Studies* 46 (1986): 119–39.

132. Almosnino, *Tefilah le-Mosheh*, 21b; *Penei Mosheh*, fol. 4v. Though Almosnino presents this view as the correct reading of Maimonides, it is in fact a marked departure from the teachings of the "master."

133. Aristotle (*Ethics* VIIII: 2, 3), as we stated in Chapter One, positied three types of love, or friendship (*philia*): love of the pleasant, love of the useful, and love of the honorable (or noble). The gist of his analysis was to show that human happiness requires life in a community of morally perfect individuals who are united by the love of the honorable, the good that is desired for its own sake. Maimonides took over this distinction in his *Eight Chapters* and stated that the love of God is the love of the noble and that it is commensurate with the knowledge of God.

Maimonides' reduction of love into knowledge yielded little discussion of the meaning of love in Jewish philosophy of the thirteenth and fourteenth centuries. But Crescas' critique of Maimonides in *Or Adonai,* as we noted in the previous chapter, changed that by making the love of God the highest religious value. During the fifteenth century Sephardic scholars such as Joseph Albo, Joel ibn Shuaib, and Joseph Hayyun followed in Crescas' footsteps to focus on the meaning of love within the framework of Aristotelian philosophy. That tradition reached its culmination in the most systematic analysis of love—Judah Abravanel's *Dialoghi d'Amore.* Following Joel ibn Shuaib, Almosnino suggests that Aristotle's analysis of love can be subsumed into two categories already known to the rabbis in Tractate Avot. Love of the pleasant and the useful are "conditional love" (*ahavah teluyah ba-davar*) and only love of the good is "unconditional love." To love God is to love Him unconditionally for the sake of the good.

134. *Penei Mosheh*, fol. 47r. Almosnino's portrayal of Man as an intermediary being between angels and beasts bears very close resemblance to Pico Della Mirandola's famous oration "On the Dignity of Man" in *The Renaissance Philosophy of Man,* ed. Ernest Cassirer et al. (Chicago: University of Chicago Press, 1948), 223–254.

135. Almosnino, *Penei Mosheh*, fols. 146v–149v. Almosnino's argumentation relies heavily on Jean Buridan's.

136. See Almosnino, *Penei Mosheh*, fol. 148r. This distinction is derived from Buridan. See James J. Walsh, "Teleology in the Ethics of Buridan," *Journal of the History of Philosophy* 18 (1980); 265–86.

137. Medieval Jewish thinkers—philosophers and kabbalists—used the term *hitbodedut* to mean either solitude and seclusion or mental concentration and meditation on God. The two meanings were often intertwined since for most Jewish thinkers, the latter depended on the former. That fusion reflects the influence of Sufism on Judaism and entered Jewish philosophy through the writings of ibn Bajja and ibn Tuafyl. See Idel, "Hitbodedut as Concentration in Ecstatic Kabbalah," 103–40. The thinkers discussed in this article employed the term *hitbodedut* to

denote mental concentration that can be attained within the social order through contemplation of Torah and performance of good deeds toward others.

138. Almosnino, *Penei Mosheh*, fol. 148r.

139. Almosnino, *Tefilah le-Mosheh*, 57b. Not surprisingly, Almosnino continues to think about the psychological make-up of human beings in genderized categories. Yet instead of talking about the intellect and the body as male and female respectively, Almosnino here discusses the intellect and the will as male and female. The "feminization" of the will is understandable given the association of the will with the body and with the practical, moral life.

140. *Penei Mosheh*, fol. 149r.

141. Almosnino, *Tefilah le-Mosheh*, 56a; *Penei Mosheh*, fol. fol. 149v; *Ma'ametz Koah*, 17b.

142. The idea that the man of prudence is the ideal man originated in Seneca, one of Johan Buridan's major sources of moral philosophy. Almosnino thus "Judaizes" moral ideals that were very common among the late Christian scholastics. On Buridan's dependence on Seneca, see James J. Walsh, "Buridan and Seneca," *Journal of the History of Ideas* 27 (1966): 23–40.

143. *Penei Mosheh*, fol. 120v. In his commentary to Book VI of the *Ethics* (no longer extant in the single manuscript), Almosnino apparently provided a full-fledged philosophical analysis of the virtue of prudence. His position can be reconstructed from the numerous (though not entirely philosophical) references to prudence in his biblical commentaries.

144. Almosnino, *Pirqei Mosheh*, 154; Cf., *Penei Mosheh*, fol. 149r–151r, where Almosnino offers a subtle analysis of love as perfection of the will and prudence.

145. Almosnino, *Yedei Mosheh*, 8b, 20b.

146. See Moses Almosnino, *Tefilah le-Mosheh*, 24a; 57a; *Penei Mosheh*, fol. 20v.

147. Almosnino, *Penei Mosheh*, fol. 149r; *Pirqei Mosheh*, 45.

148. Almosnino, *Pirqei Mosheh*, 67; 154.

149. Almosnino, *Ma'ametz Koah*, 6b.

150. See Almosnino *Ma'ametz Koah*, 216a.

151. I suspect that the fact that women such as Dona Gracia Nasi were patronesses of Jewish learning had more to do with this new appreciation of their religious merits than anything else. Almosnino's eulogies for Dona Gracia Nasi and for the wife of Meir Arama printed in *Ma'ametz Koah* bear witness to the new public respect accorded to women.

Notes to Postscript

1. For an overview of this literature see Joseph Dan, *Jewish Mysticism and Jewish Ethics* (Seattle: University of Washington Press, 1986), 76–118. For a sample of representative primary sources in an English translation consult Lawrence Fine, *Safed Spirituality* (Mahwah NJ: Paulist Press, 1986).

2. For an English translation of this influential text consult Louis Jacobs, trans.,

Rabbi Moses Cordovero: The Palm Tree of Deborah (New York: Sepher-Hermon Press, 1974). A summary and analysis of the text are provided in the Introduction, 9–45. For a detailed discussion of Cordovero's moral theory in the broader context of his mystical theology see Bracha Sack, *The Kabbalah of Rabbi Moshe Cordovero* (in Hebrew) (Jerusalem: Bialik Institute, 1995), 214–29.

3. Sack, ibid. 29. For an English translation of these ethical rules see Fine, *Safed Spirituality*, 34–38.

4. The Literature on Spinoza's biblical criticism is extensive. Very useful are Steven B. Smith, *Spinoza, Liberalism and the Question of Jewish Identity* (New Haven: Yale University Press, 1997); J. Samuel Preus, *Spinoza and the Irrelevance of Biblical Authority* (Cambridge: Cambridge University Press, 2001).

5. Seymour Feldman, "Spinoza" in *History of Jewish Philosophy*, 621.

6. On the literary activities of Isaac Satanow, see Moshe Pelli, *The Age of the Haskalah: Studies in Hebrew Literature of the Enlightenment in Germany* (Leiden: E.J.Brill, 1979), 151–70. Significantly, Satanow composed *Mishlei Asaf* (Proverbs of Asaf), which imitated biblical Wisdom literature, discussed in Chapter Two, as well as the medieval collections by Samuel ibn Naghrella, Ben Mishlei, and Ben Qohelet, discussed in Chapter Four.

7. Samson Raphael Hirsch, *The Nineteen Letters on Judaism* (New York: Feldheim Publishers, 1959), 27.

Bibliographic Essay

The following bibliographical essay provides an overview of the themes treated in this study and indicates the type of scholarly literature that shaped my approach to the subject. The sources in the bibliographical essay only partially overlap with the texts cited in the notes.

Preface:
To date, there is no comprehensive study of the concept of happiness in Judaism, although several aspects of the topic have been well researched. The most pertinent studies that cover happiness in medieval Jewish philosophy are Erwin I.J. Rosenthal, "The Concept of '*Eudaimonia*' in Medieval Islamic and Jewish Philosophy," in his *Studia Semitica*, vol. 2 (Cambridge: Cambridge University Press, 1971), 127–44 and Norman Roth, "Attaining 'Happiness' (*Eudaimonia*) in Medieval Muslim and Jewish Philosophy," *Centerpoint* 4 (1981): 21–32. It is instructive to compare these studies to Michael Fishbane, "The Inwardness of Joy in Jewish Spirituality," in *In Pursuit of Happiness*, ed. Leroy S. Rouner (Notre Dame, Ind.: University of Notre Dame Press, 1995), 71–88. Whereas the first two studies define happiness as an objective state of affairs of human flourishing, Fishbane approaches it as a subjective state of mind, or a mental attitude, and argues that in Judaism happiness is captured by the value of joy (*simhah*). These differences must not lead one to think that joy is an authentic Jewish value, whereas happiness is borrowed from Greek philosophy and imposed on Judaism by medieval Jewish philosophers. The present study argues that from its emergence, Judaism understood happiness as an objective state of affairs of human flourishing available to those who adhere to the life of Torah. Joy is an expression of human flourishing. For a thoughtful but non-academic reflection on happiness by a contemporary Jewish thinker, see Dennis Prager, *Happiness is a Serious Problem: A Human Nature Repair Manual* (New York: Regan Books for HarperCollins Publishers, 1998). Prager resonates with many elements of the Aristotelian tradition (e.g., the notion that happiness should be understood in terms of purpose and that the purpose must relate to human nature). However, for Prager human nature is often an obstacle to happiness: to be happy we must not only understand human nature correctly but also curb it.

For a philosophical discussion of the concept of happiness, see V.J. McGill, *The Idea of Happiness* (New York: Frederick A. Praeger, 1967); Wladyslaw Tatarkiewicz, *Analysis of Happiness* (The Hague: Martinus Nijhoff, 1976); David J. Depew, *The Greeks and the Good Life* (Fullerton CA: California State University of Fullerton and Indianapolis: Hacket, 1983); Elizabeth Telfer, *Happiness* (New York: St. Martin Press, 1980); Ninian Smart, "What is Happiness," in *The Good Life and Its Pursuit*, ed. Jude P. Dougherty (New York: Paragon House, 1984); Jonathan Lear,

Happiness, Death, and the Remainder of Life (Cambridge, MA: Harvard University Press, 2000). An interesting discussion of happiness by social scientists can be found in Vincent Brummer and Marcel Sarot (eds.), *Happiness, Well-Being and the Meaning of Life: A Dialogue of Social Science and Religion* (Kampen: The Netherlands: Kok Pharos Publishing House, 1996).

In ancient moral philosophy, the well-being of the individual, i.e., happiness, was predicated on the quality of the individual's character. Only the one who possesses the good character, the one who acquires the virtues, can enjoy well-being. For overviews of virtue ethics in light of alternative ethical theories, consult Burton F. Porter, *The Good Life: Alternatives in Ethics* (Lanham MD: Rowman and Littlefield, 2001). For an examination of various aspects of virtue ethics, see Robert B. Kruschwitz, *The Virtues: Contemporary Essays on Moral Character* (Belmont CA: Wadsworth Publishing Co., 1987); Michael Slote, *From Morality to Virtue* (Oxford and New York: Oxford University Press, 1992); Daniel Statman (ed.), *Virtue Ethics: A Critical Reader* (Washington DC: Georgetown University Press, 1995); Roger Crisp (ed.) *How Should One Live: Essays on the Virtues* (Oxford: Clarendon Press, 1996); Roger Crisp and Michael Slote (eds.) *Virtue Ethics* (Oxford: Oxford University Press, 1997); David Carr and Jan Steutel, *Virtue Ethics and Moral Education* (London and New York: Routledge, 1999).

Contemporary ethicists have paid relatively little attention to virtue ethics in Judaism because of the assumption that halakhah is the only source of morality in Judaism. The most sustained analysis of virtue ethics in traditional Judaism is Walter Wurzburger, *Ethics of Responsibility: Pluralistic Approaches to Covenantal Ethics* (Philadelphia: Jewish Publication Society, 1994). Wurzburger argues that Jewish law includes a virtue ethics derived from the commandment of *imitatio Dei* (Deut. 28:9). For a review of the book, see David Shatz, "Beyond Obedience: Walter Wurzburger's *Ethics of Responsibility*," *Tradition* 30 (2) (1996): 74–95. For a further elaboration of Wurzburger's approach with additional support from Jewish sources, see Yitzchak Blau, "The Implications of Jewish Virtue Ethics," *The Torah U-Madda Journal* 9 (2000): 19–41. For a recent attempt to reframe the discussion about the relationship between law and ethics in Judaism, consult Louis E. Newman, "Ethics as Law, Law as Religion: Reflections on the Problem of Law and Ethics in Judaism," in *Contemporary Jewish Ethics and Morality*, ed. Elliot N. Dorff and Louis E. Newman (New York: Oxford University Press, 1995), 79–93, reprinted in his *Past Imperatives: Studies in the History and Theory of Jewish Ethics* (Albany NY: State University of New York Press, 1998), 45–62.

Chapter One:
Useful overviews of Greek and Hellenistic moral philosophy are to be found in William J. Prior, *Virtue and Knowledge: An Introduction to Ancient Greek Ethics* (London and New York: Routledge, 1991); Julia Annas, *The Morality of Happiness* (New York: Oxford University Press, 1993); Joseph Bryant, *Moral Codes and Social*

Structure in Ancient Greece: A Sociology of Greek Ethics from Homer to the Epicureans and Stoics (Albany: State University of New Press, 1998).

Aristotle, in his *Nicomachean Ethics* and the *Eudemian Ethics,* was the first philosopher to provide a systematic analysis of the concept of happiness (*eudaimonia*). For a close study of the relationship between these two texts, consult Anthony Kenny, *The Aristotelian Ethics: A Study of the Relationship between the Eudemian and Nicomachean Ethics of Aristotle* (Oxford and New York: Clarendon Press, 1978). Our study focuses on the *Nicomachean Ethics* and ignores the subtle differences between these two texts—as well as the complex textual problems in establishing the correct text of the *Nicomachean Ethics.*

There are several English translations of the *Nicomachean Ethics.* Our study consulted the translation of David William Ross as revised by J.L. Ackrill and J.O. Urmson (Oxford and New York: Oxford University Press, 1980). An earlier version of this revised translation by J.O. Urmson alone is included in Jonathan Barnes (ed.), *The Complete Works of Aristotle: The Revised Oxford Translation* (Princeton: Princeton University Press, 1984). For other translations of the *Ethics,* consult J.A.K. Thomson (trans.), *The Ethics of Aristotle: The Nicomachean Ethics,* revised with notes and appendices by Hugh Tredennick with introduction and bibliography by Jonathan Barnes (London and New York: Penguin Books, 1976); Terence Irwin (trans.) *Nicomachean Ethics* (Indianapolis: Hacket, 1999 [1993]); Christopher Rowe (trans.), *Aristotle's Nicomachean Ethics* (with historical introduction by Christopher Rowe and philosophical introduction and commentary by Sarah Broadie) (Oxford and New York: Oxford University Press, 2002).

For discussion of Aristotle's ethics in the context of his philosophy, consult W.D. Ross, *Aristotle* (London: Methuen and New York: Barnes and Noble, 1966 [1923]); J.L. Ackrill, *Aristotle the Philosopher* (Oxford and New York: Oxford University Press, 1981); Abraham Edel, *Aristotle and His Philosophy* (Chapel Hill, NC: University of North Carolina Press, 1982); Jonathan Lear, *The Desire to Understand* (Cambridge and New York: Cambridge University Press, 1988); Jonathan Barnes (ed.), *The Cambridge Companion to Aristotle* (Cambridge and New York: Cambridge University Press, 1995).

For detailed studies of Aristotle's ethics, consult John M. Cooper, *Reason and Human Good in Aristotle* (Cambridge Mass.: Harvard University Press, 1975); Amelie Oxenberg Rorty (ed.), *Essays on Aristotle's Ethics* (Berkeley: University of California Press, 1980); W. F. R. Hardie, *Aristotle's Ethical Theory,* 2nd ed. (Oxford: Clarendon Press, 1989); Richard Kraut, *Aristotle on the Human Good* (Princeton: Princeton University Press, 1989); Sarah Broadie, *Ethics with Aristotle* (Oxford: Oxford University Press, 1991); and Anthony Kenny, *Aristotle on the Perfect Life* (Oxford: Clarendon Press and New York: Oxford University Press, 1992).

At the center of Aristotle's analysis of happiness stands the cultivation of character through the acquisition of moral and intellectual virtues. An excellent study of the fashioning of the good character according to Aristotle is Nancy Sherman, *The Fabric of Character: Aristotle's Theory of Virtue* (Oxford: Clarendon Press, 1989). For studies on the connection between virtue, knowledge, and character, see Ellen Frankel Paul, Fred D. Miller Jr., and Jeffrey Paul (eds.), *The Good Life and the Human Good* (Cambridge and New York: Cambridge University Press, 1992).

Systematic reflections about the meaning of happiness and the good life in the Hellenistic world were all rooted in the legacy of Aristotle, even if they were thought to be an alternative to Aristotle. For analysis of Hellenistic philosophical schools, consult the studies of Barnes and Annas cited above as well as Martha Nussbaum, *The Therapy of Desire: Theory and Practice in Hellenistic Ethics* (Princeton: Princeton University Press, 1994); R. W. Sharples, *Stoics, Epicureans and Sceptics: An Introduction to Hellenistic Philosophy* (London and New York: Routledge, 1996); Malcolm Schofield and Gisela Striker (eds.), *The Norms of Nature: Studies in Hellenistic Ethics* (Cambridge and New York: Cambridge University Press; Paris: Editions de la Maison des sciences de l'homme, 1986); and Gisela Striker (ed.), *Essays on Hellenist Epistemology and Ethics* (Cambridge: Cambridge University Press, 1996).

Chapter Two:
The Bible speaks in many voices about the human condition, and, therefore, it is impossible to generalize about the biblical conception of happiness. In the epic tradition, happiness is associated with prosperity, longevity, and receiving divine blessing. In the legal tradition the well-lived life is linked more specifically to observing God's commands, including the command to rejoice before God on specific occasions. On the value of joy in ancient Israelite religion, see Gary A. Anderson, *A Time to Mourn, a Time to Dance: The Expression of Grief and Joy in Israelite Religion* (University Park, PA: Pennsylvania University Press, 1991). In the Wisdom stratum of the Bible, human flourishing is predicated on the training of character, the cultivation of specific virtues, and the acquisition of prudential knowledge. The beginning of theoretical reflections on the meaning of human happiness is the Wisdom stratum, especially the Book of Proverbs, which manifests the emergence of a new human ideal in ancient Israel—the sage. For an excellent discussion of the various conceptions of the ideally wise man in the ancient Near East, the Bible, and post-biblical literature, see John G. Gammie and Leo G. Perdue (eds.), *The Sage in Israel and the Ancient Near East* (Winona Lake, IN: Eisenbrauns, 1990).

Seminal studies on the Wisdom tradition in ancient Israel include: Gerhard von Rad, *Wisdom in Israel*, trans. James D. Marton (London, S.C.M. Press, 1972); John G. Gammie (et al), *Israelite Wisdom: Theological and Literary Essays in Honor of Samuel Terrien* (Atlanta: Scholars Press, 1978); James Crenshaw, *Old Testament Wisdom: An Introduction* (Atlanta: John Knox Press, 1981); idem. *Urgent Advice and Probing Questions: Collected Writings on Old Testament Wisdom* (Macon, GA: Mercer University Press, 1995); Stuart Weeks, *Early Israelite Wisdom* (Oxford: Clarendon Press, New York: Oxford University Press, 1994); and John Day Robert Gordon and H.G.M. Williamson (eds.), *Wisdom in Ancient Israel: Essays in Honor of J.A. Emerton*, (Cambridge: Cambridge University Press, 1995).

The ideal of Wisdom is expressed most fully in the Book of Proverbs. For recent commentaries, consult William McKane, *Proverbs, A New Approach* (Philadelphia, Westminster Press, 1979); Richard J. Clifford, *Proverbs: A Commentary* (Louisville: Westminster John Knox Press, 1999). For analysis of the themes of Proverbs, see Eldon Woodcock, *Proverbs: A Topical Study* (Grand Rapids: Zondervan, 1988). For discussion of the ideal of Wisdom in Proverbs see R. N. Whybray, *Wisdom in Proverbs: The Concept of Wisdom in Proverbs 1–9* (Naperville IL: Allec R. Allenson, 1965). For an overview of modern approaches to the book of Proverbs, consult R. N. Whybray, *The Book of Proverbs: A Survey of Modern Study* (Leiden and New York: Brill, 1995).

The ideal of Wisdom in Proverbs has a clear gender identity, since Wisdom was imaged as a female. The present study excluded a systematic discussion of the gender dimension of the pursuit of happiness because I intend to devote a separate study to it, focusing on medieval commentaries on Proverbs. For now, consult Bernhard Lang, *Wisdom and the Book of Proverbs: A Hebrew Goddess Redefined* (New York: Pilgrim Press, 1968); Claudia V. Camp, *Wisdom and the Feminine in the Book of Proverbs* (Decatur, GA: Almond Press, 1985); and Athalya Brenner (ed.), *A Feminist Companion to Wisdom Literature* (Sheffield: Sheffield Academic Press, 1995).

The Wisdom ideal was expressed poetically in the so-called "Wisdom Psalms." For major studies on the Psalms, consult Sigmund Mowinckle, *The Psalms in Israel's Worship*, 2 vols. (Oxford: Basil Blackwell, 1962); Leopold Sabourin, *The Psalms: Their Origin and Meaning* (New York: Alba House, 1974); Kenneth G. Hoglund (ed. et al), *The Listening Heart: Essays in Wisdom and the Psalms in Honor of Roland E. Murphy* (Sheffield: Journal for the Study of the Old Testament Press, 1987); William L. Holladay, *The Psalms through Three Thousand Years: A Prayerbook of a Cloud of Witnesses* (Minneapolis: Fortress Press, 1993); and Nahum Sarna, *The Book of Psalms: Exploring the Prayers of Ancient Israel* (New York: Schocken, 1993). For a commentary on the Psalms, see Hans-Joachim Kraus, *Psalms 1–59: A Commentary*, trans. Hilton C. Oswald (Minneapolis: Augsburg, 1988); idem. *Psalms 60–150: A Commentary*, trans. Hilton C. Oswald (Minneapolis, Augsburg, 1989).

At some point in the Second Temple period the notion that the Torah is the peculiar Wisdom of Israel came into being when the Old Wisdom tradition was fused with the covenantal theology of the Book of Deuteronomy. On the fusion of Wisdom and Law in ancient Israel, see Leo G. Perdue, *Wisdom and Cult: A Critical Analysis of the Views of Cult in the Wisdom Literatures of Israel and the Ancient Near East* (Missoula, Mont.: Scholars Press for the Society of Biblical Literature, 1977); Joseph Blenkinsopp, *Wisdom and Law in the Old Testament: The Ordering of Life in Israel and Early Judaism* (London and New York: Oxford University Press, 1983; 1995); Donn F. Morgan, *Wisdom in the Old Testament Tradition* (Atlanta: John Knox Press, 1981); and Gerald T. Sheppard, *Wisdom as a Hermeneutical Construct: A Study in the Sapientializing of the Old Testament* (Berlin and New York: W. de Gruyter, 1980).

The fusion of Torah and Wisdom was firmly in place during the Hellenistic period, reflecting, at least to some extent, the impact of Hellenism. For overviews of the complex relationship between Judaism and Hellenism, consult Samuel Sanders, "Hellenism and Judaism," in *Great Confrontations in Jewish History*, ed. Stanley M. Wagner and Allen D. Breck (Denver: University of Denver Press, 1977), 21–38; Lee I. Levine, *Judaism and Hellenism in Antiquity: Conflict or Confluence* (Seattle and London: University of Washington Press, 1998). Among the main contributions to modern scholarship on the topic are the following studies: Saul Lieberman, *Hellenism in Jewish Palestine* (New York: Jewish Theological Seminary of America, 1950); idem. "How Much Greek in Jewish Palestine?" in *Studies and Texts, vol. I: Biblical and Other Studies*, ed. Alexander Altmann (Cambridge, Mass.: Harvard University Press, 1963), 123–41; Martin Hengel, *Judaism and Hellenism: Studies in Their Encounter in Palestine during the Early Hellenistic Period*, 2 vols. (Philadelphia: Fortress Press, 1974); John J. Collins, *Between Athens and Jerusalem* (New York: Crossroad, 1983); and Elias Bickerman, *The Jews in the Greek Age* (Cambridge Mass and London: Harvard University Press, 1988).

The Wisdom of Ben Sira (Ecclesiasticus) is a major example of the identification of Torah and Wisdom in the Second Temple period. For a new translation of Ben Sira, consult Patrick W. Skehan, *The Wisdom of Ben Sira: A New Translation*, with notes and introduction and commentary by Alexander A. Di Lella (New York: Doubleday, 1987). For analysis of Ben Sira in the larger context of Hellenistic culture, see John J. Collins, *Jewish Wisdom in the Hellenistic Age* (Louisville, KY.: Westminster John Knox Press, 1997). For discussion of Ben Sira and the context of Egyptian Wisdom tradition, see Jack T. Sanders, *Ben Sira and Demotic Wisdom* (Chico, CA: Scholars Press, 1983). The anonymous *Wisdom of Solomon* was another important Jewish text from the Hellenistic period in which we find the fusion of Torah and Wisdom. For analysis of the work, see David Winston (trans.), *The Wisdom of Solomon: With Introduction and Commentary* (Garden City, NY: Doubleday, 1979).

Philo of Alexandria was the most important and most prolific Jewish philosopher in the Hellenistic period. For a bibliography of the vast field of Philonic studies, consult David T. Runia (ed.), *Philo of Alexandria: An Annotated Bibliography 1937–1986* (Leiden: Vigiliae Christianae Supplements 8, 1992 [1988])); idem. *Philo of Alexandria: An Annotated Bibliography, 1987–1996* (Leiden and Boston: Brill, 2000). The best overview of Philo's philosophy is still Harry A. Wolfson, *Philo: Foundations of Religious Philosophy in Judaism, Christianity, and Islam* (Cambridge, MA: Harvard University Press 1982 [1968]). For a study of Philo in the context of Jewish culture in Alexandria, consult Ronald Williamson, *Jews in the Hellenistic World: Philo* (Cambridge: Cambridge University Press, 1989). On Philo's approach to biblical interpretation, see David Dawson, *Allegorical Readers and Cultural Revision in Ancient Alexandria* (Berkeley: University of California Press, 1992). On the absorption of Philo into the history of the Christian Church, see David T. Runia, *Philo in Early Christian Literature* (Assen: Van Gorcum and Minneapolis: Fortress Press, 1993); idem. *Philo and the Church Fathers: A Collection of Papers*

(Leiden and New York: E.J. Brill, 1995). For a portrayal of Philo as part of a distinctive Greek-speaking diaspora Judaism, see Peder Borgen, *Philo, John and Paul: New Perspectives on Judaism and Early Christianity* (Atlanta: Scholars Press, 1987). For a succinct discussion of the Judeo-Hellenistic philosophic sources, see David Winston, "Hellenistic Jewish Philosophy," in *History of Jewish Philosophy*, ed. Daniel H. Frank and Oliver Leaman (London and New York: Routledge, 1997), 38–61.

Chapter Three:
As a distinct social and intellectual movement, rabbinic Judaism was a response to the destruction of the Second Temple in 70 C.E., even though the religious outlook of the rabbis was rooted in the teachings of the Pharisees prior to the fall of the Temple. For a good summary of the modern scholarship on the Pharisees, consult Anthony Saldarini, "Pharisees," *Anchor Bible Dictionary*, David Noel Freedman, editor-in-chief (New York: Doubleday, 1992), vol. 5, 289–303. On the relationship between rabbinic Judaism and Pharisaism, consult Jakob J. Petuchowski, *Heirs of the Pharisees* (New York: Basic Books, 1970); Alexander Guttmann, *Rabbinic Judaism in the Making: A Chapter in the History of Halakhah from Ezra to Judah I* (Detroit: Wayne State University Press, 1970); Jacob Neusner, *The Rabbinic Traditions about the Pharisees before 70*, 5 vols. (Leiden: E.J. Brill, 1971); idem. *From Politics to Piety: The Emergence of Pharisaic Judaism* 2nd ed. (New York: Ktav, 1979); Shaye J.D. Cohen, *From the Maccabees to the Mishnah* (Philadelphia: Westminster, 1987); and Lawrence H. Schiffman, *From Text to Tradition: A History of Second Temple and Rabbinic Judaism* (Hoboken NJ: Ktav, 1991).

The rabbis after 70 C.E. constituted an intellectual elite marked by privileges, rhetorical practices, and deportment. For reconstruction of the rabbinic estate in Roman Palestine, see Lee I. Levine, *The Rabbinic Class of Roman Palestine in Late Antiquity* (Jerusalem: Yad Yitzhak ben Zvi and New York: Jewish Theological Seminary, 1989); Catherine Hezser, *The Social Structure of the Rabbinic Movement in Roman Palestine* (Tubingen: Mohr Siebeck, 1997). For a lively depiction of the rabbinic class in Babylonia, focusing on the function of the rabbis as holy men, see Jacob Neusner, *There We Sat Down: Talmudic Judaism in the Making* (New York: Ktav, 1978). The educational practices of the rabbis are analyzed in David M. Goodblatt, *Rabbinic Instruction in Sassanian Babylonia* (Leiden, The Netherlands: E.J. Brill, 1975).

The rabbis elaborated the Pharisaic ideology of dual Torah and presented Torah study as the comprehensive ideal of Jewish religious life in a world devoid of Temple. The rabbinic conception ideal of dual Torahs is best analyzed by Jacob Neusner. A good example is his *The Oral Torah: The Sacred Books of Judaism, An Introduction* (San Francisco: Harper & Row, 1986); and *From Testament to Torah: An Introduction to Judaism in Its Formative Age* (Englewood Cliffs, NJ: Prentice Hall, 1988).

While the rabbis posited the life of Torah as the happiest life, the rabbinic ethos had much in common with the social ideals and moral values of non-Jewish philosophical schools in the Greco-Roman world, especially Stoicism and Epicureanism. This line of inquiry is indebted to Henry A. Fischel, *Rabbinic Literature and Greco-Roman Philosophy: A Study of Epicurea and Rhetorica in Early Midrashic Writings* (Leiden: Brill, 1973). Like their Hellenistic and Roman counterparts, the rabbis put the training of character at the center of their experience of the happy life of Torah. Recently two doctoral dissertations have recognized the centrality of virtue ethics in rabbinic Judaism. See Jonathan Schoffer, "The Making of a Sage: The Rabbinic Ethics of Abot de Rabbi Natan" (Ph.D. dissertation, The University of Chicago, 2001). This study is now being prepared for publication under the title *The Shaping of Desire: Rabbinic Ethics in Late Antiquity* (Philadelphia: University of Pennsylvania Press, forthcoming); Dov Nelkin, "Recovering Jewish Virtue Ethics" (Ph.D. dissertation, University of Virginia, 2003).

The main sources of rabbinic virtue ethics are Tractate Avot (Chapters of the Fathers) and its kindred text, Abot de Rabbi Nathan (The Fathers according to R. Nathan), not included in the Mishnah. An English translation of Tractate Avot is available in Herbert Danby (trans.), *The Mishnah* (London: Oxford University Press, 1974 [1933]) and Jacob Neusner, *The Mishnah: A New Translation* (New Haven: Yale University Press, 1988). Abot de Rabbi Nathan is available in two versions, A and B. For an English translation of version A, consult Judah Goldin, *The Fathers according to Rabbi Nathan* (New Haven: Yale University Press, 1955); Jacob Neusner, *The Fathers According to Rabbi Nathan: An Analytic Translation and Explanation* (Atlanta: Scholars Press, 1986). Version B is available in English translation of Anthony J. Saldarini, *The Fathers According to Rabbi Nathan (Abot de rabbi Nathan): Version B* (Leiden: E.J. Brill, 1975). For analysis of the text in the context of the social ethos of the rabbinic academy see Anthony J. Saldarini, *Scholastic Rabbinism: A Literary Study of the Fathers according to Rabbi Nathan* (Chico CA: Scholars Press, 1982).

The virtue ethics of the rabbis, known as the *derekh eretz* tradition, continued to flourish in the talmudic period and was consolidated in the anthologies Seder Eliyahu Rabba and Zuta and in several small tractates in the Talmud. The best analysis of this strain in rabbinic lore are the studies of Max Kadushin: *The Theology of Seder Eliahu: A Study in Organic Thinking* (New York: Bloch, 1932); idem. *Organic Thinking: A Study in Rabbinic Thought* (New York: Jewish Theological Seminary 1938;); idem. *The Rabbinic Mind* (New York, Bloch Publishing Company, 1972). Kadushin's analysis of rabbinic thought was itself an exercise in constructive Jewish philosophy, since its analytical categories were based on the pragmatic philosophy of Charles S. Pierce. For a recent analysis of Kadushin's method and his contribution to the scholarship on rabbinic Judaism, see Peter Ochs (ed.), *Understanding the Rabbinic Mind: Essays on the Hermeneutics of Max Kadushin* (Atlanta: Scholars Press, 1990). For other attempts to systematize the rabbinic worldview, including its ethical outlook, see George Foot Moore, *Judaism in the First Centuries of the Christian Era: The Ages of the Tannaim* (Cambridge Mass.: Harvard University Press, 1966 [1927–30]); Efraim Elimelech Urbach, *The Sages: Their*

Concepts and Beliefs, trans. Israel Abraham (Cambridge Mass.: Harvard University Press 1987 [1979]).

Chapter Four:
For an overview of medieval Muslim philosophy—its main schools, thinkers, and texts—consult the essays in Seyyed Hossein Nasr and Oliver Leaman (eds.) *History of Islamic Philosophy* 2 vols. (London and New York: Routledge, 1996) and the bibliography in each chapter. Other standard surveys include W. Montgomery Watt, *Islamic Philosophy and Theology: An Extended Survey* (Edinburgh: Edinburgh University Press, 1985); Majid Fakhry, *A History of Islamic Philosophy*, 2nd ed. (New York: Columbia University Press and Longman, 1983 [1970]); Oliver Leaman, *An Introduction to Classical Islamic Philosophy* (Cambridge and New York: Cambridge University Press, 2002).

Following Aristotle's classification of science, medieval Islamic philosophers viewed ethics as part of the science of politics and, more broadly, as part of practical philosophy. Accordingly, in Islam the discourse on happiness belonged properly to political theory. For overviews of political theories in Islam, consult W. Montgomery Watt, *Islamic Political Thought: The Basic Concepts* (Edinburgh: Edinburgh University Press, 1968); Franz Rosenthal, *Greek Philosophy in the Arab World: A Collection of Essays* (Aldershot, Hampshire: Variorum and Brookfield, VA: Gower Publishing, 1990); Erwin I. J. Rosenthal, *Political Thought in Medieval Islam: An Introductory Outline* (Cambridge: Cambridge University Press, 1958; idem. *Studia Semitica*, vol. 1 "Jewish Themes;" vol 2, "Islamic Themes" (Cambridge: Cambridge University Press); idem, *Judaism, Philosophy, Culture: Selected Studies by E.I.J. Rosenthal*, with introduction by Oliver Leaman (Richmond, England: Curzon, 2001). For a more recent work that situates medieval political theories in the broader context of Islamic political thought, see Anthony Black, *The History of Islamic Political Thought: From the Prophet to the Present* (New York: Routledge, 2001). For a detailed study of "science of character" in Islam, see Majid Fakhry, *Ethical Theories in Islam* (Leiden and New York: E.J. Brill, 1991).

Medieval Jewish philosophy developed through intimate conversation with Islamic theology and philosophy. General overviews of medieval Jewish philosophy are Isaac Husik, *A History of Mediaeval Jewish Philosophy* (New York: Atheneum, 1966 [1916]); Julius Guttmann, *Philosophies of Judaism: The History of Jewish Philosophy from Biblical Times to Franz Rosenzweig*, trans. David W. Silverman with introduction by R. J. Z. Werblowsky (New York: Holt, Reinhart and Winston, 1964); and Colette Sirat, *A History of Jewish Philosophy in the Middle Ages* (Cambridge: Cambridge University Press and Paris: Editions de la maison des sciences de l'homme, 1985). Unlike the first two surveys, Sirat's book has an extended and useful bibliography that covers modern scholarship up to the early 1980s. As a reference book, Sirat's work is now superseded by the excellent *History of Jewish Philosophy*, ed. Daniel H. Frank and Oliver Leaman (London and New York: Routledge, 1997). This volume contains essays on main intellectual trends and outstanding Jewish philosophers, situated in the proper socio-cultural context. Each chapter has a bibliography of primary and secondary sources that supplements the material in Sirat's work.

Medieval Jewish philosophy emerged in response to the challenge of scholastic theology known as *Kalam*. The most systematic presentation of Kalam's doctrines is Harry A. Wolfson, *The Philosophy of the Kalam* (Cambridge, MA: Harvard University Press, 1976). On the impact of Kalam theology on Jewish religion, consult idem. *Repercussions of the Kalam in Jewish Philosophy* (Cambridge, MA.: Harvard University Press, 1979). Kalam theology influenced the rationalist critique of Karaism as much as it gave rise to the rabbinic response to Karaism. For an overview of the Jewish Kalam of both Karaite and Rabbanite variants, see Haggai Ben Shammai, "Kalam in Medieval Jewish Philosophy," in *History of Jewish Philosophy*, 115–48.

The main rabbanite Kalam thinker was Saadia Gaon. The best intellectual biography is still Henry Malter, *Saadia Gaon: His Life and Works* (Philadelphia: Jewish Publication Society of America, 1921; reprinted Hildesheim New York: G. Olms, 1978). Scholarly essays about Saadia's Gaon's literary legacy and religious philosophy are available in several anthologies. See Erwin I.J. Rosenthal, *Saadia Studies* (Manchester: Manchester University Press, 1943); Louis Finkelstein (ed.), *Rab Saadia Gaon: Studies in his Honor* (New York: Jewish Theological Seminary of America, 1944; Boaz Cohen (ed.) *Saadia Anniversary Volume* (New York: American Academy for Jewish Research, 1943); Steven T. Katz (ed.) *Saadia Gaon* (New York: Arno Press, 1980).

Like its Islamic counterpart, Jewish philosophical ethics in the Middle Ages developed in the context of *adab* culture. *Adab* was the program that enabled the semi-nomadic desert Arabs to integrate themselves into the urban and urbane culture of the Near East. In the Abbasid Empire, *adab* was the educational program and social ethos cultivated by civil servants who administered the empire and managed its court. The program consisted of vast knowledge of topics culled from diverse Hellenistic anecdotal, philosophic, and scientific sources. On *adab* culture in medieval Islam, see Marshall Hodgson, *The Venture of Islam: Conscience and History in a World Civilization* (Chicago and London: University of Chicago Press, 1974), vol. 1, 444–72.

The *adab* program was adopted by Jewish men who entered the administration of the Muslim state, especially in Andalusia. For a very readable account of Jewish history in Muslim Spain and a discussion of the courtier culture, see Jane S. Gerber, *The Jews of Spain: A History of the Sephardic Experience* (New York: The Free Press, 1992), 60–89. The standard history of the Jews in Muslim Spain is Eliyahu Ashtor, *The Jews of Moslem Spain*, 3. vols., trans. Aaron Klein and Jenny Machlowitz Klein (Philadelphia: Jewish Publication Society of American, 1973–1984). The standard history of Jews in Christian Spain is Yitzhaq F. Baer, *The Jews in Christian Spain*, 2 vols. trans. Louis Schoffman (Philadelphia: the Jewish Publication Society, 1978). The culture of the Jewish courtiers in Muslim Spain is presented most beautifully in

Ross Brann, *The Compunctious Poet: Cultural Ambiguity and Hebrew Poetry in Muslim Spain* (Baltimore: Johns Hopkins University Press, 1991). For a sample of Hebrew secular poetry in an English translation and analysis of its relationship to Arabic poetry, consult Raymond P. Scheindlin, *Wine, Women and Death: Medieval Hebrew Poems on the Good Life* (Philadelphia: The Jewish Publication Society, 1986).

Solomon Ibn Gabirol was an example of a Jewish *adib* in Muslim Spain who composed secular and religious poetry, systematic philosophy, and the first Jewish contribution to the science of character. To date, there is no comprehensive study of Gabirol's philosophy in English. For French readers, very useful is Jacques Schlanger, *La philosophie de Salomon ibn Gabirol: Etude d'un neplatonisme* (Leiden: E.J. Brill, 1968), also available in Hebrew. Aspects of Gabirol's metaphysics are discussed by several essays in Lenn E. Goodman (ed.), *Neoplatonism and Jewish Thought* (Albany: State University of New York Press, 1992). Gabirol's ethics still await a systematic study in the context of Arabic *adab* literature and the science of character. For now consult David Rosin, "The Ethics of Solomon ibn Gabirol," *Jewish Quarterly Review* 3 (1891): 159–81. For an English translation of Gabirol's ethical treatise with the original Arabic text, see Stephen S. Wise (trans.), *The Improvement of the Moral Qualities* (New York: Columbia University Press, 1902; reprinted New York: AMS Press, 1966).

A useful summary of the themes of Bahya ibn Pakuda's *Hovot Ha-Levavot* is available in the Introduction of Menachem Mansoor (ed. and trans.), *The Book of Directions of the Duties of the Heart* (London: Routledge & Kegan Paul, 1973). An earlier translation that includes both Hebrew and English text is by Moses Hayim Hyamson (trans.), *Duties of the Heart*, 2 vols. (Jerusalem: Feldheim, 1970). For a most recent translation with a commentary, see Yaakov Feldman (trans.), *Duties of the Heart* (Northvale, NJ: J. Aronson, 1996). For a systematic analysis of Bahya's religious philosophy, see George Vajda, *La Theologie ascetique de Bahya ibn Paquda* (Paris: Chahiers de la Societe Asiatique (1947).

Modern historians of Jewish philosophy regard Solomon Ibn Gabirol, Bahya ibn Paquda, Joseph ibn Zaddik, the anonymous author of *Kitab al Nafs* (attributed to Bahya ibn Paquda), Abraham ibn Ezra, and Judah Halevi as exponents of the Neoplatonic trend in medieval Jewish philosophy. For an overview, see T. M. Rudavsky, "Medieval Jewish Neoplatonism," *History of Jewish Philosophy* ed. Dan H. Frank and Oliver Leaman, 149–87. The term "Neoplatonism," however, is quite misleading since the Arabic sources from which these Jewish philosophers culled their knowledge of philosophy were themselves a fusion of elements from Platonic, Neoplatonic, and Aristotelian sources.

Chapter Five:
The scholarly literature on Maimonides is very extensive indeed. For a bibliography in English, French, German, Italian, Spanish, and Portuguese, see David R. Lachterman, "Maimonidean Studies 1950–1986: A Bibliography," *Maimonidan*

Studies, I (1990): 197–216. For a bibliographical survey of works on Maimonides in Hebrew, consult Haggai ben Shammai, "Maimonidean Studies 1965–90: Hebrew Bibliography," in Arthur Hyman (ed.), *Maimonidean Studies* 2 (1991), 17–42. Other collections of essays on Maimonides in English include: Salo Wittmayer Baron (ed.), *Essays on Maimonides: An Octocentennial Volume* (New York: AMS Press 1966 [1941]); Steven T. Katz (ed.), *Maimonides: Selected Essays* (New York: Arno Press, 1980); Joseph A. Buijs (ed.), *Maimonides: A Collection of Critical Essays* (Notre Dame: University of Notre Dame Press, 1988); Arthur A. Hyman (ed.), *Maimonidean Studies* vol. 1 (1990); vol. 2 (1991); vol. 3 (1992–93) (New York: Yeshivah University Press, 1990–); Shlomo Pines and Yirmiyahu Yovel (eds.), *Maimonides and Philosophy: Papers Presented at the Sixth Jerusalem Philosophical Encounter, May 1985* (Dordrecht and Boston: M. Nijhoff Publishers, 1986); Isadore Twersky (ed.), *Studies in Maimonides*, (Cambridge Mass.: Harvard University Press, 1990); Joel L. Kraemer (ed.), *Perspectives on Maimonides: Philosophical and Historical Studies* (Oxford and New York: Oxford University Press, 1991); Robert Cohen and Hillel Levine (eds.), *Maimonides and the Sciences* (Dordrecht and Boston: Kluwer Academic, 2000).

Maimonides was the most outstanding example of a Jewish philosopher-jurist whose philosophy of law must be understood within the context of Islamic political philosophy. His political thinking was indebted to al-Farabi and represents the Platonic tradition, in which Plato's political teachings in *The Republic* and *The Laws* were fused with Aristotle's *Nicomachean Ethics*. On Maimonides' political theory in the context of the Platonic tradition, see Leo Strauss, *Philosophy and Law*, trans. F. Bauman with a forward by Ralph Lerner (Philadelphia: Jewish Publication Society, 1987); Lawrence Berman, "Maimonides, The Disciple of Alfarabi," *Israel Oriental Studies* 4 (1974): 154–78; idem. "The Ideal State of the Philosophers and the Prophetic Laws," in A *Straight Path: Studies in Medieval Philosophy and Culture in Honor of A. Hyman*, ed. Ruth Link-Salinger (Washington, DC: Catholic University of America Press), 1987), 10–22; Miriam Galston, "Philosopher King vs. Prophet," *Israel Oriental Studies* 8 (1978): 204–18; idem. "The Purpose of the Law according to Maimonides," *Jewish Quarterly Review* 69 (1978–79): 27–51; Lenn E. Goodman," Maimonides Philosophy of Law," *Jewish Law Annual* 1 (1978): 72–107; Howard T. Kreisel, *Maimonides' Political Thought: Studies in Ethics, Law, and the Human Ideal* (Albany: State University of New York Press, 1999); and Abraham Melamed, *The Philosopher-King in Medieval and Renaissance Jewish Thought*, edited with a forward by Lenn E. Goodman (Albany: State University of New York Press, 2003).

The standard English translation of Maimonides' ethical treatises is Raymond L. Wise and Charles E. Butterworth (ed. and trans.), *Ethical Writings of Maimonides* (New York, 1975). The Eight Chapters (i.e., Maimonides' Introduction to the commentary on Tractate Avot in the Mishnah) is also available in a critical edition and English translation by Joseph I. Gorfinkle (New York: AMS Press, 1966). A useful anthology of selections from Maimonides' works, including the Eight Chapters and the Mishneh Torah: Hilkhot Deot (Laws Concerning Character Traits) is available in Isadore Twersky (ed.), *A Maimonides Reader* (New York: Behrman House, 1972).

For an analysis of Maimonides' ethical teaching and especially his reworking of Aristotle's doctrine of the mean, see Raymond L. Weiss, *Maimonides' Ethics: the Encounter of Philosophic and Religious Morality* (Chicago: University of Chicago Press, 1991); Lawrence Berman, "The Ethical Views of Maimonides within the Context of Islamicate Civilization," in *Perspectives on Maimonides*, ed. Joel L. Kraemer (Oxford: Oxford University Press), 13–32; Steven S. Schwarzschild, "Moral Radicalism and 'Middlingness' in the Ethics of Maimonides," *Studies in Medieval Culture* 11 (1977): 65–94; reprinted in *The Pursuit of the Ideal*, ed. Menachem Kellner (Albany: State University of New York Press, 1993); Marvin Fox, "Law and Morality in the Thought of Maimonides," in *Maimonides as Codifier of Jewish Law*, ed. Nahum Rakover (Jerusalem: Library of Jewish Law, 1987); idem. *Interpreting Maimonides: Studies in Methodology, Metaphysics, and Moral Philosophy* (Chicago and London: the University of Chicago Press, 1990); Bezalel Safran, "Maimonides and Aristotle on Ethical Theory," in *Alei Shefer: Studies in the Literature of Jewish Thought*, ed. Moshe Halamish (Ramat Gan, 1990), 75–93.

For a discussion of Maimonides' interpretation of the Garden of Eden narrative, see Lawrence V. Berman, "On the Fall of Man," *AJS Review* 5 (1980): 1–15. The best close reading of the relevant passages in the *Guide* is by Sara Klein-Braslavy, *Maimonides' Interpretation of the Adam Stories in Genesis: A Study of Maimonides' Anthropology* [Hebrew] (Jerusalem: Rubin Mass, 1986). On Maimonides' treatment of the Sabi'un see Salo Baron, "The Historical Outlook of Maimonides," in *History and Jewish Historians*, compiled by Arthur Hertzberg and Leon A. Feldman (Philadelphia: The Jewish Publication Society, 1964), 109–63. On Maimonides' construction of Moses as the ideal philosopher-legislator-prophet, see Kalman P. Bland, "Moses and the Law according to Maimonides," in *Mystics, Philosophers and Politicians: Essays in Jewish Intellectual History in Honor of Alexander Altmann*, ed. Yehuda Reinharz (et al) (Durham, NC: Duke University Press, 1982), 49–66. Maimonides' elaborate parable of the kingly palace has been studied by many, and, therefore, treated relatively cursorily in our study. See Daniel H. Frank, "The End of the Guide: Maimonides on the Best Life for Man," *Judaism* 34 (1985): 485–95; Menachem Kellner, *Maimonides on Human Perfection* (Atlanta: Scholars Press, 1990); Ralph Lerner, "Maimonides' Governance of the Solitary," in *Perspectives on Maimonides*, ed. Joel L. Kraemer, 33–46; Howard Kreisel, "Individual Perfection vs. Communal Welfare and the Problem of Contradictions in Maimonides' Approach to Ethics," *Proceedings of the American Academy for Jewish Research* 58 (1992): 107–41; reprinted in his *Maimonides' Political Thought*, 159–88; Steven Harvey, "Maimonides in the Sultan's Palace," in *Perspectives on Maimonides*, ed. Joel L. Kraemer (Oxford: Oxford University Press, 1991), 47–75.

For studies of Maimonides' naturalistic interpretation of the Messianic Age, see David Hartman, "Maimonides' Approach to Messianism and its Contemporary Implications," *Da'at* 1 (1978): 5–33; Jacob Dienstag (ed.), *Eschatology in Mai-*

monidean Thought: Messianism, Resurrection and the World to Come, Selected Studies (New York: Ktav, 1983) and the bibliography cited there; Joel L. Kraemer, "On Maimonides' Messianic Posture," in *Studies in Medieval Jewish History and Literature* I, ed. Isadore Twersky (Cambridge, MA: Harvard University Press, 1984); Amos Funkenstein, *Maimonides: Nature, History and Messianic Beliefs*, trans. Shmuel Himelstein (Tel Aviv: MOD Books, 1997); idem. "Maimonides' Political Theory and Realistic Messianism," in his *Perception of Jewish History* (Berkeley: University of California Press, 1993), 131–68; Aviezer Ravitzky, "To the Utmost of Human Capacity: Maimonides on the Days of the Messiah," in *Perspectives on Maimonides*, ed. Joel L. Kraemer (Oxford: Oxford University Press, 1991), 221–56.

Chapter Six:
During the 13th century, Jewish philosophy was written by followers of Maimonides, who translated philosophical texts from Arabic into Hebrew, summarized available scientific knowledge, and applied Maimonides' hermeneutical principles to the interpretation of Scriptures. An excellent description of the diffusion of philosophical learning during that century is Marc Saperstein, "The Social Cultural Context: Thirteenth to Fifteenth Centuries," in *History of Jewish Philosophy*, ed. Daniel H. Frank and Oliver Leaman, 294–330. An important venue in the dissemination of philosophical knowledge was the organization of scientific knowledge in encyclopedias. On the classification of scientific knowledge in medieval Judaism, consult Harry A. Wolfson, "The Classification of the Sciences in Medieval Jewish Philosophy in *Studies in the History of Philosophy and Religion*, ed. Isadore Twersky and George H. Williams (Cambridge Mass.: Harvard University Press, 1973), vol. 1, 493–550. For recent studies about these philosophic-scientific encyclopedias, see Steven Harvey (ed.), *The Medieval Hebrew Encyclopedias of Science and Philosophy* (Boston: Kluwer Academic Publishers, 2000).

Shem Tov Falaquera was the most important contributor to the dissemination of Maimonides' Aristotelian philosophy and popularization of his ethical teachings. The definitive study of Shem Tov Falaquera is Raphael Jospe, *Torah and Sophia: The Life and Thought of Shem Tov ibn Falaquera* (Cincinnati: Hebrew Union College Press, 1988). Jospe is the first to note the profoundly misogynist tendencies of Falaquera's intellectualist understanding of happiness. See idem. "Rejecting Moral Virtues as the Ultimate End," in *Studies in Islamic and Judaic Traditions*, ed. William Brinner and S.D. Ricks (Atlanta: Scholars Press, 1986), 185–204.

Maimonides' ideas about human happiness were debated from the end of his life throughout the 13th century and resurfaced periodically in the 15th and 16th centuries because they concerned the core issues of Jewish identity and cultural orientation. For an overview of the Maimonidean controversies during the 13th century, consult Idit Dobbs-Weinstein, "The Maimonidean Controversy," in *History of Jewish Philosophy*, 331–49. For a selection of primary sources from the debate, see Abraham S. Halkin (ed.), *After Maimonides: An Anthology of Writings by His Critics, Defenders, and Commentators* [Hebrew] (Jerusalem: The Zalman Shazar Center,

1979). A more extensive collection of relevant primary sources is available in Ben Zion Dinur, *Israel and the Diaspora: A Documentary History of the Jewish People* [Hebrew], vol. 2, book 4 (Philadelphia: Jewish Publication Society, 1969).

The first phase of the debate concerned Maimonides' alleged denial of the resurrection of the dead. The debate began in the East and then moved to the West. On the debate in East see Sarah Stroumsa, *The Beginnings of the Maimonidean Controversy in the East: Yosef ibn Shimon's Silencing Epistle Concerning the Resurrection of the Dead* [Hebrew] (Jerusalem: Ben Zvi Institute, 1999). For an analysis of the debate in the West, in which R. Meir Halevi Abulafia was the main actor, see Bernard Septimus, *Hispano-Jewish Culture in Transition: The Career and Controversies of Ramah* (Cambridge, MA: Harvard University Press, 1982). The debate about resurrection and the second Maimonidean controversy during the 1230s are discussed in Daniel Jeremy Silver, *Maimonidean Criticism and the Maimonidean Controversy, 1180–1240* (Leiden: E.J. Brill, 1965). A major proponent of the rationalist cause during the second controversy was R. David Kimhi. His activities during the debate are discussed in Frank Talmage, *David Kimhi: The Man and the Commentaries* (Cambridge, MA: Harvard University Press, 1975). On the role of Nahmanides during the debate situated against the social tensions within the Jewish community, consult Bernard Septimus, "Open Rebuke and Concealed Love: Nahmanides and the Andalusian Tradition," in *Rabbi Moses Nahmanides (Ramban): Explorations in His Religious and Literary Virtuosity*, ed. Isadore Twersky (Cambridge, MA: Harvard University Press, 1983), 11–34. The third phase in the late 1280s and early 1290s still awaits a systematic study. On the fourth phase of the debate, which resulted in the ban on the study of philosophy, consult Abraham Halkin, "Why was Levi ben Hayyim Hounded," *Proceedings of the American Academy for Jewish Research* 34 (1966): 65–76; Marc Saperstein, "The Conflict over the Rashba's Herem on Philosophical Study: A Political Perspective," *Jewish History* 1 (2) (1986): 27–38. The astrological dimension of the fourth phase of the controversy is analyzed in Dov Schwartz, "The Debate on Astral Magic in Provence in the Fourteenth Century" [Hebrew] *Zion* 58 (2) (1993): 141–74.

Chapter Seven:
An excellent introduction to kabbalah for readers with no prior exposure to this tradition is David S. Ariel, *The Mystic Quest: An Introduction to Jewish Mysticism* (New York: Schocken, 1988). A more academic study of the main themes of kabbalah is Mosheh Halamish, *An Introduction to the Kabbalah*, trans. Ruth Bar-Ilan and Ora Wiskind-Elper (Albany: State University of New York Press, 1999). The classic modern scholarship on kabbalah is still Gershom Scholem, *Major Trends in Jewish Mysticism*, with introduction by Robert Alter (New York: Schocken, 1995 [1946]). In the past two decades, Scholem's legacy has been subject to rethinking and partial revisions. For an overview, see Peter Schafer and Joseph Dan (eds.), *Gershom Scholem's Major Trends in Jewish Mysticism 50 Years After: Proceedings of the Sixth International Conference on the History of Jewish Mysticism* (Tubingen: Mohr, 1993).

For main rethinking of Scholem's legacy, see Moshe Idel, *Kabbalah: New Perspectives* (New Haven: Yale University Press, 1988); Yehudah Liebes, *Studies in Jewish Myth and Jewish Messianism,* trans. Batya Stein (Albany: State University of New York Press, 1993); idem. *Studies in the Zohar,* trans. Arnold Schwartz, Stephanie Nakache, Penina Peli (Albany: State University of New York Press, 1993); Elliot R. Wolfson, *Through the Speculum that Shines: Vision and Imagination in Medieval Jewish Mysticism* (Princeton: Princeton University Press, 1994). For a succinct overview of medieval kabbalah in continuity with the ecstatic literature of the rabbinic literature, German Pietism, and Jewish philosophy, see idem. "Jewish Mysticism: A Philosophical Overview," in *History of Jewish Philosophy,* ed. Daniel H. Frank and Oliver Leaman, pp. 450–98. That study presents kabbalah as a form of Jewish philosophy, or perhaps even, *the* philosophy of Judaism.

The *Zohar* is the *magnum opus* of 13th-century Spanish kabbalah. The standard English translation of it is by Harry Sperling and Maurice Simon, 5 vols. (London: Soncino Press, 1970 [1954]). The best anthology of Zoharic passages arranged thematically is Isaiah Tishby and Fischel Lachower (eds.), *The Wisdom of the Zohar: An Anthology of Texts,* trans. David Goldstein (London and Washington: The Littman Library of Jewish Civilization, 1991 [1989]). A small selection from the *Zohar* in English translation is available in Daniel C. Matt, *The Zohar: Book of Enlightenment* (Ramsay NJ: Paulist Press, 1983). Matt is now engaged on a new English translation of the entire *Zohar.*

The *Zohar* was most likely a product of a kabbalistic fraternity in Castile. This theory was proposed first by Yehudah Liebes, "How was the Zohar Written?" in his *Studies in the Zohar,* 85–138. For a recent, most useful and readable discussion of the Zoharic corpus, see Pinchas Giller, *Reading the Zohar: The Sacred Text of the Kabbalah* (New York: Oxford University Press, 2001). The printed Zoharic corpus includes two works—*Tiqqunei Zohar* and the *Ra'aya Mehemna*—by an anonymous kabbalist from the early 14th century. For analysis of this stratum of the Zoharic corpus, whose theological views are quite different from the bulk of the *Zohar,* consult Pinchas Giller, *The Enlightened Will Shine: Symbolization and Theurgy in the Later Strata of the Zohar* (Albany: State University Press of New York, 1993).

The most pertinent study of the *Zohar* in terms of human happiness is Elliot R. Wolfson, "Light Through Darkness: The Ideal of Human Perfection in the Zohar," *Harvard Theological Review* 81 (1988): 73–95. Wolfson has been instrumental in unpacking the hermeneutical principles of the Zohar as well as the way gender categories function in the *Zohar.* See, for example, his "Left Contained in the Right: A Study in Zoharic Hermeneutics," *AJS Review* 11 (1986): 27–52; idem. "Woman—the Feminine as Other in Theosophic Kabblah: Some Philosophical Observations on the Divine Androgyne," in *The Other in Jewish Thought and History: Constructions of Jewish Culture and Identity,* ed. Laurence J. Silberstein and Robert L. Cohn (New York: New York University Press, 1994), 166–204; and idem. *Circle in the Square: Studies in the Use of Gender in Kabbalistic Symbolism* (Albany: Statue University of New York Press, 1995).

The literary features of the *Zohar* have been studied by a few scholars. The most illuminative study is by Yehuda Liebes, "The Messiah of the Zohar," in his *Studies in the Zohar*, 1–84. In Hebrew the main contribution to the literary analysis of the Zohar are studies by Michal Oron, "Me-Omanut ha-Derush shel Ba'al Ha-Zohar," *Jerusalem Studies in Jewish Thought* 8 (1989): 299–310; idem. Iyyunim ba-Poetiqa shel Ba'al Ha-Zohar be-Parasht Mishpatim," in *Masu'ut: Studies in Kabbalistic Literature and Jewish Philosophy in Memory of Prof. Ephraim Gottlieb*, ed. Michal Oron and Amos Goldreich (Jerusalem: Bialik Institute, 1994), 1–24. Also useful is Aryeh Wineman (ed. and trans.), *Mystic Tales from the Zohar* (Philadelphia: Jewish Publication Society, 1997). The introductory essay and the notes illuminate the literary features of Zoharic story-telling technique.

To my knowledge there has been no study of the *Zohar* in the context of medieval preaching or medieval theater as I propose in this study. However, the need to interpret the *Zohar* in its Christian context has been recognized by Yehudah Liebes. See "Christian Influences in the Zohar," in his *Studies in the Zohar*, 139–61. Medieval preaching was the main vehicle for the inculcation of virtue ethics to the masses. See Siegfried Wenzel, "Vices, Virtues, and Popular Preaching," in *Medieval and Renaissance Studies*, ed. Dale B.J. Randall (Durham: Duke University, 1976, 28–54; D. L. d'Avray, *The Preaching of the Friars: Sermons Diffused from Paris before 1300* (Oxford: Clarendon Press, 1985); and C. H. Lawrence, *The Friars: The Impact of the Early Mendicant Movement on Western Society* (London and New York: Longman 1994). The portrayal of the protagonist of the *Zohar*, R. Shimon bar Yohai, and his fellow holy men should be studied in the context of medieval hagiographic literature, both oral and written.

Chapter Eight:

In the 14th century, Jewish philosophical activity was carried out primarily in Provence and in Italy. Joseph ibn Kaspi was an important philosopher-commentator who spread the rationalist outlook, his political philosophy, and his adaptation of Aristotle's *Ethics*. On the literary activity and philosophical orientation of Joseph ibn Kaspi, see Isadore Twersky, "Joseph ibn Kaspi: Portrait of a Medieval Jewish Intellectual," in *Studies in Medieval Jewish History and Literature* (Cambridge: Harvard University Press, 1979), 231–57; Barry Mesch, *Studies in Joseph Ibn Caspi: Fourteenth-Century Philosopher and Exegete* (Leiden: Brill, 1975); Basil Herring, *Joseph ibn Kaspi's Gevia' Kesef: A Study in Medieval Jewish Philosophic Bible Commentary* (New York: Ktav, 1983).

The most outstanding Jewish philosopher in the 14th century was Gersonides, who radicalized the intellectual conception of happiness among Jews: happiness means the perfection of the intellect that yields immortality. The scholarship on Gersonides is extensive. Good summaries of his philosophy in the context of the Judeo-Islamic philosophic tradition in the Middle Ages are provided by Gad Freudenthal, "Gersonides: Levi ben Gershom," in *History of Islamic Philosophy*, ed. Seyyed Hossein Nasr and Oliver Leaman (London and New York: Routledge,

1996), vol. 1, 739–54; Seymour Feldman, "Levi ben Gershom (Gersonides)," in *History of Jewish Philosophy*, ed. Daniel H. Frank and Oliver Leaman, 379–414. For collections of essays about various aspects of Gersonides' philosophy and scientific activity, consult Gilbert Dahan (ed.), *Gersonide en son temp* (Louvain-Paris: E. Peters, 1991); Gad Freudenthal (ed.), *Studies on Gersonides: A Fourteenth-Century Jewish Philosopher-Scientist* (Leiden: E.J. Brill, 1992).

For an English translation of Gersonides' main philosophical text, see Seymour Feldman (trans.), *The Wars of the Lord by Levi ben Gershom* (Gersonides), 3 vols. (Philadelphia: Jewish Publication Society, 1984–1999). The astronomical contribution of Gersonides is analyzed by Bernard R. Goldstein (ed. and trans.), *Levi ben Gerson's Prognostication for the Conjunction of 1345* (Independence Square, PA: American Philosophical Society, 1990). Gersonides' *Commentary on the Song of Songs*, the text most pertinent to his conception of happiness, is available in Menachem Kellner (trans.), *Commentary on Song of Songs by Levi Ben Gershom (Gersonides)* (New Haven: Yale University Press, 1998). The most significant study of Gersonides' biblical commentaries is Robert Eisen, *Gersonides on Providence, Covenant, and the Chosen People: A Study in Medieval Jewish Philosophy and Biblical Commentary* (Albany: State University of New York Press, 1995).

On Gersonides' theory of knowledge, which undergirds his notion of happiness as intellectual perfection, see Herbert Davidson, "Gersonides on the Material and Active Intellects," in *Studies in Gersonides: A Fourteenth-Century Jewish Philosopher Scientist*, ed. Gad Freudenthal, 195–265. The connection between Gersonides' cosmology and his notion of intellectual perfection is explored by Gad Freudenthal, "Human Felicity and Astronomy in Gersonides' Revolt against Ptolemy" [Hebrew], *Da`at* 22 (1989): 55–72. Gersonides' non-political notion of happiness is discussed in Menachem Kellner, "Gersonides on Imitatio Dei and the Dissemination of Scientific Knowledge," *Jewish Quarterly Review* 85 (3–4) (1995): 275–96; idem. "Gersonides on the Song of Songs and the Nature of Science," *The Journal of Jewish Thought and Philosophy* 4 (1994): 1–21; idem. "Politics and Perfection: Gersonides vs. Maimonides," *Jewish Political Studies Review* 6 (1–2) (1994): 49–82.

Gersonides' intellectualist conception of happiness brought to the fore the tension between determinism and choice. For an analysis of the relevant issues, consult Charles H. Manekin, "Hebrew Philosophy in the Fourteenth and Fifteenth Centuries: An Overview," in *History of Jewish Philosophy*, ed. Daniel H. Frank and Oliver Leaman, 350–78. These discussions were inseparable from the intensified Jewish-Christian confrontation in the 14th century. On the role Jewish philosophers played in the polemics against Christianity, see Daniel J. Lasker, *Jewish Philosophical Polemics against Christianity in the Middle Ages* (New York: Ktav, 1977). The involvement of Jewish philosophers was necessary because Christian polemicists, many of whom were Jewish converts to Christianity, used scholastic reasoning to debunk rabbinic Judaism. The attack on rabbinic Judaism was championed by the Dominican Order engaged in teaching to lay urban audiences. On the polemical activities of the Dominicans and their involvement in missionizing to Jews in the

13th and 14th centuries, see Jeremy Cohen, *The Friars and the Jews: The Evolution of Medieval Anti-Judaism* (Ithaca and London: Cornell University Press, 1982); Robert Chazan, *Barcelona and Beyond: The Disputation of 1263 and Its Aftermath* (Berkeley: University of California Press, 1992). For an overview of the Jewish-Christian polemics, see Hanne Trautner-Kromann, *Shield and Sword: Jewish Polemics against Christianity and the Christians in France and Spain from 1100–1500*, trans. James Manley (Tubingen: J.C.B. Mohr, 1993). The most philosophically sophisticated anti-Jewish polemicist in the 14th century was Abner of Burgos (alias, Alfonso de Valladolid). On his activities, see Robert Chazan, "Undermining the Jewish Sense of Future: Alfonso of Valladolid and the New Christian Missionizing," in *Christians, Muslims, and Jews in Medieval and Early Modern Spain*, ed. Mark Meyerson and Edward English (Notre Dame: University of Notre Dame Press, 1999), 179–94. To combat Abner's missionizing, Isaac Polleqar published his *Ezer ha-Dat*. An English translation of *Ezer Ha-Dat* is by George S. Belasco (London: J. Jacobs, 1970). This text is still awaiting a literary and philosophical analysis.

The new missionizing to the Jews in Spain was quite successful. In the persecution of 1391, thousands of Jews converted to Christianity, either under duress or by choice. The main philosophical response to the crisis of 1391 was articulated by Hasdai Crescas. For a summary of Crescas' philosophy in light of his anti-Christian polemical activities, see Daniel J. Lasker, "Chasdai Crescas," in *History of Jewish Philosophy*, ed. Daniel H. Frank and Oliver Leaman, 399–414. Crescas' anti-Christian polemical text is available in English in Daniel J. Lasker (ed. and trans), *The Refutation of the Christian Principles by Hasdai Crescas* (Albany: State University of New York Press, 1992). The most systematic analysis of Crescas' critique of Aristotle's physics remains Harry A. Wolfson, *Crescas' Critique of Aristotle* (Cambridge, MA: Harvard University Press, 1929). On the link between Crescas' critique of Aristotle and his critique of Maimonides' conception of happiness, see Warren Z. Harvey, "R. Hasdai Cresacs and His Critique of Philosophical Happiness" [Hebrew], *Proceedings of the Sixth World Congress of Jewish Studies*, vol. 3 (Jerusalem: World Union of Jewish Studies, 1977), 143–49; idem. "Hasdai Crescas' Critique of the Theory of the Acquired Intellect," Ph.D. dissertation (Columbia University, 1973). For a recent study of Crescas' philosophy in light of contemporary scholastic critique of Aristotle's physics, see Warren Z. Harvey, *Physics and Metaphysics in Hasdai Crescas* (Amsterdam: J.C. Gieben, 1998).

Chapter Nine:
Despite Crescas' critique of Aristotle, Jewish philosophers in Spain remained loyal to the Judeo-Arabic Aristotelian tradition throughout the 15th century. Jewish philosophers continued to study Aristotle and began to avail themselves of scholastic commentaries on Aristotle, with a renewed interest in the *Nicomachean Ethics*. The *Ethics* was translated anew by Meir Alguades (1405), and Joseph ibn Shem Tov composed the first full-length Hebrew commentary on the work (1455) as well as

two short commentaries/paraphrases and a systematic reconciliation of Aristotelian ethics with rabbinic Judaism in his *Kevod Elohim*. For overview of the major trends of Jewish philosophy in Spain, Italy and Ottoman Turkey during the 15th and 16th centuries, see Hava Tirosh-Rothschild, "Jewish Philosophy on the Eve of Modernity," *History of Jewish Philosophy*, pp. 499–573. For a discussion of Joseph ibn Shem Tov's literary legacy, consult Shaul Regev, "Theology and Rational Mysticism in the Writings of R. Joseph ben Shem Tov," (Ph.D. dissertation, Hebrew University of Jerusalem, 1983).

Joseph ibn Shem Tov's conception of happiness is deeply indebted to Aquinas. To date, the relationship between Aquinas and Jewish philosophy has focused on the indebtedness of Aquinas to Maimonides. See Jacob I. Dienstag (ed.), *Studies in Maimonides and St. Thomas Aquinas* (New York: Ktav, 1975); David B. Burrell, "Aquinas and Islamic and Jewish Thinkers," in Norman Kretzmann and Eleonore Stump (eds.), *The Cambridge Companion to Aquinas* (Cambridge University Press, 1993), 60–84; Idit Dobbs-Weinstein, *Maimonides and St. Thomas Aquinas on the Limits of Reason* (Albany: State University of New York Press, 1995); Alexander Broadie, "Maimonides and Aquinas," in *History of Jewish Philosophy* ed. Daniel H. Frank and Oliver Leaman, 281–93. By contrast, the impact of Aquinas on Jewish thinkers in the 15th and 16th centuries has not been sufficiently recognized, except in Hava Tirosh-Rothschild, *Between Worlds: The Life and Thought of R. David ben Judah Messer Leon* (Albany: State University of New York Press, 1991).

For analysis of Aquinas' conception of happiness, consult Ralph McInerny, *Ethica Thomistica: The Moral Philosophy of Thomas Aquinas* (Washington DC: The Catholic University of America Press, 1982); Bonnie Kent, *Virtues of the Will: The Transformation of Ethics in the Late Thirteenth Century* (Washington, DC: The Catholic University of America, 1995); Denis J.M. Bradley, *Aquinas on the Twofold Human Good: Reason and Happiness in Aquinas' Moral Science* (Washington, DC: The Catholic University of America Press, 1997); Scott MacDonald and Eleonore Stump (eds.), *Aquinas' Moral Theory: Essays in Honor of Norman Kretzmann* (Ithaca and London: Cornell University Press, 1998); Thomas S. Hibbs, *Virtue's Splendor: Wisdom, Prudence and the Human Good* (Fordham University Press, 2001); and Stephen J. Pope (ed.), *The Ethics of Aquinas*, ed. (Washington DC: Georgetown University Press, 2002).

During the 15th century, Jewish philosophers in Spain and in Italy were informed not only of Christian scholasticism but also of humanism. For excellent overviews of Renaissance humanism, consult William J. Bouwsma, *The Culture of Renaissance Humanism* (Washington: American Historical Association, 1973; published in 1959 and 1966 as *The Interpretation of Renaissance Humanism)*; Donald R. Kelley, *Renaissance Humanism* (Boston: Twayne Publishers 1991); Charles G. Nauert, Jr., *Humanism and the Culture of Renaissance Europe* (Cambridge: Cambridge University Press, 1995). An outstanding overview of the various intellectual strands in Renaissance philosophy is provided in Jill Kraye, "The Philosophy of the Italian Renaissance," in *The Renaissance and Seventeenth-Century Rationalism*, ed.

G. H. R. Parkinson (London and New York: Routledge, 1993), 16–69. An analysis of the interplay between scholasticism and humanism in the Italian Renaissance is available in Paul Oskar Kristeller, *Renaissance Thought and its Sources*, ed. Edward P. Mahoney (New York: Columbia University Press, 1979); Albert Rabil Jr., *Renaissance Humanism: Foundations, Forms, and Legacy* (Philadelphia: University of Pennsylvania Press, 1988); Erika Rummel, *The Humanist-Scholastic Debate in the Renaissance and Reformation* (Cambridge MA: Harvard University Press, 1995).

Aristotle's moral philosophy continued to thrive in the 15th and 16th centuries through new translations of the *Nicomachean Ethics* either from Greek into Latin or from Latin into vernacular languages and through new printed editions. On the proliferation of the *Ethics* in the 16th century, see Charles B. Schmitt, "Aristotle's *Ethics* in the Sixteenth Century: Some Preliminary Considerations," in his *The Aristotelian Tradition and Renaissance Universities* (London: Variorum, 1984), 87–112; Jill Kraye, "Moral Philosophy," in *The Cambridge History of Renaissance Philosophy*, ed. Charles B. Schmitt (et al) (Cambridge: Cambridge University Press, 1988), 303–86; Constance Blackwell and Sachiko Kusukawa (eds.), *Philosophy in the Sixteenth and Seventeenth Centuries: Conversations with Aristotle* (Aldershot: Ashgate, 1999); Charles H. Lohr, "Renaissance Latin Translations of the Greek Commentaries on Aristotle," in Jill Kraye and M.W. F. Stone (eds.), *Humanism and Early Modern Philosophy* (London and New York: Routledge, 2000), 24–40; Edward P. Mahoney, *Two Aristotelians of the Italian Renaissance: Nicoletto Vernia and Agostino Nifo* (Aldershot and Burlingon, VT: Ashgate/Variorum, 2000).

The humanist conception of happiness was an amalgam of themes, manifesting indebtedness to and deviation from medieval scholasticism. See Charles E. Trinkaus, *Adversity's Noblemen: The Italian Humanists on Happiness* (New York: Octagon Books, 1965); idem. *The Scope of Renaissance Humanism* (Ann Arbor: University of Michigan Press, 1983). For a more extensive discussion of the social world of the humanists see idem. *In Our Image and Likeness: Humanity and Divinity in Italian Humanist Thought* (Chicago: University of Chicago Press, 1970).

Yohanan Alemanno is the most important and original Jewish philosopher in Renaissance Italy. The literary legacy of Alemanno still awaits a systematic study. For now, consult Arthur Lesley, "*The Song of Solomon's Ascents* by Yochanan Alemanno: Love and Human Perfection According to a Jewish Colleague of Giovanni Pico" (Ph.D. dissertation University of California, Berkeley, 1976); "Some Observations on Yohanan Alemanno's Political Ideas," in *Studies in Jewish Religious and Intellectual History*, ed. Siegfried Stein and Raphael Loewe (University, Ala., and London: University of Alabama Press, 1979), 247–61; Moshe Idel, "The Study Program of Rabbi Yohanan Alemanno" [Hebrew], *Tarbiz* 48 (1979): 303–30; idem. "The Magical and Neoplatonic Interpretations of the Kabbalah in the Renaissance," in *Jewish Thought in the Sixteenth Century*, ed. Bernard D. Cooperman (Cambridge: Harvard University Press, 1983), 186–242; reprinted in *Essential Papers on Jewish Culture in Renaissance and Baroque Italy*, ed. David B. Ruderman (New York: New York University Press, 1987), 107–69; idem. "The Anthropology of Yochanan Alemanno: Sources and Influences," *Annali di storia dell'esegesi* 7 (1) (1990): 93–111; Abraham Melamed, "The Hebrew Laudatio of Yohanan Alemanno: In Praise of Lorenzo il Magnifico and the Florentine Constitution," in *Jews in Italy: Studies Dedicated to the Memory of U. Cassuto*, ed. Hayim Beinart (Jerusalem: Magnes, 1988), 1–34.

While Jewish thinkers in Italy followed the footsteps of Alemanno, fusing Aristotelianism, Platonism, Hermeticism, and kabbalah, Jewish exiles from Iberia consolidated the Hispano-Jewish philosophical tradition in their new havens in the Ottoman Empire. For a discussion of the expulsion and its impact on Sephardic Jewish intellectual creativity, consult Joseph Hacker, "The Intellectual Activity of the Jews of the Ottoman Empire during the Sixteenth and Seventeenth Centuries," in *Jewish Thought in the Seventeenth Century*, ed. Isadore Twersky and Bernard Septimus (Cambridge, MA: Harvard University Press, 1987), 95–135.

The most prolific and interesting philosopher in 16th century Ottoman Empire was Moses Almosnino. For a reconstruction of his life and communal activities, see Meir Zvi Bnaya, *Moshe Almosnino of Salonika: His Life and Work* [Hebrew] (Ramat Aviv: Tel Aviv University, 1996). A critical edition of Almosnino's popular moral treatise, *Regimiento de la vida y tratado de los suenyos* (Sefer Hanhagat Ha-Hayyim) by John Zemke will be published in the series Medieval and Renaissance Texts and Studies, vol. 255 (Tempe, Arizona: Arizona Center of Medieval and Renaissance Studies, 2003). Almosnino's commentary on Aristotle's *Nicomachean Ethics—Penei Moshe* (The Countenance of Moses) attests to the depth of Jewish knowledge of scholastic and humanist commentaries on the *Ethics*. It still awaits a systematic study.

Postscript:

By the end of the 16th century Jewish Aristotelianism was no longer a creative force, even though its main categories continued to be present in Jewish theological thinking, especially in kabbalah and in the ethical literature. For an overview of the history and trends of Jewish ethical literature, consult Joseph Dan, *Hebrew Homiletical and Ethical Literature* [Hebrew] (Jerusalem: Keter, 1974). Moses Cordovero, who systematized theosophic kabbalah in the post-Expulsion period articulated a kabbalistic virtue ethics that linked a given virtue to a particular sefirah. See Louis Jacobs (trans.), *Rabbi Moses Cordovero: The Palm Tree of Deborah* (New York: Sepher-Hermon Press, 1974). For an overview of kabbalistic ethical literature, consult Joseph Dan, *Jewish Mysticism and Jewish Ethics* (Northvale NJ: J. Aronson, 1996). For a systematic analysis of Moses Cordovero's ethical teaching in the context of his kabbalistic worldview, see Brachah Sack, *The Kabbalah of Rabbi Moshe Cordovero* [Hebrew] (Jerusalem: Bialik Institute, 1995). Cordovero was an important source for the transmission of kabbalistic virtue ethics to the following centuries. See Bracha Sack, "The Influence of Cordovero on Seventeenth Century Jewish Thought," in Isadore Twersky and Bernard Septimus, eds. *Jewish Thought in the Seventeenth Century* (Cambridge, MA: Harvard University Press, 1987), 365–72.

The philosophic discourse on happiness came to an end with the gradual dissolution of the Aristotelian worldview in the 17th century, even though traces of that worldview could be found throughout that century and well into the 18th. The most serious challenge to the premodern identification of Torah and Wisdom in Judaism—and with it to the philosophical discourse on happiness—was articulated by Spinoza. While Spinoza still defined happiness in terms of human flourishing or well-being, he denied that the life of Torah leads to happiness or that life in the perfect polity is the best way to mold the ideal character. For Spinoza, the Bible is neither a revealed text nor does it teach philosophical and scientific truths. Likewise, Spinoza replaced the medieval model of virtue and principles of right action with an internal standard of optimal functioning. Thus his critique of the Bible severed the link between Torah and Wisdom forged in the Second Temple period, and his monistic metaphysics undermined the teleological worldview in place since Aristotle. On Spinoza's biblical criticism, consult Steven B. Smith, *Spinoza, Liberalism and the Question of Jewish Identity* (New Haven: Yale University Press, 1997); J. Samuel Preus, *Spinoza and the Irrelevance of Biblical Authority* (Cambridge and New York: Cambridge University Press, 2001). On Spinoza's ethical theory, which criticized and transformed Aristotle, see Heidi Ravven, "Notes on Spinoza's Critique of Aristotle's *Ethics*: From Teleology to Process Theory," *Philosophy and Theology* 4 (1) (1989): 3–32.

The Aristotelian strain of Jewish virtue ethics and with it the philosophic reflections on human happiness were revived in the Jewish Enlightenment (Haskalah) of the 18th century. In their desire to integrate into European society, the Maskilim took their inspiration from medieval Jewish philosophers, and Isaac Satanow reissued Aristotle's *Nicomachean Ethics* in a new Hebrew translation. For overviews of the Jewish Enlightenment, see David Sorkin, *The Berlin Haskalah and German Religious Thought: Orphans of Knowledge* (London and Portland OR: Vallentine Mitchell, 2000); Shmuel Feiner and David Sorkin (eds.), *New Perspectives on the Haskalah* (London and Portland, OR: Littman Library of Jewish Civilization, 2001). On the activities of Isaac Satanow, see Moshe Peli, *The Age of Haskalah: Studies in Hebrew Literature of the Enlightenment in Germany* (Leiden: E.J. Brill, 1979), 151–70. The return of the Maskilim to Aristotle should be understood in the broader context of the German ideal of *Bildung*—namely, the self-cultivation of moral character through learning of the classics—which permeated the culture of the middle class in 19th century Germany. For Jews the adoption of this program was meant to impart "respectability" (*Sittlichkeit*) and prove that Jews deserved civic rights and social integration. See George L. Mosse, "Between *Bildung* and Respectability," in *The Jewish Response to German Culture: From the Enlightenment to the Second World War*, ed. Jehuda Reinharz and Walter Schatzberg (Hanover and London: University Press of New England, 1985), 1–16. By the 19th century, however, the thinking about human happiness in Europe was shaped not by the legacy of Aristotle but by the philosophy of either Immanuel Kant or John Stuart Mill. The rethinking of Jewish philosophy in light of their philosophies will give rise to new reflections on human happiness and a new debate about the place of happiness within Judaism.

Index

Abba Mari of Lunel, 262, 281–83, 285
Abbasid Empire, 148, 161
Abbasid revolution, 160
Abner of Burgos, 344, 373–77, 380, 389; conversion of, 373
Abrabanel, Judah (Leone Ebreo), 386, 422
Abraham, 93, 128, 140, 200, 221–23; as representation of form, 288
Abraham, Levi ben, 285–86
Abraham, R. Solomon ben, 269, 273–74, 276
Abravanel, Isaac, 391, 410–11
Abravanel, Yitzhaq, 410
Abstinence, 133, 154
Abulafia, Abraham, 278, 292, 412, 419–20, , 430
Abulafia, R. Meir Halevi: *See* Ramah
Academies, rabbinic, 103–5
Acquired intellect: impossibility of, 382–83
Action (*ma'aseh*), 126
Active Intellect, 204, 209–11, 213–14, 235, 353–54, 358–64, 419; created directly by God, 358; Gersonides' analysis of, 357–58; soul of the corporeal world, 358; source of knowledge, 358; *See also* Agent Intellect
Activity (*energia*), 44, 198
Acts, voluntary and involuntary, 29, 457 n 68
Actuality: two senses of, 22
Adab, 150, 559–60; culture, 161–63, 174; literature, 400; prose literature, 168
Adam, 86; primordial sin of, 324
Adam, 214–17, 238

Adib, 161, 171, 560
Afiya, Aaron, 423
Afterlife, 159, 167–68, 182, 188–89, 343, 386, 390; and bliss of eternal life, 404; as focus of discourse on happiness, 348; lack of, 197; Maimonidean conception of, 339; and Torah, 401
Agent Intellect, 359
Aggadic midrashim, 108
Aggadot, talmudic, 272
Agrippa, Cornelius, 422
Al-Farabi, Abu Nasr, 150–51, 208, 252, 278–79, 350, 357, 399, 417; Maimonides debt to, 196–97; and reconciliation of religion and philosophy, 192–94
Al-Ghazali, 193, 252, 350
Al Iqd al-Farid, 165
Al-Kindi, Yaakub, 150
Al-Rahman, abd I, 161
Al-Razi, Abu Bakr, 150
al-Tibb al-Ruhani (Spiritual Physics), 150
Alami, Shlomo, 379
Albert the Great, 398, 424
Albigensians, 301
Albo, Joseph, 391, 410
Alemanno, Yohanan ben Isaac, 397, 412–15, 422, 425, 430, 438
Alexander II, Pope, 248
Alexander of Aphrodisias, 145, 208–9, 279, 350, 359
Alfakar, Judah ben Joseph, 274–76
Alfonso V, 401
Alfonso X, 310, 373
Alguades, R. Meir, 398, 410, 445
Alharizi, Yehudah, 303

"Alien women", 287
Allegory: of the Mosaic Scripture, 95–97
Almohads, 248; persecution by, 297
Almosnino, Moses ben Baruch, 396–97, 423–24, 438, 445
Alphabet, Hebrew, 68
Ambiguity: between inclusive and exclusive views, 45–47; sources of, 195–98
Amoraic sources, 120
Amoraim, 105, 472 n 17
Anatoli, Jacob, 277
Anaxagoras, 39
Andalusian Jews, 248
Angels, 204
Anger, 329
Anthologies, 253
Anti-Christ, 346
Antiochus of Askalon, 106
Antisthenes of Athens, 48
Appetitive function: of the soul, 233
Appetitive power, 279
Aquinas, Thomas, 278–79, 386, 399, 401, 424; commentary on *Ethics*, 398
Aquiva, R., 117
Arama, Isaac, 391, 410–12
Arete, 11
Argyropulus, John, 399, 424
Aristeas, Letter of, 87
Aristobulus, 77–78
Aristotelianism, 47; intellectualism of, 383–84
Aristotle, 3, 77, 87, 96, 116, 119, 122, 124, 145, 194, 251, 278–79; challenges to, 379; commentaries on, 397; conception of happiness, 15–47; and conduct in this world, 404; "great-souled" man of, 128; his analysis of happiness, 196; and his perfection, 197–98; on the Human Good, 14–15; and Judaism, 438; versus Maimonides, 235–37; and Maimonides, agreement between, 237; physics of, 381–82; study of, 273; two conceptions of happiness, 9; and two-substance theory, 208; *See also Nicomachean Ethics*
Arragel, Moshe, 410
Arrogance, 185
Asceticism, 134, 182–83; goal of, 184
Ash'ariah, 146
Ashrei, 55–100, 110, 131, 312; defined, 62; in the *Zohar*, 313–15
Astral magic, 284
Astrology, 366; and happiness, 283; Jewish, 283–86; opposition by Maimonides, 283; question of, 281–83
Astronomy, 262, 352, 355, 366
Astruk, Don: *See* Abba Mari of Lunel
Ataraxia (untroubledness), 49
The Attainment of Happiness, 151
Autonomy: curbing of, 371; Jewish religious, 274, 305; of Jews in Spain, 250
Averroes: *See* Ibn Rushd
Avicenna, 203
Avodah Zarah, 110

Ba'alei ha-kabbalah (masters of the tradition), 298
Babylonian Talmud, 103, 108
Bahir, 295–98
Bahya, 166, 172–78, 297, 311–12, 328–29; intent, 177; life of, 174–75; translation of philosophy into Hebrew, 250
Bahya ben Asher, 309
Balance, 157–59; between body and soul, 153
Ban: of Rashba, 283; requirements for, 282; on study of philosophy, 262, 289; by University of Paris, 273
Banker-merchant, Jewish, 143–44

Bar Kokhba revolt, 103, 117, 136
Barcelona debate, 281, 305
Barukh, 63–64
Bedersi, Yeda'ya, 288
Being, human, 85–87
Ben Mishlei (The Son of Proverbs), 165, 167
Ben Qohelet (The Son of Ecclesiastes), 165, 167
Ben Sira, 73–77, 91, 156
Berman, Lawrence, 258, 399
Bibago, Abraham, 410–11
Bible: as God's autobiography, 297; literal reading of, 289; as a philosophic-scientific text, 351–52; Spinoza's critique of, 443
Bittul Iqqarey ha-Notzrim (Refutation of the Christian Principles), 381, 383
Black Death 1348-50, 348
Blood libels, 346
Body: corporeal, 324; domination by the soul, 429; knowledge of, 180; as an obstacle, 217; as the source of temptation, 86; status of the, 140
Body and soul: interdependence of, 231–34; relationship between, 120, 153, 157, 208, 337–38, 428–29; unity of, 334
Book of Knowledge, 206
Brethren of Purity, 175, 178, 284, 486 n 64, 486 n 66
Bruni, Leonardo of Arezzo, 399, 423
Buridan, Jean, 398, 424
Burley, Walter, 398, 424

Caution, 171
Celestial bodies, 203
Celibacy, 307
Chain of intelligences, 210
Chamber: serfs of the, 346, 552 n 10
Change: as a purposeful process, 202
Character, 23–26, 162; cultivation of, 234–35; defined, 23–24; excellence of, 27; formation of, 25; and friendship, 35; improving, 230
Charity, 436
Charles V, 398
Charters, 345
Chastisements: of love, 136
Children, 156; birth of, 308; sacrifice of, 221
Choice, 373–79; and determinism, 378–79; exercising, 216; habit of, 30; power of, 121; rational, 366; reasoned, 29; voluntary, 367
Choice (*behirah*), 365
Chrisippus, 88
Christ, messiahship of, 344
Christian Aristotelians, 210
Christian-Jewish rivalry, 343–93
Christian life: ideal, 301–2
Christiani, Pablo, 281, 305, 347
Christianity: geographic expansion of, 301; hatred for, 305; as an irrational religion, 377; and Judaism, 343, 432, 441; refuting, 401
Christians, 102–3
Church, involvement of the, 273–74
Cicero, 53, 417
Circumcision: sign of, 330
Civil life, 44–45
Classification of moral agents: *See* Hierarchy of moral agents
Cognition, 154, 157, 359
Comfort, 135
Commandments, 294; divine, 280; performance of the, 382, 387–88; rationales of the, 327; Ten, 94
Commentaries, 299
Commentary on Avot, 235
Commentary on Ecclesiastes, 267
Commentary on the Ethics, 399, 401
Commentary on the Mishnah, 214, 224, 231, 246, 265
Compassion (*middat ha-rahamim*), 130

"Completely good" community, 13
Comprehension, 237
Concentration, 434
Conditioning, moral, 124
Conduct, rabbinic code of, 104
Conflict, 218
Conjunction with God, 419
Contemplation, 37–40, 43–45, 157, 213; definition of, 37–38; of God, 407; and improved quality of life, 45; philosophic, 401
Contentment, 235
Conversion, 347, 383; to Christianity, 416; of Jews, 346; lack of interest in, 372; mass, 348, 395
Conversos, 348, 395–96
Cordoba, 161
Cordovero, Moses ben Jacob, 441–42
Corporeality: transcendence of, 238–44
Cosimo I, 424
Cosmology, 352
Counter-drama, Jewish, 302
Courage, 235; (*andreia*), 89–90; one of cardinal virtues, 13; one of the four cardinal virtues, 80; in Stoicism, 52; virtue of, 120
Court culture, 160–68
Courtier educational program, 174
Courtiers: critique of, 175; Jewish, 185, 328, 397; Jewish, in Muslim Spain, 160–61; Jewish, loss of power, 400
Covenant, the, 111–13, 293; dynamics of, 306
Covenantal theology, 55
Cowardice, in Stoicism, 52
Creation, 70, 158; biblical story of, 352; for the sake of man, 414; and Wisdom, 68–72
Creation Theology, 71–72, 402–4
Creator: and the created, 402; existence of one, 178
Crescas, Hasdai, 344, 349, 401, 405, 432; critique of Aristotelian-Maimonidean paradigm, 381–83; critique of Gersonides' divine law, 384–85; critique of Maimonides' views, 382–83; and Maimonideanism, 379–92; move to voluntarism, 383–88; philosophy of, 388–92; views of, 380

Crisippus, 51
Crusades, 248, 345; First Crusade, 346; against the Muslims, 301
Crying, joyous, 306
Culture: court, 160–68; Jewish, in Provence, 268–70; of Muslim Spain, 248
Curriculum: philosophic, 254–56
Custom, local, 282
Cynicism, 134
The Cynics, 48

Da Piera, Meshulam, 273
Dalalat al-Ha-irin (Guide of the Perplexed): See *Guide of the Perplexed*
Daniel, 253–54
David, 128, 429, 436; poetry of King, 425
David of Dinant, 273
David, R. Abraham ben: See Rabad
De Anima, 22, 38–39, 356
De Caelo et Mundo, 255
De Generatione et Corruptione, 255
Debate: of Polleqar with Abner of Burgos, 373–77; Resurrection, 263; Resurrection, in the West, 264–65
Debates, public, 147, 347, 396
Dedication, 166
Deeds: forbidden, 177; and the soul after death, 340; virtues and good, 123–25
Dehumanization of the Jews, 346
Deliberation and choice, 30
Delmedigo, Elijah, 415–16, 421
Democritus, atomistic physics of, 49

Demonization of the Jews, 346
De'ot, 233
Dependence on royal power, 249
Derekh, 62–63
Derekh Eretz Rabbah, 110
Derekh Eretz Zutta, 110
Desire, 155; control of, 157, 182–83
Desires, 96; irrational, 24; rational, 24
Determinism, 102, 373–79; astral, 365; causal, 364–67; and choice, 378–79; soft, 365–67
Deuteronomy, Book of, 56, 59–60
Devotion to God, 154, 156
Dhimma, 143, 396
Diadem (*atarah*), 308
Dialogues, dramatic, 254
Diaspora, Egyptian, 77–78
Differences, individual, 363
Diogenes of Sinope, 48
Dioscorides, 145
Divine anthropos, 321
Divine image, 205–6
Divine justice, 68
Divine law, 214, 218
Divine life, secrets of the, 316
Divine love, 434
"Divine madness", 420
Divine powers, punitive, 50
Divine ruse, 230
Divine Self, 430–31, 433
Divine Will, 436
Divinity, triune nature of, 376
Division of labor, 218
The doctrine of the mean, 26–28
Dogmas, rivalry of, 376–77
Dogmatic rationalism, 367
Dominicans, 304–5, 347, 398, 401
Donin, Nicholas, 280, 347
Double Truth theory, 351
Doubts about God, 186
Drama, didactic, 300
Dual Torahs, 148
Dualism: of body and soul, 333; of good and evil, 323; psychological, 426–28
Duality: of the deity, 307; of matter and form, 202
Duran, Simon ben Zemah, 391
Duties, classification of, 177–78
Duties of the Heart, 173–89; summary of, 178–89
Duties of the Limbs, 177–78
Duties of the members: *See* duties of the limbs
Duty: ethics of, 94; virtue as, 115

East: debate in, 278–79; Resurrection Debate (1202-1204), 263
Ecclesiastes, 170, 253, 255, 418, 424
Economic activities, 345; Jewish, 143
Eden, Garden of, 200; narrative, 89
Education: Jewish, 262, 267–77; philosophical, 288–89
Egypt, debate in, 276–77
Egyptian diaspora, 77–78
Ein ha-Qore (The Eye of the Reader), 401
Elem, Joseph Tov, 284
Element, fifth, 355
Elements, four, 203
Elements, of human *psyche*, 13
Elijah, 298, 408
Elite, Greek military, 11
Elitism, 190; philosophical, 259–61
Emanation (*shefa*), 353
Empedocles, 386
Encyclopedias, 253; medieval, 256
End of life: ideal, 276; ultimate, 343, 395
End, ultimate, 407, 436
Energia (activity), 44
Energy: spiritual, 315, 326, 517 n 61; spiritual light of Torah, 319; in Torah, 307
Enlightenment, 319
Enoch, 93

Enosh, 93
Enrique IV, 397, 399
Epictetus, 53
Epicureanism, 48–51, 399, 473 n 22
Epicurus, 48–51, 106
Epicurus' Garden, 49–51, 124
Epistle on Resurrection, 263–64, 267
ergon argument, 43
Eros, 155
Esotericism, 292; philosophical, 259–61; rabbinic, 201
Essences, 15
Essenes of Qumran, 102, 133
Eternity: blessed, 81; of the world, 221
Ether, 355
Ethical thinking, 10–11
Ethics: Aristotle's, 193; of duty, 55; interest in, 311; Jewish, 14, 193; lack of focus on, 259; and metaphysics, 176; of obedience, 60; philosophical, 157–59; science of, 398; social, 174; therapeutic function of, 233; of virtue, 6, 55, 60, 87–92, 192
Ethics. See Nicomachean Ethics
Eudaimonia, 48, 51, 97; Aristotle's view of, 352; meaning of, 11, 20–21, 454 n 38, 454 n 42
Eudemian Ethics, 3
Euphrates, 89–90
Europe, culture of thirteenth-century, 300
Eustratius, 424
Euthemia (tranquility), 49
Evil: domain of, 333; in humans, 366; problem of, 306; reality of, 325
Evil impulses, 119–21
Evil instinct, 174–75, 186
Ex-conversos, 396
Examen Vanitatis Doctrina Gentium, 380
Excellence, human, 433
Excess, avoiding, 59

Exclusive interpretation, 45–47; of Aristotle, 43–45
Excommunication: counter-ban of, 269
Exegesis, 298
Exemplum, story about the life of saints, 301
Exhortation to Virtue, 150
Exilarchate, 105
Experience, mystical, 98
Experience, sensory, 49
An Explanation of the Mosiac Scripture, 77
Expulsion: from England, 348; from France, 283; of the Jews, 249; from Kingdom of Naples, 395; from Portugal, 396; from Provence, 395; from Sicily, 395; from Spain, 395
Ezer ha-Dat (The Support of the Faith), 373

Faith, 91, 375–76, 469 n 106; religious, 364
Falaquera, Shem Tov, 253–55, 303, 373, 417
Farissol, Jacob ben Hayim, 285
Fear, of punishment, 183
Fear of the Lord, 76, 91
Female: divine, 296; elevated status of, 334; as incomplete male, 334
Ferdinand, 160
Final good, 18–21, 152–53, 392; ambiguity of, 19–20; definition of, 19; as self-sufficiency, 20
First Crusade, 346
Foreknowledge, 367
Form: of human species, 206–8; in humans, 205
Form and matter: difference between, 216
Formless matter, 354, 366
Forms, theory of, 12
Fortitude, 418
Fourth Lateran Council, 302, 346

France, expulsion of Jews from, 283
Franciscans, 304–5
Franco, Shlomo, 284
Free will, 102, 365
Friend, as another self, 36–37
Friend (*re'a*), 131
Friendship, 124–25; conditional, 132; and happiness, 33–37; marks of, 35; types of, 34–36; virtue, 132; virtuous, 34–37
Fusion of knowledge, 417

Gaius Caligula, 82
Galen, 145, 151, 169
Galileo, 391
Gamliel, Raban, 268
Gaon, Saadia: *See* Saadia
Garden of Eden, 200; narrative, 89, 206, 214–17, 362; Tree of Life, 362; Upper, 336
The Garden of Epicurus, 49–51
Gatingo, Ezra (Astruk Shlomo), 284
Gehenna: punishment in, 339; suffering in, 340
Gender imagery, 287
Generosity, 166, 186, 235
Genesis, 200, 362
Gentleness, 235
Geonim, 147
Gerondi, Nissim, 379
Gerondi, R. Jonah, 269–70, 276
Gershom, Levi ben: *See* Gersonides
Gersonides, 343–44, 349–56, 402–4; account of human knowledge, 358–64; astronomical observations of, 354; commentary on the Pentateuch, 368; doctrine of creation, 355–56; and human perfection, 364–67; life of, 349; literary activity of, 349–52; and prophecy, 369–70, 370–71; style of writing of, 350
Gestalt, divine, 296

Gihon, 89–90
Gikatilla, R. Joseph, 309
Goal, of human life, 152
God: actions of, 214; as an androgen, 296; Aristotle's conception of, 39–40; children of, 335; compassionate, 130; complete trust in, 329; conjunction with, 419; and the covenant, 111–13; and the created universe, 352–56; as creator, 158, 385; essence of, 213, 292, 331, 403; existence of, 388; fear of, 91, 122–23; as the First Intellect, 204; his ignorance of Israel, 367; his love, 385; and his perfection, 83–84; human love of, 242; image of, 129, 296; imitation of, 101, 213–14, 403; incorporeality of, 275; inner rhythm of life, 294; intellectual love of, 229, 240; Jewish conception of, 199; knowledge of, 193, 213–14, 257, 352, 364; knowledge of his essence, 352; life of, 280; limit on his knowledge, 355; limit on his omnipotence, 355; love of, 435–38, 436–37; as lover, 388; mysteries of, 299; mystical union with, 412–15; nature of, 306; omnipotence of, 324; perfecting, 294; perfection of the universe, 358; as a Prime Mover, 40; rabbinic conception of, 295–97; radical oneness of, 320; revelation from, 2, 408; service to, 175–78; sexuality of, 296; as sole object of worship, 185; soul of, 295; soul of the universe, 358; spiritual energy of, 315; in a state of imperfection, 294; submission to, 177; transcendence of, 179; trust in, 185; union with, 188–89; Unity of, 178; visualization of, 300; will of, 122
Godhead, male and female aspects of, 324

Golden Age, of Judeo-Arabic culture, 248
Good, 403; final, 152–53; human, 262; Plato's theory of the, 17
Good deeds, virtues and, 123–25
Good laws, 220
Goodness, friendship of, 34
Goods: classification of, 154–57; commonly accepted, 153–54; physical, 417; spiritual, 417
Great Chain of Being, 170, 203–4
"Great-souled man", 400
Great War (66-70 C.E.), 101–2
Greatest Happiness Principle, 1–2
Greco-Roman philosophy, 106–7
"Greek wisdom", 268
Gregory IX, Pope, 273
Grosseteste, Robert, 398, 423
Guide of the Perplexed, 273, 278; as alternative to the *Zohar*, 309–10; commentary on, 397; as an esoteric work, 195–96; *See also* Maimonides, Moses
Guide to the Guide, 257

Ha-Arokh, R. Joseph ben Shalom Ashkenazi, 309
Ha-Cohen, R. Johathan, 266
Ha-Levi, Zehariya, 391
Ha-Nagid, Samuel, 166
Ha-Nasi, R. Judah, 303
Ha-Qanah, R. Nehunya ben, 295
Ha-Sardi, Samuel, 276
Ha-Yitzhari, Matityahu, 391
Habituation, 374
Hadrianic persecution, 308
Hagar, 287
Hai ibn Yaqzan, 416
Halakhah, 113–15, 134, 259, 326, 435
Halakhic midrashim, 108
Halakhic process, 126
Halakhot, 149

Halevi, Judah, 165–66, 284–85, 379, 386, 409, 508 n 104
Halevi, Zeharyah, 410
Halfan, ben Elijah Menachem, 420
Hannina ben Tradyon, R., 117
Happiness: in the *adab* culture, 162; Aristotle's ambiguity of, 40–41; Aristotle's conception of, 398; and astrology, 283; and commandments, 344; debating the meaning of, 246–90; and the Declaration of Independence, 2; defined, 2; and evil, 322–25; "exclusive" view, 195–96, 405; during the fourteenth century, 343; and friendship, 33–37; Greek and Hellenistic views, 9–54; how to attain, 301; human, 149–52, 196, 223, 488 n 11; humanist discourses on, 414; ideals of, 37–47; as the immortality of the soul, 81–99; imperfect and perfect, 404; "inclusive" view, 76–77, 196; individual, 1; knowledge of God, 403; and knowledge of God, 404; Maimonides' view of, 205–6, 223, 289; and metaphysics, 178–80; as a pattern of living, 65; perfect, 401, 408; as perpetual "diet", 231; philosophic discourse on, 397; and philosophy, 257; in post-Aristotelian philosophy, 47–53; pursuit of, 242–44; as a pursuit of holiness, 423–24; as pursuit of perfection, 428; rabbinic conception of, 107; relationship between reason and, 82; relationship between Torah and, 82; relationship to virtue, knowledge, and wisdom, 12; as a relationship with God, 129–41; as religion perfection, 172–78; as scientific knowledge, 349–56; of the soul, 173, 386; in Stoicism, 52; and Torah, 117, 316–21, 447; Torah

study as the source of, 315–16; and tradition, 2; true, 362; two orders of, 53, 408–10; and well-being of the soul, 343; zenith of, 97–99; in the *Zohar*, 312–13; *See also* Joy; Perfection
Hardship, 134
Hasidei Ashkenaz, 295, 329
Hasidim, 134
Hatred (*sin'at hinam*), 136
Hayun, Yosef, 410
Hayyat, Judah ben Jacob, 421
Hayyun, Joseph, 410
He-Hasid, R. David ben Yehuda, 309
Health, and relation to a body, 17
Heaven, fear of, 122–23
Hedonism, moderate, 50
Heikhalot literature, 147
Hellenization, 72–73
Heresy, 273
Hermann the German, 398
Hermeneutics, 243–44, 430–31
Hesed LeAbraham (Grace to Abraham), 442
Hesheq Shelomo (The Desire of Solomon), 415, 420
Hierarchy: of being, 172, 203; of bodily functions, 232; of moral agents, 31–33; between philosophy and revealed knowledge, 409–12; of the sciences, 240; of the soul, 434; unified, 358
Hillel, 128
Hippocrates, 145, 169
Hirsch, Samson Raphael, 445
Hiyya, Abraham Bar, 284
Holiness, 129–32
Holy Luminary (*butzina qadisha*), 308
Homilies, Zoharic, 300
Honesty (*yosher*), 126
Honor, 156
Horowitz, R. Isaiah ben Abraham Halevi, 442

Hovot ha-Levavot (The Book of Direction to the Duties of the Heart): *See* Duties of the Heart
Human being, 85–87
Human existence, 214–17
Human life, end of, 263–67
Human nature, 21–23, 170–71, 206–14; and Aristotle's conception of happiness, 43–44
Human perfection, 195
Human reason, and Scriptures, 176
Human society, evolution of, 217–23
Human species, intellectual development of, 274
Humanism, 386, 396, 399; and human happiness, 413–15; Renaissance, 397, 412–13
Humanists, insecurity of, 413
Humanity, 206–14; (*philanthropeia*), 92
Humans: material and formal aspects, 205; as modes of God, 443
Humility, 127–29, 180, 186–87, 235, 328; the most cherished virtue, 61; rabbinic emphasis on, 400; types of, 187
Hymn to Zeus, 79

Ibn Abbas, Judah, 253
Ibn Abd Rabih, Mahmud, 165
Ibn Adi, Yahya, 151
Ibn Adret, R. Solomon: *See* Rashba
Ibn Ali, Samuel, 263
Ibn Bajja, 192–93, 197, 208–9, 252, 407
Ibn Daud, Abraham, 191, 297, 369
Ibn Ezra, Abraham, 165, 284, 297
Ibn Ezra, Moses, 165
Ibn Gabir, Joseph, 263
Ibn Gabirol, Solomon, 165, 168–72, 190, 297, 311–12; translation of philosophy into Hebrew, 250
Ibn Hasan, Yequtiel, 168

Ibn Hasdai, Abraham, 271, 276
Ibn Hasdai, Judah, 271, 276
Ibn Hunayn, Ishaq, 150
Ibn Ishaq, Hunayn, 145
Ibn Kaspi, Joseph, 258, 289, 445
Ibn Latif, Isaac, 422
Ibn Machir, Jacob, 282, 287
Ibn Matqah, Judah ben Solomon ha-Cohen, 253
Ibn Motot, Samuel, 284, 422
Ibn Naghrella, Samuel, 163–65, , 172, 187
Ibn Paquda, Bahya: *See* Bahya
Ibn Rushd, 193, 204, 257–58, 278–79, 344, 353, 357, 359, 361, 368, 392, 398; the Commentator, 252; super-commentaries on, 397
Ibn Sham'un, Joseph ben Judah, 263
Ibn Shaprut, Shem Tov, 284
Ibn Shem Tov, Joseph, 381, 396–412, 410, 423, 426, 438, 445
Ibn Shem Tov, Shem Tov, 379
Ibn Shuaib, Joel, 410
Ibn Sina, 192–93, 197, 200, 208, 225, 252, 279, 350, 357, 386
Ibn Tashufin, Tusuf, 248
Ibn Tibbon, Judah, 169
Ibn Tibbon, Samuel, 197, 225, 250–51, 267, 269
Ibn Tufayl, 252, 416
Ibn Yaish, Baruch, 423
Ibn Yishaq, Hunayn, 169
Ibn Zarza, Samuel, 284
Icons, 285
Idea of the Good (or Form of the Good), 16–17
Ideal person, 171; defined, 238
Ideas, world of, 92–93
Idolatry, 179, 221
Iggeret ha-Harafort (Epistle of Blasphemies), 373
Iggeret ha-Vikuah (Epistle of the Debate), 254

Iggeret Tehiyat ha-Metim (Epistle on Resurrection): *See Epistle on Resurrection*
Ihsa' al-Ulum (Catalogue of Sciences), 252
Image, divine, 129–30
Imagination, 279
Imitation (*mimesis*), 327
Imitato Dei, 441–42
Immortality, 81, 207, 361–62, 395; of the human rational soul, 363–64; individual, 387; of the soul, 80, 102, 158; in *Zohar*, 305, 514 n 35
Impulses, evil, 119–21
Inclusion, of the female into the male, 308
Inclusive interpretation, 45–47; of Aristotle, 41–43; of happiness, 76–77
Individuals (*ishim*), 356
Injustice, in Stoicism, 52
Innocent III, 346
Inquisition, papal, 246, 347, 396
Instinct, evil, 186
Intellect, 144, 181, 183, 204, 207; acquired, 209, 211–13; Active, 204, 209–11, 213–14; actual human, 209; aspects of, 38; emanated acquired, 361–63; human, 205–6, 211–13, 359; human material, 285; material, 208–9, 211; perfection of the, 193, 352, 364; potential, 209, 211; practical: *See* Reason, practical; separate, 227, 353, 405; theoretical, 28; and will, 378–79, 431–34
Intellectual activity, 126
Intellectual, status of, 260
Intelligence (*da'at*), 125–26, 237, 418; *See also* Reason
Intelligences: ten, 353; *See also* Intellect
Intemperance, in Stoicism, 52
Interaction, between Jews and others, 261

Interpretation: astrological, of the past, 284; exclusive, of Aristotle, 43–45; inclusive, of Aristotle, 41–43
Intimacy with God, 293
Involuntary acts, 29, 457 n 68
Isaac, 63, 93, 140
Isaac the Blind, 298
Isabella, 160
Isagoge, 251
Islam, happiness in, 143–91
Islamic rationalism, 192
Israel: and the covenant, 111–13; dignity of, 426; land of, 300; liberation of, 239; relations with nations, 306
Italy, Jews in, 396
IV Maccabees, 87, 468 n-97

Jacob, 63, 93, 140
Jacobus, Faber Stapulensis (Jacques Lefevre d'Etaples), 424
James I of Aragon, 281
Jerusalem, 101–2
Jerusalem Temple, 102
Jewish Aristotelianism, demise of, 394
Jewish-Christian rivalry, 343–93
Jewish status, decline of, 348
Jewry, Spanish, 145, 160, 162–63, 246, 264, 348, 373, 397; rebuilding of, 379; value of, 249–50; *See also* Conversos; Courtiers; Expulsion; Reconquest of Spain
Jews: animosity toward, 302; archenemy of Christianity, 301; as courtiers, 249–50; expulsion of Jews from France, 283; expulsion of the, 249; immortality of, 426; as slaves, 249; value of in Spain, 249; as "Witness People", 280
Job, Book of, 56, 136, 253–54, 323
John II, 379, 397
Joseph of Hamadan, R., 309
Josephus, 102, 401
Josiah, 59
Josippon, 401
Joy, 117, 125, 127, 139, 306, 362, 390; extreme, 307; in the life of Torah, 135–38; and performance of commandments, 387; *See also* Happiness
Judah I, Rabbi (Judah Ha-Nasi), 108
Judah, Samuel ben, 258, 398–99
Judah, Shlomo ben, 285
Judah, Solomon ben of Lunel, 286
Judah the Patriarch, 400–401
Judaism, 92–95; and Aristotle, 438; and Christianity, 343, 432, 441; cultural boundaries of, 261; happiness in, 3; as ideal polity, 223; path to afterlife, 348; and perfection of the intellect, 373; and philosophy, differences between, 409; as a pursuit of happiness, 9; Rabbinic, Torah in, 101–42; rationalism in, 373; rationality of, 157–59
Judea, economic ruin of, 102
Judeo-Arabic culture, Golden Age of, 248
Jurisprudence, Muslim, 145–46
"Just-right" point, 27
Justice, 418; (*dikaisyne*), 89–90; divine, 68; (*middat ha-din*), 130; one of cardinal virtues, 13; one of the four cardinal virtues, 80; in Stoicism, 52

Kabbalah, 262; as alternative to philosophy, 292–300; defined, 291; different versions of, 299; as dualistic struggle, 227; emergence of, 270; and human perfection, 280; literal meaning of, 306; Lurianic, 422; and the Maimonidean Controversy, 297–300; part of revealed tradition, 410; versus philosophy, 279–81; and

philosophy, interplay between, 292, 394–438; popularity of, 419; and prescription for happiness, 291–342; rise of, 441; studied by Christian humanists, 420; study of, 308; *See also Zohar*
Kabbalistic anthropology, 332–38
Kalam, 146, 481 n 7; Jewish, 263; Mu'tazilite, 149
Kalonimus, Meshulam ben, 275
Kant, Immanuel, 6, 445
Kantian ethics, 114
Karaites, 148–49
Kaspi, Netanel, 285–86
Keter Malkhut (Kingly Crown), 172
Kevod Elohim, 397, 399, 401–2, ; intent of, 409
Kimhi family, 250
Kimhi, R. David, 269, 271, 274–76
Kimia-yi sa'adat (The Alchemy of Happiness), 193
Kinesis (process), 44
King's palace, myth of the, 239–41
Kitab mani al-nafs, 180
Knowability, criterion for, 14
Knowledge, 162; divine, 39; Gersonides' account of, 358–64; of God, 156, 292–93, 366; of God's essence, 384; limitations of, 220; and mass availability of, 343; meditative, 165; Moses', 92–93; need of philosophic-scientific, 372; philosophic, of the sages, 287; possession of, 417; practical, 165; rational, 147, 375–76; relationship to virtue, happiness, and wisdom, 12; revealed, 147; and salvation, 343; and true opinion, 375; ultimate, 220; of the universe, 366
Krates, 51
Kuzari, 285

"Ladder of perfections", 417

Lambin, Denys, 424
Lamentations Rabbah, 130
Language: Arabic, 161, 249, 398; Armaic, 314, 517 n 60; of the Bible, 95; conception of, 422–23; divine, 422; Greek, 72; Hebrew, 299; Latin, 398; limits of, 241–42
Languedoc, 282, 301
Latin Averroists, 351
Lattes, Isaac de, 285
Law: perfect, 92–95; perfection of the, 244; revealed, study of, 256; revelation of, 158; rule of, 218; as therapy of the soul, 183–84
Law of Moses, 83, 94, 98
Laws, ceremonial, 237
Laxity in religion, 289
Leadership, 156
Learning, 209; erotic dimension of, 308
Legal system, 220
Leon, Judah Messer, 368, 412, 416
Leon, Moses de, 308–10
Letter of Aristeas, 87
Leviticus, 129
Liberality, 235
Life: Aristotle's good, 33; civil, 44–45; ideal end of, 276; ideal way of, 66, 301; Jewish, 439; moral, 435–36; philosophic, 44–45; purpose of, 306; rabbinic way of, 104; tree of, 319; ultimate end, 343
Life after death: Maimonides conception of, 338–39
Lifestyle, healthy, 232
Light of the Lord, 380
Lilith, 323
Literature, Rabbinic, 108–11
Liturgy, 131, 312
Logos, 51, 56, 93, 194; definition of, 4, 10; relationship between God and Creation, 84–85; relationship to mythos, 14

Logos and mythos: interplay of,
 198–200
Long Commentary on the Metaphysics,
 354
Lord, fear of, 76
Lovingkindness, 123–25, 130–31
Loyalty, 166
Lunel, 266
Lysimachus, Alexander, 82

Ma'amar Yiqavu ha-Mayyim (A Treatise
 on "Let the Water be Collected",
 267
Ma'arekhet ha-Elohut (The
 Constellation of the Godhead), 419
Maat, 75, 465 n 57
Maccabees, rebellion of the, 73
Magic, astral, 284–85
Magnanimity, 127, 166, 171, 236, 400
Maimon, Prat (Shlomo ben
 Menachem), 285–86
Maimonidean Controversies, 246–90,
 339, 378; Phase 1, 263–67; Phase 2,
 267–77; Phase 3, 277–81; Phase 4,
 281–89; time period of, 246
Maimonides, Moses, 3, 279, 284, 298,
 312, 401; agnosticism of, 231, 352;
 versus Aristotle, 235–37; and
 attitude toward matter, 227; critique
 of, 274–76; and his achievements,
 199; his conception of happiness,
 192–245; his narratives, 200; his
 philosophical assumptions, 201–6;
 his view of myth, 200–201;
 interpreting him, 195–201; position
 on miracles, 271; translation of
 philosophy into Hebrew, 250; *See
 also Guide of the Perplexed*
Man: perfect, 364, 417; place of, 306;
 primordial, 321; self-controlled or
 continent *See* person, self-indulgent;
 self-indulgent *See* person, self-
 indulgent; uncontrolled or
 incontinent *See* person,
 uncontrolled; vicious *See* person,
 vicious
Manetti, Gianozzo, 414
Mankind, socio-political nature of,
 217–21
Manuscript reproduction, fallibility of,
 350
Maqamah genre, 303
Mar-Hayim, Isaac, 421
Marranos, 348
Marriage, 155; childless, 307;
 heterosexual, 307; planned, 250
Martyrdom, 116
Material intellect, 360
Matter and form: composition of, 215;
 difference between, 216; interaction
 of, 170
Mean, doctrine of the, 26–28, 327,
 435
Medicine, 262
Meek person (*shefal ruah*), 126
Memory, 125
Menachem, Shlomo ben (Prat
 Maimon), 285
Meqor Hayim (Fountain of Life), 170,
 172
Merchant-banker, Jewish, 143–44
Merkabah literature, 147
Meshulam, R. Aaron ben, 266
Messiah, 370; coming of the, 437
Messiah, Days of the, 139–40
Messianic Age, 238–39, 341
Metaphysics, 176, 402; divine science
 of, 376
Metaphysics, matter and form, 201–3
Meteora, 251, 255
Middah, 118
Middle class, 270
Middle Commentary on Aristotle's Ethics,
 258, 398–400
Middle Platonism, 112
Midrash: rabbinic, 394

Midrash ha-Hokhmah (The Exposition of Wisdom), 253
Midrash Ha-Ne'elam, 310
Midrash, rabbinic, 295
Midrash Tehilim, 110
Midrashic activity, 242–44
Mikhtav ha-Hitnatzelut (A Letter of Apology), 288
Milhamot ha-Shem (The Wars of the Lord): *See* Wars of the Lord
Mimesis, linguistic, 15
Mind, 181
Minhat Qena'ot (An Offering of Zeal), 283
Minority, alienated, 344
Miracles, 264, 288–89, 367, 433; rationalist interpretation of, 267
Mirandola, Gianfrancesco Pico della, 380, 413–15
Miriam, 140
Mishnah, 103, 108, 119
Mishneh Torah (Code of Jewish Law), 195, 206, 212, 214, 224–25, 231, 233, 246, 263–66, 273
Miskawayh, Ahmad, 151
Mithridates, Flavius, 416
Mitzvot, 115, 274–75; as a path to happiness, 279–81; performance of the, 343
Mivhar ha-Peninim (Choice of Pearls), 168
Moderation, 87, 155, 158, 161, 166, 171, 184–86; ideal of, 234–35; in pleasures, 76; rejection of Maimonides' ethics of, 327–29
Modesty (*anavah*), 126, 187, 235
Monotheism, 221–23, 320
Montpelier, 282
Moral training, 168–72
Moral virtues, 172
Morality, in Proverbs, 57–59
Mordecai, Isaac ben, 278–79
Mosaic Law, 94

Mosaic Scripture: allegory of, 95–97; explanation of the, 77
Moses, 88–89, 92–95, 109, 112, 128, 140, 200, 212, 369–70; addressed by God, 225; intellectual perfection of, 371; Law of, 83, 98; as most excellent human being, 226; as most perfect human being, 377; not an angel, 227; as a prophet, 227
Moses' prophecy, uniqueness of, 224–28
Motions, of the stars, 354
Mourning, 140
Mt. Sinai, 93, 102, 109, 111, 128, 200, 223
Murder, prohibition against, 129
Muslim: jurisprudence, 145–46; sacred texts, 145; Spain, 145–91
Musrei ha-Filosofim (The Moral Teachings of the Philosophers), 169
Mu'tazilah, 146
Mu'tazilite Kalam, 149
Mysteries of the Torah, 288
Mystical kabbalah, 292
Mystical Union, 97–99, 419–21
Mysticism: and heresy, 421; intellectual, 397
Myth: of the human soul, 332; logocentric, 243; Plato's three metals, 222
Mythos, 55, 194; defined, 4, 10, 199; relationship to logos, 14
Mythos and Logos, interplay of, 246
Myths, of Judaism, 199

Nahman, R. Moses ben (Nahmanides): *See* Nahmanides
Nahmanides, 305, 339, 347; debate with Christiani, 281; expulsion of, 281; role of in the debate, 270–73
Narboni, Moses, 286, 361, 377, 416, 421
Narrative, of Garden of Eden, 206, 214

Narratives: of Maimonides, 200
Natural order, 271–72
Naturalism: Greek, 275; religious, 283–86
Nature: definition of, 16; human, 170–71, 206–14; knowledge of, 412–15; mastery of, 422–23; stability of, 238
Near-death experience, 226
Negative theology, 229–31
Neo-Orthodoxy, 445
Neoplatonists, 145
Netherlands, Jews in, 396
New Christians, 395
Newton, 391
Nicholas IV, Pope, 278
Nicholas of Giovinazzo, 278
Nicomachean Ethics, 3, 15, 17, 87, 124, 144, 150–51, 196, 234, 247, 394; after ibn Shem Tov, 410–12; among Jews and Christians, 398–401; commentaries on, 397, 423–24; status of, 257–59
Nifo, Agostino, 424
Nine hundred Theses, 415
Nineteen Letters on Judaism, 445
Nissim of Marseilles, 286
Noah, 93
Nobility, 172
Novels, philosophical, 254

Obligation, religious, 172
Obligations of the Law, 183–84
Odonis, Geraldus, 424
Olam ha-ba (world to come), 239, 263
The Old Stoa, 51
One-sex theory, 308, 515 n 46
Onemous of Gadara, 106
Opinion, true, 375
Or Ha-Shem (Light of the Lord): See *Light of the Lord*
Orderliness: of the corporeal world, 357; and Wisdom, 58

Oresme, Nicole, 380, 398, 424
Organon, 255
Orthodoxy, 113
orthos logos (right reason), 28
Other World, saint's travels to, 305–6
Ottoman Empire, 396
Oxford University, Merton College, 379

Painlessness, and pleasure, 50
Palestinian Talmud, 108
Parables, 369; of rabbis, 201
Particularism, 408–10
Particulars (*peratim*), 356
Parva Naturalia, 255
Passion narrative, 302
Passions, 96, 385; control of, 25
"Path of faith", 428
"Path of investigation", 428
Patience, 166
Patriarchate, 105
Paving the Way to Virtue, 150
Penal power, Jewish, 250
Penei Mosheh (The Countenance of Moses), 423, 431
Penis, circumcised, 308, 334
Pentateuch, 95, 113; commentaries on, 253; Gersonides' commentary on, 368, 372; midrash on, 300
Perfect law, 92–95
Perfection, 132–35, 241–42, 429–30; in afterlife, 322; of the body, 218; final, 212–13, 219–20, 240–41; and happiness, 197–98; human, 195, 294, 371, 402–4, 430–31; of the intellect, 404–6; intellectual, 207–8, 237–38, 279, 343–93, 373–79; in kabbalah, 341; masculine, 333; meanings of, 197–98; moral, 257; moral and intellectual, 194; necessary in God, 294; of opinions, 382–83; pursuit of, 129–32; religious, 192, 305–6, 394–438,

424–26; of the soul, 219, 265; of Torah, 229; *See also* Happiness
Peri Ethon, 151
Perion, Joachim, 424
Peripatetic school, 145
Peripatetics, 77, 87
Persecution, 396; Hadrianic, 308; in the Muslim world, 143
Person: ethically virtuous, 31–32; ideal, 171; ideal, defined, 238; self-controlled or continent, 32; self-indulgent, 32; uncontrolled or incontinent, 32; vicious, 32–33
Personality, virtuous, 328
Pesuqei de-Zimrah, 131
Petit, Solomon, 278–79
Phaedros, 17
Pharisees, 102–3, 133–34
Philanthropy, 400
Philip the Fair (1285-1314), 282
Philo of Alexandria, 3, 81–99, 133, 228
Philoponus, John, 158
Philosopher, reclusive, 407–8
Philosophers: Jewish, 77–81; professional, 350; social status of, 192
Philosophia (contemplation), 44
Philosophia (love of wisdom), 101
Philosophic life, 44–45
Philosophical assumptions, of Maimonides, 201–6
Philosophical sciences, 145
Philosophizing: *See* contemplation
Philosophy, 288–89; acceptance of, 281; "alien" to Judaism, 268; Aristotele's, 350; Aristotle's, critique of, 344; Bahya's definition of, 175; as a barren activity, 308; of Crescas, 388–92; as a cultural force, 251–61; difficulties of, 406; dissemination of among the Jews, 258; as female, 287; Greco-Roman, 106–7;

happiness in, 3; importance in Jewry, 222; Jewish, 4, 72–77; Jewishness of, 255; and Judaism, differences between, 409; versus kabbalah, 279–81; and kabbalah, interplay between, 292, 394–438; limits of, 394; moral, 426; primacy of, 368; and rabbinic texts, agreement between, 253; and religious worship, 172; restriction of, 282; scholastic, 349, 523 n 22; as servant of Torah, 287; as a solitary study, 251; students of, 273; study of, 222, 267; study of by middle class, 251; study of in thirteenth century, 251–54; as subordinate to revelation, 397; taught openly, 351, 524 n 27; teaching of, 261, 368, 395; and Torah, 191; in traditional Jewish society, 282
Physica, 255
Physics, 203–4; science of, 352
Pico, 421
Pietism, 91, 254; German, 269; intellectual, 172–74
Pio, Alberto, 421
Pisa, Isaac da, 421
Pisa, Yehiel da, 412
Pishon, 89–90
Plato, 12–16, , 76–77, 145, 152, 194, 197, 257, 332–33, 357; his political theory, 192
Platonism: Middle, 79, 112; Renaissance, 416
Pleasure, 135; friendship of, 34; God as source of, 181; importance of, 49
Pleasure and virtue, relationship between, 30–33
Pleasures: described, 31; physical, 154
Plessis, Philippe Le, 424
Plot-structures, 243; of Maimonides, 200

Plotinus, 145
Poetry: love, 164; secular, 163–65; wine, 164
Point, "just-right", 27
Polis, 47
Politeuma, 77
Politics, 257
Poll tax (*jizyah*), 143
Polleqar, Isaac, 344, 373–78
Post-Aristotelian Philosophy, happiness in, 47–53
Poverty, 186, 328; virtues of, 48
Power, 156; appetitive, 279; political, 156; sensitive, 279
Practical reasoning, 28–30; and formation of character, 30
Practical wisdom, in Stoicism, 52
Praxis (*ma'aseh*), 243; and *Theoria*, relationship between, 311
Praxis, primacy of, 435–38
Preaching, 278
Predictions, 369
Preparation, for spiritual energy, 286
Pressures, external, 280
Pride, 329
Primordial Torah (*torah qedumah*), 297
Privation, 202–3
Privileges, of Jews of Aragon, 379
Process (*kinesis*), 44, 198
Proclus, 145
Procreation, 155, 307
Productive, being, 156
Prognostication, and astrology, 284
Program of study, 417
Prophecy, 194, 286, 367–73; as a cognitive state, 192; Gersonides' account of, 369–70; Gersonides' de-politization of, 370–71; as highest cognitive activity, 212; intellectual, 223; Mosaic, 377–79; of Moses, 225, 228
Prophet, and imagination, 369
Prophetic kabbalah, 292

Prophets, as super-philosophers, 369
Propriety, 58
Prosperity, material, 155–56
Protection, to Jews, 248
Provence, 246, 248, 268–70
Proverbs, 58–59, 156, 170, 253, 255, 321, 418, 424
Providence, 364–67; divine, 386
Prudence, 436; one of the four cardinal virtues, 80; (*phronesis*), 89–90
Psalm 1, 64–68, 110, 122, 312, 316–17, 323; and retribution, 67
Psalm 19, 70–71, 183, 310
Psalm 119, 68–69
Psalm 145, 131, 312
Psalms, 424; study of, 429; Torah, 61; Wisdom, 61
Pseudo-Bahya, 180
Psyche (soul), 11–12
Psychology, 205–6, 414
Ptolemy, 145
Pulgar, Isaac: *See* Polleqar, Isaac
Punishment: fear of, 183; for transgressions, 349
Purification, 81
Purity: in Jewish law, 330; sexual, 328
Pythagorean-Platonic myth, 182
Pythagorean tradition, 170

Quadrivium, 256
Qumran, 102, 133
Quran, 176, 495 n 74

Rabad, 266, 298
Rabbinic academies, 103–5
Rabbinic Judaism, 145–49; Torah in, 101–42
Rabbinic literature, 108–11
Rabbis: creation of, 101; definition of, 103; as philosophers, 106–7
Ramah, 265–67, 310
Rapel, Dov, 268
Rashba, 281–83, 285; ban of, 283, 289
Rational choice, 364–67; deliberate, 35

Rational soul, 170
Rationalism: Islamic, 192; Jewish, 147; Maimonidean, 268; of Maimonides, 285; Muslim, 148; optimistic, 367–68
Rationalist interpretation, 148–49
Rationalist tradition, 159–60
Rationalists vs. Traditionalists, 286–88
Rationality, 216; of Torah, 229
Realm: sefirotic, 320–21, 326; sublunar, 356; supra-lunar, 356
Reason, 157–58, 160, 260; capacity to, 206; human, 22, 88, 147, 150; man's characteristic activity, 405; practical, 435; in Stoicism, 52; as tool, 148
Reason, theoretical: *See* intellect, theoretical
Reasoned choice, 29
Reasoning: practical, 28–30; theoretical, 238
Recanati, Menachem, 419
Reconquest of Spain, 248–51
Redemption (*ge'ulah*), 296
Regimen, necessity of, 183
Regimen of the Solitary, 407
Regulations, in the Muslim world, 143
Rejoice, commandment to, 137
Religion, as philosophic truth, 194
Religious perfection, 192
Renaissance, 396
Repentance (*teshuvah*), 136
Republic, 12, 222, 251, 257–58, 332–33
Reshit Hokhmah (Origin of Wisdom), 253, 255, 257
Respect, for master, 105
Rest, 154
Resurrection: of the body, 158, 263, 265; of the dead, 81, 102, 339, 370; Maimonides' Epistle on, 264; noncorporeal, 275
Resurrection Debate (1202-1204), 262

Retribution: divine, 158; doctrine of, 339; in Psalm 1, 67
Reuchlin, Johannes, 421
Revealed law, study of, 256
Revelation, 157–58, 394, 406, 411; divine, 298, 367–68; at Mt. Sinai, 389
Revelations, of secret knowledge, 306
Revenge, 156
Revivification, 159; of body and soul, 141
Reward: expectation of, 183; postponement of, 139
Ricius, Paulus, 416
Right reason (*orthos logos*), 28
Righteous person, 325–27
Righteousness, 68
Rimoch, Abraham, 410
Riots of 1391, 379
Ritual laws, 147
Rivalry, between Judaism and Christianity, 344–49
Rossillo, Mordekhai, 420
Rules, of human conduct, 56–57

Saadia, 144–60, 157–59, 176, 183, 297, 311–12, 369, 480 n 4; translation of philosophy into Hebrew, 250
Sabbath and Wisdom, 78
Sabians, 200, 221–23, 283, 494 n 72; purpose of story of, 223
Sacrifices, laws about, 274
Sacrificial cult, cessation of the, 137
Sadducees, 102
Sage: rabbinic, 293; (*shimush hakhamin*), 105
Sages, 109
Saintliness (*hasidut*), 133
Salutati, Caluccio, 413
Salvation: alternate programs for, 272; eternal, 301, 338–41; personal, 247, 343

Samael, 323–25
Samuel, Hillel ben, 278–79
Santification, 338
Saragossa, 168, 174, 270, 379
Sarah, 288
Satanow, Isaac, 445
Satisfaction (*sippuq*), 128
Scale of moral agents *See* hierarchy of moral agents
Scholars, itinerant preaching, 303–5
Scholem, Gershom, 311
Sciences: classification of, 252–53, 255–56, 417–19; theoretical, 256
Scotus, Duns, 356, 381, 389, 527 n 45
Scotus, Michael, 277
Scribe (*sofer*), 74
Scripture: revealed, 367–68; as source of religious obligation, 148
Scriptures, and human reason, 176
Second Sophistic movement, 106
Second Temple, 3, 55, 139
Seeskin, Kenneth, 199
Sefer ha-Bahir (The Book of Brightness): *See Bahir*
Sefer Ha-Iyyun (The Book of Contemplation), 300
Sefer ha-Mevaqesh (The Book of the Seeker), 254, 303–4
Sefer ha-Zohar (The Book of Enlightenment): *See Zohar*
Sefer Hanhagat ha-Hayyim (The Book of Management of Life), 425
Sefer Tagmulei ha-Nefesh (A Book on the Rewards of the Soul), 277, 279
Sefer Yetzirah, 295, 299
Sefirot, 291, 295; doctrine of, 421; and functions of the human soul, 335; ten, 416
Segni, Bernardo, 424
Segregation, residential, 396
Self-control, 4, 59, 119–20, 155, 157–58, 161, 165, 168–69, 172, 182, 184, 236, 418; ethos of, 160–68, 163–65; one of the four cardinal virtues, 80; (*skophrosyne*), 89–90
Self-discipline, 135
Self-government, of the Jewish minority, 194
Self-purification, 429–30
Self-sufficiency, 48; of the Stoics, 51
Seneca, 53
Sensitive power, 279
Sensory experience, 49
Separate intellects, 227
Separate Intelligence, 356–58, 427
Septimus, Bernard, 265, 410
Service, of God, 157
Seventh principle, 225–26
Sexuality, 307; centrality of, 329–31; rhythm of, 296
Sha'ar ha-Gemul (Gate of Retrubution), 272, 277
Sha'ar ha-Shamayim (The Gate of Heaven), 253
Shalom, Abraham, 391, 410–11
Shammai, 128
Sharia, 162, 193
Shekhinah, 296, 307–8, 315, 322, 324–25, 419, 437
Sheltiel, Zerahya ben, 278
Shem Tov, Isaac ben, 276
Shema, 131
Shemuel, Hillel ben, 277
Shenei Luhot ha-Berit (The Two Tablets of the Covenant), 442
Sheshet ben Isaac Benvenisti, 266
Shimon bar Yohai, R., 308–9
Shir ha-Ma'alot asher li-Shelomo (The Song of Solomon's Virtues), 412
Shlomo, Astruk (Ezra Gatingo), 284
Silence, 166; significance of, 242
Simon, Meir ben, 280
Sin: of Adam, 217; human, 296, 428; origin of, 120
Sinai: *See* Mt. Sinai

Sitra Ahra (the Other Side), 301, 323, 336, 340
Society, human, evolution of, 217–23
Socrates, 11–12, 180
Solitude, 407–8
Solomon, 57, 255, 397, 409–12, 425, 436; ideally virtuous man, 415–38; wisdom of, 421–22
Solomon, Moses ben, 278
Solomon of Arles, 253
Solomon, Wisdom of, 78–81
Song of Solomon's Virtues, 415–16
Song of Songs, 148, 253–54, 368, 415, 418
Sophia, 138
Sophists, 10–11
Sophos, 107, 161
Soul: Bahya's definition of, 181; care of, 176; definition of the human, 262; descent of the, 336–37; destiny of the, 272; doctrine of the, 333; hierarchy of, 434; human, 179–80, 359, 427; human nature and the, 332–34; immortality of the, 267, 343; incorporeal, 324; nature of, 334–36; pre-existence of, 334; rational, 170, 405; regains initial perfection, 175; salvation of the, 277, 441; substance of the, 152; vegetative, 170
Soul and body: relationship between, 120, 180–82, 337–38, 428–29; tension between, 338
Souls: of gentiles, 333; of Jews are divine, 427
Souls of the righteous, 140
Sources: Amoraic, 120; philosophic, 196; Tannaitic, 120
Spain: Jewish communities in, 160, 246; Muslim, 145–91; reconquest of, 248–51
Speculation, 126

Spinoza, Baruch de, 2, 443; excommunication of, 444
St. Augustine, 344
Stability, of nature, 238
Status, of the Jews, 249
Statutes (*huqqim*), 237
Stoicism, 51–53, 134, 399
Stoics, 77, 87–88, 96, 122, 413
Style, kabbalistic, 299
Suffering, 430
Summa Contra Gentiles, 401, 403
Summa Theologica, 401
Super-commentaries, 252; of Gersonides, 350
Superiority: of human species, 181; spiritual, 396
Supernaturalism, 49
Supreme Good, 436
Sura academy, 149
Synagogue service, 131
Synagogue, use of poetry in, 164

Tahdhib al Ahlaq, 151
Talismans, 285
Talmud, 108, 280; burning of, 281, 347; scholarship of the, 347
Tannaitic sources, 120
Taxation, of Jews in Spain, 250
Teaching, traditional oral learning, 298
Teleological Ethics, 18–19
Teleological Framework, 15–18
Telos (end), 16; of human life, 236
Temperaments, human, 169
Temperance, 96; one of cardinal virtues, 13
Tempier, Stephen, 398
Temple: destruction of, 101–2, 136; Second, 55; as a talisman, 286
Temptations, sexual, 329
Ten Commandments, 94
Tenth Treatise, 149–52
Termperance, in Stoicism, 52
Terumat ha-Kesef, 258, 445

Teshuvot la-Meharef (Refutation of the Blasphemer), 373
Textile industry, Jewish, 423
Texts, printed, 395
Themistius, 145, 208, 278–79, 350, 359, 386
Theology, 83–84; Creation, 71–72; Mu'tazilite, 146–47
Theology, covenantal, 55
Theology of Aristotle, 278
Theoretical intellect, 28
Theoretical reason: *See* intellect, theoretical
Theoria (*iyyun*), 243; and *praxis*, relationship between, 311
Theosophic kabbalah, 292
Thirteen Principles, 231, 376
Thoughtlessness, in Stoicism, 52
Tife'eret, 319, 324–25, 416, 419
Tigris, 89–90
Timaeus, 251
Time (*zeman*), 167
Tiqqun Middot ha-Nefesh (The Improvement of Moral Qualities), 168
Todros ben Joseph Halevi Abulafia, R., 310
Todros, Calonimus ben, 283
Todros, Joseph ben, 310
Toleration: of Jews, 345
Tomer Devorah (The Palm Tree of Deborah), 441–42
Torah, 55–100; author of the, 94; and the covenant, 111–13; and Derekh Eretz, 113–15; devotion to, 69, 309; divine, 406, 433; energy in, 307; as an esoteric work, 310; as a female, 287, 297, 307; as a form of law, 2; as guide for perfection, 372; and happiness, 316–21; hierarchy of, 397; holiness of, 387; joy in the life of, 135–38; knowledge of, 374–75; life of, 127, 137; link between God and Israel, 446; living by the, 61, 243; love of, 307; as manifestation of God, 280; miraculous nature of, 273; and Moses, 223–24; as most perfect law, 377; Oral, 108, 113, 347; and organization of lives, 343; paths of, 322; as perfect speech, 229; perfection and peace, 321–22; perfection of, 426; philosophic, 223–31; and philosophy, 191; Piety, 59–61; Primordial (*torah qedumah*), 297; prohibitions of the, 436; protection of, 309; rabbinic myth of dual, 298; rabbinic mythos of, 111–17; as a regimen, 231–38; relationship between happiness and, 82; rewards of, 138–41; study of, 300, 302; study of, as an erotic activity, 307; suffering in the life of, 135–38; superiority of over philosophy, 406–8; and teachings of the sciences, 256; Tree of Life as metaphor for, 362; value of, 420; way of studying, 306–8; and Wisdom, 4, 60, 64, 73–75, 112, 254–55, 317; Written, 108
Torah and Wisdom: interplay of, 246
Torah of Moses, 194, 200–201, 214, 220, 226, 367–73, 421–22; contains all truths, 288; as divine Law, 229; perfection of the, 228–29; uniqueness of, 368, 371–73
Torah study, value of, 116–17
Torahs, dual, 148
Torat Adam (Laws about Humans), 272
Tosafists, 280
Tosefta, 108
Tractate Avot, 110, 425, 431, 436
Tradition, 374; chain of, 107; and happiness, 2; Israelite Wisdom, 58; revealed, 157, 394, 425
Traditionalists vs. Rationalists, 286–88

Training, of desire, 233
Tranquility (*euthemia*), 49
Translation: of philosophic texts, 277; of philosophical texts, 250
Tree of Knowledge of Good and Evil, 89
Tree of Life, 89, 362; as metaphor for Torah, 362
Trivium, 256
Trust, and friendship, 35
Truth, 126, 194; contemplation of, 404; pursuit of, 5, 351; teaching of, 368; Torah and the pursuit of, 125–27; way of, 331–32
Two-substance theory, 427

Ultimate end of human life, 247
Umayyads, 160
Understanding (*binah*), 125–26
Union: with God, 188–89; of the separated soul, 437
Universals (*kollelim*), 356
Universe: creation of, 179, 222, 495 n 75; as hierarchy of substances, 353; structure of, 306
University of Paris: College of Navarre, 379; ecclesiastical ban by, 273
Untroubledness (*ataraxia*), 49
Utilitarians, 1, 445
Utility, friendship of, 34

Valladolid, Alfonso de: *See* Abner of Burgos
Vice, 52–53, 59, 76, 87, 89, 119, 123–24; ignorance of, 12; ornaments of, 48; soul's journey from to virtue, 95
Virtue: defined, 87, 413; as duties, 115; and ethics, 87–92, 94; as the only good, 413; relationship to happiness, knowledge, and wisdom, 12; in Stoicism, 52
Virtue and pleasure, relationship between, 30–33

Virtue ethics, 6, 192
The virtues, 23–30
Virtues: acquiring, 26; acquisition of, 291; classification of, 417–19; cultivation of, 105–6; four cardinal, 80; ideal, 293; intellectual, 90, 237; kabbalistic, 327–32; list of, 161; moral, 172, 234–35; rational, 238; religious, 185–87; and Vices, 171–72
Virtuous character, cultivation of, 117–29
Virtuous friends, characteristics of, 35
Voluntarism, 383–88, 432–33; Crescas', 388–89
Voluntary acts, 29, 457 n 68

Wars of the Lord, 276, 351, 362
Wealth, 155–56; accumulation of, 128; material, 166–67
Well-being: of the body, 219; of the soul, 219
Well-lived life, 231
West, Resurrection Debate in the, 264–65
Wicked (*rasha*), 60–61, 67
Will, 387–88; definition of, 385; divine, 271; free, 102; freedom of, 433–34; human, 383–84, 391, 414; imperfection of, 434; and intellect, 378–79, 431–34; power of the, 121–23
Will and cognition, relationship between, 389
Will and divine providence, 389–90
Will and wisdom, the same in God, 230
Wine poetry, 164
Wisdom, 38, 55–100, 126, 154, 237, 434; attributes of, 79; and Creation, 68–72; defined, 447; and Divine Providence, 79; expanding, 254–56; as a female, 75; glorification of,

75–76; (*hokhmah*), 319; love of, 242; Near Eastern, 56–57, 460 n 2; one of cardinal virtues, 13; philosophic, 397; practical, 238, 411; practical and theoretical, 165–68; practical, in Stoicism, 52; pursuit of, 167; relationship to virtue, happiness, and knowledge, 12; similar to Isis, 75; teacher of, 57–58; and Torah, 4, 73–75

Wisdom of Solomon, 78–81

Wisdom tradition, 110, 132

Wise man: privilege of, 351; training of the, 192

Witness people, 344

"Woe to", 314–15

Women: and immortality, 437–38; role of in Kabbalah, 334

World: created, 179; creation of, 264, 271; sublunar, 179, 203, 285

World Soul, 357

World (*tevel*), 167

Worship, Jewish communal, 254

Yagel, Abraham, 422

Ya'ir Nativ (Lighting the Path), 253

Yeshivah, 103

Yesod, 326

Yishmael, R., 106, 287

Yohai, R. Shimon bar, 310, 331, 341, 408, 426

Yosef, Shem Tov ben, 410

Yosse the Galilean, R., 121

Zarfati, Reuben, 419

Zealots, 102

Zeno of Citium, 51, 53

Zeus, Hymn to, 79

Zeus, *orthos logos* of, 53

Zodiac, divine, 331

Zohar, 272–73, 300–310, 394, 419; as alternative to *Guide of the Perplexed*, 309–10; as alternative to philosophy, 291–93; as discourse on happiness, 311–27; as dramatization of the well-lived life, 311; ethical teachings of the, 311–12; happiness in, 312–13; and the imagination, 340; literary structure of, 300–303; printing of, 420; as response to Christianity, 305; as response to Maimonides, 340–41; as revelation of Torah, 280; setting, 302–3; stories of the, 302